THE TRAINING OF
THE TWELVE

FOREWORD BY D. STUART BRISCOE

THE TRAINING OF
THE TWELVE

TIMELESS PRINCIPLES FOR
LEADERSHIP DEVELOPMENT

A. B. Bruce

KREGEL
CLASSICS

The Training of the Twelve: Timeless Principles for Leadership Development by Alexander Balmain Bruce

Foreword by D. Stuart Briscoe © 1988 by Kregel Publications

Published by Kregel Classics, an imprint of Kregel Publications, 2450 Oak Industrial Dr. NE, Grand Rapids, MI 49505.

Library of Congress Cataloging Card No.: 73-129738
Reproduced from the fouth edition by A. C. Armstrong and Son, 1894.

ISBN: 978-0-8254-4679-5

Printed in the United States of America

CONTENTS

vi **Contents**

THE
TRAINING
OF THE TWELVE

FOREWORD BY D. STUART BRISCOE

Alexander Balmain Bruce, a man as Scottish as his name, was born on a Perthshire farm and educated in an Edinburgh college. He ministered in Scottish country parishes and taught in a Glasgow seminary. For over forty years he devoted himself to the ministry of the Christian gospel, first as a pastor, and then as a distinguished Professor of Apologetics and New Testament Exegesis. He started writing during his pastorates and his best known book *The Training of the Twelve* was published in 1871. In keeping with the nineteenth century's love of ponderous and descriptive titles the book was subtitled, ''Passages out of the Gospels Exhibiting the Twelve Disciples of Jesus Under Discipline for the Apostleship.''

For over a hundred years *The Training of the Twelve* has been highly regarded and widely received. No less an authority than Dr. W. H. Griffith Thomas called the book, ''One of the great Christian classics of the nineteenth century,'' and Dr. Wilbur Smith, America's number one evangelical bibliophile remarked, ''There is nothing quite as important on the life of our Lord as related to the training of the twelve apostles as this book. . . .''

Now, this ''nineteenth century classic'' can expand its already rich and blessed ministry. Although over one-hundred years old, Dr. Bruce's work speaks powerfully and effectively to the contemporary Christian generation.

In recent years there has been a re-discovery of the importance of Paul's teaching in Ephesians chapter 4 concerning the pastor/teacher's responsibility to ''equip the saints for the work of the ministry.'' Many churches for long years had been ignorant of, or chose to ignore such biblical teaching, and, accordingly, a few of God's people were over-worked while the majority were under-employed. While a handful of gifts were exercised to the full, thousands of gifted people did not even know they were gifted. As a result, the potential ministry of the Church of Christ was drastically curtailed. Dr. Bruce would have felt right at home with the present emphasis on training people to minister, and his book has much to offer as a resource for such training as it shows the Master training His special team.

Seeing the church as the Body of Christ is another healthy contemporary emphasis. It serves to deliver people from the mistaken idea that the church is something people attend and introduces them to the biblical concept that the church is something people are. For Christians to see themselves as the Body of Christ and to order their lives in loving reponse to each other as fellow members, committed to mutual nurture, is potentially revolutionary. This book carefully documents the struggles and the successes of the first group of people who endeavoured so to love each other that they became recognizable as Christ's disciples.

Much has been written recently about personal Christian growth. Some of the material leans more heavily on social sciences than theological or biblical teaching and savours more of self-improvement than spiritual growth. Dr. Bruce's work will greatly benefit many modern readers because his studies carefully examine how the disciples grew as a result of their relationship with the Master. The contemporary church needs to remember that the invaluable information gleaned from the social scientist about human behaviour must never be seen as a substitute for a personal relationship with the living Lord Jesus similar to that enjoyed by the twelve as they walked the highways and byways together. How they heard His word, studied His reactions, fulfilled His commands and repsonded to His promises is faithfully recorded for us in Scripture and beautifully applied to our situations in this book.

Personally, I have found _The Training of the Twelve_ of immense value for reasons other than those listed above. When preaching through the Gospels I have constantly referred to this book and found it to be an excellent commentary. In addition, I have often sat down and read chapters for no other reason than I needed the nourishment that comes to me only from the devotional application of Scripture to my own soul. Few expositors have done more for me than A. B. Bruce in this regard.

Perhaps the best recommendation that I can give the book, however, is to tell you that although I have many hundreds of books in my growing library, all carefully catalogued and filed, shelved and ordered, I have just realised that _The Training of the Twelve_ has never been officially included in my library! The reason is simple. Ever since I purchased my copy, years ago, it has stayed either on my desk or at my elbow with a handful of other books which I need to refer to constantly. I just haven't been able to part with it long enough to let my secretary put it in its proper place! On second thought, it is in its proper place right where I can get hold of it quickly. I hope your copy will find such a place in your life and experience.

D. STUART BRISCOE

PREFACE TO THE SECOND EDITION

ON receiving notice from the publisher that a second edition of *The Training of the Twelve* which first appeared in 1871, was called for, I was obliged to consider the question what alterations should be made on a work which, though written with care, was too obviously, to my maturer judgment, stamped with imperfection. Two alternatives suggested themselves to my mind. One was to recast the whole, so as to give it a more critical and scientific character, and make it bear more directly on current controversies respecting the origin of Christianity. The other was to allow the book to remain substantially as it was, retaining its popular form, and limiting alterations to details susceptible of improvement without change of plan. After a little hesitation, I decided for the latter course, for the following reasons. From expressions of opinion that reached me from many and very diverse quarters, I had come to be convinced that the book was appreciated and found useful, and I thence concluded that, notwithstanding its faults, it might continue to be of service in its primitive shape. Then, considering how difficult in all things it is to serve two masters or accomplish at once two ends, I saw that the adoption of the former of the two alternative courses was tantamount to writing a new book, which could be done, if necessary, independently of the present publication. I confess to having a vague plan of such a work in my head, which may or may not be carried into effect. The Tübingen school of critics, with whose works English readers are now becoming acquainted through translations, maintain that catholic Christianity was the result of a compromise or reconciliation between two radically opposed tendencies, represented respectively by the original apostles and by Paul, the two tendencies being Judaistic exclusiveness on the one hand, and Pauline universalism on the other. The twelve said : Christianity for Jews, and all who are willing to become Jews by compliance with Jewish custom ; Paul said : Christianity for the whole world, and for all on the same terms. Now the material dealt with in *The Training of the Twelve*, must, from the nature of the case, have some bearing on this conflict-hypothesis of Dr. Baur and his friends. The question arises, What was to be expected of *the men that were with Jesus ?* and the consideration of this question would form an important division of such a controversial work as I have in view. Another chapter might consider the part assigned to Peter in the Acts of the Apostles (alleged by the same school of critics to be a part invented for him by the writer for an apologetic purpose), seeking especially to determine whether it was a likely part for him to play — likely in view of his idiosyncrasies, or the training he had received. Another appropriate topic would be the character of the Apostle John, as portrayed in the synoptical Gospels, in its bearing on the questions of the authorship of the fourth Gospel, and the hostility to Paul and his universalism alleged to be manifested in the Book of Revelation. In such a work there would further fall to be considered the materials bearing on the same theme in other parts of the New Testament, especially those to be found in the Epistle to the Galatians. Finally, there might not inappropriately be found a place in such a work for a discussion of the question, How far do the synoptical Gospels — the principal sources of information regarding the teaching and public actions of Christ — bear traces of the influence of controversial or conciliatory tendencies ? e.g. what ground is there for the assertion that the mission of the seventy is an invention in the interest of

Pauline universalism intended to throw the original apostles
into the shade?

In the present work I have not attempted to develop the
argument here outlined, but have merely indicated the places
at which the different points of the argument might come in,
and the way in which they might be used. The conflict-
hypothesis was not absent from my mind in writing the
book at first; but I was neither so well acquainted with
the literature relating thereto, nor so sensible of its importance, as I am now.

In preparing this new edition for the press, I have not lost
sight of any hints from friendly critics which might tend to
make it more acceptable and useful. In particular, I have
kept steadily in view retrenchment of the homiletic element,
though I am sensible that I may still have retained too much
for some tastes, but I hope not too much for the generality
of readers. I have had to remember, that while some friends
called for condensation, others have complained that the
matter was too closely packed. I have also had occasion to
observe in my reading of books on the Gospel history that it
is possible to be so brief and sketchy as to miss not only the
latent connections of thought, but even the thoughts themselves. The changes have not all been in the direction of
retrenchment. While not a few paragraphs have been cancelled or reduced in bulk, other new ones have been added,
and in one or two instances whole pages have been rewritten.
Among the more important additions may be mentioned a
note at the end of the chapter relating to the farewell discourse, giving an analysis of the discourse into its compo-
nent parts; and a concluding paragraph at the end of the
work summing up the instructions which the twelve had
received from Jesus during the time they had been with
Him. Besides these, a feature of this edition is a series of
footnotes referring to some of the principal recent publications, British and foreign, whose contents relate more or less
to the Gospel history, such as the works of Keim, Pfleiderer,
Golani, Farrar, Sanday, and *Supernatural Religion*. The

notes referring to Mr. Sanday's work bear on the important question, how far we have in John's Gospel a reliable record of the words spoken by Jesus to His disciples on the eve of His passion.

Besides the index of passages discussed which appeared in the first edition, this edition contains a carefully-prepared table of contents at the end, which it is hoped will add to the utility of the work. To make the bearing of the contents on the training of the disciples more apparent, I have in several instances changed the titles of chapters, or supplied alternative titles.

With these explanations, I send forth this new edition, with grateful feelings for the kind reception which the work has already received, and in the hope that by the divine blessing it may continue to be of use as an attempt to illustrate an interesting and important theme.

A. B. B.

1

BEGINNINGS

John 1:29-51

THE section of the Gospel history above indicated, possesses the interest peculiar to the beginnings of all things that have grown to greatness. Here are exhibited to our view the infant church in its cradle, the petty sources of the River of Life, the earliest blossoms of Christian faith, the humble origin of the mighty empire of the Lord Jesus Christ.

All beginnings are more or less obscure in appearance, but none were ever more obscure than those of Christianity. What an insignificant event in the history of the church, not to say of the world, this first meeting of Jesus of Nazareth with five humble men, Andrew, Peter, Philip, Nathanael, and another unnamed! It actually seems almost too trivial to find a place even in the evangelic narrative. For we have here to do not with any formal solemn call to the great office of the apostleship, or even with the commencement of an uninterrupted discipleship, but at the utmost with the beginnings of an acquaintance with and of faith in Jesus on the part of certain individuals who subsequently became constant attendants on His person, and ultimately apostles of His religion. Accordingly we find no mention made in the three first Gospels of the events here recorded.

Far from being surprised at the silence of the synoptical

evangelists, one is rather tempted to wonder how it came
to pass that John, the author of the fourth Gospel, after the
lapse of so many years, thought it worth while to relate
incidents so minute, especially in such close proximity to
the sublime sentences with which his Gospel begins. But
we are kept from such incredulous wonder by the reflection,
that facts objectively insignificant may be very important to
the feelings of those whom they personally concern. What
if John were himself one of the five who on the present
occasion became acquainted with Jesus? That would make
a wide difference between him and the other evangelists,
who could know of the incidents here related, if they knew
of them at all, only at second hand. In the case supposed, it
would not be surprising that to his latest hour John remembered with emotion the first time he saw the Incarnate
Word, and deemed the minutest memorials of that time
unspeakably precious. First meetings are sacred as well as
last ones, especially such as are followed by a momentous
history, and accompanied, as is apt to be the case, with
omens prophetic of the future.[1] Such omens were not
wanting in connection with the first meeting between Jesus
and the five disciples. Did not the Baptist then first give
to Jesus the name "Lamb of God," so exactly descriptive
of His earthly mission and destiny? Was not Nathanael's
doubting question, "Can any good thing come out of Nazareth?" an ominous indication of a conflict with unbelief
awaiting the Messiah? And what a happy omen of an
opening era of wonders to be wrought by divine grace and
power was contained in the promise of Jesus to the pious,
though at first doubting, Israelite : "Henceforth ye shall see
heaven open, and the angels of God ascending and descending upon the Son of man"!
    That John, the writer of the fourth Gospel, really was the
fifth unnamed disciple, may be regarded as certain. It is his
way throughout his Gospel, when alluding to himself, to use
a periphrasis, or to leave, as here, a blank where his name
should be. One of the two disciples who heard the Baptist
call Jesus the Lamb of God was the evangelist himself,
Andrew, Simon Peter's brother, being the other.[2]

---

[1] Omina principiis inesse solent. — Ovid. *Fast.* i. 178.   [2] Ver. 41.

The impressions produced on our minds by these little anecdotes of the infancy of the Gospel must be feeble, indeed, as compared with the emotions awakened by the memory of them in the breast of the aged apostle by whom they are recorded. It would not, however, be creditable either to our intelligence or to our piety if we could peruse this page of the evangelic history unmoved, as if it were utterly devoid of interest. We should address ourselves to the study of the simple story with somewhat of the feeling with which men make pilgrimages to sacred places; for indeed the ground is holy.

The scene of the occurrences in which we are concerned was in the region of Peræa, on the banks of the Jordan, at the lower part of its course. The persons who make their appearance on the scene were all natives of Galilee, and their presence here is due to the fame of the remarkable man whose office it was to be the forerunner of the Christ. John, surnamed the Baptist, who had spent his youth in the desert as a hermit, living on locusts and wild honey, and clad in a garment of camel's hair, had come forth from his retreat, and appeared among men as a prophet of God. The burden of his prophecy was, " Repent, for the kingdom of heaven is at hand." In a short time many were attracted from all quarters to see and hear him. Of those who flocked to his preaching, the greater number went as they came; but not a few were deeply impressed, and, confessing their sins, underwent the rite of baptism in the waters of the Jordan. Of those who were baptized, a select number formed themselves into a circle of disciples around the person of the Baptist, among whom were at least two, and most probably the whole, of the five men mentioned by the evangelist. Previous converse with the Baptist had awakened in these disciples a desire to see Jesus, and prepared them for believing in Him. In his communications to the people around him John made frequent allusions to One who should come after himself. He spoke of this coming One in language fitted to awaken great expectations. He called himself, with reference to the coming One, a mere voice in the wilderness, crying, " Prepare ye the way of the Lord." At another time he said, " I baptize with water; but there standeth One among you whom ye know not : He it is who, coming after me, is preferred before me, whose shoe's latchet I am not worthy to unloose." This great One was none other than the Messiah, the Son of God, the King of Israel.

Such discourses were likely to result, and by the man of God who uttered them they were intended to result, in the disciples of the Baptist leaving him and going over to Jesus. And we see here the process of transition actually com- mencing. We do not affirm that the persons here named finally quitted the Baptist's company at this time, to become henceforth regular followers of Jesus. But an acquaintance now begins which will end in that. The bride is introduced to the Bridegroom, and the marriage will come in due season ; not to the chagrin but to the joy of the Bridegroom's friend.[1]

How easily and artlessly does the mystic bride, as repre- sented by these five disciples, become acquainted with her heavenly Bridegroom ! The account of their meeting is idyllic in its simplicity, and would only be spoiled by a com- mentary. There is no need of formal introduction : they all introduce each other. Even John and Andrew were not formally introduced to Jesus by the Baptist ; they rather introduced themselves. The exclamation of the desert prophet on seeing Jesus, " Behold the Lamb of God, which taketh away the sin of the world !" repeated next day in an abbreviated form, was the involuntary utterance of one absorbed in his own thoughts, rather than the deliberate speech of one who was directing his disciples to leave himself and go over to Him of whom he spake. The two disciples, on the other hand, in going away after the personage whose presence had been so impressively announced, were not obey- ing an order given by their old master, but were simply follow- ing the dictates of feelings which had been awakened in their breasts by all they had heard him say of Jesus, both on the present and on former occasions. They needed no injunction to seek the acquaintance of one in whom they felt so keenly interested : all they needed was to know that this was He. They were as anxious to see the Messianic King as the world is to see the face of a secular prince.

[1] John iii. 29.

It is natural that we should scan the evangelic narrative for indications of character with reference to those who, in the way so quaintly described, for the first time met Jesus. Little is said of the five disciples, but there is enough to show that they were all pious men. What they found in their new friend indicates what they wanted to find. They evidently belonged to the select band who waited for the consolation of Israel, and anxiously looked for Him who should fulfil God's promises and realize the hopes of all devout souls. Besides this general indication of character supplied in their common confession of faith, a few facts are stated respecting these first believers in Jesus tending to make us a little better acquainted with them. Two of them certainly, all of them probably, had been disciples of the Baptist. This fact is decisive as to their moral earnestness. From such a quarter none but spiritually earnest men were likely to come. For if the followers of John were at all like himself, they were men who hungered and thirsted after real righteousness, being sick of the righteousness then in vogue ; they said Amen in their hearts to the preacher's withering exposure of the hollowness of current religious profession and of the worthlessness of fashionable good works, and sighed for a sanctity other than that of pharisaic superstition and ostentation ; their conscience acknowledged the truth of the prophetic oracle, " We are all as an unclean thing, and all our righteousnesses are as filthy rags ; and we all do fade as a leaf, and our iniquities like the wind have taken us away ; " and they prayed fervently for the reviving of true religion, for the coming of the divine kingdom, for the advent of the Messianic King with fan in His hand to separate chaff from wheat, and to put right all things which were wrong. Such, without doubt, were the sentiments of those who had the honor to be the first disciples of Christ.

Simon, best known of all the twelve under the name of Peter, is introduced to us here, through the prophetic insight of Jesus, on the good side of his character as the man of rock. When this disciple was brought by his brother Andrew into the presence of his future Master, Jesus, we are told, " beheld him and said, Thou art Simon the son of Jona : thou shalt be called Cephas " — Cephas meaning in Syriac, as the evangelist explains, the same which Petros signifies in Greek. The penetrating glance of Christ discerned in this disciple latent capacities of faith and devotion, the rudiments of ultimate strength and power.

What manner of man Philip was the evangelist does not directly tell us, but merely whence he came. From the present passage, and from other notices in the Gospels, the conclusion has been drawn that he was characteristically deliberate, slow in arriving at decision ; and for proof of this view, reference has been made to the "phlegmatic circumstantiality" [1] with which he described to Nathanael the person of Him with whom he had just become acquainted.[2] But these words of Philip, and all that we elsewhere read of him, rather suggest to us the idea of the earnest inquirer after truth, who has thoroughly searched the Scriptures and made himself acquainted with the Messiah of promise and prophecy, and to whom the knowledge of God is the *summum bonum*. In the solicitude manifested by this disciple to win his friend Nathanael over to the same faith we recognize that generous sympathetic spirit, characteristic of earnest inquirers, which afterwards revealed itself in him when he became the bearer of the request of devout Greeks for permission to see Jesus.[3]

The notices concerning Nathanael, Philip's acquaintance, are more detailed and more interesting than in the case of any other of the five ; and it is not a little surprising that we should be told so much in this place about one concerning whom we otherwise know almost nothing. It is even not quite certain that he belonged to the circle of the twelve, though the probability is, that he is to be identified with the Bartholomew of the synoptical catalogues — his full name in that case being Nathanael the son of Tolmai. It is strongly in favor of this supposition that the name Bartholomew comes immediately after Philip in the lists of the apostles.[4] Be this as it may, we know on the best authority that Nathanael was a man of great moral excellence. No sooner had Jesus seen him than He exclaimed, "Behold an Israelite

[1] Luthardt, *Das Johan. Evang.* i. 102.   [2] Ver. 45.   [3] John xii. 22.
[4] Ewald lays stress on this in proof of the identity of the two, *Geschichte Christus*, p. 327. In Acts i. 13 Thomas comes between Philip and Bartholomew.

indeed, in whom is no guile!" The words suggest the idea of one whose heart was pure ; in whom was no doubleminded-ness, impure motive, pride, or unholy passion : a man of gentle, meditative spirit, in whose mind heaven lay reflected like the blue sky in a still lake on a calm summer day. He was a man much addicted to habits of devotion : he had been engaged in spiritual exercises under cover of a fig-tree just before he met with Jesus. So we are justified in concluding, from the deep impression made on his mind by the words of Jesus, " Before that Philip called thee, when thou wast under the fig-tree, I saw thee." Nathanael appears to have understood these words as meaning, " I saw into thy heart, and knew how thou wast occupied, and therefore I pronounced thee an Israelite indeed." He accepted the statement made to him by Jesus as an evidence of preternatural knowledge, and therefore he forthwith made the confession, " Rabbi ! Thou art the Son of God ; Thou art the *King* of Israel" — the King of that sacred commonwealth whereof you say I am a citizen.

It is remarkable that this man, so highly endowed with the moral dispositions necessary for seeing God, should have been the only one of all the five disciples who manifested any hesitancy about receiving Jesus as the Christ. When Philip told him that he had found the Messiah in Jesus of Nazareth, he asked incredulously, " Can there any good thing come out of Nazareth ? " One hardly expects such prejudice in one so meek and amiable ; and yet, on reflection, we per-ceive it to be quite characteristic. Nathanael's prejudice against Nazareth sprung not from pride, as in the case of the people of Judæa who despised the Galileans in general, but from humility. He was a Galilean himself, and as much an object of Jewish contempt as were the Nazarenes. His inward thought was, " Surely the Messiah can never come from among a poor despised people such as we are — from Nazareth or any other Galilean town or village ! " [1] He tim-idly allowed his mind to be biassed by a current opinion origi-nating in feelings with which he had no sympathy ; a fault

---

[1] Stanley thinks Nathanael meant to single out Nazareth from the rest of Galilee as of specially bad notoriety. In that case the argument would be *à fortiori:* Can any good come out of Galilee, and specially from Nazareth, infamous even there? — *Sinai and Palestine,* p. 366.

common to men whose piety, though pure and sincere, defers too much to human authority, and who thus become the slaves of sentiments utterly unworthy of them.

While Nathanael was not free from prejudices, he showed his guilelessness in being willing to have them removed. He came and saw. This openness to conviction is the mark of moral integrity. The guileless man dogmatizes not, but investigates, and therefore always comes right in the end. The man of bad, dishonest heart, on the contrary, does not come and see. Deeming it his interest to remain in his present mind, he studiously avoids looking at aught which does not tend to confirm his foregone conclusions. He may, indeed, *profess* a desire for inquiry, like certain Israelites of whom we read in this same Gospel, of another stamp than Nathanael, but sharing with him the prejudice against Galilee. " Search and look," said these Israelites not without guile, in reply to the ingenuous question of the honest but timid Nicodemus : "Doth our law judge any man before it hear him, and know what he doeth ?" "Search and look," said they, appealing to observation and inviting inquiry ; but they added : " For out of Galilee ariseth no prophet " [1] — a dictum which at once prohibited inquiry in effect, and intimated that it was unnecessary. " Search and look ; but we tell you beforehand you cannot arrive at any other conclusion than ours ; nay, we warn you, you had better not."

Such were the characters of the men who first believed in Jesus. What, now, was the amount and value of their belief ? On first view the faith of the five disciples, leaving out of account the brief hesitation of Nathanael, seems unnaturally sudden and mature. They believe in Jesus on a moment's notice, and they express their faith in terms which seem appropriate only to advanced Christian intelligence. In the present section of John's Gospel we find Jesus called not merely the Christ, the Messiah, the King of Israel, but the Son of God and the Lamb of God — names expressive to us of the cardinal doctrines of Christianity, the Incarnation and the Atonement.

The haste and maturity which seem to characterize the

---

[1] John vii. 52. The Revised Version has : " Search and see that out of Galilee ariseth no prophet."

faith of the five disciples are only superficial appearances. As to the former : these men believed that Messiah was to come some time ; and they wished much it might be then, for they felt He was greatly needed. They were men who waited for the consolation of Israel, and they were prepared at any moment to witness the advent of the Comforter. Then the Baptist had told them that the Christ was come, and that He was to be found in the person of Him whom he had baptized, and whose baptism had been accompanied with such remarkable signs from heaven ; and what the Baptist said they implicitly believed. Finally, the impression produced on their minds by the bearing of Jesus when they met, tended to confirm John's testimony, being altogether worthy of the Christ.

The appearance of *maturity* in the faith of the five brethren is equally superficial. As to the name Lamb of God, it was given to Jesus by John, not by them. It was, so to speak, the *baptismal* name which the preacher of repentance had learned by reflection, or by special revelation, to give to the Christ. What the name signified even he but dimly comprehended, the very repetition of it showing him to be but a learner striving to get up his lesson ; and we know that what John understood only in part, the men whom he introduced to the acquaintance of Jesus, now and for long after, understood not at all.[1]

The title Son of God was given to Jesus by one of the five disciples as well as by the Baptist, a title which even the apostles in after years found sufficient to express their mature belief respecting the Person of their Lord. But it does not follow that the name was used by them at the beginning with the same fulness of meaning as at the end. It was a name which could be used in a sense coming far short of that which it is capable of conveying, and which it did convey in apostolic preaching — merely as one of the Old Testament titles

[1] The use of such a title by John at such an early period does certainly give one a surprise. And yet is it not more surprising to find such a passage as the fifty-third chapter of Isaiah, on *any* interpretation of it, in an Old Testament book? And being there, why wonder that this title was in John's mouth ? That John understood the full import of his own words we are not bound, or even entitled, to believe. Why should not the utterance be as much a mystery for him as, according to the Apostle Peter, similar utterances by older prophets were to them ?

of Messiah, a synonyme for Christ. It was doubtless in this rudimentary sense that Nathanael applied the designation to Him, whom he also called the King of Israel.

The faith of these brethren was, therefore, just such as we should expect in beginners. In substance it amounted to this, that they recognized in Jesus the Divine Prophet, King, Son of Old Testament prophecy; and its value lay not in its maturity, or accuracy, but in this, that however imperfect, it brought them into contact and close fellowship with Him, in whose company they were to see greater things than when they first believed, one truth after another assuming its place in the firmament of their minds, like the stars appearing in the evening sky as daylight fades away.

2

FISHERS OF MEN

Matt. 4:18-22; Mark 1:16-20; Luke 5:1-11

THE twelve arrived at their final intimate relation to Jesus only by degrees, three stages in the history of their fellowship with Him being distinguishable. In the first stage they were simply believers in Him as the Christ, and His occasional companions at convenient, particularly festive, seasons. Of this earliest stage in the intercourse of the disciples with their Master we have some memorials in the four first chapters of John's Gospel, which tell how some of them first became acquainted with Jesus, and represent them as accompanying Him at a marriage in Cana,[1] at a passover in Jerusalem,[2] on a visit to the scene of the Baptist's ministry,[3] and on the return journey through Samaria from the south to Galilee.[4]

In the second stage, fellowship with Christ assumed the form of an uninterrupted attendance on His person, involving entire, or at least habitual abandonment of secular occupations.[5] The present narratives bring under our view certain of the disciples entering on this second stage of discipleship. Of the four persons here named, we recognize three, Peter, Andrew, and John, as old acquaintances, who have already passed through the first stage of discipleship. One of them, James the brother of John, we meet with for the first time ; a fact which suggests the remark, that in some cases the first and second stages may have been blended together — professions of faith in Jesus as the Christ being immediately followed by the renunciation of secular callings

---

[1] John ii. 1.　　　　　　　[2] John ii. 13, 17, 22.
[3] John iii. 22.　　　　　　[4] John iv. 1-27, 31, 43-45.
[5] Entire in Matthew's case, of course; in the case of the fishers, not necessarily so.

for the purpose of joining His company. Such cases, however, were probably exceptional and few.

The twelve entered on the last and highest stage of discipleship when they were chosen by their Master from the mass of His followers, and formed into a select band, to be trained for the great work of the apostleship. This important event probably did not take place till all the members of the apostolic circle had been for some time about the person of Jesus.

From the evangelic records it appears that Jesus began at a very early period of His ministry to gather round Him a company of disciples, with a view to the preparation of an agency for carrying on the work of the divine kingdom. The two pairs of brothers received their call at the commencement of the first Galilean ministry, in which the first act was the selection of Capernaum by the seaside as the centre of operations and ordinary place of abode.[1] And when we think what they were called unto, we see that the call could not come too soon. The twelve were to be Christ's witnesses in the world after He Himself had left it; it was to be their peculiar duty to give to the world a faithful account of their Master's words and deeds, a just image of His character, a true reflection of His spirit.[2] This service obviously could be rendered only by persons who had been, as nearly as possible, eye-witnesses and servants of the Incarnate Word from the beginning. While, therefore, except in the cases of Peter, James, John, Andrew, and Matthew, we have no particulars in the Gospels respecting the calls of those who afterwards became apostles, we must assume that they all occurred in the first year of the Saviour's public ministry.

That these calls were given with conscious reference to an ulterior end, even the apostleship, appears from the remarkable terms in which the earliest of them was expressed. " Follow Me," said Jesus to the fishermen of Bethsaida, "and I will make you fishers of men." These words (whose origi-

---

[1] Matt. iv. 13.

[2] It is not assumed here that the Gospels, as we have them, were written by apostles. The statement in the text implies only that the teaching of the apostles, whether oral or written, was the ultimate source of the evangelic traditions recorded in the Gospels.

nality stamps them as a genuine saying of Jesus) show that the great Founder of the faith desired not only to have disciples, but to have about Him men whom He might train to make disciples of others : to cast the net of divine truth into the sea of the world, and to land on the shores of the divine kingdom a great multitude of believing souls. Both from His words and from His actions we can see that He attached supreme importance to that part of His work which consisted in training the twelve. In the intercessory prayer,[1] *e.g.*, He speaks of the training He had given these men as if it had been the principal part of His own earthly ministry. And such, in one sense, it really was. The careful, painstaking education of the disciples secured that the Teacher's influence on the world should be permanent ; that His kingdom should be founded on the rock of deep and indestructible convictions in the minds of the few, not on the shifting sands of superficial evanescent impressions on the minds of the many. Regarding that kingdom, as our Lord Himself has taught us in one of His parables to do,[2] as a thing introduced into the world like a seed cast into the ground and left to grow according to natural laws, we may say that, but for the twelve, the doctrine, the works, and the image of Jesus might have perished from human remembrance, nothing remaining but a vague mythical tradition, of no historical value, and of little practical influence.

Those on whom so much depended, it plainly behoved to possess very extraordinary qualifications. The mirrors must be finely polished that are designed to reflect the image of Christ ! The apostles of the Christian religion must be men of rare spiritual endowment. It is a *catholic* religion, intended for all nations ; therefore its apostles must be free from Jewish narrowness, and have sympathies wide as the world. It is a *spiritual* religion, destined ere long to antiquate Jewish ceremonialism ; therefore its apostles must be emancipated in conscience from the yoke of ordinances.[3] It is a religion, once more, which is to proclaim the Cross, pre-

---

[1] John xvii. 6.   [2] Mark iv. 26.
[3] Universality and Spirituality are admitted by the Tübingen school to have been attributes of the religion of Jesus as set forth by Himself. This is an important fact in connection with their conflict-hypothesis.

viously an instrument of cruelty and badge of infamy, as the hope of the world's redemption, and the symbol of all that is noble and heroic in conduct ; therefore its heralds must be superior to all conventional notions of human and divine dignity, capable of glorying in the cross of Christ, and willing to bear a cross themselves. The apostolic character, in short, must combine freedom of conscience, enlargement of heart, enlightenment of mind, and all in the superlative degree.

The humble fishermen of Galilee had much to learn before they could satisfy these high requirements ; so much, that the time of their apprenticeship for their apostolic work, even reckoning it from the very commencement of Christ's ministry, seems all too short. They were indeed godly men, who had already shown the sincerity of their piety by forsaking all for their Master's sake. But at the time of their call they were exceedingly ignorant, narrow-minded, superstitious, full of Jewish prejudices, misconceptions, and animosities. They had much to unlearn of what was bad, as well as much to learn of what was good, and they were slow both to learn and to unlearn. Old beliefs already in possession of their minds made the communication of new religious ideas a difficult task. Men of good honest heart, the soil of their spiritual nature was fitted to produce an abundant harvest ; but it was stiff, and needed much laborious tillage before it would yield its fruit. Then, once more, they were poor men, of humble birth, low station, mean occupations, who had never felt the stimulating influence of a liberal education, or of social intercourse with persons of cultivated minds.[1]

We shall meet with abundant evidence of the crude spiritual condition of the twelve, even long after the period when they were called to follow Jesus, as we proceed with the studies on which we have entered. Meantime we may discover significant indications of the religious immaturity of at

[1] Throughout this work great prominence is given to the moral and spiritual defects of the twelve. But we must protest at the outset against the inference that such men must remain permanently disqualified for the task of being the apostles of the universal religion, the religion of humanity. Everything may be hoped of men who could leave all for Christ's society. Where there is a noble soul, there is an indefinite capacity of growth.

least one of the disciples — Simon, son of Jonas — in Luke's account of the incidents connected with his call. Pressed by the multitude who had assembled on the shore of the lake to hear Him preach, Jesus, we read, entered into a ship (one of two lying near at hand), which happened to be Simon's, and requesting him to thrust out a little from the land, sat down, and taught the people from the vessel. Having finished speaking, Jesus said unto the owner of the boat, "Launch out into the deep, and let down your nets for a draught." Their previous efforts to catch fish had been unsuccessful; but Simon and his brother did as Jesus directed, and were rewarded by an extraordinary take, which appeared to them and their fishing companions, James and John, nothing short of miraculous. Simon, the most impressible and the most demonstrative of the four, gave utterance to his feelings of astonishment by characteristic words and gestures. He fell down at Jesus' knees, saying, "Depart from me, for I am a sinful man, O Lord!"

This exclamation opens a window into the inner man of him who uttered it through which we can see his spiritual state. We observe in Peter at this time that mixture of good and evil, of grace and nature, which so frequently reappears in his character in the subsequent history. Among the good elements discernible are reverential awe in presence of Divine Power, a prompt calling to mind of sin betraying tenderness of conscience, and an unfeigned self-humiliation on account of unmerited favor. Valuable features of character these; but they did not exist in Peter without alloy. Along with them were associated superstitious dread of the supernatural and a slavish fear of God. The presence of the former element is implied in the reassuring exhortation addressed to the disciple by Jesus, "Fear not; from henceforth thou shalt catch men." Slavish fear of God is even more manifest in his own words, "Depart from me, O Lord." Powerfully impressed with the superhuman knowledge revealed in connection with the great draught of fishes, he regards Jesus for the moment as a supernatural being, and as such dreads Him as one whom it is not safe to be near, especially for a poor sinful mortal like himself. This state of mind shows how utterly unfit

Peter is, as yet, to be an apostle of a Gospel which magnifies the grace of God even to the chief of sinners. His piety, sufficiently strong and decided, is not of a Christian type; it is legal, one might almost say pagan, in spirit.

With all their imperfections, which were both numerous and great, these humble fishermen of Galilee had, at the very outset of their career, one grand distinguishing virtue, which, though it may co-exist with many defects, is the cardinal virtue of Christian ethics, and the certain forerunner of ultimate high attainment. They were animated by a devotion to Jesus and to the divine kingdom which made them capable of any sacrifice. Believing Him who bade them follow Him to be the Christ, come to set up God's kingdom on earth, they " straightway " left their nets and joined his company, to be thenceforth His constant companions in all His wanderings. The act was acknowledged by Jesus Himself to be meritorious; and we cannot, without injustice, seek to disparage it by ascribing it to idleness, discontent, or ambition as its motive. The Gospel narrative shows that the four brethren were not idle, but hard-working, industrious men. Neither were they discontented, if for no other reason than that they had no cause for discontent. The family of James and John at least seems to have been in circumstances of comfort; for Mark relates that, when called by Jesus, they left their father Zebedee in the ship with the hired servants, and went after Him. But ambition, had it no place among their motives ? Well, we must admit that the twelve, and especially James and John, were by no means free from ambitious passions, as we shall see hereafter. But to whatever extent ambition may have influenced their conduct at a later period, it was not the motive which determined them to leave their nets. Ambition needs a temptation : it does not join a cause which is obscure and struggling, and whose success is doubtful; it strikes in when success is assured, and when the movement it patronizes is on the eve of its glorification. The cause of Jesus had not got to that stage yet.

One charge only can be brought against those men, and it can be brought with truth, and without doing their memory any harm. They were *enthusiasts:* their hearts were fired, and, as an unbelieving world might say, their heads were turned by a dream about a divine kingdom to be set up in Israel, with Jesus of Nazareth for its king. That dream possessed them, and imperiously ruled over their minds and shaped their destinies, compelling them, like Abraham, to leave their kindred and their country, and to go forth on what might well appear beforehand to be a fool's errand. Well for the world that they were possessed by the idea of the kingdom! For it was no fool's errand on which they went forth, leaving their nets behind. The kingdom they sought turned out to be as real as the land of Canaan, though not such altogether as they had imagined. The fishermen of Galilee did become fishers of men on a most extensive scale, and, by the help of God, gathered many souls into the church of such as should be saved. In a sense they are casting their nets into the sea of the world still, and, by their testimony to Jesus in Gospel and Epistle, are bringing multitudes to become disciples of Him among whose first followers they had the happiness to be numbered.

The four, the twelve, forsook *all* and followed their Master. Did the "all" in any case include wife and children? It did in at least one instance — that of Peter; for the Gospels tell how Peter's mother-in-law was healed of a fever by the miraculous power of Christ.[1] From a passage in Paul's first epistle to the Corinthian church, it appears that Peter was not the only one among the apostles who was married.[2] From the same passage we further learn, that forsaking of wives for Christ's sake did not mean literal desertion. Peter the apostle led his wife about with him, and Peter the disciple may sometimes have done the same. The likelihood is that the married disciples, like married soldiers, took their wives with them or left them at home, as circumstances might require or admit. Women, even married women, did sometimes follow Jesus; and the wife of Simon, or of any other married disciple, may occasionally have been among the number. At an advanced period in the history we find the *mother* of James and John in Christ's company far from home; and where mothers were, wives, if they wished, might also be. The infant church, in its original nomadic or itinerant state,

---

[1] Matt. viii. 14; Mark i. 29-31; Luke iv. 38, 39. [2] 1 Cor. ix. 5.

seems to have been a motley band of pilgrims, in which all sorts of people as to sex, social position, and moral character were united, the bond of union being ardent attachment to the person of Jesus.

This church itinerant was not a regularly organized society, of which it was necessary to be a constant member in order to true discipleship.   Except in the case of the twelve, following Jesus from place to place was optional, not compulsory ; and in most cases it was probably also only occasional.[1] It was the natural consequence of faith, when the object of faith, the centre of the circle, was Himself in motion. Believers would naturally desire to see as many of Christ's works and hear as many of His words as possible.   When the object of faith left the earth, and His presence became spiritual, all occasion for such nomadic discipleship was done away.   To be present with Him thereafter, men needed only to forsake their *sins.*

---

[1] The words recorded in Luke xxii. 28, as spoken by Jesus to the disciples on the night before His death, " Ye are they who have continued with me in my temptations," might be referred to as tending to prove both the continuousness of the companionship of *the twelve* with Jesus and the early date of its commencement.   The saying is directly intended to bear testimony to the fidelity of the disciples, but it bears indirect testimony on the other points also.   They had been with their Master, if not as a constituted body of twelve, at least as individuals, from the time He began to have "temptations," which was very early, and they had been with Him throughout them all.

3

MATTHEW THE PUBLICAN

Matt. 9:9-13; Mark 2:15-17; Luke 5:27-32

THE call of Matthew signally illustrates a very prominent feature in the public action of Jesus, viz., His utter disregard of the maxims of worldly wisdom. A publican disciple, much more a publican apostle, could not fail to be a stumbling-block to Jewish prejudice, and therefore to be, for the time at least, a source of weakness rather than of strength. Yet, while perfectly aware of this fact, Jesus invited to the intimate fellowship of disciplehood one who had pursued the occupation of a tax-gatherer, and at a later period selected him to be one of the twelve. His procedure in this case is all the more remarkable when contrasted with the manner in which He treated others having outward advantages to recommend them to favorable notice, and who showed their readiness to follow by volunteering to become disciples ; of whom we have a sample in the scribe who came and said, " Master, I will follow Thee whithersoever Thou goest." [1] This man, whose social position and professional attainments seemed to point him out as a very desirable acquisition, the " Master" deliberately scared away by a gloomy picture of his own destitute condition, saying, " The foxes have holes, and the birds of the air have nests,[2] but the Son of man hath not where to lay His head."

The eye of Jesus was single as well as omniscient : He looked on the heart, and had respect solely to spiritual fitness. He had no faith in any discipleship based on misapprehensions and by-ends ; and, on the other hand, He had no fear of the drawbacks arising out of the external connections or past history of true believers, but was entirely indifferent

---

[1] Matt. viii. 18· 20.   [2] More correctly, roosts, or lodging-places.

to men's antecedents. Confident in the power of truth, He chose the base things of the world in preference to things held in esteem, assured that they would conquer at the last. Aware that both He and His disciples would be despised and rejected of men for a season, He went calmly on His way, choosing for His companions and agents "whom He would," undisturbed by the gainsaying of His generation — *like one who knew that His work concerned all nations and all time.*

The publican disciple bears two names in the Gospel history. In the first Gospel he is called Matthew, while in the second and third Gospels he is called Levi. That the same person is intended, may, we think, be regarded as a matter of certainty.[1] It is hardly conceivable that two publicans should have been called to be disciples at the same place and time, and with all accompanying circumstances, and these so remarkable, precisely similar. We need not be surprised that the identity has not been notified, as the fact of the two names belonging to one individual would be so familiar to the first readers of the Gospels as to make such a piece of information superfluous.

It is not improbable that Levi was the name of this disciple before the time of his call, and that Matthew was his name as a disciple, — the new name thus becoming a symbol and memorial of the more important change in heart and life. Similar emblematic changes of name were of frequent occurrence in the beginning of the Gospel. Simon son of Jonas was transformed into Peter, Saul of Tarsus became Paul, and Joses the Cypriot got from the apostles the beautful Christian name of Barnabas (son of consolation or prophecy), by his philanthropy, and magnanimity, and spiritual wisdom, well deserved.

Matthew seems to have been employed as a collector of revenue, at the time when he was called, in the town of Capernaum, which Jesus had adopted as His place of abode. For it was while Jesus was at home "in His own city,"[2] as

---

[1] Ewald (*Christus*, pp. 364, 397) denies the identity, and asserts that Levi was not one of the twelve; yet he admits the far less certain identity of Nathanael and Bartholomew.

[2] Matt. ix. 1.

Capernaum came to be called, that the palsied man was brought to Him to be healed ; and from all the evangelists [1] we learn that it was on His way out from the house where that miracle was wrought that He saw Matthew, and spoke to him the word, " Follow Me." The inference to be drawn from these facts is plain, and it is also important, as helping to explain the apparent abruptness of the call, and the promptitude with which it was responded to. Jesus and His new disciple being fellow-townsmen, had opportunities of seeing each other before.

The time of Matthew's call cannot be precisely determined, but there is good reason for placing it before the Sermon on the Mount, of which Matthew's Gospel contains the most complete report. The fact just stated is of itself strong evidence in favor of this chronological arrangement, for so full an account of the sermon was not likely to emanate from one who did not hear it. An examination of the third Gospel converts probability into something like certainty. Luke prefixes to his abbreviated account of the sermon a notice of the constitution of the apostolic society, and represents Jesus as proceeding " with them " [2] — the twelve, whose names he has just given — to the scene where the sermon was delivered. Of course the act of constitution must have been preceded by the separate acts of calling, and by Matthew's call in particular, which accordingly is related by the third evangelist in an earlier part of his Gospel.[3] It is true the position of the call in Luke's narrative in itself proves nothing, as Matthew relates his own call after the sermon ; and as, moreover, neither one nor other systematically adheres to the chronological principle of arrangement in the construction of his story. We base our conclusion on the assumption, that when any of the evangelists professes to give the order of sequence, his statement may be relied on ; and on the observations, that Luke does manifestly commit himself to a chronological datum in making the ordination of the twelve antecedent to the preaching of the Sermon on the Mount, and that Matthew's arrangement in the early part of his Gospel is as manifestly unchronological, his matter being massed on the topical

[1] Matt. ix. 9; Mark ii. 13; Luke v. 27.   [2] Luke vi. 13-17.   [3] Luke v. 27.

principle, — ch. v.-vii. showing Jesus as a great ethical teacher; ch. viii. and ix. as a worker of miracles ; ch. x. as a master, choosing, instructing, and sending forth on an evangelistic mission the twelve disciples ; ch. xi. as a critic of His contemporaries and assertor of His own prerogatives ; ch. xii. as exposed to the contradictions of unbelief ; and ch. xiii. as teaching the doctrines of the kingdom by parables.

Passing from these subordinate points to the call itself, we observe that the narratives of the event are very brief and fragmentary. There is no intimation of any previous acquaintance such as might prepare Matthew to comply with the invitation addressed to him by Jesus. It is not to be inferred, however, that no such acquaintance existed, as we can see from the case of the four fishermen, whose call is narrated with equal abruptness in the synoptical Gospels, while we know from John's Gospel that three of them at least were previously acquainted with Jesus. The truth is, that, in regard to both calls, the evangelists concerned themselves only about the *crisis*, passing over in silence all preparatory stages, and not deeming it necessary to inform intelligent readers that, of course, neither the publican nor any other disciple blindly followed one of whom he knew nothing merely because asked or commanded to follow. The fact already ascertained, that Matthew, while a publican, resided in Capernaum, makes it absolutely certain that he knew of Jesus before he was called. No man could live in that town in those days without hearing of " mighty works " done in and around it. Heaven had been opened right above Capernaum, in view of all, and the angels had been thronging down upon the Son of man. Lepers were cleansed, and demoniacs dispossessed ; blind men received their sight, and palsied men the use of their limbs ; one woman was cured of a chronic malady, and another, daughter of a distinguished citizen, — Jairus, ruler of the synagogue, — was brought back to life from the dead. These things were done publicly, made a great noise, and were much remarked on. The evangelists relate how the people " were all amazed, insomuch that they questioned among themselves, saying, What thing is this ? what new doctrine is this ? for with authority commandeth He even the unclean spirits, and they do obey

Him ;"[1] how they glorified God, saying, "We never saw it on this fashion,"[2] or, "We have seen strange things to-day."[3] Matthew himself concludes his account of the raising of Jairus' daughter with the remark : "The fame hereof went abroad into all that land."[4]

We do not affirm that all these miracles were wrought before the time of the publican's call, but some of them certainly were. Comparing one Gospel with another, to determine the historical sequence,[5] we conclude that the greatest of all these mighty works, the last mentioned, though narrated by Matthew after his call, really occurred before it. Think, then, what a powerful effect that marvellous deed would have in preparing the tax-gatherer for recognizing, in the solemnly uttered word, "Follow me," the command of One who was Lord both of the dead and of the living, and for yielding to His bidding, prompt, unhesitating obedience!

In crediting Matthew with some previous knowledge of Christ, we make his conversion to discipleship appear reasonable without diminishing its moral value. It was not a matter of course that he should become a follower of Jesus merely because he had heard of, or even seen, His wonderful works. Miracles of themselves could make no man a believer, otherwise all the people of Capernaum should have believed. How different was the actual fact, we learn from the complaints afterwards made by Jesus concerning those towns along the shores of the Lake of Gennesareth, wherein most of His mighty works were done, and *of Capernaum in particular*. Of this city He said bitterly : "Thou, Capernaum, shalt thou be exalted unto heaven ? thou shalt go down unto Hades : for if the mighty works which have been done in thee had been done in Sodom, it would have remained until this day.[6] Christ's complaint against the inhabitants of these favored cities was that they did not *repent*, that is,

[1] Mark i. 27.   [3] Luke v. 26.
[2] Mark ii. 12.   [4] Matt. ix. 26.
[5] See Ebrard, *Gospel History*, on the subject of sequence.
[6] Matt. xi. 23. There can be little doubt that the reading μὴ ὑψωθήσῃ, in the first clause, adopted in the R. V., is the correct one. It brings Christ's prophetic word into closer correspondence with Isa. xiv. 13-15, to which there is an obvious allusion : " Thou hast said in thine heart, I will ascend unto heaven. . . . Yet thou shalt be brought down to hell."

make the kingdom of heaven their chief good and chief end.
They wondered sufficiently at His miracles, and talked abundantly of them, and ran after Him to see more works of the
same kind, and enjoy anew the sensation of amazement ; but
after a while they relapsed into their old stupidity and list-
lessness, and remained morally as they had been before He
came among them, not children of the kingdom, but children
of this world.

It was not so with the collector of customs. He not
merely wondered and talked, but he "repented." Whether
he had more to repent of than his neighbors, we cannot tell.
It is true that he belonged to a class of men who, seen
through the colored medium of popular prejudice, were all
bad alike, and many of whom were really guilty of fraud and
extortion ; but he may have been an exception. His farewell
feast shows that he possessed means, but we must not take
for granted that they were dishonestly earned. This only
we may safely say, that if the publican disciple had been
covetous, the spirit of greed was now exorcised ; if he had
ever been guilty of oppressing the poor, he now abhorred
such work. He had grown weary of collecting revenue from
a reluctant population, and was glad to follow One who had
come to take burdens off instead of laying them on, to remit
debts instead of exacting them with rigor. And so it came
to pass that the voice of Jesus acted on his heart like a spell :
" He left all, rose up, and followed Him."

This great decision, according to the account of all the
evangelists, was followed shortly after by a feast in Matthew's
house at which Jesus was present.[1] From Luke we learn
that this entertainment had all the character of a great
occasion, and that it was given in honor of Jesus. The
honor, however, was such as few would value, for the other
guests were peculiar. " There was a great company of publicans, and of others that sat down with them ; "[2] and among
the "others" were some who either were or were esteemed,
in a superlative degree, "sinners."[3]

This feast was, as we judge, not less rich in moral significance than in the viands set on the board. For the host

[1] Matthew says modestly, "in *the* house " (ix. 10).   [3] Luke v. 29.
[2] Matt. ix. 10.

himself it was, without doubt, a jubilee feast commemorative of his emancipation from drudgery and uncongenial society and sin, or, at all events, temptation to sin, and of his entrance on the free, blessed life of fellowship with Jesus. It was a kind of poem, saying for Matthew what Doddridge's familiar lines say for many another, perhaps not so well —

> "Oh happy day, that fixed my choice
> On Thee, my Saviour, and my God!
> Well may this glowing heart rejoice,
> And tell its raptures all abroad!
>
> 'Tis done; the great transaction's done:
> I am my Lord's, and He is mine;
> He drew me, and I followed on,
> Charmed to confess the voice divine."

The feast was also, as already said, an act of homage to Jesus. Matthew made his splendid feast in honor of his new master, as Mary of Bethany shed her precious ointment. It is the way of those to whom much grace is shown and given, to manifest their grateful love in deeds bearing the stamp of what a Greek philosopher called magnificence,[1] and churls call extravagance; and whoever might blame such acts of devotion, Jesus always accepted them with pleasure.

The ex-publican's feast seems further to have had the character of a farewell entertainment to his fellow-publicans. He and they were to go different ways henceforth, and he would part with his old comrades in peace.

Once more: we can believe that Matthew meant his feast to be the means of introducing his friends and neighbors to the acquaintance of Jesus, seeking with the characteristic zeal of a young disciple to induce others to take the step which he had resolved on himself, or at least hoping that some sinners present might be drawn from evil ways into the paths of righteousness. And who can tell but it was at this very festive gathering, or on some similar occasion, that the gracious impressions were produced whose final outcome was that affecting display of gratitude unutterable at that other feast in Simon's house, to which neither publicans nor sinners were admitted?

---

[1] μεγαλοπρέπεια. — ARISTOTLE'S *Ethic. Nicomach.* iv. 2.

Matthew's feast was thus, looked at from within, a very joyous, innocent, and even edifying one. But, alas! looked at from without, like stained windows, it wore a different aspect : it was, indeed, nothing short of scandalous. Certain Pharisees observed the company assemble or disperse, noted their character, and made, after their wont, sinister reflec tions. Opportunity offering itself, they asked the disciples of Jesus the at once complimentary and censorious question : "Why eateth your master with publicans and sinners ?" The interrogants were for the most part local members of the pharisaic sect, for Luke calls them "*their* scribes and Phari sees," [1] which implies that Capernaum was important enough to be honored with the presence of men representing that religious party. It is by no means unlikely, however, that among the unfriendly spectators were some Pharisees all the way from Jerusalem, the seat of ecclesiastical government, already on the track of the Prophet of Nazareth, watching His doings, as they watched those of the Baptist before Him. The news of Christ's wondrous works soon spread over all the land, and attracted spectators from all quarters — from Decapolis, Jerusalem, Judæa, and Peræa, as well as Galilee : [2] and we may be sure that the scribes and Pharisees of the holy city were not the last to go and see, for we must own they performed the duty of religious espionage with exemplary diligence.

The presence of ill-affected men belonging to the pharisaic order was almost a standing feature in Christ's public minis try. But it never disconcerted Him. He went calmly on His way doing His work ; and when His conduct was called in question, He was ever ready with a conclusive answer. Among the most striking of His answers or apologies to them who examined Him, were those in which He vindicated Himself for mixing with publicans and sinners. They are three in number, spoken on as many occasions: the first in connection with Matthew's feast ; the second in the house of Simon the Pharisee ;[3] and the third on an occasion not minutely defined, when certain scribes and Pharisees brought against Him the grave charge, " This man receiveth sinners, and eateth with them." [4] These apologies for loving the

[1] Luke v. 30.   [2] Matt. iv. 25.   [3] Luke vii. 36.   [4] Luke xv.

unloved and the morally unlovely are full of truth and grace, poetry and pathos, and not without a touch of quiet, quaint satire directed against the sanctimonious fault-finders. The first may be distinguished as the *professional* argument, and is to this effect : " I frequent the haunts of sinners, because I am a *physician*, and they are sick and need healing. Where should a physician be but among his patients ? where often-est, but among those most grievously afflicted?" The second may be described as the *political* argument, its drift being this : " It is good policy to be the friend of sinners who have much to be forgiven ; for when they are restored to the paths of virtue and piety, how great is their love ! See that penitent woman, weeping for sorrow and also for joy, and bathing her Saviour's feet with her tears. Those tears are refreshing to my heart, as a spring of water in the arid desert of pharisaic frigidity and formalism." The third may be denominated the argument from *natural instinct*, and runs thus : " I receive sinners, and eat with them, and seek by these means their moral restoration, for the same reason which moves the shepherd to go after a lost sheep, leaving his unstrayed flock in the wilderness, viz. because it is natural to seek the lost, and to have more joy in finding things lost than in possessing things which never have been lost. Men who understand not this feeling are solitary in the universe ; for angels in heaven, fathers, housewives, shepherds, all who have human hearts on earth, understand it well, and act on it every day."

In all these reasonings Jesus argued with His accusers on their own premises, accepting their estimate of themselves, and of the class with whom they deemed it discreditable to associate, as righteous and sinful respectively. But He took care, at the same time, to let it appear that His judgment concerning the two parties did not coincide with that of His interrogators. This He did on the occasion of Matthew's feast, by bidding them go study the text, " I will have mercy, and not sacrifice ;" meaning by the quotation to insinuate, that while very religious, the Pharisees were also very inhuman, full of pride, prejudice, harshness, and hatred ; and to proclaim the truth, that this character was in God's sight far more detestable than that of those who were addicted to the coarse vices of the multitude, not to speak of those who were "sinners" mainly in the pharisaic imagination, and within inverted commas.

Our Lord's last words to the persons who called His con-duct in question at this time were not merely apologetic, but judicial. " I came not," He said, "to call the righteous, but sinners ;" [1] intimating a purpose to let the self-righteous alone and to call to repentance and to the joys of the kingdom those who were not too self-satisfied to care for the benefits offered, and to whom the gospel feast would be a real enter-tainment. The word, in truth, contained a significant hint of an approaching religious revolution in which the last should become first and the first last ; Jewish outcasts, Gen-tile dogs, made partakers of the joys of the kingdom and the "righteous" shut out. It was one of the pregnant sayings by which Jesus made known to those who could understand, that His religion was an universal one, a religion for humanity, a gospel for mankind, because a gospel for sinners. And what this saying declared in word, the conduct it apologized for proclaimed yet more expressively by deed. It was an ominous thing that loving sympathy for "publicans and sinners" — the pharisaic instinct discerned it to be so, and rightly took the alarm. It meant death to privileged monopolies of grace and to Jewish pride and exclusivism — all men equal in God's sight, and welcome to salvation on the same terms. In fact it was a virtual announcement of the Pauline programme of an universalistic gospel, which the twelve are supposed by a certain school of theologians to have opposed as determinedly as the Pharisees themselves. Strange that the men who had been with Jesus were so obtuse as not to understand, even at the last, what was involved in their Master's fellowship with the low and the lost ! Was Buddha more fortunate in his disciples than Jesus in His ? Buddha said, " My law is a law of grace for all," directing the saying immediately against Brahminical caste prejudice ; and his followers understood that it meant, Buddhism a missionary religion, a religion even for Sudras, and therefore for all mankind !

[1] εἰς μετάνοιαν seems to be genuine only in Luke, and the words express only a part of Christ's meaning. He called men not merely to repentance, but to participation in all the blessedness of the kingdom.

4

THE TWELVE

Matt. 10:1-4; Mark 3:13-19; Luke 6:12-16; Acts 1:13

THE selection by Jesus of the twelve from the band of disciples who had gradually gathered around His person is an important landmark in the Gospel history. It divides the ministry of our Lord into two portions, nearly equal, probably, as to duration, but unequal as to the extent and importance of the work done in each respectively. In the earlier period Jesus labored single-handed; His miraculous deeds were confined for the most part to a limited area, and His teaching was in the main of an elementary character. But by the time when the twelve were chosen, the work of the kingdom had assumed such dimensions as to require organization and division of labor; and the teaching of Jesus was beginning to be of a deeper and more elaborate nature, and His gracious activities were taking on ever-widening range.

It is probable that the selection of a limited number to be His close and constant companions had become a necessity to Christ, in consequence of His very success in gaining disciples. His followers, we imagine, had grown so numerous as to be an incumbrance and an impediment to his movements, especially in the long journeys which mark the later part of His ministry. It was impossible that all who believed could continue henceforth to follow Him, in the literal sense, whithersoever He might go: the greater number could now only be occasional followers. But it was His wish that certain selected men should be with Him at all times and in all places, — His travelling companions in all His wanderings, witnessing all His work, and ministering to His daily needs. And so, in the quaint words of Mark, "Jesus calleth unto Him whom He would, and they came unto Him, and He made twelve, that they should be with Him." [1]

These twelve, however, as we know, were to be something more than travelling companions or menial servants of the Lord Jesus Christ. They were to be, in the mean time, students of Christian doctrine, and occasional fellow-laborers in the work of the kingdom, and eventually Christ's chosen trained agents for propagating the faith after He Himself had left the earth. From the time of their being chosen, indeed, the twelve entered on a regular apprenticeship for the great office of apostleship, in the course of which they were to learn, in the privacy of an intimate daily fellowship with their Master, what they should be, do, believe, and teach, as His witnesses and ambassadors to the world. Henceforth the training of these men was to be a constant and prominent part of Christ's personal work. He was to make it His business to tell them in darkness what they should afterwards speak in the daylight, and to whisper in their ear what in after years they should preach upon the housetops. [2]

The time when this election was made, though not absolutely determined, is fixed in relation to certain leading events in the Gospel history. John speaks of the twelve as an organized company at the period of the feeding of the five thousand, and of the discourse on the bread of life in the synagogue of Capernaum, delivered shortly after that miracle. From this fact we learn that the twelve were chosen at least one year before the crucifixion; for the miracle of the feeding took place, according to the fourth evangelist, shortly before a Passover season. [3] From the words spoken by Jesus to the men whom He had chosen, in justification of His seeming doubt of their fidelity after the multitude had deserted Him, "Did I not choose you the twelve, and one of you is a devil?" [4] we conclude that the choice was then not quite a recent event. The twelve had been long enough together to give the false disciple opportunity to show his real character.

---

[1] Mark iii. 13. The verb ἐποίησε, "made," is used here in the same sense as in Heb. iii. 2, "who was faithful to Him that made Him" (τῷ ποιήσαντι αὐτόν). There it is rendered "appointed," which the R. V. introduces here also.

[2] Matt. x. 27. [4] John vi. 70, as in R. V.

[3] John vi. 4.

Turning now to the synoptical evangelists, we find them fixing the position of the election with reference to two other most important events. Matthew speaks for the first time of the twelve as a distinct body in connection with their *mission in Galilee*. He does not, however, say that they were chosen immediately before, and with direct reference to, that mission. He speaks rather as if the apostolic fraternity had been previously in existence, his words being, " When He had called unto Him His twelve disciples." Luke, on the other hand, gives a formal record of the election, as a preface to his account of the *Sermon on the Mount*, so speaking as to create the impression that the one event immediately preceded the other.[1] Finally, Mark's narrative confirms the view suggested by these observations on Matthew and Luke, viz. that the twelve were called just before the Sermon on the Mount was delivered, and some considerable time before they were sent forth on their preaching and healing mission. There we read : " Jesus goeth up into the mountain (τὸ ὄρος),[2] and calleth unto Him whom He would " — the ascent referred to evidently being that which Jesus made just before preaching His great discourse. Mark continues : " And He ordained twelve, that they should be with Him, and that He might send them forth to preach, and to have power to heal sicknesses and to cast out devils." Here allusion is made to an *intention* on Christ's part to send forth His disciples on a mission, but the intention is not represented as immediately realized. Nor can it be said that immediate realization is implied, though not expressed ; for the evangelist gives an account of the mission as actually carried out several chapters further on in his Gospel, commencing with the words, " And He calleth unto Him the twelve, and began to send them forth."[3]

It may be regarded, then, as tolerably certain, that the calling of the twelve was a prelude to the preaching of the great sermon on the kingdom, in the founding of which they were afterwards to take so distinguished a part. At what

---

[1] Luke vi. 13 compared with 17, where note that Luke represents the name "apostle" as originating with Christ : " Whom also He named apostles " (ver. 13).

[2] This expression is used by all the Synoptics. It seems to signify a mountain district rather than a particular hill.

[3] Mark vi. 7.

precise period in the ministry of our Lord the sermon itself is to be placed, we cannot so confidently determine. Our opinion, however, is, that the Sermon on the Mount was delivered towards the close of Christ's first lengthened minis- try in Galilee, during the time which intervened between the two visits to Jerusalem on festive occasions mentioned in the second and fifth chapters of John's Gospel.[1]

The *number* of the apostolic company is significant, and was doubtless a matter of choice, not less than was the com- position of the selected band. A larger number of eligible men could easily have been found in a circle of disciples which afterwards supplied not fewer than seventy auxiliaries for evangelistic work ;[2] and a smaller number might have served all the present or prospective purposes of the apostle- ship. The number twelve was recommended by obvious symbolic reasons. It happily expressed in figures what Jesus claimed to be, and what He had come to do, and thus fur- nished a support to the faith and a stimulus to the devotion of His followers. It significantly hinted that Jesus was the divine Messianic King of Israel, come to set up the kingdom whose advent was foretold by prophets in glowing language, suggested by the palmy days of Israel's history, when the theocratic community existed in its integrity, and all the tribes of the chosen nation were united under the royal house of David. That the number twelve was designed to bear such a mystic meaning, we know from Christ's own words to the apostles on a later occasion, when, describing to them the rewards awaiting them in the kingdom for past services and sacrifices, He said, " Verily I say unto you, that ye which have followed me, in the regeneration, when the Son of man shall sit in the throne of His glory, ye also shall sit upon twelve thrones, judging the twelve tribes of Israel." [3]

It is possible that the apostles were only too well aware of

[1] So Ebrard, *Gosp. Hist.*   Ewald places the election after the feast of John v.

[2] This mission of the seventy is regarded by Baur, and others of the same school, as a pure invention of the third Evangelist's, meant to throw the twelve into the shade, and to serve the cause of Pauline universalism.   This opinion is entirely arbitrary ; but even supposing we were to concede the point, it would still remain true, as stated in the text, that Christ could have had more than twelve apostles had He desired.

[3] Matt. xix. 28.   Keim recognizes the number twelve as bearing a symbolic meaning, as stated in the text, against Schleiermacher, who regarded it as purely accidental. — *Geschichte Jesu von Nazara*, ii. 304.

the mystic significance of their number, and found in it an encouragement to the fond delusive hope that the coming kingdom should be not only a spiritual realization of the promises, but a literal restoration of Israel to political integrity and independence. The risk of such misapprehension was one of the drawbacks connected with the particular number twelve, but it was not deemed by Jesus a sufficient reason for fixing on another. His method of procedure in this, as in all things, was to abide by that which in itself was true and right, and then to correct misapprehensions as they arose.

From the number of the apostolic band, we pass to the persons composing it. Seven of the twelve — the first seven in the catalogues of Mark and Luke, assuming the identity of Bartholomew and Nathanael — are persons already known to us. With two of the remaining five — the first and the last — we shall become well acquainted as we proceed in the history. Thomas called Didymus, or the Twin, will come before us as a man of warm heart but melancholy temperament, ready to die with his Lord, but slow to believe in His resurrection. Judas Iscariot is known to all the world as the Traitor. He appears for the first time, in these catalogues of the apostles, with the infamous title branded on his brow, "Judas Iscariot, who also betrayed Him." The presence of a man capable of treachery among the elect disciples is a mystery which we shall not now attempt to penetrate. We merely make this historical remark about Judas here, that he seems to have been the only one among the twelve who was not a Galilean. He is surnamed, from his native place apparently, the man of Kerioth ; and from the Book of Joshua we learn that there was a town of that name in the southern border of the tribe of Judah.[1]

The three names which remain are exceedingly obscure. On grounds familiar to Bible scholars, it has often been attempted to identify James of Alphæus with James the brother or kinsman of the Lord. The next on the lists of

[1] Josh. xv. 24. See Renan, *Vie de Jésus*, p. 160 (13th ed.). Ewald (*Christus*, p. 398) thinks Kerioth is Kartah, in the tribe of Zebulun (Josh. xxi. 34). If Judas was a Judæan, he may have become a disciple at the time of Christ's visit to the Jordan, mentioned in John iii. 22.

Matthew and Mark has been supposed by many to have been a brother of this James, and therefore another brother of Jesus. This opinion is based on the fact, that in place of the Lebbæus or Thaddæus of the two first Gospels, we find in Luke's catalogues the name Judas "of James." The ellipsis in this designation has been filled up with the word brother, and it is assumed that the James alluded to is James the son of Alphæus. However tempting these results may be, we can scarcely regard them as ascertained, and must content ourselves with stating that among the twelve was a second James, besides the brother of John and son of Zebedee, and also a second Judas, who appears again as an interlocutor in the farewell conversation between Jesus and His disciples on the night before His crucifixion, carefully distinguished by the evangelist from the traitor by the parenthetical remark "not Iscariot." [1]   This Judas, being the same with Lebbæus Thaddæus, has been called the three-named disciple.[2]

The disciple whom we have reserved to the last place, like the one who stands at the head of all the lists, was a Simon. This second Simon is as obscure as the first is celebrated, for he is nowhere mentioned in the Gospel history, except in the catalogues ; yet, little known as he is, the epithet attached to his name conveys a piece of curious and interesting information. He is called the Kananite (not Canaanite), which is a political, not a geographical designation, as appears from the Greek word substituted in the place of this Hebrew one by Luke, who calls the disciple we now speak of Simon Zelotes ; that is, in English, Simon the Zealot. This epithet Zelotes connects Simon unmistakably with the famous party which rose in rebellion under Judas in the days of the taxing,[3] some twenty years before Christ's ministry began, when Judæa and Samaria were brought under the direct government of Rome, and the census of the population was taken with a view to subsequent taxation. How singular a phenomenon is this ex-zealot among the disciples of Jesus ! No two men could differ more widely in their spirit, ends,

---

[1] John xiv. 22.

[2] Ewald (*Christus*, p. 399) thinks Lebbæus and Judas different persons, and supposes that the former had died in Christ's lifetime, and that Judas had been chosen in his place.

[3] Acts v. 37.

and means, than Judas of Galilee and Jesus of Nazareth. The one was a political malcontent; the other would have the conquered bow to the yoke, and give to Cæsar Cæsar's due. The former aimed at restoring the kingdom to Israel, adopting for his watchword, " We have no Lord or Master but God ; " the latter aimed at founding a kingdom not national, but universal, not "of this world," but purely spirit-ual. The means employed by the two actors were as diverse as their ends. One had recourse to the carnal weapons of war, the sword and the dagger ; the other relied solely on the gentle but omnipotent force of truth.

What led Simon to leave Judas for Jesus we know not ; but he made a happy exchange for himself, as the party he forsook were destined in after years to bring ruin on them-selves and on their country by their fanatical, reckless, and unavailing patriotism. Though the insurrection of Judas was crushed, the fire of discontent still smouldered in the breasts of his adherents ; and at length it burst out into the blaze of a new rebellion, which brought on a death-struggle with the gigantic power of Rome, and ended in the destruc-tion of the Jewish capital, and the dispersion of the Jewish people.

The choice of this disciple to be an apostle supplies another illustration of Christ's disregard of prudential wis-dom. An ex-zealot was not a safe man to make an apostle of, for he might be the means of rendering Jesus and His followers objects of political suspicion. But the Author of our faith was willing to take the risk. He expected to gain many disciples from the dangerous classes as well as from the despised, and He would have them, too, represented among the twelve.

It gives one a pleasant surprise to think of Simon the zealot and Matthew the publican, men coming from so oppo-site quarters, meeting together in close fellowship in the little band of twelve. In the persons of these two disciples extremes meet — the tax-gatherer and the tax-hater : the unpatriotic Jew, who degraded himself by becoming a ser-vant of the alien ruler ; and the Jewish patriot, who chafed under the foreign yoke, and sighed for emancipation. This union of opposites was not accidental, but was designed by

Jesus as a prophecy of the future. He wished the twelve to be the church in miniature or germ; and therefore He chose them so as to intimate that, as among them distinctions of publican and zealot were unknown, so in the church of the future there should be neither Greek nor Jew, circumcision nor uncircumcision, bond nor free, but only Christ — all to each, and in each of the all.

These were the names of the twelve as given in the catalogues. As to the order in which they are arranged, on closely inspecting the lists we observe that they contain three groups of four, in each of which the same names are always found, though the order of arrangement varies. The first group includes those best known, the second the next best, and the third those least known of all, or, in the case of the traitor, known only too well. Peter, the most prominent character among the twelve, stands at the head of all the lists, and Judas Iscariot at the foot, carefully designated, as already observed, the traitor. The apostolic roll, taking the order given in Matthew, and borrowing characteristic epithets from the Gospel history at large, is as follows : —

FIRST GROUP

Simon Peter	The man of rock.
Andrew	Peter's brother.
James and } John }	{ Sons of Zebedee, and sons of { thunder.

SECOND GROUP

Philip	The earnest inquirer.
Bartholomew, or Nathanael . .	The guileless Israelite.
Thomas	The melancholy.
Matthew	The publican (so called by himself only).

THIRD GROUP

James (the son) of Alphæus . .	(James the Less? Mark xv. 40.)
Lebbæus, Thaddæus, Judas of James,	The three-named disciple.
Simon	The Zealot.
Judas, the man of Kerioth . . .	The Traitor.

Such were the men whom Jesus chose to be with Him while He was on this earth, and to carry on His work after He left it. Such were the men whom the church celebrates as the "glorious company of the apostles." The praise is merited; but the glory of the twelve was not of this world. In a worldly point of view they were a very insignificant company indeed, — a band of poor illiterate Galilean provincials, utterly devoid of social consequence, not likely to be chosen by one having supreme regard to prudential considerations. Why did Jesus choose such men? Was He guided by feelings of antagonism to those possessing social advantages, or of partiality for men of His own class? No; His choice was made in true wisdom. If He chose Galileans mainly, it was not from provincial prejudice against those of the south; if, as some think, He chose two or even four [1] of his own kindred, it was not from nepotism; if He chose rude, unlearned, humble men, it was not because He was animated by any petty jealousy of knowledge, culture, or good birth. If any rabbi, rich man, or ruler had been willing to yield himself unreservedly to the service of the kingdom, no objection would have been taken to him on account of his acquirements, possessions, or titles. The case of Saul of Tarsus, the pupil of Gamaliel, proves the truth of this statement. Even Gamaliel himself would not have been objected to, could he have stooped to become a disciple of the unlearned Nazarene. But, alas! neither he nor any of his order would condescend so far, and therefore the despised One did not get an opportunity of showing His willingness to accept as disciples and choose for apostles such as they were.

The truth is, that Jesus was obliged to be content with fishermen, and publicans, and quondam zealots, for apostles. They were the best that could be had. Those who deemed themselves better were too proud to become disciples, and thereby they excluded themselves from what all the world now sees to be the high honor of being the chosen princes of the kingdom. The civil and religious aristocracy boasted of their unbelief.[2] The citizens of Jerusalem did feel for a moment interested in the zealous youth who had purged the temple with a whip of small cords; but their faith was super-

---

[1] Matthew or Levi, being a son of Alphæus, has been supposed to be a brother of James, and Simon the Zealot to be the Simon mentioned in Matt. xiii. 55.

[2] John vii. 48.

ficial, and their attitude patronizing, and therefore Jesus did not commit Himself unto them, because He knew what was in them.[1] A few of good position were sincere sympathizers, but they were not so decided in their attachment as to be eligible for apostles. Nicodemus was barely able to speak a timid apologetic word in Christ's behalf, and Joseph of Arimathea was a disciple " secretly," for fear of the Jews. These were hardly the persons to send forth as missionaries of the cross — men so fettered by social ties and party connections, and so enslaved by the fear of man. The apostles of Christianity must be made of sterner stuff.

And so Jesus was obliged to fall back on the rustic, but simple, sincere, and energetic men of Galilee. And He was quite content with His choice, and devoutly thanked His Father for giving Him even such as they. Learning, rank, wealth, refinement, freely given up to his service, He would not have despised; but He preferred devoted men who had none of these advantages to undevoted men who had them all. And with good reason; for it mattered little, except in the eyes of contemporary prejudice, what the social position or even the previous history of the twelve had been, provided they were spiritually qualified for the work to which they were called. What tells ultimately is, not what is without a man, but what is within. John Bunyan was a man of low birth, low occupation, and, up till his conversion, of low habits; but he was by nature a man of genius, and by grace a man of God, and he would have made — he was, in fact — a most effective apostle.

But it may be objected that all the twelve were by no means gifted like Bunyan; some of them, if one may judge from the obscurity which envelops their names, and the silence of history regarding them, having been undistinguished either by high endowment or by a great career, and in fact, to speak plainly, all but useless. As this objection virtually impugns the wisdom of Christ's choice, it is necessary to examine how far it is according to truth.[2] We submit the following considerations with this view : —

[1] John ii. 23–25.
[2] Keim says that Jesus was in a genuinely human way (*ächt menschlich*) deceived in His disciples to a certain extent. They turned out not the men He had hoped. The remark occurs in connection with the Galilean mission. — *Geschichte Jesu von Nazara*, ii. 332.

1. That some of the apostles were comparatively obscure, inferior men, cannot be denied ; but even the obscurest of them may have been most useful as *witnesses* for Him with whom they had companied from the beginning. It does not take a *great* man to make a good witness, and to be witnesses of Christian facts was the main business of the apostles. That even the humblest of them rendered important service in that capacity we need not doubt, though nothing is said of them in the apostolic annals. It was not to be expected that a history so fragmentary and so brief as that given by Luke should mention any but the principal actors, especially when we reflect how few of the characters that appear on the stage at any particular crisis in human affairs are prominently noticed even in histories which go elaborately into detail. The purpose of history is served by recording the words and deeds of the representative men, and many are allowed to drop into oblivion who did nobly in their day. The less distinguished members of the apostolic band are entitled to the benefit of this reflection.

2. Three eminent men, or even two (Peter and John), out of twelve, is a good proportion ; there being few societies in which superior excellence bears such a high ratio to respectable mediocrity. Perhaps the number of " Pillars " [1] was as great as was desirable. Far from regretting that all were not Peters and Johns, it is rather a matter to be thankful for, that there were diversities of gifts among the first preachers of the gospel. As a general rule, it is not good when all are leaders. Little men are needed as well as great men ; for human nature is one-sided, and little men have their peculiar virtues and gifts, and can do some things better than their more celebrated brethren.

3. We must remember how little we know concerning any of the apostles. It is the fashion of biographers in our day, writing for a morbidly or idly curious public, to enter into the minutest particulars of outward event or personal peculiarity regarding their heroes. Of this fond idolatrous minuteness there is no trace in the evangelic histories. The writers of

---

[1] This title is given to Peter, James, and John by Paul in his Epistle to the Galatians (ii. 9). Hence in the Tübingen literature devoted to the maintenance of the conflict-theory, these three are called the " Pillar Apostles."

the Gospels were not afflicted with the biographic mania. Moreover, the apostles were not their theme. Christ was their hero ; and their sole desire was to tell what they knew of Him. They gazed steadfastly at the Sun of Righteousness, and in His effulgence they lost sight of the attendant stars. Whether they were stars of the first magnitude, or of the second, or of the third, made little difference.

5

HEARING AND SEEING

Luke1:1-4; Matt. 13:16-17; Luke 10:23,24; Matt. 5-7; Luke 6:17-49;
Matt. 13:1-52; Matt. 8:16,17; Mark 4:33, 34

IN the training of the twelve for the work of the apostleship, hearing and seeing the words and works of Christ
necessarily occupied an important place. Eye and ear witnessing of the facts of an unparalleled life was an indispensable preparation for future witness-bearing. The apostles
could secure credence for their wondrous tale only by being
able to preface it with the protestation : " That which we
have seen and heard declare we unto you." None would
believe their report, save those who, at the very least, were
satisfied that it emanated from men who had been with Jesus.
Hence the third evangelist, himself not an apostle, but only
a companion of apostles, presents his Gospel with all confidence to his friend Theophilus as a genuine history, and no
mere collection of fables, because its contents were attested
by men who "from the beginning were eye-witnesses and
ministers of the Word."

In the early period of their discipleship hearing and seeing
seem to have been the main occupation of the twelve. They
were then like children born into a new world, whose first
and by no means least important course of lessons consists
in the use of their senses in observing the wonderful objects
by which they are surrounded.

The things which the twelve saw and heard were wonderful
enough. The great Actor in the stupendous drama was
careful to impress on His followers the magnitude of their
privilege. " Blessed," said He to them on one occasion, "are
the eyes which see the things that ye see : for I tell you, that
many prophets and kings desired to see the things which ye

see, and saw them not ; and to hear the things which ye hear, and heard them not." [1]   Yet certain generations of Israel had seen very remarkable things : one had seen the wonders of the Exodus, and the sublimities connected with the lawgiving at Sinai ; another, the miracles wrought by Elijah and Elisha ; and successive generations had been privileged to listen to the not less wonderful oracles of God, spoken by David, Solomon, Isaiah, and the rest of the prophets.   But the things witnessed by the twelve eclipsed the wonders of all bygone ages ; for a greater than Moses, or Elijah, or David, or Solomon, or Isaiah, was here, and the promise to Nathanael was being fulfilled.   Heaven had been opened, and the angels of God — the spirits of wisdom, and power, and love — were ascending and descending on the Son of man.

We may here take a rapid survey of the *mirabilia* which it was the peculiar privilege of the twelve to see and hear, more or less during the whole period of their discipleship, and specially just after their election.   These may be comprehended under two heads : the Doctrine of the Kingdom, and the Philanthropic Work of the Kingdom.

    1. Before the ministry of Jesus commenced, His forerunner had appeared in the wilderness of Judæa, preaching, and saying, " Repent ye, for the kingdom of heaven is at hand ; " and some time after their election the twelve disciples were sent forth among the towns and villages of Galilee to repeat the Baptist's message.   But Jesus Himself did something more than proclaim the advent of the kingdom.   He expounded the nature of the divine kingdom, described the character of its citizens, and discriminated between genuine and spurious members of the holy commonwealth.   This He did partly in what is familiarly called the Sermon on the Mount, preached shortly after the election of the apostles ; and partly in certain parables uttered about the same period. [2]

    In the great discourse delivered on the mountain-top, the qualifications for citizenship in the kingdom of heaven were

---

[1] Luke x. 23, 24.   The authors of the Revised Version have introduced many changes in the A. V. by stricter rendering of tenses, and especially of the aorists, which in the old version are frequently treated as perfects.   They may have carried this too far, but on the whole they have rendered good service in this department.

[2] That the election of the twelve preceded the utterance of the parables is plain from Mark iv. 10, " They that were about Him *with the twelve*, asked of Him the parable."

set forth, first positively, and then comparatively. The positive truth was summed up in seven golden sentences called the Beatitudes, in which the felicity of the kingdom was represented as altogether independent of the outward conditions with which worldly happiness is associated. The blessed, according to the preacher, were the poor, the hungry, the mournful, the meek, the merciful, the pure in heart, the peaceable, the sufferers for righteousness' sake. Such were blessed themselves, and a source of blessing to the human race: the salt of the earth, the light of the world raised above others in spirit and character, to draw them upwards, and lead them to glorify God.

Next, with more detail, Jesus exhibited the righteousness of the kingdom, and of its true citizens, in contrast to that which prevailed. "Except your righteousness," He went on to say with solemn emphasis, "shall exceed the righteousness of the scribes and Pharisees, ye shall in no case enter into the kingdom of heaven;" and then He illustrated and enforced the general proposition by a detailed description of the counterfeit in its moral and religious aspects : in its moae of interpreting the moral law, and its manner of performing the duties of piety, such as prayer, alms, and fasting. In the one aspect He characterized pharisaic righteousness as superficial and technical ; in the other as ostentatious, self-complacent, and censorious. In contrast thereto, He described the *ethics* of the kingdom as a pure stream of life, having charity for its fountainhead ; a morality of the heart, not merely of outward conduct ; a morality also broad and catholic, overleaping all arbitrary barriers erected by legal pedantry and natural selfishness. The *religion* of the kingdom He set forth as humble, retiring, devoted in singleness of heart to God and things supernal ; having faith in God as a benignant gracious Father for its root, and contentment, cheerfulness, and freedom from secular cares for its fruits ; and, finally, as reserved in its bearing towards the profane, yet averse to severity in judging, yea, to judging at all, leaving men to be judged by God.

The discourse, of which we have given a hasty outline, made a powerful impression on the audience. "The people," we read, "were astonished at His doctrine; for He taught them as one having authority (the authority of wisdom and truth), and not as the scribes," who had merely the authority of office. It is not probable that either the multitude or the twelve understood the sermon ; for it was both deep and lofty, and their minds were pre-occupied with very different ideas of the coming kingdom. Yet the drift of all that had been said was clear and simple. The kingdom whereof Jesus was both King and Lawgiver was not to be a kingdom of this world : it was not to be here or there in space, but within the heart of man ; it was not be the monopoly of any class or nation, but open to all possessed of the requisite spiritual endowments *on equal terms*. It is nowhere said, indeed, in the sermon, that ritual qualifications, such as circumcision, were not indispensable for admission into the kingdom. But circumcision is ignored here, as it was ignored thoughout the teaching of Jesus. It is treated as something simply out of place, which cannot be dove-tailed into the scheme of doctrine set forth ; an incongruity the very mention of which would create a sense of the grotesque. How truly it was so any one can satisfy himself by just imagining for a moment that among the Beatitudes had been found one running thus : Blessed are the circumcised, for no uncircumcised ones shall enter into the kingdom of heaven. This significant silence concerning the seal of the national covenant could not fail to have its effect on the minds of the disciples, as a hint at eventual antiquation.

The weighty truths thus taught first in the didactic form of an ethical discourse, Jesus sought at other times to popularize by means of *parables*. In the course of His ministry He uttered many parabolic sayings, the parable being with Him a favorite form of instruction. Of the thirty [1] parables preserved in the Gospels, the larger number were of an occasional character, and are best understood when viewed in connection with the circumstances which called them forth. But there is a special group of eight which appear to have been spoken about the same period, and to have been designed to serve one object, viz. to exhibit in simple pictures

---

[1] This number is only an approximate estimate. The number of the parables is estimated differently by different writers, according to their definition of a parable and method of treating the collection.

the outstanding features of the kingdom of heaven in its nature and progress, and in its relations to diverse classes of men. One of these, the parable of the sower, apparently the first spoken, shows the different reception given to the word of the kingdom by various classes of hearers, and the varied issues in their life. Two — the parables of the tares and of the net cast into the sea — describe the mixture of good and evil that should exist in the kingdom till the end, when the grand final separation would take place. Another pair of short parables — those of the treasure hid in a field and of the precious pearl — set forth the incomparable importance of the kingdom, and of citizenship therein. Other two — the grain of mustard seed, and the leaven hid in three measures of meal — explain how the kingdom advances from small beginnings to a great ending. An eighth parable, found in Mark's Gospel only, teaches that growth in the divine kingdom proceeds by stages, analogous to the blade, the ear, and the full corn in the ear, in the growth of grain.[1]

These parables, or the greater number of them, were spoken in the hearing of a miscellaneous audience ; and from a reply of Jesus to a question put by the disciples, it might appear that they were intended mainly for the ignorant populace. The question was, " Why speakest Thou unto them in parables ? " and the reply, " Because it is given unto you to know the mysteries of the kingdom of heaven, but to them it is not given ; " which seems to imply, that in the case of the twelve such elementary views of truth — such children's sermons, so to speak — might be dispensed with. Jesus meant no more, however, than that for them the parables were not so important as for common hearers, being only one of several means of grace through which they were to become eventually scribes instructed in the kingdom, acquainted with all its mysteries, and able, like a wise householder, to bring out of their treasures things new and old ;[2] while for the multitude the parables were indispensable, as affording their only chance of getting a little glimpse into the mysteries of the kingdom.

That the twelve were not *above* parables yet appears from the fact that they asked and received explanations of them

[1] Mark iv. 26.   [2] Matt. xiii. 52.

in private from their Master: of all, probably, though the interpretations of two only, the parables of the sower and the tares, are preserved in the Gospels.[1] They were still only children; the parables were pretty pictures to them, but of what they could not tell. Even after they had received private expositions of their meaning, they were probably not much wiser than before, though they professed to be satisfied.[2] Their profession was doubtless sincere : they spake as they felt; but they spake as children, they understood as children, they thought as children, and they had much to learn yet of these divine mysteries.

When the children had grown to spiritual manhood, and fully understood these mysteries, they highly valued the happiness they had enjoyed in former years, in being privi- leged to hear the parables of Jesus. We have an interesting memorial of the deep impression produced on their minds by these simple pictures of the kingdom, in the reflection with, which the first evangelist closes his account of Christ's parabolic teaching. "All these things," he remarks, "spake Jesus unto the multitude in parables, . . . that it might be fulfilled which was spoken by the prophet, saying, I will open my mouth in parables, I will utter things which have been kept secret from the foundation of the world."[3] The quota- tion (from the seventy-eighth Psalm) significantly diverges both from the Hebrew original and from the Septuagint version.[4] Matthew has consciously adapted the words so as to express the absolute originality of the teaching in which he found their fulfilment. While the Psalmist uttered dark sayings from the ancient times of Israel's history, Jesus in the parables had spoken things that had been hidden from the creation. Nor was this an exaggeration on the part of the evangelist. Even the use of the parable as a vehicle of instruction was all but new, and the truths expressed in the parables were altogether new. They were indeed the eternal verities of the divine kingdom, but till the days of Jesus they had remained unannounced. Earthly things had always been fit to emblem forth heavenly things ; but, till the

---

[1] Mark iv. 34.　　　　[2] Matt. xiii. 51.　　　　[3] Matt. xiii. 34, 35.

[4] ἐρεύξομαι κεκρυμμένα ἀπὸ καταβολῆς κόσμου (Matt.); אַבִּיעָה חִידוֹת מִנִּי־קֶדֶם (Hebrew); φθέγξομαι προβλήματα ἀπ᾽ ἀρχῆς (Sept.).

great Teacher appeared, no one had ever thought of linking them together, so that the one should become a mirror of the other, revealing the deep things of God to the common eye: even as no one before Isaac Newton had thought of connecting the fall of an apple with the revolution of the heavenly bodies, though apples had fallen to the ground from the creation of the world.

2. The things which the disciples had the happiness to see in connection with the philanthropic work of the kingdom were, if possible, still more marvellous than those which they heard in Christ's company. They were eye-witnesses of the events which Jesus bade the messengers of John report to their master in prison as unquestionable evidence that He was the Christ who should come.[1] In their presence, as spectators, blind men received their sight, lame men walked, lepers were cleansed, the deaf recovered hearing, dead persons were raised to life again. The performance of such wonderful works was for a time Christ's daily occupation. He went about in Galilee and other districts, "doing good, and healing all that were oppressed of the devil."[2] The "miracles" recorded in detail in the Gospels give no idea whatever of the extent to which these wondrous operations were carried on. The leper cleansed on the descent from the mountain, when the great sermon was preached, the palsied servant of the Roman centurion restored to health and strength, Peter's mother-in-law cured of a fever, the demoniac dispossessed in the synagogue of Capernaum, the widow's son brought back to life while he was being carried out to burial, — these, and the like, are but a few samples selected out of an innumerable multitude of deeds not less remarkable, whether regarded as mere miracles or as acts of kindness. The truth of this statement appears from paragraphs of frequent recurrence in the Gospels, which relate not individual miracles, but an indefinite number of them taken *en masse*. Of such paragraphs take as an example the following, cursorily rehearsing the works done by Jesus at the close of a busy day: "And at even, when the sun did set, they brought unto Him all that were diseased, and them that were possessed with devils ; and all the city was gath-

[1] Matt. xi. 2.   [2] Acts xi. 38.

ered together at the door. And He healed many that were sick of divers diseases, and cast out many devils."[1] This was what happened on a single Sabbath evening in Capernaum, shortly after the Sermon on the Mount was preached; and such scenes appear to have been common at this time: for we read a little farther on in the same Gospel, that "Jesus spake unto His disciples, that a small ship should wait on Him because of the multitude, lest they should throng Him; for He had healed many; insomuch that they pressed upon Him for to touch Him, as many as had plagues."[2] And yet again Mark tells how "they went into an house, and the multitude cometh together again, so that they could not so much as eat bread."[3]

The inference suggested by such passages as to the vast extent of Christ's labors among the suffering, is borne out by the impressions these made on the minds both of friends and foes. The ill-affected were so struck by what they saw, that they found it necessary to get up a theory to account for the mighty influence exerted by Jesus in curing physical, and especially psychical maladies. "This fellow," they said, "doth not cast out devils but by Beelzebub the prince of devils." It was a lame theory, as Jesus showed; but it was at least conclusive evidence that devils were cast out, and in great numbers.

The thoughts of the well-affected concerning the works of Jesus were various, but all which have been recorded involve a testimony to His vast activity and extraordinary zeal. Some, apparently relatives, deemed him mad, fancying that enthusiasm had disturbed His mind, and compassionately sought to save Him from doing Himself harm through excessive solicitude to do good to others.[4] The sentiments of the people who received benefit were more devout. "They marvelled, and glorified God, which had given such power unto men;"[5] and they were naturally not inclined to criticise an "enthusiasm of humanity" whereof they were themselves the objects.

The contemporaneous impressions of the twelve concern-

---

[1] Mark i. 32-34.   [4] Mark iii. 21.
[2] Mark iii. 9.   [5] Matt. ix. 8.
[3] Mark iii. 19, 20.

ing their Master's deeds are not recorded ; but of their subsequent reflections as apostles we have an interesting sample
in the observations appended by the first evangelist to his
account of the transactions of that Sabbath evening in Capernaum already alluded to. The devout Matthew, according
to his custom, saw in these wondrous works Old Testament
Scripture fulfilled ; and the passage whose fulfilment he
found therein was that touching oracle of Isaiah, " Surely
He hath borne our griefs and carried our sorrows ; " which,
departing from the Septuagint, he made apt to his purpose
by rendering, " Himself took our infirmities and bore our
sicknesses." [1] The Greek translators interpreted the text
as referring to men's spiritual maladies — their sins ; [2] but
Matthew deemed it neither a misapplication nor a degradation of the words to find in them a prophecy of Messiah's
deep sympathy with such as suffered from any disease,
whether spiritual or mental, or merely physical. He knew
not how better to express the intense compassion of his Lord
towards all sufferers, than by representing Him in prophetic
language as taking their sicknesses on Himself. Nor did he
wrong the prophet's thought by this application of it. He
but laid the foundation of an *à fortiori* inference to a still
more intense sympathy on the Saviour's part with the spiritually diseased. For surely He who so cared for men's bodies
would care yet more for their souls. Surely it might safely
be anticipated, that He who was so conspicuous as a healer
of bodily disease would become yet more famous as a Saviour
from sin.

The works which the twelve were privileged to see were
verily worth seeing, and altogether worthy of the Messianic
King. They served to demonstrate that the King and the
kingdom were not only coming, but come ; for what could
more certainly betoken their presence, than mercy dropping
like the " gentle rain from heaven upon the place beneath " ?
John, indeed, seems to have thought otherwise, when he sent
to inquire of Jesus if He were the Christ who was to come.
He desiderated, we imagine, a work of judgment on the
impenitent as a more reliable proof of Messiah's advent than
these miracles of mercy. The prophetic infirmity of queru-

---

[1] Matt. viii. 17.   [2] οὗτος τὰς ἁμαρτίας ἡμῶν φέρει.

lousness and the prison air had got the better of his judgment and his heart, and he was in the truculent humor of
Jonah, who was displeased with God, not because He was too
stern, but rather because He was too gracious, too ready to
forgive.

The least in the kingdom of heaven is incapable now of
being offended with these works of our Lord on account of
their mercifulness.   The offence in our day lies in a different
direction.   Men stumble at the miraculousness of the things
seen by the disciples and recorded by the evangelists.   Mercy,
say they, is God-like, but miracles are impossible ; and they
think they do well to be sceptical.   An exception is made,
indeed, in favor of some of the healing miracles, because it is
not deemed impossible that they might fall within the course
of nature, and so cease to belong to the category of the
miraculous.   " Moral therapeutics " might account for them
— a department of medical science which Mr. Matthew
Arnold thinks has not been at all sufficiently studied yet.[1]
All other miracles besides those wrought by moral therapeutics are pronounced fabulous.   But why not extend the
dominion of the moral over the physical, and say without
qualification : Mercy is God-like, therefore such works as
those wrought by Jesus were matters of course ?   So they
appeared to the writers of the Gospels.   What they wondered
at was not the supernaturalness of Christ's healing operations, but the unfathomable depth of divine compassion which
they revealed.   There is no trace of the love of the marvellous either in the Gospels or in the Epistles.   The disciples
may have experienced such a feeling when the era of wonders
first burst on their astonished view, but they had lost it
entirely by the time the New Testament books began to be
written.[2]   Throughout the New Testament miracles are
spoken of in a sober, almost matter-of-fact, tone.   How is
this to be explained ?   The explanation is that the apostles
had seen too many miracles while with Jesus to be excited
about them.   Their sense of wonder had been deadened by

[1] *Literature and Dogma*, p. 143, ed. 4.

[2] Isaac Taylor, in *The Restoration of Belief*, founds on this fact an argument for the
reality of miracles, contending that the calm, matter-of-fact tone in which miracles are
spoken of in the Epistles can be accounted for only by their being a great outstanding
fact of that age (*vide* pp. 128–211.)

being sated. But though they ceased to marvel at the power of their Lord, they never ceased to wonder at His grace. The love of Christ remained for them throughout life a thing passing knowledge; and the longer they lived, the more cordially did they acknowledge the truth of their Master's words : " Blessed are the eyes which see the things that ye see."

6

LESSONS ON PRAYER

Matt. 6:5-13; 7:7-11; Luke 11:1-13; 18:1-5

IT would have been matter for surprise if, among the manifold subjects on which Jesus gave instruction to His disciples, prayer had not occupied a prominent place. Prayer is a necessity of spiritual life, and all who earnestly try to pray soon feel the need of teaching how to do it. And what theme more likely to engage the thoughts of a Master who was Himself emphatically a man of prayer, spending occasionally whole nights in prayerful communion with His heavenly Father?[1]

We find, accordingly, that prayer was a subject on which Jesus often spoke in the hearing of His disciples. In the Sermon on the Mount, for example, He devoted a paragraph to that topic, in which He cautioned His hearers against pharisaic ostentation and heathenish repetition, and recited a form of devotion as a model of simplicity, comprehensiveness, and brevity.[2] At other times He directed attention to the necessity, in order to acceptable and prevailing prayer, of perseverance,[3] concord,[4] strong faith,[5] and large expectation.[6]

The passage cited from the eleventh chapter of Luke's Gospel gives an account of what may be regarded as the most complete and comprehensive of all the lessons communicated by Jesus to His disciples on the important subject to which it relates. The circumstances in which this lesson was given are interesting. The lesson on prayer was itself an answer to prayer. A disciple, in all probability one of the twelve,[7]

---

[1] Mark i. 35; Luke vi. 12; Matt. xiv. 23.
[2] Matt. vi. 5-13.
[3] Luke xi. 1-13, xviii. 1-5.
[4] Matt. xviii. 19.
[5] Matt. xxi. 22.
[6] John xvi. 23, 24.
[7] The twelve are not named; but the lesson must, from its nature, have been given to a close circle of disciples.

after hearing Jesus pray, made the request : " Lord, teach us to pray, as John also taught his disciples." The request and its occasion taken together convey to us incidentally two pieces of information. From the latter we learn that Jesus, besides praying much alone, also prayed in company with His disciples, practising family prayer as the head of a household, as well as secret prayer in personal fellowship with God His Father. From the former we learn that the social prayers of Jesus were most impressive. Disciples hearing them were made painfully conscious of their own incapacity, and after the Amen were ready instinctively to proffer the request, " Lord, teach us to pray," as if ashamed any more to attempt the exercise in their own feeble, vague, stammering words.

When this lesson was given we know not, for Luke introduces his narrative of it in the most indefinite manner, without noting either time or place. The reference to John in the past tense might seem to indicate a date subsequent to his death ; but the mode of expression would be sufficiently explained by the supposition that the disciple who made the request had previously been a disciple of the Baptist.[1] Nor can any certain inference be drawn from the contents of the lesson. It is a lesson which might have been given to the twelve at any time during their disciplehood, so far as their spiritual necessities were concerned. It is a lesson for children, for spiritual minors, for Christians in the crude stage of the divine life, afflicted with confusion of mind, dumbness, dejection, unable to pray for want of clear thought, apt words, and above all, of faith that knows how to wait in hope ; and it meets the wants of such by suggesting topics, supplying forms of language, and furnishing their weak faith with the props of cogent arguments for perseverance. Now such was the state of the twelve during all the time they were with Jesus ; till He ascended to heaven, and power descended from heaven on them, bringing with it a loosed tongue and an enlarged heart. During the whole period of their discipleship, they needed prompting in prayer such as a mother gives her child, and exhortations to perseverance in the habit of praying, even as do the humblest followers of Christ. Far

---

[1] The request, in that case, might be pharaphrased : " Lord, teach (Thou also) us to pray, as John taught us when we were *his* disciples."

from being exempt from such infirmities, the twelve may even have experienced them in a superlative degree. The heights correspond to the depths in religious experience. Men who are destined to be apostles must, as disciples, know more than most of the chaotic, speechless condition, and of the great, irksome, but most salutary business of Waiting on God for light, and truth, and grace, earnestly desired but long withheld.

It was well for the church that her first ministers needed this lesson on prayer; for the time comes in the case of most, if not all, who are spiritually earnest, when its teaching is very seasonable. In the spring of the divine life, the beautiful blossom-time of piety, Christians may be able to pray with fluency and fervor, unembarrassed by want of words, thoughts, and feelings of a certain kind. But that happy stage soon passes, and is succeeded by one in which prayer often becomes a helpless struggle, an inarticulate groan, a silent, distressed, despondent waiting on God, on the part of men who are tempted to doubt whether God be indeed the hearer of prayer, whether prayer be not altogether idle and useless. The three wants contemplated and provided for in this lesson — the want of ideas, of words, and of faith — are as common as they are grievous. How long it takes most to fill even the simple petitions of the Lord's Prayer with definite meanings! the second petition, e.g., "Thy kingdom come," which can be presented with perfect intelligence only by such as have formed for themselves a clear conception of the ideal spiritual republic or commonwealth. How difficult, and therefore how rare, to find out acceptable words for precious thoughts slowly reached! How many, who have never got any thing on which their hearts were set without needing to ask for it often, and to wait for it long (no uncommon experience), have been tempted by the delay to give up asking in despair! And no wonder; for delay is hard to bear in all cases, especially in connection with spiritual blessings, which are in fact, and are by Christ here assumed to be, the principal object of a Christian man's desires. Devout souls would not be utterly confounded by delay, or even refusal, in connection with mere temporal goods; for they know that such things as health, wealth, wife, children, home, position,

are not unconditionally good, and that it may be well sometimes not to obtain them, or not easily and too soon. But it
is most confounding to desire with all one's heart the Holy
Ghost, and yet seem to be denied the priceless boon ; to pray
for light, and to get instead deeper darkness ; for faith, and
to be tormented with doubts which shake cherished convictions to their foundations ; for sanctity, and to have the mud
of corruption stirred up by temptation from the bottom of
the well of eternal life in the heart.   Yet all this, as every
experienced Christian'knows, is part of the discipline through
which scholars in Christ's school have to pass ere the desire
of their heart be fulfilled.[1]

The lesson on prayer taught by Christ, in answer to
request, consists of two parts, in one of which thoughts and
words are put into the mouths of immature disciples, while
the other provides aids to faith in God as the answerer of
prayer.   There is first a form of prayer, and then an argument enforcing perseverance in prayer.

The form of prayer commonly called the Lord's Prayer,
which appears in the Sermon on the Mount as a sample of
the right kind of prayer, is given here as a summary of the
general heads under which all special petitions may be comprehended.   We may call this form the *alphabet* of all possible prayer.   It embraces the elements of all spiritual desire,
summed up in a few choice sentences, for the benefit of those
who may not be able to bring their struggling aspirations to
birth in articulate language.   It contains in all six petitions,
of which three — the first three, as was meet — refer to
God's glory, and the remaining three to man's good.   We
are taught to pray, first for the advent of the divine kingdom,
in the form of universal reverence for the divine name, and
universal obedience to the divine will ; and then, in the
second place, for daily bread, pardon, and protection from
evil for ourselves.   The whole is addressed to God as Father,
and is supposed to proceed from such as realize their fellowship one with another as members of a divine family, and
therefore say, "Our Father."   The prayer does not end, as

---

[1] Readers may be reminded here of the well-known hymn of Newton, beginning —

"I asked the Lord that I might grow
In faith, and love, and every grace." — (No. 25, F. C. Hymn-Book.)

our prayers now commonly do, with the formula, "for Christ's sake;" nor could it, consistently with the supposition that it proceeded from Jesus. No prayer given by Him for the present use of His disciples, before His death, could have such an ending, because the plea it contains was not intelligible to them previous to that event. The twelve did not yet know what Christ's sake (*sache*) meant, nor would they till after their Lord had ascended, and the Spirit had descended and revealed to them the true meaning of the facts of Christ's earthly history. Hence we find Jesus, on the eve of His passion, telling His disciples that up to that time they had asked nothing in His name, and representing the use of His name as a plea to be heard, as one of the privileges awaiting them in the future. "Hitherto," He said, "have ye asked nothing in my name; ask, and ye shall receive, that your joy may be full."[1]   And in another part of His discourse: "Whatsoever ye shall ask in my name, that will I do, that the Father may be glorified in the Son."[2]

To what extent the disciples afterwards made use of this beautifully simple yet profoundly significant form, we do not know; but it may be assumed that they were in the habit of repeating it as the disciples of the Baptist might repeat the forms taught them by *their* master. There is, however, no reason to think that the " Lord's Prayer," though of permanent value as a part of Christ's teaching, was designed to be a stereotyped, binding method of addressing the Father in heaven. It was meant to be an aid to inexperienced disciples, not a rule imposed upon apostles.[3] Even after they had attained to spiritual maturity, the twelve might use this form if they pleased, and possibly they did occasionally use it; but Jesus expected that by the time they came to be teachers in the church they should have outgrown the need of it as an aid to devotion. Filled with the Spirit, enlarged in heart, mature in spiritual understanding, they should then be able to pray as their Lord had prayed when He was with them; and while the six petitions of the model prayer would still

[1] John xvi. 24.
[2] John xiv. 13.
[3] Jeremy Taylor, in his *Apology for Authorized and Set Forms of Liturgy*, makes no distinction between disciples and apostles. When the distinction is attended to, much of his argument falls to the ground. *Vid.* §§ 86-112.

enter into all their supplications at the throne of grace, they would do so only as the alphabet of a language enters into the most extended and eloquent utterances of a speaker, who never thinks of the letters of which the words he utters are composed.[1]

In maintaining the provisional, *pro tempore* character of the Lord's Prayer, so far as the twelve were concerned, we lay no stress on the fact already adverted to, that it does not end with the phrase, "for Christ's sake." That defect could easily be supplied afterwards mentally or orally, and therefore was no valid reason for disuse. The same remark applies to our use of the prayer in question. To allow this form to fall into desuetude merely because the customary concluding plea is wanting, is as weak on one side as the too frequent repetition of it is on the other. The Lord's Prayer is neither a piece of Deism unworthy of a Christian, nor a magic charm like the "Pater noster" of Roman Catholic devotion. The most advanced believer will often find relief and rest to his spirit in falling back on its simple, sublime sentences, while mentally realizing the manifold particulars which each of them includes ; and he is but a tyro in the art of praying, and in the divine life generally, whose devotions consist exclusively, or even mainly, in repeating the words which Jesus put into the mouths of immature disciples.

The view now advocated regarding the purpose of the Lord's Prayer is in harmony with the spirit of Christ's whole teaching. Liturgical forms and religious methodism in general were much more congenial to the strict ascetic school of the Baptist than to the free school of Jesus. Our Lord evidently attached little importance to forms of prayer, any more than to fixed periodic fasts, else He would not have waited till He was asked for a form, but would have made systematic provision for the wants of His followers, even as the Baptist did, by, so to speak, compiling a book of devotion or composing a liturgy. It is evident, even from the present instructions on the subject of praying, that Jesus considered

---

[1] Keim takes the same view : he thinks the *Mustergebet* was not meant to be an *Alltagsgebet*, and in proof adduces the facts that no trace of its use appears in the history of Christ's own life, in the times of the Jerusalem Church, in the recollections of the Apostle Paul, and that only in the second century it began to be the object of a regular " ja mechanisch-katholischen " use. — *Jesu von Nazara*, ii. 280.

the form He supplied of quite subordinate importance: a mere temporary remedy for a minor evil, the want of utterance, till the greater evil, the want of faith, should be cured ; for the larger portion of the lesson is devoted to the purpose of supplying an antidote to unbelief.[1]

The second part of this lesson on prayer is intended to convey the same moral as that which is prefixed to the

[1] From the design of the Lord's Prayer as now explained we may determine the proper place and use of all fixed forms of devotion. Liturgical forms are for private rather than for public use ; for those who are in the dumb, arid stage of the spiritual life, rather than for those who have attained the power and utterance of spiritual maturity. To the private use of such forms by persons who desire to pray, yet cannot do it, no reasonable objection can be taken. Advantage justifies use. The less experienced Christian may ask the more experienced to teach him to pray, and the more experienced may reply, " After this manner pray ye." If we may read and repeat the sacred songs of Christian poets to find expression for emotions which are common to us and them, but which we cannot, like them, adequately express, why may we not read and repeat the prayers of the saints for a similar purpose? The superficial, who have not earnestness and sincerity enough to know what it is to stammer, may despise such aids as suited only for children ; and those who are yet in the first flush of religious fervor may turn away from written forms as cold and dead, however classical. Well, let all do without such aids who can ; only the time may come, even for the fervent, when, forsaken of emotion, deficient in experience, discouraged by failure, disappointed in ardent youthful hopes, tormented by speculative doubts concerning the utility and the reasonableness of prayer coming over the soul like chill east winds in the winter of its religious history, they may be very glad to read over forms of devotion which, by their simplicity and dignity, serve to inspire a sense of reality, and to produce a soothing, sedative effect on their diseased, restless spirits. For all in such a plight, we, having respect to the example of Christ, are entitled to plead that they shall not be required to remain prayerless because they cannot for the time pray without book.

But when we pass from the closet to the church, the case is altered. There we ought to find pastors capable of doing, each one for his fellow-worshippers, what Christ did for His disciples, and of praying with the freedom and force to which the disciples themselves afterwards attained. It may be asserted, indeed, that this, though the desirable, is not the actual state of matters. A recent writer, in advocating the introduction of written forms of prayer into the Presbyterian Church, says : " I feel persuaded that a *verbatim* report of all the public prayers uttered in Scotland any one Sunday in the year would settle the question forever in the mind of every person who was capable of forming a rational judgment on such a matter." * It is to be hoped that this is an exaggerated view of existing ministerial incapacity ; but even granting its accuracy, it is a fair question whether the remedy proposed would not be worse than the evil, and the gain in propriety more than counterbalanced by a loss in the more important quality of fervor. This much we may say, even if not disposed to take up high ground of principle in opposition to liturgical forms, but rather to concur in the moderate sentiments of Richard Baxter, when he says : " I cannot be of their opinion who think God will not accept him that prayeth by the common Prayer-book, and that such forms are a self-invented worship which God rejecteth ; nor yet can I be of their mind that say the use of extemporary prayers." † In Baxter's time religious controversy ran very high, and opposed views were stated in extreme form. The Churchman derided the extempore effusions of the Puritan ; the Puritan went so far in his opposition to liturgical prayer as even to maintain that the Lord's Prayer itself should never be repeated. Baxter, not being a partisan,

* *The Reform of the Church of Scotland*, by Robert Lee, D.D., p. 76.
† Baxter's Life, from his own original MS., lib. i. part i § 213.

parable of the unjust judge — "that men ought always to pray, and not to faint." The supposed cause of fainting is also the same, even delay on the part of God in answering our prayers. This is not, indeed, made so obvious in the earlier lesson as in the later. The parable of the ungenerous neighbor is not adapted to convey the idea of long delay ; for the favor asked, if granted at all, must be granted in a

but a lover of truth, sympathized with neither party, but regarded the question at issue as one of policy rather than of principle, to be settled not by abstract reasoning, but by a calm consideration of what on the whole was most conducive to edification ; in which point of view his judgment and his practice were both on the side of extempore prayer.

Looking at the question, with Baxter, as one of policy, we are fully persuaded that the existing practice of Presbyterian and other churches can be justified on such good grounds as should make them contented, to say the least, with their own way, and indisposed to imitate those whose way is different in this matter. The ministers of religion, like the apostles, ought to be able to dispense with liturgical forms ; and the best way to secure that they shall possess such ability, is.to throw them on their own resources, and on God, and so convert the ideal into a requirement applicable to all, making no provision for exceptions. The full benefit of a system cannot be obtained unless it be rigidly enforced ; and while such enforcement may involve occasional disadvantages, the relaxation of the rule would probably produce greater damage to the church. Allowance made for timidity, inexperience, or extraordinary incapacity, would be abused by the indolent and the careless ; and many would remain permanently in a state similar to that of the disciples, who, if compelled to stir up the gift of God which is in them, or to seek earnestly gifts and graces not possessed, might ere long attain to apostolic freedom and power. The same remarks might be applied to preaching. In individual instances congregations might benefit by the preacher being allowed to use foreign materials of instruction ; but under such a permission, how many would content themselves with reading sermons out of books, or from manuscripts purchased at so much per dozen, who, under a system aiming at turning to the utmost account individual talent, and therefore requiring all teachers of truth to give their hearers the benefit of their own thoughts, would through practice attain to a fair measure of preaching power.

On the whole, therefore, the Presbyterian Church has reason to be satisfied with its existing **system** of public worship, whatever reason there may be for dissatisfaction with the existing state of worship in particular instances. The ideal is good, however far short the reality may come of it. The aim and effect of the liturgical system is to make the mass of worshippers as independent as possible of the individual minister ; the aim, if not the effect of our system, is to make individual ministers as valuable as possible to the worshippers, for their instruction and edification. The one system may secure a uniform solemnity and decency, but the other system tends to secure the more important qualities of fervor, energy, and life; and we believe, whatever fastidious critics may allege, it does to a considerable extent secure them. At lowest, the non-liturgical method secures that the worship of the church shall be a true reflection of her life, and therefore, however beggarly, at least sincere. Men who preach their own sermons and pray their own prayers are more likely to preach and pray as they believe and live, than those who merely read compositions provided to their hand. It only remains to add, that while having no objection on principle to an attempt at amalgamating the two methods so as to reap the advantages of both — a scheme favored by some respected brethren in all the churches — we confess to grave doubts, for the reasons above explained, as to the utility of such an attempt. [We leave the above as in the second edition. Our present impression, however, is that a mixture of the liturgical system, with fixed forms, with the free extempore method, is not impracticable, and might yield better results than either separately. — Note to third edition.]

very few minutes.   But the lapse of time between the presenting and the granting of our requests is implied and
presupposed as a matter of course.   It is by delay that God
seems to say to us what the ungenerous neighbor said to
his friend, and that we are tempted to think that we pray
to no purpose.

Both the parables spoken by Christ to inculcate perseverance in prayer seek to effect their purpose by showing the
power of importunity in the most unpromising circumstances.
The characters appealed to are both bad — one is ungenerous,
and the other unjust ; and from neither is any thing to be
gained except by working on his selfishness.   And the point
of the parable in either case is, that importunity has a power
of annoyance which enables it to gain its object.

It is important again to observe what is supposed to be
the leading subject of prayer in connection with the argument now to be considered.   The thing upon which Christ
assumes His disciples to have set their hearts is personal
sanctification.[1]   This appears from the concluding sentence
of the discourse: "How much more shall your heavenly
Father give the Holy Spirit to them that ask Him !"   Jesus
takes for granted that the persons to whom He addresses
Himself here seek first the kingdom of God and His righteousness.   Therefore, though He inserted a petition for
daily bread in the form of prayer, He drops that object out
of view in the latter part of His discourse ; both because it is
by hypothesis not the chief object of desire, and also because,
for all who truly give God's kingdom the first place in their
regards, food and raiment are thrown into the bargain.[2]

To such as do not desire the Holy Spirit above all things,
Jesus has nothing to say.   He does not encourage them to
hope that they shall receive any thing of the Lord ; least of
all, the righteousness of the kingdom, personal sanctification.
He regards the prayers of a double-minded man, who has

---

[1] The supposed subject of prayer in Luke xviii. is the general interest of the divine
kingdom on the earth.

[2] In Matt. vii. 11, which answers to Luke xi. 13, the phrase expressive of the object
of desire is ἀγαθὰ, "good things," instead of πνεῦμα ἅγιον.   The Pauline character of the
latter expression has been remarked on, as one of many traces of the apostle's influence
on the third Evangelist.   The doctrine that the Holy Spirit is the immanent ground of
Christian sanctity is emphatically Pauline.   But the doctrine of *gradual* sanctification
is not prominent in Paulinism.

two chief ends in view, as a hollow mockery — mere words, which never reach Heaven's ear.

The supposed cause of fainting being delay, and the supposed object of desire being the Holy Spirit, the spiritual situation contemplated in the argument is definitely determined. The Teacher's aim is to succor and encourage those who feel that the work of grace goes slowly on within them, and wonder why it does so, and sadly sigh because it does so. Such we conceive to have been the state of the twelve when this lesson was given them. They had been made painfully conscious of incapacity to perform aright their devotional duties, and they took that incapacity to be an index of their general spiritual condition, and were much depressed in consequence.

The argument by which Jesus sought to inspire His discouraged disciples with hope and confidence as to the ultimate fulfilment of their desires, is characterized by boldness, geniality, wisdom, and logical force. Its boldness is evinced in the choice of illustrations. Jesus has such confidence in the goodness of His cause, that He states the case as disadvantageously for Himself as possible, by selecting for illustration not good samples of men, but persons rather below than above the ordinary standard of human virtue. A man who, on being applied to at any hour of the night by a neighbor for help in a real emergency, such as that supposed in the parable, or in a case of sudden sickness, should put him off with such an answer as this, "Trouble me not, the door is now shut, and my children are with me in bed : I cannot rise and give thee," would justly incur the contempt of his acquaintances, and become a byword among them for all that is ungenerous and heartless. The same readiness to take an extreme case is observable in the second argument, drawn from the conduct of fathers towards their children. "If a son shall ask bread of *any* of you" — so it begins.[1] Jesus does not care what father may be selected ; He is willing to take any one they please : He will take the very worst as readily as the best ; nay, more readily, for the argument turns not on the goodness of the parent, but rather on his

---

[1] Or "of which of you that is a father shall his son ask a loaf," as in R. V. The sense is the same.

want of goodness, as it aims to show that no special goodness is required to keep all parents from doing what would
be an outrage on natural affection, and revolting to the
feelings of all mankind.

The genial, kindly character of the argument is manifest
from the insight and sympathy displayed therein.   Jesus
divines what hard thoughts men think of God under the
burden of unfulfilled desire ; how they doubt His goodness,
and deem Him indifferent, heartless, unjust.   He shows His
intimate knowledge of their secret imaginations by the cases
He puts ; for the unkind friend and unnatural father, and we
may add, the unjust judge, are pictures not indeed of what
God is, or of what He would have us believe God to be, but
certainly of what even pious men sometimes think Him to
be.[1]   And He cannot only divine, but sympathize.   He
does not, like Job's friends, find fault with those who harbor
doubting and apparently profane thoughts, nor chide them
for impatience, distrust, and despondency.   He deals with
them as men compassed with infirmity, and needing sympathy, counsel, and help.   And in supplying these, He comes
down to their level of feeling, and tries to show that, even
if things were as they seem, there is no cause for despair.
He argues from their own thoughts of God, that they should
still hope in Him.   "Suppose," He says in effect, "God to
be what you fancy, indifferent and heartless, still pray on ;
see, in the case I put, what perseverance can effect.   Ask
as the man who wanted loaves asked, and ye shall also
receive from Him who seems at present deaf to your petitions.   Appearances, I grant, may be very unfavorable, but
they cannot be more so in your case than in that of the
petitioner in the parable ; and yet you observe how he fared
through not being too easily disheartened."

Jesus displays His wisdom in dealing with the doubts of
His disciples, by avoiding all elaborate explanations of the
causes or reasons of delay in the answering of prayer, and
using only arguments adapted to the capacity of persons
weak in faith and in spiritual understanding.   He does not
attempt to show why sanctification is a slow, tedious work,
not a momentary act : why the Spirit is given gradually and

[1] See the Book of Job, *passim*, and Ps. lxxiii., lxxvii., etc.

in limited measure, not at once and without measure. He simply urges His hearers to persevere in seeking the Holy Spirit, assuring them that, in spite of trying delay, their desires will be fulfilled in the end. He teaches them no philosophy of waiting on God, but only tells them that they shall not wait in vain.

This method the Teacher followed not from necessity, but from choice. For though no attempt was made at explaining divine delays in providence and grace, it was not because explanation was impossible. There were many things which Christ might have said to His disciples at this time if they could have borne them ; some of which they afterwards said themselves, when the Spirit of Truth had come, and guided them into all truth, and made them acquainted with the secret of God's way. He might have pointed out to them, e.g., that the delays of which they complained were according to the analogy of nature, in which gradual growth is the universal law ; that time was needed for the production of the ripe fruits of the Spirit, just in the same way as for the production of the ripe fruits of the field or of the orchard ; that it was not to be wondered at if the spiritual fruits were peculiarly slow in ripening, as it was a law of growth that the higher the product in the scale of being, the slower the process by which it is produced ;[1] that a momentary sanctification, though not impossible, would be as much a miracle in the sense of a departure from law, as was the immediate transformation of water into wine at the marriage in Cana ; that if instantaneous sanctification were the rule instead of the rare exception, the kingdom of grace would become too like the imaginary worlds of children's dreams, in which trees, fruits, and palaces spring into being full-grown, ripe, and furnished, in a moment as by enchantment, and too unlike the real, actual world with which men are conversant, in which delay, growth, and fixed law are invariable characteristics.

Jesus might further have sought to reconcile His disciples to delay by descanting on the virtue of patience. Much could be said on that topic. It could be shown that a char-

[1] This idea is well worked out in a sermon by H. W. Beecher on " Waiting for the Lord." — *Sermons,* vol. 1.

acter cannot be perfect in which the virtue of patience has no place, and that the gradual method of sanctification is best adapted for its development, as affording abundant scope for its exercise.   It might be pointed out how much the ultimate enjoyment of any good thing is enhanced by its having to be waited for ; how in proportion to the trial is the triumph of faith ; how, in the quaint words of one who was taught wisdom in this matter by his own experience, and by the times in which he lived, " It is fit we see and feel the shaping and sewing of every piece of the wedding garment, and the framing and moulding and fitting of the crown of glory for the head of the citizen of heaven ;" how "the repeated sense and frequent experience of grace in the ups and downs in the way, the falls and risings again of the traveller, the revolutions and changes of the spiritual condition, the new moon, the darkened moon, the full moon in the Spirit's ebbing and flowing, raiseth in the heart of saints on their way to the country a sweet smell of the fairest rose and lily of Sharon ;" how, " as travellers at night talk of their foul ways, and of the praises of their guide, and battle being ended, soldiers number their wounds, extol the valor, skill, and courage of their leader and captain," so "it is meet that the glorified soldiers may take loads of experience of free grace to heaven with them, and there speak of their way and their country, and the praises of Him that hath redeemed them out of all nations, tongues, and languages.[1]"

Such considerations, however just, would have been wasted on men in the spiritual condition of the disciples.   Children have no sympathy with growth in any world, whether of nature or of grace.   Nothing pleases them but that an acorn should become an oak at once, and that immediately after the blossom should come the ripe fruit.   Then it is idle to speak of the uses of patience to the inexperienced ; for the moral value of the discipline of trial cannot be appreciated till the trial is past.   Therefore, as before stated, Jesus abstained entirely from reflections of the kind suggested, and adopted a simple, popular style of reasoning which even a child could understand.

The reasoning of Jesus, while very simple, is very cogent

[1] Samuel Rutherford, *Trial and Triumph of Faith*, Sermon xviii.

and conclusive. The first argument — that contained in the parable of the ungenerous neighbor — is fitted to inspire hope in God, even in the darkest hour, when He appears indifferent to our cry, or positively unwilling to help, and so to induce us to persevere in asking. "As the man who wanted the loaves knocked on louder and louder, with an importunity that knew no shame,' and would take no refusal, and thereby gained his object, the selfish friend being glad at last to get up and serve him out of sheer regard to his own comfort, it being simply impossible to sleep with such a noise; *so* (such is the drift of the argument), so continue thou knocking at the door of heaven, and thou shalt obtain thy desire if it were only to be rid of thee. See in this parable what a power importunity has, even at a most unpromising time — midnight — and with a most unpromising person, who prefers his own comfort to a neighbor's good: ask, therefore, persistently, and it shall be given unto you also; seek, and ye shall find; knock, and it shall be opened unto you."

At one point, indeed, this most pathetic and sympathetic argument seems to be weak. The petitioner in the parable had the selfish friend in his power by being able to annoy him and keep him from sleeping. Now, the tried desponding disciple whom Jesus would comfort may rejoin: "What power have I to annoy *God*, who dwelleth on high, far beyond my reach, in imperturbable felicity? 'Oh that I knew where I might find Him, that I might come even to His seat! But, behold, I go forward, but He is not there; and backward, but I cannot perceive Him: on the left hand, where He doth work, but I cannot behold Him: He hideth Himself on the right hand, that I cannot see Him.'"[2] The objection is one which can hardly fail to occur to the subtle spirit of despondency, and it must be admitted that it is not frivolous. There is really a failure of the analogy at this point. We can annoy a man, like the ungenerous neighbor in bed, or the unjust judge, but we cannot annoy God. The parable does not suggest the true explanation of divine delay, or of the ultimate success of importunity. It merely proves, by a homely instance, that delay, apparent refusal, from whatever cause

---

[1] The Greek word is ἀναίδειαν = shamelessness. [2] Job xxiii. 3, 8, 9.

it may arise, is not necessarily final, and therefore can be no good reason for giving up asking.

This is a real if not a great service rendered. But the doubting disciple, besides discovering with characteristic acuteness what the parable fails to prove, may not be able to extract any comfort from what it does prove. What is he to do then? Fall back on the strong asseveration with which Jesus follows up the parable: "And *I* say unto you." Here, doubter, is an oracular dictum from One who can speak with authority; One who has been in the bosom of the eternal God, and has come forth to reveal His inmost heart to men groping in the darkness of nature after Him, if haply they might find Him. When He addresses you in such emphatic, solemn terms as these, "I say unto you, Ask, and it shall be given you; seek, and ye shall find; knock, and it shall be opened unto you," you may take the matter on His word, at least *pro tempore*. Even those who doubt the reasonableness of prayer, because of the constancy of nature's laws and the unchangeableness of divine purposes, might take Christ's word for it that prayer is not vain, even in relation to daily bread, not to speak of higher matters, until they arrive at greater certainty on the subject than they can at present pretend to. Such may, if they choose, despise the parable as childish, or as conveying crude anthropopathic ideas of the Divine Being, but they cannot despise the deliberate declarations of One whom even they regard as the wisest and best of men.

The second argument employed by Jesus to urge perseverance in prayer is of the nature of a *reductio ad absurdum*, ending with a conclusion *à fortiori*. "If," it is reasoned, "God refused to hear His children's prayers, or, worse still, if He mocked them by giving them something bearing a superficial resemblance to the things asked, only to cause bitter disappointment when the deception was discovered, then were He not only as bad as, but far worse than, even the most depraved of mankind. For, take fathers at random, which of them, if a son were to ask bread, would give him a stone? or if he asked a fish, would give him a serpent? or if he asked an egg, would offer him a scorpion? The very supposition is monstrous. Human nature is largely vitiated by moral evil; there is, in particular, an evil spirit of selfishness in the heart which comes into conflict with the generous affections, and leads men ofttimes to do base and unnatural things. But men taken at the average are not diabolic; and nothing short of a diabolic spirit of mischief could prompt a father to mock a child's misery, or deliberately to give him things fraught with deadly harm. If, then, earthly parents, though evil in many of their dispositions, give good, and, so far as they know, only good, gifts to their children, and would shrink with horror from any other mode of treatment, is it to be credited that the Divine Being, that Providence, can do what only devils would think of doing? On the contrary, what is only barely possible for man is for God altogether impossible, and what all but monsters of iniquity will not fail to do God will do much more. He will most surely give good gifts, and only good gifts, to His asking children; most especially will He give His best gift, which His true children desire above all things, even the Holy Spirit, the enlightener and the sanctifier. Therefore again I say unto you: Ask, and ye shall receive; seek, and ye shall find; knock, and it shall be opened."

Yet it is implied in the very fact that Christ puts such cases as a stone given for bread, a serpent for a fish, or a scorpion for an egg, that God seems at least sometimes so to treat His children. The time came when the twelve thought they had been so treated in reference to the very subject in which they were most deeply interested, after their own personal sanctification, viz., the restoration of the kingdom to Israel. But their experience illustrates the general truth, that when the Hearer of prayer seems to deal unnaturally with His servants, it is because they have made a mistake about the nature of good, and have not known what they asked. They have asked for a stone, thinking it bread, and hence the true bread seems a stone; for a shadow, thinking it a substance, and hence the substance seems a shadow. The kingdom for which the twelve prayed was a shadow, hence their disappointment and despair when Jesus was put to death: the egg of hope, which their fond imagination had been hatching, brought forth the scorpion of the cross, and they fancied that God had mocked and

deceived them. But they lived to see that God was true
and good, and that they had deceived themselves, and that
all which Christ had told them had been fulfilled. And all
who wait on God ultimately make a similar discovery, and
unite in testifying that "the Lord is good unto them that
wait for Him, to the soul that seeketh Him." [1]

For these reasons should all men pray, and not faint.
Prayer is rational, even if the Divine Being were like men
in the average, not indisposed to do good when self-interest
does not stand in the way — the creed of heathenism. It is
still more manifestly rational if, as Christ taught and Christians believe, God be better than the best of men — the one
supremely good Being — the *Father* in heaven. Only in
either of two cases would prayer really be irrational: if God
were no living being at all, — the creed of atheists, with
whom Christ holds no argument; or if He were a being
capable of doing things from which even bad men would
start back in horror, *i.e.*, a being of diabolic nature, — the
creed, it is to be hoped, of no human being.

---

[1] Lam. iii. 25.

7

LESSONS IN RELIGIOUS LIBERTY;
or, the Nature of True Holiness

SECTION I — FASTING

Matt. 9:14-17; Mark 2:16-22; Luke 5:33-39

WE have learnt in the last chapter how Jesus taught His disciples to pray, and we are now to learn in the present chapter how He taught them to live.

Christ's *ratio vivendi* was characteristically simple ; its main features being a disregard of minute mechanical rules, and a habit of falling back in all things on the great principles of morality and piety.

The practical carrying out of this rule of life led to considerable divergence from prevailing custom. In three respects especially, according to the Gospel records, were our Lord and His disciples chargeable, and actually charged, with the offence of nonconformity. They departed from existing practice in the matters of fasting, ceremonial purifications as prescribed by the elders, and Sabbath sanctification. The first they neglected for the most part, the second altogether; the third they did not neglect, but their mode of observing the weekly rest was in spirit totally, and in detail widely, diverse from that which was in vogue.

These divergences from established custom are historically interesting as the small beginnings of a great moral and religious revolution. For in teaching His disciples these new habits, Jesus was inaugurating a process of spiritual emancipation which was to issue in the complete deliverance of the apostles, and through them of the Christian church, from the burdensome yoke of Mosaic ordinances, and from the still more galling bondage of a "vain conversation received by tradition from the fathers."

The divergences in question have much biographical interest also in connection with the religious experience of the
twelve. For it is a solemn crisis in any man's life when he
first departs in the most minute particulars from the religious
opinions and practices of his age. The first steps in the
process of change are generally the most difficult, the most
perilous, and the most decisive. In these respects, learning
spiritual freedom is like learning to swim. Every expert
in the aquatic art remembers the troubles he experienced in
connection with his first attempts, — how hard he found it to
make arms and legs keep stroke ; how he floundered and
plunged ; how fearful he was lest he should go beyond his
depth and sink to the bottom. At these early fears he may
now smile, yet were they not altogether groundless ; for the
tyro does run some risk of drowning though the bathing-
place be but a small pool or dam built by schoolboys on a
burn flowing through an inland dell, remote from broad rivers
and the great sea.

It is well both for young swimmers and for apprentices in
religious freedom when they make their first essays in the
company of an experienced friend, who can rescue them
should they be in danger. Such a friend the twelve had in
Christ, whose presence was not only a safeguard against all
inward spiritual risks, but a shield from all assaults which
might come upon them from without. Such assaults were
to be expected. Nonconformity invariably gives offence to
many, and exposes the offending party to interrogation at
least, and often to something more serious. Custom is a
god to the multitude, and no one can withhold homage from
the idol with impunity. The twelve accordingly did in fact
incur the usual penalties connected with singularity. Their
conduct was called in question, and censured, in every
instance of departure from use and wont. Had they been
left to themselves, they would have made a poor defence
of the actions impugned ; for they did not understand the
principles on which the new practice was based, but simply
did as they were directed. But in Jesus they had a friend
who did understand those principles, and who was ever ready
to assign good reasons for all He did Himself, and for all
He taught His followers to do. The reasons with which he

defended the twelve against the upholders of prevailing usage were specially good and telling; and they constitute, taken together, an apology for nonconformity not less remarkable than that which He made for graciously receiving publicans and sinners,[1] consisting, like it, of three lines of defence corresponding to the charges which had to be met. That apology we propose to consider in the present chapter under three divisions, in the first of which we take up the subject of *fasting*.

From Matthew's account we learn that the conduct of Christ's disciples in neglecting fasting was animadverted on by the disciples of John the Baptist. "Then," we read, "came to Him the disciples of John" — those, that is, who happened to be in the neighborhood — "saying, Why do we and the Pharisees fast oft, but Thy disciples fast not?"[2] From this question we learn incidentally that in the matter of fasting the school of the Baptist and the sect of the Pharisees were agreed in their general practice. As Jesus told the Pharisees at a later date, John came in their own "way" of legal righteousness."[3] But it was a case of extremes meeting; for no two religious parties could be more remote in some respects than the two just named. But the difference lay rather in the motives than in the external acts of their religious life. Both did the same things — fasted, practised ceremonial ablutions, made many prayers — only they did them with a different mind. John and his disciples performed their religious duties in simplicity, godly sincerity, and moral earnestness; the Pharisees, as a class, did all their works ostentatiously, hypocritically, and as matters of mechanical routine.

From the same question we further learn that the disciples of John, as well as the Pharisees, were very zealous in the practice of fasting. They fasted *oft, much* (πυκνὰ, Luke; πολλὰ, Matthew). This statement we otherwise know to be strictly true of such Pharisees as made great pretensions to piety. Besides the annual fast on the great day of atone-

---

[1] *Vide* pp. 26, 27.

[2] Matt. ix. 14. From Mark and Luke it might be inferred that some Pharisees were joint interrogators; but it is not asserted, neither is it likely.

[3] Matt. xxi. 32.

ment appointed by the law of Moses, and the four fasts which had become customary in the time of the Prophet Zechariah, in the fourth, fifth, seventh, and tenth months of the Jewish year, the stricter sort of Jews fasted twice every week, viz., on Mondays and Thursdays.[1] This bi-weekly fast is alluded to in the parable of the Pharisee and the publican.[2] It is not to be assumed, of course, that the practice of the Baptist's disciples coincided in this respect with that of the strictest sect of the pharisaic party. Their system of fasting may have been organized on an independent plan, involving different arrangements as to times and occasions. The one fact known, which rests on the certain basis of their own testimony, is that, like the Pharisees, John's disciples fasted often, if not on precisely the same days and for the same reasons.

It does not clearly appear what feelings prompted the question put by John's disciples to Jesus. It is not impossible that party spirit was at work, for rivalry and jealousy were not unknown, even in the environment of the forerunner.[3] In that case, the reference to pharisaic practice might be explained by a desire to overwhelm the disciples of Jesus by numbers, and put them, as it were, in a hopeless minority on the question. It is more likely, however, that the uppermost feeling in the mind of the interrogators was one of surprise, that in respect of fasting they should approach nearer to a sect whose adherents were stigmatized by their own master as a "generation of vipers," than to the followers of One for whom that master cherished and expressed the deepest veneration. In that case, the object of the question was to obtain information and instruction. It accords with this view that the query was addressed to Jesus. Had disputation been aimed at, the questioners would more naturally have applied to the disciples.

If John's followers came seeking instruction, they were not disappointed. Jesus made a reply to their question, remarkable at once for originality, point, and pathos, setting forth in lively parabolic style the great principles by which

---

[1] See Buxtorf, *De Synagoga Judaica*, c. xxx. ; also Zech. viii. 19.
[2] Luke xviii. 12.
[3] John iii. 26.

the conduct of His disciples could be vindicated, and by which He desired the conduct of all who bore His name to be regulated. Of this reply it is to be observed, in the first place, that it is of a purely defensive character. Jesus does not blame John's disciples for fasting, but contents Himself with defending His own disciples for abstaining from fasting. He does not feel called on to disparage the one party in order to justify the other, but takes up the position of one who virtually says : " To fast may be right for you, the followers of John : not to fast is equally right for my followers." How grateful to Christ's feelings it must have been that He could assume this tolerant attitude on a question in which the name of John was mixed up ! For He had a deep respect for the forerunner and his work, and ever spoke of him in most generous terms of appreciation ; now calling him a burning and a shining lamp,[1] and at another time declaring him not only a prophet but something more.[2] And we may remark in passing, that John reciprocated these kindly feelings, and had no sympathy with the petty jealousies in which his disciples sometimes indulged. The two great ones, both of them censured for different reasons by their degenerate contemporaries, ever spoke of each other to their disciples and to the public in terms of affectionate respect ; the lesser light magnanimously confessing his inferiority, the greater magnifying the worth of His humble fellow-servant. What a refreshing contrast was thus presented to the mean passions of envy, prejudice, and detraction so prevalent in other quarters, under whose malign influence men of whom better things might have been expected spoke of John as a madman, and of Jesus as immoral and profane ![3]

Passing from the manner to the matter of the reply, we notice that, for the purpose of vindicating His disciples, Jesus availed Himself of a metaphor suggested by a memorable word uttered concerning Himself at an earlier period by the master of those who now examined Him. To certain disciples who complained that men were leaving him and going to Jesus, John had said in effect : " Jesus is the Bridegroom, I am but the Bridegroom's friend ; therefore it is

---

[1] John v. 35.   [2] Matt. xi. 7-15.
[3] Matt. xi. 16, 19.

right that men should leave me and join Jesus."[1]   Jesus
now takes up the Baptist's words, and turns them to account
for the purpose of defending the way of life pursued by His
disciples.   His reply, freely paraphrased, is to this effect :
" I *am* the Bridegroom, as your master said ; it is right that
the children of the bride-chamber come to me ; and it is also
right that, when they have come, they should adapt their
mode of life to their altered circumstances.   Therefore they
do well not to fast, for fasting is the expression of sadness,
and how should they be sad in my company ?   As well might
men be sad at a marriage festival.   The days *will* come when
the children of the bride-chamber shall be sad, for the Bridegroom will not always be with them ; and at the dark hour
of His departure it will be natural and seasonable for them
to fast, for then they shall be in a fasting mood — weeping,
lamenting, sorrowful, and disconsolate."

The principle underlying this graphic representation is,
that fasting should not be a matter of fixed mechanical rule,
but should have reference to the state of mind ; or, more
definitely, that men should fast when they are sad, or in a
state of mind akin to sadness — absorbed, pre-occupied — as
at some great solemn crisis in the life of an individual or a
community, such as that in the history of Peter, when he
was exercised on the great question of the admission of the
Gentiles to the church, or such as that in the history of
the Christian community at Antioch, when they were about to
ordain the first missionaries to the heathen world.   Christ's
doctrine, clearly and distinctly indicated here, is that fasting
in any other circumstances is forced, unnatural, unreal ; a
thing which men may be made to do as a matter of form, but
which they do not with their heart and soul.   " Can ye make
the children of the bride-chamber fast while the bridegroom
is with them ? "[2] He asked, virtually asserting that it was
impossible.

By this rule the disciples of our Lord were justified, and
yet John's were not condemned.   It was admitted to be
natural for them to fast, as they were mournful, melancholy,
unsatisfied.   They had not found Him who was the Desire
of all nations, the Hope of the future, the Bridegroom of

---

[1] John iii. 29.   [2] Luke v. 34, μὴ δύνασθε . . . ποιῆσαι νηστεύειν.

the soul. They only knew that all was wrong; and in their querulous, despairing mood they took pleasure in fasting, and wearing coarse raiment, and frequenting lonely, desolate regions, living as hermits, a practical protest against an ungodly age. The message that the kingdom was at hand had indeed been preached to them also; but as proclaimed by John the announcement was *awful* news, not good news, and made them anxious and dispirited, not glad. Men in such a mood could not do otherwise than fast; though whether they did well to *continue* in that mood after the Bridegroom had come, and had been announced to them as such by their own master, is another matter. Their grief was wilful, idle, causeless, when He had appeared who was to take away the sin of the world.

Jesus had yet more to say in reply to the questions addressed to Him. Things new and unusual need manifold apology, and therefore to the beautiful similitude of the children of the bride-chamber He added two other equally suggestive parables: those, viz., of the *new patch on the old garment*, and the *new wine in old skins*. The design of these parables is much the same as that of the first part of His reply, viz., to enforce the *law of congruity* in relation to fasting and similar matters; that is, to show that in all *voluntary* religious service, where we are free to regulate our own conduct, the outward act should be made to correspond with the inward condition of mind, and that no attempt should be made to force particular acts or habits on men without reference to that correspondence. " In natural things," He meant to say, "we observe this law of congruity. No man putteth a piece of unfulled cloth [1] on an old garment. Neither do men put new wine into old skins, and that not merely out of regard to propriety, but to avoid bad consequences. For if the rule of congruity be neglected, the patched garment will be torn by the contraction of the new cloth; [2] and the old skin bottles will burst under the fermenting force of the new liquor, and the wine will be spilled and lost."

[1] Matt. ix. 16, ῥάκους ἀγνάφου.

[2] Luke v. 36 gives the thought a different turn. The cloth is merely new (καινὸν), and two objections to patching are hinted at. *First*, good cloth is wasted in patching, which would have been better employed in making a new garment. *Second*, the patchwork is unseemly and unsatisfactory. The old and the new do not *agree* (οὐ συμφωνεῖ).

The old cloth and old bottles in these metaphors represent old ascetic fashions in religion ; the new cloth and the new wine represent the new joyful life in Christ, not possessed by those who tenaciously adhered to the old fashions. The parables were applied primarily to Christ's own age, but they admit of application to all transition epochs ; indeed, they find new illustration in almost every generation.

The force of these homely parables as arguments in vindication of departure from current usage in matters of religion may be evaded in either of two ways. First, their relevancy may be denied ; *i.e.*, it may be denied that religious beliefs are of such a nature as to demand congenial modes of expression, under penalties if the demand is not complied with. This position is usually assumed virtually or openly by the patrons of use and wont. Conservative minds have for the most part a very inadequate conception of the vital force of belief. Their own belief, their spiritual life altogether, is often a feeble thing, and they imagine tameness or pliancy must be an attribute of other men's faith also. Nothing but dire experience will convince them that they are mistaken ; and when the proof comes in the shape of an irrepressible revolutionary outburst, they are stupefied with amazement. Such men learn nothing from the history of previous generations ; for they persist in thinking that their own case will be an exception. Hence the *vis inertiæ* of established custom evermore insists on adherence to what is old, till the new wine proves its power by producing an explosion needlessly wasteful, by which both wine and bottles often perish, and energies which might have quietly wrought out a beneficent reformation are perverted into blind powers of indiscriminate destruction.

Or, in the second place, the relevancy of these metaphors being admitted in general terms, it may be denied that a new wine (to borrow the form of expression from the second, more suggestive metaphor) has come into existence. This was virtually the attitude assumed by the Pharisees towards Christ. " What have you brought ? " they asked Him in effect, " to your disciples, that they cannot live as others do, but must needs invent new religious habits for themselves ? This new life of which you boast is either a vain pretence, or an illegitimate, spurious thing, not worthy of toleration, and the waste of which would be no matter for regret." Similar was the attitude assumed towards Luther by the opponents of the Reformation. They said to him in effect : " If this new revelation of yours, that sinners are justified by faith alone, were true, we admit that it would involve very considerable modification in religious opinion, and many alterations in religious practice. But we deny the truth of your doctrine, we regard the peace and comfort you find in it as a hallucination ; and therefore we insist that you return to the time-honored faith, and then you will have no difficulty in acquiescing in the long-established practice." The same thing happens to a greater or less extent every generation ; for new wine is always in course of being produced by the eternal vine of truth, demanding in some particulars of belief and practice new bottles for its preservation, and receiving for answer an order to be content with the old ones.

Without going the length of denunciation or direct attempt at suppression, those who stand by the old often oppose the new by the milder method of disparagement. They eulogize the venerable past, and contrast it with the present, to the disadvantage of the latter. " The old wine is vastly superior to the new : how mellow, mild, fragrant, wholesome, the one ! how harsh and fiery the other ! " Those who say so are not the worst of men : they are often the best, — the men of taste and feeling, the gentle, the reverent, and the good, who are themselves excellent samples of the old vintage. Their opposition forms by far the most formidable obstacle to the public recognition and toleration of what is new in religious life ; for it naturally creates a strong prejudice against any cause when the saintly disapprove of it.

Observe, then, how Christ answers the honest admirers of the old wine. He concedes the point : He admits that their preference is natural. Luke represents Him as saying, in the conclusion of His reply to the disciples of the Baptist : " No man also, having drunk old wine, desireth the new ; for he saith, The old is good." [1] This striking sentiment exhibits

---

[1] Luke v. 39. The version given in the text is in accordance with the reading approved by critics, in which εὐθέως (straightway) is omitted, and instead of χρηστότερος (better) stands χρηστός (good). The sense, however, is the same. It is implied that the new wine will be desired by and by, and *good* is an emphatic positive which virtually asserts superiority.

rare candor in stating the case of opponents, and not less rare modesty and tact in stating the case of friends. It is as if Jesus had said : " I do not wonder that you love the old wine of Jewish piety, fruit of a very ancient vintage ; or even that you dote upon the very bottles which contain it, covered over with the dust and cobwebs of ages. But what then ? Do men object to the existence of new wine, or refuse to have it in their possession, because the old is superior in flavor ? No : they drink the old, but they carefully preserve the new, knowing that the old will get exhausted, and that the new, however harsh, will mend with age, and may ultimately be superior even in flavor to that which is in present use. Even so should you behave towards the new wine of my kingdom. You may not straightway desire it, because it is strange and novel ; but surely you might deal more wisely with it than merely to spurn it, or spill and destroy it ! "

Too seldom for the church's good have lovers of old ways understood Christ's wisdom, and lovers of new ways sympathized with His charity. A celebrated historian has remarked : " It must make a man wretched, if, when on the threshold of old age, he looks on the rising generation with uneasiness, and does not rather rejoice in beholding it ; and yet this is very common with old men. Fabius would rather have seen Hannibal unconquered than see his own fame obscured by Scipio." [1] There are always too many Fabii in the world, who are annoyed because things will not remain stationary, and because new ways and new men are ever rising up to take the place of the old. Not less rare, on the other hand, is Christ's charity among the advocates of progress. Those who affect freedom despise the stricter sort as fanatics and bigots, and drive on changes without regard to their scruples, and without any appreciation of the excellent qualities of the " old wine." When will young men and old men, liberals and conservatives, broad Christians and narrow, learn to bear with one another ; yea, to recognize each in the other the necessary complement of his own one-sidedness ?

[1] Niebuhr, *Lectures on Roman History*, ii. 77, 78.

SECTION II — RITUAL ABLUTIONS

MATT. xv. 1-20; MARK vii. 1-23; LUKE xi. 37-41

The happy free society of Jesus, which kept bridal high-tide when others fasted, was in this further respect singular in its manners, that its members took their meals unconcerned about existing usages of purification. They ate bread with "defiled, that is to say, with unwashen hands." Such was their custom, it may be assumed, from the beginning, though the practice does not appear to have become the subject of animadversion till an advanced period in the ministry of our Lord,[1] at least in a way that gave rise to incidents worthy of notice in the Gospel records. Even at the marriage in Cana, where were set six water-pots of stone for the purposes of purifying, Christ and His disciples are to be conceived as distinguished from the other guests by a certain inattention to ritual ablutions. This we infer from the reasons by which the neglect was defended when it was impugned, which virtually take up the position that the habit condemned was not only lawful, but incumbent — a positive duty in the actual circumstances of Jewish society, and therefore, of course, a duty which could at no time be neglected by those who desired to please God rather than men. But indeed it needs no proof that one of such grave earnest spirit as Jesus could never have paid any regard to the trifling regulations about washing before eating invented by the "elders."

These regulations were no trifles in the eyes of the Pharisees ; and therefore we are not surprised to learn that the indifference with which they were treated by Jesus and the twelve provoked the censure of that zealous sect of religionists on at least two occasions, adverted to in the Gospel narratives. On one of these occasions, certain Pharisees and scribes, who had followed Christ from Jerusalem to the north, seeing some of His disciples eat without previously going through the customary ceremonial ablutions, came to Him, and asked, "Why walk not Thy disciples according to the traditions of the elders, but eat bread with unwashen

---

[1] During the last stay in Galilee, within six months of the crucifixion.

hands ? "¹   In the other instance Jesus Himself was the
direct object of censure.   " A certain Pharisee," Luke relates,
"besought Jesus to dine with him ; and He went in, and
sat (directly) down to meat : and when the Pharisee saw it,
he marvelled that He had not first washed before dinner."²
Whether the host expressed his surprise by words or by
looks only is not stated ; but it was observed by his guest,
and was made an occasion for exposing the vices of the
pharisaic character.   " Now," said the accused, in holy zeal
for true purity, "now do ye Pharisees make clean the outside
of the cup and platter, but your inward part is full of raven-
ing and wickedness.   Ye fools, did not He that made that
which is without make that which is within also ?   But
rather give alms of such things as ye have ; and, behold, all
things are clean unto you."³   That is to say, the offending
guest charged His scandalized host, and the sect he belonged
to, with sacrificing inward to outward purity, and at the same
time taught the important truth that to the pure all things
are pure, and showed the way by which inward real purity
was to be reached, viz., by the practice of that sadly neglected
virtue, humanity or charity.

The Lord's reply in the other encounter with pharisaic
adversaries on the subject of washings was similar in its
principle, but different in form.   He told the zealots for
purifications, without periphrasis, that they were guilty of
the grave offence of sacrificing the commandments of God
to the commandments of men — to these pet traditions of
the elders.   The statement was no libel, but a simple melancholy fact, though its truth does not quite lie on the surface.
This we hope to show in the following remarks ; but before
we proceed to that task, we must force ourselves, however
reluctantly, to acquire a little better acquaintance with the
contemptible senilities whose neglect once seemed so heinous
a sin to persons deeming themselves holy.

The aim of the rabbinical prescriptions respecting washings was not physical cleanliness, but something thought to
be far higher and more sacred.   Their object was to secure,
not physical, but ceremonial purity ; that is, to cleanse the

¹ Mark vii. 1, 2, 5.   ² Luke xi. 37.
³ Luke xi. 39-41.   *Vide*, for a similar passage, Matt. xxiii. 25, 26.

person from such impurity as might be contracted by contact with a Gentile, or with a Jew in a ceremonially unclean state, or with an unclean animal, or with a dead body or any part thereof. To the regulations in the law of Moses respecting such uncleanness the rabbis added a vast number of additional rules on their own responsibility, in a self-willed zeal for the scrupulous observance of the Mosaic precepts. They issued *their* commandments, as the Church of Rome has issued hers, under the pretext that they were necessary as means towards the great end of fulfilling strictly the commandments of God.

The burdens laid on men's shoulders by the scribes on this plausible ground were, by all accounts, indeed most grievous. Not content with purifications prescribed in the law for uncleanness actually contracted, they made provision for merely possible cases. If a man did not remain at home all day, but went out to market, he must wash his hands on his return, because it was *possible* that he might have touched some person or thing ceremonially unclean. Great care, it appears, had also to be taken that the water used in the process of ablution was itself perfectly pure ; and it was necessary even to apply the water in a particular manner to the hands, in order to secure the desired result. Without travelling beyond the sacred record, we find, in the items of information supplied by Mark respecting prevailing Jewish customs of purification, enough to show to what ridiculous lengths this momentous business of washing was carried. " Many other things," remarks he quaintly, and not without a touch of quiet satire, " there be which they have received to hold, as the washing of cups and pots, brazen vessels, and of tables." [1] All things, in short, used in connection with food — in cooking it, or in placing it on the table — had to be washed, not merely as people might wash them now to remove actual impurity, but to deliver them from the more serious uncleanness which they might possibly have contracted since last used, by touching some person or thing not technically clean. A kind and measure of purity, in fact, were aimed at incompatible with life in this world. The

[1] Mark vii. 4. κλινῶν means " couches " rather than tables. But the right of the word to be in the text is very doubtful, and it is omitted in R. V.

very air of heaven was not clean enough for the doting patrons of patristic traditions; for, not to speak of other more real sources of contamination, the breeze, in blowing over *Gentile* lands to the sacred land of Jewry, had contracted defilement which made it unfit to pass into ritualistic lungs till it had been sifted by a respirator possessing the magic power to cleanse it from its pollution.

The extravagant fanatical zeal of the Jews in these matters is illustrated in the Talmud by stories which, although belonging to a later age, may be regarded as a faithful reflection of the spirit which animated the Pharisees in the time of our Lord. Of these stories the following is a sample: "Rabbi Akiba was thrown by the Christians into prison, and Rabbi Joshua brought him every day as much water as sufficed both for washing and for drinking. But on one occasion it happened that the keeper of the prison got the water to take in, and spilled the half of it. Akiba saw that there was too little water, but nevertheless said, Give me the water for my hands. His brother rabbi replied, My master, you have not enough for drinking. But Akiba replied, He who eats with unwashed hands perpetrates a crime that ought to be punished with death. Better for me to die of thirst than to transgress the traditions of my ancestors." [1]   Rabbi Akiba would rather break the sixth commandment, and be guilty of self-murder, than depart from the least punctilio of a fantastic ceremonialism; illustrating the truth of the declaration made by Christ in His reply to the Pharisees, which we now proceed to consider.

It was not to be expected that, in defending His disciples from the frivolous charge of neglecting the washing of hands, Jesus would show much respect for their accusers. Accordingly, we observe a marked difference between the tone of His reply in the present case, and that of His answer to John's disciples. Towards them the attitude assumed was respectfully defensive and apologetic; towards the present interrogants the attitude assumed is offensive and denunciatory. To John's disciples Jesus said, "Fasting is right for

[1] Buxtorf, *De Syn. Jud.* pp. 236, 237. This author quotes the following saying of another rabbi: "Qui illotis manibus panem comedit, idem est ac si scorto accubaret" (p. 236).

you: not to fast is equally right for my disciples." To the Pharisees He replies by a retort which at once condemns their conduct and justifies the behavior which they challenged. "Why," ask they, "do Thy disciples transgress the traditions of the elders?" "Why," asked He in answer, "do ye also transgress the commandments of God by your traditions?" as if to say, "It becomes not you to judge; you, who see the imaginary mote in the eye of a brother, have a beam in your own."

This spirited answer was something more than a mere retort or *et tu quoque* argument. Under an interrogative form it enunciated a great principle, viz., that the scrupulous observance of human traditions in matters of practice leads by a sure path to a corresponding negligence and unscrupulousness in reference to the eternal laws of God. Hence Christ's defence of His disciples was in substance this: "I and my followers despise and neglect those customs because we desire to keep the moral law. Those washings, indeed, may not seem seriously to conflict with the great matters of the law, but to be at worst only trifling and contemptible. But the case is not so. To treat trifles as serious matters, as matters of conscience, which ye do, is degrading and demoralizing. No man can do that without being or becoming a moral imbecile, or a hypocrite: either one who is incapable of discerning between what is vital and what not in morals, or one who finds his interest in getting trifles, such as washing of hands, or paying tithe of herbs, to be accepted as the important matters, and the truly great things of the law — justice, mercy, and faith — quietly pushed aside as if they were of no moment whatever."

The whole history of religion proves the truth of these views. A ceremony and tradition ridden time is infallibly a morally corrupt time. Hypocrites ostensibly zealots, secretly atheists; profligates taking out their revenge in licentiousness for having been compelled, by tyrannous custom or intolerant ecclesiastical authorities, to conform outwardly to practices for which they have no respect; priests of the type of the sons of Eli, gluttonous, covetous, wanton: such are the black omens of an age in which ceremonies are every thing, and godliness and virtue nothing. Ritualistic practices, artificial duties of all kinds, whether originating with Jewish rabbis or with doctors of the Christian church, are utterly to be abjured. Recommended by their zealous advocates, often sincerely, as eminently fitted to promote the culture of morality and piety, they ever prove, in the long run, fatal to both. Well are they called in the Epistle to the Hebrews "dead works." They are not only dead, but death-producing; for, like all dead things, they tend to putrefy, and to breed a spiritual pestilence which sweeps thousands of souls into perdition. If they have any life at all, it is life feeding on death, the life of *fungi* growing on dead trees; if they have any beauty, it is the beauty of decay, of autumnal leaves sere and yellow, when the sap is descending down to the earth, and the woods are about to pass into their winter state of nakedness and desolation. Ritualism at its best is but the shortlived after-summer of the spiritual year! very fascinating it may be, but when it cometh, be sure winter is at the doors. "We all do fade as a leaf, and our iniquities, like the wind, have taken us away."

Having brought a grave countercharge against the Pharisees, that of sacrificing morality to ceremonies, the commandments of God to the traditions of men, Jesus proceeded forthwith to substantiate it by a striking example and a Scripture quotation. The example selected was the evasion of the duties arising out of the fifth commandment, under pretence of a previous religious obligation. God said, "Honor thy father and mother," and attached to a breach of the commandment the penalty of death. The Jewish scribes said, "Call a thing *Corban*, and you will be exempt from all obligation to give it away, even for the purpose of assisting needy parents." The word Corban in the Mosaic law signifies a gift or offering to God, of any kind, bloody or bloodless, presented on any occasion, as in the fulfilment of a vow.[1] In rabbinical dialect it signified a thing devoted to sacred purposes, and therefore not available for private or secular use. The traditional doctrine on the subject of Corban was mischievous in two ways. It encouraged men to make religion an excuse for neglecting morality, and it opened a wide door to knavery and hypocrisy. It taught

[1] Num. vi. 14.

that a man might not only by a vow deny *himself* the use of things lawful, but that he might, by devoting a thing to God, relieve himself of all obligation to give to *others* what, but for the vow, it would have been his duty to give them. Then, according to the pernicious system of the rabbis, it was not necessary really to give the thing to God in order to be free of obligation to give it to man. It was enough to *call* it Corban. Only pronounce that magic word over any thing, and forthwith it was sealed over to God, and sacred from the use of others at least, if not from your own use. Thus self-willed zeal for the honor of God led to the dishonoring of God, by taking His name in vain ; and practices which at best were chargeable with setting the first table of the law over against the second, proved eventually to be destructive of both tables. They made the whole law of God of none effect by their traditions. The disannulling of the fifth commandment was but a sample of the mischief the zealots for the commandments of men had wrought, as is implied in Christ's concluding words, " Many such like things do ye." [1]

The Scripture quotation [2] made by our Lord in replying to the Pharisees was not less apt than the example was illustrative, as pointing out their characteristic vices, hypocrisy and superstition. They were near to God with their mouth, they honored Him with their lips, but they were far from Him in their hearts. Their religion was all on the outside. They scrupulously washed their hands and their cups, but they took no care to cleanse their polluted souls. Then, in the second place, their fear of God was taught by the precept of men. Human prescriptions and traditions were their guide in religion, which they followed blindly, heedless how far these commandments of men might lead them from the paths of righteousness and true godliness.

The prophetic word was quick, powerful, sharp, searching, and conclusive. Nothing more was needed to confound the Pharisees, and nothing more was said to them at this time. The sacred oracle was the fitting conclusion of an unanswerable argument against the patrons of tradition. But Jesus had compassion on the poor multitude who were being misled

---

[1] Mark vii. 13.   [2] Isa. xxix. 13.

to their ruin by their blind spiritual guides, and therefore He took the opportunity of addressing a word to those who stood around on the subject of dispute. What He had to say to them He expressed in the terse, pointed form of a proverb: "Hear and understand: not that which goeth into the mouth defileth a man; but that which cometh out of the mouth, this defileth a man." This was a riddle to be solved, a secret of wisdom to be searched out, a lesson in religion to be conned. Its meaning, though probably understood by few at the moment, was very plain. It was simply this: "Pay most attention to the cleansing of the heart, not, like the Pharisees, to the cleansing of the hands. When the heart is pure, all is pure; when the heart is impure, all outward purification is vain. The defilement to be dreaded is not that from meat ceremonially unclean, but that which springs from a carnal mind, the defilement of evil thoughts, evil passions, evil habits."

This passing word to the bystanders became the subject of a subsequent conversation between Jesus and His disciples, in which He took occasion to justify Himself for uttering it, and explained to them its meaning. The Pharisees had heard the remark, and were naturally offended by it, as tending to weaken their authority over the popular conscience. The twelve observed their displeasure, perhaps they overheard their comments; and, fearing evil consequences, they came and informed their Master, probably with a tone which implied a secret regret that the speaker had not been less outspoken. Be that as it may, Jesus gave them to understand that it was not a case for forbearance, compromise, or timid, time-serving, prudential policy; the ritualistic tendency being an evil plant which must be uprooted, no matter with what offence to its patrons. He pleaded, in defence of His plainness of speech, His concern for the souls of the ignorant people whose guides the Pharisees claimed to be. "Let them alone, what would follow? Why, the blind leaders and the blindly led would fall together into the ditch. Therefore if the leaders be so hopelessly wedded to their errors that they cannot be turned from them, let us at least try to save their comparatively ignorant victims."

The explanation of the proverbial word spoken to the

people Jesus gave to His disciples by request of Peter.[1] It is rudely plain and particular, because addressed to rudely ignorant hearers. It says over again, in the strongest possible language, that to eat with unwashen hands defileth not a man, because nothing entering the mouth can come near the soul; that the defilement to be dreaded, the only defilement worth speaking of, is that of an evil, unrenewed heart, out of which proceed thoughts, words, and acts which are offences against the holy, pure law of God. The concluding words, "purging all meats," have, however, a peculiar significance, if we adopt the reading approved by critics: "This He said, purging all meats." In that case we have the evangelist giving his own opinion of the effect of Christ's words, viz., that they amounted to an abrogation of the ceremonial distinction between clean and unclean. A very remarkable comment, as coming from the man to whom we are indebted for the report of the preaching of that apostle who in his disciple days called forth the declaration, and who had the vision of the sheet let down from heaven.

The evangelist having given us his comment, we may add ours. We observe that our Lord is here silent concerning the ceremonial law of Moses (to which the traditions of the elders were a supplement), and speaks only of the commandments of God, *i.e.* the precepts of the decalogue. The fact is significant, as showing in what direction He had come to destroy, and in what to fulfil. Ceremonialism was to be abolished, and the eternal laws of morality were to become áll in all. Men's consciences were to be delivered from the burden of outward positive ordinances, that they might be free to serve the living God, by keeping His ten words, or the one royal law of love. And it is the duty of the church to stand fast in the liberty Christ designed and purchased for her, and to be jealous of all human traditions out of holy zeal for the divine will, shunning superstition on the one side, and the licentious freedom of godless libertinism on the other. Christ's true followers wish to be free, but not to do as they like; rather to do what God requires of them. So minded, they reject unceremoniously all human authority in religion, thereby separating themselves from the devotees to

---

[1] Matt. xv. 17–20; Mark vii. 18–23.

tradition; and at the same time, as God's servants, they reverence His word and His law, thereby putting a wide gulf between them and the lawless and disobedient, who side with movements of religious reform, not in order to get something better in the place of what is rejected, but to get rid of all moral restraint in matters human or divine.

SECTION III — SABBATH OBSERVANCE

MATT. xii. 1-14; MARK ii. 23—iii. 1-6; LUKE vi. 1-11, xiii. 10-16,
xiv. 1-6; JOHN v. 1-18, ix. 13-17

In no part of their conduct were Jesus and His disciples more frequently found fault with than in respect to their mode of observing the Sabbath. Six distinct instances of offence given or taken on this score are recorded in the Gospel history; in five of which Jesus Himself was the offender, while in the remaining instance His disciples were at least the ostensible objects of censure.

The offences of Jesus were all of one sort; His crime was, that on the Sabbath-day He wrought works of healing on the persons of men afflicted respectively with palsy, a withered hand, blindness, dropsy, and on the body of a poor woman "bowed together" by an infirmity of eighteen years' standing. The offence of the disciples, on the other hand, was that, while walking along a way which lay through a corn-field, they stepped aside and plucked some ears of grain for the purpose of satisfying their hunger. This was not theft, for it was permitted by the law of Moses;[1] but nevertheless it was, in the judgment of the Pharisees, Sabbath-breaking. It was contrary to the command, "Thou shalt not work;" for to pluck some ears was reaping on a small scale, and to rub them was a species of threshing!

These offences, deemed so grave when committed, seem very small at this distance. All the transgressions of the Sabbath law charged against Jesus were works of mercy; and the one transgression of the disciples was for them a work of necessity, and the toleration of it was for others a duty of mercy, so that in condemning them the Pharisees had

[1] Deut. xxiii. 24, 25

forgotten that divine word: "I will have mercy, and not sacrifice." It is, indeed, hard for us now to conceive how any one could be serious in regarding such actions as breaches of the Sabbath, especially the harmless act of the twelve. There is a slight show of plausibility in the objection taken by the ruler of the synagogue to miraculous cures wrought on the seventh day : "There are six days on which men ought to work ; in them therefore come and be healed, and not on the Sabbath-day." [1] The remark was specially plausible with reference to the case which had provoked the ire of the dignitary of the synagogue. A woman who had been a sufferer for eighteen years might surely bear her trouble one day more, and come and be healed on the morrow ! But on what pretence could the disciples be blamed as Sabbath-breakers for helping themselves to a few ears of corn ? To call such an act working was too ridiculous. Men who found a Sabbatic offence here must have been very anxious to catch the disciples of Jesus in a fault.

On the outlook for faults we have no doubt the Pharisees were ; and yet we must admit that, in condemning the act referred to, they were acting faithfully in accordance with their theoretical views and habitual tendencies. Their judg-ment on the conduct of the twelve was in keeping with their traditions concerning washings, and their tithing of mint and other garden herbs, and their straining of gnats out of their wine-cup. Their habit, in all things, was to degrade God's law by framing innumerable petty rules for its better obser-vance, which, instead of securing that end, only made the law appear base and contemptible. In no case was this miser-able micrology carried greater lengths than in connection with the fourth commandmemt. With a most perverse ingenuity, the most insignificant actions were brought within the scope of the prohibition against labor. Even in the case put by our Lord, that of an animal fallen into a pit, it was deemed lawful to lift it out — so at least those learned in rabbinical lore tell us — only when to leave it there till Sabbath was past would involve risk to life. When delay was not dangerous, the rule was to give the beast food sufficient for the day ; and if there was water in the bottom of the pit,

[1] Luke xiii. 14

to place straw and bolsters below it, that it might not be drowned.[1]

Yet with all their strictness in abstaining from every thing bearing the faintest resemblance to work, the Jews were curiously lax in another direction. While scrupulously observing the law which prohibited the cooking of food on Sabbath,[2] they did not make the holy day by any means a day of fasting. On the contrary, they considered it their duty to make the Sabbath a day of feasting and good cheer.[3] In fact, it was at a Sabbath feast, given by a chief man among the Pharisees, that one of the Sabbath miracles was wrought for which Jesus was put upon His defence. At this feast were numerous guests, Jesus Himself being one,— invited, it is to be feared, with no friendly feelings, but rather in the hope of finding something against Him concerning the Sabbatic law. "It came to pass," we read in Luke, "as He (Jesus) went into the house of one of the rulers of the Pharisees to eat bread on a Sabbath-day, that they were watching Him.[4] They set a trap, and hoped to catch in it Him whom they hated without cause ; and they got for their pains such searching, humbling table-talk as they had probably never heard before.[5] This habit of feasting had grown to a great abuse in the days of Augustine, as appears from the description he gives of the mode in which contemporary Jews celebrated their weekly holiday. "To-day," he writes, "is the Sabbath, which the Jews at the present time keep in loose, luxurious ease, for they occupy their leisure in frivolity ; and wherers God commanded a Sabbath, they spend it in those things which God forbids. Our rest is from evil works, theirs is from good works ; for it is better to plough than to dance. They rest from good work, they rest not from idle work."[6]

[1] Buxtorf, *De Syn. Jud.* pp. 352–356. The same author states that it was a breach of the law to let a cock wear a piece of ribbon round its leg on Sabbath : it was making it bear something. It was also forbidden to walk through a stream on stilts, because, though the stilts appear to bear you, you really carry the stilts. These were probably later refinements.

[2] Ex. xvi. 23.

[3] They appealed, in justification of this practice, to Neh. viii. 10.

[4] Luke xiv. 1.

[5] Luke xiv. 7-24.

[6] *Enarratio in Psalmum* xci. (xcii.) 2. Similar complaints were made by other Fathers, such as Prudentius and Chrysostom. *Vide* Bingham, B. xx. c. ii.

From the folly and pedantry of scribes and Pharisees we gladly turn to the wisdom of Jesus, as revealed in the animated, deep, and yet sublimely simple replies made by Him to the various charges of Sabbath-breaking brought against Himself and His disciples. Before considering these replies in detail, we premise one general remark concerning them all. In none of these apologies or defences does Jesus call in question the obligation of the Sabbath law. On that point He had no quarrel with His accusers. His argument in this instance is entirely different from the line of defence adopted in reference to fasting and purifications. In regard to fasting, the position He took up was : Fasting is a voluntary matter, and men may fast or not as they are disposed. In regard to purification His position was : Ceremonial ablutions at best are of secondary moment, being mere types of inward purity, and as practised now, lead inevitably to the utter ignoring of spiritual purity, and therefore must be neglected by all who are concerned for the great interests of morality. But in reference to the alleged breaches of the Sabbath, the position Jesus took up was this : These acts which you condemn are not transgressions of the law, rightly apprehended, in its spirit and principle. The importance of the law was conceded, but the pharisaic interpretation of its meaning was rejected. An appeal was made from their pedantic code of regulations about Sabbath observance to the grand design and principle of the law ; and the right was asserted to examine all rules in the light of the principle, and to reject or disregard those in which the principle had either been mistakenly applied, or, as was for the most part the case with the Pharisees, lost sight of altogether.

The key to all Christ's teaching on the Sabbath, therefore, lies in His conception of the *original design* of that divine institution. This conception we find expressed with epigrammatic point and conciseness, in contrast to the pharisaic idea of the Sabbath, in words uttered by Jesus on the occasion when He was defending His disciples. "The Sabbath," said He, "was made for man, and not man for the Sabbath." In other words, His doctrine was this : The Sabbath was meant to be a *boon* to man, not a *burden;* it was not a day taken from man by God in an exacting spirit, but a day given by

God in mercy to man — God's holiday to His subjects; all
legislation enforcing its observance having for its end to
insure that all should really get the benefit of the boon —
that no man should rob himself, and still less his fellow-
creatures, of the gracious boon.

This difference between Christ's mode of regarding the
Sabbath and the pharisaic involves of necessity a corresponding difference in the spirit and the details of its observance.
Take Christ's view, and your principle becomes : That is the
best way of observing the Sabbath which is most conducive
to man's physical and spiritual well-being — in other words,
which is best for his body and for his soul; and in the light
of this principle, you will keep the holy day in a spirit of
intelligent joy and thankfulness to God the Creator for His
gracious consideration towards His creatures.   Take the
pharisaic view, and your principle of observance becomes :
He best keeps the Sabbath who goes greatest lengths in mere
abstinence from any thing that can be construed into labor,
irrespective of the effect of this abstinence either on his own
well-being or on that of others.   In short, we land in the
silly, senseless minuteness of a rabbinical legislation, which
sees in such an act as that of the disciples plucking and rub-
bing the ears of corn, or that of the healed man who carried
his bed home on his shoulders,[1] or that of one who should
walk a greater distance than two thousand cubits, or three-
fourths of a mile,[2] on a Sabbath, a heinous offence against
the fourth commandment and its Author.

A Sabbath observance regulated by the principle that the
institution was made for man's good, obviously involves two
great general uses — rest for the body, and worship as the
solace of the spirit.   We should rest from servile labor on
the divinely given holiday, and we should lift up our hearts
in devout thought to Him who made all things at the first,
who "worketh hitherto," preserving the creation in being
and well-being, and whose tender compassion towards sinful
men is great, passing knowledge.   These things are both

[1] John v. 10.
[2] This was the limit of a Sabbath-day journey according to the scribes.   It was fixed
by the distance between the wall of a Levitical city and the outside boundary of its
suburb.   There were casuistical contrivances for lengthening the journey.   See Num.
xxxv. 5 ; and Buxtorf, *De Syn. Jud.* c. xvi.

necessary to man's true good, and therefore must enter as essential elements of a worthy Sabbath observance.

But, on the other hand, the Sabbath being made for man, the two general requirements of rest and worship may not be so pressed that they shall become hostile to man's well-being, and in effect self-destructive, or mutually destructive. The rule, "Thou shalt rest," must not be so applied as to exclude *all* action and all work ; for absolute inaction is *not* rest, and entire abstinence from work of every description would often-times be detrimental both to private and to public well-being. Room must be left for acts of "necessity and mercy ;" and too peremptory as well as too minute legislation as to what are and what are not acts of either description must be avoided, as these may vary for different persons, times, and circum-stances, and men may honestly differ in opinion in such details who are perfectly loyal to the great broad principles of Sabbath sanctification. In like manner, the rule, "Thou shalt worship," must not be so enforced as to make religious duties irksome and burdensome — a mere mechanical, legal service ; or so as to involve the sacrifice of the other great practical end of the Sabbath, viz., rest to the animal nature of man. Nor may men dictate to each other as to the means of worship any more than as to the amount ; for one may find helps to devotion in means which to another would prove a hindrance and a distraction.

It was only in regard to cessation from work that pharisaic legislation and practice anent Sabbath observance were carried to superstitious and vexatious excess. The Sabbatic mania was a *monomania*, those affected thereby being mad simply on one point, the stringent enforcement of *rest*. Hence the peculiar character of all the charges brought against Christ and His disciples, and also of His replies. The offences committed were all works deemed unlawful ; and the defences all went to show that the works done were not contrary to law when the law was interpreted in the light of the principle that the Sabbath was made for man. They were works of necessity or of mercy, and therefore lawful on the Sabbath-day.

Jesus drew His proofs of this position from three sources : Scripture history, the everyday practice of the Pharisees themselves, and the providence of God. In defence of His disciples, He referred to the case of David eating the shew-bread when he fled to the house of God from the court of King Saul,[1] and to the constant practice of the priests in doing work for the service of the temple on Sabbath-days, such as offering double burnt-offerings, and removing the stale shewbread from the holy place, and replacing it by hot loaves. David's case proved the general principle that necessity has no law, hunger justifying his act, as it should also have justified the act of the disciples even in pharisaic eyes. The practice of the priests showed that work merely as work is not contrary to the law of the Sabbath, some works being not only lawful, but incumbent on that day.

The argument drawn by Jesus from common practice was well fitted to silence captious critics, and to suggest the prin-ciple by which His own conduct could be defended. It was to this effect: "You would lift an ox or an ass out of a pit on Sabbath, would you not? Why? To save life? Why then should not I heal a sick person for the same reason? Or is a beast's life of more importance than that of a human being? Or again: Would you scruple to loose your ox or your ass from the stall on the day of rest, and lead him away to watering?[2] If not, why object to me when on the Sabbath-day I release a poor human victim from a bondage of eighteen years' duration, that she may draw water out of the wells of salvation?" The argument is irresistible, the conclusion inevitable; that it is lawful, dutiful, most seasonable, *to do well* on the Sabbath-day. How blind they must have been to whom so obvious a proposition needed to be proved! how oblivious of the fact that love is the foundation and ful-filment of all law, and that therefore no particular precept could ever be meant to suspend the operation of that divine principle!

The argument from providence used by Jesus on another occasion[3] was designed to serve the same purpose with the others, viz., to show the lawfulness of certain kinds of work

---

[1] 1 Sam. xxi. 6. This occurred on Sabbath, for the old shewbread was replaced by new on that day (hot loaves baked on Sabbath). But this is not the point insisted on by Christ.

[2] Luke xiii. 14, 15.

[3] John v. 17.

on the day of rest. "My Father worketh even until now," said
He to His accusers, "and I work." The Son claimed the
right to work *because* and *as* the Father worked on all days
of the week. The Father worked incessantly for beneficent,
conservative ends, most holily, wisely, and powerfully preserving and governing all His creatures and all their actions,
keeping the planets in their orbits, causing the sun to rise
and shine, and the winds to circulate in their courses, and
the tides to ebb and flow on the seventh day as on all the
other six. So Jesus Christ, the son of God, claimed the
right to work, and did work — saving, restoring, healing ; as
far as might be bringing fallen nature back to its pristine
state, when God the Creator pronounced all things good,
and rested, satisfied with the world He had brought into
being. Such works of beneficence, by the doctrine of Christ,
may always be done on the Sabbath-day : works of humanity,
like those of the physician, or of the teacher of neglected
children, or of the philanthropist going his rounds among
the poor and needy, or of the Christian minister preaching the
gospel of peace, and many others, of which men filled with
love will readily bethink themselves, but whereof too many,
in the coldness of their heart, do not so much as dream.
Against such works there is no law save that of churlish,
ungenial, pharisaic custom.

One other saying our Lord uttered on the present subject,
which carries great weight for Christians, though it can have
had no apologetic value in the opinion of the Pharisees, but
must rather have appeared an aggravation of the offence it was
meant to excuse. We refer to the word, "The Son of man is
Lord even of the Sabbath-day," uttered by Jesus on the occasion when He defended His disciples against the charge of
Sabbath-breaking. This statement, remarkable, like the claim
made at the same time to be greater than the temple, as an
assertion of superhuman dignity on the part of the meek and
lowly One, was not meant as a pretension to the right to
break the law of rest without cause, or to abrogate it altogether. This is evident from Mark's account,[1] where the words
come in as an inference from the proposition that the Sabbath
was made for man, which could not logically be made the

[1] Mark ii. 27, 28.

foundation for a repeal of the statute, seeing it is the most powerful argument for the perpetuity of the weekly rest. Had the Sabbath been a mere burdensome restriction imposed on men, we should have expected its abrogation from Him who came to redeem men from all sorts of bondage. But was the Sabbath made *for* man — for man's good? Then should we expect Christ's function to be not that of a repealer, but that of a universal philantnropic legislator, making what had previously been the peculiar privilege of Israel a common blessing to all mankind. For the Father sent His Son into the world to deliver men indeed from the yoke of ordinances, but not to cancel any of His gifts, which are all "without repentance," and, once given, can never be withdrawn.

What, then, does the lordship of Christ over the Sabbath signify? Simply this: that an institution which is of the nature of a boon to man properly falls under the control of Him who is the King of grace and the administrator of divine mercy. He is the best judge how such an institution should be observed; and He has a right to see that it shall not be perverted from a boon into a burden, and so put in antagonism to the royal imperial law of love. The Son of man hath authority to cancel all regulations tending in this direction emanating from men, and even all by-laws of the Mosaic code savoring of legal rigor, and tending to veil the beneficent design of the fourth commandment of the decalogue.[1] He may, in the exercise of His mediatorial prerogative, give the old institution a new name, alter the day of its celebration, so as to invest it with distinctively Christian associations congenial to the hearts of believers, and make it in all the details of its observance subservient to the great ends of His incarnation.

[1] The position of the Sabbath in the decalogue (where nothing is placed which was of merely Jewish concern, and which was not of fundamental importance) is a presumption of perpetuity for every candid mind. The much disputed question of the ethical nature of the Sabbath law is not of so great moment as has been imagined. Moral or not, the weekly rest is to all men, and at all times, of vital importance; therefore practically, if not philosophically, of ethical value. The fourth commandment certainly differs from the others in this respect, that it is not written on the natural conscience. The utmost length reason could go would be to determine that rest is needful. Whether rest should be periodical or at irregular intervals, on the seventh day or on the tenth, as in revolutionary France, with its mania for the decimal system, the light of nature could not teach. But the decalogue settles that point, and settles it forever, for all who believe in the divine origin of the Mosaic legislation. The fourth commandment is a revelation for all time of God's mind on the universally important question of the proper relation between labor and rest.

To such effect did the Son of man claim to be Lord of the Sabbath-day; and His claim, so understood, was acknowledged by the church, when, following the traces of the apostolic usage, she changed the weekly rest from the seventh day to the first,[1] that it might commemorate the joyful event of the resurrection of the Saviour, which lay nearer the heart of a believer than the old event of the creation, and called the first day by His name, the Lord's day.[2] That claim all Christians acknowledge who, looking at the day in the light of God's original design, and of Christ's teaching, example and work, so observe it as to keep the golden mean between the two extremes of pharisaic rigor and of Sadducaic laxity: recognizing on the one hand the beneficent ends served by the institution, and doing their utmost to secure that these ends shall be fully realized, and, on the other hand, avoiding the petty scrupulosity of a cheerless legalism, which causes many, especially among the young, to stumble at the law as a statute of unreasonable arbitrary restriction; avoiding also the bad pharisaic habit of indulging in over-confident judgments on difficult points of detail, and on the conduct of those who in such points do not think and act as they do themselves.

We may not close this chapter, in which we have been studying the lessons in free yet holy living given by our Lord to His disciples, without adding a reflection applicable to all the three. By these lessons the twelve were taught a virtue very necessary for the apostles of a religion in many

[1] How this change was brought about we do not well know. Probably it was accomplished by degrees, and without full consciousness of the transition which was being made, or of its import. From the beginning believers seem to have met for worship on the first day of the week; but there is no evidence that they rested entirely from work on that day. In many cases they could not have done so if they wished, *e.g.* in the case of slaves of heathen masters. Hence, probably, we may account for the church in Troas meeting in the evening, and worshipping till midnight. The likelihood is that the first Christians rested on the seventh day as Jews, and as Christians worshipped on the morning or evening of the first day, before or after their daily toil. In course of time, as Jewish believers became more weaned from Judaism, the Gentile worshippers multiplied, so as to have a preponderating influence on the customs of the church, the seventh-day rest would disappear, and the first-day rest, the Lord's day, would take its place. To prevent misapprehension, it is necessary to explain that the seventh day continued to be observed as a fast-day or a festival, with religious services, long after it had ceased to be regarded as a day on which men ought entirely to rest from labor. *Vide* on this, Bingham, *Origines Ecclesiasticæ*, B. xx. c. iii.

[2] In Greek κυριακὴ ἡμέρα, or simply ἡ κυριακή; in Latin *Dies Dominicus*. Thus in Tertullian, *De Corona*, iii., "Die Dominico jejunium nefas ducimus."

respects new — the power to bear isolation and its consequences.   When Peter and John appeared before the
Sanhedrim, the rulers marvelled at their boldness, till they
recognized in them companions of Jesus the Nazarene.
They seem to have imagined that His followers were fit for
any thing requiring audacity.   They were right.   The
apostles had strong nerves, and were not easily daunted ;
and the lessons which we have been considering help us to
understand whence they got their rare moral courage.
They had been accustomed for years to stand alone, and to
disregard the fashion of the world, till at length they
could do what was right, heedless of human criticism, without effort, almost without thought.

8

FIRST ATTEMPTS AT EVANGELISM

SECTION I — THE MISSION

Matt. 10; Mark 6:7-13, 30-32; Luke 9:1-11

THE twelve are now to come before us as active agents in advancing the kingdom of God. Having been for some time in Christ's company, witnessing His miraculous works, hearing His doctrine concerning the kingdom, and learning how to pray and how to live, they were at length sent forth to evangelize the towns and villages of their native province, and to heal the sick in their Master's name, and by His power. This mission of the disciples as evangelists or miniature apostles was partly, without doubt, an educational experiment for their own benefit ; but its direct design was to meet the spiritual necessities of the people, whose neglected condition lay heavy on Christ's heart. The compassionate Son of man, in the course of His wanderings, had observed how the masses of the population were, like a shepherdless flock of sheep, scattered and *torn*,[1] and it was His desire that all should know that a good Shepherd had come to care for the lost sheep of the house of Israel. The multitudes were ready enough to welcome the good news ; the difficulty was to meet the pressing demand of the hour. The harvest, the grain, ready for reaping, was plenteous, but the laborers were few.[2]

In connection with this mission four things call for special notice : The sphere assigned for the work, the nature of the work, the instructions for carrying it on, the results of the mission, and the return of the missionaries. These points

---

[1] ἐσκυλμένοι, Matt. ix. 36, the reading preferred by critics = flayed, harassed. The idea suggested is that of sheep whose fleeces are torn by thorns.

[2] Matt. ix. 37.

we shall consider in their order, except that, for convenience, we shall reserve Christ's instructions to His disciples for the last place, and give them a section to themselves.

1. The sphere of the mission, as described in general terms, was the whole land of Israel. "Go," said Jesus to the twelve, " to the lost sheep of the house of Israel ; " and further on, in Matthew's narrative, He speaks to them as if the plan of the mission involved a visit to all the cities of Israel.[1] Practically, however, the operations of the disciples seem to have been restricted to their native province of Galilee, and even within its narrow limits to have been carried on rather among the villages and hamlets, than in considerable towns or cities like Tiberias. The former of these statements is supported by the fact that the doings of the disciples attracted the attention of Herod the tetrarch of Galilee,[2] which implies that they took place in his neighborhood ;[3] while the latter is proved by the words of the third evangelist in giving a summary account of the mission : " They departed and went through the villages (towns, Eng. Ver.), preaching the gospel, and healing everywhere." [4]

While the apprentice missionaries were permitted by their instructions to go to any of the lost sheep of Israel, to all if practicable, they were expressly forbidden to extend their labors beyond these limits. They were not to go into the way of the Gentiles, nor enter into any city or town of the Samaritans.[5] This prohibition arose in part out of the general plan which Christ had formed for founding the kingdom of God on the earth. His ultimate aim was the conquest of the world ; but in order to that, He deemed it necessary first to secure a strong base of operations in the Holy Land and among the chosen people. Therefore He ever regarded Himself personally as a Messenger of God to the Jewish nation, seriously giving that as a reason why He should not work among the heathen,[6] and departing occasionally from the rule only in order to supply in His own ministry prophetic intimations of an approaching time

---

[1] Matt. x. 6, 23.

[2] Mark vi. 14 ; Luke ix. 7.

[3] Herod resided at Tiberias.

[4] Luke ix. 6, κατὰ τὰς κώμας = " villages," R.V.

[5] Matt. x. 5.

[6] Matt. xv. 24.

when Jew and Samaritan and Gentile should be united on
equal terms in one divine commonwealth.[1] But the principal
reason of the prohibition lay in the present spiritual condition of the disciples themselves. The time would come
when Jesus might say to His chosen ones, " Go ye into all
the world, and preach the gospel to every creature ; "[2] but
that time was not yet. The twelve, at the period of their
first trial mission, were not fit to preach the gospel, or to do
good works, either among Samaritans or Gentiles. Their
hearts were too narrow, their prejudices too strong : there
was too much of the Jew, too little of the Christian, in their
character. For the catholic work of the apostleship they
needed a new divine illumination and a copious baptism
with the benignant spirit of love. Suppose these raw
evangelists had gone into a Samaritan village, what would
have happened ? In all probability they would have been
drawn into disputes on the religious differences between
Samaritans and Jews, in which, of course, they would have
lost their temper ; so that, instead of seeking the salvation
of the people among whom they had come, they would rather
be in a mood to call down fire from heaven to consume them,
as they actually proposed to do at a subsequent period.[3]

2. The work intrusted to the twelve was in one department very extensive, and in the other very limited. They
were endowed with unlimited powers of healing, but their
commission was very restricted so far as preaching was concerned. In regard to the former their instructions were :
" Heal the sick, cleanse the lepers, raise the dead, cast out
devils : freely ye have received, freely give ; " in regard to
the latter: " As ye go, preach, saying, The kingdom of
heaven is at hand."[4] The commission in the one case seems
too wide, in the other too narrow ; but in both the wisdom
of Jesus is apparent to a deeper consideration. In so far
as miraculous works were concerned, there was no need for
restriction, unless it were to avoid the risk of producing

[1] John iv. 7 – 24.   [2] Mark xvi. 15.
[3] Luke ix. 54. Some have imagined that the restriction proceeded from the limitation
of Christ's own aims. But had His aim been as limited as is supposed, there would
have been no mention of restrictions, and no need for them, for the disciples would never
have thought of going among the Samaritans or Gentiles to preach and heal.
[4] Matt. x. 7, 8.

elation and vanity in those who wielded such wonderful power —a risk which was certainly not imaginary, but which could be remedied when it assumed tangible form. All the miracles wrought by the twelve were really wrought by Jesus Himself, their sole function consisting in making a believing use of His name. This seems to have been perfectly understood by all ; for the works done by the apostles did not lead the people of Galilee to wonder who *they* were, but only who and what He was in whose name all these things were done.[1] Therefore, it being Christ's will that such miracles should be wrought through the instrumentality of His disciples, it was just as easy for them to do the greatest works as to do the smaller ; if, indeed, there be any sense in speaking of degrees of difficulty in connection with miracles, which is more than doubtful.

As regards the preaching, on the other hand, there was not only reason, but necessity, for restriction. The disciples could do no more than proclaim the fact that the kingdom was at hand, and bid men everywhere repent, by way of a preparation for its advent. This was really all they knew themselves. They did not as yet understand, in the least degree, the doctrine of the cross ; they did not even know the nature of the kingdom. They had, indeed, heard their Master discourse profoundly thereon, but they had not comprehended his words. Their ideas respecting the coming kingdom were nearly as crude and carnal as were those of other Jews, who looked for the restoration of Israel's political independence and temporal prosperity as in the glorious days of old. In one point only were they in advance of current notions. They had learned from John and from Jesus that repentance was necessary in order to citizenship in this kingdom. In all other respects they and their hearers were pretty much on a level. Far from wondering, therefore, that the preaching programme of the disciples was so limited, we are rather tempted to wonder how Christ could trust them to open their mouths at all, even on the one topic of the kingdom. Was there not a a danger that men with such crude ideas might foster delusive hopes, and give rise to political excitement ? Nay,

---

[1] Mark vi. 14, "His name was spread abroad" (φανερὸν ἐγένετο).

may we not discover actual traces of such excitement in the notice taken of their movements at Herod's court, and in the proposal of the multitude not long after, to take Jesus by force to make Him a king?[1] Doubtless there was danger in this direction; and therefore, while He could not, to avoid it, leave the poor perishing people uncared for, Jesus took all possible precautions to obviate mischief as far as might be, by in effect prohibiting His messengers from entering into detail on the subject of the kingdom, and by putting a sound form of words into their mouths. They were instructed to announce the kingdom as a kingdom of *heaven;*[2] a thing which some might deem a lovely vision, but which all worldly men would guess to be quite another thing from what they desired. A kingdom of heaven! What was that to them? What they wanted was a kingdom of earth, in which they might live peaceably and happily under just government, and, above all, with plenty to eat and drink. A kingdom of heaven! That was only for such as had no earthly hope; a refuge from despair, a melancholy consolation in absence of any better comfort. Even so, ye worldlings! Only for such as ye deem miserable was the message meant. To the poor the kingdom was to be preached. To the laboring and heavy laden was the invitation "Come to me" addressed, and the promise of rest made; of rest from ambition and discontent, and scheming, carking care, in the blessed hope of the supernal and the eternal.

3. The impression produced by the labors of the twelve seems to have been very considerable. The fame of their doings, as already remarked, reached the ears of Herod, and great crowds appear to have accompanied them as they moved from place to place. On their return, *e.g.* from the mission to rejoin the company of their Master, they were thronged by an eager, admiring multitude who had witnessed or experienced the benefits of their work, so that it was necessary for them to withdraw into a desert place in order

[1] John vi. 15.
[2] This is the name usually given to the kingdom in Matthew, as distinct from the other evangelists, who employ the title "kingdom of God." It is a curious fact that the most Hebrew Gospel should thus use the most spiritual designation for the kingdom.

to obtain a quiet interval of rest. "There were many," the second evangelist informs us, "coming and going, and they had no leisure so much as to eat. And they departed unto a desert place by ship privately." [1] Even in the desert solitudes on the eastern shore of the Sea of Galilee they failed to secure the desired privacy. "The people saw them departing, and ran afoot thither (round the end of the sea) out of all cities, and outwent them, and came together unto Him." [2]

In quality the results of the mission appear to have been much less satisfactory than in their extent. The religious impressions produced seem to have been in a great measure superficial and evanescent. There were many blossoms, so to speak, on the apple-tree in the springtide of this Galilean "revival;" but only a comparatively small number of them set in fruit, while of these a still smaller number ever reached the stage of ripe fruit. This we learn from what took place shortly after, in connection with Christ's discourse on the bread of life, in the synagogue of Capernaum. Then the same men who, after the miraculous feeding in the desert, would have made Christ a king, deserted Him in a body, scandalized by His mysterious doctrine; and those who did this were, for the most part, just the men who had listened to the twelve while they preached repentance. [3]

Such an issue to a benevolent undertaking must have been deeply disappointing to the heart of Jesus. Yet it is remarkable that the comparative abortiveness of the first evangelistic movement did not prevent Him from repeating the experiment some time after on a still more extensive scale. "After these things," writes the third evangelist, "the Lord appointed other seventy also, and sent them two and two before His face, into every city and place whither He Himself would come." [4] The Tübingen school of critics, indeed, as we have already indicated, [5] assure us that this mission had no existence, being a pure invention of the third evangelist, intended to thrust into the shade the mission of

1 Mark vi. 31, 32.
2 Mark vi. 33.
3 Compare Mark vi. 30–35 with John vi. 22–25.
4 Luke x. 1.
5 *Vide* note, p. 32.

the twelve, and to exhibit the Christian religion as a religion
for humanity, represented by the Samaritans as the
recipients, and by the *seventy* as the preachers of the faith,
the number corresponding to the number of the nations.
The theory is not devoid of plausibility, and it must be
owned the history of this mission is very obscure ; but the
assumption of invention is violent, and we may safely take
for granted that Luke's narrative rests on an authentic
tradition. The motive of this second mission was the same
as in the case of the first, as were also the instructions to
the missionaries. Jesus still felt deep compassion for the
perishing multitude, and hoping against hope, made a new
attempt to save the lost sheep. He would have all men
called at least to the fellowship of the kingdom, even though
few should be chosen to it. And when the immediate
results were promising He was gratified, albeit knowing,
from past experience as well as by divine insight, that the
faith and repentance of many were only too likely to be
evanescent as the early dew. When the seventy returned
from their mission, and reported their great success, He
hailed it as an omen of the downfall of Satan's kingdom,
and, rejoicing in spirit, gave thanks to the Supreme Ruler in
heaven and earth, His Father, that while the things of the
kingdom were hid from the wise and the prudent, the people
of intelligence and discretion, they were by His grace
revealed unto babes — the rude, the poor, the ignorant.[1]

The reference in the thanksgiving prayer of Jesus to the
"wise and prudent" suggests the thought that these
evangelistic efforts were regarded with disfavor by the
refined, fastidious classes of Jewish religious society. This
is in itself probable. There are always men in the church,
intelligent, wise, and even good, to whom popular religious
movements are distasteful. The noise, the excitement, the
extravagances, the delusions, the misdirection of zeal, the
rudeness of the agents, the instability of the converts — all
these things offend them. The same class of minds would
have taken offence at the evangelistic work of the twelve
and the seventy, for undoubtedly it was accompanied with
the same drawbacks. The agents were ignorant ; they had

1 Luke x. 17-21.

few ideas in their heads; they understood little of divine truth; their sole qualification was, that they were earnest and could preach repentance well. Doubtless, also, there was plenty of noise and excitement among the multitudes who heard them preach; and we certainly know that their zeal was both ill-informed and short-lived. These things, in fact, are standing features of all popular movements. Jonathan Edwards, speaking with reference to the "revival" of religion which took place in America in his day, says truly: "A great deal of noise and tumult, confusion and uproar, darkness mixed with light, and evil with good, is always to be expected in the beginning of something very glorious in the state of things in human society or the church of God. After nature has long been shut up in a cold, dead state, when the sun returns in the spring, there is, together with the increase of the light and heat of the sun, very tempestuous weather before all is settled, calm, and serene, and all nature rejoices in its bloom and beauty." [1]

None of the "wise and prudent" knew half so well as Jesus what evil would be mixed with the good in the work of the kingdom. But He was not so easily offended as they. The Friend of sinners was ever like Himself. He sympathized with the multitude, and could not, like the Pharisees, contentedly resign them to a permanent condition of ignorance and depravity. He rejoiced greatly over even one lost sheep restored; and He was, one might say overjoyed, when not one, but a whole flock, even *began* to return to the fold. It pleased Him to see men repenting even for a season, and pressing into the kingdom even rudely and violently; [2] for His love was strong, and where strong love is, even wisdom and refinement will not be fastidious.

Before passing from this topic, let us observe that there is another class of Christians, quite distinct from the wise and prudent, in whose eyes such evangelistic labors as those of the twelve stand in no need of vindication. Their tendency, on the contrary, is to regard such labors as the whole work of the kingdom. Revival of religion among the neglected masses is for them the sum of all good-doing. Of the more still, less observable work of instruction going on in the

---

[1] *Thoughts on Revival,* Part I. sec iii.   [2] Matt xi 12.

church they take no account. Where there is no obvious
excitement, the church in their view is dead, and her ministry
inefficient. Such need to be reminded that there were *two*
religious movements going on in the days of the Lord Jesus.
One consisted in rousing the mass out of the stupor of
indifference; the other consisted in the careful, exact training of men already in earnest, in the principles and truths
of the divine kingdom. Of the one movement the disciples,
that is, both the twelve and the seventy, were the agents;
of the other movement they were the subjects. And the
latter movement, though less noticeable, and much more
limited in extent, was by far more important than the
former; for it was destined to bring forth fruit that should
remain — to tell not merely on the present time, but on the
whole history of the world. The deep truths which the great
Teacher was now quietly and unobservedly, as in the dark,
instilling into the minds of a select band, the recipients of
His confidential teaching were to speak in the broad daylight ere long; and the sound of their voice would not stop
till it had gone through all the earth. There would have
been a poor outlook for the kingdom of heaven if Christ had
neglected this work, and given Himself up entirely to vague
evangelism among the masses.

4. When the twelve had finished their mission, they
returned and told their Master all that they had done and
taught. Of their report, or of His remarks thereon, no
details are recorded. Such details we do find, however, in
connection with the later mission of the seventy. "The
seventy," we read, "returned again with joy, saying, Lord,
even the devils are subject unto us through Thy name."[1]
The same evangelist from whom these words are quoted,
informs us that, after congratulating the disciples on their
success, and expressing His own satisfaction with the facts
reported, Jesus spoke to them the warning word: "Notwithstanding in this rejoice not, that the spirits are subject unto
you; but rather rejoice because your names are written in
heaven."[2] It was a timely caution against elation and
vanity. It is very probable that a similar word of caution
was addressed to the twelve also after their return. Such a

[1] Luke x. 17.   [2] Luke x. 20.

word would certainly not have been unseasonable in their case. They had been engaged in the same exciting work, they had wielded the same miraculous powers, they had been equally successful, they were equally immature in character, and therefore it was equally difficult for them to bear success. It is most likely, therefore, that when Jesus said to them on their return, " Come ye yourselves apart into a desert place, and rest awhile," [1] He was not caring for their bodies alone, but was prudently seeking to provide repose for their heated minds as well as for their jaded frames.

The admonition to the seventy is indeed a word in season to all who are very zealous in the work of evangelism, especially such as are crude in knowledge and grace. It hints at the possibility of their own spiritual health being injured by their very zeal in seeking the salvation of others. This may happen in many ways. Success may make the evangelists vain, and they may begin to sacrifice unto their own net. They may fall under the dominion of the devil through their very joy that he is subject unto them. They may despise those who have been less successful, or denounce them as deficient in zeal. The eminent American divine already quoted gives a lamentable account of the pride, presumption, arrogance, conceit, and censoriousness which characterized many of the more active promoters of religious revival in his day. [2] Once more, they may fall into carnal security respecting their own spiritual state, deeming it impossible that any thing can go wrong with those who are so devoted, and whom God has so greatly owned. An obvious as well as dangerous mistake ; for doubtless Judas took part in this Galilean mission, and, for aught we know to the contrary, was as successful as his fellow-disciples in casting out devils. Graceless men may for a season be employed as agents in promoting the work of grace in the hearts of others. Usefulness does not necessarily imply goodness, according to the teaching of Christ Himself. " Many," He declares in the Sermon on the Mount," will say unto me on that day, Lord, Lord, did we not prophesy by Thy name, and by Thy name cast out devils, and by Thy

---

[1] Mark vi. 31.   [2] *Thoughts on Revival*, Part iv.

name do many wonderful works?" And mark the answer which He says He will give such. It is not: I call in question the correctness of your statement — that is tacitly admitted; it is: "I never knew you; depart from me, ye that work iniquity."[1]

These solemn words suggest the need of watchfulness and self-examination; but they are not designed to discourage or discountenance zeal. We must not interpret them as if they meant, "Never mind *doing* good, only *be* good;" or, "Care not for the salvation of others: look to your own salvation." Jesus Christ did not teach a listless or a selfish religion. He inculcated on His disciples a large-hearted generous concern for the spiritual well-being of men. To foster such a spirit He sent the twelve on this trial mission, even when they were comparatively unfitted for the work, and notwithstanding the risk of spiritual harm to which it exposed them. At all hazards He would have His apostles be filled with enthusiasm for the advancement of the kingdom; only taking due care, when the vices to which young enthusiasts are liable began to appear, to check them by a warning word and a timely retreat into solitude.

Section II — The Instructions

The instructions given by Jesus to the twelve in sending them forth on their first mission, are obviously divisible into two parts. The first, shorter part, common to the narratives of all the three first evangelists, relates to the present; the second and much the longer part, peculiar to Matthew's narrative, relates mainly to the distant future. In the former, Christ tells His disciples what to do now in their apprentice apostleship; in the latter, what they must do and endure when they have become apostles on the great scale, preaching the gospel, not to Jews only, but to all nations.

It has been doubted whether the discourse included in the second part of the apostolic or missionary instructions, as given by Matthew, was really uttered by Jesus on this occasion. Stress has been laid by those who take the

---

[1] Matt vii. 22. See, for views similar to those above stated, Edwards' *Thoughts on Revival*, Part ii. sec. ii.

negative view of this question on the facts that the first evangelist alone gives the discourse in connection with the trial mission, and that the larger portion of its contents are given by the other evangelists in other connections. Reference has also been made, in support of this view, to the statement made by Jesus to His disciples, in His farewell address to them before the crucifixion, that He had not till then spoken to them of coming persecutions, and for this reason, that while He was with them it was unnecessary.[1] Finally, it has been deemed unlikely that Jesus would frighten His inexperienced disciples by alluding to dangers not imminent at the time of their mission in Galilee. These doubts, in view of the topical method of grouping his materials undoubtedly followed by Matthew, are legitimate, but they are not conclusive. It was natural that Jesus should signalize the first missionary enterprise of the twelve chosen men by some such discourse as Matthew records, setting forth the duties, perils, encouragements, and rewards of the apostolic vocation. It was His way, on solemn occasions, to speak as a prophet who in the present saw the future, and from small beginnings looked forward to great ultimate issues. And this Galilean mission, though humble and limited compared with the great undertaking of after years, was really a solemn event. It was the beginning of that vast work for which the twelve had been chosen, which embraced the world in its scope, and aimed at setting up on earth the kingdom of God. If the Sermon on the Mount was appropriately delivered on the occasion when the apostolic company was formed, this discourse on the apostolic vocation was not less appropriate when the members of that company first put their hands to the work unto which they had been called. Even the allusions to distant dangers contained in the discourse appear on reflection natural and seasonable, and calculated to re-assure rather than to frighten the disciples. It must be remembered that the execution of the Baptist had recently occurred, and that the twelve were about to commence their missionary labors within the dominions of the tyrant by whose command the barbarous murder had been committed. Doubtless these humble men

[1] John xvi. 4.

who were to take up and repeat the Baptist's message, "Repent," ran no present risk of his fate; but it was natural that they should fear, and it was also natural that their Master should think of their future when such fears would be any thing but imaginary; and on both accounts it was seasonable to say to them in effect: Dangers are coming, but fear not.

Such, in substance, is the burden of the second part of Christ's instructions to the twelve. Of the first part, on the other hand, the burden is, *Care not.* These two words, Care not, Fear not, are the soul and marrow of all that was said by way of prelude to the first missionary enterprise, and we may add, to all which might follow. For here Jesus speaks to all ages and to all times, telling the Church in what spirit all her missionary enterprises must be undertaken and carried on, that they may have His blessing.

1. The duty of entering on their mission without carefulness, relying on Providence for the necessaries of life, was inculcated on the twelve by their Master in very strong and lively terms. They were instructed to procure nothing for the journey, but just to go as they were. They must provide neither gold nor silver, nor even so much as brass coin in their purses, no scrip or wallet to carry food, no change of raiment; not even sandals for their feet, or a staff for their hands. If they had the last-mentioned articles, good and well; if not, they could do without them. They might go on their errand of love barefooted, and without the aid even of a staff to help them on their weary way, having their feet shod only with the preparation of the gospel of peace, and leaning their weight upon God's words of promise, "As thy days, so shall thy strength be." [1]

In these directions for the way, it is the spirit, and not the mere letter, which is of intrinsic and permanent value. The truth of this statement is evident from the very variations of the evangelists in reporting Christ's words. One, for example (Mark), makes Him say to His disciples in effect: "If you have a staff in your hand, and sandals on your feet, and one coat on your back, let that suffice." Another (Matthew) represents Jesus as saying: "Provide

[1] Deut. xxxiii. 25.

nothing for this journey, neither coat, shoes, nor staff." [1] In spirit the two versions come to the same thing ; but if we insist on the letter of the injunctions with legal strictness, there is an obvious contradiction between them. What Jesus meant to say, in whatever form of language He expressed Himself, was this : Go at once, and go as you are, and trouble not yourselves about food or raiment, or any bodily want ; trust in God for these. His instructions proceeded on the principle of division of labor, assigning to the servants of the kingdom military duty, and to God the commissariat department.

So understood, the words of our Lord are of permanent validity, and to be kept in mind by all who would serve Him in His kingdom. And though the circumstances of the church have greatly altered since these words were first spoken, they have not been lost sight of. Many a minister and missionary has obeyed those instructions almost in their letter, and many more have kept them in their spirit. Nay, has not every poor student fulfilled these injunctions, who has gone forth from the humble roof of his parents to be trained for the ministry of the gospel, without money in his pocket either to buy food or to pay fees, only with simple faith and youthful hope in his heart, knowing as little how he is to find his way to the pastoral office, as Abraham knew how to find his way to the promised land when he left his native abode, but, with Abraham, trusting that He who said to him, "Leave thy father's house," will be his guide, his shield, and his provider ? And if those who thus started on their career do at length arrive at a wealthy place, in which their wants are abundantly supplied, what is that but an indorsement by Providence of the law enunciated by the Master : " The workman is worthy of his meat " ? [2]

The directions given to the twelve with respect to temporalities, in connection with their first mission, were meant to be an education for their future work. On entering on the duties of the apostolate, they should have to live literally by faith, and Jesus mercifully sought to inure them to the

---

[1] The first evangelist may be reconciled with the second by laying stress on the word " provide " (μὴ κτήσησθε). See Alford, *in loco.*

[2] Matt. x. 10.

habit while He was with them on earth. Therefore, in
sending them out to preach in Galilee, He said to them
in effect : " Go and learn to seek the kingdom of God with a
single heart, unconcerned about food or raiment ; for till ye
can do that ye are not fit to be my apostles." They had
indeed been learning to do that ever since they began to
follow Him ; for those who belonged to His company literally
lived from day to day, taking no thought for the morrow.
But there was a difference between their past state and that
on which they were about to enter. Hitherto Jesus had
been with them ; now they were to be left for a season to
themselves. Hitherto they had been like young children in
a family under the care of their parents, or like young birds
in a nest sheltered by their mother's wing, and needing only
to open their mouths wide in order to get them filled; now
they were to become like boys leaving their father's house
to serve an apprenticeship, or like fledglings leaving the
warm nest in which they were nursed, to exercise their
wings and seek food for themselves.

While requiring His disciples to walk by faith, Jesus gave
their faith something to rest on, by encouraging them to
hope that what they provided not for themselves God would
provide for them through the instrumentality of His people.
" Into whatsoever city or town ye shall enter, inquire who in
it is worthy, and there abide till ye go thence." [1] He took
for granted, we observe, that there would always be found at
every place at least one good man with a warm heart, who
would welcome the messengers of the kingdom to his house
and table for the pure love of God and of the truth. Surely
no unreasonable assumption ! It were a wretched hamlet,
not to say town, that had not a single worthy person in it.
Even wicked Sodom had a Lot within its walls who could
entertain angels unawares.

To insure good treatment of His servants in all ages
wherever the gospel might be preached, Jesus made it
known that He put a high premium on all acts of kindness
done towards them. This advertisement we find at the
close of the address delivered to the twelve at this time :
" He that receiveth you," He said to them, "receiveth me ;

[1] Matt. x. 11.

and he that receiveth me, receiveth Him that sent me. He
that receiveth a prophet in the name of a prophet, shall
receive a prophet's reward ; and he that receiveth a righteous
man in the name of a righteous man, shall receive a
righteous man's reward." And then, with increased pathos
and solemnity, He added : " Whosoever shall give to drink
unto one of these little ones a cup of cold water only in the
name of a disciple, verily I say unto you, he shall in no wise
lose his reward." [1] How easy to go forth into Galilee, yea,
into all the world, serving such a sympathetic Master on
such terms !

But while thus encouraging the young evangelists, Jesus
did not allow them to go away with the idea that all things
would be pleasant in their experience. He gave them to
understand that they should be ill received as well as kindly
received. They should meet with churls who would refuse
them hospitality, and with stupid, careless people who would
reject their message ; but even in such cases, He assured
them, they should not be without consolation If their
peaceful salutation were not reciprocated, they should at all
events get the benefit of their own spirit of good-will : their
peace would return to themselves. If their words were not
welcomed by any to whom they preached, they should at least
be free from blame ; they might shake off the dust from
their feet, and say : " Your blood be upon your own heads,
we are clean; we leave you to your doom, and go elsewhere." [2] Solemn words, not to be uttered, as they are too
apt to be, especially by young and inexperienced disciples,
in pride, impatience, or anger, but humbly, calmly, deliber
ately, as a part of God's message to men. When uttered in
any other spirit, it is a sign that the preacher has been as
much to blame as the hearer for the rejection of his message.
Few have any right to utter such words at all ; for it requires
rare preaching indeed to make the fault of unbelieving
hearers so great that it shall be more tolerable for Sodom
and Gomorrah in the day of judgment than for them. But
such preaching has been. Christ's own preaching was such,
and hence the fearful doom He pronounced on those who
rejected His words. Such also the preaching of the apostles

[1] Matt x 40–42.   [2] Matt. x. 13, 14.

was to be ; and therefore to uphold their authority, Jesus solemnly declared that the penalty for despising their word would be not less than for neglecting His own.[1]

2. The remaining instructions, referring to the future rather than to the present, while much more copious, do not call for lengthened explanation. The burden of them all, as we have said, is "Fear not." This exhortation, like the refrain of a song, is repeated again and again in the course of the address.[2] From that fact the twelve might have inferred that their future lot was to be of a kind fitted to inspire fear. But Jesus did not leave them to learn this by inference ; He told them of it plainly. "Behold," He said, with the whole history of the church in His view, "Behold, I send you forth as sheep in the midst of wolves." Then He went on to explain in detail, and with appalling vividness, the various forms of danger which awaited the messengers of truth ; how they should be delivered up to councils, scourged in synagogues, brought before governors and kings (like Felix, Festus, Herod), and hated of all for His name's sake.[3] He explained to them, at the same time, that this strange treatment was inevitable in the nature of things, being the necessary consequence of divine truth acting in the world like a chemical solvent, and separating men into parties, according to the spirit which ruled in them. The truth would divide even members of the same family, and make them bitterly hostile to each other ;[4] and however deplorable the result might be, it was one for which there was no remedy. Offences must come : "Think not," He said to His disciples, horrified at the dark picture, and perhaps secretly hoping that their Master had painted it in too sombre colors, "Think not that I am come to send peace on earth : I came not to send peace, but a sword. For I am come to set a man at variance against his father, and the daughter against her mother, and the daughter-in-law against her mother-in-law. And a man's foes shall be they of his own household."[5]

Amid such dangers two virtues are specially needful —

[1] Matt. x. 15.
[2] Matt. x. 26, 28, 31.
[3] Matt. x. 16–18.
[4] Matt. x. 21.
[5] Matt. x. 34–36.

caution and fidelity; the one, that God's servants may not be cut off prematurely or unnecessarily, the other, that while they live, they may really do God's work, and fight for the truth. In such times Christ's disciples must not fear, but be brave and true; and yet, while fearless, they must not be foolhardy. These qualities it is not easy to combine; for conscientious men are apt to be rash, and prudent men are apt to be unfaithful. Yet the combination is not impossible, else it would not be required, as it is in this discourse. For it was just the importance of cultivating the apparently incompatible virtues of caution and fidelity that Jesus meant to teach by the remarkable proverb-precept: "Be wise as serpents, harmless as doves."[1] The serpent is the emblem of cunning, the dove of simplicity. No creatures can be more unlike; yet Jesus requires of His disciples to be at once serpents in cautiousness, and doves in simplicity of aim and purity of heart. Happy they who can be both; but if we cannot, let us at least be doves. The dove must come before the serpent in our esteem, and in the development of our character. This order is observable in the history of all true disciples. They begin with spotless sincerity; and after being betrayed by a generous enthusiasm into some acts of rashness, they learn betimes the serpent's virtues. If we invert the order, as too many do, and begin by being prudent and judicious to admiration, the effect will be that the higher virtue will not only be postponed, but sacrificed. The dove will be devoured by the serpent: the cause of truth and righteousness will be betrayed out of a base regard to self-preservation and worldly advantage.

On hearing a general maxim of morals announced, one naturally wishes to know how it applies to particular cases. Christ met this wish in connection with the deep, pregnant maxim, "Be wise as serpents, harmless as doves," by giving examples of its application. The first case supposed is that of the messengers of truth being brought up before civil or ecclesiastical tribunals to answer for themselves. Here the dictate of wisdom is, "Beware of men,"[2] "Do not be so simple as to imagine all men good, honest, fair, tolerant. Remember there are wolves in the world — men full of

---

[1] Matt. x. 16.   [2] Matt. x 17.

malice, falsehood, and unscrupulousness, capable of inventing
the most atrocious charges against you, and of supporting
them by the most unblushing mendacity. Keep out of their
clutches if you can ; and when you fall into their hands,
expect neither candor, justice, nor generosity." But how
are such men to be answered ? Must craft be met with craft,
lies with lies ? No ; here is the place for the simplicity of
the dove. Cunning and craft boot not at such an hour ;
safety lies in trusting to Heaven's guidance, and telling the
truth. "When they deliver you up, take no (anxious)
thought how or what ye shall speak ; for it shall be given
you in that same hour what ye shall speak. For it is not ye
that speak, but the Spirit of your Father which speaketh in
you." [1] The counsel given to the apostles has been justified
by experience. What a noble book the speeches uttered by
confessors of the truth under the inspiration of the Divine
Spirit, collected together, would make ! It would be a sort
of Martyrs' Bible.

Jesus next puts the case of the heralds of His gospel being
exposed to popular persecutions, and shows the bearing of
the maxim upon it likewise. Such persecutions, as distinct
from judicial proceedings, were common in apostolic
experience, and they are a matter of course in all critical
eras. The ignorant, superstitious populace, filled with
prejudice and passion, and instigated by designing men,
play the part of obstructives to the cause of truth, mobbing,
mocking, and assaulting the messengers of God. How,
then, are the subjects of this ill-treatment to act ? On the
one hand, they are to show the wisdom of the serpent by
avoiding the storm of popular ill-will when it arises ; and on
the other hand, they are to exhibit the simplicity of the
dove by giving the utmost publicity to their message, though
conscious of the risk they run. "When they persecute you
in this city, flee ye into the next ; " [2] yet, undaunted by
clamor, calumny, and violence, "what I tell you in darkness,
that speak ye in light ; what ye hear in the ear, that preach
ye upon the house-tops." [3]

To each of these injunctions a reason is annexed. Flight
is justified by the remark, "Verily I say unto you, Ye shall

[1] Matt. x. 19, 20.   [2] Matt. x. 23.   [3] Matt. x. 27.

not have gone over the cities of Israel till the Son of man
be come." [1]   The coming alluded to is the destruction of
Jerusalem and the dispersion of the Jewish nation ; and the
meaning is, that the apostles would barely have time, before
the catastrophe came, to go over all the land, warning the
people to save themselves from the doom of an untoward
generation, so that they could not well afford to tarry in any
locality after its inhabitants had heard and rejected the
message.   The souls of all were alike precious ; and if one
city did not receive the word, perhaps another would.[2]   The
reason annexed to the injunction to give the utmost
publicity to the truth, in spite of all possible dangers, is :
" The disciple is not above his master, nor the servant above
his lord." [3]   That is to say : To be evil entreated by the
ignorant and violent multitude is hard to bear, but not
harder for you than for me, who already, as ye know, have
had experience of popular malice at Nazareth, and am
destined, as ye know not, to have yet more bitter experience
of it at Jerusalem.   Therefore see that ye hide not your
light under a bushel to escape the rage of wolfish men.

The disciples are supposed, lastly, to be in peril not
merely of trial, mocking, and violence, but even of their
life, and are instructed how to act in that extremity.   Here
also the maxim, " Wise as serpents, harmless as doves,"
comes into play in both its parts.   In this case the wisdom
of the serpent lies in knowing what to fear.   Jesus reminds
His disciples that there are two kinds of deaths, one caused
by the sword, the other by unfaithfulness to duty ; and tells
them in effect, that while both are evils to be avoided, if
possible, yet if a choice must be made, the latter death is
most to be dreaded.   " Fear not," He said, "them which
kill the body, but are not able to kill the soul ; but rather
fear him who is able to destroy both soul and body in hell,"
— the tempter, that is, who, when one is in danger, whispers :
Save thyself at any sacrifice of principle or conscience.[4]
The simplicity of the dove in presence of extreme peril

[1] Matt. x. 23.
[2] Paul and Barnabas acted on this principle at Antioch of Pisidia.   Acts xiii. 46.
[3] Matt. x. 24, 25.
[4] Matt. x. 28.   It has been much disputed who is referred to here — God or Satan
It may be either : God as Judge ; Satan as tempter.   We prefer the latter.

consists in childlike trust in the watchful providence of the Father in heaven. Such trust Jesus exhorted His disciples to cherish in charmingly simple and pathetic language. He told them that God cared even for sparrows, and reminded them that, however insignificant they might seem to themselves, they were at least of more value than many sparrows, not to say than two, whose money value was just one farthing. If God neglected not even a pair of sparrows, but provided for them a place in His world where they might build their nest and safely bring forth their young, would He not care for them as they went forth two and two preaching the doctrine of the kingdom? Yea! He would; the very hairs of their head were numbered. Therefore they might go forth without fear, trusting their lives to His care; remembering also that, at worst, death was no great evil, seeing that for the faithful was reserved a crown of life, and, for those who confessed the Son of man, the honor of being confessed by Him in turn before His Father in heaven.[1]

Such were the instructions of Christ to the twelve when He sent them forth to preach and to heal. It was a rare, unexampled discourse, strange to the ears of us moderns, who can hardly imagine such stern requirements being seriously made, not to say exactly complied with. Some readers of these pages may have stood and looked up at Mont Blanc from Courmayeur or Chamounix. Such is our attitude towards this first missionary sermon. It is a mountain at which we gaze in wonder from a position far below, hardly dreaming of climbing to its summit. Some noble ones, however, have made the arduous ascent; and among these the first place of honor must be assigned to the chosen companions of Jesus.

---

[1] Matt. x. 32, 33.

9

THE GALILEAN CRISIS

SECTION I — THE MIRACLE

John 6:1-15; Matt. 14:13-21; Mark 6:33-34; Luke 9:11-17

THE sixth chapter of John's Gospel is full of marvels. It tells of a great miracle, a great enthusiasm, a great storm, a great sermon, a great apostasy, and a great trial of faith and fidelity endured by the twelve. It contains, indeed, the compendious history of an important crisis in the ministry of Jesus and the religious experience of His disciples, — a crisis in many respects foreshadowing the great final one, which happened little more than a year afterwards,[1] when a more famous miracle still was followed by a greater popularity, to be succeeded in turn by a more complete desertion, and to end in the crucifixion, by which the riddle of the Capernaum discourse was solved, and its prophecy fufilled.[2]

---

[1] John vi 4: "The passover, a feast of the Jews, was nigh."

[2] Keim, while admitting the reality of a Galilean crisis, thinks the account of it in John vi. unhistorical, though he praises it as one of the finest compositions in the whole book. The historical account he finds in Matt. xvi.; and he discovers in the fourth Gospel manifest points of correspondence to the synoptical version. Peter's utterance in the close of the chapter is simply his famous confession in another form. The devil in John's account corresponds to the Satan of the synoptical, only John's devil is in Judas, while the synoptical one is in Peter. Keim says that in John's account of the crisis the rise and fall of the star of Jesus is compressed into a single chapter, and treated as the work of a day. Through feeding and storm Jesus mounts at once to the highest popularity, and loses it again as suddenly in consequence of the repulsive discourse in Capernaum. But this is a most incorrect representation. John does indeed dispose of the *crisis* in one chapter, but he does not make the enthusiasm of the people appear as the result of the miracle of feeding or of any one act. He takes up the Galilean ministry (of which he knows, though he does not relate it) at the point where it has already reached the result of making Jesus a popular idol (see ver. 2), and then proceeds to relate the story of the crisis. And the history which he gives, consistent and intelligible in itself, as we hope to show, helps to explain things in the synoptical account not in themselves clear, *e.g.* Christ's compelling the disciples to go away across the lake in great haste, of which we shall speak farther on. *Vide Jesu von Nazara*, ii. 578.

The facts recorded by John in this chapter of his Gospel may all be comprehended under these four heads : the miracle in the wilderness, the storm on the lake, the sermon in the synagogue, and the subsequent sifting of Christ's disciples. These, in their order, we propose to consider in four distinct sections.

The scene of the miracle was on the eastern shore of the Galilean Sea. Luke fixes the precise locality in the neighborhood of a city called Bethsaida.[1] This, of course, could not be the Bethsaida on the western shore, the city of Andrew and Peter. But there was, it appears, another city of the same name at the north-eastern extremity of the lake, called by way of distinction, Bethsaida Julias.[2] The site of this city, we are informed by an eye-witness, "is discernible on the lower slope of the hill which overhangs the rich plain at the mouth of the Jordan" (that is, at the place where the waters of the Upper Jordan join the Sea of Galilee). "The 'desert place,'" the same author goes on to say, by way of proving the suitableness of the locality to be the scene of this miracle, "was either the green tableland which lies half-way up the hill immediately above Bethsaida, or else in the parts of the plain not cultivated by the hand of man would be found the 'much green grass,' still fresh in the spring of the year when this event occurred, before it had faded away in the summer sun : the tall grass which, broken down by the feet of the thousands then gathered together, would make 'as it were, 'couches' for them to recline upon."[3]

To this place Jesus and the twelve had retired after the return of the latter from their mission, seeking rest and privacy. But what they sought they did not find. Their movements were observed, and the people flocked along the shore toward the place whither they had sailed, running all the way, as if fearful that they might escape, and so arriving at the landing place before them.[4] The multitude which thus gathered around Jesus was very great. All the evangelists agree in stating it at five thousand ; and as the arrangement

[1] Luke ix. 10.
[2] Rebuilt by Philip the tetrarch, and referred to by Josephus.
[3] Stanley, *Sinai and Palestine*. p. 382 The "desert place" is spoken of in Luke ix. 10, the "much green grass" in Mark vi 39 and John vi. 10 combined.
[4] Mark vi. 33.

of the people at the miraculous repast in groups of hundreds and fifties [1] made it easy to ascertain their number, we may accept this statement not as a rough estimate, but as a tolerably exact calculation.

Such an immense assemblage testifies to the presence of a great excitement among the populations living by the shore of the Sea of Galilee. A fervid enthusiasm, a hero-worship, whereof Jesus was the object, was at work in their minds. Jesus was the idol of the hour : they could not endure his absence ; they could not see enough of His work, nor hear enough of His teaching. This enthusiasm of the Galileans we may regard as the cumulative result of Christ's own past labors, and in part also of the evangelistic mission which we considered in the last chapter.[2] The infection seems to have spread as far south as Tiberias, for John relates that boats came from that city "to the place where they did eat bread." [3] Those who were in these boats came too late to witness the miracle and share in the feast, but this does not prove that their errand was not the same as that of the rest ; for, owing to their greater distance from the scene, the news would be longer in reaching them, and it would take them longer to go thither.

The great miracle wrought in the neighborhood of Bethsaida Julias consisted in the feeding of this vast assemblage of human beings with the utterly inadequate means of "five barley loaves and two small fishes." [4] It was truly a stupendous transaction, of which we can form no conception ; but no event in the Gospel history is more satisfactorily attested. All the evangelists relate the miracle with much minuteness, with little even apparent discrepancy, and with such graphic detail as none but eye-witnesses could have supplied. Even John, who records so few of Christ's miracles, describes this one with as careful a hand as any of his brother evangelists, albeit introducing it into his narative merely as a preface to the sermon on the Bread of Life found in his Gospel only.

This wonderful work, so unexceptionably attested, seems open to exception on another ground. It *appears* to be a

---

[1] Mark vi. 40.
[2] *Vide* p. 104.
[3] John vi. 23.
[4] John vi. 9.

miracle without a sufficient reason It cannot be said to have been urgently called for by the necessities of the multitude. Doubtless they were hungry, and had brought no victuals with them to supply their bodily wants. But the miracle was wrought on the afternoon of the day on which they left their homes, and most of them might have returned within a few hours. It would, indeed, have been somewhat hard to have undertaken such a journey at the end of the day without food; but the hardship, even if necessary, was far within the limits of human endurance. But it was not necessary; for food could have been got on the way without going far, in the neighboring towns and villages, so that to disperse them as they were would have involved no considerable inconvenience. This is evident from the terms in which the disciples made the suggestion that the multitude should be sent away. We read: " When the day began to wear away, then came the twelve, and said unto Him, Send the multitude away, that they may go into the villages and country round about, and lodge and get victuals." [1] In these respects there is an obvious difference between the *first* miraculous feeding and the *second*, which occurred at a somewhat later period at the south-eastern extremity of the Lake. On that occasion the people who had assembled around Jesus had been three days in the wilderness without aught to eat, and there were no facilities for procuring food, so that the miracle was demanded by considerations of humanity.[2] Accordingly we find that compassion is assigned as the motive for that miracle: " Jesus called His disciples unto Him, and saith unto them, I have compassion on the multitude, because they have now been with me three days, and have nothing to eat; and if I send them away fasting to their own houses, they will faint by the way; for some of them are come from far." [3]

If our object were merely to get rid of the difficulty of assigning a sufficient motive for the first great miracle of feeding, we might content ourselves with saying that Jesus did not need any very urgent occasion to induce Him to use His power for the benefit of others. For His own benefit He would not use it in case even of extreme need, not even

[1] Luke ix. 12.   [2] Mark viii. 3, 4.   [3] Mark viii. 1-3.

after a fast of forty days. But when the *well-being* (not to say the *being*) of others was concerned, He dispensed miraculous blessings with a liberal hand. He did not ask Himself : Is this a grave enough occasion for the use of divine power? Is this man ill enough to justify a miraculous interference with the laws of nature by healing him? Are these people here assembled hungry enough to be fed, like their fathers in the wilderness, with bread from heaven? But we do not insist on this, because we believe that something else and higher was aimed at in this miracle than to satisfy physical appetite. It was a symbolic, didactic, *critical* miracle. It was meant to teach, and also to test ; to supply a text for the subsequent sermon, and a touchstone to try the character of those who had followed Jesus with such enthusiasm. The miraculous feast in the wilderness was meant to say to the multitude just what our sacramental feast says to us : "I, Jesus the Son of God Incarnate, am the bread of life. What this bread is to your bodies, I myself am to your souls." And the communicants in that feast were to be tested by the way in which they regarded the transaction. The spiritual would see in it a sign of Christ's divine dignity, and a seal of His saving grace ; the carnal would rest simply in the outward fact that they had eaten of the loaves and were filled, and would take occasion from what had happened to indulge in high hopes of temporal felicity under the benign reign of the Prophet and King who had made His appearance among them.

The miracle in the desert was in this view not merely an act of mercy, but an act of judgment. Jesus mercifully fed the hungry multitude in order that He might sift it, and separate the true from the spurious disciples. There was a much more urgent demand for such a sifting than for food to satisfy merely physical cravings. If those thousands were all genuine disciples, it was well ; but if not — if the greater number were following Christ under misapprehension — the sooner that became apparent the better. To allow so large a mixed multitude to follow Himself any longer without sifting would have been on Christ's part to encourage false hopes, and to give rise to serious misapprehensions as to the nature of His kingdom and His earthly mission. And no better method of separating the chaff from the wheat in that large company of professed disciples could have been devised, than first to work a miracle which would bring to the surface the latent carnality of the greater number, and then to preach a sermon which could not fail to be offensive to the carnal mind.

That Jesus freely chose, for a reason of His own, the miraculous method of meeting the difficulty that had arisen, appears to be not obscurely hinted at in the Gospel narra-tives. Consider, for example, in this connection, John's note of time, " The passover, a feast of the Jews, was nigh." Is this a merely chronological statement ? We think not. What further purpose, then, is it intended to serve ? To explain how so great a crowd came to be gathered around Jesus ? — Such an explanation was not required, for the true cause of the great gathering was the enthusiasm which had been awakened among the people by the preaching and healing work of Jesus and the twelve. The evangelist refers to the approaching passover, it would seem, not to explain the movement of the people, but rather to explain the acts and words of His Lord about to be related. " The passover was nigh, and " — so may we bring out John's meaning — " Jesus was thinking of it, though He went not up to the feast that season. He thought of the paschal lamb, and how He, the true Paschal Lamb, would ere long be slain for the life of the world ; and He gave expression to the deep thoughts of His heart in the symbolic miracle I am about to relate, and in the mystic discourse which followed." [1]

The view we advocate respecting the motive of the miracle in the wilderness seems borne out also by the tone adopted by Jesus in the conversation which took place between Him-self and the twelve as to how the wants of the multitude might be supplied. In the course of that conversation, of which fragments have been preserved by the different evangelists, two suggestions were made by the disciples. One was to dismiss the multitude that they might procure supplies for themselves ; the other, that they (the disciples)

---

[1] For the view of John vi. 4 above given, see Luthardt, *Das Johan. Evangelium*, i 80, ii. 41.

should go to the nearest town (say Bethsaida Julias, probably not far off) and purchase as much bread as they could get for two hundred denarii, which would suffice to alleviate hunger at least, if not to satisfy appetite.[1] Both these proposals were feasible, otherwise they would not have been made ; for the twelve had not spoken thoughtlessly, but after consideration, as appears from the fact that one of their number, Andrew, had already ascertained how much provision could be got on the spot. The question how the multitude could be provided for had evidently been exercising the minds of the disciples, and the two proposals were the result of their deliberations. Now, what we wish to point out is, that Jesus does not appear to have given any serious heed to these proposals. He listened to them, not displeased to see the generous concern of His disciples for the hungry people, yet with the air of one who meant from the first to pursue a different line of action from any they might suggest. He behaved like a general in a council of war whose own mind is made up, but who is not unwilling to hear what his subordinates will say. This is no mere inference of ours, for John actually explains that such was the manner in which our Lord acted on the occasion. After relating that Jesus addressed to Philip the question, Whence shall we buy bread, that these may eat ? he adds the parenthetical remark, " This He said to prove him, for He Himself knew what He would do." [2]

Such, then, was the design of the miracle ; what now was its result ? It raised the swelling tide of enthusiasm to its full height, and induced the multitude to form a foolish and dangerous purpose — even to crown the wonder-working Jesus, and make Him their king instead of the licentious despot Herod. They said, " This is of a truth that Prophet that should come into the world ; " and they were on the point of coming and taking Jesus by force to make Him a king, insomuch that it was necessary that He should make His escape from them, and depart into a mountain Himself alone.[3] Such are the express statements of the fourth

[1] Mark vi. 37 ; John vi. 7. A denarius (Eng. Ver. a penny) seems to have been a day's wages (Matt. xx. 9), and was about the eighth part of an ounce of silver.

[2] John vi. 6.

[3] John vi. 14, 15. The prophet meant was one like Moses (Deut. xviii. 15).

Gospel, and what is there stated is obscurely implied in the narratives of Matthew and Mark. They tell how, after the miracle in the desert, Jesus *straightway constrained* His disciples to get into a ship and to go to the other side.[1] Why such haste, and why such urgency? Doubtless it was late, and there was no time to lose if they wished to get home to Capernaum that night. But why go home at all, when the people, or at least a part of them, were to pass the night in the wilderness? Should the disciples not rather have remained with them, to keep them in heart and take a charge of them? Nay, was it dutiful in disciples to leave their Master alone in such a situation? Doubtless the reluctance of the twelve to depart sprang from their asking themselves these very questions; and, as a feeling having such an origin was most becoming, the constraint put on them presupposes the existence of unusual circumstances, such as those recorded by John. In other words, the most natural explanation of the fact recorded by the synoptical evangelists is, that Jesus wished to extricate both Himself and His disciples from the foolish enthusiasm of the multitude, an enthusiasm with which, beyond question, the disciples were only too much in sympathy, and for that purpose arranged that they should sail away in the dusk across the lake, while He retired into the solitude of the mountains.[2]

What a melancholy result of a hopeful movement have we here! The kingdom has been proclaimed, and the good news has been extensively welcomed. Jesus, the Messianic King, is become the object of most ardent devotion to an enthusiastic population. But, alas! their ideas of the kingdom are radically mistaken. Acted out, they would mean rebellion and ultimate ruin. Therefore it is necessary that Jesus should save Himself from His own friends, and hide Himself from His own followers. How certainly do Satan's tares get sown among God's wheat! How easily does enthusiasm run into folly and mischief!

The result of the miracle did not take Jesus by surprise. It was what He expected; nay, in a sense, it was what He aimed at. It was time that the thoughts of many hearts

---

[1] Matt. xiv. 22; Mark i. 45, Εὐθέως ἠνάγκασεν.
[2] John vi. 15, 16. *Vide* p. 116, note 2.

should be revealed; and the certainty that the miracle would help to reveal them was one reason at least for its being worked. Jesus furnished for the people a table in the wilderness, and gave them of the corn of heaven, and sent them meat to the full,[1] that He might prove them, and know what was in their heart,[2] — whether they loved Him for His own sake, or only for the sake of expected worldly advantage. That many followed Him from by-ends He knew beforehand, but He desired to bring the fact home to their own consciences. The miracle put that in His power, and enabled Him to say, without fear of contradiction, "Ye seek me, not because ye saw the miracles, but because ye did eat of the loaves and were filled."[3] It was a searching word, which might well put all His professed followers, not only then, but now, on self-examining thoughts, and lead each man to ask himself, Why do I profess Christianity? is it from sincere faith in Jesus Christ as the Son of God and Saviour of the world, or from thoughtless compliance with custom, from a regard to reputation, or from considerations of worldly advantage?

SECTION II — THE STORM

MATT. xiv. 24-33; MARK vi. 45-52; JOHN vi. 16-21

"In perils in the wilderness, in perils in the sea," wrote Paul, describing the varied hardships encountered by himself in the prosecution of his great work as the apostle of the Gentiles. Such perils meet together in this crisis in the life of Jesus. He has just saved himself from the dangerous enthusiasm manifested by the thoughtless multitude after the miraculous repast in the desert; and now, a few hours later, a still greater disaster threatens to befall Him. His twelve chosen disciples, whom He had hurriedly sent off in a boat, that they might not encourage the people in their foolish project, have been overtaken in a storm while He is alone on the mountain praying, and are in imminent danger of being drowned. His contrivance for escaping one evil has involved Him in a worse; and it seems as if, by a combination of mischances, He were to be suddenly deprived of all

---

[1] Ps. lxxviii. 19, 24, 25.   [2] Deut. viii. 2.   [3] John vi. 26.

His followers, both true and false, at once, and left utterly
alone, as in the last great crisis. The Messianic King
watching on those heights, like a general on the day of
battle, is indeed hard pressed, and the battle is going against
Him. But the Captain of salvation is equal to the emergency ; and however sorely perplexed He may be for a
season, He will be victorious in the end.

The Sea of Galilee, though but a small sheet of water,
some thirteen miles long by six broad, is liable to be visited
by sharp, sudden squalls, probably due to its situation. It
lies in a deep hollow of volcanic origin, bounded on either
side by steep ranges of hills rising above the water-level
from one to two thousand feet. The difference of temperature at the top and bottom of these hills is very considerable.
Up on the tablelands above the air is cool and bracing ;
down at the margin of the lake, which lies seven hundred
feet below the level of the ocean, the climate is tropical.
The storms caused by this inequality of temperature are
tropical in violence. They come sweeping down the ravines
upon the water ; and in a moment the lake, calm as glass
before, becomes from end to end white with foam, whilst the
waves rise into the air in columns of spray.[1]

Two such storms of wind were encountered by the twelve
after they had become disciples, probably within the same
year ; the one with which we are concerned at present, and
an earlier one on the occasion of a visit to Gadara.[2] Both
happened by night, and both were exceedingly violent. In
the first storm, we are told, the ship was covered with the
waves, and filled almost to sinking, so that the disciples
feared they should perish. The second storm was equally
violent, and was of much longer duration. It caught the
twelve apparently when they were half-way across, and after
the gray of dusk had deepened into the darkness of night.
From that time the wind blew with unabated force till
daybreak, in the fourth watch, between the hours of three
and six in the morning. Some idea of the fury of the blast
may be gathered from the fact recorded, that even then they
were still little more than half-way over the sea. They had

[1] Stanley, *Sinai and Palestine*, p. 380.
[2] Matt. viii. 23; Mark iv. 35 ; Luke viii. 22.

rowed in all only a distance of twenty-five or thirty furlongs,[1] the whole distance in a slanting direction, from the eastern to the western shore, being probably about fifty. During all those weary hours they had done little more, pulling with all their might, than hold their own against wind and waves.

All this while what was Jesus doing ? In the first storm He had been with His disciples in the ship, sweetly sleeping after the fatigues of the day, "rocked in cradle of the imperious surge." This time He was absent, and not sleeping ; but away up among the mountains alone, watching unto prayer. For He, too, had His own struggle on that tempestuous night ; not with the howling winds, but with sorrowful thoughts. That night He, as it were, rehearsed the agony in Gethsemane, and with earnest prayer and absorbing meditation studied the passion sermon which He preached on the morrow. So engrossed was His mind with His own sad thoughts, that the poor disciples were for a season as if forgotten ; till at length, at early dawn, looking seawards,[2] He saw them toiling in rowing against the contrary wind, and without a moment's further delay made haste to their rescue.

This storm on the Sea of Galilee, besides being important as a historical fact, possesses also the significance of an emblem. When we consider the time at which it occurred, it is impossible not to connect it in our thoughts with the untoward events of the next day. For the literal storm on the water was succeeded by a spiritual storm on the land, equally sudden and violent, and not less perilous to the souls of the twelve than the other had been to their bodies. The bark containing the precious freight of Christ's true discipleship was then overtaken by a sudden gust of unpopularity, coming down on it like a squall on a highland loch, and all but upsetting it. The fickle crowd which but the day before would have made Jesus their king, turned away abruptly from Him in disappointment and disgust ; and it was not without an effort, as we shall see,[3] that the twelve maintained their steadfastness. They had to pull hard against wind and waves, that they might not be carried headlong to ruin by the tornado of apostasy.

---

[1] John vi. 19.   [2] Mark vi. 48.   [3] See Section IV. of the present chapter.

There can be little doubt that the two storms, — on the lake and on the shore, — coming so close one on the other, would become associated in the memory of the apostles ; and that the literal storm would be stereotyped in their minds as an expressive emblem of the spiritual one, and of all similar trials of faith. The incidents of that fearful night — the watching, the wet, the toil without result, the fatigue, the terror and despair — would abide indelibly in their recollection, the symbolic representation of all the perils and tribulations through which believers must pass on their way to the kingdom of heaven, and especially of those that come upon them while they are yet immature in the faith. Symbolic significance might be discovered specially in three features. The storm took place *by night ;* in the *absence of Jesus ;* and while it lasted *all progress was arrested.* Storms at sea may happen at all hours of the day, but trials of faith always happen in the night. Were there no darkness there could be no trial. Had the twelve understood Christ's discourse in Capernaum, the apostasy of the multitude would have seemed to them a light matter. But they did not understand it, and hence the solicitude of their Master lest they too should forsake Him. In all such trials, also, the absence of the Lord to feeling is a constant and most painful feature. Christ is not in the ship while the storm rages by night, and we toil on in rowing unaided, as we think, by His grace, uncheered by His spiritual presence. It was so even with the twelve next day on shore. Their Master, present to their eyes, had vanished out of sight to their understanding. They had not the comfort of comprehending His meaning, while they clung to Him as one who had the words of eternal life. Worst of all, in these trials of faith, with all our rowing, we make no progress ; the utmost we can effect is to hold our own, to keep off the rocky shore in the midst of the sea. Happily that is something, yea, it is every thing. For it is not always true that if not going forward we must be going backward. This is an adage for fair weather only. In a time of storm there is such a thing as standing still, and then to do even so much is a great achievement. Is it a small thing to weather the storm, to keep off the rocks, the sands, and the breakers ? Vex not the soul of him who is already vexed enough by the buffeting winds, by retailing wise saws about progress and backsliding indiscriminately applied.   Instead of playing thus the part of a Job's friend, rather remind him that the great thing for one in his situation is to endure, to be immovable, to hold fast his moral integrity and his profession of faith, and to keep off the dangerous coasts of immorality and infidelity ; and assure him that if he will only pull a little longer, however weary his arm, God will come and calm the wind, and he will forthwith reach the land.

The storm on the lake, besides being an apt emblem of the trial of faith, was for the twelve an important lesson in faith, helping to prepare them for the future which awaited them.   The temporary absence of their Master was a preparation for His perpetual absence.   The miraculous interposition of Jesus at the crisis of their peril was fitted to impress on their minds the conviction that even after He had ascended He would still be with them in the hour of danger.   From the ultimate happy issue of a plan which threatened for a time to miscarry, they might further learn to cherish a calm confidence in the government of their exalted Lord, even in midst of most untoward events.   They probably concluded, when the storm came on, that Jesus had made a mistake in ordering them to sail away across the lake while He remained behind to dismiss the multitude.   The event, however, rebuked this hasty judgment, all ending happily.   Their experience in this instance was fitted to teach a lesson for life : not rashly to infer mismanagement or neglect on Christ's part from temporary mishaps, but to have firm faith in His wise and loving care for His cause and people, and to anticipate a happy issue out of all perplexities ; yea, to glory in tribulation, because of the great deliverance which would surely follow.

Such strong faith the disciples were far enough from possessing at the time of the storm.   They had no expectation that Jesus would come to their rescue ; for when He did come, they thought He was a spirit flitting over the water, and cried out in an agony of superstitious terror. Here also we note, in passing, a curious correspondence between the incidents of this crisis and those connected with the final one. The disciples had then as little expectation of seeing their Lord return from the dead as they had now of seeing Him come to them over the sea ; and therefore His re-appearance at first frightened rather than comforted them. "They were terrified and affrighted, and supposed that they had seen a spirit." [1] Good, unlooked for in either case, was turned into evil ; and what to faith would have been a source of intense joy, became, through unbelief, only a new cause of alarm.

The fact of His not being expected seems to have imposed on Jesus the necessity of using artifice in His manner of approaching His storm-tossed disciples. Mark relates that "He would have passed by then," [2] affecting strangeness, as we understand it, out of delicate consideration for their weakness. He knew what He would be taken for when first observed ; and therefore He wished to attract their attention at a safe distance, fearing lest, by appearing among them at once, He might drive them distracted. He found it needful to be as cautious in announcing His advent to save as men are wont to be in communicating evil tidings : first appearing, as the spectre, as far away as He could be seen ; then revealing Himself by His familiar voice uttering the words of comfort, "It is I ; be not afraid," and so obtaining at length a willing reception into the ship. [3]

The effects which followed the admission of Jesus into the vessel betrayed the twelve into a new manifestation of the weakness of their faith. "The wind ceased : and they were sore amazed in themselves beyond measure, and wondered." [4] They ought not to have wondered so greatly, after what had happened once before on these same waters, and especially after such a miracle as had been wrought in the wilderness on the previous day. But the storm had blown all thoughts of such things out of their mind, and driven them utterly stupid. "They reflected not on the loaves (nor on the rebuking of the winds), for their heart was hardened." [5]

But the most interesting revelation of the mental state of the disciples at the time when Jesus came to their relief,

---

[1] Luke xxiv. 37.
[2] Mark vi. 48.
[3] John vi. 21.
[4] Mark vi. 51.
[5] Mark vi. 52.

is to be found in the episode concerning Peter related in Matthew's Gospel. When that disciple understood that the supposed spectre was his beloved Master, he cried, "Lord, if it be Thou, bid me come unto Thee on the water;"[1] and on receiving permission, he forthwith stepped out of the ship into the sea. This was not faith, but simple rashness. It was the rebound of an impetuous, headlong nature from one extreme of utter despair to the opposite extreme of extravagant, reckless joy. What in the other disciples took the tame form of a willingness to receive Jesus into the ship, after they were satisfied it was He who walked on the waters,[2] took, in the case of Peter, the form of a romantic, adventurous wish to go out to Jesus where He was, to welcome Him back among them again. The proposal was altogether like the man — generous, enthusiastic, and well-meant, but inconsiderate.

Such a proposal, of course, could not meet with Christ's approval, and yet He did not negative it. He rather thought good to humor the impulsive disciple so far, by inviting him to come, and then to allow him, while in the water, to feel his own weakness. Thus would He teach him a little self-knowledge, and, if possible, save him from the effects of his rash, self-confident temper. But Peter was not to be made wise by one lesson, nor even by several. He would go on blundering and erring, in spite of rebuke and warning, till at length he fell into grievous sin, denying the Master whom he loved so well. The denial at the final crisis was just what might be looked for from one who so behaved at the minor crisis preceding it. The man who said, "Bid me come to Thee," was just the man to say, "Lord, I am ready to go with Thee both into prison and to death." He who was so courageous on deck, and so timid amid the waves, was the one of all the disciples most likely to talk boldly when danger was not at hand, and then play the coward when the hour of trial actually arrived. The scene on the lake was but a foreshadowing or rehearsal of Peter's fall.

And yet that scene showed something more than the weakness of that disciple's faith. It showed also what is possible to those who believe. If the tendency of weak

---

[1] Matt. xiv. 28.   [2] John vi. 21.

faith be to sink, the triumph of strong faith is to walk on the waves, glorying in tribulation, and counting it all joy when exposed to divers temptations. It is the privilege of those who are weak in faith, and the duty of all, mindful of human frailty, to pray, "Lead us not into temptation." But when storms come not of their inviting, and when their ship is upset in midst of the sea, then may Christians trust to the promise, "When thou passest through the waters, I will be with thee;" and if only they have faith, they shall be enabled to tread the rolling billows as if walking on firm land.

> "He bids me come; His voice I know,
> And boldly on the waters go,
>   And brave the tempest's shock.
> O'er rude temptations now I bound;
> The billows yield a solid ground,
>   The wave is firm as rock."

SECTION III. — THE SERMON

JOHN vi. 32-58

The task now before us is to study that memorable address delivered by Jesus in the synagogue of Capernaum on the bread of life, which gave so great offence at the time, and which has ever since been a stone of stumbling, a subject of controversy, and a cause of division in the visible church, and, so far as one can judge from present appearances, will be to the world's end. On a question so vexed as that which relates to the meaning of this discourse, one might well shrink from entering. But the very confusion which prevails here points it out as our plain duty to disregard the din of conflicting interpretations, and, humbly praying to be taught of God, to search for and set forth Christ's own mind.

The sermon on the bread of life, however strangely it sounds, was appropriate both in matter and manner to the circumstances in which it was delivered. It was natural and seasonable that Jesus should speak to the people of the meat that endureth unto everlasting life after miraculously providing perishable food to supply their physical wants. It was even natural and seasonable that He should speak of this high topic in the startling, apparently gross, harsh style which He adopted on the occasion. The form of thought suited the situation. Passover time was approaching, when the paschal lamb was slain and eaten; and if Jesus desired to say in effect, without saying it in so many words, " I am the true Paschal Lamb," what more suitable form of language could He employ than this : " The bread that I will give is my flesh, which I will give for the life of the world " ? The style was also adapted to the peculiar complexion of the speaker's feelings at the moment. Jesus was in a sad, austere mood when He preached this sermon. The foolish enthusiasm of the multitude had saddened Him. Their wish to force a crown on His head made Him think of His cross; for He knew that this idolatrous devotion to a political Messiah meant death sooner or later to one who declined such carnal homage. He spoke, therefore, in the synagogue of Capernaum with Calvary in view, setting Himself forth as the life of the world in terms applicable to a sacrificial victim, whose blood is shed, and whose flesh is eaten by those presenting the offering; not mincing His words, but saying every thing in the strongest and intensest manner possible.

The theme of this memorable address was very naturally introduced by the preceding conversation between Jesus and the people who came from the other side of the lake, hoping to find Him at Capernaum, His usual place of abode.[1] To their warm inquiries as to how He came thither, He replied by a chilling observation concerning the true motive of their zeal, and an exhortation to set their hearts on a higher food than that which perisheth.[2] Understanding the exhortation as a counsel to cultivate piety, the persons to whom it was addressed inquired what they should do that they might work the works of God, *i.e.* please God.[3] Jesus replied by declaring that the great testing work of the hour was to receive Himself as one whom God had sent.[4] This led to a demand on their part for evidence in support of this high claim to be the divinely missioned Messiah. The miracle just wrought on the other side of the lake was great, but not

---

[1] John vi. 24. Luthardt very properly points out that the fact of the people expecting to find Jesus in Capernaum implies such a residence there as the synoptical Gospels inform us of. — *Das Joh. Evang.* ii. 50.

[2] Vers. 26, 27.

[3] Ver. 28.   [4] Ver. 29.

great enough, they thought, to justify such lofty pretensions. In ancient times a whole nation had been fed for many years by bread brought down from heaven by Moses. What was the recent miracle compared to that? He must show a sign on a far grander scale, if He wished them to believe that a greater than Moses was here.[1] Jesus took up the challenge, and boldly declared that the manna, wonderful as it was, was not the true heavenly bread. There was another bread, of which the manna was but the type : like it, coming down from heaven ;[2] but unlike it, giving life not to a nation, but to a world, and not life merely for a few short years, but life for eternity. This announcement, like the similar one concerning the wonderful water of life made to the woman of Samaria, provoked desire in the hearts of the hearers, and they exclaimed, " Lord, evermore give us this bread." Then said Jesus unto them, " I am the bread of life : he that cometh unto me shall never hunger ; and he that believeth on me shall never thirst." [3]

In these words Jesus briefly enunciated the doctrine of the true bread, which He expounded and inculcated in His memorable Capernaum discourse. The doctrine, as stated, sets forth what the true bread is, what it does, and how it is appropriated.

1. The true bread is He who here speaks of it — Jesus Christ. "I am the bread." The assertion implies, on the speaker's part, a claim to have descended from heaven ; for such a descent is one of the properties by which the true bread is defined.[4] Accordingly we find Jesus, in the sequel of His discourse, expressly asserting that He had come down from heaven.[5] This declaration, understood in a super-natural sense, was the first thing in His discourse with which His hearers found fault. " The Jews then murmured at Him, because He said, I am the bread *which came down from heaven.* And they said, Is not this Jesus, the son of Joseph, whose father and mother we know? how is it then that He saith, I came down from heaven ? " [6] It was natural

---

[1] Vers. 30, 31. Moses is not named, but he is in their thoughts.
[2] ὁ καταβαίνων, ver. 33, refers to ἄρτος, not the speaker directly.
[3] John vi. 32-35.   [5] Vers. 38, 51, 58, 62.
[4] Ver. 33.   [6] Vers. 41, 42.

they should murmur if they did not know or believe that there was any thing out of course in the way in which Jesus came into the world. For such language as He here employs could not be used without blasphemy by a mere man born after the fashion of other men. It is language proper only in the mouth of a Divine Being who, for a purpose, hath assumed human nature.

In setting Himself forth, therefore, as the bread which came down from heaven, Jesus virtually taught the doctrine of the incarnation. The solemn assertion, "I am the bread of life," is equivalent in import to that made by the evangelist respecting Him who spoke these words : " The Word became flesh, and dwelt among us, full of grace and truth." [1]

It is, however, not *merely* as incarnate that the Son of God is the bread of eternal life. Bread must be broken in order to be eaten. The Incarnate One must die as a sacrificial victim that men may truly feed upon Him. The Word become flesh, and crucified in the flesh, is the life of the world. This special truth Jesus went on to declare, after having stated the general truth that the heavenly bread was to be found in Himself. " The bread," said He, " that I will give is my flesh, (which I will give) for the life of the world." [2] The language here becomes modified to suit the new turn of thought. " I am " passes into " I will give," and " bread " is transformed into " flesh."

Jesus evidently refers here to His death. His hearers did not so understand Him, but we can have no doubt on the matter. The verb " give," suggesting a sacrificial act, and the future tense both point that way. In words dark and mysterious before the event, clear as day after it, the speaker declares the great truth, that His death is to be the life of men ; that His broken body and shed blood are to be as meat and drink to a perishing world, conferring on all who shall partake of them the gift of immortality. How He is to die, and why His death shall possess such virtue, He does not here explain. The Capernaum discourse makes no men-

---

[1] John i. 14.
[2] John vi. 51. The words in the original represented by those within brackets are of doubtful authority, but the sense is the same whether they be erased or retained. The first δώσω contains the idea.

tion of the cross; it contains no theory of atonement, the time is not come for such details; it simply asserts in broad, strong terms that the flesh and blood of the incarnate Son of God, severed as in death, are the source of eternal life.

This mention by Jesus of His flesh as the bread from heaven gave rise to a new outburst of murmuring among His hearers. "They strove among themselves, saying, How can this man give us His flesh to eat?"[1] Jesus had not yet said that His flesh must be eaten, but they took for granted that such was His meaning. They were right; and accordingly He went on to say, with the greatest solemnity and emphasis, that they must even eat His flesh and drink His blood. Unless they did that, they should have no life in them; if they did that, they should have life in all its fulness — life eternal both in body and in soul. For His flesh was the true food, and His blood was the true drink. They who partook of these would share in His own life. He should dwell in them, incorporated with their very being; and they should dwell in Him as the ground of their being. They should live as secure against death by Him, as He lived from everlasting to everlasting by the Father. "This, therefore," said the speaker, reverting in conclusion to the proposition with which he started, "this (even my flesh) is that bread which came down from Heaven; not as your fathers did eat manna and are dead: he that eateth of this bread shall live forever."[2]

A third expression of disapprobation ensuing led Jesus to put the copestone on His high doctrine of the bread of life, by making a concluding declaration, which must have appeared at the time the most mysterious and unintelligible of all: that the bread which descended from heaven must ascend up thither again, in order to be to the full extent the bread of everlasting life. Doth this offend you? asked He at His hearers: this which I have just said about your eating my flesh and blood; what will ye say "if ye shall see the Son of man ascend up where He was before?"[3] The question

---

[1] John vi. 52.

[2] John vi. 53-58. In ver. 55 the reading vibrates between ἀληθῶς and ἀληθής. Ver. 57, διὰ τὸν πατέρα means literally "on account of," but "by" gives the practical sense. So with δι' ἐμέ.

[3] John vi. 61, 62.

was in effect an affirmation, and it was also a prophetic hint, that only after He had left the world would He become on an extensive scale and conspicuously a source of life to men ; because then the manna of grace would begin to descend not only on the wilderness of Israel, but on all the barren places of the earth ; and the truth in Him, the doctrine of His life, death, and resurrection, would become meat indeed and drink indeed unto a multitude, not of murmuring hearers, but of devout, enlightened, thankful believers ; and no one would need any longer to ask for a sign when he could find in the Christian church, continuing steadfastly in the apostles' doctrine and fellowship, and in breaking bread and in prayers, the best evidence that He had spoken truth who said, "I am the bread of life."

2. This, then, is the heavenly bread : even the God-man incarnate, crucified, and glorified. Let us now consider more attentively the marvellous virtue of this bread. It is the bread of *life*. It is the office of all bread to sustain life, but it is the peculiarity of this divine bread to give eternal life. "He that cometh to me," said the speaker, "shall never hunger, and he that believeth on me, shall never thirst."[1] With reference to this life-giving power He called the bread of which He spake "living bread," and meat indeed, and declared that he who ate thereof should not die, but should live forever.[2]

In commending this miraculous bread to His hearers, Jesus, we observe, laid special stress on its power to give eternal life even to the body of man. Four times over He declared in express terms that all who partook of this bread of life should be raised again at the last day.[3] The prominence thus given to the resurrection of the body is due in part to the fact that throughout His discourse Jesus was drawing a contrast between the manna which fed the Israelites in the desert and the true bread of which it was the type. The contrast was most striking just at this point. The manna was merely a substitute for ordinary food ; it had no power to ward off death : the generation which had been so miraculously supported passed away from the earth, like all other generations of mankind. Therefore, argued

[1] John vi. 35.   [2] John vi. 51, 55, 50.   [3] John vi. 39, 40, 44, 54.

Jesus, it could not be the true bread from heaven ; for the true bread must be capable of destroying death, and endowing the recipients with the power of an endless existence. A man who eats thereof must not die ; or dying, must rise again. " Your fathers did eat manna in the wilderness, and are dead. This is the bread which cometh down from heaven, that a man may eat thereof, and not die." [1]

But the prominence given to the resurrection of the body is due mainly to its intrinsic importance. For if the dead rise not, then is our faith vain, and the bread of life degenerates into a mere quack nostrum, pretending to virtues which it does not possess. True, it may still give spiritual life to those who eat thereof, but what is that without the hope of a life hereafter ? Not much, according to Paul, who says, " If in this life only we have hope in Christ, we are of all men most miserable." [2] Many, indeed, in our day do not concur in the apostle's judgment. They think that the doctrine of the life everlasting may be left out of the creed without loss — nay, even with positive advantage, to the Christian faith. The life of a Christian seems to them so much nobler when all thought of future reward or punishment is dismissed from the mind. How grand, to pass through the wilderness of this world feeding on the manna supplied in the high, pure teaching of Jesus, without caring whether there be a land of Canaan on the other side of Jordan ! Very sublime indeed ! but why, in that case, come into the wilderness at all ? why not remain in Egypt, feeding on more substantial and palatable viands ? The children of Israel would not have left the house of bondage unless they had hoped to reach the promised land. An immortal hope is equally necessary to the Christian. He must believe in a world to come in order to live above the present evil world. If Christ cannot redeem the body from the power of the grave, then it is in vain that He promises to redeem us from guilt and sin. The bread of life is unworthy of the name, unless it hath power to cope with physical as well as with moral corruption.

Hence the prominence given by Jesus in this discourse to the resurrection of the body. He knew that here lay the crucial experiment by which the value and virtue of the bread

[1] John vi. 49, 50.   [2] 1 Cor. xv. 19.

He offered to His hearers must be tested. " You call this bread the bread of life, in contrast to the manna of ancient times : — do you mean to say that, like the tree of life in the garden of Eden, it will confer on those who eat thereof the gift of a blessed immortality ? " " Yes, I do," replied the Preacher in effect to this imaginary question : " this bread I offer you will not merely quicken the soul to a higher, purer life ; it will even revivify your bodies, and make the corruptible put on incorruption, and the mortal put on immortality."

3. And how, then, is this wondrous bread to be appropriated that one may experience its vitalizing influences ? Bread, of course, is eaten ; but what does eating in this case mean ? It means, in one word, *faith.* " He that *cometh* to me shall never hunger, and he that *believeth* in me shall never thirst." [1] Eating Christ's flesh and drinking His blood, and, we may add, drinking the water of which he spake to the woman by the well, all signify believing in Him as He is offered to men in the gospel : the Son of God manifested in the flesh, crucified, raised from the dead, ascended into glory ; the Prophet, the Priest, the King, and the Mediator between God and man. Throughout the Capernaum discourse eating and believing are used interchangeably as equivalents. Thus, in one sentence, we find Jesus saying, " Verily, verily, I say unto you, He that *believeth* on me hath everlasting life : I am that bread of life ; " [2] and shortly after remarking, " I am the living bread which came down from heaven : If any man *eat* of this bread he shall live forever." [3] If any further argument were necessary to justify the identifying of eating with believing, it might be found in the instruction given by the Preacher to His hearers before He began to speak of the bread of life : " This is the work of God, that ye believe on Him whom He hath sent." [4] That sentence furnishes the key to the interpretation of the whole subsequent discourse. " Believe," said Jesus, with reference to the foregoing inquiry, What shall we do, that we might work the works of God ? — " Believe, and thou hast done God's work." " Believe," we may understand Him as saying with reference to an inquiry,

---

[1] John vi. 35.
[2] Vers. 47, 48.
[3] Ver. 51.
[4] Ver. 29.

How shall we eat this bread of life ? — " Believe, and thou
hast eaten."

Believe, and thou hast eaten : such was the formula in
which Augustine expressed his view of Christ's meaning in
the Capernaum discourse.[1]   The saying is not only terse, but
true, in our judgment ; but it has not been accepted by all
interpreters.   Many hold that eating and faith are something
distinct, and would express the relation between them thus :
Believe, and thou shalt eat.   Even Calvin objected to the
Augustinian formula. Distinguishing his own views from those
held by the followers of Zwingli, he says : " To them to eat
is simply to believe.   I say that Christ's flesh is eaten in
believing because it is made ours by faith, and that that eating
is the fruit and effect of faith.   Or more clearly : To them
eating is faith, to me it seems rather to follow from faith."[2]

The distinction taken by Calvin between eating and
believing seems to have been verbal rather than real.   With
many other theologians, however, it is far otherwise.   All
upholders of the magical doctrines of transubstantiation
and consubstantiation contend for the literal interpretation
of the Capernaum discourse even in its strongest statements.
Eating Christ's flesh and drinking His blood are, for such,
acts of the mouth, *accompanied* perhaps with acts of faith,
but not *merely* acts of faith.   It is assumed for the most
part as a matter of course, that the discourse recorded in
the sixth chapter of John's Gospel has reference to the
sacrament of the Supper, and that only on the hypothesis
of such a reference can the peculiar phraseology of the discourse be explained.   Christ spoke then of eating His flesh
and drinking His blood, so we are given to understand,
because He had in His mind that mystic rite ere long to be
instituted, in which bread and wine should not merely represent, but become, the constituent elements of His crucified
body.

While the sermon on the bread of life continues to be
mixed up with sacramentarian controversies, agreement in
its interpretation is altogether hopeless.   Meantime, till a
better day dawn on a divided and distracted church, every

[1] Crede et manducasti. — In Joannis Evangelium Tract. xxv. § 12.
[2] Calv. Institutio IV. xvii. 5.

man must endeavor to be fully persuaded in his own mind. Three things are clear to our mind. First, it is incorrect to say that the sermon delivered in the Capernaum synagogue refers to the sacrament of the Supper. The true state of the case is, that both refer to a third thing, viz. the death of Christ, and both declare, in different ways, the same thing concerning it. The sermon says in symbolic words what the Supper says in a symbolic act : that Christ crucified is the life of men, the world's hope of salvation. The sermon says more than this, for it speaks of Christ's ascension as well as of His death ; but it says this for one thing.

A second point on which we are clear is, that it is quite unnecessary to assume a mental reference by anticipation to the Holy Supper, in order to account for the peculiarity of Christ's language in this famous discourse. As we saw at the beginning, the whole discourse rose naturally out of the present situation. The mention by the people of the manna naturally led Jesus to speak of the bread of life ; and from the bread He passed on as naturally to speak of the flesh and the blood, because he could not fully be bread until He had become flesh and blood dissevered, *i.e.* until He had endured death. All that we find here might have been said, in fact, although the sacrament of the Supper had never existed. The Supper is of use not so much for interpreting the sermon as for establishing its credibility as an authentic utterance of Jesus. There is no reason to doubt that He who instituted the mystic feast, could also have preached this mystic sermon.

The third truth which shines clear as a star to our eye is, — that through faith alone we may attain all the blessings of salvation. Sacraments are very useful, but they are not necessary. If it had pleased Christ not to institute them, we could have got to heaven notwithstanding. Because He has instituted them, it is our duty to celebrate them, and we may expect benefit from their celebration. But the benefit we receive is simply an aid to faith, and nothing which cannot be received by faith. Christians eat the flesh and drink the blood of the Son of man at all times, not merely at communion times, simply by believing in Him.

They eat His flesh and drink His blood at His table in the same sense as at other times ; only perchance in a livelier manner, their hearts being stirred up to devotion by remembrance of His dying love, and their faith aided by seeing, handling, and tasting the bread and the wine.

SECTION IV — THE SIFTING

JOHN vi. 66 - 71

The sermon on the bread of life produced decisive effects. It converted popular enthusiasm for Jesus into disgust ; like a fan, it separated true from false disciples ; and like a winnowing breeze, it blew the chaff away, leaving a small residuum of wheat behind. " From that time many of His disciples went back, and walked no more with Him."

This result did not take Jesus by surprise. He expected it ; in a sense He wished it, though He was deeply grieved by it. For while His large, loving human heart yearned for the salvation of all, and desired that all should come and get life, He wanted none to come to Him under misapprehension, or to follow Him from by-ends. He sought disciples God-given,[1] God-drawn,[2] God-taught,[3] knowing that such alone would continue in His word.[4] He was aware that in the large mass of people who had recently followed Him were many disciples of quite another description ; and He was not unwilling that the mixed multitude should be sifted. Therefore He preached that mystic discourse, fitted to be a savor of life or of death according to the spiritual state of the hearer. Therefore, also, when offence was taken at the doctrine taught, He plainly declared the true cause,[5] and expressed His assurance that only those whom His Father taught and drew would or could really come unto Him.[6] These things He said not with a view to irritate, but He deemed it right to say them though they should give rise to irritation, reckoning that true believers would take all in good part, and that those who took umbrage would thereby reveal their true character.

The apostatizing disciples doubtless thought themselves

[1] John vi. 37.   [3] John vi. 45.   [5] John vi. 36, 37.
[2] John vi. 44.   [4] John viii. 31.   [6] John vi. 44.

fully justified in withdrawing from the society of Jesus. They turned their back on Him, we fancy, in most virtuous indignation, saying in their hearts — nay, probably saying aloud to one another: " Who ever heard the like of that ? how absurd ! how revolting ! The man who can speak thus is either a fool, or is trying to make fools of his hearers." And yet the hardness of His doctrine was not the real reason which led so many to forsake Him ; it was simply the pretext, the most plausible and respectable reason that they could assign for conduct springing from other motives. The grand offence of Jesus was this : He was not the man they had taken Him for ; He was not going to be at their service to promote the ends they had in view. Whatever He meant by the bread of life, or by eating His flesh, it was plain that He was not going to be a bread-king, making it His business to furnish supplies for their physical appetites, ushering in a golden age of idleness and plenty. That ascertained, it was all over with Him so far as they were concerned : He might offer His heavenly food to whom He pleased ; they wanted none of it.

Deeply affected by the melancholy sight of so many human beings deliberately preferring material good to eternal life, Jesus turned to the twelve, and said, " Will ye also go away ? " or more exactly, " You do not wish to go away too, do you ? "[1] The question may be understood as a virtual expression of confidence in the persons to whom it was addressed, and as an appeal to them for sympathy at a discouraging crisis. And yet, while a negative answer was expected to the question, it was not expected as a matter of course. Jesus was not without solicitude concerning the fidelity even of the twelve. He interrogated them, as conscious that they were placed in trying circumstances, and that if they did not actually forsake Him now, as at the great final crisis, they were at least *tempted* to be offended in Him.

A little reflection suffices to satisfy us that the twelve were indeed placed in a position at this time calculated to try their faith most severely. For one thing, the mere fact of their Master being deserted wholesale by the crowd of

---

[1] John vi. 67. The particle μή implies that a negative answer is looked for. See Winer, *Neutest. Grammatik*, § 57, Moulton's translation, p. 641.

quondam admirers and followers involved for the chosen band a temptation to apostasy. How mighty is the power of sympathy! how ready are we all to follow the multitude, regardless of the way they are going! and how much moral courage it requires to stand alone! How difficult to witness the spectacle of thousands, or even hundreds, going off in sullen disaffection, without feeling an impulse to imitate their bad example! how hard to keep one's self from being carried along with the powerful tide of adverse popular opinion! Especially hard it must have been for the twelve to resist the tendency to apostatize if, as is more than probable, they sympathized with the project entertained by the multitude when their enthusiasm for Jesus was at full-tide. If it would have gratified them to have seen their beloved Master made king by popular acclamation, how their spirits must have sunk when the bubble burst, and the would-be subjects of the Messianic Prince were dispersed like an idle mob, and the kingdom which had seemed so near vanished like a cloudland!

Another circumstance trying to the faith of the twelve was the strange, mysterious character of their Master's discourse in the synagogue of Capernaum. That discourse contained hard, repulsive, unintelligible sayings for them quite as much as for the rest of the audience. Of this we can have no doubt when we consider the repugnance with which some time afterward they received the announcement that Jesus was destined to be put to death.[1] If they objected even to the fact of His death, how could they understand its meaning, especially when both fact and meaning were spoken of in such a veiled and mystic style as that which pervades the sermon on the bread of life? While, therefore, they believed that their Master had the words of eternal life, and perceived that His late discourse bore on that high theme, it may be regarded as certain that the twelve did not understand the words spoken any more than the multitude, however much they might try to do so. They knew not what connection existed between Christ's flesh and eternal life, how eating that flesh could confer any benefit, or even what eating it might mean. They had quite lost sight of the

[1] Matt. xvi. 22.

Speaker in His eagle flight of thought; and they must have looked on in distress as the people melted away, painfully conscious that they could not altogether blame them.

Yet, however greatly tempted to forsake their Master, the twelve did abide faithfully by His side. They did come safely through the spiritual storm. What was the secret of their steadfastness? what were the anchors that preserved them from shipwreck? These questions are of practical interest to all who, like the apostles at this crisis, are tempted to apostasy by evil example or by religious doubt; by the fashion of the world they live in, whether scientific or illiterate, refined or rustic; or by the deep things of God, whether these be the mysteries of providence, the mysteries of revelation, or the mysteries of religious experience: we may say, indeed, to all genuine Christians, for what Christian has not been tempted in one or other of these ways at some period in his history?

Sufficient materials for answering these questions are supplied in the words of Simon Peter's response to Jesus. As spokesman for the whole company, that disciple promptly said: " Lord, to whom shall we go? Thou hast the words of eternal life. And we believe and know that Thou art that Christ, the Son of the living God," [1] or, according to the reading preferred by most critics, " that Thou art the Holy One of God." [2]

Three anchors, we infer from these words, helped the twelve to ride out the storm : *Religious earnestness or sincerity ; a clear perception of the alternatives before them ; and implicit confidence in the character and attachment to the person of their Master.*

1. The twelve, as a body, were sincere and thoroughly in earnest in religion. Their supreme desire was to know "the words of eternal life," and actually to gain possession of that life. Their concern was not about the meat that perisheth, but about the higher heavenly food of the soul which Christ had in vain exhorted the majority of His hearers to labor for. As yet they knew not clearly wherein

---

[1] John vi. 68, 69.
[2] See Alford *in loc.* The confession of Christ's holiness was appropriate, as meeting an implied charge of having uttered language shocking to the moral feelings.

that food consisted, but according to their light they sincerely prayed, "Lord, evermore give us *this* bread." Hence it was no disappointment to them that Jesus declined to become a purveyor of mere material food : they had never expected or wished Him to do so ; they had joined His company with entirely different expectations. A certain element of error might be mingled with truth in their conceptions of His Mission, but the gross, carnal hopes of the multitude had no place in their breasts. They became not disciples to better their worldly circumstances, but to obtain a portion which the world could neither give them nor take from them.

What we have now stated was true of all the twelve save *one;* and the crisis we are at present considering is memorable for this, among other things, that it was the first occasion on which Jesus gave a hint that there was a false disciple among the men whom He had chosen. To justify Himself for asking a question which seemed to cast a doubt upon their fidelity, He replied to Peter's protestation by the startling remark : "Did not I choose you the twelve, and one of you is a devil?"[1] as if to say: "It is painful to me to have to use this language of suspicion, but I have good cause : there is one among you who has had *thoughts* of desertion, and who is capable even of treachery." With what sadness of spirit must He have made such an intimation at this crisis ! To be forsaken by the fickle crowd of shallow, thoughtless followers had been a small matter, could He have reckoned all the members of the select band good men and true friends. But to have an enemy in one's own house, a *diabolus* capable of playing Satan's part in one's small circle of intimate companions :—it was hard indeed !

But how could a man destined to be a traitor, and deserving to be stigmatized as a devil, manage to pass creditably through the present crisis ? Does not the fact seem to imply that, after all, it is possible to be steadfast without being single-minded ? Not so ; the only legitimate inference is, that the crisis was not searching enough to bring out the true character of Judas. Wait till you see the end. A little religion will carry a man through many trials, but there is

[1] John vi. 70.

an *experimentum crucis* which nothing but sincerity can stand. If the mind be double, or the heart divided, a time comes that compels men to act according to the motives that are deepest and strongest in them. This remark applies especially to creative, revolutionary, or transition epochs. In quiet times a hypocrite may pass respectably through this world, and never be detected till he get to the next, whither his sins follow him to judgment. But in critical eras the sins of the double-minded find them out in this life. True, even then some double-minded men can stand more temptation than others, and are not to be bought so cheaply as the common herd. But all of them have their price, and those who fall less easily than others fall in the end most deeply and tragically.

Of the character and fall of Judas we shall have another opportunity to speak. Our present object is simply to point out that from such as he Jesus did not expect constancy. By referring to that disciple as He did, He intimated His conviction that no one in whom the love of God and truth was not the deepest principle of his being would continue faithful to the end. In effect He inculcated the necessity, in order to steadfastness in faith, of moral integrity, or godly sincerity.

2. The second anchor by which the disciples were kept from shipwreck at this season was a clear perception of the alternatives. " To whom shall we go ? " asked Peter, as one who saw that, for men having in view the aim pursued by himself and his brethren, there was no course open but to remain where they were. He had gone over rapidly in his mind all the possible alternatives, and this was the conclusion at which he had arrived. " To whom *shall* we go — we who seek eternal life ? John, our former master, is dead ; and even were he alive, he would send us back to Thee. Or shall we go to the scribes and Pharisees ? We have been too long with Thee for that ; for Thou hast taught us the superficiality, the hypocrisy, the ostentatiousness, the essential ungodliness of their religious system. Or shall we follow the fickle multitude there, and relapse into stupidity and indifference ? It is not to be thought of. Or, finally, shall we go to the Sadducees, the idolaters of the material

and the temporal, who say there is no resurrection, neither any angels nor spirits ? God forbid ! That were to renounce a hope dearer than life, without which life to an earnest mind were a riddle, a contradiction, and an intolerable burden."

We may understand what a help this clear perception of the alternatives was to Peter and his brethren, by reflecting on the help we ourselves might derive from the same source when tempted by dogmatic difficulties to renounce Christianity. It would make one pause if he understood that the alternatives open to him were to abide with Christ, or to become an atheist, ignoring God and the world to come ; that when he leaves Christ, he must go to school to some of the great masters of thoroughgoing unbelief. In the works of a well-known German author is a dream, which portrays with appalling vividness the consequences that would ensue throughout the universe should the Creator cease to exist. The dream was invented, so the gifted writer tells us, for the purpose of frightening those who discussed the being of God as coolly as if the question respected the existence of the Kraken or the unicorn, and also to check all atheistic thoughts which might arise in his own bosom. " If ever," he says, "my heart should be so unhappy and deadened as to have all those feelings which affirm the being of a God destroyed, I would use this dream to frighten myself, and so heal my heart, and restore its lost feelings." [1] Such benefit as Richter expected from the perusal of his own dream, would any one, tempted to renounce Christianity, derive from a clear perception that in ceasing to be a Christian he must make up his mind to accept a creed which acknowledges no God, no soul, no hereafter.

Unfortunately it is not so easy for us now as it was for Peter to see clearly what the alternatives before us are. Few are so clear-sighted, so recklessly logical, or so frank as the late Dr. Strauss, who in his latest publication, *The Old and the New Faith*, plainly says that he is no longer a Christian. Hence many in our day call themselves Christians whose theory of the universe (or Weltanschauung, as the Germans call it) does not allow them to believe in the

[1] J. F. Richter, *Siebenkäs*, viii.

miraculous in any shape or in any sphere ; with whom it is an
axiom that the continuity of nature's course cannot be broken,
and who therefore cannot even go the length of Socinians in
their view of Christ and declare Him to be, without qualification, the Holy One of God, the morally sinless One. Even
men like Renan claim to be Christians, and, like Balaam,
bless Him whom their philosophy compels them to blame.
Our modern Balaams all confess that Jesus is at least the
holiest of men, if not the absolutely Holy One. They are
constrained to bless the Man of Nazareth. They are spell-
bound by the Star of Bethlehem, as was the Eastern
soothsayer by the Star of Jacob, and are forced to say in
effect : " How shall I curse, whom God hath not cursed ? or
how shall I defy, whom the Lord hath not defied? Behold,
I have received commandment to bless : and He hath
blessed ; and I cannot reverse it." [1]   Others not going so
far as Renan, shrinking from thoroughgoing naturalism,
believing in a perfect Christ, a moral miracle, yet affect a
Christianity independent of dogma, and as little as possible
encumbered by miracle, a Christianity purely ethical,
consisting mainly in admiration of Christ's character and
moral teaching ; and, as the professors of such a Christianity, regard themselves as exemplary disciples of Christ.
Such are the men of whom the author of *Supernatural
Religion* speaks as characterized by "a tendency to eliminate
from Christianity, with thoughtless dexterity, every supernatural element which does not quite accord with current
opinions," and as endeavoring " to arrest for a moment the
pursuing wolves of doubt and unbelief by practically throwing
to them scrap by scrap the very doctrines which constitute
the claims of Christianity to be regarded as a divine revelation
at all." [2]   Such men can hardly be said to have a consistent
theory of the universe, for they hold opinions based on
incompatible theories, are naturalistic in tendency, yet will
not carry out naturalism to all its consequences. They are
either not able, or are disinclined, to *realize the alternatives*
and to obey the voice of logic, which like a stern policeman
bids them " Move on ; " but would rather hold views which

[1] Numb. xxiii. 8, 20.
[2] *Supernatural Religion*, i. 92 (6th ed.).

unite the alternatives in one compound eclectic creed, like Schleiermacher, — himself an excellent example of the class, — of whom Strauss remarks that he ground down Christianity and Pantheism to powder, and so mixed them that it is hard to say where Pantheism ends and Christianity begins. In presence of such a spirit of compromise, so widespread, and recommended by the example of many men of ability and influence, it requires some courage to have and hold a definite position, or to resist the temptation to yield to the current and adopt the watchword : Christianity without dogma and miracle. 'But perhaps it will be easier by and by to realize the alternatives, when time has more clearly shown whither present tendencies lead. Meantime it is the evening twilight, and for the moment it seems as if we could do without the sun, for though he is below the horizon, the air is still full of light. But wait awhile ; and the deepening of the twilight into the darkness of night will show how far Christ the Holy One of the Church's confession can be dispensed with as the Sun of the spiritual world.

3. The third anchor whereby the twelve were enabled to ride out the storm, was confidence in the character of their Master. They believed, yea, they knew, that He was the Holy One of God. They had been with Jesus long enough to have come to very decided conclusions respecting Him. They had seen Him work many miracles ; they had heard Him discourse with marvellous wisdom, in parable and sermon, on the divine kingdom ; they had observed His wondrously tender, gracious concern for the low and the lost ; they had been present at His various encounters with Pharisees, and had noted His holy abhorrence of their falsehood, pride, vanity, and tyranny. All this blessed fellowship had begotten a confidence in, and reverence for, their beloved Master, too strong to be shaken by a single address containing some statements of an incomprehensible character, couched in questionable or even offensive language. Their intellect might be perplexed, but their heart remained true ; and hence, while others who knew not Jesus well went off in disgust, they continued by His side, feeling that such a friend and guide was not to be parted with for a trifle.

" We believe and know," said Peter. He believed because

he knew. Such implicit confidence as the twelve had in Jesus is possible only through intimate knowledge ; for one cannot thus trust a stranger. All, therefore, who desire to get the benefit of this trust, must be willing to spend time and take trouble to get into the heart of the Gospel story, and of its great subject. The sure anchorage is not attainable by a listless, random reading of the evangelic narratives, but by a close, careful, prayerful study, pursued it may be for years. Those who grudge the trouble are in imminent danger of the fate which befell the ignorant multitude, being liable to be thrown into panic by every new infidel book, or to be scandalized by every strange utterance of the Object of faith. Those, on the other hand, who do take the trouble, will be rewarded for their pains. Storm-tossed for a time, they shall at length reach the harbor of a creed which is no nondescript compromise between infidelity and scriptural Christianity, but embraces all the cardinal facts and truths of the faith, as taught by Jesus in the Capernaum discourse, and as afterwards taught by the men who passed safely through the Capernaum crisis.

May God in His mercy guide all souls now out in the tempestuous sea of doubt into that haven of rest !

10

THE LEAVEN OF THE PHARISEES
AND SADDUCEES

Matt. 16:1-12; Mark 8:10-21

THIS new collision between Jesus and His opponents took
place shortly after a second miracle of feeding similar to
that performed in the neighborhood of Bethsaida Julias.
What interval of time elapsed between the two miracles
cannot be ascertained;[1] but it was long enough to admit
of an extended journey on the part of our Lord and His
disciples to the coasts of Tyre and Sidon, the scene of the
pathetic meeting with the Syrophenician woman, and round
from thence through the region of the ten cities, on the
eastern border of the Galilean lake. It was long enough
also to allow the cause and the fame of Jesus to recover
from the low state to which they sank after the sifting
sermon in the synagogue of Capernaum. The unpopular
One had again become popular, so that on arriving at the
south-eastern shore of the lake He found Himself attended
by thousands, so intent on hearing Him preach, and on
experiencing His healing power, that they remained with
Him three days, almost, if not entirely, without food, thus
creating a necessity for the second miraculous repast.

After the miracle on the south-eastern shore, Jesus, we
read, sent away the multitude; and taking ship, came into
the coasts of Magdala, on the western side of the sea.[2] It
was on His arrival there that He encountered the party who
came seeking of Him a sign from heaven. These persons
had probably heard of the recent miracle, as of many others

---

[1] The chronological relation of the events recorded in Matt. xv. and xvi. to the feast
of tabernacles spoken of in John vii. is an important question. It is one, however, on
which the learned differ, and certainly is unattainable.

[2] Matt. xv. 39.

wrought by Him; but, unwilling to accept the conclusion to which these wondrous works plainly led, they affected to regard them as insufficient evidence of His Messiahship, and demanded still more unequivocal proof before giving in their adherence to His claim. "Show us a sign from heaven," said they; meaning thereby, something like the manna brought down from heaven by Moses, or the fire called down by Elijah, or the thunder and rain called down by Samuel;[1] it being assumed that such signs could be wrought only by the power of God, whilst the signs on earth, such as Jesus supplied in His miracles of healing, might be wrought by the power of the devil![2] It was a demand of a sort often addressed to Jesus in good faith or in bad;[3] for the Jews sought after such signs — miracles of a singular and startling character, fitted to gratify a superstitious curiosity, and astonish a wonder-loving mind — miracles that were merely signs, serving no other purpose than to display divine power; like the rod of Moses, converted into a serpent, and reconverted into its original form.

These demands of the sign-seekers Jesus uniformly met with a direct refusal. He would not condescend to work miracles of any description merely as certificates of His own Messiahship, or to furnish food for a superstitious appetite, or materials of amusement to sceptics. He knew that such as remained unbelievers in presence of His ordinary miracles, which were not naked signs, but also works of beneficence, could not be brought to faith by any means; nay, that the more evidence they got, the more hardened they should become in unbelief. He regarded the very demand for these signs as the indication of a fixed determination on the part of those who made it not to believe in Him, even if, in order to rid themselves of the disagreeable obligation, it should be necessary to put Him to death. Therefore, in refusing the signs sought after, He was wont to accompany the refusal with a word of rebuke or of sad foreboding; as when He said, at a very early period of His ministry, on His first visit

---

[1] See Alford. Stier refers to the apocryphal books to explain the nature of the signs demanded.

[2] Matt. xii. 24 et par.

[3] John ii. 18, vi. 30; Matt. xii. 38.

to Jerusalem, after His baptism : " Destroy this temple, and in three days I will raise it up." [1]

On the present occasion the soul of Jesus was much perturbed by the renewed demands of the sign-seekers. " He sighed deeply in His spirit," knowing full well what these demands meant, with respect both to those who made them and to Himself ; and He addressed the parties who came tempting Him in excessively severe and bitter terms, — reproaching them with spiritual blindness, calling them a wicked and adulterous generation, and ironically referring them now, as He had once done before,[2] to the sign of the prophet Jonas. He told them, that while they knew the weather signs, and understood what a red sky in the morning or evening meant, they were blind to the manifest signs of the times, which showed at once that the Sun of righteousness had arisen, and that a dreadful storm of judgment was coming like a dark night on apostate Israel for her iniquity. He applied to them, and the whole generation they represented, the epithet " wicked," to characterize their false-hearted, malevolent, and spiteful behavior towards Himself ; and He employed the term " adulterous," to describe them, in relation to God, as guilty of breaking their marriage covenant, pretending great love and zeal with their lip, but in their heart and life turning away from the living God to idols — forms, ceremonies, signs. He gave them the story of Jonah the prophet for a sign, in mystic allusion to His death ; meaning to say, that one of the most reliable evidences that He was God's servant indeed, was just the fact that He was rejected, and ignominiously and barbarously treated by such as those to whom He spake : that there could be no worse sign of a man than to be well received by them — that he could be no true Christ who was so received.[3]

---

[1] John ii. 19. 　　　　　[2] Matt. xii. 40.

[3] Pfleiderer (*Die Religion*, ii. 447) recognizes so fully the importance of this encounter between Jesus and the Pharisees, that he fixes on it as the historical germ of the Temptation-history. He looks on the demand as made in earnest by persons ready to receive Jesus as the Christ, if He gave the necessary miracle-sign, and to form a friendly alliance with Him. Jesus, on the other hand, he represents as unwilling to take the Messiah sceptre out of hands sin-stained, and preferring to reach by another path His throne. That He was not, however, insensible to the temptation, Pfleiderer thinks was shown by the word of warning He afterwards uttered about the leaven of the Pharisees.

Having thus freely uttered His mind, Jesus left the sign-seekers; and entering into the ship in which He had just crossed from the other side, departed again to the same eastern shore, anxious to be rid of their unwelcome presence. On arriving at the land, He made the encounter which had just taken place the subject of instruction to the twelve. "Take heed," He said as they walked along the way, "and beware of the leaven of the Pharisees and Sadducees." The word was spoken abruptly, as the utterance of one waking out of a revery. Jesus, we imagine, while His disciples rowed Him across the lake, had been brooding over what had occurred, sadly musing on prevailing unbelief, and the dark, lowering weather-signs, portentous of evil to Him and to the whole Jewish people. And now, recollecting the presence of the disciples, He communicates His thoughts to them in the form of a warning, and cautions them against the deadly influence of an evil time, as a parent might bid his child beware of a poisonous plant whose garish flowers attracted its eye.

In this warning, it will be observed, pharisaic and sadducaic tendencies are identified. Jesus speaks not of two leavens, but of one common to both sects, as if they were two species of one genus, two branches from one stem.[1] And such indeed they were. Superficially, the two parties were very diverse. The one was excessively zealous, the other was "moderate" in religion; the one was strict, the other easy in morals; the one was exclusively and intensely Jewish in feeling, the other was open to the influence of pagan civilization. Each party had a leaven peculiar to itself: that of the Pharisees being, as Christ was wont to declare, hypocrisy;[2] that of the Sadducees, an engrossing interest in merely material and temporal concerns, assuming in some a political form, as in the case of the partisans of the Herod family, called in the Gospels Herodians, in others wearing the guise of a philosophy which denied the existence of spirit and the reality of the future life, and made that denial an excuse for exclusive devotion to the interests of time. But here, as elsewhere, extremes met. Phariseeism, Sadduceeism,

---

[1] In this connection, the omission of the article before Σαδδουκαίων is significant.
[2] Luke xii. 1.

Herodianism, though distinguished by minor differences, were radically one. The religionists, the philosophers, the politicians, were all members of one great party, which was inveterately hostile to the divine kingdom. All alike were worldly-minded (of the Pharisees it is expressly remarked that they were covetous[1]); all were opposed to Christ for fundamentally the same reason, viz. because He was not of this world; all united fraternally at this time in the attempt to vex Him by unbelieving, unreasonable demands;[2] and they all had a hand in His death at the last. It was thus made apparent, once for all, that a Christian is not one who merely differs superficially either from Pharisees or from Sadducees separately, but one who differs radically from both. A weighty truth, not yet well understood; for it is fancied by many that right believing and right living consist in going to the opposite extreme from any tendency whose evil influence is apparent. To avoid pharisaic strictness and superstition, grown odious, men run into sadducaic scepticism and license; or, frightened by the excesses of infidelity and secularity, they seek salvation in ritualism, infallible churches, and the revival of mediæval monkery. Thus the two tendencies continue ever propagating each other on the principle of action and reaction; one generation or school going all lengths in one direction, and another making a point of being as unlike its predecessor or its neighbor as possible, and both being equally far from the truth.

What the common leaven of Phariseeism and Sadduceeism was, Jesus did not deem it necessary to state. He had already indicated its nature with sufficient plainness in His severe reply to the sign-seekers. The radical vice of both sects was just ungodliness: blindness, and deadness of heart to the Divine. They did not know the true and the good when they saw it; and when they knew it, they did not love it. All around them were the evidences that the King and the kingdom of grace were among them; yet here were they asking for arbitrary outward signs, "external evidences" in the worst sense, that He who spake as never man spake, and worked wonders of mercy such as had never before

[1] Luke xvi. 14.   [2] In Mark (viii. 15) the "leaven of Herod" is mentioned.

been witnessed, was no impostor, but a man wise and good, a prophet, and the Son of God. Verily the natural man, religious or irreligious, is blind and dead! What these seekers after a sign needed was not a new sign, but a new heart ; not mere evidence, but a spirit willing to obey the truth.

The spirit of unbelief which ruled in Jewish society Jesus described as a leaven, with special reference to its diffusiveness ; and most fitly, for it passes from sire to son, from rich to poor, from learned to unlearned, till a whole generation has been vitiated by its malign influence. Such was the state of things in Israel as it came under His eye. Spiritual blindness and deadness, with the outward symptom of the inward malady, — a constant craving for evidence, — met him on every side. The common people, the leaders of society, the religious, the sceptics, the courtiers, and the rustics, were all blind, and yet apparently all most anxious to see ; ever renewing the demand, " What sign showest Thou, that we may see and believe Thee ? What dost Thou work ? "

Vexed an hour ago by the sinister movements of foes, Jesus next found new matter for annoyance in the stupidity of friends. The disciples utterly, even ludicrously, misunderstood the warning word addressed to them. In conversation by themselves, while their Master walked apart, they discussed the question, what the strange words, so abruptly and earnestly spoken, might mean ; and they came to the sapient conclusion that they were intended to caution them against buying bread from parties belonging to either of the offensive sects. It was an absurd mistake, and yet, all things considered, it was not so very unnatural : for, in the first place, as already remarked, Jesus had introduced the subject very abruptly ; and secondly, some time had elapsed since the meeting with the seekers of a sign, during which no allusion seems to have been made to that matter. How were they to know that during all that time their Master's thoughts had been occupied with what took place on the western shore of the lake ? In any case, such a supposition was not likely to occur to their mind ; for the demand for a sign had, doubtless, not appeared to them an event of much consequence, and it was probably forgotten as soon as their backs were turned upon the men who made it. And then, finally, it so happened that, just before Jesus began to speak, they remembered that in the hurry of a sudden departure they had forgotten to provide themselves with a stock of provisions for the journey. That was what *they* were thinking about when *He* began to say, "Take heed, and beware of the leaven of the Pharisees and of the Sadducees." The momentous circumstance that they had with them but one loaf was causing them so much concern, that when they heard the caution against a particular kind of leaven, they jumped at once to the conclusion, "It is because we have no bread."

Yet the misunderstanding of the disciples, though simple and natural in its origin, was blameworthy. They could not have fallen into the mistake had the interest they took in spiritual and temporal things respectively been proportional to their relative importance. They had treated the incident on the other side of the lake too lightly, and they had treated their neglect to provide bread too gravely. They should have taken more to heart the ominous demand for a sign, and the solemn words spoken by their Master in reference thereto ; and they should not have been troubled about the want of loaves in the company of Him who had twice miraculously fed the hungry multitude in the desert. Their thoughtlessness in one direction, and their over-thoughtfulness in another, showed that food and raiment occupied a larger place in their minds than the kingdom of God and its interests. Had they possessed more faith and more spirituality, they would not have exposed themselves to the reproachful question of their Master : "How is it that ye do not understand that I spake it not to you concerning bread, that ye should beware of the leaven of the Pharisees and Sadducees ?"[1]

And yet, Jesus can hardly have expected these crude disciples to appreciate as He did the significance of what had occurred on the other side of the lake. It needed no common insight to discern the import of that demand for a sign ; and the faculty of reading the signs of the times

[1] Matt. xvi. 11.

possessed by the disciples, as we shall soon see, and as all we have learned concerning them already might lead us to expect, was very small indeed. One of the principal lessons to be learned from the subject of this chapter, indeed, is just this : how different were the thoughts of Christ in reference to the future from the thoughts of His companions. We shall often have occasion to remark on this hereafter, as we advance towards the final crisis. At this point we are called to signalize the fact prominently for the first time.

11

PETER'S CONFESSION;
or, Current Opinion and Eternal Truth

Matt. 16:13-20; Mark 8-27-30; Luke 9:18-21

FROM the eastern shore of the lake Jesus directed His course northwards along the banks of the Upper Jordan, passing Bethsaida Julias, where, as Mark informs us, He restored eyesight to a blind man. Pursuing His journey, He arrived at length in the neighborhood of a town of some importance, beautifully situated near the springs of the Jordan, at the southern base of Mount Hermon. This was Cæsarea Philippi, formerly called Paneas, from the heathen god Pan, who was worshipped by the Syrian Greeks in the limestone cavern near by, in which Jordan's fountains bubble forth to light. Its present name was given to it by Philip, tetrarch of Trachonitis, in honor of Cæsar Augustus; his own name being appended (Cæsarea *Philippi*, or Philip's Cæsarea) to distinguish it from the other town of the same name on the Mediterranean coast. The town so named could boast of a temple of white marble, built by Herod the Great to the first Roman Emperor, besides villas and palaces, built by Philip, Herod's son, in whose territories it lay, and who, as we have just stated, gave it its new name.

Away in that remote secluded region, Jesus occupied Himself for a season in secret prayer, and in confidential conversations with His disciples on topics of deepest interest. One of these conversations had reference to His own Person. He introduced the subject by asking the twelve the question, " Whom do men say that I, the Son of man, am ? " This question He asked, not as one needing to be informed, still less from any morbid sensitiveness, such as vain men feel respecting the opinions entertained of them by their

fellow-creatures. He desired of His disciples a recital of
current opinions, merely by way of preface to a profession
of their own faith in the eternal truth concerning Himself.
He deemed it good to draw forth from them such a profession at this time, because He was about to make communications to them on another subject, viz. His sufferings,
which He knew would sorely try their faith. He wished
them to be fairly committed to the doctrine of His *Messiahship* before proceeding to speak in plain terms on the
unwelcome theme of His *death*.

From the reply of the disciples, it appears that their
Master had been the subject of much talk among the people.
This is only what we should have expected. Jesus was a
very public and a very extraordinary person, and to be much
talked about is one of the inevitable penalties of prominence.
The merits and the claims of the Son of man were accordingly freely and widely canvassed in those days, with gravity
or with levity, with prejudice or with candor, with decision
or indecision, intelligently or ignorantly, as is the way of
men in all ages. As they mingled with the people, it was
the lot of the twelve to hear many opinions concerning
their Lord which never reached His ear ; sometimes kind
and favorable, making them glad ; at other times unkind and
unfavorable, making them sad.

The opinions prevalent among the masses concerning
Jesus — for it was with reference to these that He interrogated His disciples [1] — seem to have been mainly favorable.
All agreed in regarding Him as a prophet of the highest
rank, differing only as to which of the great prophets of
Israel He most nearly resembled or personated. Some said
He was John the Baptist revived, others Elias, while others
again identified Him with one or other of the great prophets,
as Jeremiah. These opinions are explained in part by an
expectation then commonly entertained, that the advent of
the Messiah would be preceded by the return of one of the
prophets by whom God had spoken to the fathers, partly
by the perception of real or supposed resemblances between
Jesus and this or that prophet ; His tenderness reminding
one hearer of the author of the Lamentations, His sternness

---

[1] Luke ix. 18, οἱ ὄχλοι.

in denouncing hypocrisy and tyranny reminding another of the prophet of fire, while perhaps His parabolic discourses led a third to think of Ezekiel or of Daniel.

When we reflect on the high veneration in which the ancient prophets were held, we cannot fail to see that these diverse opinions current among the Jewish people concerning Jesus imply a very high sense of His greatness and excellence. To us, who regard Him as the Sun, while the prophets were at best but lamps of greater or less brightness, such comparisons may well seem not only inadequate, but dishonoring. Yet we must not despise them, as the testimonies of open-minded but imperfectly-formed contemporaries to the worth of Him whom we worship as the Lord. Taken separately, they show that in the judgment of candid observers Jesus was a man of surpassing greatness; taken together, they show the many-sidedness of His character, and its superiority to that of any one of the prophets; for He could not have reminded those who witnessed His works, and heard Him preach, of all the prophets in turn, unless He had comprehended them all in His one person. The very diversity of opinion respecting Him, therefore, showed that a greater than Elias, or Jeremiah, or Ezekiel, or Daniel, had appeared.

These opinions, valuable still as testimonials to the excellence of Christ, must be admitted further to be indicative, so far, of good dispositions on the part of those who cherished and expressed them. At a time when those who deemed themselves in every respect immeasurably superior to the multitude could find no better names for the Son of man than Samaritan, devil, blasphemer, glutton and drunkard, companion of publicans and sinners, it was something considerable to believe that the calumniated One was a prophet as worthy of honor as any of those whose sepulchres the professors of piety carefully varnished, while depreciating, and even putting to death, their living successors. The multitude who held this opinion might come short of true discipleship; but they were at least far in advance of the Pharisees and Sadducees, who came in tempting mood to ask a sign from heaven, and whom no sign, whether in heaven or in earth, would conciliate or convince.

How, then, did Jesus receive the report of His disciples?
Was He satisfied with these favorable, and in the circumstances really gratifying, opinions current among the people?
He was not. He was not content to be put on a level with
even the greatest of the prophets. He did not indeed
express any displeasure against those who assigned Him
such a rank, and He may even have been pleased to hear
that public opinion had advanced so far on the way to the
true faith. Nevertheless He declined to accept the position
accorded. The meek and lowly Son of man claimed to be
something more than a great prophet. Therefore He turned
to His chosen disciples, as to men from whom He expected
a more satisfactory statement of the truth, and pointedly
asked what they thought of Him. "But you — whom say
ye that I am?"

In this case, as in many others, Simon son of Jonas
answered for the company. His prompt, definite, memorable reply to his Master's question was this: "Thou art the
Christ, the Son of the living God." [1]

With this view of His person Jesus *was* satisfied. He
did not charge Peter with extravagance in going so far
beyond the opinion of the populace. On the contrary, He
entirely approved of what the ardent disciple had said, and
expressed His satisfaction in no cold or measured terms.
Never, perhaps, did He speak in more animated language,
or with greater appearance of deep emotion. He solemnly
pronounced Peter "blessed" on account of His faith; He
spake for the first time of a church which should be founded,
professing Peter's faith as its creed; He promised that
disciple great power in that church, as if grateful to him
for being the first to put the momentous truth into words,
and for uttering it so boldly amid prevailing unbelief, and
crude, defective belief; and He expressed, in the strongest
possible terms, His confidence that the church yet to be
founded would stand to all ages proof against all the assaults
of the powers of darkness.

[1] So in Matthew; in the other Gospels the reply is abbreviated, and the confession
of Messiahship alone mentioned. Matthew's account of this memorable incident is
throughout the fullest, a fact of importance when it is considered that Matthew's,
according even to Dr. Baur, is the oldest and most historical Gospel.

Simon's confession, fairly interpreted, seems to contain
these two propositions, — that Jesus was the *Messiah*, and
that He was *divine*. " Thou art the Christ," said he in the
first place, with conscious reference to the reported opinions
of the people, — " Thou art the Christ," and not merely a
prophet come to prepare Christ's way. Then he added :
"the Son of God," to explain what he understood by the
term Christ. The Messiah looked for by the Jews in general
was merely a man, though a very superior one, the ideal
man endowed with extraordinary gifts. The Christ of Peter's
creed was more than man — a superhuman, a divine being.
This truth he sought to express in the second part of his
confession. He called Jesus Son of God, with obvious
reference to the name His Master had just given Himself —
Son of man. " Thou," he meant to say, "art not only what
Thou hast now called Thyself, and what, in lowliness of
mind, Thou art wont to call Thyself — the Son of man ; [1]
Thou art also Son of God, partaking of the divine nature
not less really than of the human." Finally, he prefixed
the epithet "living" to the divine name, to express his
consciousness that he was making a very momentous declaration, and to give that declaration a solemn, deliberate
character. It was as if he said : " I know it is no light
matter to call any one, even Thee, Son of God, of the One
living eternal Jehovah. But I shrink not from the assertion,
however bold, startling, or even blasphemous it may seem.
I cannot by any other expression do justice to all I know
and feel concerning Thee, or convey the impression left on
my mind by what I have witnessed during the time I have
followed Thee as a disciple." In this way was the disciple
urged on, in spite of his Jewish monotheism, to the
recognition of his Lord's divinity.[2]

That the famous confession, uttered in the neighborhood
of Cæsarea Philippi, really contains *in germ* [3] the doctrine of
Christ's divinity, might be inferred from the simple fact that

[1] For a fuller exposition of the view we take of this title, which has occasioned so
much discussion, we may refer our readers to *The Humiliation of Christ*, note, p. 225
(*Cunningham Lectures*, sixth series, 2d ed.).
[2] On this topic consult Wace, *Christianity and Morality*, the *Boyle Lectures* fcr
1874-75, Lecture V., second course.
[3] Of course all that was implied was not yet present to Peter's mind.

Jesus was satisfied with it; for He certainly claimed to be
Son of God in a sense predicable of no mere man, even
according to synoptical accounts of His teaching.[1]   But
when we consider the peculiar terms in which He expressed
Himself respecting Peter's faith, we are still further confirmed
in this conclusion.   "Flesh and blood," said He to the
disciple, "hath not revealed it unto thee, but my Father
which is in heaven."   These words evidently imply that the
person addressed had said something very extraordinary;
something he could not have learned from the traditional
established belief of his generation respecting Messiah;
something new even for himself and his fellow-disciples,
if not in word, at least in meaning,[2] to which he could not
have attained by the unaided effort of his own mind.   The
confession is virtually represented as an inspiration, a revelation, a flash of light from heaven, — the utterance not of the
rude fisherman, but of the divine Spirit speaking, through
his mouth, a truth hitherto hidden, and yet but dimly
comprehended by him to whom it hath been revealed.   All
this agrees well with the supposition that the confession
contains not merely an acknowledgment of the Messiahship
of Jesus in the ordinary sense, but a proclamation of the
true doctrine concerning Messiah's person — viz. that He
was a divine being manifest in the flesh.

The remaining portion of our Lord's address to Simon
shows that He assigned to the doctrine confessed by that
disciple the place of fundamental importance in the Christian
faith.   The object of these remarkable statements [3] is not to
assert the supremacy of Peter, as Romanists contend, but to
declare the supremely important nature of the truth he has
confessed.   In spite of all difficulties of interpretation, this
remains clear and certain to us.   Who or what the "rock"
is we deem doubtful; it may be Peter, or it may be his confession: it is a point on which scholars equally sound in the
faith, and equally innocent of all sympathy with Popish
dogmas, are divided in opinion, and on which it would ill
become us to dogmatize.   Of this only we are sure, that not

---

[1] *E.g.* in Matthew xi. 27, though we cannot go into the discussion here.
[2] The words, with exception of the epithet "living," are found in John i. 49.
[3] Matt. xvi. 18, 19.

Peter's person, but Peter's faith, is the fundamental matter in Christ's mind. When He says to that disciple, "Thou art Petros," He means, "Thou art a man of rock, worthy of the name I gave thee by anticipation the first time I met thee, because thou hast at length got thy foot planted on the rock of the eternal truth." He speaks of the church that is to be, for the first time, in connection with Simon's confession, because that church is to consist of men adopting that confession as their own, and acknowledging Him to be the Christ, the Son of God.[1] He alludes to the keys of the kingdom of heaven in the same connection, because none but those who homologate the doctrine first solemnly enunciated by Simon, shall be admitted within its gates. He promises Peter the power of the keys, not because it is to belong to him alone, or to him more than others, but by way of honorable mention, in recompense for the joy he has given his Lord by the superior energy and decision of his faith. He is grateful to Peter, because he has believed most emphatically that He came out from God ;[2] and He shows His gratitude by promising first to him individually a power which He afterwards conferred on all His chosen disciples.[3] Finally, if it be true that Peter is here called the rock on which the church shall be built, this is to be understood in the same way as the promise of the keys. Peter is called the foundation of the church only in the same sense as all the apostles are called the foundation by the Apostle Paul,[4] viz. as the first preachers of the true faith concerning Jesus as the Christ and Son of God ; and if the man who *first* professed that faith be honored by being called individually the rock, that only shows that the *faith*, and not the man, is after all the true foundation. That which makes Simon a *Petros*, a rock-like man, fit to build on, is the real *Petra* on which the Ecclesia is to be built.

After these remarks we deem it superfluous to enter minutely into the question to what the term "rock" refers in the sentence, "Thou art Peter, and on this rock I will build my church." At the same time, we must say that it

---

[1] This was the usual formula by which converts confessed their faith in the apostolic age.

[2] John xvi. 27.   [3] Matt. xviii. 18 ; John xx. 23.   [4] Eph. ii. 20.

is by no means so clear to us that the rock must be Peter,
and can be nothing else, as it is the fashion of modern
commentators to assert. To the rendering, "Thou art
Petros, a man of rock ; and on *thee*, as on a rock, I will build
my church," it is possible, as already admitted, to assign
an intelligible scriptural meaning. But we confess our
preference for the old Protestant interpretation, according
to which our Lord's words to His disciple should be thus
paraphrased : "Thou, Simon Barjonas, art Petros, a man
of rock, worthy of thy name Peter, because thou hast made
that bold, good confession ; and on the truth thou hast now
confessed, as on a rock, will I build my church ; and so long
as it abides on that foundation it will stand firm and
unassailable against all the powers of hell." So rendering,
we make Jesus say not only what He really thought, but
what was most worthy to be said. For divine truth is the
sure foundation. Believers, even Peters, may fail, and prove
any thing but stable ; but truth is eternal, and faileth never.
This we say not unmindful of the counterpart truth, that
"the truth," unless confessed by living souls, is dead, and
no source of stability. Sincere personal conviction, with
a life corresponding, is needed to make the faith in the
objective sense of any virtue.

We cannot pass from these memorable words of Christ
without adverting, with a certain solemn awe, to the strange
fate which has befallen them in the history of the church. This
text, in which the church's Lord declares that the powers of
darkness shall not prevail against her, has been used by these
powers as an instrument of assault, and with only too much
success. What a gigantic system of spiritual despotism
and blasphemous assumption has been built on these two
sentences concerning the rock and the keys ! How nearly,
by their aid, has the kingdom of God been turned into a
kingdom of Satan ! One is tempted to wish that Jesus,
knowing beforehand what was to happen, had so framed His
words as to obviate the mischief. But the wish were vain.
No forms of expression, however carefully selected, could
prevent human ignorance from falling into misconception,
or hinder men who had a purpose to serve, from finding in
Scripture what suited that purpose. Nor can any Christian,

on reflection, think it desirable that the Author of our faith had adopted a studied prudential style of speech, intended not so much to give faithful expression to the actual thoughts of His mind and feelings of His heart, as to avoid giving occasion of stumbling to honest stupidity, or an excuse for perversion to dishonest knavery. The spoken word in that case had been no longer a true reflection of the Word incarnate. All the poetry and passion and genuine human feeling which form the charm of Christ's sayings would have been lost, and nothing would have remained but prosaic platitudes, like those of the scribes and of theological pedants. No; let us have the precious words of our Master in all their characteristic intensity and vehemence of unqualified assertion; and if prosaic or disingenuous men will manufacture out of them incredible dogmas, let them answer for it. Why should the children be deprived of their bread, and only the dogs be cared for?

One remark more ere we pass from the subject of this chapter. The part we find Peter playing in this incident at Cæsarea Philippi prepares us for regarding as historically credible the part assigned to him in the Acts of the Apostles in some momentous scenes, as, *e.g.*, in that brought before us in the tenth chapter. The Tübingen school of critics tell us that the Acts is a composition full of invented situations adapted to an apologetic design; and that the plan on which the book proceeds is to make Peter act as like Paul as possible in the first part, and Paul, on the other hand, as much like Peter as possible in the second. The conversion of the Roman centurion by Peter's agency they regard as a capital instance of Peter being made to pose as Paul, *i.e.*, as an universalist in his views of Christianity. Now, all we have to say on the subject here is this. The conduct ascribed to Peter the apostle in the tenth chapter of the Acts is credible in the light of the narrative we have been studying. In both we find the same man the recipient of a revelation; in both we find him the first to receive, utter, and act on a great Christian truth. Is it incredible that the man who received one revelation as a disciple should receive another as an apostle? Is it not psychologically probable that the man who now appears so original and audacious in connection with one great truth, will again show the same attributes of originality and audacity in connection with some other truth? For our part, far from feeling sceptical as to the historic truth of the narrative in the Acts, we should have been very much surprised if in the history of the nascent church Peter had been found playing a part altogether devoid of originalities and audacities. He would in that case have been very unlike his former self.

12

FIRST LESSON ON THE CROSS

Matt. 16:21-28; Mark 8:31-38; Luke 9:22-27

NOT till an advanced period in His public ministry — not, in fact, till it was drawing to a close — did Jesus speak in plain, unmistakable terms of His *death*. The solemn event was foreknown by Him from the first; and He betrayed His consciousness of what was awaiting Him by a variety of occasional allusions. These earlier utterances, however, were all couched in mystic language. They were of the nature of riddles, whose meaning became clear after the event, but which before, none could, or at least did, read. Jesus spake now of a temple, which, if destroyed, He should raise again in three days;[1] at another time of a lifting up of the Son of man, like unto that of the brazen serpent in the wilderness;[2] and on yet other occasions, of a sad separation of the bridegroom from the children of the bridechamber,[3] of the giving of His flesh for the life of the world,[4] and of a sign like that of the prophet Jonas, which should be given in His own person to an evil and adulterous generation.[5]

At length, after the conversation in Cæsarea Philippi, Jesus changed His style of speaking on the subject of His sufferings, substituting for dark, hidden allusions, plain, literal, matter - of - fact statements.[6] This change was naturally adapted to the altered circumstances in which He was placed. The signs of the times were growing

---

[1] John ii. 19.
[2] John iii. 14.
[3] Matt. ix. 15.
[4] John vi.
[5] Matt. xvi. 4.
[6] " He spake that saying openly " (παῤῥησίᾳ), Mark viii. 32.

ominous ; storm-clouds were gathering in the air ; all things were beginning to point towards Calvary. His work in Galilee and the provinces was nearly done ; it remained for Him to bear witness to the truth in and around the holy city ; and from the present mood of the ecclesiastical authorities and the leaders of religious society, as manifested by captious question and unreasonable demand,[1] and a constant espionage on His movements, it was not difficult to foresee that it would not require many more offences, or much longer time, to ripen dislike and jealousy into murderous hatred. Such plain speaking, therefore, concerning what was soon to happen, was natural and seasonable. Jesus was now entering the valley of the shadow of death, and in so speaking He was but adapting His talk to the situation.

Plain-speaking regarding His death was now not only natural on Christ's part, but at once necessary and safe in reference to His disciples. It was necessary, in order that they might be prepared for the approaching event, as far as that was possible in the case of men who, to the last, persisted in hoping that the issue would be different from what their Master anticipated. It was safe ; for now the subject might be spoken of plainly without serious risk to their faith. Before the disciples were established in the doctrine of Christ's person, the doctrine of the cross might have scared them away altogether. Premature preaching of a Christ to be crucified might have made them unbelievers in the *fundamental* truth that Jesus of Nazareth was the Christ. Therefore, in consideration of their weakness, Jesus maintained a certain reserve respecting His sufferings, till their faith in Him as the Christ should have become sufficiently rooted to stand the strain of the storm soon to be raised by a most unexpected, unwelcome, and incomprehensible announcement. Only after hearing Peter's confession was He satisfied that the strength necessary for enduring the trial had been attained.

Wherefore, "from that time forth began Jesus to show unto His disciples how that He must go unto Jerusalem, and suffer many things of the elders and chief priests and scribes, and be killed, and be raised again the third day."

[1] Matt. xv. 1 sqq., xvi. 1 sqq.

Every clause in this solemn announcement demands our reverent scrutiny.

Jesus showed unto His disciples —

1. "That He must go unto Jerusalem." Yes! there the tragedy must be enacted: that was the fitting scene for the stupendous events that were about to take place. It was dramatically proper that the Son of man should die in that "holy," unholy city, which had earned a most unenviable notoriety as the murderess of the prophets, the stoner of them whom God sent unto her. "It cannot be " — it were incongruous — "that a prophet perish out of Jerusalem." [1] It was due also to the dignity of Jesus, and to the design of His death, that He should suffer there. Not in an obscure corner or in an obscure way must He die, but in the most public place, and in a formal, judicial manner. He must be lifted up in view of the whole Jewish nation, so that all might see Him whom they had pierced, and by whose stripes also they might yet be healed. The "Lamb of God " must be slain in the place where all the legal sacrifices were offered.

2. "And suffer many things." Too many to enumerate, too painful to speak of in detail, and better passed over in silence for the present. The bare fact that their beloved Master was to be put to death, without any accompanying indignities, would be sufficiently dreadful to the disciples; and Jesus mercifully drew a veil over much that was present to His own thoughts. In a subsequent conversation on the same sad theme, when His passion was near at hand, He drew aside the veil a little, and showed them some of the "many things." But even then He was very sparing in His allusions, hinting only by a passing word that He should be mocked, and scourged, and spit upon.[2] He took no delight in expatiating on such harrowing scenes. He was willing to bear those indignities, but He cared not to speak of them more than was absolutely necessary.

3. "Of the elders and chief priests and scribes." Not of them alone, for Gentile rulers and the people of Israel were to have a hand in evil-entreating the Son of man as well as Jewish ecclesiastics. But the parties named were to be

---

[1] Luke xiii. 33.   [2] Mark x. 34; Luke xviii. 32.

the prime movers and most guilty agents in the nefarious transaction. The men who ought to have taught the people to recognize in Jesus the Lord's Anointed, would hound them on to cry, " Crucify Him, crucify Him," and by importunities and threats urge heathen authorities to perpetrate a crime for which they had no heart. Gray-haired elders sitting in council would solemnly decide that He was worthy of death ; high priests would utter oracles, that one man must die for the people, that the whole nation perish not ; scribes learned in the law would use their legal knowledge to invent plausible grounds for an accusation involving capital punishment. Jesus had suffered many petty annoyances from such persons already ; but the time was approaching when nothing would satisfy them but getting the object of their dislike cast forth out of the world. Alas for Israel, when her wise men, and her holy men, and her learned men, knew of no better use to make of the stone chosen of God, and precious, than thus contemptuously and wantonly to fling it away !

4. " And be killed." Yes, and for blessed ends pre-ordained of God. But of these Jesus speaks not now. He simply states, in general terms, the fact, in this first lesson on the doctrine of the cross.[1] Any thing more at this stage had been wasted words. To what purpose speak of the theology of the cross, of God's great design in the death which was to be brought about by man's guilty instrumentality, to disciples unwilling to receive even the matter of fact ? The rude shock of an unwelcome announcement must first be over before any thing can be profitably said on these higher themes. Therefore not a syllable here of salvation by the death of the Son of man ; of Christ crucified *for* man's guilt as well as *by* man's guilt. The hard bare fact alone is stated, theology being reserved for another season, when the hearers should be in a fitter frame of mind for receiving instruction.

5. Finally, Jesus told His disciples that He should "be raised again the third day." To some so explicit a reference

[1] The cross is not even named here ; but it was in Christ's thoughts, as the following address to the disciples plainly shows. The *fact*, without the *mode*, of death was enough for the first lesson.

to the resurrection at this early date has appeared improbable.[1] To us, on the contrary, it appears eminently seasonable. When was Jesus more likely to tell His disciples that He would rise again shortly after His death, than just on the occasion when He first told them plainly that He should die? He knew how harsh the one announcement would be to the feelings of His faithful ones, and it was natural that He should add the other, in the hope that when it was understood that His death was to be succeeded, after a brief interval of three days, by resurrection, the news would be much less hard to bear. Accordingly, after uttering the dismal words "be killed," He, with characteristic tenderness, hastened to say, "and be raised again the third day;" that, having torn, He might heal, and having smitten, He might bind up.[2]

The grave communications made by Jesus were far from welcome to His disciples. Neither now nor at any subsequent time did they listen to the forebodings of their Lord with resignation even, not to speak of cheerful acquiescence or spiritual joy. They never heard Him speak of His death without pain ; and their only comfort, in connection with such announcements as the present, seems to have been the hope that He had taken too gloomy a view of the situation, and that His apprehensions would turn out groundless. They, for their part, could see no grounds for such dark anticipations, and their Messianic ideas did not dispose them to be on the outlook for these. They had not the slightest conception that it behoved the Christ to suffer. On the contrary, a crucified Christ was a scandal and a contradiction to them, quite as much as it continued to be to the majority of the Jewish people after the Lord had ascended to glory. Hence the more firmly they believed that Jesus was the Christ, the more confounding it was to be told that He must

---

[1] The three synoptical evangelists agree in adding this reference to the resurrection to the first announcement of Christ's death. Their agreement in the whole of this announcement is very striking, yet only what was to be expected, considering its contents.

[2] Pfleiderer regards the pre-intimations by Jesus of a supernatural restitution of His person as the Messiah of the kingdom of God, as not less historical than any of the words ascribed to Him in the synoptical Gospel. He only thinks the definite fixation of the interval between death and resurrection due to later redaction. — *Die Religion*, ii. 433.

be put to death. "How," they asked themselves, "can these things be? How can the Son of God be subject to such indignities? How can our Master be the Christ, as we firmly believe, come to set up the divine kingdom, and to be crowned its King with glory and honor, and yet at the same time be doomed to undergo the ignominious fate of a criminal execution?" These questions the twelve could not now, nor until after the Resurrection, answer; nor is this wonderful, for if flesh and blood could not reveal the doctrine of Christ's person, still less could it reveal the doctrine of His cross. Not without a very special illumination from heaven could they understand the merest elements of that doctrine, and see, *e.g.*, that nothing was more worthy of the Son of God than to humble Himself and become subject unto death, *even* the death of the cross; that the glory of God consists not merely in being the highest, but in this, that being high, He stoops in lowly love to bear the burden of His own sinful creatures; that nothing could more directly and certainly conduce to the establishment of the divine kingdom than the gracious self-humiliation of the King; that only by ascending the cross could Messiah ascend the throne of His mediatorial glory; that only so could He subdue human hearts, and become Lord of men's affections as well as of their destinies. Many in the church do not understand these blessed truths, even at this late era: what wonder, then, if they were hid for a season from the eyes of the first disciples! Let us not reproach them for the veil that was on their faces; let us rather make sure that the same veil is not on our own.

On this occasion, as at Cæsarea Philippi, the twelve found a most eloquent and energetic interpreter of their sentiments in Simon Peter. The action and speech of that disciple at this time were characteristic in the highest degree. He took Jesus, we are told (laid hold of Him, we suppose, by His hand or His garment), and began to *rebuke* Him, saying, "Be it far from Thee, Lord;" or more literally, "God be merciful to Thee: God forbid! this shall not be unto Thee." What a strange compound of good and evil is this man! His language is dictated by the most intense affection: he cannot bear the thought of any harm befalling his Lord; yet how irreverent and disrespectful he is towards Him whom he has just acknowledged to be the Christ, the Son of the living God! How he overbears, and contradicts, and domineers, and, as it were, tries to bully his Master into putting away from His thoughts those gloomy forebodings of coming evil! Verily he has need of chastisement to teach him his own place, and to scourge out of his character the bad elements of forwardness, and undue familiarity, and presumptuous self-will.

Happily for Peter, he had a Master who, in His faithful love, spared not the rod when it was needful. Jesus judged that it was needed now, and therefore He administered a rebuke not less remarkable for severity than was the encomium at Cæsarea Philippi for warm, unqualified approbation, and curiously contrasting with that encomium in the terms in which it was expressed. He turned round on His offending disciple, and sternly said: "Get thee behind me, Satan; thou art an offence unto me: for thou savorest not the things that be of God, but those that be of men." The same disciple who on the former occasion had spoken by inspiration of Heaven is here represented as speaking by inspiration of mere flesh and blood — of mere natural affection for his Lord, and of the animal instinct of self-preservation, thinking of self-interest merely, not of duty. He whom Christ had pronounced a man of rock, strong in faith, and fit to be a foundation-stone in the spiritual edifice, is here called an offence, a stumbling-stone lying in his Master's path. Peter, the noble confessor of that fundamental truth, by the faith of which the church would be able to defy the gates of hell, appears here in league with the powers of darkness, the unconscious mouthpiece of Satan the tempter. "Get thee behind me, Satan!" What a downcome for him who but yesterday got that promise of the power of the keys! How suddenly has the novice church dignitary, too probably lifted up with pride or vanity, fallen into the condemnation of the devil!

This memorable rebuke seems mercilessly severe, and yet on consideration we feel it was nothing more than what was called for. Christ's language on this occasion needs no apology, such as might be drawn from supposed excitement

of feeling, or from a consciousness on the speaker's part
that the infirmity of His own sentient nature was
whispering the same suggestion as that which came from
Peter's lips. Even the hard word Satan, which is the sting
of the speech, is in its proper place. It describes exactly
the character of the advice given by Simon. That advice
was substantially this : " Save thyself at any rate ; sacrifice
duty to self-interest, the cause of God to personal
convenience." An advice truly Satanic in principle and
tendency ! For the whole aim of Satanic policy is to get
self-interest recognized as the chief end of man. Satan's
temptations aim at nothing worse than this. Satan is
called the Prince of this world, because self-interest rules
the world ; he is called the accuser of the brethren, because
he does not believe that even the sons of God have any
higher motive. He is a sceptic ; and his scepticism consists
in determined, scornful unbelief in the reality of any chief
end other than that of personal advantage. "Doth Job, or
even Jesus, serve God for naught ? Self-sacrifice, suffering
for righteousness' sake, fidelity to truth even unto death : —
it is all romance and youthful sentimentalism, or hypocrisy
and hollow cant. There is absolutely no such thing as a
surrender of the lower life for the higher ; all men are
selfish at heart, and have their price : some may hold out
longer than others, but in the last extremity every man
will prefer his own things to the things of God. All that a
man hath will he give for his life, his moral integrity and
his piety not excepted." Such is Satan's creed.

The suggestion made by Peter, as the unconscious tool
of the spirit of evil, is identical in principle with that made
by Satan himself to Jesus in the temptation in the
wilderness. The tempter said then in effect : "If Thou be
the Son of God, use Thy power for Thine own behoof ;
Thou art hungry, *e.g.*, make bread for Thyself out of the
stones. If Thou be the Son of God, presume on Thy
privilege as the favorite of Heaven ; cast Thyself down
from this elevation, securely counting on protection from
harm, even where other men would be allowed to suffer the
consequences of their foolhardiness. What better use canst
Thou make of Thy divine powers and privileges than to

promote Thine own advantage and glory?" Peter's feeling
at the present time seems to have been much the same :
"If Thou be the Son of God, why shouldst Thou suffer
an ignominious, violent death? Thou hast power to save
Thyself from such a fate ; surely Thou wilt not hesitate to
use it!" The attached disciple, in fact, was an unconscious
instrument employed by Satan to subject Jesus to a second
temptation, analogous to the earlier one in the desert of
Judæa. It was the god of this world that was at work in
both cases ; who, being accustomed to find men only too
ready to prefer safety to righteousness, could not believe
that he should find nothing of this spirit in the Son of God,
and therefore came again and again seeking an open point
in His armor through which he might shoot his fiery darts ;
not renouncing hope till his intended victim hung on the
cross, apparently conquered by the world, but in reality a
conqueror both of the world and of its lord.

The severe language uttered by Jesus on this occasion,
when regarded as addressed to a dearly beloved disciple,
shows in a striking manner His holy abhorrence of every
thing savoring of self-seeking. "Save Thyself," counsels
Simon : "Get thee behind me, Satan," replies Simon's Lord.
Truly Christ was not one who pleased Himself. Though
He were a Son, yet would He learn obedience by the things
which He had to suffer. And by this mind He proved
Himself to be the Son, and won from His Father the
approving voice : "Thou art my beloved Son, in Thee I am
well pleased," — Heaven's reply to the voice from hell
counselling Him to pursue a course of self-pleasing. Persevering in this mind, Jesus was at length lifted up on the
cross, and so became the Author of eternal salvation unto
all them that obey Him. Blessed now and forevermore be
His name, who so humbled Himself, and became obedient
as far as *death!*

SECTION II — CROSS-BEARING THE LAW OF DISCIPLESHIP

MATT. xvi. 24 - 28 ; MARK viii. 34 - 38 ; LUKE ix. 23 - 27

After one hard announcement, comes another not less hard. The Lord Jesus has told His disciples that He must one day be put to death ; He now tells them, that as it fares with Him, so it must fare with them also. The second announcement was naturally occasioned by the way in which the first had been received. Peter had said, and all had felt, " This shall not be unto Thee." Jesus replies in effect, " Say you so ? I tell you that not only shall I, your Master, be crucified, — for such will be the manner of my death,[1] — but ye too, faithfully following me, shall most certainly have your crosses to bear. 'If any man will come after me, let him deny himself, and take up his cross, and follow me.'"

The second announcement was not, like the first, made to the twelve only. This we might infer from the terms of the announcement, which are general, even if we had not been informed, as we are by Mark and Luke, that before making it Jesus called the people unto Him, with His disciples, and spake in the hearing of them all.[2] The doctrine here taught, therefore, is for all Christians in all ages : not for apostles only, but for the humblest disciples ; not for priests or preachers, but for the laity as well ; not for monks living in cloisters, but for men living and working in the outside world. The King and Head of the church here proclaims a universal law binding on all His subjects, requiring all to bear a cross in fellowship with Himself.

We are not told how the second announcement was received by those who heard it, and particularly by the twelve. We can believe, however, that to Peter and his brethren it sounded less harsh than the first, and seemed, at least theoretically, more acceptable. Common experience might teach them that crosses, however unpleasant to flesh and blood, were nevertheless things that might be looked

---

[1] The cross, though not mentioned, was evidently in Christ's thoughts when He spake of His death at this time. *Vide* last section, note, p. 176.

[2] Mark viii. 34, προσκαλεσάμενος τὸν ὄχλον ; Luke ix. 23, ἔλεγε δὲ πρὸς πάντας.

for in the lot of mere men. But what had Christ the Son
of God to do with crosses? Ought He not to be exempt
from the sufferings and indignities of ordinary mortals? If
not, of what avail was His divine Sonship? In short, the
difficulty for the twelve was probably, not that the servant
should be no better than the Master, but that the Master
should be no better than the servant.

Our perplexity, on the other hand, is apt to be just the
reverse of this. Familiar with the doctrine that Jesus died
on the cross in our room, we are apt to wonder what occasion
there can be for our bearing a cross. If He suffered for us
vicariously, what need, we are ready to inquire, for suffering
on our part likewise? We need to be reminded that Christ's
sufferings, while in some respects peculiar, are in other
respects common to Him with all in whom His spirit abides;
that while, as redemptive, His death stands alone, as suffering for righteousness' sake it is but the highest instance of
a universal law, according to which all who live a true godly
life must suffer hardship in a false evil world.[1] And it is
very observable that Jesus took a most effectual method
of keeping this truth prominently before the mind of His
followers in all ages, by proclaiming it with great emphasis
on the first occasion on which He plainly announced that He
Himself was to die, *giving it, in fact, as the first lesson on
the doctrine of His death: the first of four to be found in the
Gospels.*[2] Thereby He in effect declared that only such as
were willing to be crucified with Him should be saved by
His death; nay, that willingness to bear a cross was indispensable to the right understanding of the doctrine of
salvation through Him. It is as if above the door of the
school in which the mystery of redemption was to be taught,
He had inscribed the legend: Let no man who is unwilling
to deny himself, and take up his cross, enter here.

In this great law of discipleship the cross signifies not
merely the external penalty of death, but all troubles that
come on those who earnestly endeavor to live as Jesus lived

---

[1] Plato had a glimpse of this law. " The just," he writes, " will be scourged, racked,
bound, will have his eyes put out, and after suffering many ills will be *crucified* "
(ἀνασχινδιλευθήσεται). — *De Republica*, lib. ii.

[2] *Vide* chaps. xvii., xviii., xxii.

in this world, and in *consequence* of that endeavor. Many and various are the afflictions of the righteous, differing in kind and degree, according to times and circumstances, and the callings and stations of individuals. For the righteous One, who died not only by the unjust, but *for* them, the appointed cup was filled with all possible ingredients of shame and pain, mingled together in the highest degree of bitterness. Not a few of His most honored servants have come very near their Master in the manner and measure of their afflictions for His sake, and have indeed drunk of His cup, and been baptized with His bloody baptism. But for the rank and file of the Christian host the hardships to be endured are ordinarily less severe, the cross to be borne less heavy. For one the cross may be the calumnies of lying lips, "which speak grievous things proudly and contemptuously against the righteous;" for another, failure to attain the much-worshipped idol success in life, so often reached by unholy means not available for a man who has a conscience; for a third, mere isolation and solitariness of spirit amid uncongenial, unsympathetic neighbors, not minded to live soberly, righteously, and godly, and not loving those who do so live.

The cross, therefore, is not the same for all. But that there is a cross of some shape for all true disciples is clearly implied in the words : "*If any one* will come after me, let him deny himself, and take up his cross." The plain meaning of these words is, that there is no following Jesus on any other terms —a doctrine which, however clearly taught in the Gospel, spurious Christians are unwilling to believe and resolute to deny. They take the edge off their Lord's statement by explaining that it applies only to certain critical times, happily very different from their own ; or that if it has some reference to all times, it is only applicable to such as are called to play a prominent part in public affairs as leaders of opinion, pioneers of progress, prophets denouncing the vices of the age, and uttering unwelcome oracles, — a proverbially dangerous occupation, as the Greek poet testified who said : " Apollo alone should prophesy, for he fears nobody." [1] To maintain that all who would live devoutly in Christ Jesus

---

[1] Φοῖβον ἀνθρώποις μόνον
Χρῆν θεσπιῳδεῖν ὃς δέδοικεν οὐδένα. — EŲRIP. *Phœnissæ*, 958, 959.

must suffer somehow, is, they think, to take too gloomy and morose a view of the wickedness of the world, or too high and exacting a view of the Christian life.   The righteousness which in ordinary times involves a cross is in their view folly and fanaticism.   It is speaking when one should be silent, meddling in matters with which one has no concern; in a word, it is being righteous overmuch.   Such thoughts as these, expressed or unexpressed, are sure to prevail extensively when religious profession is common.   The fact that fidelity involves a cross, as also the fact that Christ was crucified just because He was righteous, are well understood by Christians when they are a suffering minority, as in primitive ages.   But these truths are much lost sight of in peaceful, prosperous times.   Then you shall find many holding most sound views of the cross Christ bore for them, but sadly ignorant concerning the cross they themselves have to bear in fellowship with Christ.   Of this cross they are determined to know nothing.   What it can mean, or whence it can come, they cannot comprehend; though had they the true spirit of self-denial required of disciples by Christ, they might find it for themselves in their daily life, in their business, in their home, nay, in their own heart, and have no need to seek for it in the ends of the earth, or to manufacture artificial crosses out of ascetic austerities.

To the law of the cross Jesus annexed three reasons designed to make the obeying of it easier, by showing disciples that, in rendering obedience to the stern requirement, they attend to their own true interest.   Each reason is introduced by a " For."

The first reason is : " For whosoever will save his life shall lose it ; but whosoever will lose his life for my sake shall find it."   In this startling paradox the word "life" is used in a double sense.   In the first clause of each member of the sentence it signifies natural life, with all the adjuncts that make it pleasant and enjoyable ; in the second, it means the spiritual life of a renewed soul.   The deep, pregnant saying may therefore be thus expanded and paraphrased : Whosoever *will* save, *i.e.*, make it his first business to save or preserve, his natural life and worldly wellbeing, shall lose the higher life, the life indeed ; and whosoever is willing to

lose his natural life for my sake shall find the true eternal
life. According to this maxim we must lose something, it is
not possible to live without sacrifice of some kind ; the only
question being what shall be sacrificed — the lower or the
higher life, animal happiness or spiritual blessedness. If we
choose the higher, we must be prepared to deny ourselves
and take up our cross, though the actual amount of the loss
we are called on to bear may be small ; for godliness is
profitable unto all things, having promise of the life that
now is, as well as of that which is to come.[1] If, on the other
hand, we choose the lower, and resolve to have it at all
hazards, we must inevitably lose the higher. The soul's life,
and all the imperishable goods of the soul, — righteousness,
godliness, faith, love, patience, meekness,[2] — are the price
we pay for worldly enjoyment.

This price is too great: and that is what Jesus next told
His hearers as the second persuasive to cross-bearing. "For
what," He went on to ask, "is a man profited if he shall
gain the whole world, and lose his own soul? or what
shall a man give in exchange for his soul?" The two
questions set forth the incomparable value of the soul on
both sides of a commercial transaction. The soul, or life,
in the true sense of the word,[3] is too dear a price to pay even
for the whole world, not to say for that small portion of
it which falls to the lot of any one individual. He who
gains the world at such a cost is a loser by the bargain. On
the other hand, the whole world is too small, yea, an utterly
inadequate price, to pay for the ransom of the soul once lost.
What shall a man give in exchange for the priceless thing
he has foolishly bartered away? "Wherewith shall I come
before the Lord, and bow myself before the high God? shall
I come before Him with burnt-offerings, with calves of a
year old? will the Lord be pleased with thousands of rams, or
with ten thousands of rivers of oil? shall I give my firstborn
for my transgression, the fruit of my body for the sin of my
soul?"[4] No! O man ; not any of these things, nor any thing

[1] 1 Tim. iv. 8.
[2] 1 Tim. vi. 11.
[3] The word rendered "soul" in ver. 26 is the same which is rendered "life" in ver.
25 (ψυχή). The two meanings are blended here.
[4] Micah vi. 6.

else thou hast to give ; not the fruit of thy merchandise, not
ten thousands of pounds sterling. Thou canst not buy back
thy soul, which thou hast bartered for the world, with all
that thou hast of the world. The redemption of the soul is
indeed precious ; it cannot be delivered from the bondage of
sin by corruptible things, such as silver and gold : the
attempt to purchase pardon and peace and life that way can
only make thy case more hopeless, and add to thy condemnation.

The appeal contained in these solemn questions comes
home with irresistible force to all who are in their right
mind. Such feel that no outward good can be compared in
value to having a "saved soul," *i.e.* being a right-minded
Christian man. All, however, are not so minded. Multitudes
account their souls of very small value indeed. Judas sold
his soul for thirty pieces of silver ; and not a few who
probably deem themselves better than he would part with
theirs for the most paltry worldly advantage. The great
ambition of the million is to be happy as animals, not to be
blessed as "saved," noble-spirited, sanctified men. "Who
will show us any good ?" is that which the many say. "Give
us health, wealth, houses, lands, honors, and we care not for
righteousness, either imputed or personal, peace of conscience,
joy in the Holy Ghost. These may be good also in their
way, and if one could have them along with the other, without trouble or sacrifice, it were perhaps well ; but we cannot
consent, for their sakes, to deny ourselves any pleasure, or
voluntarily endure any hardship."

The third argument in favor of cross-bearing is drawn
from the second advent. "For the Son of man shall come
in the glory of His Father, with His angels ; and then shall
He reward every man according to his works." [1] These
words suggest a contrast between the present and the future
state of the speaker, and imply a promise of a corresponding
contrast between the present and the future of His faithful
followers. *Now* Jesus is the Son of man, destined ere many
weeks pass to be crucified at Jerusalem. At the end of the
days He will appear invested with the manifest glory of
Messiah, attended with a mighty host of ministering spirits ;

[1] Matt. xvi. 17. Ver. 28 presents a difficulty on which we cannot enter here.

His reward for enduring the cross, despising the shame.
Then will He reward every man according to the tenor of his
present life. To the cross-bearers He will grant a crown of
righteousness ; to the cross-spurners He will assign, as their
due, shame and everlasting contempt. Stern doctrine,
distasteful to the modern mind on various grounds, specially
on these two : because it sets before us alternatives in the
life beyond, and because it seeks to propagate heroic virtue
by hope of reward, instead of exhibiting virtue as its own
reward. As to the former, the alternative of the promised
reward is certainly a great mystery and burden to the spirit ;
but it is to be feared that an alternative is involved in any
earnest doctrine of moral distinctions or of human freedom
and responsibility. As to the other, Christians need not
be afraid of degenerating into moral vulgarity in Christ's
company. There is no vulgarity or impurity in the virtue
which is sustained by the hope of eternal life. That hope
is not selfishness, but simply self-consistency. It is simply
believing in the *reality* of the kingdom for which you labor
and suffer ; involving, of course, the reality of each individual Christian's interest therein, your own not excepted.
And such faith is necessary to heroism. For who would
fight and suffer for a dream ? What patriot would risk his
life for his country's cause who did not hope for the
restoration of her independence ? And who but a pedant
would say that the purity of his patriotism was sullied,
because his hope for the whole nation did not exclude all
reference to himself as an individual citizen ? Equally
necessary is it that a Christian should believe in the kingdom of glory, and equally natural and proper that he should
cherish the hope of a personal share in its honors and
felicities. Where such faith and hope are not, little
Christian heroism will be found. For as an ancient Church
Father said, "There is no certain work where there is an
uncertain reward." [1] Men cannot be heroes in doubt or
despair. They cannot struggle after perfection and a divine
kingdom, sceptical the while whether these things be more
than devout imaginations, unrealizable ideals. In such a

---

[1] Nullum opus certum est mercedis incertæ. Tertulliani *De Resurrectione Carnis*,
cap. xxi. See also Clark's Ante-Nicene Library : Tertullian, ii. 251.

mood they will take things easy, and make secular happiness
their chief concern.[1]

---

[1] Pfleiderer, who occupies the standpoint of a speculative theism which recognizes no miraculous breach of the world's continuity, and who maintains the doctrine of universal restitution, the ultimate unconditional victory of good over evil, in his work, *Die Religion*, advocates the views above expressed in reference to the moral quality of virtue stimulated by the Eternal Hope. He bases the doctrine of immortality on this, that a belief in the realizableness of the kingdom of God is a necessary condition of heroism, and he resolves the hope of the individual Christian, as we have done, into that belief. With reference to the value of this hope to the heroes of the race, he remarks: "Look at the real heroes of good in the world, as distinct from the vain prattlers about virtue: is not in all these the ground-tone a deep elegiac rather than a cheerful one? do not they all speak more of the bitterness than of the happiness of life?" Having pointed out the cause of this in the frustration of noble aims in reference to the present life, he asks whether a fight begun and carried on *with the consciousness of its hopelessness* has a rational sense. The whole argument is very well worth perusal. *Vide Die Religion*, ii. 238, 239. In his more recent work, *Religionsphilosophie*, published in 1878, this author expresses himself in a more unfavorable manner respecting the life to come, treating the fact as doubtful, and faith in it as not indispensable.

13

THE TRANSFIGURATION

Matt. 17:1-13; Mark 9:2-13; Luke 9:28-36

THE transfiguration is one of those passages in the Saviour's earthly history which an expositor would rather pass over in reverent silence. For such silence the same apology might be pleaded which is so kindly made in the Gospel narrative for Peter's foolish speech concerning the three tabernacles : " He wist not what to say." Who does know what to say any more than he ? Who is able fully to speak of that wondrous night-scene among the mountains,[1] during which heaven was for a few brief moments let down to earth, and the mortal body of Jesus being transfigured shone with celestial brightness, and the spirits of just men made perfect appeared and held converse with Him respecting His approaching passion, and a voice came forth from the excellent glory, pronouncing Him to be God's well-beloved Son ? It is too high for us, this august spectacle, we cannot attain unto it ; its grandeur oppresses and stupefies ; its mystery surpasses our comprehension ; its glory is ineffable. Therefore, avoiding all speculation, curious questioning, theological disquisition, and ambitious word-picturing in connection with the remarkable occurrence here recorded, we confine ourselves in this chapter to the humble task of explaining briefly its significance for Jesus Himself, and its lesson for His disciples.

The "transfiguration," to be understood, must be viewed in connection with the announcement made by Jesus shortly before it happened, concerning His death. This is evident from the simple fact, that the three evangelists who relate the event so carefully note the time of its occurrence with

---

[1] Of Hermon ? The traditional scene of the transfiguration was Mount Tabor.

reference to that announcement, and the conversation which accompanied it. All tell how, within six or eight days thereafter,[1] Jesus took three of His disciples, Peter, James, and John, and brought them into an high mountain apart, and was transfigured before them. The Gospel historians are not wont to be so careful in their indications of time, and their minute accuracy here signifies in effect : " While the foregoing communications and discourses concerning the cross were fresh in the thoughts of all the parties, the won-drous events we are now to relate took place." The relative date, in fact, is a fingerpost pointing back to the conversation on the passion, and saying : " If you desire to understand what follows, remember what went before."

This inference from the note of time given by all the evangelists is fully borne out by a statement made by Luke alone, respecting the subject of the conversation on the holy mount between Jesus and His celestial visitants. " And," we read, " behold, there talked with Him two men, which were Moses and Elias ; who appeared in glory, and spake of His decease (or exodus) which He should accomplish at Jerusalem."[2] That exit, so different from their own in its circumstances and consequences, was *the* theme of their talk. They had appeared to Jesus to converse with Him thereon ; and when they ceased speaking concerning it, they took their departure for the abodes of the blessed. How long the conference lasted we know not, but the subject was sufficiently suggestive of interesting topics of conversa-tion. There was, *e.g.*, the surprising contrast between the death of Moses, immediate and painless, while his eye was not dim nor his natural force abated, and the painful and ignominious death to be endured by Jesus. Then there was the not less remarkable contrast between the manner of Elijah's departure from the earth — translated to heaven without tasting death at all, making a triumphant exit out of the world in a chariot of fire, and the way by which Jesus should enter into glory — the *via dolorosa* of the cross. Whence this privilege of exemption from death, or from its

---

[1] μεθ' ἡμέρας ἑξ, Matthew and Mark ; ὡσεὶ ἡμέραι ὀκτὼ, Luke. The two expressions may easily mean the same period of time.

[2] Luke ix. 31, ἔλεγον τὴν ἔξοδον αὐτοῦ.

bitterness, granted to the representatives of the law and the prophets, and wherefore denied to Him who was the end both of law and of prophecy? On these points, and others of kindred nature, the two celestial messengers, enlightened by the clear light of heaven, may have held intelligent and sympathetic converse with the Son of man, to the refreshment of His weary, saddened, solitary soul.

The same evangelist who specifies the subject of conversation on the holy mount further records that, previous to His transfiguration, Jesus had been engaged in prayer. We may therefore see, in the honor and glory conferred on Him there, the Father's answer to His Son's supplications; and from the nature of the answer we may infer the subject of prayer. It was the same as afterwards in the garden of Gethsemane. The cup of death was present to the mind of Jesus now, as then; the cross was visible to His spiritual eye; and He prayed for nerve to drink, for courage to endure. The attendance of the three confidential disciples, Peter, James, and John, significantly hints at the similarity of the two occasions. The Master took these disciples with Him into the mount, as He afterwards took them into the garden, that He might not be altogether destitute of company and kindly sympathy as He walked through the valley of the shadow of death, and felt the horror and the loneliness of the situation.

It is now clear how we must view the transfiguration scene in relation to Jesus. It was an aid to faith and patience, specially vouchsafed to the meek and lowly Son of man, in answer to His prayers, to cheer Him on His sorrowful path towards Jerusalem and Calvary. Three distinct aids to His faith were supplied in the experiences of that wondrous night. The first was a foretaste of the glory with which He should be rewarded after His passion, for His voluntary humiliation and obedience unto death. For the moment He was, as it were, rapt up into heaven, where He had been before He came into the world; for His face shone like the sun, and His raiment was white as the pure untrodden snow on the high alpine summits of Hermon. "Be of good cheer," said that sudden flood of celestial light: "the suffering will soon be past, and Thou shalt enter into Thine eternal joy!"

A second source of comfort to Jesus in the experiences on the mount, was the assurance that the mystery of the cross was understood and appreciated by saints in heaven, if not by the darkened minds of sinful men on earth. He greatly needed such comfort; for among the men then living, not excepting His chosen disciples, there was not one to whom He could speak on that theme with any hope of eliciting an intelligent and sympathetic response. Only a few days ago, He had ascertained by painful experience the utter incapacity of the twelve, even of the most quick-witted and warm-hearted among them, to comprehend the mystery of His passion, or even to believe in it as a certain fact. Verily the Son of man was most lonely as He passed through the dark valley! the very presence of stupid, unsympathetic companions serving only to enhance the sense of solitariness. When He wanted company that could understand His passion thoughts, He was obliged to hold converse with spirits of just men made perfect; for, as far as mortal men were concerned, He had to be content to finish His great work without the comfort of being understood until it was accomplished.

The talk of the great lawgiver and of the great prophet of Israel on the subject of His death was doubtless a real solace to the spirit of Jesus. We know how He comforted Himself at other times with the thought of being understood in heaven if not on earth. When heartless Pharisees called in question His conduct in receiving sinners, He sought at once His defence and His consolation in the blessed fact that there was joy in heaven at least, whatever there might be among them, over one penitent sinner, more than over ninety and nine just persons that needed no repentance. When He thought how "little ones," the weak and helpless, were despised and trampled under foot in this proud inhuman world, He reflected with unspeakable satisfaction that in heaven their angels did always behold the face of His Father; yea, that in heaven there were angels who made the care of little ones their special business, and were therefore fully able to appreciate the doctrine of humility and kindness which He strove to inculcate on ambitious and quarrelsome disciples. Surely, then, we may believe that when He looked forward to His own decease — the crowning evidence of His

love for sinners — it was a comfort to His heart to think :
"Up yonder they know that I am to suffer, and comprehend
the reason why, and watch with eager interest to see how I
move on with unfaltering step, with my face steadfastly set to
go to Jerusalem." And would it not be specially comforting
to have sensible evidence of this, in an actual visit from two
denizens of the upper world, deputed as it were and commissioned to express the general mind of the whole community
of glorified saints, who understood that their presence in
heaven was due to the merits of that sacrifice which He was
about to offer up in His own person on the hill of Calvary ?

A third, and the chief solace to the heart of Jesus, was
the approving voice of His heavenly Father : "This is
my beloved Son, in whom I am well pleased." That voice,
uttered then, meant : "Go on Thy present way, self-devoted to
death, and shrinking not from the cross. I am pleased with
Thee, because Thou pleasest not Thyself. Pleased with Thee
at all times, I am most emphatically delighted with Thee when,
in a signal manner, as lately in the announcement made to
Thy disciples, Thou dost show it to be Thy fixed purpose
to save others, and not to save Thyself."

This voice from the excellent glory was one of three
uttered by the divine Father in the hearing of His Son
during His life on earth. The first was uttered by the
Jordan, after the baptism of Jesus, and was the same as
the present, save that it was spoken to Him, not concerning
Him, to others. The last was uttered at Jerusalem shortly
before the crucifixion, and was of similar import with the
two preceding, but different in form. The soul of Jesus
being troubled with the near prospect of death, He prayed :
"Father, save me from this hour ; but for this cause came
I unto this hour. Father, glorify Thy name." Then, we
read, came there a voice from heaven, saying : "I have both
glorified it (by Thy life), and will glorify it again" (more
signally by Thy death). All three voices served one end.
Elicited at crises in Christ's history, when He manifested in
peculiar intensity His devotion to the work for which He
had come into the world, and His determination to finish it,
however irksome the task might be to flesh and blood, these
voices expressed, for His encouragement and strengthening,

the complacency with which His Father regarded His self-humiliation and obedience unto death. At His baptism, He, so to speak, confessed the sins of the whole world; and by submitting to the rite, expressed His purpose to fulfil all righteousness as the Redeemer from sin. Therefore the Father then, for the first time, pronounced Him His beloved Son. Shortly before the transfiguration He had energetically repelled the suggestion of an affectionate disciple, that He should save Himself from His anticipated doom, as a temptation of the devil; therefore the Father renewed the declaration, changing the second person into the third, for the sake of those disciples who were present, and specially of Peter, who had listened to the voice of his own heart rather than to his Master's words. Finally, a few days before His death, He overcame a temptation of the same nature as that to which Peter had subjected Him, springing this time out of the sinless infirmity of His own human nature. Beginning His prayer with the expression of a wish to be saved from the dark hour, He ended it with the petition, "Glorify Thy name." Therefore the Father once more repeated the expression of His approval, declaring in effect His satisfaction with the way in which His Son had glorified His name hitherto, and His confidence that He would not fail to crown His career of obedience by a God-glorifying death.

Such being the meaning of the vision on the mount for Jesus, we have now to consider what lesson it taught the disciples who were present, and through them their brethren and all Christians.

The main point in this connection is the injunction appended to the heavenly voice: "Hear Him." This command refers specially to the doctrine of the cross preached by Jesus to the twelve, and so ill received by them. It was meant to be a solemn, deliberate indorsement of all that He had said then concerning His own sufferings, and concerning the obligation to bear their cross lying on all His followers. Peter, James, and John were, as it were, invited to recall all that had fallen from their Master's lips on the unwelcome topic, and assured that it was wholly true and in accordance with the divine mind.

Nay, as these disciples had received the doctrine with murmurs of disapprobation, the voice from heaven addressed to them was a stern word of rebuke, which said : " Murmur not, but devoutly and obediently hear."

This rebuke was all the more needful, that the disciples had just shown that they were still of the same mind as they had been six days ago. Peter at least was as yet in no cross-bearing humor. When, on wakening up to clear consciousness from the drowsy fit which had fallen on him, that disciple observed the two strangers in the act of departing, he exclaimed : " Master, it is good for us to be here, and let us make three tabernacles ; one for Thee, and one for Moses, and one for Elias." He was minded, we perceive, to enjoy the felicities of heaven without any preliminary process of cross-bearing. He thought to himself : " How much better to abide up here with the saints than down below amidst unbelieving captious Pharisees and miserable human beings, enduring the contradiction of sinners, and battling with the manifold ills wherewith the earth is cursed ! Stay here, my Master, and you may bid good-by to all those dark forebodings of coming sufferings, and will be beyond the reach of malevolent priests, elders, and scribes. Stay here, on this sun-lit, heaven-kissing hill ; go no more down into the depressing, sombre valley of humiliation. Farewell, earth and the cross : welcome, heaven and the crown ! "

We do not forget, while thus paraphrasing Peter's foolish speech, that when he uttered it he was dazed with sleep and the splendors of the midnight scene. Yet, when due allowance has been made for this, it remains true that the idle suggestion was an index of the disciple's present mind. Peter *was* drunken, though not with wine ; but what men say, even when drunken, is characteristic. There was a sober meaning in his senseless speech about the tabernacle. He really meant that the celestial visitants should remain, and not go away, as they were in the act of doing when he spoke.[1] This appears from the conversation which took place between Jesus and the three disciples while descending the mountain.[2] Peter and his two companions asked their Master : " Why then say the scribes that Elias must first

[1] Luke ix. 33, ἐν τῷ διαχωρίζεσθαι.   [2] Matt. xvii. 9-13 ; Mark ix. 9-13.

come?" The question referred, we think, not to the injunction laid on the disciples by Jesus just before, "Tell the vision to no man until the Son of man be risen again from the dead," but rather to the fugitive, fleeting character of the whole scene on the mountain. The three brethren were not only disappointed, but perplexed, that the two celestials had been so like angels in the shortness of their stay and the suddenness of their departure. They had accepted the current notion about the advent of Elias before, and in order to, the restoration of the kingdom; and they fondly hoped that this was he come at last in company with Moses, heralding the approaching glory, as the advent of swallows from tropical climes is a sign that summer is nigh, and that winter with its storms and rigors is over and gone. In truth, while their Master was preaching the cross they had been dreaming of crowns. We shall find them continuing so to dream till the very end.

" Hear ye Him : " — this voice was not meant for the three disciples alone, or even for the twelve, but for all professed followers of Christ as well as for them. It says to every Christian : " Hear Jesus, and strive to understand Him while He speaks of the mystery of His sufferings and the glory that should follow — those themes which even angels desire to look into. Hear Him when He proclaims cross-bearing as a duty incumbent on all disciples, and listen not to self-indulgent suggestions of flesh and blood, or the temptations of Satan counselling thee to make self-interest or self-preservation thy chief end. Hear Him, yet again, and weary not of the world, nor seek to lay down thy burden before the time. Dream not of tabernacles where thou mayest dwell secure, like a hermit in the wild, having no share in all that is done beneath the circuit of the sun. Do thy part manfully, and in due season thou shalt have, not a tent, but a temple to dwell in : an house not made with hands, eternal in the heavens.

It is true, indeed, that we who are in this tabernacle of the body, in this world of sorrow, cannot but groan now and then, being burdened. This is our infirmity, and in itself it is not sinful; neither is it wrong to heave an occasional sigh, and utter a passing wish that the time of cross-bearing were over. Even the holy Jesus felt at times this weariness of life. An expression of something like impatience escaped His lips at this very season. When He came down from the mount and learned what was going on at its base, He exclaimed, with reference at once to the unbelief of the scribes who were present, to the weak faith of the disciples, and to the miseries of mankind suffering the consequences of the curse: "O faithless and perverse generation, how long shall I be with you? how long shall I suffer you?" Even the loving Redeemer of man felt tempted to be weary in well-doing — weary of encountering the contradiction of sinners and of bearing with the spiritual weakness of disciples. Such weariness therefore, as a momentary feeling, is not necessarily sinful: it may rather be a part of our cross. But it must not be indulged in or yielded to. Jesus did not give Himself up to the feeling. Though He complained of the generation amidst which He lived, He did not cease from His labors of love for its benefit. Having relieved His heart by this utterance of a reproachful exclamation, He gave orders that the poor lunatic should be brought to Him that he might be healed. Then, when He had wrought this new miracle of mercy, He patiently explained to His own disciples the cause of their impotence to cope successfully with the maladies of men, and taught them how they might attain the power of casting out all sorts of devils, even those whose hold of their victims was most obstinate, viz. by faith and prayer.[1] So He continued laboring in helping the miserable and instructing the ignorant, till the hour came when He could truly say, "It is finished."

---

[1] Matt. xvii. 19-21; Mark ix. 28, 29 Ver 21 in Matthew is not genuine, being borrowed by copyists from Mark. In Mark ix. 29 the true text is, "This kind can come forth by nothing but by prayer." The addition, καὶ νηστείᾳ, "and fasting," is a gloss, due to the ascetic spirit which early crept into the church.

14

TRAINING IN TEMPER:
or, Discourse on Humility

SECTION I — AS THIS LITTLE CHILD !

Matt. 18:1-14; Mark 9:33-37; 42-50; Luke 9:46-48

FROM the Mount of Transfiguration Jesus and the twelve returned through Galilee to Capernaum. On this homeward journey the Master and His disciples were in very different moods of mind. He sadly mused on His cross ; they vainly dreamed of places of distinction in the approaching kingdom. The diversity of spirit revealed itself in a corresponding diversity of conduct. Jesus for the second time began to speak on the way of His coming sufferings, telling His followers how the Son of man should be *betrayed* into the hands of men, and how they should kill Him, and how the third day He should be raised again.[1] The twelve, on the other hand, began as they journeyed along to dispute among themselves who should be the greatest in the kingdom of heaven.[2] Strange, humiliating contrast exhibited again and again in the evangelic history ; jealous, angry altercations respecting rank and precedence, on the part of the disciples, following new communications respecting His passion on the part of their Lord, as comic follows tragic in a dramatic representation.

This unseemly and unseasonable dispute shows clearly what need there was for that injunction appended to the voice from heaven, " Hear Him ; " and how far the disciples were as yet from complying therewith. They heard Jesus only when He spake things agreeable. They listened with pleasure when He assured them that ere long they should see the Son of man come in His kingdom ; they were deaf

---

[1] Matt. xvii. 22, 23; Mark ix. 30-32; Luke ix. 44, 45.   [2] Mark ix. 33.

to all He said concerning the suffering which must precede
the glory. They forgot the cross, after a momentary fit of
sorrow when their Lord referred to it, and betook themselves
to dreaming of the crown ; as a child forgets the death of
a parent, and returns to its play. " How great," thought
they, "shall we all be when the kingdom comes ! " Then
by an easy transition they passed from idle dreams of the
common glory to idle disputes as to who should have the
largest share therein ; for vanity and jealousy lie very near
each other. " Shall we all be equally distinguished in the
kingdom, or shall one be higher than another ? Does
the favor shown to Peter, James, and John, in selecting
them to be eye-witnesses of the prefigurement of the coming
glory, imply a corresponding precedence in the kingdom
itself ? " [1] The three disciples probably hoped it did ; the
other disciples hoped not, and so the dispute began. It was
nothing that they should all be great together ; the question of questions was, who should be the greatest — a question
hard to settle when vanity and presumption contend on one
side, and jealousy and envy on the other.

Arrived at Capernaum, Jesus took an early opportunity
of adverting to the dispute in which His disciples had been
engaged, and made it the occasion of delivering a memorable
discourse on humility and kindred topics, designed to serve
the purpose of *disciplining their temper and will.* The task
to which He now addressed Himself was at once the most
formidable and the most needful He had as yet undertaken
in connection with the training of the twelve. Most formidable, for nothing is harder than to train the human will into
loyal subjection to universal principles, to bring men to
recognize the claims of the law of love in their mutual
relations, to expel pride, ambition, vainglory, and jealousy,
and envy from the hearts even of the good. Men may
have made great progress in the art of prayer, in religious
liberty, in Christian activity, may have shown themselves
faithful in times of temptation, and apt scholars in Christian
doctrine, and yet prove signally defective in temper : self-

---

[1] The three disciples were forbidden to tell any man what they had seen on the holy
mount. The prohibition was probably not meant to refer to their brethren. Even if it
did, they must have found it very hard to keep silent about such a wondrous scene.

willed, self-seeking, having an eye to their own glory, even
when seeking to glorify God. Most needful, for what good
could these disciples do as ministers of the kingdom so long
as their main concern was about their own place therein?
Men full of ambitious passions and jealous of each other
could only quarrel among themselves, bring the cause they
sought to promote into contempt, and breed all around them
confusion and every evil work. No wonder then that Jesus
from this time forth devoted Himself with peculiar earnestness to the work of casting out from His disciples the devil
of self-will, and imparting to them as a salt His own spirit
of meekness, humility, and charity. He knew how much
depended on His success in this effort to salt the future
apostles, to use His own strong figure,[1] and the whole tone
and substance of the discourse before us reveal the depth
of His anxiety. Specially significant in this respect is the
opening part in which He makes use of a child present in
the chamber as the vehicle of instruction ; so, out of the
mouth of a babe and suckling, perfecting the praise of a
lowly mind. Sitting in the midst of ambitious disciples
with the little one in His arms for a text, He who is the
greatest in the kingdom proceeds to set forth truths mortifying to the spirit of pride, but sweeter than honey to the
taste of all renewed souls.

The first lesson taught is this : To be great in the kingdom, yea, to gain admission into it at all, it is necessary to
become like a little child. "Except ye be converted, and
become as little children, ye shall not enter into the kingdom
of heaven. Whosoever, therefore, shall humble himself
as this little child, the same is greatest in the kingdom of
heaven." The feature of child-nature which forms the
special point of comparison is its unpretentiousness. Early
childhood knows nothing of those distinctions of rank which
are the offspring of human pride, and the prizes coveted by
human ambition. A king's child will play without scruple
with a beggar's, thereby unconsciously asserting the insig-
nificance of the things in which men differ, compared with

---

[1] Mark ix. 49. The words " and every sacrifice shall be salted with salt," are a gloss
from Lev. ii. 13, introduced to explain the saying. For remarks on this passage see note
at close of Section III. of the present chapter.

the things that are common to all. What children are
unconsciously, that Jesus requires His disciples to be voluntarily and deliberately. They are not to be pretentious and
ambitious, like the grown children of the world, but meek
and lowly of heart ; disregarding rank and distinctions,
thinking not of their place in the kingdom, but giving themselves up in simplicity of spirit to the service of the King.
In this sense, the greatest one in the kingdom, the King Himself, was the humblest of men. Of humility in the form of
self-depreciation or self-humiliation on account of sin Jesus
could know nothing, for there was no defect or fault in His
character. But of the humility which consists in self-forget-
fulness He was the perfect pattern. We cannot say that
He thought *little* of Himself, but we may say that He
thought not of Himself at all : He thought only of the
Father's glory and of man's good. Considerations of
personal aggrandizement had no place among His motives.
He shrank with holy abhorrence from all who were influenced
by such considerations ; no character appearing so utterly
detestable in His eye as that of the Pharisee, whose religion
was a theatrical exhibition, always presupposing the presence
of spectators, and who loved the uppermost rooms at feasts
and the chief seats in the synagogues, and to be called of
men Rabbi, Rabbi. For Himself He neither desired nor
received honor from men. He came not to be ministered
unto, but to minister : He, the greatest, humbled Himself
to be the least — to be a child born in a stable and laid in a
manger ; to be a man of sorrow, lightly esteemed by the
world ; yea, to be nailed to a cross. By such wondrous
self-humiliation He showed His divine greatness.

The higher we rise in the kingdom the more we shall be
like Jesus in this humbling of Himself. Childlikeness such
as He exhibited is an invariable characteristic of spiritual
advancement, even as its absence is the mark of moral
littleness. The little man, even when well-intentioned, is
ever consequential and scheming, — ever thinking of himself,
his honor, dignity, reputation, even when professedly doing
good. He always studies to glorify God in a way that
shall at the same time glorify himself. Frequently above
the love of gain, he is never above the feeling of self-

importance. The great ones in the kingdom, on the other hand, throw themselves with such unreservedness into the work to which they are called, that they have neither time nor inclination to inquire what place they shall obtain in this world or the next. Leaving consequences to the great Governor and Lord, and forgetful of self-interest, they give their whole soul to their appointed task ; content to fill a little space or a large one, as God shall appoint, if only He be glorified.

This is the true road to a high place in the eternal kingdom. For be it observed, Jesus did not summarily dismiss the question, who is greatest in the kingdom, by negativing the existence of distinctions therein. He said not on this occasion, He said not on any other, " It is needless to ask who is the greatest in the kingdom : there is no such thing as a distinction of greater and less there." On the contrary, it is implied here, and it is asserted elsewhere, that there is such a thing. According to the doctrine of Christ, the supernal commonwealth has no affinity with jealous radicalism, which demands that all shall be equal. There are grades of distinction there as well as in the kingdoms of this world. The difference between the divine kingdom and all others lies in the principle on which promotion proceeds. Here the proud and the ambitious gain the post of honor ; there honors are conferred on the humble and the self-forgetful. He that on earth was willing to be the least in lowly love will be the great one in the kingdom of heaven.

The next lesson Jesus taught His disciples was the duty of *receiving* little ones ; that is, not merely children in the literal sense, but all that a child represents — the weak, the insignificant, the helpless. The child which He held in His arms having served as a type of the humble in spirit, next became a type of the humble in station, influence, and importance ; and having been presented to the disciples in the former capacity as an object of imitation, was commended to them in the latter as an object of kind treatment. They were to receive the little ones graciously and lovingly, careful not to offend them by harsh, heartless, contemptuous conduct. All such kindness He, Jesus, would receive as done to Himself.

This transition of thought from *being* like a child to receiving all that of which childhood in its weakness is the emblem, was perfectly natural; for there is a close connection between the selfish struggle to be great and an offensive mode of acting towards the little. Harshness and contemptuousness are vices inseparable from an ambitious spirit. An ambitious man is not, indeed, necessarily cruel in his disposition, and capable of cherishing heartless designs in cold blood. At times, when the demon that possesses him is quiescent, the idea of hurting a child, or any thing that a child represents, may appear to him revolting; and he might resent the imputation of any such design, or even a hint at the possibility of his harboring it, as a wanton insult. "Is thy servant a dog?" asked Hazael indignantly at Elisha, when the prophet described to him his own future self, setting the strongholds of Israel on fire, slaying their young men with the sword, dashing their children to the earth, and ripping up their women with child. At the moment his horror of these crimes was quite sincere, and yet he was guilty of them all. The prophet rightly divined his character, and read his future career of splendid wickedness in the light of it. He saw that he was ambitious, and all the rest followed as a matter of course. The king of Syria, his master, about whose recovery he affected solicitude, he should first put to death; and once on the throne, the same ambition that made him a murderer would goad him on to schemes of conquest, in the prosecution of which he should perpetrate all the barbarous cruelties in which Oriental tyrants seemed to take fiendish delight.

The crimes of ambition, and the lamentations with which it has filled the earth, are a moral commonplace. Full well aware of the fact, Jesus exclaimed, as the havoc already wrought and yet to be wrought by the lust for place and power rose in vision before His eye: "Woe to the world because of offences!" Woe indeed, but not merely to the wrong-sufferer; the greater woe is reserved for the wrong-doer. So Jesus taught His disciples, when He added: "But woe to that man by whom the offence cometh!" Nor did He leave His hearers in the dark as to the nature of the offender's doom. "Whoso," He declared, in language which came forth from His lips like a flame of righteous indignation at thought of the wrongs inflicted on the weak and helpless, — "Whoso shall offend one of these little ones which believe in me, it were better for him that a mill-stone were hanged about his neck, and that he were drowned in the depth of the sea." "It were better for him" — or, it suits him, it is what he deserves; and it is implied, though not expressed, that it is what he gets when divine vengeance at length overtakes him. The mill-stone is no idle figure of speech, but an appropriate emblem of the ultimate doom of the proud. He who *will* mount to the highest place, regardless of the injuries he may inflict on little ones, shall be cast down, not to earth merely, but to the very lowest depths of the ocean, to the very abyss of hell, with a heavy weight of curses suspended on his neck to sink him down, and keep him down, so that he shall rise no more.[1] "They sank as lead in the mighty waters!"

Such being the awful doom of selfish ambition, it were wise in the high-minded to fear, and to anticipate God's judgment by judging themselves. This Jesus counselled His disciples to do by repeating a stern saying uttered once before in the Sermon on the Mount, concerning the cutting off offending members of the body.[2] At first view that saying appears irrelevant here, because the subject of discourse is offences against others, not offences against one's self. But its relevancy becomes evident when we consider that all offences against a brother are offences against ourselves. That is the very point Christ wishes to impress on His disciples. He would have them understand that self-interest dictates scrupulous care in avoiding offences to the little ones. "Rather than harm one of these," says the great Teacher in effect, "by hand, foot, eye, or tongue, have recourse to self-mutilation; for he that sinneth against even the least in the kingdom, sinneth also against his own soul."

---

[1] μύλος ὀνικός, stone of a mill turned by an ass, larger than one belonging to a hand-mill, selected to make sure that the wicked shall sink to rise no more. How Christ's words fulfil themselves from age to age! Think of the "Bulgarian atrocities" of 1876, the execrations they awakened in Britain, and the all too probable fate which awaits Turkey in the near future!

[2] Matt. xviii. 8, 9; compare v. 29, 30.

One thing more Jesus taught His disciples while He held
the child in His arms, viz. that those who injured or despised
little ones were entirely out of harmony with the mind of
Heaven. "Take heed," said He, "that ye despise not one
of these little ones ; " and then He proceeded to enforce the
warning by drawing aside the veil, and showing them a
momentary glimpse of that very celestial kingdom in which
they were all so desirous to have prominence. "Lo, there !
see those angels standing before the throne of God — these
be ministering spirits to the little ones ! And lo, here am I,
the Son of God, come all the way from heaven to save them !
And behold how the face of the Father in heaven smiles on
the angels and on me because we take such loving interest
in them !" [1]   How eloquent the argument ! how powerful the
appeal ! "The inhabitants of heaven," such is its drift, "are
loving and humble ; ye are selfish and proud. What hope
can ye cherish of admission into a kingdom, the spirit of
which is so utterly diverse from that by which ye are
animated ?   Nay, are ye not ashamed of yourselves when ye
witness this glaring contrast between the lowliness of the
celestials and the pride and pretensions of puny men ?   Put
away, henceforth and forever, vain, ambitious thoughts, and
let the meek and gentle spirit of Heaven get possession of
your hearts."

In the beautiful picture of the upper world one thing is
specially noteworthy, viz. the introduction by Jesus of a
reference to His work as the Saviour of the lost, into an
argument designed to enforce care for the little ones.[2]   The
reference is not an irrelevance ; it is of the nature of an
argument *à fortiori*.   If the Son of man cared for the *lost*,

---

[1] Matt. xviii. 10-14.

[2] Matt. xviii. 11 is not found in the best critical authorities, and is regarded by scholars
as interpolated from Luke xix. 10 ; and the parable of the good shepherd is also regarded
by many as foreign to the connection of thought.   As to the former point, we agree with
Alford in thinking that ver. 11 cannot be interpolated from Luke, " 1st, from the absence
of any sufficient reason (apparent on the surface) for insertion ; 2d, from the nearly unani-
mous omission of Luke's ζητῆσαι καὶ, which would have exactly suited the ζητεῖ of ver.
12." That it should form a part of the text in a critical edition of the Greek Testament we
do not assert, but it is quite credible to us that Christ uttered such a sentiment on this
occasion.   The thought is germain to the connection, however awkwardly it may come in
in the narrative.   For a similar reason, we think it quite likely that the parable of the good
shepherd was spoken at this time.   It was just as much needed to rebuke the ambitious
spirit of disciples as to ward off the assaults of censorious Pharisees.

the *low*, the morally degraded, how much more will He care for those who are merely little! It is a far greater effort of love to seek the salvation of the wicked than to interest one's self in the weak ; and He who did the one will certainly not fail to do the other. In adverting to His love as the Saviour of the sinful, as set forth in the parable of the good shepherd going after the straying sheep,[1] Jesus further directed the attention of His disciples to the sublimest example of humility. For that love shows that there was not only no pride of greatness in the Son of God, but also no pride of *holiness*. He could not only condescend to men of humble estate, but could even become the brother of the vile : one with them in sympathy and lot, that they might become one with Him in privilege and character. Once more, in making reference to His own love as the Saviour, Jesus pointed out to His disciples the true source of that charity which careth for the weak and despiseth not the little. No one who rightly appreciated His love could deliberately offend or heartlessly contemn any brother, however insignificant, who had a place in His Saviour-sympathies. The charity of the Son of man, in the eyes of all true disciples, surrounds with a halo of sacredness the meanest and vilest of the human race.

SECTION II — CHURCH DISCIPLINE

MATT. xviii. 15-20

Having duly cautioned His hearers against offending the little ones, Jesus proceeded (according to the account of His words in the Gospel of Matthew) to tell them how to act when they were not the givers, but the receivers or the judges, of offences. In this part of His discourse He had in view the future rather than the present. Contemplating the time when the kingdom — that is, the church — should be in actual existence as an organized community, with the twelve exercising in it authority as apostles, He gives directions for the exercise of discipline, in order to the purity and wellbeing of the Christian brotherhood ;[2] confers on the

---

[1] Matt. xviii. 12, 13.
[2] Matt. xviii. 15-17. Keim views the whole discourse (which he regards as substantially one continuous utterance as recorded in Matt. xviii. with the supplement in the

twelve collectively what He had already granted to Peter singly — the power to bind and loose, that is, to inflict and remove church censures;[1] and makes a most encouraging promise of His own spiritual presence, and of prevailing power with His heavenly Father in prayer, to all assembled in His name, and agreeing together in the objects of their desires.[2] His aim throughout is to insure beforehand that the community to be called after His name shall be indeed a holy, loving, united society.

The rules here laid down for the guidance of the apostles in dealing with offenders, though simple and plain, have given rise to much debate among religious controversialists interested in the upholding of diverse theories of church government.[3] Of these ecclesiastical disputes we shall say nothing here; nor do we deem it needful to offer any expository comments on our Lord's words, save a sentence of explanation on the phrase employed by Him to describe the state of excommunication: " Let him " (that is, the impenitent brother about to be cast out of the church) " be unto thee as an heathen man and a publican." These words, luminous without doubt at the time they were spoken, are not quite so clear to us now; but yet their meaning in the main is sufficiently plain. The idea is, that the persistently impenitent offender is to become at length to the person he has offended, and to the whole church, one with whom is to be held no religious, and as little as possible social fellowship. The religious aspect of excommunication is pointed at by the expression " as an heathen man," and the social side of it is expressed in the second clause of the sentence, "and a publican." Heathens were excluded from the temple, and had no part in Jewish religious rites. Publicans were not excluded from the temple, so far as we know; but they were regarded as social pariahs by all Jews affecting patriotism and

other evangelists) as meant by Jesus to serve the purpose of organizing the disciples into a religious community (*Gemeinde*) in view of His probable death. This piece of work Keim calls Christ's last Galilean task, and he represents it as in accordance with Christ's wisdom and love that He attended to the duty then. *Vide Geschichte Jesu,* ii. 605.

[1] Ver. 18.
[2] Vers. 19, 20.
[3] Persons curious concerning these controversies will find abundant information in Gillespie's *Aaron's Rod Blossoming.*

religious strictness. This indiscriminate dislike of the whole class was not justifiable, nor is any approval of it implied here. Jesus refers to it simply as a familiar matter of fact, which conveniently and clearly conveyed His meaning to the effect : Let the impenitent offender be to you what heathens are to all Jews by law — persons with whom to hold no religious fellowship ; and what publicans are to Pharisees by inveterate prejudice — persons to be excluded from all but merely unavoidable social intercourse."

Whatever obscurity may attach to the letter of the rules for the management of discipline, there can be no doubt at all as to the loving, holy spirit which pervades them.

The spirit of love appears in the conception of the church which underlies these rules. The church is viewed as a commonwealth, in which the concern of one is the concern of all, and *vice versa*. Hence Jesus does not specify the class of offences He intends, whether private and personal ones, or such as are of the nature of scandals, that is, offences against the church as a whole. On His idea of a church such explanations were unnecessary, because the distinction alluded to in great part ceases to exist. An offence against the conscience of the whole community is an offence against each individual member, because he is jealous for the honor of the body of believers ; and on the other hand, an offence which is in the first place private and personal, becomes one in which all are concerned so soon as the offended party has failed to bring His brother to confession and reconciliation. A chronic alienation between two Christian brethren will be regarded, in a church after Christ's mind, as a scandal not to be tolerated, because fraught with deadly harm to the spiritual life of all.

Very congenial also to the spirit of charity is the order of proceeding indicated in the directions given by Jesus. First, strictly private dealing on the part of the offended with his offending brother is prescribed ; then, after such dealing has been fairly tried and has failed, but not till then, third parties are to be brought in as witnesses and assistants in the work of reconciliation ; and finally, and only as a last resource, the subject of quarrel is to be made public, and brought before the whole church. This method of pro-

cedure is obviously most considerate as towards the offender.
It makes confession as easy to him as possible by sparing
him the shame of exposure. It is also a method which
cannot be worked out without the purest and holiest motives
on the part of him who seeks redress. It leaves no room
for the reckless talkativeness of the scandalmonger, who
loves to divulge evil news, and speaks to everybody of a
brother's faults rather than to the brother himself. It
puts a bridle on the passion of resentment, by compelling
the offended one to go through a patient course of dealing
with his brother before he arrive at the sad issue at which
anger jumps at once, viz. total estrangement. It gives no
encouragement to the officious and over-zealous, who make
themselves busy in ferreting out offences ; for the way of
such is not to begin with the offender, and then go to the
church, but to go direct to the church with severe charges,
based probably on hearsay information gained by dishon-
orable means.

Characteristic of the loving spirit of Jesus, the Head of
the church, is the horror with which He contemplates, and
would have His disciples contemplate, the possibility of any
one, once a brother, becoming to his brethren as a heathen
or a publican. This appears in His insisting that no expedient shall be left untried to avert the sad catastrophe. How
unlike in this respect is His mind to that of the world,
which can with perfect equanimity allow vast multitudes of
fellow-men to be what heathens were to Jews, and publicans
to Pharisees — persons excluded from all kindly communion !
Nay, may we not say, how unlike the mind of Jesus in this
matter to that of many even in the church, who treat
brethren in the same outward fellowship with most perfect
indifference, and have become so habituated to the evil
practice, that they regard it without compunction as a quite
natural and right state of things !

Such heartless indifferentism implies a very different ideal
of the church from that cherished by its Founder. Men
who do not regard ecclesiastical fellowship as imposing any
obligation to love their Christian brethren, think, consciously
or unconsciously, of the church as if it were a hotel, where
all kinds of people meet for a short space, sit down together

at the same table, then part, neither knowing nor caring any thing about each other; while, in truth, it is rather a family, whose members are all brethren, bound to love each other with pure heart fervently. Of course this hotel theory involves as a necessary consequence the disuse of discipline. For, strange as the idea may seem to many, the law of love is the basis of church discipline. It is because I am bound to take every member of the church to my arms as a brother, that I am not only entitled, but bound, to be earnestly concerned about his behavior. If a brother in Christ, according to ecclesiastical standing, may say to me, "You must love me with all your heart," I am entitled to say in reply, "I acknowledge the obligation in the abstract, but I demand of you in turn that you shall be such that I can love you as a Christian, however weak and imperfect; and I feel it to be both my right and my duty to do all I can to make you worthy of such brotherly regard, by plain dealing with you anent your offences. I am willing to love *you*, but I cannot, I dare not, be on friendly terms with your *sins;* and if you refuse to part with these, and virtually require me to be a partaker in them by connivance, then our brotherhood is at an end, and I am free from my obligations." To such a language and such a style of thought the patron of the hotel theory of church fellowship is an utter stranger. Disclaiming the obligation to love his brethren, he at the same time renounces the right to insist on Christian virtue as an indispensable attribute of church membership, and declines to trouble himself about the behavior of any member, except in so far as it may affect himself personally. All may think and act as they please — be infidels or believers, sons of God or sons of Belial: it is all one to him.

Holy severity finds a place in these directions, as well as tender, considerate love. Jesus solemnly sanctions the excommunication of an impenitent offender. "Let him," saith He, with the tone of a judge pronouncing sentence of death, "be unto thee as an heathen man and a publican." Then, to invest church censures righteously administered with all possible solemnity and authority, He proceeds to declare that they carry with them eternal consequences; adding in His most emphatic manner the awful words —

awful both to the sinner cast out and to those who are responsible for his ejection : "Verily I say unto you, Whatsoever ye shall bind on earth shall be bound in heaven ; and whatsoever ye shall loose on earth, shall be loosed in heaven." The words may be regarded in one sense as a caution to ecclesiastical rulers to beware how they use a power of so tremendous a character ; but they also plainly show that Christ desired His church on earth, as nearly as possible, to resemble the church in heaven : to be holy in her membership, and not an indiscriminate congregation of righteous and unrighteous men, of believers and infidels, of Christians and reprobates ; and for that end committed the power of the keys to those who bear office in His house, authorizing them to deliver over to Satan's thrall the proud, stubborn sinner who refuses to be corrected, and to give satisfaction to the aggrieved consciences of his brethren.

Such rigor, pitiless in appearance, is really merciful to all parties. It is merciful to the faithful members of the church, because it removes from their midst a mortifying limb, whose presence imperils the life of the whole body. Scandalous open sin cannot be tolerated in any society without general demoralization ensuing ; least of all in the church, which is a society whose very *raison d'être* is the culture of Christian virtue. But the apparently pitiless rigor is mercy even towards the unfaithful who are the subjects thereof. For to keep scandalous offenders inside the communion of the church is to do your best to damn their souls, and to exclude them ultimately from heaven. On the other hand, to deliver them over to Satan may be, and it is to be hoped will be, but giving them a foretaste of hell now that they may be saved from hell-fire forever. It was in this hope that Paul insisted on the excommunication of the incestuous person from the Corinthian church, that by the castigation of his fleshly sin "his spirit might be saved in the day of the Lord Jesus." It is this hope which comforts those on whom the disagreeable task of enforcing church censures falls in the discharge of their painful duty. They can cast forth evil-doers from the communion of saints with less hesitation, when they know that as "publicans and sinners" the excommunicated are nearer the kingdom of

God than they were as church members, and when they consider that they are still permitted to seek the good of the ungodly, as Christ sought the good of all the outcasts of His day ; that it is still in their power to pray for them, and to preach to them, as they stand in the outer court of the Gentiles, though they may not put into their unholy hands the symbols of the Saviour's body and blood.

Such considerations, indeed, would go far to reconcile those who are sincerely concerned for the spiritual character of the church, and for the safety of individual souls, to very considerable reductions of communion rolls. There cannot be a doubt that, if church discipline were upheld with the efficiency and vigor contemplated by Christ, such reductions would take place on an extensive scale. It is indeed true that the purging process might be carried to excess, and with very injurious effects. Tares might be mistaken for wheat, and wheat for tares. The church might be turned into a society of Pharisees, thanking God that they were not as other men, or as the poor publicans who stood without, hearing and praying, but not communicating ; while among those outside the communion rails might be not only the unworthy, but many timid ones who dared not come nigh, but, like the publican of the parable, could only stand afar off, crying, " God be merciful to me, a sinner," yet all the while were justified rather than the others. A system tending to bring about such results is one extreme to be avoided. But there is another yet more pernicious extreme still more sedulously to be shunned : a careless laxity, which allows sheep and goats to be huddled together in one fold, the goats being thereby encouraged to deem themselves sheep, and deprived of the greatest benefit they can enjoy — the privilege of being spoken to plainly as " unconverted sinners."

Such unseemly mixtures of the godly and the godless are too common phenomena in these days. And the reason is not far to seek. It is not indifference to morality, for that is not generally a characteristic of the church in our time. It is the desire to multiply members. The various religious bodies value members still more than morality or high-toned Christian virtue, and they fear lest by discipline they may

lose one or two names from their communion roll. The fear
is not without justification. Fugitives from discipline are
always sure of an open door and a hearty welcome in some
quarter. This is one of the many curses entailed upon us by
that greatest of all scandals, religious division. One who
has become, or is in danger of becoming, as a heathen man
and a publican to one ecclesiastical body, has a good chance
of becoming a saint or an angel in another. Rival churches
play at cross purposes, one loosing when another binds ; so
doing their utmost to make all spiritual sentences null and
void, both in earth and heaven, and to rob religion of all
dignity and authority. Well may libertines pray that the
divisions of the church may continue, for while these last
they fare well ! Far otherwise did it fare with the like of
them in the days when the church was catholic and one ;
when sinners repenting worked their way, in the slow course
of years, from the *locus lugentium* outside the sanctuary,
through the *locus audientium* and the *locus substratorum* to
the *locus fidelium :* in that painful manner learning what an
evil and a bitter thing it is to depart from the living God.[1]

The promise made to consent in prayer[2] comes in appropriately in a discourse delivered to disciples who had been
disputing who should be the greatest. In this connection the
promise means : " So long as ye are divided by dissensions
and jealousies, ye shall be impotent alike with men and with
God ; in your ecclesiastical procedure as church rulers, and
in your supplications at the throne of grace. But if ye be
united in mind and heart, ye shall have power with God, and
shall prevail : my Father will grant your requests, and I
myself will be in the midst of you."

It is not necessary to assume any very close connection
between this promise and the subject of which Jesus had
been speaking just before. In this familiar discourse transition is made from one topic to another in an easy conver-
sational manner, care being taken only that all that is said
shall be relevant to the general subject in hand. The meeting, supposed to be convened in Christ's name, need not

[1] See Bingham's *Origines Ecclesiasticæ* for an account of the ancient church
discipline.
[2] Matt. xviii. 19, 20.

therefore be one of church officers assembled for the transaction of ecclesiastical business : it may be a meeting, in a
church or in a cottage, purely for the purposes of worship.
The promise avails for all persons, all subjects of prayer, all
places, and all times ; for all truly Christian assemblies great
and small.

The promise avails for the smallest number that can make
a meeting — even for two or three.   This minimum number
is condescended on for the purpose of expressing in the
strongest possible manner the importance of brotherly concord.   Jesus gives us to understand that two agreed are
better, stronger, than twelve or a thousand divided by enmities and ambitious passions.   " The Lord, when He would
commend unanimity and peace to His disciples, said, ' If two
of you shall agree on earth,' etc., to show that most is granted
not to the multitude, but to the concord of the supplicants." [1]
It is an obvious inference, that if by agreement even two be
strong, then a multitude really united in mind would be proportionally stronger.   For we must not fancy that God has any
partiality for a little meeting, or that there is any virtue in a
small number.   Little strait sects are apt to fall into this
mistake, and to imagine that Christ had them specially in
His eye when He said two or three, and that the kind of
agreement by which they are distinguished — agreement in
whim and crotchet — is what He desiderated.   Ridiculous
caricature of the Lord's meaning !   The agreement He
requires of His disciples is not entire unanimity in opinion,
but consent of mind and heart in the ends they aim at, and
in unselfish devotion to these ends.   When He spake of two
or three, He did not contemplate, as the desirable state of
things, the body of His church split up into innumerable
fragments by religious opinionativeness, each fragment in
proportion to its minuteness imagining itself sure of His
presence and blessing.   He did not wish His church to consist of a collection of clubs having no intercommunion with
each other, any more than He desired it to be a monster
hotel, receiving and harboring all comers, no questions being
asked.   He made the promise now under consideration, not
to stimulate sectarianism, but to encourage the cultivation

[1] Cyprianus, *De Unitate Ecclesiæ.*

of virtues which have ever been too rare on earth — brotherly-kindness, meekness, charity. The thing He values, in a word, is not paucity of numbers, due to the *want* of charity, but union of hearts in lowly love among the greatest number possible.

SECTION III — FORGIVING INJURIES

MATT. xviii. 21-35

A lesson on forgiveness fitly ended the solemn discourse on humility delivered in the hearing of disputatious disciples. The connection of thought between beginning and end is very real, though it does not quite lie on the furface. A vindictive temper, which is the thing here condemned, is one of the vices fostered by an ambitious spirit. An ambitious man is sure to be the receiver of many offences, real or imaginary. He is quick to take offence, and slow to forgive or forget wrong. Forgiving injuries is not in his way: he is more in his element when he lays hold of his debtor by the throat, and with ruffian fierceness demands payment.

The concluding part of the discourse was occasioned by a question put by Peter, the usual spokesman of the twelve, who came to Jesus and said : " Lord, how oft shall my brother sin against me, and I forgive him ? till seven times ? " By what precise association of ideas the question was suggested to Peter's mind we know not ; perhaps he did not know himself, for the movements of the mind are often mysterious, and in impulsive mercurial natures they are also apt to be sudden. Thoughts shoot into consciousness like meteors into the upper atmosphere ; and suddenly conceived, are as abruptly uttered, with physical gestures accompanying, indicating the force with which they have taken possession of the soul. Suffice it to say, that the disciple's query, however suggested, was relevant to the subject in hand, and had latent spiritual affinities with all that Jesus had said concerning humility and the giving and receiving of offences. It showed on Peter's part an intelligent attention to the words of his Master, and a conscientious solicitude to conform his conduct to those heavenly precepts by which he felt for the moment subdued and softened.

The question put by Peter further revealed a curious

mixture of childlikeness and childishness. To be so earnest about the duty of forgiving, and even to think of practising the duty so often as seven times towards the same offender, betrayed the true child of the kingdom ; for none but the graciously-minded are exercised in that fashion. But to imagine that pardon repeated just so many times would exhaust obligation and amount to something magnanimous and divine, was very simple. Poor Peter, in his ingenuous attempt at the magnanimous, was like a child standing on tiptoe to make himself as tall as his father, or climbing to the top of a hillock to get near the skies.

The reply of Jesus to His honest but crude disciple was admirably adapted to put him out of conceit with himself, and to make him feel how puny and petty were the dimensions of his charity. Echoing the thought of the prophetic oracle, it tells those who would be like God that they must multiply pardons :[1] " I say not unto thee, Until seven times ; but, Until seventy times seven." Alas for the rarity of such charity under the sun ! Christ's thoughts are not man's thoughts, neither are His ways common among men. As the heavens are higher than the earth, so are His thoughts and ways higher than those current in this world. For many, far from forgiving times without number a brother confessing his fault, do not forgive even so much as once, but act so that we can recognize their portrait drawn to the life in the parable of the *unmerciful servant.*

In this parable, whose minutest details are fraught with instruction, three things are specially noteworthy : the contrast between the two debts ; the corresponding contrast between the two creditors ; and the doom pronounced on those who, being forgiven the large debt owed by them, refuse to forgive the small debt owed to them.

The two debts are respectively ten thousand talents and a hundred denarii, being to each other in the proportion of, say, a million to one. The enormous disparity is intended to represent the difference between the shortcomings of all men towards God, and those with which any man can charge a fellow-creature. The representation is confessed to be just by all who know human nature and their own hearts ; and the

[1] Isa. lv. 7.

consciousness of its truth helps them greatly to be gentle and forbearing towards offenders. Yet the parable seems to be faulty in this, that it makes the unmerciful servant answerable for such a debt as it seems impossible for any man to run up. Who ever heard of a private debt amounting in British money to millions sterling? The difficulty is met by the suggestion that the debtor is a person of high rank, like one of the princes whom Darius set over the kingdom of Persia, or a provincial governor of the Roman Empire. Such an official might very soon make himself liable for the huge sum here specified, simply by retaining for his own benefit the revenues of his province as they passed through his hands, instead of remitting them to the royal treasury.

That it was some such unscrupulous minister of state, guilty of the crime of embezzlement, whom Jesus had in His eye, appears all but certain when we recollect what gave rise to the discourse of which this parable forms the conclusion. The disciples had disputed among themselves who should be greatest in the kingdom, each one being ambitious to obtain the place of distinction for himself. Here, accordingly, their Master holds up to their view the conduct of a great one, concerned not about the faithful discharge of his duty, but about his own aggrandizement. "Behold," He says to them in effect, "what men who wish to be great ones do! They rob their king of his revenue, and abuse the opportunities afforded by their position to enrich themselves; and while scandalously negligent of their own obligations, they are characteristically exacting towards any little one who may happen in the mose innocent way, not by fraud, but by misfortune, to have become their debtor."

Thus understood, the parable faithfully represents the guilt and criminality of those at least who are animated by the spirit of pride, and deliberately make self-advancement their chief end: a class by no means small in number. Such men are great sinners, whoever may be little ones. They not merely come short of the glory of God, the true chief end of man, but they deliberately rob the Supreme of His due, calling in question His sovereignty, denying their accountability to Him for their actions, and by the spirit

which animates them, saying every moment of their lives,
"Who is Lord over us?" It is impossible to over-estimate
the magnitude of their guilt.

The contrast between the two creditors is not less striking
than that between the two debts. The king forgives the
enormous debt of his unprincipled satrap on receiving a
simple promise to pay; the forgiven satrap relentlessly
exacts the petty debt of some three pounds sterling from
the poor hapless underling who owes it, stopping his ear
to the identical petition for delay which he had himself successfully presented to his sovereign lord. Here also the
coloring of the parable appears too strong. The great
creditor seems lenient to excess: for surely such a crime as
the satrap had been guilty of ought not to go unpunished;
and surely it had been wise to attach little weight to a
promise of future payment made by a man who, with unbounded extravagance, had already squandered such a
prodigious sum, so that he had nothing to pay! Then this
great debtor, in his character as small creditor, seems
incredibly inhuman; for even the meanest, most greedy, and
grasping churl, not to speak of so great a gentleman, might
well be ashamed to show such eagerness about so trifling a
sum as to seize the poor wight who owed it by the throat
and drag him to prison, to lie there till he paid it.

The representation is doubtless extreme, and yet in both
parts it is in accordance with truth. God does deal with His
debtors as the king dealt with the satrap. He is slow to
anger, and of great kindness, and repenteth Him of the evil
He hath threatened. He giveth men space to repent, and
by providential delays accepts promises of amendment,
though He knoweth full well that they will be broken, and
that those who made them will go on sinning as before. So
He dealt with Pharaoh, with Israel, with Nineveh; so He
deals with all whom He calls to account by remorse of
conscience, by a visitation of sickness, or by the apprehension
of death, when, on their exclaiming, in a passing penitential
mood, "Lord, have patience with me, and I will pay Thee all,"
He grants their petition, knowing that when the danger or the
fit of repentance is over, the promise of amendment will be
utterly forgotten. Truly was it written of old: "He hath

not dealt with us after our sins, nor rewarded us according to our iniquities."

Nor is the part played by the unmerciful servant, however infamous and inhuman, altogether unexampled ; although its comparative rarity is implied in that part of the parabolic story which represents the fellow-servants of the relentless one as shocked and grieved at his conduct, and as reporting it to the common master. It would not be impossible to find originals of the dark picture, even among professors of the Christian religion, who believe in the forgiveness of sins through the blood of Jesus, and hope to experience all the benefits of divine mercy for His sake. It is, indeed, precisely by such persons that the crime of unmercifulness is, in the parable, supposed to be committed. The exacting creditor meets his debtor just as he himself comes out from the presence of the king after craving and receiving remission of his own debt. This feature in the story at once adapts its lesson specially to believers in the gospel, and points out the enormity of their guilt. All such, if not really forgiven, do at least consciously live under a reign of grace, in which God is assuming the attitude of one who desires all to be reconciled unto Himself, and for that end proclaims a gratuitous pardon to all who will receive it. In men so situated the spirit of unmercifulness is peculiarly offensive. Shameful in a pagan, — for the light of nature teacheth the duty of being merciful, — such inhuman rigor as is here portrayed in a Christian is utterly abominable. Think of it ! he goes out from the presence of the King of grace ; rises up from the perusal of the blessed gospel, which tells of One who received publicans and sinners, even the chief ; walks forth from the house of prayer where the precious evangel is proclaimed, yea, from the communion table, which commemorates the love that moved the Son of God to pay the debt of sinners ; and he meets a fellow-mortal who has done him some petty wrong, and seizes him by the throat, and truculently demands reparation on pain of imprisonment or something worse if it be not forthcoming. May not the most gracious Lord righteously say to such an one : "O thou wicked servant ! I forgave thee all that debt, because thou desiredst me ; shouldest thou not also have had compassion on thy fellow-servant, even as I had pity on thee?" What can the miscreant who showed no mercy expect, but to receive judgment without mercy, and to be delivered over to the tormentors, to be kept in durance and put to the rack, without hope of release, till he shall have paid his debt to the uttermost farthing?

This very doom Jesus, in the closing sentences of His discourse, solemnly assured His disciples awaited all who cherish an unforgiving temper, even if they themselves should be the guilty parties. "So likewise shall my heavenly Father do also unto you if ye from your *hearts* forgive not every one his brother." [1] Stern words these, which lay down a rule of universal application, not relaxable in the case of favored parties. Were partiality admissible at all, such as the twelve would surely get the benefit of it; but as if to intimate that in this matter there is no respect of persons, the law is enunciated with direct, emphatic reference to them. And harsh as the law might seem, Jesus is careful to indicate His cordial approval of its being enforced with Rhadamanthine rigor. For that purpose He calls God the Judge by the endearing name "My heavenly Father;" as if to say: "The great God and King does not seem to me unduly stern in decreeing such penalties against the unforgiving. I, the merciful, tender-hearted Son of man, thoroughly sympathize with such judicial severity. I should solemnly say Amen to that doom pronounced even against you if you behaved so as to deserve it. Think not that because ye are my chosen companions, therefore violations of the law of love by you will be winked at. On the contrary, just because ye are great ones in the kingdom, so far as privilege goes, will compliance with its fundamental laws be especially expected of you, and non-compliance most severely punished. To whom much is given, of him shall much be required. See, then, that ye forgive every one his brother their trespasses, and that ye do so really, not in pretence, *even from your very hearts.*" By such severe plainness of speech did Jesus educate His disciples for being truly great ones in His kingdom : great not in pride, preten- sion, and presumption, but in loyal obedience to the behests

[1] The remaining words, "their trespasses," are probably a gloss.

of their King, and particularly to this law of forgiveness, on which He insisted in His teaching so earnestly and so frequently.[1] And we cannot but remark here, at the close of our exposition of the discourse on humility, that if the apostles in after days did not rise superior to petty passions, it was not the fault of their Master in neglecting their training. "With holy earnestness," — to quote the language of a German scholar, — "springing equally out of solicitude for the new community, zeal for the cause of God and of men; nay, for the essential truths of the new religion of divine grace and of the brotherhood of mankind, Jesus sought to ward off the dark shadow of petty, ungodly feelings which He saw creeping stealthily into the circle of His disciples, and of whose still more extensive and mischievous influence, after His departure, He could not but be apprehensive."[2] We cannot believe that all this earnestness had been manifested in vain; that the disciples did not at length get the salt thoroughly into them.[3]

SECTION IV — THE TEMPLE TAX: AN ILLUSTRATION OF THE SERMON

MATT. xvii. 24–27

This story is a nut with a dry, hard shell, but a very sweet kernel. Superficial readers may see in it nothing more than a curious anecdote of a singular fish with a piece of money in its mouth turning up opportunely to pay a tax, related

---

[1] See Matt. vi. 14.

[2] Keim, *Geschichte Jesu*, ii. 611.

[3] Mark ix. 49, 50. This passage, peculiar to Mark, and forming without doubt a most authentic part of the discourse on humility, is difficult to interpret. But while we may hesitate as to the precise exposition, we can have little difficulty in getting at the leading thoughts contained. They are these three: —

1. The necessity of a more or less painful process of purification in order to salvation.

2. The need of constant care lest the salt of grace, already possessed, become insipid.

3. The wholesome influence of the salt of grace when it hath not lost its savor in maintaining a state of mutual concord among Christians.

The first thought is expressed by the words, "Every one shall be salted with fire," the form of expression being naturally determined by the previous reference to *hell* fire. The meaning is, put yourselves through a *purgatorial* fire, that ye may escape the fire that is *penal*. A fire salting of some kind is inevitable: choose the one that is saving. The third of the above thoughts is expressed in the words, "Have salt in yourselves, and be at peace with each other." The salt meant is that of a severe self-discipline that wrestles with the evil passion in the heart, and resolutely lops off every member that offendeth. Where this salt is, all occasion for quarrelling arising out of ambitious, vain, self-willed thoughts and desires is taken away.

by Matthew, alone of the evangelists, not because of its
intrinsic importance, but simply because, being an ex-tax-
gatherer, he took kindly to the tale. Devout readers, though
unwilling to acknowledge it, may be secretly scandalized by
the miracle related, as not merely a departure from the rule
which Jesus observed of not using His divine power to help
Himself, but as something very like a piece of sport on His
part, or an expression of a humorous sense of incongruity,
reminding one of the grotesque figures in old cathedrals, in
the carving of which the builders delighted to show their
skill, and find for themselves amusement.

Breaking the shell of the story, we discover within, as its
kernel, a most pathetic exhibition of the humiliation and
self-humiliation of the Son of man, who appears exposed
to the indignity of being dunned for temple dues, and so
oppressed with poverty that He cannot pay the sum
demanded, though its amount is only fifteenpence; yet
neither pleading poverty nor insisting on exemption on the
score of privilege, but quietly meeting the claims of the collectors in a manner which, if sufficiently strange, as we admit,[1]
was at all events singularly meek and peaceable.

The present incident supplies, in truth, an admirable illustration of the doctrine taught in the discourse on humility.
The greatest in the kingdom here exemplifies by anticipation
the lowliness He inculcated on His disciples, and shows
them in exercise a holy, loving solicitude to avoid giving
offence not only to the little ones within the kingdom, but
even to those without. He stands not on His dignity as
the Son of God, though the voice from heaven uttered on the
holy mount still rings in His ears, but consents to be treated
as a subject or a stranger; desiring to live peaceably with
men whose ways He does not love, and who bear Him no
good-will, by complying with their wishes in all things

---

[1] Jesus, we believe, did work miracles expressive of humor, not however in levity, but
in holy earnest. Such were the cursing of the fig-tree; the healing of blindness by
putting clay on the eyes, as a satire on the blind guides; and the present one, expressing
a sense of the incongruity between the outward condition and the intrinsic dignity of the
Son of God. But Dr. Farrar doubts whether a miracle was wrought at all. He thinks
the translation of our Lord's words concerning the fish might run, "On opening its
mouth thou shalt *get* or *obtain* a stater;" such a use of the verb εὑρίσκω being quite
classical; and suggests the possibility of some essential particular having been omitted
or left unexplained. — *The Life of Christ*, ii. 46.

lawful. We regard, in short, this curious scene at Capernaum (with the Mount of Transfiguration in the distant
background!) as a historical frontispiece to the sermon we
have been studying. We think ourselves justified in taking
this view of it, by the consideration that, though the scene
occurred before the sermon was delivered, it happened *after*
the dispute which supplied the preacher with a text. The
disciples fell to disputing on the way home from the Mount
of Transfiguration, while the visit of the tax-gatherers took
place on their arrival in Capernaum. Of course Jesus knew
of the dispute at the time of the visit, though He had not
yet expressly adverted to it. Is it too much to assume that
His knowledge of what had been going on by the way
influenced His conduct in the affair of the tribute money,
and led Him to make it the occasion for teaching by action
the same lesson which He meant to take an early opportunity
of inculcating by words?[1]

This assumption, so far from being unwarranted, is, we
believe, quite necessary in order to make Christ's conduct
on this occasion intelligible. Those who leave out of account
the dispute by the way are not at the right point of view for
seeing the incident at Capernaum in its natural light, and
they fall inevitably into misunderstandings. They are forced,
e.g., to regard Jesus as arguing seriously against payment
of the temple tax, as something not legally obligatory, or as
lying out of the ordinary course of His humiliation as the
Son of man. Now it was neither one nor other of these
things. The law of Moses ordained that every man above
twenty years should pay the sum of half a shekel as an atonement for his soul, and to meet the expenses connected with
the service of the tabernacle rendered to God for the common
benefit of all Israelites; and Jesus, as a Jew, was just as
much under obligation to comply with this particular law as
with any other. Nor was there any peculiar indignity, either

---

[1] We invite the special attention of our readers to the above indicated connection, as
for want of insight into the connection the incident now under consideration has received
very scant justice. Weizsäcker, *e.g.*, no extreme critic, holds that the incident in question
has no connection with the group of incidents amid which it occurs, and says Matthew,
brings it in here because it happened at Capernaum, because he could not get it in sooner,
and must put it here or leave it out altogether. — *Vide Untersuchungen über die
evangelische Geschichte*, p. 73.

in kind or degree, involved in obeying that law. Doubtless
it was a great indignity and humiliation to the Son of God
to be paying taxes for the maintenance of His own Father's
house! All that He said to Peter, pointing out the incongruity of such a state of things, was sober truth. But the
incongruity does not meet us here alone; it runs through
the whole of our Lord's earthly experience. His life, in all
respects, departed from the analogy of kings' sons. Though
He were a Son, yet learned He obedience; though He were
a Son, yet came He not to be ministered unto, but to minister;
though He were a Son, yet became He subject to the law,
not merely the moral but the ceremonial, and was circumcised, and took part in the temple worship, and frequented
the sacred feasts, and offered sacrifices, though these were
all only shadows of good things, whereof He Himself was
the substance. Surely, in a life containing so many indignities and incongruities, — which was, in fact, one grand
indignity from beginning to end, — it was a small matter to
be obliged to pay annually, for the benefit of the temple, the
paltry sum of fifteenpence! He who with marvellous patience
went through all the rest, could not possibly mean to stumble
and scruple at so trifling a matter. He who did nothing
towards destroying the temple and putting an end to legal
worship before the time, could not be a party to the mean
policy of starving out its officials, or grudging the funds
necessary to keep the sacred edifice in good repair. He
might say openly what He thought of existing ecclesiastical
abuses, but He would do no more.

The truth is, that the words spoken by Jesus to Simon
were not intended as an argument against paying the tax,
but as an explanation of what was meant by His paying it,
and of the motive which guided Him in paying it. They
were a lesson for Simon, and through him for the twelve, on
a subject wherein they had great need of instruction; not a
legal defence against the demands of the tax-gatherer. But
for that dispute by the way, Jesus would probably have taken
the quietest means for getting the tax paid, as a matter of
course, without making any remarks on the subject. That
He had already acted thus on previous occasions, Peter's
prompt affirmative reply to the question of the collectors

seems to imply. The disciple said "yes," as knowing what his Master had done in past years, and assuming as a thing of course that His practice would be the same now. But Jesus did not deem it, in present circumstances, expedient to let His disciples regard His action with respect to the tax as a mere vulgar matter of course ; He wanted them to understand and reflect on *the moral meaning* and *the motive* of His action for their own instruction and guidance.

He wished them to understand, *in the first place*, that for Him to pay the temple dues *was* a humiliation and an incongruity, similar to that of a king's son paying a tax for the support of the palace and the royal household ; that it was not a thing of course that He should pay, any more than it was a thing of course that He should become man, and, so to speak, leave His royal state behind and assume the rank of a peasant ; that it was an act of voluntary humiliation, forming one item in the course of humiliation to which He voluntarily submitted, beginning with His birth, and ending with His death and burial. He desired His disciples to think of these things in the hope that meditation on them would help to rebuke the pride, pretension, and self-assertion which had given rise to that petty dispute about places of distinction. He would say to them, in effect : " Were I, like you, covetous of honors, and bent on asserting my importance, I would stand on my dignity, and haughtily reply to these collectors of tribute : Why trouble ye me about temple dues ? Know ye not who I am ? I am the Christ, the Son of the living God : the temple is my Father's house ; and I, His Son, am free from all servile obligations. But, note ye well, I do nothing of the kind. With the honors heaped upon me on the Mount of Transfiguration fresh in my recollection, with the consciousness of who I am, and whence I came, and whither I go, abiding deep in my soul, I submit to be treated as a mere common Jew, suffering my honors to fall into abeyance, and making no demands for a recognition which is not voluntarily conceded. The world knows me not ; and while it knows me not, I am content that it should do with me, as with John, whatsoever it lists. Did the rulers know who I am, they would be ashamed to ask of me temple dues ; but since they do not, I accept and bear all the indignities consequent on their ignorance."

All this Jesus said in effect to His disciples, by first adverting to the grounds on which a refusal to pay the didrachmon might plausibly be defended, and then after all paying it. The manner of payment also was so contrived by Him as to re-enforce the lesson. He said not to Simon simply: "Go and catch fish, that with the proceeds of their sale we may satisfy our creditors." He gave him directions as the Lord of nature, to whom all creatures in land or sea were subject, and all their movements familiar, while yet so humbled as to need the services of the meanest of them. By drawing on His omniscience in giving these instructions to His disciple, He did, in a manner, what He never did either before or after, viz. wrought a miracle for His own behoof. The exception, however, had the same reason as the rule, and therefore proved the rule. Jesus abstained from using His divine faculties for His own benefit, that He might not impair the integrity of His humilation; that His human life might be a real *bona fide* life of hardship, unalleviated by the presence of the divine element in His personality. But what was the effect of the lightning-flash of divine knowledge emitted by Him in giving those directions to Peter? To impair the integrity of His humiliation? Nay, but only to make it glaringly conspicuous. It said to Simon, and to us, if he and we had ears to hear: " Behold who it is that pays this tax, and that is reduced to such straits in order to pay it! It is He who knoweth all the fowls of the mountain, and whatsoever passeth through the paths of the sea!"

The other point on which Jesus desired to fix the attention of His disciples, was the reason which moved Him to adopt the policy of submission to what was in itself an indignity. That reason was to avoid giving offence: " Notwithstanding, lest we should offend them." This was not, of course, the only reason of His conduct in this case. There were other comprehensive reasons applicable to His whole experience of humiliation, and to this small item therein in particular; a full account of which would just amount to an answer to the great question put by Anselm: "Cur Deus Homo;" Why did God become man? On that great question we do not enter here, however, but confine ourselves to the remark, that while the reason assigned by Jesus to Peter for the payment of the temple dues was by no means the only one, or even the chief, it was the reason to which, for the disciples' sake, He deemed it expedient just then to give prominence. He was about to discourse to them largely on the subject of giving and receiving offences ; and He wished them, and specially their foremost man, first of all to observe how very careful He Himself was not to offend, — what a prominent place the desire to avoid giving offence occupied among His motives.

Christ's declared reason for paying the tribute is strikingly expressive of His lowliness and His love. The mark of His lowliness is that there is no word here of *taking* offence. How easily and plausibly might He have taken up the position of one who did well to be angry ! " I am the Christ, the Son of God," He might have said, "and have substantiated my claims by a thousand miracles in word and deed, yet they wilfully refuse to recognize me ; I am a poor homeless wanderer, yet they, knowing this, demanded the tribute, as if more for the sake of annoying and insulting me than of getting the money. And for what purpose do they collect these dues ? For the support of a religious establishment thoroughly effete, to repair an edifice doomed to destruction, to maintain a priesthood scandalously deficient in the cardinal virtues of integrity and truth, and whose very existence is a curse to the land. I cannot in conscience pay a didrachmon, no, not even so much as a farthing, for any such objects."

The lowly One did not assume this attitude, but gave what was asked without complaint, grudging, or railing ; and His conduct conveys a lesson for Christians in all ages, and in our own age in particular. It teaches the children of the kingdom not to murmur because the world does not recognize their status and dignity. The world knew not when He came, even God's eternal Son ; what wonder if it recognize not His younger brethren ! The kingdom of heaven itself is not believed in, and its citizens should not be surprised at any want of respect towards them individually. The manifestation of the sons of God is one of the things for which Christians wait in hope. For the present they are not the children, but the strangers : instead of exemption from burdens, they should rather expect oppression ; and they should be thankful when they are put on a level with their fellow-creatures, and get the benefit of a law of toleration.

As the humility of Jesus was shown by His not *taking*, so His love was manifested by His solicitude to avoid *giving* offence. He desired, if possible, to conciliate persons who for the most part had treated Him all along as a heathen and a publican, and who ere long, as He knew well, would treat Him even as a felon. How like Himself was the Son of man in so acting! How thoroughly in keeping His procedure here with His whole conduct while He was on the earth! For what was His aim in coming to the world, what His constant endeavor after He came, but to cancel offences, and to put an end to enmities — to reconcile sinful men to God and to each other? For these ends He took flesh; for these ends He was crucified. His earthly life was all of a piece — a life of lowly love.

"Lest *we* should offend," said Jesus, using the plural to hint that He meant His conduct to be imitated by the twelve and by all His followers. How happy for the world and the church were this done! How many offences might have been prevented had the conciliatory spirit of the Lord always animated those called by His name! How many offences might be removed were this spirit abundantly poured out on Christians of all denominations now! Did this motive, "Notwithstanding, lest we should offend," bulk largely in all minds, what breaches might be healed, what unions might come! A national church *morally*, if not legally, established in unity and peace, might be realized in Scotland in the present generation. Surely a consummation devoutly to be wished! Let us wish for it; let us pray for it; let us cherish a spirit tending to make it possible; let us hope for it against hope, in spite of increasing tendencies on all sides to indulge in an opposite spirit.

SECTION V — THE INTERDICTED EXORCIST: ANOTHER ILLUSTRATION
OF THE SERMON

MARK ix. 38-41 ; LUKE ix. 49, 50

The discourses of our Lord were not continuous, unbroken
addresses on formally announced themes, such as we are
wont to hear, but rather for the most part of the nature of
Socratic dialogues, in which He was the principal speaker,
His disciples contributing their part in the form of a question asked, an exclamation uttered, or a case of conscience
propounded.   In the discourse or dialogue on humility,
two of the disciples acted as interlocutors, viz. Peter and
John.   Towards the close the former of these two disciples,
as we saw, asked a question concerning the forgiving of
injuries ; and near the commencement the other disciple,
John, related an anecdote which was brought up to his
recollection by the doctrine of his Master, respecting receiving little ones in His name, and on which the truth therein
set forth seemed to have a bearing.   The facts thus brought
under his notice led Jesus to make reflections, which supply
an interesting illustration of the bearing of the doctrine He
was inculcating on a particular class of cases or questions.
These reflections, with the incident to which they relate,
now solicit attention.

The story told by John was to the effect that on one
occasion he and his brethren had found a man unknown to
them engaged in the work of casting out devils, and had
served him with an interdict, because, though he used the
name of Jesus in practising exorcism, he did not follow or
identify himself with them, the twelve.   At what particular
time this happened is not stated ; but it may be conjectured
with much probability that the incident was a reminiscence
of the Galilean mission, during which the disciples were
separated from their Master, and were themselves occupied
in healing the sick, and casting out evil spirits, and in preaching the gospel of the kingdom.

John, it will be observed, does not disclaim joint responsibility for the high-handed proceeding he relates, but speaks
as if the twelve had acted unanimously in the matter.   It

may surprise some to find *him*, the apostle of love,[1] consenting to so uncharitable a deed ; but such surprise is founded on superficial views of his character, as well as on ignorance of the laws of spiritual growth. John is not now what he will be, but differs from his future self, as much as an orange in its second year differs from the same orange in its third final year of growth. The fruit of the Spirit will ultimately ripen in this disciple into something very sweet and beautiful ; but meantime it is green, bitter, and fit only to set the teeth on edge. Devoted in mind, tender and intense in his attachment to Jesus, scrupulously conscientious in all his actions, he is even now ; but he is also bigoted, intolerant, ambitious. Already he has played the part of a very high churchman in suppressing the nonconforming exorcist ; ere long we shall see him figuring, together with his brother, as a persecutor, proposing to call down fire from heaven to destroy the enemies of his Lord ; and yet again we shall find him, along with the same brother and their common mother, engaged in an ambitious plot to secure those places of distinction in the kingdom about which all the twelve have lately been wrangling.

In refusing to recognize the exorcist fellow-worker, however humble, as a brother, the disciples proceeded on very narrow and precarious grounds. The test they applied was purely external. What sort of man the person interdicted might be they did not inquire ; it was enough that he was not of their company : as if all inside that charmed circle — Judas, for example — were good ; and all outside, not excepting a Nicodemus, utterly Christless ! Two good things, on their own showing, could be said of him whom they silenced : he was well occupied, and he seemed to have a most devout regard for Jesus ; for he cast out devils, and he did it in Jesus' name. These were not indeed decisive marks of discipleship, for it was possible that a man might practise exorcism for gain, and use the name of Christ because it had been proved to be a good name to conjure by ;

---

[1] The Tübingen school regard this designation as without foundation, and hold that the true character of John is to be learnt from the synoptical Gospels and the Book of Revelation. In this paragraph, as in other passages (*vide* next chapter), our aim is to supply hints of a proof that it is psychologically possible that John might be both the son of thunder and the apostle of love.

but they ought to have been regarded as at least presumptive evidence in favor of one in whose conduct they appeared. Judging by the facts, it was probable that the silenced exorcist was an honest and sincere man, whose heart had been impressed by the ministry of Jesus and His disciples, and who desired to imitate their zeal in doing good. It was even possible that he was more than this — a man possessing higher spiritual endowment than his censors, some provincial prophet as yet unknown to fame. How preposterous, in view of such a possibility, that narrow outward test, " Not with us " !

As an illustration of what this way of judging lands in, one little fact in the history of the celebrated Sir Matthew Hale, whose *Contemplations* are familiar to all readers of devout literature, may here be introduced. Richard Baxter relates that the good people in the part of the country where the distinguished judge resided, after his retirement from the judicial bench, did not entertain a favorable opinion of his religious character, their notion being that he was certainly a very moral man, but *not converted*. It was a serious conclusion to come to about a fellow-creature, and one is curious to know on what so solemn a judgment was based. The author of the *Saint's Rest* gives us the needful information on this momentous point. The pious folks about Acton, he tells us, ranked the ex-judge among the unconverted, because he did not frequent their private weekly prayer-meetings ! It was the old story of the twelve and the exorcist under a new Puritanic form. Baxter, it is needless to say, did not sympathize with the harsh, uncharitable opinion of his less enlightened brethren. His thoughts breathed the gentle, benignant, humble, charitable spirit of Christian maturity. " I," he adds, after relating the fact above stated, " I that have heard and read his serious expressions of the concernments of eternity, and seen his love to all good men, and the blamelessness of his life, thought better of his piety than of mine own." [1]

In silencing the exorcist the twelve were probably actuated by a mixture of motives — partly by jealousy, and partly by conscientious scruples. They disliked, we imagine, the idea

[1] *Reliquiæ Baxterianæ*, Part iii. p. 47.

of any one using Christ's name but themselves, desiring a monopoly of the power conferred by that name to cast out evil spirits; and they probably thought it unlikely, if not impossible, that any one who kept aloof from them could be sincerely devoted to their Master.

In so far as the disciples acted under the influence of jealousy, their conduct towards the exorcist was morally of a piece with their recent dispute who should be the greatest. The same spirit of pride revealed itself on the two occasions under different phases. The silencing of the exorcist was a display of arrogance analogous to that of those who advance for their church the claim to be exclusively the church of Christ. In their dispute among themselves, the disciples played on a humble scale the game of ambitious, self-seeking ecclesiastics contending for seats of honor and power. In the one case the twelve said in effect to the man whom they found casting out devils: We are the sole commissioned, authorized agents of the Lord Jesus Christ; in the other case they said to each other: We are all members of the kingdom and servants of the King; but I deserve to have a higher place than thou, even to be a prelate sitting on a throne.

In so far as the intolerance of the twelve was due to honest scrupulosity, it is deserving of more respectful consideration. The plea of conscience, *honestly* advanced, must always be listened to with serious attention, even when it is mistaken. We say "honestly" with emphasis, because we cannot forget that there is much scrupulosity that is not honest. Conscience is often used as a stalking-horse by proud, quarrelsome, self-willed men to promote their own private ends. Pride, says one, speaking of doctrinal disputes, "is the greatest enemy of moderation. This makes men stickle for their opinions to make them fundamental. Proud men, having deeply studied some additional point in divinity, will strive to make the same necessary to salvation, to enhance the value of their own worth and pains; and it must needs be fundamental in religion, because it is fundamental to their reputation."[1] These shrewd remarks hold good of other things besides doctrine. Opinionative, pragmatic persons,

---

[1] Thomas Fuller, *Holy State*, bk. iii. c. 20.

would make every thing in religion fundamental on which they have decided views; and if they could get their own way, they would exclude from the church all who held not with them in the very minutiæ of belief and practice. But there is such a thing also as honest scrupulosity, and it is more common than many imagine. There is a certain tendency to intolerant exaction, and to severity in judging, in the unripe stage of every earnest life. For the conscience of a young disciple is like a fire of green logs, which smokes first before it burns with a clear blaze. And a Christian whose conscience is in this state must be treated as we treat a dull fire: he must be borne with, that is, till his conscience clear itself of bitter, cloudy smoke, and become a pure, genial, warm flame of zeal tempered by charity.

That the scrupulosity of the twelve was of the honest kind, we believe for this reason, that they were willing to be instructed. They told their Master what they had done, that they might learn from Him whether it was right or wrong. This is not the way of men whose plea of conscience is a pretext.

The instruction honestly desired by the disciples, Jesus promptly communicated in the form of a clear, definite judgment on the case, with a reason annexed. "Forbid him not," He replied to John, "for he that is not against us is for us." [1]

The reason assigned for this counsel of tolerance reminds us of another maxim uttered by Jesus on the occasion when the Pharisees brought against Him the blasphemous charge of casting out devils by aid of Beelzebub.[2] The two sayings have a superficial aspect of contradiction: one seeming to say, The great matter is not to be decidedly against; the other, The great matter is to be decidedly for. But they are harmonized by a truth underlying both — that the cardinal matter in spiritual character is the bias of the heart. Here Jesus says: "If the heart of a man be with me, then, though by ignorance, error, isolation from those who are avowedly my friends, he may seem to be against me, he is really for me." In the other case He meant to say: "If a man be not in heart with me (the case of the Pharisees), then, though

---

[1] Mark ix. 39, 40 (Luke has "you" for "us").   [2] Matt. xii. 30.

by his orthodoxy and his zeal he may seem to be on God's side, and therefore on mine, he is in reality against me."

To the words just commented on, Mark adds the following, as spoken by Jesus at this time: "There is no man that shall do a miracle in my name that can lightly speak evil of me." The voice of wisdom and charity united is audible here. The emphasis is on the word ταχὺ, lightly or readily. This word, in the first place, involves the admission that the case supposed might happen; an admission demanded by historical truth, for such cases did actually occur in after days. Luke tells, *e.g.*, of certain vagabond Jews (in every sense well named) who took upon them to call over demoniacs the name of the Lord Jesus, without any personal faith in Him, but simply in the way of trade, being vile traffickers in exorcism for whom even the devils expressed their contempt, exclaiming, "Jesus I know, and Paul I know, but who are ye?"[1] Our Lord knowing before that such cases would happen, and being acquainted with the depths of human depravity, could not do otherwise than admit the possibility of the exorcist referred to by John being animated by unworthy motives. But while making the admission, He took care to indicate that, in His judgment, the case supposed was very improbable, and that it was very unlikely that one who did a miracle in His name would speak evil of Him. And He desired His discples to be on their guard against readily and lightly believing that any man could be guilty of such a sin. Till strong reasons for thinking otherwise appeared, He would have them charitably regard the outward action as the index of sincere faith and love (which they might the more easily do then, when nothing was to be gained by the use or profession of Christ's name, but the displeasure of those who had the characters and lives of men in their power).

Such were the wise, gracious words spoken by Jesus with reference to the case brought up for judgment by John. Is it possible to extract any lessons from these words of general application to the church in all ages, or specially applicable to our own age in particular? It is a question on which one must speak with diffidence; for while all bow to the judgment

[1] Acts xix. 13.

of Jesus on the conduct of His disciples, as recorded in the
Gospels, there is much difference among Christians as to
the inferences to be drawn therefrom, in reference to cases in
which their own conduct is concerned. The following reflections, may, however, safely be hazarded : —

1. We may learn from the discreet, loving words of the
great Teacher to beware of hasty conclusions concerning
men's spiritual state based on merely external indications.
Say not with the Church of Rome, "Out of our communion
is no possibility of salvation or of goodness;" but rather
admit that even in that corrupt communion may be many
building on the true foundation, though, for the most part,
with very combustible materials ; nay, that Christ may have
not a few friends outside the pale of all the churches. Ask
not with Nathanael, "Can any good thing come out of
Nazareth?" but remember that the best things may come
out of most unexpected quarters. Be not forgetful to entertain strangers, for thereby some have entertained angels
unawares. Bear in mind that, by indulging in the cry, "Not
with us," in reference to trifles and crotchets, you may tempt
God, while giving His Holy Spirit to those whom you un-
church, to withdraw His influences from you for your pride,
exclusiveness, and self-will, and may turn your creed into a
prison, in which you shall be shut out from the fellowship
of saints, and doomed to experience the chagrin of seeing
through the window-bars of your cell God's people walking
at large, while you lie immured in a jail.

2. In view of that verdict, "Forbid him not," one must
read with a sad, sorrowful heart, many pages of church
history, in which the predominating spirit is that of the
twelve rather than that of their Master. One may confidently say, that had Christ's mind dwelt more in those called
by His name, many things in that history would have been
different. Separatism, censoriousness, intolerance of nonconformity, persecution, would not have been so rife ; Con-
venticle Acts and Five-mile Acts would not have disgraced
the statute-book of the English Parliament ; Bedford jail
would not have had the honor of receiving the illustrious
dreamer of the *Pilgrim's Progress* as a prisoner ; Baxter, and
Livingstone of Ancrum, and thousands more like-minded, by

whose stirring words multitudes had been quickened to a new spiritual life, would not have been driven from their parishes and their native lands, and forbidden under heavy penalties to preach that gospel they understood and loved so well, but would have enjoyed the benefit of that law of toleration which they purchased so dearly for us, their children.

3. The divided state of the church has ever been a cause of grief to good men, and attempts have been made to remedy the evil by schemes of union. All honest endeavors having in view the healing of breaches, which, since the days of the Reformation, have multiplied so greatly as to be the opprobrium of Protestantism, deserve our warmest sympathies and most earnest prayers. But we cannot be blind to the fact that through human infirmity such projects are apt to miscarry; it being extremely difficult to get a whole community, embracing men of different temperaments and in different stages of Christian growth, to take the same view of the terms of fellowship. What, then, is the duty of Christians meanwhile? We may learn from our Lord's judgment in the case of the exorcist. If those who are not of our company cannot be brought to enter into the same ecclesiastical organization, let us still recognize them *from the heart* as fellow-disciples and fellow-laborers, and avail ourselves of all lawful or open ways of showing that we care infinitely more for those who truly love Christ, in whatever church they be, than for those who are with us ecclesiastically, but in spirit and life are not with Christ, but against Him. So shall we have the comfort of feeling that, though separated from brethren beloved, we are not schismatical, and be able to speak of the divided state of the church as a thing that we desire not, but merely endure because we cannot help it.

Many religious people are at fault here. There are Christians not a few who do not believe in these two articles of the Apostles' Creed, "the holy catholic church" and "the communion of saints." They care little or nothing for those who are outside the pale of their own communion: they practise brotherly-kindness most exemplarily, but they have no charity. Their church is their club, in which they enjoy the comfort of associating with a select number of persons,

whose opinions, whims, hobbies, and ecclesiastical politics
entirely agree with their own; every thing beyond in the
wide wide world being regarded with cold indifference, if
not with passionate aversion or abhorrence. It is one of
the many ways in which the spirit of religious legalism, so
prevalent amongst us, reveals itself. The spirit of adoption
is a catholic spirit. The legal spirit is a dividing, sectarian
spirit, multiplying fundamentals, and erecting scruples into
principles, and so manufacturing evermore new religious
sects or clubs. Now a club, ecclesiastical or other, is a
very pleasant thing by way of a luxury; but it ought to be
remembered that, besides the club, and including all the
clubs, there is the great Christian commonwealth. This fact
will have to be more recognized than it has been if church
life is not to become a mere imbecility. To save us from this
doom one of two things must take place. Either religious
people must overcome their doting fondness for the mere
club fellowship of denominationalism, involving absolute
uniformity in opinion and practice ; or a sort of Amphictyonic
council must be set on foot as a counterpoise to sectarianism, in which all the sects shall find a common meeting-
place for the discussion of great catholic questions bearing
on morals, missions, education, and the defence of cardinal
truths. Such a council (utopian it will be deemed) would
have many open questions in its constitution. In the ancient
Amphictyonic council men were not known as Athenians or
Spartans, but as Greeks; and in our modern utopian one
men would be known only as Christians, not as Episcopalians,
Presbyterians, Independents, Churchmen, and Dissenters.
It would be such a body, in fact, as the " Evangelical
Alliance " of recent origin, created by the craving for some
visible expression of the feeling of catholicity; but not, like
it, amateur, self-constituted, and patronized (to a certain
extent) by persons alienated from all existing ecclesiastical
organizations, and disposed to substitute it as a new church
in their place, but consisting of representatives belonging
to, and regularly elected and empowered by, the different
sections of the church.[1]

[1] In recent years the phenomenon of " Pan-presbyterianism " has made its appearance.
It is to be feared that this movement will not serve the cause of catholicity, but will

One remark more we make on this club theory of church fellowship. Worked out, it secures at least one object. It breaks Christians up into small companies, and insures that they shall meet in twos and threes! Unhappily, it does not at the same time procure the blessing promised to the two or three. The spirit of Jesus dwells not in coteries of self-willed, opinionative men, but in the great commonwealth of saints, and especially in the hearts of those who love the whole body more than any part, not excepting that to which they themselves belong; to whom the Lord and Head of the church fulfils His promise, by enriching them with magnanimous heroic graces, and causing them to rise like cedars above the general level of contemporary character, and endowing them with a moral power which exercises an ever-widening influence long after the strifes of their age, and the men who delighted in them, have sunk into oblivion.

rather work in a purely antiquarian direction, and serve the purpose of those who would bind the reformed churches to the seventeenth century. Our Amphictyonic council is yet, like Plato's Republic, *in nubibus*. Perhaps disintegration must go farther before the era of reconstruction arrives. Or is it ever to arrive? Is the day for catholic Christianity past?

15

THE SONS OF THUNDER
Luke 9:51-56

THE delivery of the discourse on humility appears to have been the closing act of our Lord's ministry in Galilee; for immediately after finishing their accounts of the discourse, the two first evangelists proceed to speak of what we have reason to regard as His final departure from His native province for the south. "It came to pass," says Matthew, "that when Jesus had finished these sayings, He departed from Galilee, and came into the coasts of Judea."[1] Of this journey neither Matthew nor Mark gives any details: they do not even mention Christ's visit to Jerusalem at the feast of dedication in winter, referred to by John,[2] from which we know that the farewell to Galilee took place at least some four months before the crucifixion. The journey, however, was not without its interesting incidents, as we know from Luke, who has preserved several of them in his Gospel.[3]

Of these incidents, that recorded in the passage above cited is one. For the words with which the evangelist introduces his narrative obviously allude to the same journey from Galilee to the south, of which Matthew and Mark speak in the passages already referred to. The journey though Samaria adverted to here by Luke occurred "when the time was come (or rather coming)[4] that He (Jesus) should be

[1] Matt. xix. 1, 2; Mark x. 1.

[2] John x. 22, 23.

[3] The journey through Samaria, with all accompanying incidents, including the mission of the seventy, the Tübingen critics regard as an invention of the third evangelist, designed to promote the cause of universalism. But such a journey, with all that relates to it, is just as probable intrinsically as Christ's intercourse with publicans and sinners, which was equally unconventional, and equally universalistic in principle and tendency. It is of course freely admitted that Luke's pronounced universalism accounts for these incidents finding a place in his Gospel while they do not appear in Matthew and Mark.

[4] ἐν τῷ συμπληροῦσθαι.

received up," that is, towards the close of His life. Then the peculiar expression, " He steadfastly set His face to go to Jerusalem," hints not obscurely at a final transference of the scene of Christ's work from the north to the south. It refers not merely to the geographical direction in which He was going, but also, and chiefly, to the state of mind in which He journeyed. He went towards Jerusalem, feeling that His duty lay in and near it henceforth, as a victim self-consecrated to death, His countenance wearing a solemn, earnest, dignified aspect, expressive of the great lofty purpose by which His soul was animated.

It was natural that Luke, the companion of Paul and evangelist to the Gentiles, should carefully preserve this anecdote from the last journey of Jesus to Judea through Samaria. It served admirably the purpose he kept in view throughout in compiling his Gospel — that, viz., of illustrating the catholicity of the Christian dispensation ; and therefore he gathered it into his basket, that it might not be lost. He has brought it in at a very suitable place, just after the anecdote of the exorcist ; for, not to speak of the link of association supplied in the name of John, the narrator in one case and an actor in the other, this incident, like the one recorded immediately before, exhibits a striking contrast between the harsh spirit of the disciples and the gentle, benignant spirit of their Master. That contrast forms the moral interest of the story.

The main fact in the story was this. The inhabitants of a certain Samaritan village at which Jesus and His travelling companions arrived at the close of a day's journey having declined, on being requested, to give them quarters for the night, James and John came to their Master, and proposed that the offending villagers should be destroyed by fire from heaven.

It was a strange proposal to come from men who had been for years disciples of Jesus, and especially from one who, like John, had been in the Master's company at the time of that meeting with the woman by the well, and heard the rapturous words with which He spoke of the glorious new era that was dawning.[1] It shows how slow the best are to learn the

[1] John iv.

heavenly doctrine and practice of charity. How startling, again, to think of this same John, a year or two after the date of this savage suggestion, going down from Jerusalem and preaching the gospel of Jesus the crucified in "many of the villages of the Samaritans,"[1] possibly in this very village which he desired to see destroyed!

Such are the contrasts which growth in grace brings. In the green, crude stage of the divine life, whose characteristics are opinionativeness, censoriousness, scrupulosity, intolerance, blind passionate zeal, John would play the part of a mimic Elijah; in his spiritual maturity, after the summer sun of Pentecost had wrought its effects in his soul, and sweetened all its acid juices, he became an ardent apostle of salvation, and exhibited in his character the soft, luscious fruits of "love, joy, peace, long-suffering, gentleness, goodness, faith, meekness, and self-control." Such contrasts in the same character at different periods, however surprising, are perfectly natural. Amid all changes the elements of the moral being remain the same. The juice of the ripe apple is the same that was in the green fruit, *plus* sun-light and sun-heat. The zeal of the son of thunder did not disappear from John's nature after he became an apostle; it only became tempered by the light of wisdom, and softened by the heat of love. He did not even cease to hate, and become an indiscriminately amiable individual, whose charity made no distinction between good and evil. To the last, John was what he was at the first, an intense hater as well as an intense lover. But in his later years he knew better what to hate — the objects of his abhorrence being hypocrisy, apostasy, and Laodicean insincerity;[2] not, as of old, mere ignorant rudeness and clownish incivility. He could distinguish then between wickedness and weakness, malice and prejudice;

---

[1] Acts viii.

[2] *Vide* Book of Revelation, chaps. ii. and iii., commonly regarded as the latest of John's writings. (Reuss, however (*Théologie Chrétienne*), maintains it was his earliest.) Baur and the Tübingen school generally hold that in the Apocalypse (which they reckon the work of the Apostle John) the old narrowness appears unmitigated in bitter hatred of the Apostle Paul, who is supposed to be aimed at in the words, "Thou hast tried them which say they are apostles and are not, and hast found them liars," out of the Epistle to the Church of Ephesus. This passage, and the quarrel between Peter and Paul at Antioch (Gal. ii.), are the principal Biblical supports adduced by the school for their famous conflict-hypothesis.

and while cherishing strong antipathy towards the one, he felt only compassion towards the other.

To some it may seem a matter of wonder how a man capable of entertaining so revolting a purpose as is here ascribed to James and John could ever be the disciple whom Jesus loved. To understand this, it must be remembered that Jesus, unlike most men, could love a disciple not merely for what he was, but for what he should become. He could regard with complacency even sour grapes in their season for the sake of the goodly fruit into which they should ripen. Then, further, we must not forget that John, even when possessed by the devil of resentment, was animated by a purer and holier spirit. Along with the smoke of carnal passion there was some divine fire in his heart. He loved Jesus as intensely as he hated the Samaritans; it was his devoted attachment to his Master that made him resent their incivility so keenly. In his tender love for the Bridegroom of his soul, he was beautiful as a mother overflowing with affection in the bosom of her family; though in his hatred he was terrible as the same mother can be in her enmity against her family's foes. John's nature, in fact, was feminine both in its virtues and in its faults, and, like all feminine natures, could be both exquisitely sweet and exquisitely bitter.[1]

Passing now from personal remarks on John himself to the truculent proposal emanating from him and his brother, we must beware of regarding it in the light of a mere extravagant ebullition of temper consequent upon a refusal of hospitality. No doubt the two brethren and all their fellow-disciples were annoyed by the unexpected incivility, nor can one wonder if it put them out of humor. Weary men are easily irritated, and it was not pleasant to be obliged to trudge on to another village after the fatigues of a day's journey. But we have too good an opinion of the twelve to fancy any of them capable of revenging rudeness by murder.

The savage mood of James and John is not even thoroughly explained by the recollection that the churlish villagers were *Samaritans,* and that they were Jews. The chronic ill-will between the two races had unquestionably its own influence

---

[1] *Conf.* remarks on John at pp. 230, 231.

in producing ill-feeling on both sides. The nationality of the travellers was one, if not the sole reason, why the villagers refused them quarters. They were Galilean Jews going southwards to Jerusalem, and that was enough. Then the twelve, as Jews, were just as ready to take offence as the Samaritan villagers were to give it. The powder of national enmity was stored up in their breasts ; and a spark, one rude word or insolent gesture, was enough to cause an explosion. Though they had been for years with Jesus, there was still much more of the old Jewish man than of the new Christian man in them. If they had been left to the freedom of their own will, they would probably have avoided the Samaritan territory altogether, and, like the rest of their countrymen, taken a roundabout way to Jerusalem by cross-ing to the eastward of the Jordan. Between persons so affected towards each other offences are sure to arise. When Guelph and Ghibeline, Orangemen and Ribbonmen, Cavalier and Roundhead meet, it does not take much to make a quarrel.

But there was something more at work in the minds of the two disciples than party passion. There was *conscience* in their quarrel as well as temper and hereditary enmities. This is evident, both from the deliberate manner in which they made their proposal to Jesus, and from the reason by which they sought to justify it. They came to their Master, and said, "Wilt Thou that we command fire to come down from heaven, and consume them?" entertaining no doubt appar-ently of obtaining His approval, and of procuring forthwith the requisite fire from heaven for the execution of their dire intent. Then they quoted the precedent of Elijah, who, refusing to have any dealings with the idolatrous king of Samaria, called down fire from heaven to consume his messengers, as a signal mark of divine displeasure.[1] The conscious motive by which they were actuated was evidently sincere, though ill-informed, jealousy for the honor of their Lord. As the prophet of fire was indignant at the conduct of King Ahaziah in sending messengers to the god of Ekron, Baalzebub by name, to inquire whether he should recover

---

[1] The words ὡς καὶ Ἠλίας ἐποίησε are a doubtful reading. It is evident, however, that the two disciples must have had Elias in *mind* when they made their proposal.

from the disease with which he was afflicted;[1] so the sons of thunder were indignant because inhabitants of the same godless territory over which Ahaziah ruled had presumed to insult their revered Master by refusing a favor which they ought to have been only too proud to have an opportunity of granting.

The two brothers thought they did well to be angry; and, if they had been minded to defend their conduct after it was condemned by Jesus, which they do not seem to have been, they might have made a defence by no means destitute of plausibility. For consider who these Samaritans were. They belonged to a mongrel race, sprung from heathen Assyrians, whose presence in the land was a humiliation, and from base, degenerate Israelites unworthy of the name. Their forefathers had been the bitter enemies of Judah in the days of Nehemiah, spitefully obstructing the building of Zion's walls, instead of helping the exiles in their hour of need, as neighbors ought to have done. Then, if it was unfair to hold the present generation responsible for the sins of past generations, what was the character of the Samaritans then living? Were they not blasphemous heretics, who rejected all the Old Testament Scriptures save the five books of Moses? Did they not worship at the site of the rival temple on Gerizim,[2] which their fathers had with impious effrontery erected in contempt of the true temple of God in the holy city? And finally, had not these villagers expressed their sympathy with all the iniquities of their people, and repeated them all in one act by doing dishonor to Him who was greater than even the true temple, and worthy not only to receive common civility, but even divine worship?

Ruthless persecutors and furious zealots, furnished with such plausible pleas, have always been confident, like the two disciples, that they did God service. It is of the very nature of zealotry to make the man of whom it has taken possession believe that the Almighty not only approves, but shares his fierce passions, and fancy himself intrusted with a *carte blanche* to launch the thunders of the Most High against all

---

[1] 2 Kings i.
[2] The temple was destroyed a hundred years before Christ by Hyrcanus the high priest. — JOSEPH. *Antiq. Jud.* xiii. 9. 1.

in whom his small, peering, inhuman eye can discern aught
not approved by his tyrannic conscience.   What a world
were this if the fact were so indeed !

> " Every pelting, petty officer
> Would use God's heaven for thunder ; nothing but thunder."

Thank God the fact is not so !   The Almighty does thunder
sometimes, but not in the way His petty officers would wish.

> " Merciful Heaven!
> Thou rather, with Thy sharp and sulphurous bolt,
> Splitt'st the unwedgeable and gnarled oak
> Than the soft myrtle."

Jesus too, all gentle as He was, had His thunderbolts ; but
He reserved them for other objects than poor, benighted,
prejudiced Samaritans.   His zeal was directed against great
sins, and powerful, privileged, presumptuous sinners ; not
against little sins, or poor, obscure, vulgar sinners.   He
burst into indignation at the sight of His Father's house
turned into a den of thieves by those who ought to have
known, and did know better ; He only felt compassion for
those who, like the woman by the well, knew not what they
worshipped, and groped after God in semi-heathen darkness.
His spirit was kindled within Him at the spectacle of ostentatious orthodoxy and piety allied to the grossest worldliness ;
He did not, like the Pharisee, blaze up in sanctimonious wrath
against irreligious publicans, who might do no worship at all,
or who, like the heretical Samaritans, did not worship in the
right place.   Would that zeal like that of Jesus, aiming its
bolts at the proud oak and sparing the humble shrub, were
more common ! But such zeal is dangerous, and therefore it
will always be rare.

The Master, in whose vindication the two disciples wished
to call down heaven's destroying fire, lost no time in making
known His utter want of sympathy with the monstrous
proposal.   He turned and rebuked them.   According to the
old English version, He said, " Ye know not what manner
of spirit ye are of." [1]   It is a doubtful reading, and as such is
omitted in our Revised Version, but it is a true saying.

[1] Luke ix. 55.

The saying was true in more senses than one. The spirit of James and John was, in the first place, not such as they fancied. They thought themselves actuated by zeal for the glory of their Lord, and so they were in part. But the flame of their zeal was not pure : it was mixed up with the bitter smoke of carnal passions, anger, pride, self-will. Then, again, their spirit was not such as became the apostles of the gospel, the heralds of a new era of grace. They were chosen to preach a message of mercy to every creature, even to the chief of sinners ; to tell of a love that suffered not itself to be overcome of evil, but sought to overcome evil with good; to found a kingdom composed of citizens from every nation, wherein should be neither Jew nor Samaritan, but Christ all and in all. What a work to be achieved by men filled with the fire-breathing spirit of the "sons of thunder" ! Obviously a great change must be wrought within them to fit them for the high vocation wherewith they have been called. Yet again, the spirit of James and John was, of course, not that of their Master. He "came not to destroy men's lives, but to save them."[1] To see the difference between the mind of the disciples and that of Jesus, put this scene side by side with that other which happened on Samaritan ground — the meeting by the well. We know what we have seen here : what see we there ? The Son of man, as a Jew, speaking to and having dealings with a Samaritan, so seeking to abolish inveterate and deep-seated enmities between man and man ; as the Friend of sinners seeking to restore a poor, erring, guilty creature to God and holiness ; as the Christ announcing the close of an old time, in which the worship even of the true God was ritualistic, exclusive, and local, and the advent of a new religious era characterized by the attributes of spirituality, universality, and catholicity. And we see Jesus rejoicing, enthusiastic in His work ; deeming it His very meat and drink to reveal to men one God and Father, one Saviour, one life, for all without distinction ; to regenerate individual character, society, and religion ; to break down all barriers separating man from God and from his fellow-men, and so to become the great Reconciler and Peacemaker.

---

[1] The words quoted are regarded by critics as a gloss ; but, like those referred to in the previous note, they are true and appropriate.

Thinking of this work as exhibited by sample in the conversion of the woman by the well, He speaks to His surprised and unsympathetic disciples as one who perceives on the eastern horizon the first faint streaks of light heralding the advent of a new glorious day, and all around, in the field of the world, yellow crops of grain ripe for the sickle. " It is coming on apace," He says in effect, "the blessed, long-expected era, after a long night of spiritual darkness ; the new world is about to begin : lift up your eyes and look on the fields of Gentile lands, and see how they be white already for the harvest ! "

At the time of the meeting by the well, the disciples who were with Jesus neither understood nor sympathized with His high thoughts and hopes. The bright prospect on which His eyes were riveted was not within their horizon. For them, as for children, the world was still small, a narrow valley bounded by hills on either side ; while their Master, up on the mountain-top, saw many valleys beyond, in which He was interested, and out of which He believed many souls would find their way into the eternal kingdom.[1] For the disciples God was yet the God of the Jews only ; salvation was *for* the Jews as well as *of* them : they knew of only one channel of grace — Jewish ordinances ; only one way to heaven — that which lay through Jerusalem.

At the later date to which the present scene belongs, the disciples, instead of progressing, seem to have retrograded. Old bad feelings seem to be intensified, instead of being replaced by new and better ones.   They are now not merely out of sympathy with, but in direct antagonism to, their Lord's mind ; not merely apathetic or sceptical about the salvation of Samaritans, but bent on their destruction. Aversion and prejudice have grown into a paroxysm of enmity.

Yes, even so ; things must get to the worst before they begin to mend.   There will be no improvement till the Lamb shall have been slain to take away sin, to abolish enmities, and to make of twain one new man.   It is the knowledge of that which makes Jesus set His face so steadfastly towards Jerusalem.   He is eager to drink the cup of suffering, and to be baptized with the baptism of blood, because He knows

[1] This thought was suggested by a passage in Richter's *Flegeljahre*.

that only thereby can He finish the work whereof He spoke in such glowing language on the earlier occasion to His disciples. The very wrath of His devoted followers against the Samaritan villagers makes Him quicken His pace on His crossward way, saying to Himself sadly as He advances, " Let me hasten on, for not till I am lifted up can these things end."

16

IN PEREA:
or, the Doctrine of Self-Sacrifice

SECTION I — COUNSELS OF PERFECTION

Matt. 19; 1-26; Mark 10:1-27; Luke 18:15-27

AFTER His final departure from Galilee, Jesus found for Himself a new place of abode and scene of labor for the brief remainder of His life, in the region lying to the eastward of the Jordan, at the lower end of its course. "He departed from Galilee, and came into the borders of Judæa beyond Jordan."[1] We may say that He ended His ministry where it began, healing the sick, and teaching the high doctrines of the kingdom in the place which witnessed His consecration by baptism to His sacred work, and where He gained His first disciples.[2]

This visit of Jesus to Peræa towards the close of His career is a fact most interesting and significant in itself, apart altogether from its accompanying incidents. It was evidently so regarded by John, who not less carefully than the two first evangelists records the fact of the visit, though, unlike them, he gives no details concerning it. The terms in which he alludes to this event are peculiar. Having briefly explained how Jesus had provoked the ill-will of the Jews in Jerusalem at the feast of dedication, he goes on to say: "Therefore they sought again to take Him; but He escaped out of their hands, and went away *again* beyond Jordan, into the place *where John at first baptized.*"[3] The word "again," and the reference to the Baptist, are indicative of reflection and recollection — windows letting us see into John's heart. He is thinking with emotion of his personal experiences connected with the first visit of Jesus to those sacred regions, of his

---

[1] Matt. xix. 1.   [2] See ch. i.   [3] John x. 40.

first meeting with his beloved Master, and of the mystic name given to Him by the Baptist, "the Lamb of God" then uncomprehended by the disciples, now on the eve of being expounded by events; and to the evangelist writing his Gospel, clear as day in the bright light of the cross.

It was hardly possible that the disciple whom Jesus loved could do other than think of the first visit when speaking of the second. Even the multitude, as he records, reverted mentally to the earlier occasion while following Jesus in the later. They remembered what John, His forerunner, had said of One among them whom they knew not, and who yet was far greater than himself; and they remarked that his statements, however improbable they might have appeared at the time, had been verified by events, and he himself proved to be a true prophet by Christ's miracles, if not by his own. "John," said they to each other, "did no miracle; but all things that John said of this man were true."[1]

If John the disciple, and even the common people, thought of the first visit of Jesus to Peræa at the time of His second, we may be sure that Jesus Himself did so also. He had His own reasons, doubt it not, for going back to that hallowed neighborhood. His journey to the Jordan, we believe, was a pilgrimage to holy ground, on which He could not set His foot without profound emotion. For there lay His Bethel, where He had made a solemn baptismal vow, not, as Jacob, to give a tithe of His substance, but to give Himself, body and soul, a sacrifice to His Father, in life and in death; there the Spirit had descended on Him like a dove; there He had heard a celestial voice of approval and encouragement, the reward of His entire self-surrender to His Father's holy will. All the recollections of the place were heart-stirring, recalling solemn obligations, inspiring holy hopes, urging Him on to the grand consummation of His life-work; charging Him by His baptism, His vows, the descent of the Spirit, and the voice from heaven, to crown His labors of love, by drinking of the cup of suffering and death for man's redemption. To these voices of the past He willingly opened His ear. He wished to hear them, that by their hallowed tones His spirit might be braced and solemnized for the coming agony.

[1] John x. 41.

While retiring to Peræa for these private reasons, that He might muse on the past and the future, and link sacred memories to solemn anticipations, Jesus did not by any means live there a life of seclusion and solitary meditation. On the contrary, during His sojourn in that neighborhood, He was unusually busy healing the sick, teaching the multitude "as He was wont" (so Mark states, with a mental reference to the past ministry in Galilee), answering inquiries, receiving visits, granting favors. "Many resorted unto Him" there on various errands. Pharisees came, asking entangling questions about marriage and divorce, hoping to catch Him in a trap, and commit Him to the expression of an opinion which would make Him unpopular with some party or school, Hillel's or Shammai's,[1] it did not matter which. A young ruler came with more honorable intent, to inquire how he might obtain eternal life. Mothers came with their little ones, beseeching for them His blessing, thinking it worth getting, and not fearing denial; and messengers came with sorrowful tidings from friends, who looked to Him as their comfort in the time of trouble.[2]

Though busily occupied among the thronging crowd, Jesus contrived to have some leisure hours with His chosen disciples, during which He taught them some new lessons on the doctrine of the divine kingdom. The subject of these lessons was sacrifice for the sake of the kingdom — a theme congenial to the place, the time, the situation, and the mood of the Teacher. The external occasion suggesting that topic was supplied by the interviews Jesus had had with the Pharisees and the young ruler. These interviews naturally led Him to speak to His disciples on the subject of self-sacrifice under two special forms, — abstinence from marriage and renunciation of property, — though He did not confine His discourse to these points, but went on to set forth the rewards of self-sacrifice in any form, and the spirit in which all sacrifices must be performed, in order to possess value in God's sight.

The Pharisees, we read, "came unto Him, tempting Him,

---

[1] The question of divorce was a subject of dispute between these two schools, the loose and the strict schools of morals respectively.

[2] John xi.

and saying, Is it lawful for a man to put away his wife for every cause?" To this question Jesus replied, by laying down the primitive principle, that divorce was justified only by conjugal infidelity, and by explaining, that any thing to the contrary in the law of Moses was simply an accommodation to the hardness of men's hearts. The disciples heard this reply, and they made their own remarks on it. They said to Jesus: "If the case of the man be so with his wife, it is not good to marry." The view enunciated by their Master, which took no account of incompatibility of temper, involuntary dislike, uncongeniality of habits, differences in religion, quarrels among relatives, as pleas for separation, seemed very stringent even to them ; and they thought that a man would do well to consider what he was about before committing himself to a life-long engagement with such possibilities before him, and to ask himself whether it would not be better, on the whole, to steer clear of such a sea of troubles, by abstaining from wedlock altogether.

The *impromptu* remark of the disciples, viewed in connection with its probable motives, was not a very wise one ; yet it is to be observed that Jesus did not absolutely disapprove of it. He spoke as if He rather sympathized with the feeling in favor of celibacy, — as if to abstain from marriage were the better and wiser way, and only not to be required of men because for the majority it was impracticable. "But he said unto them, All men cannot receive this saying, save they to whom it is given." Then going on to enumerate the cases in which, from any cause, men remained unmarried, He spoke with apparent approbation of some who voluntarily, and from high and holy motives, denied themselves the comfort of family relationships : "There be eunuchs which have made themselves eunuchs for the kingdom of heaven's sake." Such, He finally gave His disciples to understand, were to be imitated by all who felt called and able to do so. "He that is able to receive (this high virtue), let him receive it," He said ; hinting that, while many men could not receive it, but could more easily endure all possible drawbacks of married life, even on the strictest views of conjugal obligation, than preserve perfect chastity in an unmarried state, it was well for him who could make himself a eunuch for the kingdom of heaven, as he would not only escape much trouble, but be free from carefulness, and be able to serve the kingdom without distraction.

The other form of self-sacrifice — the renunciation of property — became the subject of remark between Jesus and His disciples, in consequence of the interview with the young man who came inquiring about eternal life. Jesus, reading the heart of this anxious inquirer, and perceiving that he loved this world's goods more than was consistent with spiritual freedom and entire singleness of mind, had concluded His directions to him by giving this counsel : " If thou wilt be perfect, go and sell that thou hast, and give to the poor, and then thou shalt have treasure in heaven : and come, and follow me." The young man having thereon turned away sorrowful, because, though desiring eternal life, he was unwilling to obtain it at such a price, Jesus proceeded to make his case a subject of reflection for the instruction of the twelve. In the observations He made He did not expressly say that to part with property was necessary to salvation, but He did speak in a manner which seemed to the disciples almost to imply that. Looking round about, He remarked to them first, " How hardly shall they that have riches enter into the kingdom of God ! " The disciples being astonished at this hard saying, He softened it somewhat by altering slightly the form of expression. " Children," he said, " how hard is it for them that trust in riches to enter into the kingdom of God ! " [1] hinting that the thing to be renounced in order to salvation was not money, but the inordinate love of it. But then He added a third reflection, which, by its austerity, more than cancelled the mildness of the second. " It is easier," He declared, "for a camel to go through the eye of a needle, than for a rich man to enter into the kingdom of God." That assertion, literally interpreted, amounts to a declaration that the salvation of a rich

---

[1] Mark x. 24. The reading here, however, is doubtful ; some copies giving a reading to this effect : " How hard it is to enter into the kingdom of God " ($\pi\hat{\omega}\varsigma$ $\delta\acute{\upsilon}\sigma\kappa o\lambda\acute{o}\nu$ $\grave{\epsilon}\sigma\tau\iota\nu$ $\epsilon\grave{\iota}\varsigma$ $\tau\grave{\eta}\nu$ $\beta\alpha\sigma\iota\lambda\acute{\epsilon}\acute{\iota}\alpha\nu$ $\tauο\hat{\upsilon}$ $\theta\epsilonο\hat{\upsilon}$ $\epsilon\grave{\iota}\sigma\epsilon\lambda\theta\epsilon\hat{\iota}\nu$). Alford regards this reading as a mistake of the copyist, due to similar ending of $\grave{\epsilon}\sigma\tau\iota\nu$ and $\chi\rho\acute{\eta}\mu\alpha\sigma\iota\nu$ (the words omitted being $\tauο\grave{\upsilon}\varsigma$ $\pi\epsilon\pi o\iota\theta\acute{o}\tau\alpha\varsigma$ $\grave{\epsilon}\pi\grave{\iota}$ $\chi\rho\acute{\eta}\mu\alpha\sigma\iota\nu$). The abbreviated reading is adopted by Tischendorf (8th ed.), and by Westcott and Hort in their valuable edition of the Greek Testament. The revisers adhere to the old text.

man is an impossibility, and seems to teach by plain impli-
cation, that the only way for a rich man to get into heaven
is to cease to be rich, and become poor by a voluntary
renunciation of property.   Such seems to have been the
impression made thereby on the minds of the disciples : for
we read that they were astonished above measure, and said
among themselves, "Who then can be saved?"[1]

It is an inquiry of vital moment what our Lord really
meant to teach on the subjects of marriage and money.   The
question concerns not merely the life to come, but the whole
character of our present life.   For if man's life on earth doth
not consist wholly in possessions and family relations, these
occupy a very prominent place therein.   Family relations are
essential to the existence of society, and without wealth there
could be no civilization.   Did Jesus, then, frown or look down
on these things, as at least unfavorable to, if not incompatible
with, the interests of the divine kingdom and the aspirations
of its citizens ?

This question up till the time of the Reformation was for the
most part answered by the visible church in the affirmative.
From a very early period the idea began to be entertained that
Jesus meant to teach the intrinsic superiority, in point of
Christian virtue, of a life of celibacy and voluntary poverty,
over that of a married man possessing property.   Abstinence
from marriage and renunciation of earthly possessions came,
in consequence, to be regarded as essential requisites for high
Christian attainments.   They were steps of the ladder by
which Christians rose to higher grades of grace than were
attainable by men involved in family cares and ties, and in
the entanglements of worldly substance.   They were not,
indeed, necessary to salvation, — to obtain, that is, a simple
admission into heaven, — but they were necessary to obtain
an abundant entrance.   They were trials of virtue appointed
to be undergone by candidates for honors in the city of God.
They were indispensable conditions of the higher degrees of
spiritual fruitfulness.   A married or rich Christian might
produce thirty-fold, but only those who denied themselves the
enjoyments of wealth and wedlock could bring forth sixty-
fold or an hundred-fold.   While, therefore, these virtues of

[1] Mark x. 23–27.

abstinence were not to be demanded of all, they were to be commended as "counsels of perfection" to such as, not con-tent to be commonplace Christians, would rise to the heroic pitch of excellence, and, despising a simple admission into the divine kingdom, wished to occupy first places there.

This style of thought is now so antiquated that it is hard to believe it ever prevailed. As a proof, however, that it is no invention of ours, take two brief extracts from a distinguished bishop and martyr of the third century, Cyprian of Carthage, which are samples of much of the same kind to be found in the early Fathers of the church. The one quotation proclaims the superior virtue of voluntary virginity in these terms : "Strait and narrow is the way which leads to life, hard and arduous is the path (*limes*, narrower still than the narrow way) which tends to glory. Along this path of the way go the martyrs, go virgins, go all the just. For the first (degree of fruitful-ness), the hundred-fold, is that of the martyrs ; the second, the sixty-fold, is yours (ye virgins)." [1] The second extract, while ascribing, like the first, superior merit to virginity, indicates the *optional* character of that high-class virtue. Referring to the words of Christ, " There be eunuchs which have made themselves eunuchs for the kingdom of heaven's sake," Cyprian says : "This the Lord commands not, but exhorts ; He imposes not the yoke of necessity, that the free choice of the will might remain. But whereas he says (John xiv. 2), that there are many mansions with His Father, He here points out the lodging quarters of the better mansion (*melioris habitaculi hospitia*). Seek ye, O virgins, those better mansions. Crucifying (*castrantes*) the desires of the flesh, obtain for yourselves the reward of greater grace in the celestial abodes." [2]

Similar views were entertained in those early ages respect-ing the meaning of Christ's words to the young man. The inevitable results of such interpretations in due course were monastic institutions and the celibacy of the clergy. The direct connection between an ascetic interpretation of the counsel given by Jesus to the rich youth who inquired after

[1] *De Disciplinâ et Habitu Virginum, sub finem* (Clark's Ante-Nicene Library, *Cyprian*, i. 333).
[2] *Ex eodem libro.*

eternal life, and the rise of monasticism, is apparent in the history of Antony, the father of the monastic system. It is related of him, that going into the church on one occasion when the Gospel concerning the rich young man was read before the assembly, he, then also young, took the words as addressed by Heaven to himself. Going out of the church, he forthwith proceeded to distribute to the inhabitants of his native village his large, fertile, and beautiful landed estates which he inherited from his fathers, reserving only a small portion of his property for the benefit of his sister. Not long after he gave away that also, and placed his sister to be educated with a society of pious virgins, and settling down near his paternal mansion, began a life of rigid asceticism.[1]

The ascetic theory of Christian virtue, which so soon began to prevail in the church, has been fully tested by time, and proved to be a huge and mischievous mistake. The verdict of history is conclusive, and to return to an exploded error, as some seem disposed to do, is utter folly. At this time of day, the views of those who would find the *beau-ideal* of Christian life in a monk's cell appear hardly worthy of serious refutation. It may, however, be useful briefly to indicate the leading errors of the monkish theory of morals ; all the more that, in doing this, we shall at the same time be explaining the true meaning of our Lord's words to His disciples.

This theory, then, is in the first place based on an erroneous assumption — viz., that abstinence from things lawful is intrinsically a higher sort of virtue than temperance in the use of them. This is not true. Abstinence is the virtue of the weak, temperance is the virtue of the strong. Abstinence is certainly the safer way for those who are prone to inordinate affection, but it purchases safety at the expense of moral culture ; for it removes us from those temptations connected with family relationships and earthly possessions, through which character, while it may be imperilled, is at the same time developed and strengthened. Abstinence is also inferior to temperance in healthiness of tone. It tends inevitably to morbidity, distortion, exaggeration. The ascetic virtues

---

[1] *Vita S. Antonii* (Athanasii). See also Neander, *Church History*, Clark's edition, ii. 308.

were wont to be called by their admirers *angelic*. They are certainly angelic in the negative sense of being unnatural and inhuman. Ascetic abstinence is the ghost or disembodied spirit of morality, while temperance is its soul, embodied in a genuine human life transacted amid earthly relations, occupations, and enjoyments. Abstinence is even inferior to temperance in respect to what seems its strong point — self-sacrifice. There is something morally sublime, doubtless, in the spectacle of a man of wealth, birth, high office, and happy domestic condition, leaving rank, riches, office, wife, children, behind, and going away to the deserts of Sinai and Egypt to spend his days as a monk or anchoret.[1] The stern resolution, the absolute mastery of the will over the natural affections, exhibited in such conduct, is very imposing. Yet how poor, after all, is such a character compared with Abraham, the father of the faithful, and model of temperance and singleness of mind; who could use the world, of which he had a large portion, without abusing it; who kept his wealth and state, and yet never became their slave, and was ready at God's command to part with his friends and his native land, and even with an only son! So to live, serving ourselves heir to all things, yet maintaining unimpaired our spiritual freedom; enjoying life, yet ready at the call of duty to sacrifice life's dearest enjoyments: this is true Christian virtue, the higher Christian life for those who would be perfect. Let us have many Abrahams so living among our men of wealth, and there is no fear of the church going back to the Middle Ages. Only when the rich, as a class, are luxurious, vain, selfish, and proud, is there a danger of the tenet gaining credence among the serious, that there is no possibility of living a truly Christian life except by parting with property altogether.

The ascetic theory is also founded on an error in the interpretation of Christ's sayings. These do not assert or necessarily imply any intrinsic superiority of celibacy and voluntary poverty over the conditions to which they are opposed. They only imply, that in certain circumstances the unmarried dispossessed state affords peculiar facilities for

---

[1] We have in view here Nilus of Constantinople. See Isaac Taylor's *Logic in Theology*, p. 130.

attending without distraction to the interests of the divine kingdom. This is certainly true. It is less easy sometimes to be single-minded in the service of Christ as a married person than as an unmarried, as a rich man than as a poor man. This is especially true in times of hardship and danger, when men must either not be on Christ's side at all, or be prepared to sacrifice all for His sake. The less one has to sacrifice in such a case, the easier it is for him to bear his cross and play the hero; and he may be pronounced happy at such a crisis who has no family to forsake and no worldly concerns to distract him. Personal character may suffer from such isolation: it may lose geniality, tenderness, and grace, and contract something of inhuman sternness; but the particular tasks required will be more likely to be thoroughly done. On this account, it may be said with truth that "the forlorn hope in battle, as well as in the cause of Christianity, must consist of men who have no domestic relations to divide their devotion, who will leave no wife nor children to mourn over their loss."[1] Yet this statement cannot be taken without qualification. For it is not impossible for married and wealthy Christians to take their place in the forlorn hope: many have done so, and those who do are the greatest heroes of all. The advantage is not necessarily and invariably on the side of those who are disengaged from all embarrassing relationships, *even in time of war;* and in times of peace it is all on the other side. Monks, like soldiers, are liable to frightful degeneracy and corruption when there are no great tasks for them to do. Men who in emergencies are capable, in consequence of their freedom from all domestic and secular embarrassments, of rising to an almost superhuman pitch of self-denial, may at other seasons sink to a depth of self-indulgence in sloth and sensuality which is rarely seen in those who enjoy the protecting influence of family ties and business engagements.[2]

But not to insist further on this, and conceding frankly all that can be said in favor of the unmarried and dispossessed state in connection with the service of the kingdom in certain

[1] Robertson of Brighton. Sermons, series iii.: *On Marriage and Celibacy.*
[2] For a dark picture of the corruption prevalent among the monastics in early ages, see Isaac Taylor's *Ancient Christianity.*

circumstances, what we are concerned to maintain is, that nowhere in the Gospel do we find the doctrine taught that such a state is in itself and essentially virtuous. It is absurd to say, as Renan does,[1] that the monk is in a sense the only true Christian. The natural type of the Christian is not the monk, but the soldier, both of whom are often placed in the same position in relation to marriage and property ties, but for altogether different reasons. The watchword of Christian ethics is not *devoteeism*, but *devotion*. Consuming devotion to the kingdom is the one cardinal virtue required of all citizens, and every stern word enjoining self-sacrifice is to be interpreted in relation thereto. " Let the dead bury their dead;" "No man having put his hand to the plough, and looking back, is fit for the kingdom of God;" " If any man hate not father and mother, he cannot be my disciple;" " Sell all that thou hast, and come follow me" — these and many other sayings of kindred import all mean one thing: the kingdom first, every thing else second, and when the interest of the holy state demands it, military promptitude in leaving all and repairing to the standards. Essentially the same idea is the key to the meaning of a difficult parable spoken to "the apostles," and recorded in Luke's Gospel, which we may call the parable of *extra service*.[2] The thought intended is that the service of the kingdom is very exacting, involving not only hard toil in the field through the day, but extra duties in the evening when the weary laborer would gladly rest, having no fixed hours of labor, eight, ten, or twelve, but claiming the right to summon to work at any hour of all the twenty-four, as in the case of soldiers in time of war, or of farm-laborers in time of harvest. And the extra service, or overtime duty, is not monkish asceticism, but extraordinary demands in unusual emergencies, calling men weary from age or from over-exertion to still further efforts and sacrifices.

The theory under consideration is guilty, in the third place, of an error in logic. On the assumption that abstinence is necessarily and intrinsically a higher virtue than temperance, it is illogical to speak of it as optional. In that case, our Lord should have given not counsels, but

[1] *Vie de Jésus*, p. 328.   [2] Luke xvii. 7–10.

commands. For no man is at liberty to choose whether he shall be a good Christian or an indifferent one, or is excused from practising certain virtues merely because they are difficult. It is absolutely incumbent on all to press on towards perfection ; and if celibacy and poverty be necessary to perfection, then all who profess godliness should renounce wedlock and property. The church of Rome, consistently with her theory of morals, forbids her priests to marry. But why stop there? Surely what is good for priests is good for people as well.

The reason why the prohibition is not carried further, is of course that the laws of nature and the requirements of society render it impracticable. And this brings us to the last objection to the ascetic theory, viz. that, consistently carried out, it lands in absurdity, by involving the destruction of society and the human race. A theory which involves such consequences cannot be true. For the kingdom of grace and the kingdom of nature are not mutually destructive. One God is the sovereign of both ; and all things belonging to the lower kingdom — every relation of life, every faculty, passion, and appetite of our nature, all material possessions — are capable of being made subservient to the interests of the higher kingdom, and of contributing to our growth in grace and holiness.

The grand practical difficulty is to give the kingdom of God and His righteousness their due place of supremacy, and to keep all other things in strict subordination. The object of those hard sayings uttered by Jesus in Peræa was to fix the attention of the disciples and of all on that difficulty. He spoke so strongly, that men compassed by the cares of family and the comforts of wealth might duly lay to heart their danger ; and, conscious of their own helplessness, might seek grace from God, to do that which, though difficult, is not impossible, viz. while married, to be as if unmarried, caring for the things of the Lord ; and while rich, to be humble in mind, free in spirit, and devoted in heart to the service of Christ.

One word may here aptly be said on the beautiful incident of the little children brought to Jesus to get His blessing. Who can believe that it was His intention to teach a monkish theory of morals after reading that story? How opportunely those mothers came to Him seeking a blessing for their little ones, just after He had uttered words which might be interpreted, and were actually interpreted in after ages, as a disparagement of family relations. Their visit gave Him an opportunity of entering His protest by anticipation against such a misconstruction of His teaching. And the officious interference of the twelve to keep away the mothers and their offspring from their Master's person only made that protest all the more emphatic. The disciples seem to have taken from the words Jesus had just spoken concerning abstaining from marriage for the sake of the kingdom, the very impression out of which monasticism sprang. "What does He care," thought they, "for you mothers and your children? His whole thoughts are of the kingdom of heaven, where they neither marry nor are given in marriage: go away, and don't trouble Him at this time." The Lord did not thank His disciples for thus guarding His person from intrusion like a band of over-zealous policemen. "He was much displeased, and said unto them, Suffer the little children to come unto me, and forbid them not: for of such is the kingdom of God." [1]

SECTION II — THE REWARDS OF SELF-SACRIFICE

MATT. xix. 27-30; MARK x. 28-31; LUKE xviii. 28-30

The remarks of Jesus on the temptations of riches, which seemed so discouraging to the other disciples, had a different effect on the mind of Peter. They led him to think with self-complacency of the contrast presented by the conduct of himself and his brethren to that of the youth who came inquiring after eternal life. "We," thought he to himself, have done what the young man could not do, — what, according to the statement just made by the Master, rich men find very hard to do; we have left all to follow Jesus. Surely an act so difficult and so rare must be very meritorious." With his characteristic frankness, as he thought so he spoke. "Behold," said he with a touch of brag in his tone and

[1] Mark x. 14. For an admirable defence of the anti-ascetic interpretation of Christ's words to the young rich man, see the tract of Clement of Alexandria, *Quis dives salvetur*.

manner, "we have forsaken all, and followed Thee : what shall we have therefore ?"

To this question of Peter, Jesus returned a reply full at once of encouragement and of warning for the twelve, and for all who profess to be servants of God. First, with reference to the subject-matter of Peter's inquiry, He set forth in glowing language the great rewards in store for him and his brethren ; and not for them only, but for all who made sacrifices for the kingdom. Then, with reference to the self-complacent or calculating spirit which, in part at least, had prompted the inquiry, He added a moral reflection, with an illustrative parable appended, conveying the idea that rewards in the kingdom of God were not determined merely by the fact, or even by the amount, of sacrifice. Many that were first in these respects might be last in real merit, for lack of another element which formed an essential ingredient in the calculation, viz. *right motive ;* while others who were last in these respects might be first in recompense in virtue of the spirit by which they were animated. We shall consider these two parts of the reply in succession. Our present theme is the *rewards of self-sacrifice in the divine kingdom.*

The first thing which strikes one in reference to these rewards, is the utter disproportion between them and the sacrifices made. The twelve had forsaken fishing-boats and nets, and they were to be rewarded with thrones ; and every one that forsakes any thing for the kingdom, no matter what it .may be, is promised an hundred-fold in return, in this present life, of the very thing he has renounced, and in the world to come life everlasting.

These promises strikingly illustrate the generosity of the Master whom Christians serve. How easy it would have been for Jesus to depreciate the sacrifices of His followers, and even to turn their glory into ridicule ! "You have forsaken all ! What was your all worth, pray ? If the rich young man had parted with his possessions as I counselled, he might have had something to boast of ; but as for you poor fishermen, any sacrifices you have made are hardly deserving of mention." But such words could not have been uttered by Christ's lips. It was never His way to despise things small in outward bulk, or to disparage services rendered to Himself, as if with a view to diminish His own obligations. He rather loved to make Himself a debtor to His servants, by generously exaggerating the value of their good deeds, and promising to them, as their *fit* recompense, rewards immeasurably exceeding their claims. So He acted in the present instance. Though the "all" of the disciples was a very little one, He still remembered that it was their all; and with impassioned earnestness, with a "verily" full of tender, grateful feeling, He promised them thrones as if they had been fairly earned!

These great and precious promises, if believed, would make sacrifices easy. Who would not part with a fishing-boat for a throne? and what merchant would stick at an investment which would bring a return, not of five per cent., or even of a hundred per cent., but of a hundred to one?

The promises made by Jesus have one other excellent effect when duly considered. They tend to humble. Their very magnitude has a sobering effect on the mind. Not even the vainest can pretend that their good deeds deserve to be rewarded with thrones, and their sacrifices to be recompensed an hundred-fold. At this rate, all must be content to be debtors to God's grace, and all talk of merit is out of the question. That is one reason why the rewards of the kingdom of heaven are so great. God bestows His gifts so as at once to glorify the Giver and to humble the receiver.

Thus far of the rewards in general. Looking now more narrowly at those specially made to the twelve, we remark that on the surface they seem fitted to awaken or foster false expectation. Whatever they meant in reality, there can be little doubt as to the meaning the disciples would put on them at the time. The "regeneration" and the "thrones" of which their Master spake would bring before their imagination the picture of a kingdom of Israel restored, — regenerated in the sense in which men speak of a regenerated Italy, — the yoke of foreign domination thrown off; alienated tribes reconciled and re-united under the rule of Jesus, proclaimed by popular enthusiasm their hero King; and themselves, the men who had first believed in His royal pretensions and shared His early fortunes, rewarded for their fidelity by being made provincial governors, each ruling over a separate tribe. These romantic ideas were never to be realized: and we naturally ask why Jesus, knowing that, expressed Himself in language fitted to encourage such baseless fancies? The answer is, that He could not accomplish the end He designed, which was to inspire His disciples with hope, without expressing His promise in terms which involved the risk of illusion. Language so chosen as to obviate all possibility of misconception would have had no inspiring influence whatever. The promise, to have any charm, must be like a rainbow, bright in its hues, and solid and substantial in its appearance. This remark applies not only to the particular promise now under consideration, but more or less to all God's promises in Scripture or in nature. In order to stimulate, they must to a certain extent deceive us, by promising that which, as we conceive it, and cannot at the time help conceiving it, will never be realized.[1] The rainbow is painted in such colors as to draw us, children as we are, irresistibly on ; and then, having served that end, it fades away. When this happens, we are ready to exclaim, " O Lord, Thou hast deceived me ! " but we ultimately find that we are not cheated out of the blessing, though it comes in a different form from what we expected. God's promises are never delusive, though they may be illusive. Such was the experience of the twelve in connection with the dazzling promise of thrones. They did not get what they expected; but they got something analogous, something which to their mature spiritual judgment appeared far greater and more satisfying than that on which they had first set their hearts.[2]

What, then, was this Something? A real glory, honor, and power in the kingdom of God, conferred on the twelve as the reward of their self-sacrifice, partially in this life, perfectly in the life to come. In so far as the promise referred to this present life, it was shown by the event to signify the judicial legislative influence of the companions of Jesus as apostles and founders of the Christian church. The twelve,

[1] See a striking sermon on this point by Rev. F. W. Robertson, in third series of his Sermons. Subject — *The Illusiveness of Life.*

[2] The question, What was Christ's doctrine concerning the kingdom in its future final form, is one of the most difficult in the whole range of gospel studies. Some have maintained that that doctrine was ambiguous, not self-consistent, variable ; now apocalyptic and sensuous, now ideal and spiritual. Pfleiderer says that the kingdom, as Christ set it forth, was both spiritual-inward and sensuous-outward, purely human and religious and Judaico-theocratic. We cannot go critically into the matter here.

as the first preachers of the gospel trained by the Lord for that end, occupied a position in the church that could be filled by none that came after them. The keys of the kingdom of heaven were put into their hands. They were the foundation-stones on which the walls of the church were built. They sat, so to speak, on episcopal thrones, judging, guiding, ruling the twelve tribes of the true Israel of God, the holy commonwealth embracing all who professed faith in Christ. Such a sovereign influence the twelve apostles exerted in their lifetime; yea, they continue to exert it still. Their word not only was, but still is, law; their example has ever been regarded as binding on all ages. From their epistles, as the inspired expositions of their Master's pregnant sayings, the church has derived the system of doctrine embraced in her creed. All that remains of their writings forms part of the sacred canon, and all their recorded words are accounted by believers "words of God." Surely here is power and authority nothing short of regal! The reality of sovereignty is here, though the trappings of royalty, which strike the vulgar eye, are wanting. The apostles of Jesus were princes indeed, though they wore no princely robes; and they were destined to exercise a more extensive sway than ever fell to the lot of any monarch of Israel, not to speak of governors of single tribes.

The promise to the twelve had doubtless a reference to their position in the church in heaven as well as in the church on earth. What they will be in the eternal kingdom we know not, any more than we know what we ourselves shall be, our notions of heaven altogether being very hazy. We believe, however, on the ground of clear Scripture statements, that men will not be on a dead level in heaven any more than on earth. Radicalism is not the law of the supernal commonwealth, even as it is not the law in any well-ordered society in this world. The kingdom of glory will be but the kingdom of grace perfected, the regeneration begun here brought to its final and complete development. But the regeneration, in its imperfect state, is an attempt to organize men into a society based on the possession of spiritual life, all being included in the kingdom who are new creatures in Christ Jesus, and the highest place being assigned to those who have attained the highest stature as spiritual men. This ideal has never been more than approximately realized. The "visible" church, the product of the attempt to realize it, is, and ever has been, a most disappointing embodiment, in outward visible shape, of the ideal city of God. Ambition, selfishness, worldly wisdom, courtly arts, have too often procured thrones for false apostles, who never forsook any thing for Christ. Therefore we still look forward and upward with longing eyes for the true city of God, which shall as far exceed our loftiest conceptions as the visible church comes short of them. In that ideal commonwealth perfect moral order will prevail. Every man shall be in his own true place there; no vile men shall be in high places, no noble souls shall be doomed to obstruction, obscurity, and neglect ; but the noblest will be the highest and first, even though now they be the lowest and last. "There shall be true glory, where no one shall be praised by mistake or in flattery ; true honor, which shall be denied to no one worthy, granted to no one unworthy ; nor shall any unworthy one ambitiously seek it, where none but the worthy are permitted to be." [1]

Among the noblest in the supernal commonwealth will be the twelve men who cast in their lot with the Son of man, and were His companions in His wanderings and temptations. There will probably be many in heaven greater than they in intellect and otherwise ; but the greatest will most readily concede to them the place of honor as the first to believe in Jesus, the personal friends of the Man of Sorrow, and the chosen vessels who carried His name to the nations, and in a sense opened the kingdom of heaven to all who believe.[2]

Such we conceive to be the import of the promise made to the apostles, as leaders of the white-robed band of martyrs and confessors who suffer for Christ's sake. We have next to notice the general promise made to all the faithful indiscriminately. "There is no man," so it runs in Mark, "that hath left house, or brethren, or sisters, or father, or mother, or wife, or children, or lands, for my sake and the gospel's,

---

[1] Augustini *de Civitate Dei*, xxii. 30.

[2] The superior rank of the twelve in the eternal kingdom is recognized in the Book of Revelation, chap. xxi. 14 : "The walls of the city had twelve foundations, and in them the names of the twelve apostles of the Lamb."

but he shall receive an hundred-fold now in this time, houses, and brethren, and sisters, and mothers, and children, and lands, with persecutions ; and in the world to come eternal life."

This promise also, like the special one to the twelve, has a twofold reference. Godliness is represented as profitable for both worlds. In the world to come the men who make sacrifices for Christ will receive eternal life ; in the present they shall receive, along with persecutions, an hundred-fold of the very things which have been sacrificed. As to the former of these, eternal life, it is to be understood as the minimum reward in the great Hereafter. All the faithful will get that at least. What a *maximum* is that *minimum !* How blessed to be assured on the word of Christ that there is such a thing as eternal life *attainable* on any terms ! We may well play the man for truth and conscience, and fight the good fight of faith, when, by so doing, it is possible for us to gain such a prize. "A hope so great and so divine may trials well endure." To win the crown of an imperishable life of bliss, we should not deem it an unreasonable demand on the Lord's part that we be faithful even unto death. Life sacrificed on these terms is but a river emptying itself into the ocean, or the morning star losing itself in the perfect light of day. Would that we could lay hold firmly of the blessed hope set before us here, and through its magic influence become transformed into moral heroes ! We in these days have but a faint belief in the life to come. Our eyes are dim, and we cannot see the land that is afar off. Some of us have become so philosophical as to imagine we can do without the future reward promised by Jesus, and play the hero on atheistical principles. That remains to be seen. The annals of the martyrs tell us what men have been able to achieve who earnestly believed in the life everlasting. Up to this date we have not heard of any great heroisms enacted or sacrifices made by *unbelievers.* The martyrology of scepticism has not yet been written.[1]

[1] Some have referred to Buddhism as a system which produces moral heroism without an eternal hope for motive. But Buddhism has an eternal hope. *Nirvana*, even if it mean annihilation, was as much an object of hope to Buddha as heaven and everlasting life is to a Christian. The dogma of transmigration had made continued life such a horror, that extinction appeared a boon. Further, *Nirvana* is not, like annihilation to the materialist, a matter of physical necessity irrespective of character : it is the high reward of virtue.

That part of Christ's promise which respects hereafter must be taken on trust ; but the other part, which concerns the present life, admits of being tested by observation. The question, therefore, may competently be put : Is it true, as matter of fact, that sacrifices are recompensed by an hundredfold — that is, a manifold [1] — return in kind in this world ? To this question we may reply, *first,* that the promise will be found to hold good with the regularity of a law, if we do not confine our view to the *individual* life, but include successive generations. When providence has had time to work out its results, the meek do, at least by their heirs and representatives, inherit the earth, and delight themselves in the abundance of peace. The persecuted cause at length conquers the world's homage, and receives from it such rewards as it can bestow. The words of the prophet are then fulfilled : " The children which thou shalt have, after thou hast lost the other (by persecutor's hands), shall say again in thine ears, The place is too strait for me : give place to me that I may dwell." [2] And again : " Lift up thine eyes round about, and see ; all they gather themselves together, they come to thee : thy sons shall come from far, and thy daughters shall be nursed at thy side. Then thou shalt see, and flow together, and thine heart shall throb and swell ; because the abundance of the sea shall be converted unto thee, the wealth of the Gentiles shall come unto thee. Thou shalt also suck the milk of the Gentiles, and shalt suck the breast of kings. For brass I will bring gold, and for iron I will bring silver, and for wood brass, and for stones iron." [3] These prophetic promises, extravagant though they seem, have been fulfilled again and again in the history of the church : in the early ages, under Constantine, after the fires of persecution kindled by pagan zeal for hoary superstitions and idolatries had finally died out ; [4] in Protestant Britain, once famous for men who were ready to lose all, and who did actually lose much, for Christ's sake, now mistress of the seas, and heiress of the

---

[1] πολλαπλασίονα, Luke xviii. 30.
[2] Isa. xlix. 20.
[3] Isa. lx. 4, 5, 16, 17.
[4] See sermon of Paulinus of Tyre at the consecration of his church, rebuilt, like many others, after the last persecution, the churches having been destroyed by the edict of Diocletian. Euseb. *Hist. Eccl.* x. 4.

wealth of all the world ; in the new world across the Atlantic, with its great, powerful, populous nation, rivalling England in wealth and strength, grown from a small band of Puritan exiles who loved religious liberty better than country, and sought refuge from despotism in the savage wildernesses of an unexplored continent.

Still it must be confessed that, taken strictly and literally, the promise of Christ does not hold good in every instance. Multitudes of God's servants have had what the world would account a miserable lot. Does the promise, then, simply and absolutely fail in their case ? No ; for, *secondly*, there are more ways than one in which it can be fulfilled. Blessings, for example, may be multiplied an hundred-fold without their external bulk being altered, simply by the act of renouncing them. Whatever is sacrificed for truth, whatever we are willing to part with for Christ's sake, becomes from that moment immeasurably increased in value. Fathers and mothers, and all earthly friends, become unspeakably dear to the heart when we have learned to say : " Christ is first, and these must be second." Isaac was worth an hundred sons to Abraham when he received him back from the dead. Or, to draw an illustration from another quarter, think of John Bunyan in jail brooding over his poor blind daughter, whom he left behind at home. "Poor child, thought I," thus ne describes his feelings in that inimitable book, *Grace Abounding*, "what sorrow art thou like to have for thy portion in this world ! Thou must be beaten, must beg, suffer hunger, cold, nakedness, and a thousand calamities, though I cannot now endure the wind should blow upon thee. But yet, thought I, I must venture you all with God, though it goeth to the quick to leave you. Oh ! I saw I was as a man who was pulling down his house upon the heads of his wife and children ; yet I thought on those two milch kine that were to carry the ark of God into another country, and to leave their calves behind them." If the faculty of enjoyment be, as it is, the measure of real possession, here was a case in which to forsake wife and child was to multiply them an hundred-fold, and in the multiplied value of the things renounced to find a rich solatium for sacrifice and persecutions. The soliloquy of the Bedford prisoner is the very poetry of natural affection.

What pathos is in that allusion to the milch kine! what a depth of tender feeling it reveals!   The power to feel so is the reward of self-sacrifice; the power to *love* so is the reward of "hating" our kindred for Christ's sake.   You shall find no such love among those who make natural affection an excuse for moral unfaithfulness, thinking it a sufficient apology for disloyalty to the interests of the divine kingdom to say, "I have a wife and family to care for."

Without undue spiritualizing, then, we see that a valid meaning can be assigned to the strong expression, "an hundred-fold."   And from the remarks just made, we see further why "persecutions" are thrown into the account, as if they were not drawbacks, but a part of the gain.   The truth is, the hundred-fold is realized, not in spite of persecutions, but to a great extent because of them.   Persecutions are the salt with which things sacrificed are salted, the condiment which enhances their relish.   Or, to put the matter arithmetically, persecutions are the factor by which earthly blessings given up to God are multiplied an hundred-fold, if not in quantity, at least in virtue.

Such are the rewards provided for those who make sacrifices for Christ's sake.   Their sacrifices are but a seed sown in tears, from which they afterwards reap a plentiful harvest in joy.   But what now of those who have made no sacrifices, who have received no wounds in battle?   If this has proceeded not from lack of will, but from lack of opportunity, they shall get a share of the rewards.   David's law has its place in the divine kingdom: "As his part is that goeth down to the battle, so shall his part be that tarrieth by the stuff: they shall part alike."   Only all must see to it that they remain not by the stuff from cowardice, or indolence and self-indulgence.   They who act thus, declining to put themselves to any trouble, to run any risk, or even so much as to part with a sinful lust for the kingdom of God, cannot expect to find a place therein at the last.

SECTION III — THE FIRST LAST, AND THE LAST FIRST

MATT. xix. 30, xx. 1-20; MARK x. 31

Having declared the rewards of self-sacrifice, Jesus proceeded to show the risk of forfeiture or partial loss arising
out of the indulgence of unworthy feelings, whether as
motives to self-denying acts, or as self-complacent reflections on such acts already performed. "But," He said in a
warning manner, as if with upraised finger, "many that are
first shall be last, and the last shall be first." Then, to
explain the profound remark, He uttered the parable preserved in Matthew's Gospel only, which follows immediately
after.

The explanation is in some respects more difficult than the
thing to be explained, and has given rise to much diverse
interpretation. And yet the main drift of this parable seems
clear enough. It is not, as some have supposed, designed to
teach that all will share alike in the eternal kingdom, which
is not only irrelevant to the connection of thought, but *untrue*.
Neither is the parable intended to proclaim the great
evangelic truth that salvation is of grace and not of merit,
though it may be very proper in preaching to take occasion
to discourse on that fundamental doctrine. The great outstanding thought set forth therein, as it seems to us, is this,
that in estimating the value of work, the divine Lord whom
all serve takes into account not merely quantity, but quality;
that is, the spirit in which the work is done.

The correctness of this view is apparent when we take a
comprehensive survey of the whole teaching of Jesus on the
important subject of *work and wages* in the divine kingdom,
from which it appears that the relation between the two
things is fixed by righteous law, caprice being entirely
excluded; so that if the first in work be last in wages in any
instances, it is for very good reasons.

There are, in all, three parables in the Gospels on the
subject referred to, each setting forth a distinct idea, and, in
case our interpretation of the one at present to be specially
considered is correct, all combined presenting an exhaustive
view of the topic to which they relate. They are the parables

of the Talents[1] and of the Pounds,[2] and the one before us, called by way of distinction "the Laborers in the Vineyard."

In order to see how these parables are at once distinct and mutually complementary, it is necessary to keep in view the principles on which the value of work is to be determined. Three things must be taken into account in order to form a just estimate of men's works, viz. the quantity of work done, the ability of the worker, and the motive. Leaving out of view meantime the motive : when the ability is equal, quantity determines relative merit ; and when ability varies, then it is not the absolute amount, but the relation of the amount to the ability that ought to determine value.

The parables of the Pounds and of the Talents are designed to illustrate respectively these two propositions. In the former parable the ability is the same in all, each servant receiving one pound ; but the quantity of work done varies, one servant with his pound gaining ten pounds, while another with the same amount gains only five. Now, by the above rule, the second should not be rewarded as the first, for he has not done what he might. Accordingly, in the parable a distinction is made, both in the rewards given to the two servants, and in the manner in which they are respectively addressed by their employer. The first gets ten cities to govern, and these words of commendation in addition : " Well, thou good servant ; because thou hast been faithful in a very little, have thou authority over ten cities." The second, on the other hand, gets only five cities, and what is even more noticeable, no praise. His master says to him dryly, " Be thou also over five cities." He had done somewhat, in comparison with idlers even something considerable, and therefore his service is acknowledged and proportionally rewarded. But he is not pronounced a good and faithful servant ; and the eulogy is withheld, simply because it was not deserved : for he had not done what he could, but only half of what was possible, taking the first servant's work as the measure of possibility.

In the parable of the Talents the conditions are different. There the amount of work done varies, as in the parable of the Pounds ; but the ability varies in the same proportion,

---

[1] Matt. xxv. 14–30   [2] Luke xix. 12–28

so that the ratio between the two is the same in the case of both servants who put their talents to use.   One receives five, and gains five ; the other receives two, and gains two According to our rule, these two should be equal in merit ; and so they are represented in the parable.   The same reward is assigned to each, and both are commended in the very same terms ; the master's words in either case being : " Well done, good and faithful servant ; thou hast been faithful over a few things, I will make thee ruler over many things ; enter thou into the joy of thy lord."

Thus the case stands when we take into account only the two elements of ability to work and the amount of work done ; or, to combine both into one, the element of zeal. But there is more than zeal to be considered, at least in the kingdom of God.   In this world men are often commended for their diligence irrespective of their motives ; and it is not always necessary even to be zealous in order to gain vulgar applause.   If one do something that looks large and liberal, men will praise him without inquiring whether for him it was a great thing, a heroic act involving self-sacrifice, or only a respectable act, not necessarily indicative of earnestness or devotion.   But in God's sight many bulky things are very little, and many small things are very great.   The reason is, that He seeth the heart, and the hidden springs of action there, and judges the stream by the fountain.   Quantity is nothing to Him, unless there be zeal ; and even zeal is nothing to Him, unless it be purged from all vainglory and self-seeking — a pure spring of good impulses ; cleared of all smoke of carnal passion — a pure flame of heaven-born devotion.   A base motive vitiates all.

To emphasize *this* truth, and to insist on the necessity of right motives and emotions in connection with work and sacrifices, is the design of the parable spoken by Jesus in Peræa.   It teaches that a small quantity of work done in a right spirit is of greater value than a large quantity done in a wrong spirit, however zealously it may have been performed. One hour's work done by men who make no bargain is of greater value than twelve hours' work done by men who have borne the heat and burden of the day, but who regard their doings with self-complacency.   Put in preceptive form, the lesson of the parable is : Work not as hirelings basely calculat-ing, or as Pharisees arrogantly exacting, the wages to which you deem yourselves entitled ; work humbly, as deeming yourselves unprofitable servants at best ; generously, as men superior to selfish calculations of advantage ; trustfully, as men who confide in the generosity of the great Employer, regarding Him as one from whom you need not to protect yourselves by making beforehand a firm and fast bargain.

In this interpretation, it is assumed that the spirit of the first and of the last to enter the vineyard was respectively such as has been indicated ; and the assumption is justified by the manner in which the parties are described. In what spirit the last worked may be inferred from their making no bargain ; and the temper of the first is manifest from their own words at the end of the day : "These last," said they, "have wrought but one hour, and thou hast made them equal to us, which have borne the burden and heat of the day." This is the language of envy, jealousy, and self-esteem, and it is in keeping with the conduct of these laborers at the commencement of the day's work ; for they entered the vine-yard as hirelings, having made a bargain, agreeing to work for a stipulated amount of wages.

The first and last, then, represent two classes among the professed servants of God. The first are the calculating and self-complacent ; the last are the humble, the self-forgetful, the generous, the trustful. The first are the Jacobs, plodding, conscientious, able to say for themselves, "Thus I was : in the day the drought consumed me, and the frost by night, and the sleep departed from mine eyes ;" yet ever studious of their own interest, taking care even in their religion to make a sure bargain for themselves, and trusting little to the free grace and unfettered generosity of the great Lord. The last are Abraham-like men, not in the lateness of their service, but in the magnanimity of their faith, entering the vineyard without bargaining, as Abraham left his father's house, know-ing not whither he was to go, but knowing only that God had said, "Go to a land that I shall show thee." The first are the Simons, righteous, respectable, exemplary, but hard, prosaic, ungenial ; the last are the women with alabaster boxes, who for long have been idle, aimless, vicious, wasteful of life, but at last, with bitter tears of sorrow over an unprofitable past, begin life in earnest, and endeavor to redeem lost time by the passionate devotion with which they serve their Lord and Saviour.   The first, once more, are the elder brothers who stay at home in their father's house, and never transgress any of his commandments, and have no mercy on those who do; the last are the prodigals, who leave their father's house and waste their substance on riotous living, but at length come to their senses, and say, "I will arise, and go to my father;" and having met him, exclaim, "Father, I have sinned, and am no more worthy to be called thy son : make me as one of thy hired servants."

The two classes differing thus in character are treated in the parable precisely as they ought to be.   The last are made first, and the first are made last.   The last are paid first, to signify the pleasure which the master has in rewarding them. They are also paid at a much higher rate ; for, receiving the same sum for one hour's work that the others receive for twelve, they are paid at the rate of twelve pence *per diem*. They are treated, in fact, as the prodigal was, for whom the father made a feast ; while the "first" are treated as the elder brother, whose service was acknowledged, but who had to complain that his father never had given him a kid to make merry with his friends.   Those who deem themselves unworthy to be any thing else than hired servants, and most unprofitable in that capacity, are dealt with as sons ; and those who deem themselves most meritorious are treated coldly and distantly, as hired servants.

Reverting now from the parable to the apophthegm it was designed to illustrate, we observe that the degradation of such as are first in ability, zeal, and length of service, to the last place as regards the reward, is represented as a thing likely to happen often.   "*Many* that are first shall be last." This statement implies that self-esteem is a sin which easily besets men situated as the twelve, *i.e.* men who have made sacrifices for the kingdom of God.   Now, that this is a fact observation proves ; and it further teaches us that there are certain circumstances in which the laborious and self-denying are specially liable to fall into the vice of self-righteousness. It will serve to illustrate the deep and, to most minds on first view, obscure saying of Jesus, if we indicate here what these circumstances are.

1. Those who make sacrifices for Christ's sake are in danger of falling into a self-righteous mood of mind, when the spirit of self-denial manifests itself in rare occasional acts, rather than in the form of a habit. In this case Christians rise at certain emergencies to an elevation of spirit far above the usual level of their moral feelings ; and therefore, though at the time when the sacrifice was made they may have behaved heroically, they are apt afterwards to revert self-complacently to their noble deeds, as an old soldier goes back on his battles, and with Peter to ask, with a proud consciousness of merit for having forsaken all, What shall we have therefore ? Verily, a state of mind greatly to be feared. A society in which spiritual pride and self-complacency prevails is in a bad way. One possessed of prophetic insight into the moral laws of the universe can foretell what will happen. The religious community which deems itself first will gradually fall behind in gifts and graces, and some other religious community which it despises will gradually advance onward, till the two have at length, in a way manifest to all men, changed places.

2. There is great danger of degeneracy in the spirit of those who make sacrifices for the kingdom of God, when any particular species of service has come to be much in demand, and therefore to be held in very high esteem. Take, as an example, the endurance of physical tortures and of death in times of persecution. It is well known with what a *furor* of admiration martyrs and confessors were regarded in the suffering church of the early centuries. Those who suffered martyrdom were almost deified by popular enthusiasm : the anniversaries of their death — of their birthdays,[1] as they were called, into the eternal world — were observed with religious solemnity, when their doings and sufferings in this world were rehearsed with ardent admiration in strains of extravagant eulogy. Even the confessors, who had suffered, but not died for Christ, were looked up to as a superior order of beings, separated by a wide gulf from the common herd of untried Christians. They were saints, they had a halo of

---

[1] The festival of a martyr was called his *natalitia*.

glory round their heads; they had power with God, and
could, it was believed, bind or loose with even more authority
than the regular ecclesiastical authorities. Absolution was
eagerly sought for from them by the lapsed; admission to
their communion was regarded as an open door by which sinners might return into the fellowship of the church. They
had only to say to the erring, "Go in peace," and even
bishops must receive them. Bishops joined with the
populace in this idolatrous homage to the men who suffered
for Christ's sake. They petted and flattered the confessors,
partly from honest admiration, but partly also from policy, to
induce others to imitate their example, and to foster the
virtue of hardihood, so much needed in suffering times.

This state of feeling in the church was obviously fraught
with great danger to the souls of those who endured hardship
for the truth, as tempting them to fanaticism, vanity, spiritual
pride, and presumption. Nor were they all by any means
temptation-proof. Many took all the praise they received
as their due, and deemed themselves persons of great consequence. The soldiers, who had been flattered by their
generals to make them brave, began to act as if they were
the masters, and could write, for example, to one who had
been a special offender in the extravagance of his eulogies,
such a letter as this: "All the confessors to Cyprian the
bishop: Know that we have granted peace to all those of
whom you have had an account what they have done: how
they have behaved since the commission of their crimes; and
we would that these presents should be by you imparted to
the rest of the bishops. We wish you to maintain peace
with the holy martyrs."[1] Thus was fulfilled in these confessors the saying, "Many that are first shall be last." First in
suffering for the truth and in reputation for sanctity, they
became last in the judgment of the great Searcher of hearts.
They gave their bodies to be scourged, maimed, burned, and
it profited them little or nothing.[2]

[1] Cave, *Primitive Christianity*, Part iii. cap. v. For the original, *vide* Cypriani *Opera* [Clark's Ante-Nicene Library, *Cyprian*, i. 54].
[2] The virtue *now* in request is that of giving liberally to missions and to philanthropic enterprises of all sorts. The same degeneracy of motive may take place in connection with giving as in connection with suffering in early times, and the first in our subscription-lists may be last in the book of life.

3. The first are in danger of becoming the last when self-denial is reduced to a system, and practised ascetically, not for Christ's sake, but for one's own sake. That in respect of the amount of self-denial the austere ascetic is entitled to rank first, nobody will deny. But his right to rank first in intrinsic spiritual worth, and therefore in the divine kingdom, is more open to dispute. Even in respect to the fundamental matter of getting rid of self, he may be, not first, but last. The self-denial of the ascetic is in a subtle way intense self-assertion. True Christian self-sacrifice signifies hardship, loss undergone, not for its own sake, but for Christ's sake, and for truth's sake, at a time when truth cannot be maintained without sacrifice. But the self-sacrifice of the ascetic is not of this kind. It is all endured for his own sake, for his own spiritual benefit and credit. He practises self-denial after the fashion of a miser, who is a total abstainer from all luxuries, and even grudges himself the necessaries of life because he has a passion for hoarding. Like the miser, he deems himself rich ; yet both he and the miser are alike poor : the miser, because with all his wealth he cannot part with his coin in exchange for enjoyable commodities ; the ascetic, because his coins, "good works," so called, painful acts of abstinence, are counterfeit, and will not pass current in the kingdom of heaven. All his labors to save his soul will turn out to be just so much rubbish to be burned up ; and if he be saved at all, it will be as by fire.

Recalling now for a moment the three classes of cases in which the first are in danger of becoming last, we perceive that the word "many" is not an exaggeration. For consider how much of the work done by professing Christians belongs to one or other of these categories : occasional spasmodic efforts ; good works of liberality and philanthropy, which are in fashion and in high esteem in the religious world ; and good works done, not so much from interest in the work, as from their reflex bearing on the doer's own religious interests. Many are called to work in God's vineyard, and many are actually at work. But few are chosen ; few are *choice* workers ; few work for God in the spirit of the precepts taught by Jesus.

But though there be few such workers, there are some. Jesus does not say *all* who are first shall be last, and all who are last shall be first : His word is *many*. There are numerous exceptions to the rule in both its parts. Not all who bear the heat and burden of the day are mercenary and self-righteous. No ; the Lord has always had in His spiritual vineyard a noble band of workers, who, if there were room for boasting in any case, might have boasted on account of the length, the arduousness, and the efficiency of their service, yet cherished no self-complacent thoughts, nor indulged in any calculations how much more they should receive than others. Think of devoted missionaries to heathen lands ; of heroic reformers like Luther, Calvin, Knox, and Latimer ; of eminent men of our own day, recently taken from amongst us. Can you fancy such men talking like the early laborers in the vineyard ? Nay, verily ! all through life their thoughts of themselves and their service were very humble indeed ; and at the close of life's day their day's work seemed to them a very sorry matter, utterly undeserving of the great reward of eternal life. Such first ones shall not be last.

If there be some first who shall not be last, there are doubtless also some last who shall not be first. If it were otherwise ; if to be last in length of service, in zeal and devotion, gave a man an advantage, it would be ruinous to the interests of the kingdom of God. It would, in fact, be in effect putting a premium on indolence, and encouraging men to stand all the day idle, or to serve the devil till the eleventh hour ; and then in old age to enter the vineyard, and give the Lord the poor hour's work, when their limbs were stiff and their frames feeble and tottering. No such demoralizing law obtains in the divine kingdom. Other things being equal, the longer and the more earnestly a man serves God, the sooner he begins, and the harder he works, the better for himself hereafter. If those who begin late in the day are graciously treated, it is in spite, not in consequence, of their tardiness. That they have been so long idle is not a commendation, but a sin ; not a subject of self-congratulation, but of deep humiliation. If it be wrong for those who have served the Lord much to glory in the greatness of their service, it is surely still more unbecoming, even ridiculous, for any one to pride himself in the littleness of his. If the first has no cause for boasting and self-righteousness, still less has the last.

17

THE SONS OF ZEBEDEE AGAIN:
or, Second Lesson on the Doctrine of the Cross

Matt. 20:17-28; Mark 10:32-45; Luke 18:31-34

THE incident recorded in these sections of Matthew's and Mark's Gospels happened while Jesus and His disciples were going up to Jerusalem for the last time, journeying *via* Jericho, from Ephraim in the wilderness, whither they had retired after the raising of Lazarus.[1] The ambitious request of the two sons of Zebedee for the chief places of honor in the kingdom was therefore made little more than a week before their Lord was crucified. How little must they have dreamed what was coming! Yet it was not for want of warning; for just before they presented their petition, Jesus had for the third time explicitly announced His approaching passion, indicating that His death would take place in connection with this present visit to Jerusalem, and adding other particulars respecting His last sufferings not specified before fitted to arrest attention; as that His death should be the issue of a judicial process, and that He should be delivered by the Jewish authorities to the Gentiles, to be mocked, and scourged, and crucified.[2]

After recording the terms of Christ's third announcement, Luke adds, with reference to the disciples: " They understood none of these things; and this saying was hid from them, neither knew they the things which were spoken."[3] The truth of this statement is sufficiently apparent from the scene which ensued, not recorded by Luke, as is also the cause of the fact stated. The disciples, we perceive, were thinking of other matters while Jesus spake to them of His

---

[1] John xi. 54.
[2] Matt. xx. 17-19. Mark (x. 34) adds spitting to the catalogue of indignities.
[3] Luke xviii. 34.

approaching sufferings. They were dreaming of the thrones they had been promised in Peræa, and therefore were not able to enter into the thoughts of their Master, so utterly diverse from their own. Their minds were completely possessed by romantic expectations, their heads giddy with the sparkling wine of vain hope ; and as they drew nigh the holy city their firm conviction was, "that the kingdom of God should immediately appear."[1]

While all the disciples were looking forward to their thrones, James and John were coveting the most distinguished ones, and contriving a scheme for securing these to themselves, and so getting the dispute who should be the greatest settled in their own favor. These were the two disciples who made themselves so prominent in resenting the rudeness of the Samaritan villagers. The greatest zealots among the twelve were thus also the most ambitious, a circumstance which will not surprise the student of human nature. On the former occasion they asked fire from heaven to consume their adversaries ; on the present occasion they ask a favor from Heaven to the disadvantage of their friends. The two requests are not so very dissimilar.

In hatching and executing their little plot, the two brothers enjoyed the assistance of their mother, whose presence is not explained, but may have been due to her having become an attendant on Jesus in her widowhood,[2] or to an accidental meeting with Him and His disciples at the junction of the roads converging on Jerusalem, whither all were now going to keep the feast. Salome was the principal actor in the scene, and it must be admitted she acted her part well. Kneeling before Jesus, as if doing homage to a king, she intimated her humble wish to proffer a petition ; and being gently asked, "What wilt thou ?" said, "Grant that these my two sons may sit, the one on Thy right hand, and the other on the left, in Thy kingdom."

This prayer had certainly another origin than the inspiration of the Holy Ghost, and the scheme of which it was the outcome was not one which we should have expected com-

---

[1] Luke xix. 11.
[2] Salome was one of the women who followed Christ in Galilee, and served Him. Mark xv. 41.

panions of Jesus to entertain. And yet the whole proceeding is so true to human nature as it reveals itself in every age, that we cannot but feel that we have here no myth, but a genuine piece of history. We know how much of the world's spirit is to be found at all times in religious circles of high reputation for zeal, devotion, and sanctity ; and we have no right to hold up our hands in amazement when we see it appearing even in the immediate neighborhood of Jesus. The twelve were yet but crude Christians, and we must allow them time to become sanctified as well as others. Therefore we neither affect to be scandalized at their conduct, nor, to save their reputation, do we conceal its true character. We are not surprised at the behavior of the two sons of Zebedee, and yet we say plainly that their request was foolish and offensive : indicative at once of bold presumption, gross stupidity, and unmitigated selfishness.

It was an irreverent, presumptuous request, because it virtually asked Jesus their Lord to become the tool of their ambition and vanity. Fancying that He would yield to mere solicitation, perhaps calculating that He would not have the heart to refuse a request coming from a female suppliant, who as a widow was an object of compassion, and as a contributor to His support had claims to His gratitude, they begged a favor which Jesus could not grant without being untrue to His own character and His habitual teaching, as exemplified in the discourse on humility in the house at Capernaum. In so doing they were guilty of a disrespectful, impudent forwardness most characteristic of the ambitious spirit, which is utterly devoid of delicacy, and pushes on towards its end, reckless what offence it may give, heedless how it wounds the sensibilities of others.

The request of the two brothers was as ignorant as it was presumptuous. The idea implied therein of the kingdom was utterly wide of truth and reality. James and John not only thought of the kingdom that was coming as a kingdom of this world, but they thought meanly of it even under that view. For it is an unusually corrupt and unwholesome condition of matters, even in a secular state, when places of highest distinction can be obtained by solicitation and favor, and not on the sole ground of fitness for the duties of

the position.   When family influence or courtly arts are the
pathway to power, every patriot has cause to mourn.   How
preposterous, then, the idea that promotion can take place
in the divine, ideally-perfect kingdom by means that are
inadmissible in any well-regulated secular kingdom!   To
cherish such an idea is in effect to degrade and dishonor the
Divine King, by likening Him to an unprincipled despot,
who has more favor for flatterers than for honest men ; and
to caricature the divine kingdom by assimilating it to the
most misgoverned states on earth, such as those ruled over
by a Bomba or a Nero.

The request of the brethren was likewise intensely selfish.
It was ungenerous as towards their fellow-disciples ; for it
was an attempt to overreach them, and, like all such attempts,
produced mischief, disturbing the peace of the family circle,
and giving rise to a most unseemly embitterment of feeling
among its members.   "When the ten heard it, they were
moved with indignation."   No wonder ; and if James and
John did not anticipate such a result, it showed that they
were very much taken up with their own selfish thoughts ;
and if they did anticipate it, and nevertheless shrank not
from a course of action which was sure to give offence, that
only made their selfishness the more heartless and inexcusable.

But the petition of the two disciples was selfish in a far
wider view, viz. with reference to the public interests of
the divine kingdom.   It virtually meant this : "Grant us the
places of honor and power, come what may ; even though
universal discontent and disaffection, disorder, disaster, and
chaotic confusion ensue."   These are the sure effects of
promotion by favor instead of by merit, both in church and
in state, as many a nation has found to its cost in the day of
trial.   James and John, it is true, never dreamt of disaster
resulting from their petition being granted.   No self-seekers
and place-hunters ever do anticipate evil results from their
promotion.   But that does not make them less selfish.   It
only shows that, besides being selfish, they are vain.

The reply of Jesus to this ambitious request, considering
its character, was singularly mild.   Offensive though the
presumption, forwardness, selfishness, and vanity of the two
disciples must have been to His meek, holy, self-forgetful

spirit, He uttered not a word of direct rebuke, but dealt with them as a father might deal with a child that had made a senseless request. Abstaining from animadversion on the grave faults brought to light by their petition, He noticed only the least culpable — their ignorance. "Ye know not," He said to them quietly, "what ye ask;" and even this remark He made in compassion rather than in the way of blame. He pitied men who offered prayers whose fulfilment, as He knew, implied painful experiences of which they had no thought. It was in this spirit that He asked the explanatory question : "Are ye able to drink of the cup that I am about to drink, and to be baptized with the baptism that I am baptized with ? " [1]

But there was more than compassion or correction in this question, even instruction concerning the true way of obtaining promotion in the kingdom of God. In interrogatory form Jesus taught His disciples that advancement in His kingdom went not by favor, nor was obtainable by clamorous solicitation ; that the way to thrones was the *via dolorosa* of the cross ; that the palm-bearers in the realms of glory should be they who had passed through great tribulation, and the princes of the kingdom they who had drunk most deeply of His cup of sorrow ; and that for those who refused to drink thereof, the selfish, the self-indulgent, the ambitious, the vain, there would be no place at all in the kingdom, not to speak of places of honor on His right or left hand.

The startling question put to them by Jesus did not take James and John by surprise. Promptly and firmly they replied, "We are able." Had they then really taken into account the cup and the baptism of suffering, and deliberately made up their minds to pay the costly price for the coveted prize ? Had the sacred fire of the martyr spirit already been kindled in their hearts ? One would be happy to think so, but we fear there is nothing to justify so favorable an opinion. It is much more probable that, in their eagerness to obtain the object of their ambition, the two brothers were ready to promise any thing, and that, in fact, they neither knew nor cared what they were promising. Their confident declaration bears a suspiciously close resemblance to the bravado uttered

---

[1] The second clause is a doubtful reading, and is omitted in R. V.

by Peter a few days later : "Though all men shall be offended because of Thee, yet will I never be offended."

Jesus, however, did not choose, in the case of the sons of Zebedee, as in the case of their friend, to call in question the heroism so ostentatiously professed, but adopted the course of assuming that they were not only able, but willing, yea, eager, to participate in His sufferings.   With the air of a king granting to favorites the privilege of drinking out of the royal wine-cup, and of washing in the royal ewer, He replied : "Ye shall drink indeed of my cup, and be baptized with the baptism that I am baptized with."   It was a strange favor which the King thus granted!   Had they only known the meaning of the words, the two brethren might well have fancied that their Master was indulging in a stroke of irony at their expense.   Yet it was not so.   Jesus was not mocking His disciples when He spake thus, offering them a stone instead of bread : He was speaking seriously, and promising what He meant to bestow, and what, when the time of bestowal came — for it did come — they themselves regarded as a real privilege ; for all the apostles agreed with Peter that they who were reproached for the name of Christ were to be accounted happy, and had the spirit of glory and of God resting on them.   Such, we believe, was the mind of James when Herod killed him with the persecutor's sword : such, we know, was the mind of John when he was in the isle of Patmos "for the word of God, and for the testimony of Jesus Christ."

Having promised a favor not coveted by the two disciples, Jesus next explained that the favor they did covet was not unconditionally at His disposal : "But to sit on my right hand and on my left is not mine to give, save to those for whom it is prepared of my Father."   The Authorized Version suggests the idea that the bestowal of rewards in the kingdom is not in Christ's hands at all.   That, however, is not what Jesus meant to say ; but rather this, that though it is Christ's prerogative to assign to citizens their places in His kingdom, it is not in His power to dispose of places by partiality and patronage, or otherwise than in accordance with fixed principles of justice and the sovereign ordination of His Father.   The words, paraphrased, signify : "I can

say to any one, Come, drink of my cup, for there is no risk
of mischief arising out of favoritism in that direction.   But
there my favors must end.   I cannot say to any one, as I
please, Come, sit beside me on a throne ; for each man must
get the place prepared for him, and for which he is prepared."

Thus explained, this solemn saying of our Lord furnishes
no ground for an inference which, on first view, it seems not
only to suggest, but to necessitate, viz. that one may taste
of the cup, yet lose the crown ; or, at least, that there is no
connection between the measure in which a disciple may
have had fellowship with Christ in His cross, and the place
which shall be assigned to him in the eternal kingdom.   That
Jesus had no intention to teach such a doctrine is evident
from the question He had asked just before He made the
statement now under consideration, which implies a natural
sequence between the cup and the throne, the suffering and
the glory.   The sacrifice and the great reward so closely
conjoined in the promise made to the twelve in Peræa are
disjoined here, merely for the purpose of signalizing the
rigor with which all corrupt influences are excluded from
the kingdom of heaven.   It is beyond doubt, that those on
whom is bestowed in high measure the favor of being companions with Jesus in tribulation shall be rewarded with high
promotion in the eternal kingdom.   Nor does this statement
compromise the sovereignty of the Father and Lord of all ;
on the contrary, it contributes towards its establishment.
There is no better argument in support of the doctrine of
election than the simple truth that affliction is the education
for heaven.   For in what does the sovereign hand of God
appear more signally than in the appointment of crosses ? If
crosses would let us alone, we would let them alone.   We
choose not the bitter cup and the bloody baptism : we are
chosen for them, and in them.   God impresses men into the
warfare of the cross ; and if any come to glory in this way,
as many an impressed soldier has done, it will be to glory to
which, in the first place at least, they did not aspire.

The asserted connection between suffering and glory serves
to defend as well as to establish the doctrine of election.
Looked at in relation to the world to come, that doctrine

seems to lay God open to the charge of partiality, and is
certainly very mysterious.   But look at election in its bearing
on the *present* life.   In that view it is a privilege for which
the elect are not apt to be envied.   For the elect are not the
happy and the prosperous, but the toilers and sufferers.[1]   In
fact, they are elected not for their own sake, but for the
world's sake, to be God's pioneers in the rough, unwelcome
work of turning the wilderness into a fruitful field ; to be
the world's salt, leaven, and light, receiving for the most part
little thanks for the service they render, and getting often
for reward the lot of the destitute, the afflicted, and the
tormented.   So that, after all, election is a favor to the non-
elect : *it is God's method of benefiting men at large ;* and
whatever peculiar benefit may be in store for the elect is
well earned, and should not be grudged.   Does any one envy
them their prospect ?   He may be a partaker of their future
joy if he be willing to be companion to such forlorn beings,
and to share their tribulations now.

It is hardly needful to explain that, in uttering these
words, Jesus did not mean to deny the utility of prayer, and
to say, "You may ask for a place in the divine kingdom,
and not get it ; for all depends on what God has ordained."
He only wished the two disciples and all to understand that
to obtain their requests they must know what they ask, and
accept all that is implied, in the present as well as in the
future, in the answering of their prayers.   This condition is
too often overlooked.   Many a bold, ambitious prayer, even
for spiritual blessing, is offered up by petitioners who have
no idea what the answer would involve, and if they had,
would wish their prayer unanswered.   Crude Christians ask,
e.g., to be made holy.   But do they know what doubts,
temptations, and sore trials of all kinds go to the making of
great saints ?   Others long for a full assurance of God's love ;
desire to be perfectly persuaded of their election.   Are they

---

[1] The lines of Euripides may be appropriated here to the true sons of God —

Οὔτ' ἐπὶ κερκίσιν οὔτε λόγοις
φάτιν ἄϊον' εὐτυχίας μετέχειν
θεόθεν τέκνα θνατοῖς (*Ion*, 510) ;

the meaning being, I have never heard it said that sons born to mortals of divine paternity
were happy.

willing to be deprived of the sunshine of prosperity, that in the dark night of sorrow they may see heaven's stars? Ah me! how few do know what they ask! how much all need to be taught to pray for right things with an intelligent mind and in a right spirit!

Having said what was needful to James and John, Jesus next addressed a word in season to their brethren inculcating humility; most appropriately, for though the ten were the offended party, not offenders, yet the same ambitious spirit was in them, else they would not have felt and resented the wrong done so keenly. Pride and selfishness may vex and grieve the humble and the self-forgetful, but they provoke resentment only in the proud and the selfish; and the best way to be proof against the assaults of other men's evil passions is to get similar affections exorcised out of our own breasts. " Let this mind be in you which was also in Christ Jesus;" then shall nothing be done by you at least in strife or vainglory.

" When the ten heard it," we read, " they were moved with indignation against the two brethren." Doubtless it was a very unedifying scene which ensued; and it is very disappointing to witness such scenes where one might have looked to see in perfection the godly spectacle of brethren dwelling together in unity. But the society of Jesus was a real thing, not the imaginary creation of a romance-writer; and in all real human societies, in happy homes, in the most select brotherhoods, scientific, literary, or artistic, in Christian churches, there will arise tempests now and then. And let us be thankful that the twelve, even by their folly, gave their Master an occasion for uttering the sublime words here recorded, which shine down upon us out of the serene sky of the gospel story like stars appearing through the tempestuous clouds of human passion — manifestly the words of a Divine Being, though spoken out of the depths of an amazing self-humiliation.

The manner of Jesus, in addressing His heated disciples, was very tender and subdued. He collected them all around Him, the two and the ten, the offenders and the offended, as a father might gather together his children to receive admonition, and He spoke to them with the calmness and solemnity of one about to meet death. Throughout this whole scene death's solemnizing influence is manifestly on the Saviour's spirit. For does He not speak of His approaching sufferings in language reminding us of the night of His betrayal, describing His passion by the poetic sacramental name " my cup," and for the first time revealing the secret of His life on earth — the grand object for which He is about to die ?

In moral significance, the doctrine of Jesus at this time was a repetition of His teaching in Capernaum, when He chose the little child for His text. As He said then, Who would be great must be childlike, so He says here, Whosoever will be great among you, let him be your minister. In the former discourse His model and His text was an infant ; now it is a slave, another representative of the mean and despicable. Now, as before, He quotes His own example to enforce His precept ; stimulating His disciples to seek distinction in a path of lowly love by representing the Son of man as come not to be ministered unto, but to minister, even to the length of giving His life a ransom for the many, as He then reminded them, that the Son of man came like a shepherd, to seek and to save the lost sheep.

The single new feature in the lesson which Jesus gave His disciples at this season is, the contrast between His kingdom and the kingdoms of earth in respect to the mode of acquiring dominion, to which He directed attention, by way of preface, to the doctrine about to be communicated. " Ye know," He said, " that the princes of the Gentiles exercise dominion over them, and they that are great (provincial governors, often more tyrannical than their superiors) exercise authority upon them. But it shall not be so among you." There is a hint here at another contrast besides the one mainly intended, viz. that between the harsh despotic sway of worldly potentates, and the gentle dominion of love alone admissible in the divine kingdom. But the main object of the words quoted is to point out the difference in the way of acquiring rather than in the manner of using power. The idea is this : earthly kingdoms are ruled by a class of persons who possess hereditary rank — the aristocracy, nobles, or princes. The governing class are those whose birthright it is to rule, and whose boast it is never to have been in a servile position, but always to have been served. In my kingdom, on the other hand, a man becomes a great one, and a ruler, by being first the servant of those over whom he is to bear rule. In other states, they rule whose privilege it is to be ministered unto ; in the divine commonwealth, they rule who account it a privilege to minister.

In drawing this contrast, Jesus had, of course, no intention to teach politics ; no intention either to recognize or to call in question the divine right of the princely cast to rule over their fellow-creatures. He spoke of things as they were, and as His hearers knew them to be in secular states, and especially in the Roman Empire. If any political inference might be drawn from His words, it would not be in favor of absolutism and hereditary privilege, but rather in favor of power being in the hands of those who have earned it by faithful service, whether they belong to the governing class by birth or not. For what is beneficial in the divine kingdom cannot be prejudicial to secular commonwealths. The true interests, one would say, of an earthly kingdom should be promoted by its being governed as nearly as possible in accordance with the laws of the kingdom which cannot be moved. Thrones and crowns may, to prevent disputes, go by hereditary succession, irrespective of personal merit ; but the reality of power should ever be in the hands of the ablest, the wisest, and the most devoted to the public good.

Having explained by contrast the great principle of the spiritual commonwealth, that he who would rule therein must first serve, Jesus proceeded next to enforce the doctrine by a reference to His own example. "Whosoever will be chief among you," said He to the twelve, "let him be your servant ;" and then He added the memorable words : "Even as the Son of man came not to be ministered unto, but to minister, and to give His life a ransom for many."

These words were spoken by Jesus as one who claimed to be a King, and aspired to be the first in a great and mighty kingdom. At the end of the sentence we must mentally supply the clause — which was not expressed simply because it was so obviously implied in the connection of thought — "so seeking to win a kingdom." Our Lord sets Himself forth here not merely as an example of humility, but as one whose case illustrates the truth that the way to power in the spiritual world is service ; and in stating that He came not to be ministered unto, but to minister, He expresses not the whole truth, but only the present fact.   The whole truth was, that He came to minister in the first place, that He might be ministered to in turn by a willing, devoted people, acknowledging Him as their sovereign.   The point on which He wishes to fix the attention of His disciples is the peculiar way He takes to get His crown ; and what He says in effect is this : "I am a King, and I expect to have a kingdom ; James and John were not mistaken in that respect.   But I shall obtain my kingdom in another way than secular princes get theirs.   They get their thrones by succession, I get mine by personal merit ; they secure their kingdom by right of birth, I hope to secure mine by the right of service ; they inherit their subjects, I buy mine, the purchase-money being mine own life."

What the twelve thought of this novel plan of getting dominion and a kingdom, and especially what ideas the concluding word of their Master suggested to their minds when uttered, we know not.   We are sure, however, that they did not comprehend that word ; and no marvel, for the thought of Jesus was very deep.   Who can understand it fully even now?   Here we emphatically see through a glass, in enigmas.

This memorable saying has been the subject of much doubtful disputation among theologians, nor can we hope by any thing that we can say to terminate controversy.   The word is a deep well which has never yet been fathomed, and probably never will.   Brought in so quietly as an illustration to enforce a moral precept, it opens up a region of thought which takes us far beyond the immediate occasion of its being uttered.   It raises questions in our minds which it does not solve ; and yet there is little in the New Testament on the subject of Christ's death which might not be comprehended within the limits of its possible significance.

First of all, let us say that we have no sympathy with that school of critical theologians who call in question the authen-

ticity of this word.[1]   It is strange to observe how unwilling
some are to recognize Christ as the original source of great
thoughts which have become essential elements in the faith
of the church.   This idea of Christ's death as a ransom is
here now.   With whom did it take its rise? was the mind of
Jesus not original enough to conceive it, that it must be
fathered on some one else?   Another thing has to be considered in connection with this saying, and the kindred one
uttered at the institution of the supper.   After Jesus had
begun to dwell much in thought, accompanied with deep
emotion, on the fact that He must die, it was inevitable that
His mind should address itself to the task of investing the
harsh, prosaic fact with poetic, mystic meanings.   We speak
of Jesus for the moment simply as a man of wonderful
spiritual genius, whose mind was able to cope with death,
and rob it of its character of a mere fate, and invest it with
beauty, and clothe the skeleton with the flesh and blood of an
attractive system of spiritual meanings.

Regarding, then, this precious saying as unquestionably
authentic, what did Christ mean to teach by it?   First this,
at least, in general, that there was a causal connection
between His act in laying down His life and the desired
result, viz. spiritual sovereignty.   And without having any
regard to the term *ransom*, even supposing it for the moment
absent from the text, we can see for ourselves that there is
such a connection.   However original the method adopted
by Jesus for getting a kingdom — and when compared with
other methods of getting kingdoms, *e.g.* by inheritance, the
most respectable way, or by the sword, or, basest of all, by
paying down a sum of money, as in the last days of the
Roman Empire, its originality is beyond dispute — however
original the method of Jesus, it has proved strangly successful.   The event has proved that there must be a connection
between the two things, — the death on the cross and the
sovereignty of souls.   Thousands of human beings, yea,
millions, in every age, have said Amen with all their hearts
to the doxology of John in the Apocalypse : " Unto Him
that loved us and washed us from our sins in His own blood,

---

[1] Baur expresses doubts in his *Neutestamentliche Theologie*, p. 100. Keim, on the
other hand, defends the authenticity.

and hath made us kings and priests unto God and His
Father, unto Him be glory and dominion forever." Without
doubt this result of His self-devotion was present to the
mind of Jesus when He uttered the words before us, and
in uttering them He meant for one thing to emphasize the
power of divine love in self-sacrifice, to assert its sway over
human hearts, and to win for the King of the sacred commonwealth a kind of sovereignty not attainable otherwise than
by humbling Himself to take upon Him the form of a
servant.   Some assert that to gain this power was the sole
end of the Incarnation.   We do not agree with this view,
but we have no hesitation in regarding the attainment of
such moral power by self-sacrifice as one end of the Incarnation.   The Son of God wished to charm us away from self-
indulgence and self-worship, to emancipate us from sin's
bondage by the power of His love, that we might acknowledge
ourselves to be His, and devote ourselves gratefully to His
services.

But there is more in the text than we have yet found, for
Jesus says not merely that He is to lay down His life for the
many, but that He is to lay down His life in the form of a
ransom.   The question is, what are we to understand by this
form in which the fact of death is expressed ?   Now it may
be assumed that the word "ransom " was used by Jesus in a
sense having affinity to Old Testament usage.   The Greek
word (λύτρον) is employed in the Septuagint as the equivalent
for the Hebrew word *copher* (כֹּפֶר), about whose meaning
there has been much discussion, but the general sense of
which is a covering.   How the idea of covering is to be
taken, whether in the sense of shielding, or in the sense of
exactly covering the same surface, as one penny covers
another, *i.e.* as an equivalent, has been disputed, and must
remain doubtful.[1]   The theological interest of the question
is this, that if we accept the word in the general sense of
protection, then the ransom is not offered or accepted as a
legal equivalent for the persons or things redeemed, but
simply as something of a certain value which is received as a
matter of favor.   But leaving this point on one side, what

[1] Ritschl takes the former view (*vide Lehre von der Rechtfertigung*, ii. 80), Hofmann
the other (*vide Schriftbeweis*).

we are concerned with in connection with this text is the broader thought that Christ's life is given and accepted for the lives of many, whether as an exact equivalent or otherwise being left indeterminate. Jesus represents His death voluntarily endured as a means of delivering from death the souls of the many; how or why does not clearly appear. A German theologian, who energetically combats the Anselmian theory of satisfaction, finds in the word these three thoughts: *First*, the ransom is offered as a gift to God, not to the devil. Jesus, having undoubtedly the train of thought in Psalm xlix. in His mind, speaks of devoting His life to God in the pursuit of His vocation, not of subjecting Himself to the might of sin or of the devil. *Second*, Jesus not only presupposes that no man can offer either for himself or for others a valuable gift capable of warding off death unto God, as the Psalmist declares; but He asserts that in this view He Himself renders a service in the place of many which no one of them could render either for himself or for another. *Third*, Jesus, having in mind also, doubtless, the words of Elihu in the Book of Job concerning an angel, one of a thousand, who may avail to ransom a man from death, distinguishes Himself from the mass of men liable to death in so far as He regards Himself as excepted from the natural doom of death, and conceives of His death as a voluntary act by which He surrenders His life to God, as in the text John x. 17, 18.[1] In taking so much out of the saying we do not subject it to undue straining. The assumption that there is a mental reference to the Old Testament texts in the forty-ninth Psalm and in the thirty-third chapter of Job, as also to the redemption of the males among the children of Israel by the payment of a half-shekel, seems reasonable; and in the light of these passages it does not seem going too far to take out of our Lord's words these three ideas: The ransom is given to God (Psalm xlix. 7: "Nor give to God a ransom for him"); it is given for the lives of men doomed to die; and it is available for such a purpose because the thing given is the life of an exceptional being, one among a thousand, not a brother mortal doomed to die, but an angel assuming flesh that He may freely die. Thus the text contains, besides

[1] Ritschl, *Lehre von der Rechtfertigung*, ii. 84.

the general truth that by dying in self-sacrificing love the Son of man awakens in the many a sense of grateful devotion that carries Him to a throne, this more special one, that by His death He puts the many doomed to death as the penalty of sin somehow in a different relation to God, so that they are no longer criminals, but sons of God, heirs of eternal life, members of the holy commonwealth, enjoying all its privileges, redeemed by the life of the King Himself, as the half-shekel offered as the price of redemption.

These few hints must suffice as an indication of the probable meaning of the autobiographical saying in which Jesus conveyed to His disciples *their second lesson on the doctrine of the cross.*[1] With two additional reflections thereon we end this chapter. When He said of Himself that He came not to be ministered unto, but to minister, Jesus alluded not merely to His death, but to His whole life. The statement is an epitome in a single sentence of His entire earthly history. The reference to His death has the force of a superlative. He came to minister, even to the extent of giving His life a ransom. Then this saying, while breathing the spirit of utter lowliness, at the same time betrays the consciousness of superhuman dignity. Had Jesus not been more than man, His language would not have been humble, but presumptuous. Why should the son of a carpenter say of Himself, I came not to be ministered unto? servile position and occupation was a matter of course for such an one. The statement before us is rational and humble, only as coming from one who, being in the form of God, freely assumed the form of a servant, and became obedient unto death for our salvation.

[1] *Vide* p. 183.

18

THE ANOINTING IN BETHANY:
or, Third Lesson on the Doctrine of the Cross

Matt. 26:6-13; Mark 14:3-9; John 12:1-8

THE touching story of the anointing of Jesus by Mary
at Bethany forms part of the preface to the history of the
passion, as recorded in the synoptical Gospels. That preface,
as given most fully by Matthew, includes four particulars:
first, a statement made by Jesus to His disciples two days
before the passover concerning His betrayal; *second*, a meeting of the priests in Jerusalem to consult when and how
Jesus should be put to death; *third*, the anointing by Mary;
fourth, the secret correspondence between Judas and the
priests. In Mark's preface the first of these four particulars
is omitted; in Luke's both the first and the third.

The four facts related by the first evangelist had this in
common, that they were all signs that the end so often
foretold was at length at hand. Jesus now says, not "the
Son of man shall be betrayed," but "the Son of man is
betrayed to be crucified." The ecclesiastical authorities of
Israel are assembled in solemn conclave, not to discuss the
question what should be done with the object of their dislike
— that is already determined — but how the deed of darkness
may be done most stealthily and most securely. The Victim
has been anointed by a friendly hand for the approaching
sacrifice. And, finally, an instrument has been found to
relieve the priests from their perplexity, and to pave the way
in a most unexpected manner for the consummation of their
wicked purpose.

The grouping of the incidents in the introduction to the
tragic history of the crucifixion is strikingly dramatic in its
effect. First comes the Sanhedrim in Jerusalem plotting

against the life of the Just One. Then comes Mary at
Bethany, in her unutterable love breaking her alabaster box,
and pouring its contents on the head and feet of her beloved
Lord. Last comes Judas, offering to sell his Master for less
than Mary wasted on a useless act of affection! Hatred and
baseness on either hand, and true love in the midst.[1]

This memorable transaction of Mary with her alabaster
box belongs to the history of the passion, in virtue of the
interpretation put upon it by Jesus, which gives to it the
character of a lyric prelude to the great tragedy enacted on
Calvary. It belongs to the history of the twelve disciples,
because of the unfavorable construction which they put on
it. All the disciples, it seems, disapproved of the action, the
only difference between Judas and the rest being that he
disapproved on hypocritical grounds, while his fellow-disciples
were honest both in their judgment and in their motives.
By their fault-finding the twelve rendered to Mary a good
service. They secured for her a present defender in Jesus,
and future eulogists in themselves. Their censure drew from
the Lord the extraordinary statement, that wheresoever the
gospel might be preached in the whole world, what Mary
had done would be spoken of for a memorial of her. This
prophecy the fault-finding disciples, when they became apostles, helped to fulfil. They felt bound by the virtual commandment of their Master, as well as by the generous
re-action of their own hearts, to make amends to Mary for
former wrong done, by telling the tale of her true love to
Jesus wherever they told the story of His true love to men.
From their lips the touching narrative passed in due course
into the gospel records, to be read with a thrill of delight by
true Christians to the end of time. Verily one might be
content to be spoken against for a season for the sake of
such chivalrous championship as that of Jesus, and such
magnanimous recantations as those of His apostles!

When we consider from whom Mary's defence proceeds,
we must be satisfied that it was not merely generous, but
just. And yet surely it is a defence of a most surprising
character! Verily it seems as if, while the disciples went to

---

[1] On the apparent discrepancy between the synoptists and John as to time, and on
all other points belonging to harmony, see the commentaries, especially Alford and Stier.

one extreme in blaming, their Lord went to the other extreme in praising ; as if, in so lauding the woman of Bethany, He were but repeating her extravagance in another form. You feel tempted to ask : Was her action, then, so pre-eminently meritorious as to deserve to be associated with the gospel throughout all time? Then, as to the explanation of the action given by Jesus, the further questions suggest them-selves : Was there really any reference in Mary's mind to His death and burial while she was performing it ? Does not Jesus rather impute to her His own feeling, and invest her act with an ideal poetic significance, which lay not in it, but in His own thoughts ? And if so, can we indorse the judgment He pronounced ; or must we, on the question as to the intrinsic merit of Mary's act, give our vote on the side of the twelve against their Master ?

We, for our part, cordially take Christ's side of the question ; and in doing so, we can afford to make two admissions. In the first place, we admit that Mary had no thought of embalming, in the literal sense, the dead body of Jesus, and possibly was not thinking of His death at all when she anointed Him with the precious ointment. Her action was simply a festive honor done to one whom she loved unspeak-ably, and which she might have rendered at another time.[1] We admit further, that it would certainly have been an extravagance to speak of Mary's deed, however noble, as entitled to be associated with the gospel everywhere and throughout all time, unless it were fit to be spoken of not merely for her sake, but more especially for the gospel's sake ; that is to say, unless it were capable of being made use of to expound the nature of the gospel. In other words, the breaking of the alabaster box must be worthy to be employed as an emblem of the deed of love performed by Jesus in dying on the cross.

Such, indeed, we believe it to be. Wherever the gospel is truly preached, the story of the anointing is sure to be prized as the best possible illustration of the spirit which moved

---

[1] It is natural to connect the anointing with the raising of Lazarus, and to find in gratitude for the restoration of a brother to life the motive to that deed of love. It has been suggested that the ointment may originally have been provided for the burial rites of Lazarus.

Jesus to lay down His life, as also of the spirit of Christianity as it manifests itself in the lives of sincere believers. The breaking of the alabaster box is a beautiful symbol at once of Christ's love to us and of the love we owe to Him. As Mary broke her box of ointment and poured forth its precious contents, so Christ broke His body and shed His precious blood; so Christians pour forth their hearts before their Lord, counting not their very lives dear for His sake. Christ's death was a breaking of an alabaster box for us; our life should be a breaking of an alabaster box for Him.

This relation of spiritual affinity between the deed of Mary and His own deed in dying is the true key to all that is enigmatical in the language of Jesus in speaking of the former. It explains, for example, the remarkable manner in which He referred to the gospel in connection therewith. "This gospel," He said, as if it had been already spoken of; nay, as if the act of anointing were the gospel. And so it was *in a figure*. The one act already done by Mary naturally suggested to the mind of Jesus the other act about to be done by Himself. "There," He thought within Himself, "in that broken vessel and outpoured oil is my death fore-shadowed; in the hidden motive from which that deed proceeded is the eternal spirit in which I offer myself a sacrifice revealed." This thought He meant to express when He used the phrase "this gospel;" and in putting such a construction on Mary's deed He was in effect giving His disciples *their third lesson on the doctrine of the cross.*

In the light of this same relation of spiritual affinity, we clearly perceive the true meaning of the statement made by Jesus concerning Mary's act: "In that she hath poured this ointment on my body, she did it for my burial." It was a mystic, poetic explanation of a most poetic deed, and as such was not only beautiful, but *true*. For the anointing in Bethany has helped to preserve, to embalm so to speak, the true meaning of the Saviour's death. It has supplied us with a symbolic act through which to understand that death; it has shed around the cross an imperishable aroma of self-forgetting love; it has decked the Saviour's grave with flowers that never shall wither, and reared for Jesus, as well as for Mary, a memorial-stone that shall endure throughout all generations. Might it not be fitly said of such a deed, She did it for my burial? Was it not most unfitly said of a deed capable of rendering so important a service to the gospel, that it was wasteful and useless?

These questions will be answered in the affirmative by all who are convinced that the spiritual affinity asserted by us really did exist. What we have now to do, therefore, is to show, by going a little into detail, that our assertion is well founded.

There are three outstanding points of resemblance between Mary's "good work" in anointing Jesus, and the good work wrought by Jesus Himself in dying on the cross.

There was first a resemblance in motive. Mary wrought her good work out of pure love. She loved Jesus with her whole heart, for what He was, for what He had done for the family to which she belonged, and for the words of instruction she had heard from His lips when He came on a visit to their house. There was such a love in her heart for her friend and benefactor as imperatively demanded expression, and yet could not find expression in words. She must do something to relieve her pent-up emotions: she must get an alabaster box and break it, and pour it on the person of Jesus, else her heart will break.

Herein Mary's act resembles closely that of Jesus in dying on the cross, and in coming to this world that He might die. For just such a love as that of Mary, only far deeper and stronger, moved Him to sacrifice Himself for us. The simple account of Christ's whole conduct in becoming man, and undergoing what is recorded of Him, is this: He *loved sinners*. After wearying themselves in studying the philosophy of redemption, learned theologians come back to this as the most satisfactory explanation that can be given. Jesus so loved sinners as to lay down His life for them; nay, we might almost say, He so loved them that He must needs come and die for them. Like Nehemiah, the Jewish patriot in the court of the Persian king, He could not stay in heaven's court while His brethren far away on earth were in an evil case; He must ask and obtain leave to go down to their assistance.[1] Or, like Mary, He must procure an

---

[1] See Neh. i. and ii. Nehemiah, like Mary, may be spoken of wherever the gospel is preached, to illustrate the heart of the Redeemer and interpret His thoughts.

alabaster box — a human body — fill it with the fine essence of a human soul, and pour out His soul unto death on the cross for our salvation. The spirit of Jesus, yea, the spirit of the Eternal God, is the spirit of Mary and of Nehemiah, and of all who are like-minded with them. In reverence we ought rather to say, the spirit of such is the spirit of Jesus and of God ; and yet it is needful at times to put the matter in the inverse way. For somehow we are slow to believe that love is a reality for God. We almost shrink, as if it were an impiety, from ascribing to the Divine Being attributes which we confess to be the noblest and most heroic in human character. Hence the practical value of the sanction here given by Jesus to the association of the anointing in Bethany with the crucifixion on Calvary. He, in effect, says to us thereby : Be not afraid to regard my death as an act of the same kind as that of Mary : an act of pure, devoted love. Let the aroma of her ointment circulate about the neighborhood of my cross, and help you to discern the sweet savor of my sacrifice. Amid all your speculations and theories on the grand theme of redemption, take heed that ye fail not to see in my death my loving heart, and the loving heart of my Father, revealed.[1]

Mary's "good work" further resembled Christ's in its self-sacrificing character. It was not without an effort and a sacrifice that that devoted woman performed her famous act

---

[1] There is a tendency among theologians of an ultra-scholastic habit of mind to treat all that is said of love in connection with the atonement as sentimental, or at most, as available only for popular purposes, and to represent the judicial aspect of the atonement as alone of scientific validity. Thus a recent writer on the History of Doctrines (Shedd) says : " All true scientific development of the doctrine of the atonement, it is very evident, must take its departure from the idea of divine justice. This conception is the primary one in the biblical representation of this doctrine." This author is greatly in love with " soteriologies " of scientific pretensions. He idolizes Anselm as the author of the " first metaphisique of the Christian doctrine of atonement," and as the first to challenge for the doctrine of vicarious satisfaction " both a rational necessity and a scientific rationality." Anselm did certainly carry the passion for *à priori* reasoning on the subject of redemption to its extreme limit. He aimed to demonstrate not only a hypothetical necessity for an atonement in order to salvation, but an absolute necessity. A certain number of sinners, he maintained, must be saved to fill up the numbers of the fallen angels, as " it is indubitable that rational nature which is or is to be happy in the contemplation of God is foreknown by God in a certain rational and perfect number which can neither be more nor less " (*Cur Deus Homo*, i. c. 16). How happy is one to get away from such science so called to the supper-room in Bethany ! Let the august attribute of justice get its due place in the theology of the atonement, but let not " love " be relegated from theology to popular sermons. Christ's death satisfied both divine justice and divine love, and the glory of the gospel is that the *same* event satisfied both.

of homage.   All the evangelists make particular mention of the costliness of the ointment.   Mark and John represent the murmuring disciples as estimating its value at the round sum of three hundred pence; equal, say, to the wages of a laboring man for a whole year at the then current rate of a denarius per day.   This was a large sum in itself; but what is more particularly to be noted, it was a very large sum for Mary.   This we learn from Christ's own words, as recorded by the second evangelist.   "She hath done what she could," He kindly remarked of her, in defending her conduct against the harsh censures of His disciples.   It was a remark of the same kind as that which He made a day or two after in Jerusalem concerning the poor widow whom He saw casting two mites into the temple treasury; and it implied that Mary had expended all her resources on that singular tribute of respect to Him whom her soul loved.   All her earnings, all her little hoard, had been given in exchange for that box, whose precious contents she poured on the Saviour's person. Hers was no ordinary love: it was a noble, heroic, self-sacrificing devotion, which made her do her utmost for its object.

Herein the woman of Bethany resembled the Son of man. He, too, did what He could.   Whatever it was possible for a holy being to endure in the way of humiliation, temptation, sorrow, suffering, yea, even in the way of becoming "sin" and "a curse," He willingly underwent.   All through His life on earth He scrupulously abstained from doing aught that might tend to make his cup of affliction come short of absolute fulness.   He denied Himself all the advantages of divine power and privilege; He emptied Himself; He made Himself poor; He became in all possible respects like His sinful brethren, that He might qualify Himself for being a merciful and trustworthy High Priest to them in things pertaining to God.   Such sacrifices in life and death did His love impose on Him.

While imposing sacrifices, love, by way of compensation, makes them easy.   It is not only love's destiny, but it is love's delight, to endure hardships, to bear burdens for the object loved.   It is not satisfied till it has found an opportunity of embodying itself in a service involving cost, labor, pain. The things from which selfishness shrinks love ardently longs for. These reflections, we believe, are applicable to Mary. With her love to Jesus, it was more easy for her to do what she did than to refrain from doing it. But love's readiness and eagerness to sacrifice herself are most signally exemplified in the case of Jesus Himself. It was indeed His pleasure to suffer for our redemption. Far from shrinking from the cross, He looked forward to it with earnest desire ; and when the hour of His passion approached, He spoke of it as the hour of His glorification. He had no thought of achieving our salvation at the smallest possible cost to Himself. His feeling was rather akin to this : " The more I suffer the better : the more thoroughly shall I realize my identity with my brethren ; the more completely will the sympathetic, burden - bearing, help - bringing instincts and yearnings of my love be satisfied." Yes : Jesus had more to do than to purchase sinners for as small a price as would be accepted for their ransom. He had to do justice to His own heart ; He had adequately to express its deep *compassion ;* and no act of limited or calculated dimensions would avail to exhaust the contents of that whose dimensions were immeasurable. Measured suffering, especially when endured by so august a personage, might satisfy divine justice, but it could not satisfy divine love.

A third feature which fitted Mary's " good work " to be an emblem of the Saviour's, was its *magnificence.* This also appeared in the expenditure connected with the act of anointing, which was not only such as involved a sacrifice for a person of her means, but very liberal with reference to the purpose in hand. The quantity of oil employed in the service was, according to John, not less than a pound weight. This was much more than could be said to be necessary. There was an appearance of waste and extravagance in the manner of the anointing, even admitting the thing in itself to be right and proper. Whether the disciples would have objected to the ceremony, however performed, does not appear ; but it was evidently the extravagant amount of ointment expended which was the prominent object of their displeasure. We conceive them as saying in effect : " Surely less might have done ; the greater part at least, if not the whole of this ointment, might have been saved for other uses. This is simply senseless, prodigal expenditure."

What to the narrow-hearted disciples seemed prodigality was but the princely magnificence of love, which, as even a heathen philosopher could tell, considers not for how much or how little this or that can be done, but how it can be done most gracefully and handsomely.[1] And what seemed to them purposeless waste served at least one good purpose. It symbolized a similar characteristic of Christ's good work as the Saviour of sinners. *He* did *His* work magnificently, and in no mean, economical way. He accomplished the redemption of "many" by means adequate to redeem all. "With Him is plenteous redemption." He did not measure out His blood in proportion to the number to be saved, nor limit His sympathies as the sinner's friend to the elect. He shed bitter tears for doomed souls; He shed His blood without measure, and without respect to numbers, and offered an atonement which was sufficient for the sins of the world. Nor was this attribute of universal sufficiency attaching to His atoning work one to which He was indifferent. On the contrary, it appears to have been in His thoughts at the very moment He uttered the words authorizing the association of Mary's deed of love with the gospel. For He speaks of that gospel, which was to consist in the proclamation of His deed of love in dying for sinners, as a gospel for the whole world; evidently desiring that, as the odor of Mary's ointment filled the room in which the guests were assembled, so the aroma of His sacrifice might be diffused as an atmosphere of saving health among all the nations.

We may say, therefore, that in defending Mary against the charge of waste, Jesus was at the same time defending Himself; replying by anticipation to such questions as these : To what purpose weep over doomed Jerusalem ? why sorrow for souls that are after all to perish ? why trouble Himself about men not elected to salvation ? why command His gospel to be preached to every creature, with an emphasis which seems to say He wishes every one saved, when He knows only a definite number will believe the report ? why not

[1] *Vide* p. 25.

confine His sympathies and His solicitudes to those who shall be effectually benefited by them ? why not restrict His love to the channel of the covenant ? why allow it to overflow the embankments like a river in full flood ? [1]

Such questions betray ignorance of the conditions under which even the elect are saved. Christ could not save any unless He were heartily willing to save all, for that willing-ness is a part of the perfect righteousness which it behoved Him to fulfil. The sum of duty is, Love God supremely, and thy neighbor as thyself ; and "neighbor" means, for Christ as for us, every one who needs help, and whom He can help. But not to dwell on this, we remark that such questions show ignorance of the nature of love. Magnifi-cence, misnamed by churls extravagance and waste, is an invariable attribute of all true love. David recognized this truth when he selected the profuse anointing of Aaron with the oil of consecration at his installation into the office of high priest as a fit emblem of brotherly love.[2] There was "waste" in that anointing too, as well as in the one which took place at Bethany. For the oil was not *sprinkled* on the head of Aaron, though that might have been sufficient for the purpose of a mere ceremony. The vessel was emptied on the high priest's person, so that its contents flowed down from the head upon the beard, and even to the skirts of the sacerdotal robes. In that very waste lay the point of the resemblance for David. It was a feature that was likely to strike his mind, for he, too, was a wasteful man in his way. He had loved God in a manner which exposed him to the charge of extravagance. He had danced before the Lord, for example, when the ark was brought up from the house of Obed-edom to Jerusalem, forgetful of his dignity, exceeding the bounds of decorum, and, as it might seem, without excuse, as a much less hearty demonstration of his feelings would have served the purpose of a religious solemnity.[3]

David, Mary, Jesus, all loving, devoted beings, prophets,

---

[1] On the apparent waste in the economy of redemption, there are some good remarks in the writings of Andrew Fuller, and especially in *Three Conversations on Particular Redemption.* He says : "It accords with the general conduct of God to impart His favors with a kind of profusion which, to the mind of man that sees only one or two ends to be answered by them, may have the appearance of waste."

[2] Ps. cxxxiii.   [3] 2 Sam. vi.

apostles, martyrs, confessors, belong to one company, and come all under one condemnation. They must all plead guilty to a waste of affection, sorrow, labor, tears; all live so as to earn for themselves the blame of extravagance, which is their highest praise. David dances, and Michal sneers; prophets break their hearts for their people's sins and miseries, and the people make sport of their grief; Marys break their alabaster boxes, and frigid disciples object to the waste; men of God sacrifice their all for their religious convictions, and the world calls them fools for their pains, and philosophers bid them beware of being martyrs by mistake; Jesus weeps over sinners that will not come to Him to be saved, and thankless men ask, Why shed tears over vessels of wrath fitted for destruction?

We have thus seen that Mary's good deed was a fit and worthy emblem of the good deed of Jesus Christ in dying on the cross. We are now to show that Mary herself is in some important respects worthy to be spoken of as a model Christian. Three features in her character entitle her to this honorable name.

First among these is her enthusiastic attachment to the person of Christ. The most prominent feature in Mary's character was her power of loving, her capacity of self-devotion. It was this virtue, as manifested in her action, that elicited the admiration of Jesus. He was so delighted with the chivalrous deed of love, that He, so to speak, canonized Mary on the spot, as a king might confer knighthood on the battle-field on a soldier who had performed some noble feat of arms. "Behold," He said in effect, "here is what I understand by Christianity: an unselfish and uncalculating devotion to me as the Saviour of sinners, and as the Sovereign of the kingdom of truth and righteousness. Therefore, wherever the gospel is preached, let this that this woman hath done be spoken of, not merely as a memorial of her, but to intimate what I expect of all who believe in me."

In so commending Mary, Jesus gives us to understand in effect that devotion is the chief of Christian virtues. He proclaims the same doctrine afterwards taught by one who, though last, was the first of all the apostles in his comprehension of the mind of Christ — the Apostle Paul. That glowing panegyric on charity, so well known to all readers of his epistles, in which he makes eloquence, knowledge, faith, the gift of tongues, and the gift of prophecy, do obeisance to her, as the sovereign virtue, is but the faithful interpretation in general terms of the encomium pronounced on the woman of Bethany. The story of the anointing and the thirteenth chapter of the First Epistle to the Corinthians may be read with advantage together.

In making love the test and measure of excellence, Jesus and Paul, and the rest of the apostles (for they all shared the Master's mind at last), differ widely from the world religious and irreligious. Pharisees and Sadducees, scrupulous religionists, and unscrupulous men of no religion, agree in disliking ardent, enthusiastic, chivalrous devotion, even in the most noble cause. They are wise and prudent, and their philosophy might be embodied in such maxims as these: "Be not too catholic in your sentiments, too warm in your sympathies, too keen in your sense of duty; never allow your heart to get the better of your head, or your principles to interfere with your interest." So widely diffused is the dislike to earnestness, especially in good, that all nations have their proverbs against enthusiasm. The Greeks had their μηδὲν ἄγαν, the Latins their *Ne quid nimis;* [1] expressing scepticism in proverb-maker and proverb-quoter as to the possibility of wisdom being enthusiastic about any thing. The world is prosaic, not poetic, in temperament — prudential, not impulsive: it abhors eccentricity in good or in evil; it prefers a dead level of mediocrity, moderation, and self-possession; its model man is one who never forgets himself, either by sinking below himself in folly or wickedness, or by rising above himself, and getting rid of meanness, pride, selfishness, cowardice, and vanity in devotion to a noble cause.

The twelve were like the world in their temperament at the time of the anointing: they seem to have regarded Mary as a romantic, quixotic, crazy creature, and her action as absurd and indefensible. They objected not, of course, to her love of Jesus; but they deemed the manner of its manifestation foolish, as the money spent on the ointment might have been applied to a better purpose — say, to the relief of the

---

[1] The Scotch proverb to the same effect is, " Nae owers are guid."

destitute — and Jesus loved nothing the less, seeing that, according to His own teaching, all philanthropic actions were deeds of kindness to Himself. And, on first thoughts, one is half inclined to say that they had reason on their side, and were far wiser, while not less devoted to Jesus than Mary. But look at their behavior on the day of their Lord's crucifixion, and learn the difference between them and her. Mary loved so ardently as to be beyond calculations of consequences or expenses ; they loved so coldly, that there was room for fear in their hearts : therefore, while Mary spent her all on the ointment, they all forsook their Master, and fled to save their own lives. Whence we can see that, despite occasional extravagances, apparent or real, that spirit is wisest as well as noblest which makes us incapable of calculation, and proof against temptations arising therefrom. One rash, blundering, but heroic Luther is worth a thousand men of the Erasmus type, unspeakably wise, but cold, passionless, timid, and time-serving. Scholarship is great, but action is greater ; and the power to do noble actions comes from love.

How great is the devoted Mary compared with the cold-hearted disciples ! She does noble deeds, and they criticise them. Poor work for a human being, criticism, especially the sort that abounds in fault-finding ! Love does not care for such occupation ; it is too petty for her generous mind. If there be room for praise, she will give that in unstinted measure ; but rather than carp and blame, she prefers to be silent. Then observe again how love in Mary becomes a substitute for prescience. She does not know that Jesus is about to die, but she acts as if she did. Such as Mary can divine ; the *instincts* of love, the inspiration of the God of love, teach them to do the right thing at the right time, which is the very highest attainment of true wisdom. On the other hand, we see in the case of the disciples how coldness of heart consumes knowledge and makes men stupid. They had received far more information than Mary concerning the future. If they did not know that Jesus was about to be put to death, they ought to have known from the many hints and even plain intimations which had been given them. But, alas ! they had forgot all these. And why ? For the same reason which makes all men so forgetful of things

pertaining to their neighbors. The twelve were too much
taken up with their own affairs. Their heads were filled
with vain dreams of worldly ambition, and so their Master's
words were forgotten almost as soon as they were uttered,
and it became needful that He should tell them pathetically
and reproachfully : " The poor ye have always with you, but
me ye have not always." Men so minded never understand
the times, so as to know what Israel ought to do, or to
approve the conduct of those who do know.

A second admirable feature in Mary's character was the
freedom of her spirit. She was not tied down to methods
and rules of well-doing. The disciples, judging from their
language, seem to have been great methodists, servile in
their adherence to certain stereotyped modes of action.
" This ointment," said they, " might have been sold for much,
and given to the *poor*." They understand that charity to the
poor is a very important duty : they know that their Master
often referred to it ; and they make it every thing. " Charity,"
in the sense of almsgiving,[1] is their hobby. When Judas
went out to betray his Lord, they fancied that he was gone
to distribute what remained of the supper among some poor
persons of his acquaintance. Their very ideas of well-doing
appear to be method-ridden. Good works with them do not
seem to be co-extensive with noble deeds of all sorts. The
phrase is technical, and limited in its application to a confined
circle of actions of an expressly and obviously religious and
benevolent nature.

Not so with Mary. She knows of more ways of doing
good than one. She can invent ways of her own. She is
original, creative, not slavishly imitative. And she is as
fearless as she is original. She cannot only imagine forms
of well-doing out of the beaten track, but she has the courage
to realize her conceptions. She is not afraid of the public.
She does not ask beforehand, What will the twelve think

---

[1] We cannot regard as an improvement the exclusion of the word charity from the
Revised Version. The motive is obvious enough, the fact that it is often employed in
the sense of alms-giving. But it has a well-understood sense besides that, viz. " catholic
love ; " and it is altogether too precious a word in our religious vocabulary to be thrown
away. The effect of the omission on the style of the R. V. is sometimes very unhappy.
Thus in 2 Pet. i. 7, for " to brotherly kindness charity," in the A. V., we have in R. V.,
" in your love of the brethren love." What could be more helpless ?

of this ? With a free mind she forms her plan, and with prompt, free hand she forthwith executes it.

For this freedom Mary was indebted to her large heart. Love made her original in thought and conduct. People without heart cannot be original as she was. They may addict themselves to good works from one motive or another ; but they go about them in a very slavish, mechanical way. They have to be told by some individual in whom they confide, or more commonly, by custom or fashión, what to do ; and hence they never do any good which is not in vogue. But Mary needed no counsellor : she took counsel of her own heart. Love told her infallibly what was the duty of the hour ; that her business for the present was not to give alms, but to anoint the person of the great High Priest.

We may learn from the example of Mary that love is, not less than necessity, the mother of invention. A great heart has fully as much to do with spiritual originality as a clever head. What is needed to fill the church with original preachers, original givers, original actors in all departments of Christian work, is not more brains, or more training, or more opportunities, but above all, more *heart*. When there is little love in the Christian community, it resembles a river in dry weather, which not only keeps within its banks, but does not even occupy the whole of its channel, leaving large beds of gravel or sand lying high and dry on both sides of the current. But when the love of God is shed abroad in the hearts of her members, the church becomes like the same river in time of rain. The stream begins to rise, all the gravel beds gradually disappear, and at length the swollen flood not only fills its channel, but overflows its banks, and spreads over the meadows. New methods of well-doing are then attempted, and new measures of well-doing reached ; new songs are indited and sung ; new forms of expression for old truths are invented, not for the sake of novelty, but in the creative might of a new spiritual life.

It was love that made Mary free from fear, as well as from the bondage of mechanical custom. "Love," saith one who knew love's power well, "casteth out fear." Love can make even shrinking, sensitive women bold — bolder even than men. It can teach us to disregard that thing called public

opinion, before which all mankind cowers.   It was love that
made Peter and John so bold when they stood before the
Sanhedrim.   They had been with Jesus long enough to love
Him more than their own life, and therefore they quailed not
before the face of the mighty.   It was love that made Jesus
Himself so indifferent to censure, and so disregardful of
conventional restraints in the prosecution of His work.   His
heart was so devoted to His philanthropic mission, that He
set at defiance the world's disapprobation ; nay, probably did
not so much as think of it, except when it obtruded itself
upon His notice.   And what love did for Mary, and for Jesus,
and for the apostles in after days, it does for all.   Wherever
it exists in liberal measure, it banishes timidity and shyness,
and the imbecility which accompanies these, and brings along
with it power of character and soundness of mind.   And
to crown the encomium, we may add, that while it makes
us bold, love does not make us impudent.   Some men are
bold because they are too selfish to care for other people's
feelings.   Those who are bold through love may dare to do
things which will be found fault with ; but they are always
anxious, as far as possible, to please their neighbors, and to
avoid giving offence.

One remark more let us make under this head.   The liberty
which springs from love can never be dangerous.   In these
days many people are greatly alarmed at the progress of
broad school theology.   And of the breadth that consists in
sceptical indifference to catholic Christian truth we do well to
be jealous.   But, on the other hand, of the breadth and
freedom due to consuming love for Christ, and all the grand
interests of His kindgom, we cannot have too much.   The
spirit of charity may indeed treat as comparatively light
matters, things which men of austere mind deem of almost
vital importance, and may be disposed to do things which
men more enamoured of order and use and wont than of
freedom may consider licentious innovations.   But the harm
done will be imaginary rather than real ; and even if it were
otherwise, the impulsive Marys are never so numerous in the
church that they may not safely be tolerated.   There are
always a sufficient number of prosaic, order-loving disciples
to keep their quixotic brethren in due check.

Finally, the *nobility* of Mary's spirit was not less remarkable than its freedom. There was no taint of vulgar utilitarianism about her character. She thought habitually, not of the immediately, obviously, and materially useful, but of the honorable, the lovely, the morally beautiful. Hard, practical men might have pronounced her a romantic, sentimental, dreamy mystic; but a more just, appreciative estimate would represent her as a woman whose virtues were heroic and chivalrous rather than commercial. Jesus signalized the salient point in Mary's character by the epithet which He employed to describe her action. He did not call it a useful work, but a good, or, better still, a *noble* work.

And yet, while Mary's deed was characteristically noble, it was not the less useful. All good deeds are useful in some way and at some time or other. All noble and beautiful things — thoughts, words, deeds — contribute ultimately to the benefit of the world. Only the uses of such deeds as Mary's — of the best and noblest needs — are not always apparent or appreciable. If we were to make immediate, obvious, and vulgar uses the test of what is right, we should exclude not only the anointing in Bethany, but all fine poems and works of art, all sacrifices of material advantage to truth and duty; every thing, in fact, that has not tended directly to increase outward wealth and comfort, but has merely helped to redeem the world from vulgarity, given us glimpses of the far-off land of beauty and goodness, concerning which we now and then but faintly dream, brought us into contact with the divine and the eternal, made the earth classic ground, a field where heroes have fought, and where their bones are buried, and where the moss-grown stone stands to commemorate their valor.

In this nobility of spirit Mary was pre-eminently *the Christian*. For the genius of Christianity is certainly not utilitarian. Its counsel is: "Whatsoever things are true, whatsoever things are venerable, whatsoever things are just, whatsoever things are pure, whatsoever things are lovely, think of these things." All these things are emphatically useful; but it is not of their utility, but of themselves, we are asked to think, and that for a very good reason. Precisely in order to be useful, we must aim at something higher than usefulness; just as, in order to be happy, we must aim at something higher than happiness. We must make right revealed to us by an enlightened conscience and a loving pure heart our rule of duty, and then we may be sure that uses of all kinds will be served by our conduct, whether we foresee them or not; whereas, if we make calculations of utility our guide in action, we shall leave undone the things which are noblest and best, because as a rule the uses of such things are least obvious, and longest in making their appearance. Supremely useful to the world is the heroic devotion of the martyr; but it takes centuries to develop the benefits of martyrdom; and if all men had followed the maxims of utilitarian philosophy, and made utility their motive to action, there would never have been any martyrs at all. Utilitarianism tends to trimming and time-serving; it is the death of heroism and self-sacrifice; it walks by sight, and not by faith; it looks only to the present, and forgets the future; it seats prudence on the throne of conscience; it produces not great characters, but at best petty busybodies. These things being considered, it need not surprise us to find that the term "usefulness," of such frequent recurrence in the religious vocabulary of the present day, has no place in the New Testament.[1]

Four further observations may fitly close these meditations on the memorable transactions in Bethany.

1. In all the attributes of character hitherto enumerated, Mary was a model of genuinely evangelic piety. The evangelic spirit is a spirit of noble love and fearless *liberty*. It is a counterfeit evangelicism that is a slave to the past, to tradition, to fixed customs and methods in religion. The true name for this temper and tendency is *legalism*.

2. From Christ's defence of Mary we may learn that being found fault with is not infallible evidence of being wrong. A much-blamed man is commonly considered to have done something amiss, as the only possible reason for his being censured. But, in truth, he may only have done something unusual; for all unusual things are found fault with — the unusually good as well as, nay, more than, the unusually bad. Hence it comes

---

[1] On the defects of utilitarian morality see Sir James Macintosh's *Dissertation*, under Jeremy Bentham.

that Paul makes the apparently superfluous remark, that there
is no law against love and its kindred graces. In point of
fact, these virtues are treated as if illegal and criminal when-
ever they exceed the usual stinted niggard measure in which
such precious metals are found in the world. Was not He
who perfectly embodied all the heavenly graces flung out of
existence by the world as a person not to be tolerated ?
Happily the world ultimately comes round to a juster opinion,
though often too late to be of service to those who have
suffered wrong. The barbarians of the island of Malta, who,
when they saw the viper fastened on Paul's hand, thought
he must needs be a murderer, changed their minds when he
shook off the reptile unharmed, and exclaimed, "He is a
god." Hence we should learn this maxim of prudence, not
to be too hasty in criticising if we want to have credit for
insight and consistency. But we should discipline ourselves
to slowness in judging from far higher considerations. We
ought to cherish a reverence for the character and for the
personality of all intelligent responsible beings, and to be
under a constant fear of making mistakes, and calling good
evil, and evil good. In the words of an ancient philosopher,
"We ought always to be very careful when about to blame
or praise a man, lest we speak not rightly. For this purpose
it is necessary to learn to discriminate between good and
bad men. For God is displeased when one blames a person
like Himself, or praises one unlike Himself. Do not imagine
that stones and sticks, and birds and serpents, are holy, and
that men are not. For of all things the holiest is a good
man, and the most detestable a bad." [1]

3. If we cannot be Christians like Mary, let us at all events
not be disciples like Judas. Some may think it would not
be desirable that all should be like the woman of Bethany :
plausibly alleging that, considering the infirmity of human
nature, it is necessary that the romantic, impulsive, mystic
school of Christians should be kept in check by another
school of more prosaic, conservative, and so to say, plebeian
character; while perhaps admitting that a few Christians
like Mary in the church help to preserve religion from
degenerating into coarseness, vulgarity, and formalism. Be

[1] Plato, *Minos*.

this as it may, the church has certainly no need for Judases. Judas and Mary! these two represent the two extremes of human character. The one exemplifies Plato's πάντων μιαρώτατον (hatefullest of all things), the other his πάντων ἱερώτατον (holiest of all things). Characters so diverse compel us to believe in a heaven and a hell. Each one goeth to his and her own place: Mary to the "land of the leal;" Judas to the land of the false, who sell their conscience and their God for gold.

4. It is worthy of notice how naturally and appropriately Jesus, in His magnanimous defence of Mary's generous, large-hearted deed, rises to the full height of prophetic prescience, and anticipates for His gospel a world-wide diffusion: "Wheresoever this gospel shall be preached *in the whole world.*" Such a gospel could be nothing less than world-wide in sympathy, and no one who understood it and its Author could fail to have a burning desire to go into all the world and preach it unto every creature. This universalistic touch in Christ's utterance at this time, far from taking us by surprise, rather seems a matter of course. Even critics of the naturalistic school allow its genuineness. "This word in Bethany," says one of the ablest writers on the Gospel history belonging to this school, "is the solitary quite reliable word of the last period of Christ's life concerning the world-wide career which Jesus saw opening up for Himself and His cause."[1] If therefore the twelve remained narrow Judaists to the end, it was not due to the absence of the universalistic element in their Master's teaching, but simply to this, that they remained permanently as incapable of appreciating Mary's act, and the gospel whereof it was an emblem, as they showed themselves at this time. That they did so continue, however, we do not believe; and the best evidence of this is that the story of Mary of Bethany has attained a place in the evangelic records.

---

[1] Keim, *Geschichte Jesu*, iii. 224.

19

FIRSTFRUITS OF THE GENTILES

John 12:20-23

THIS narrative presents interesting points of affinity with that contained in the fourth chapter of John's Gospel, — the story of the woman by the well. In both Jesus comes into contact with persons outside the pale of the Jewish church; in both He takes occasion from such contact to speak in glowing language of an hour that is coming, yea, now is, which shall usher in a glorious new era for the kingdom of God; in both He expresses, in the most intense, emphatic terms, His devotion to His Father's will, His faith in the future spread of the gospel, and His lively hope of a personal reward in glory;[1] in both, to note yet one other point of resemblance, He employs, for the expression of His thought, agricultural metaphors: in one case, the earlier, borrowing His figure from the process of reaping; in the other, the later, from that of sowing.

But, besides resemblances, marked differences are observable in these two passages from the life of the Lord Jesus. Of these the most outstanding is this, that while on the earlier occasion there was nothing but enthusiasm, joy, and hope in the Saviour's breast, on the present occasion these feelings are blended with deep sadness. His soul is not only elated with the prospect of coming glory, but troubled as with the prospect of impending disaster. The reason is that His death is nigh: it is within three days of the time when He must be lifted up on the cross; and sentient nature shrinks from the bitter cup of suffering.

---

[1] John iv. 34–36. Ver. 34 expresses Christ's devotion; ver. 35 His faith, making visible and present things not seen and future; ver. 36 His hope of a great reward in common with all sowers and reapers.

But while we observe the presence of a new emotion here, we also see that its presence produces no abatement in the old emotions manifested by Jesus in connection with His interview with the woman of Samaria. On the contrary, the near prospect of death only furnishes the Saviour with the means of giving enhanced intensity to the expression of His devotion and His faith and hope. Formerly He said that the doing of His Father's will was more to Him than *meat;* now He says in effect that it is more to Him than *life.*[1] At the beginning He had seen by the eye of faith a vast extent of fields, white already to the harvest, in the wide wilderness of Gentile lands ; now He not only continues to see these fields in spite of His approaching passion, but He sees them as the *effect* thereof — a whole world of golden grain growing out of one corn of wheat cast into the ground, and rendered fruitful of life by its own death.[2] At the well of Sychar He had spoken with lively hope of the wages in store for Himself, and all fellow-laborers in the kingdom of God, whether sowers or reapers ; here death is swallowed up in victory, through the power of His hope. To suffer is to enter into glory ; to be lifted up on the cross is to be exalted to heaven, and seated on the throne of a world-wide dominion.[3]

The men who desired to see Jesus while He stood in one of the courts of the temple were, the evangelist informs us, Greeks. Whence they came, whether from east or from west, or from north or from south, we know not ; but they were evidently bent on entering into the kingdom of God. They had got so far on the way to the kingdom already. The presumption, at least, is that they had left Paganism behind, and had embraced the faith of One living, true God, as taught by the Jews, and were come at this time up to Jerusalem to worship at the Passover as Jewish proselytes.[4] But they had not, it would seem, found rest to their souls : there was something more to be known about God which was still hid from them. This they hoped to learn from Jesus, with whose name and fame they had somehow become

---

[1] John xii. 28.   [2] Ver. 24.   [3] Vers. 23, 32.
[4] This is the natural inference even from the A. V., "there were certain Greeks *among* them that came up to worship," retained in R. V. The true rendering is, "there were certain Greeks of the number of those " (Greeks), etc. (ἐκ τῶν ἀναβαινόντων, not ἐν τοῖς). So Dr. Field of Norwich in *Otium Norvicense*, Part iii.

acquainted. Accordingly, an opportunity presenting itself to them of communicating with one of those who belonged to His company, they respectfully expressed to him their desire to meet his Master. " Sir," said they, " we would see Jesus." In themselves the words might be nothing more than the expression of a curious wish to get a passing glimpse of one who was understood to be a remarkable man. Such an interpretation of the request, however, is excluded by the deep emotion it awakened in the breast of Jesus. Idle curiosity would not have stirred His soul in such a fashion. Then the notion that these Greeks were merely curious strangers is entirely inconsistent with the connection in which the story is introduced. John brings in the present narrative immediately after quoting a reflection made by the Pharisees respecting the popularity accruing to Jesus from the resurrection of Lazarus. " Perceive ye," said they to each other, " how ye prevail nothing ? Behold, the world has gone after Him." " Yes, indeed," rejoins the evangelist in effect, " and that to an extent of which ye do not dream. He whom ye hate is beginning to be inquired after, even by Gentiles from afar, as the following history will show."

We do right, then, to regard the Greek strangers as earnest inquirers. They were true seekers after God. They were genuine spiritual descendants of their illustrious countrymen Socrates and Plato, whose utterances, written or unwritten, were one long prayer for light and truth, one deep unconscious sigh for a sight of Jesus. They wanted to see the Saviour, not with the eye of the body merely, but, above all, with the eye of the spirit.

The part played by the two disciples named in the narrative, in connection with this memorable incident, claims a brief notice. Philip and Andrew had the honor to be the medium of communication between the representatives of the Gentile world and Him who had come to fulfil the desire and be the Saviour of all nations. The devout Greeks addressed themselves to the former of these two disciples, and he in turn took his brother-disciple into his counsels. How Philip came to be selected as the bearer of their request by these Gentile inquirers, we do not know. Reference has been made to the fact that the name Philip is Greek, as implying the probability that the disciple who bore it had Greek connections, and the possibility of a previous acquaintance between him and the persons who accosted him on this occasion. There may be something in these conjectures, but it is more important to remark that the Greeks were happy in their choice of an intercessor. Philip was himself an inquirer, and had an inquirer's sympathy with all who might be in a similar state of mind. The first time he is named in the Gospel history he is introduced expressing his faith in Jesus, as one who had carefully sought the truth, and who, having at length found what he sought, strove to make others partakers of the blessing. "Philip findeth Nathanael, and saith unto him, We have found Him of whom Moses, in the law and the prophets, did write, Jesus of Nazareth, the son of Joseph." The exactness and fulness of this confession speaks to careful and conscientious search. And Philip has still the inquirer's temper. A day or two subsequent to this meeting with the Greeks, we find him making for himself the most important request: "Lord, show us the Father, and it sufficeth us."

But why, then, does this sympathetic disciple not convey the request of the Greeks direct to Jesus? Why take Andrew with him, as if afraid to go alone on such an errand? Just because the petitioners are Greeks and Gentiles. It is one thing to introduce a devout Jew like Nathanael to Jesus, quite another to introduce Gentiles, however devout. Philip is pleased that his Master should be inquired after in such a quarter, but he is not sure about the propriety of acting on his first impulse. He hesitates, and is in a flurry of excitement in presence of what he feels to be a new thing, a significant event, the beginning of a religious revolution.[1] His inclination is to play the part of an intercessor for the Greeks; but he distrusts his own judgment, and, before acting on it, lays the case before his brother-disciple and fellow-townsman Andrew, to see how it will strike him. The result of the consultation was, that the two disciples came and told their Master. They felt that they were perfectly

---

[1] Luthardt (*Das Joh. Evan.* i. 102) thinks this hesitancy specially characteristic of Philip, and contrasts with it the promptitude of Andrew, as exhibited here, and also in John vi. 9. This is possible. Thoughtful, inquiring men are often unready in practical ma ters.

safe in mentioning the matter to Him, and then leaving Him to do as He pleased.

From the narrative of the evangelist we learn that the communication of the two disciples mightily stirred the soul of Jesus. Manifestations of spiritual susceptibility, by persons who were aliens from the commonwealth of Israel, did always greatly move His feelings. The open-mindedness of the people of Sychar, the simple faith of the Roman centurion, the quick-witted faith of the Syro-Phœnician woman, the gratitude of the Samaritan leper, touched Him profoundly. Such exhibitions of spiritual life in unexpected quarters came upon His spirit like breezes on an Æolian harp, drawing forth from it sweetest tones of faith, hope, joy, charity ; and, alas ! also sometimes sad, plaintive tones of disappointment and sorrow, like the sighing of the autumn wind among Scottish pines, when He thought of the unbelief and spiritual deadness of the chosen people for whom He had done so much.[1] Never was His heart more deeply affected than on the present occasion. No marvel ! What sight more moving than that of a human being seeking after God, the fountain of light and of life ! Then the spontaneity of these Greek inquirers is beautiful. It is something to be thankful for in this unspiritual, unbelieving world, when one and another, here and there, responds to God's call, and receives a divine word which has been spoken to him. But here we have the rare spectacle of men coming uncalled : not sought after by Christ, and accepting Him offering Himself to them as a Saviour and Lord, but seeking Him, and begging it as a great favor to be admitted to His presence, that they may offer Him their sincere homage, and hear Him speak words of eternal life. They come, too, from a most unusual quarter ; and, what is still more worthy to be noticed, at a most critical time. Jesus is just about to be conclusively rejected by His own people ; just on the point of being crucified by them. Some have shut their eyes, and stopped their ears, and hardened their hearts in the most determined manner against Him and His teaching ; others,

[1] John xii. 37-43. See next chapter of this work, the perusal of which may help the reader to understand the emotion awakened in Christ's breast by the request of these Greek strangers.

not insensible to His merits, have meanly and heartlessly concealed their convictions, fearing the consequences of an open profession. The saying of the Prophet Esaias has been fulfilled in His bitter experience, " Who hath believed our report? and to whom hath the arm of the Lord been revealed?" Pharisaism, Sadduceeism, ignorance, indifference, fickleness, cowardice, have confronted Him on every side. How refreshing, amidst abounding contradiction, stupidity, and dull insusceptibility, this intimation brought to Him at the eleventh hour : " Here are certain Greeks who are interested in you, and want to see you!" The words fall on His ear like a strain of sweet music ; the news is reviving to His burdened spirit like the sight of a spring to a weary traveller in a sandy desert ; and in the fulness of His joy He exclaims : " The hour is come that the Son of man should be glorified." Rejected by His own people, He is consoled by the inspiring assurance that He shall be believed on in the world, and accepted by the outlying nations as all their salvation and all their desire.

The thoughts of Jesus at this time were as deep as His emotions were intense. Specially remarkable is the first thought to which He gave utterance in these words : " Verily, verily, I say unto you, Except a corn of wheat fall into the ground and die, it abideth alone ; but if it die, it bringeth forth much fruit." He speaks here with the solemnity of one conscious that he is announcing a truth new and strange to his hearers. His object is to make it credible and comprehensible to His disciples, that death and increase may go together. He points out to them that the fact is so in the case of grain ; and He would have them understand that the law of increase, not only in *spite* but in *virtue* of death, will hold true equally in His own case. " A grain of wheat, by dying, becometh fruitful ; so I must die in order to become, on a large scale, an object of faith and source of life. During my lifetime I have had little success. Few have believed, many have disbelieved ; and they are about to crown their unbelief by putting me to death. But my death, so far from being, as they fancy, my defeat and destruction, will be but the beginning of my glorification. After I have been crucified, I shall begin to be believed in extensively as the Lord and Saviour of men."

Having by the analogy of the corn of wheat set forth death as the condition of fruitfulness, Jesus, in a word subsequently spoken, proclaimed His approaching crucifixion as the secret of His future *power.* " I," said He, " if I be lifted up from the earth, will *draw* all men unto me." He used the expression "lifted up" in a double sense, — partly, as the evangelist informs us, in allusion to the manner of His death, partly with reference to His ascension into heaven ; and He meant to say, that after He had been taken up into glory, He would, through His cross, attract the eyes and hearts of men towards Himself. And, strange as such a statement might appear before the event, the fact corresponded to the Saviour's expectation. The cross — symbol of shame ! — did become a source of glory ; the sign of weakness became an instrument of moral power. Christ crucified, though to unbelieving Jews a stumbling-block, and to philosophic Greeks foolishness, became to many believers the power of God and the wisdom of God. By His voluntary humiliation and meek endurance of suffering the Son of God *drew* men to Him in sincerest faith, and devoted reverential love.

The largeness of Christ's desires and expectations is very noteworthy. He speaks of "much fruit," and of drawing "all men" unto Him. Of course we are not to look here for an exact definition of the extent of redemption. Jesus speaks as a man giving utterance, in the fulness of his heart, to his high, holy hope ; and we may learn from His ardent words, if not the theological extent of atonement, at least the *extensiveness* of the Atoner's good wishes. He would have all men believe in Him and be saved. He complained with deep melancholy of the fewness of believers among the Jews ; He turned with unspeakable longing to the Gentiles, in hope of a better reception from them. The greater the number of believers at any time and in any place, the better He is pleased ; and He certainly does not contemplate with indifference the vast amount of unbelief which still prevails in all quarters of the world. His heart is set on the complete expulsion of the prince of this world from his usurped dominion, that He Himself may reign over all the kingdoms of the earth.

The narrative contains a word of application addressed by Jesus to His disciples in connection with the law of increase by death, saying in effect that it applied to them as well as to Himself.[1] This appears at first surprising, insomuch that we are tempted to think that the sayings alluded to are brought in here by the evangelist out of their true historical connection. But on reconsideration we come to think otherwise. We observe that in all cases, wherever it is possible, Christ in His teaching takes His disciples into partnership with Himself. He does not insist on those aspects of truth which are peculiar to Himself, but rather on those which are common to Him with His followers. If there be any point of contact at all, any sense in which what He states of Himself is true of those who believe in Him, He seizes on that, and makes it a prominent topic of discourse. So He did on the occasion of the meeting by the well; so when He first plainly announced to His disciples that He was to be put to death. And so also He does here. Here, too, He asserts a fellowship between Himself and His followers in respect to the necessity of death as a condition of fruitfulness. And the fellowship asserted is not a far-fetched conceit: it is a great practical reality. The principle laid down is this, that in proportion as a man is a partaker of Christ's suffering in His estate of humiliation shall he be a partaker of the glory, honor, and power which belong to His estate of exaltation. This principle holds true even in this life. The bearing of the cross, the undergoing of death, is the condition of fruit-bearing both in the sense of personal sanctification and in the sense of effective service in the kingdom of God. In the long-run the measure of a man's power is the extent to which he is baptized into Christ's death. We must fill up that which is behind of the afflictions of Christ in our flesh for His body's sake, which is the church, if we would be the honored instruments of advancing that great work in the world for which He was willing, like a corn of wheat, to fall into the ground and die.

Striking as this saying is, it is not to be reckoned among

[1] John xii. 25, 26.

those which contain a distinct contribution to the doctrine of the cross. No new principle or view is contained therein, only old views restated, the views taught in the first and second lessons being combined — death a condition of *life*[1] and of *power*.[2] Even the very original word concerning the corn of wheat shows us no new aspect of Christ's death, but only helps by a familiar analogy to understand how death can be a means of increase. The main use of the foregoing chapter is to show us the beginnings of that Christian universalism which Jesus anticipated in speaking of Mary's act of anointing, and to serve as a foil to the chapter that follows concerning the doom of Jerusalem.

---

[1] Matt. xvi. 25; cf. John xii. 25.   [2] Matt. xx. 28; cf. John xii. 24.

20

O JERUSALEM, JERUSALEM!
or, Discourse on the Last Things

Matt. 21-25, Mark 11-13; Luke 19:29-48; 20, 21

THE few days intervening between the anointing and the Passover were spent by Jesus in daily visits to Jerusalem in company with His disciples, returning to Bethany in the evening. During that time He spoke much in public and in private, on themes congenial to His feelings and situation: the sin of the Jewish nation, and specially of its religious leaders; the doom of Jerusalem, and the end of the world. The record of His sayings during these last days fills five chapters of Matthew's Gospel — a proof of the deep impressions which they made on the mind of the twelve.

Prominent among these utterances, which together form the dying testimony of the "Prophet of Nazareth," stands the great philippic delivered by Him against the scribes and Pharisees of Jerusalem. This terrible discourse had been preceded by various encounters between the speaker and His inverate foes, which were as the preliminary skirmishes that form the prelude to a great engagement. In these petty fights Jesus had been uniformly victorious, and had overwhelmed His opponents with confusion. They had asked Him concerning His authority for taking upon Him the office of a reformer, in clearing the temple precincts of traders; and he had silenced them by asking in reply their opinion of John's mission, and by speaking in their hearing the parables of *the Two Sons, the Vinedressers, and the Rejected Stone*,[1] wherein their hypocrisy, unrighteousness, and ultimate damnation were vividly depicted. They had tried to catch Him in a trap by an insnaring question concerning the tribute paid to the Roman government; and

[1] Matt. xxi. 23-46.

he had extricated Himself with ease, by simply asking for a penny, and pointing to the emperor's head on it, demanding of His assailants, "Whose is this image and superscription?" and on receiving the reply, "Cæsar's," giving His judgment in these terms: "Render therefore unto Cæsar the things which are Cæsar's, and unto God the things that are God's." [1] Twice foiled, the Pharisees (with their friends the Herodians) gave place to their usual foes, but present allies, the Sadducees, who attempted to puzzle Jesus on the subject of the resurrection, only to be ignominiously discomfited; [2] whereupon the pharisaic brigade returned to the charge, and through the mouth of a lawyer not yet wholly perverted inquired, "Which is the great commandment in the law?" To this question Jesus gave a direct and serious reply, summing up the whole law in love to God and love to man, to the entire contentment of His interrogator. Then, impatient of further trifling, He blew a trumpet-peal, the signal of a grand offensive attack, by propounding the question, "What think ye of Christ, whose son is He?" and taking occasion from the reply to quote the opening verse of David's martial psalm, asking them to reconcile it with their answer.[3] In appearance fighting the Pharisees with their own weapons, and framing a mere theological puzzle, He was in reality reminding them who *He* was, and intimating to them the predicted doom of those who set themselves against the Lord's anointed.

Thereupon David's Son and David's Lord proceeded to fulfil the prophetic figure, and to make a footstool of the men who sat in Moses' seat, by delivering that discourse in which, to change the figure, the Pharisee is placed in a moral pillory, a mockery and a byword to all after ages; and a sentence is pronounced on the pharisaic character inexorably severe, yet justified by fact, and approved by the conscience of all true Christians.[4] This anti-pharisaic speech may be regarded as the final, decisive, comprehensive, dying testimony of Jesus against the most deadly and damning form of evil prevailing in His age, or that can prevail in any age — religious hypocrisy; and as such it

[1] Matt. xxii. 15–22.   [3] Matt. xxii. 41–45.
[2] Matt. xxii. 23–33.   [4] Matt. xxiii.

forms a necessary part of the Righteous One's witness-bearing in behalf of the truth, to which His disciples are expected to say Amen with no faltering voice. For the spirit of moral resentment is as essential in Christian ethics as the spirit of mercy; nor can any one who regards the anti-pharisaic polemic of the Gospel history as a scandal to be ashamed of, or a blemish to be apologized for, or at least as a thing which, however necessary at the time, propriety now requires us to treat with neglect, — a practice too common in the religious world, — be cleared of the suspicion of having more sympathy at heart with the men by whom the Lord was crucified than with the Lord Himself. Blessed is he who is not ashamed of Christ's sternest words ; who, far from stumbling at those bold prophetic utterances, has rather found in them an aid to faith at the crisis of his religious history, as evincing an identity between the moral sentiments of the Founder of the faith and his own, and helping him to see that what he may have mistaken for, and what claimed to be, Christianity, was not that at all, but only a modern reproduction of a religious system which the Lord Jesus Christ could not endure, or be on civil terms with. Yea, and blessed is the church which sympathizes with, and practically gives effect to, Christ's warning words in the opening of this discourse against clerical ambition, the source of the spiritual tyrannies and hypocrisies denounced. Every church needs to be on its guard against this evil spirit. The government of the Jewish church, theoretically theocratic, degenerated at last into *Rabbinism ;* and it is quite possible for a church which has for its motto, "One is your Master, even Christ," to fall into a state of abject subjection to the power of ambitious ecclesiastics.

Without for a moment admitting that there is any thing in these invectives against hypocrisy to be apologized for, we must nevertheless advert to the view taken of them by some recent critics of the sceptical school. These speeches, then, we are told, are the rash, unqualified utterances of a young man, whose spirit was unmellowed by years and experience of the world ; whose temperament was poetic, therefore irritable, impatient, and unpractical ; and whose temper was that of a Jew, morose, and prone to bitterness in controversy.

At this time, we are further to understand, provoked by persevering opposition, He had lost self-possession, and had abandoned Himself to the violence of anger, His bad humor having reached such a pitch as to make Him guilty of actions seemingly absurb, such as that of cursing the fig-tree. He had, in fact, become reckless of consequences, or even seemed to court such as were disastrous ; and, weary of conflict, sought by violent language to precipitate a crisis, and provoke His enemies to put Him to death.[1]

These are blasphemies against the Son of man as unfounded as they are injurious. The last days of Jesus were certainly full of intense excitement, but to a candid mind no traces of passion are discernible in His conduct. All His recorded utterances during those days are in a high key, suited to one whose soul was animated by the most sublime feelings. Every sentence is eloquent, every word tells ; but all throughout is natural, and appropriate to the situation. Even when the terrible attack on the religious leaders of Israel begins, we listen awestruck, but not shocked. We feel that the speaker has a right to use such language, that what He says is true, and that all is said with commanding authority and dignity, such as became the Messianic King. When the speaker has come to an end, we breathe freely, sensible that a delicate though necessary task has been performed with not less wisdom than fidelity. Deep and undisguised abhorrence is expressed in every sentence, such as it would be difficult for any ordinary man, yea, even for an extraordinary one, to cherish without some admixture of that wrath which worketh not the righteousness of God. But in the antipathies of a Divine Being the weakness of passion finds no place : His abhorrence may be deep, but it is also ever calm ; and we challenge unbelievers to point out a single feature in this discourse inconsistent with the hypothesis that the speaker is divine. Nay, leaving out

---

[1] See Renan, *Vie de Jésus*, chap. xix. Keim also thinks there was something faulty in Christ's temper, though admitting that His faults were infirmities springing out of His virtues. Two defects he specifies : *Passionateness*, as shown in His invectives against the Pharisees ; and *Hardness*, inhuman severity, shown in His bearing towards His mother (John ii.), towards John the Baptist (Matt. xi.), and towards the Syro-Phœnician woman (Matt. xv. 21.), — faults both of a noble soul devoted to duty, but choleric in temperament as a true-born Jew. *Vide Geschichte Jesu*, iii. 649.

of view Christ's divinity, and criticising His words with a freedom unfettered by reverence, we can see no traces in them of a man carried headlong by a tempest of anger. We find, after strictest search, no loose expressions, no passionate exaggerations, but rather a style remarkable for artistic precision and accuracy. The pictures of the ostentatious, place-hunting, title-loving rabbi; of the hypocrite, who makes long prayers and devours widows' houses; of the zealot, who puts himself to infinite trouble to make converts, only to make his converts worse rather than better men; of the Jesuitical scribe, who teaches that the gold of the temple is a more sacred, binding thing to swear by than the temple itself; of the Pharisee, whose conscience is strict or lax as suits his convenience; of the whited sepulchres, fair without, full within of dead men's bones; of the men whose piety manifests itself in murdering living prophets and garnishing the sepulchres of dead ones, — are moral daguerreotypes which will stand the minutest inspection of criticism, drawn by no irritated, defeated man, feeling sorely and resenting keenly the malice of his adversaries, but by one who has gained so complete a victory, that He can make sport of His foes, and at all events runs no risk of losing self-control.

The aim of the discourse, equally with its style, is a sufficient defence against the charge of bitter personality. The direct object of the speaker was not to expose the blind guides of Israel, but to save from delusion the people whom they were misguiding to their ruin. The audience consisted of the disciples and the multitude who heard Him gladly. It is most probable that many of the blind guides were present; and it would make no difference to Jesus whether they were or not, for He had not two ways of speaking concerning men — one before their faces, another behind their backs. It is told of Demosthenes, the great Athenian orator, and the determined opponent of Philip of Macedon, that he completely broke down in that king's presence on the occasion of his first appearance before him as an ambassador from his native city. But a greater than Demosthenes is here, whose sincerity and courage are as marvellous as His wisdom and eloquence, and who can say all He thinks of the religious heads of the people in their own hearing. Still, in the present instance, the parties formally addressed were not the heads of the people, but the people themselves; and it is worthy of notice how carefully discriminating the speaker was in the counsel which He gave them. He told them that what He objected to was not so much the teaching of their guides, as their lives : they might follow all their precepts with comparative impunity, but it would be fatal to follow their example. How many reformers in similar circumstances would have joined doctrine and practice together in one indiscriminate denunciation ! Such moderation is not the attribute of a man in a rage.

But the best clew of all to the spirit of the speaker is the manner in which His discourse ends : "O Jerusalem, Jerusalem !" Strange ending for one filled with angry passion ! O Jesus, Jesus ! how Thou risest above the petty thoughts and feelings of ordinary men ! Who shall fathom the depths of Thy heart ? What mighty waves of righteousness, truth, pity, and sorrow roll through Thy bosom !

Having uttered that piercing cry of grief, Jesus left the temple, never, so far as we know, to return. His last words to the people of Jerusalem were : "Behold, your house is left unto you desolate. For I say unto you, Ye shall not see me henceforth, till ye shall say, Blessed is He that cometh in the Name of the Lord." On the way from the city to Bethany, by the Mount of Olives, the rejected Saviour again alluded to its coming doom. The light-hearted disciples had drawn His attention to the strength and beauty of the temple buildings, then in full view. In too sad and solemn a mood for admiring mere architecture, He replied in the spirit of a prophet : "See ye not all these things ? Verily I say unto you, There shall not be left here one stone upon another, that shall not be thrown down." [1]

Arrived at Mount Olivet, the company sat down to take a leisurely view of the majestic pile of which they had been speaking. How different the thoughts and feelings suggested by the same object to the minds of the spectators ! The twelve look with merely outward eye ; their Master looks

[1] Matt. xxiv. 1, 2.

with the inward eye of prophecy. They see nothing before them but the goodly stones ; He sees the profanation in the interior, greedy traders within the sacred precincts, religion so vitiated by ostentation, as to make a poor widow casting her two mites into the treasury, in pious simplicity, a rare and pleasing exception. The disciples think of the present only ; Jesus looks forward to an approaching doom, fearful to contemplate, and doubtless backward too, over the long and checkered history through which the once venerable, now polluted, house of God had passed. The disciples are elated with pride as they gaze on this national structure, the glory of their country, and are happy as thoughtless men are wont to be ; the heart of Jesus is heavy with the sadness of wisdom and prescience, and of love that would have saved, but can now do nothing but weep, and proclaim the awful words of doom.

Yet, with all their thoughtlessness, the twelve could not quite forget those dark forebodings of their Master. The weird words haunted their minds, and made them curious to know more. Therefore they came to Jesus, or some of them — Mark mentions Peter, James, John, and Andrew [1] — and asked two questions : when Jerusalem should be destroyed ; and what should be the signs of His coming, and of the end of the world. The two events referred to in the questions — the end of Jerusalem, and the end of the world — were assumed by the questioners to be contemporaneous. It was a natural and by no means a singular mistake. Local and partial judgments are wont to be thus mixed up with the universal one in men's imaginations ; and hence almost every great calamity which inspires awe leads to anticipations of the last day. Thus Luther, when his mind was clouded by the dark shadow of present tribulation, would remark : "The world cannot stand long, perhaps a hundred years at the outside. At the last will be great alterations and commotions, and already there are great commotions among men. Never had the men of law so much occupation as now. There are vehement dissensions in our families, and discord in the church." [2] In apostolic times Christians expected the immediate coming of Christ with such confidence and ardor, that

[1] Mark xiii. 3.   [2] Luther's *Table Talk*, Bohn's edition, p. 325.

some even neglected their secular business, just as towards the close of the tenth century people allowed churches to fall into disrepair because the end of the world was deemed close at hand.

In reality, the judgment of Jerusalem and that of the world at large were to be separated by a long interval. Therefore Jesus treated the two things as distinct in His prophetic discourse, and gave separate answers to the two questions which the disciples had combined into one, that respecting the end of the world being disposed of first.[1]

The answer He gave to this question was general and negative. He did not fix a time, but said in effect: "The end will not be till such and such things have taken place," specifying six antecedents of the end in succession, the first being the appearance of false Christs.[2] Of these He assured His disciples there would be many, deceiving many; and most truly, for several quack Messiahs did appear even before the destruction of Jerusalem, availing themselves of, and imposing on, the general desire for deliverance, even as quack doctors do in reference to bodily ailments, and succeeding in deceiving many, as unhappily in such times is only too easy. But among the number of their dupes were found none of those who had been previously instructed by the true Christ to regard the appearance of pseudo-Christs merely as one of the signs of an evil time. The deceivers of others were for them a preservative against delusion.

The second antecedent is, "wars and rumors of wars." Nation must rise against nation: there must be times of upheaving and dissolution; declines and falls of empires, and risings of new kingdoms on the ruins of the old. This second sign would be accompanied by a third, in the shape of commotions in the physical world, emblematic of those in

[1] Matt. xxiv. 4-14. The eschatological discourse delivered on the Mount of Olives is confessedly difficult to interpret. Keim remarks that the perplexities are equally great whether we deal with it critically or uncritically, believe or deny its genuineness (vide Geschichte, iii. 193). Two important questions arise in reference to the discourse — (1) Are the end of Jerusalem and the end of the world really kept apart in the discourse as we have it? (2) Granting that the disciples and evangelists confounded the two, is it credible that Jesus also confounded them? Did He not reckon on a long future for His gospel? If He did, and yet no recognition of the fact is to be found in the eschatological discourse as we have it, then the inference would be that the discourse is in some respects not exactly reported. The following exposition sufficiently indicates our view.

[2] Matt. xxiv. 5.

the political.   Famines, earthquakes, pestilences, etc., would occur in divers places.[1]

Yet these things, however dreadful, would be but the beginning of sorrows ; nor would the end come till those signs had repeated themselves again and again.   No one could tell from the occurrence of such phenomena that the end would be now ; he could only infer that it *was not yet.*[2]

Next in order come persecutions, with all the moral and social phenomena of persecuting times.[3]   Christians must undergo a discipline of hatred among the nations because of the Name they bear, and as the reputed authors of all the disasters which befall the people among whom they live. Times must come when, if the Tiber inundate Rome, if the Nile overflow not his fields, if drought, earthquake, famine, or plague visit the earth, the cry of the populace will forthwith be, " The Christians to the lions ! "

Along with persecutions, as a fifth antecedent of the end, would come a sifting of the church.[4]   Many would break down or turn traitors ; there would spring up manifold animosities, schisms, and heresies, each named from its own false prophet.   The prevalence of these evils in the church would give rise to much spiritual declension.   " Because iniquity shall abound, the love of many shall wax cold."[5]

The last thing that must happen ere the end come is the evangelization of the world ; [6] which being achieved, the end would at length arrive.   From this sign we may guess that the world will last a long while yet ; for, according to the law of historical probability, it will be long ere the gospel shall have been preached to all men for a witness.   Ardent Christians or enthusiastic students of prophecy who think otherwise must remember that sending a few missionaries to a heathen country does not satisfy the prescribed condition. The gospel has not been preached to a nation for a witness, that is, so as to form a basis of moral judgment, till it has been preached to the whole people as in Christendom.   This has never yet been done for all the nations, and at the present rate of progress it is not likely to be accomplished for centuries to come.

---

[1] Vers. 6, 7.   [3] Ver. 9.   [5] Ver. 12.
[2] Ver. 8.   [4] Matt. xxiv. 10.   [6] Ver. 14.

Having rapidly sketched an outline of the events that must precede the end of the world, Jesus addressed Himself to the more special question which related to the destruction of Jerusalem.   He could now speak on that subject with more freedom, after He had guarded against the notion that the destruction of the holy city was a sign of His own immediate final coming.   "When, then," He began, — the introductory formula signifying, to answer *now* your first question, — "ye shall see the abomination of desolation spoken of by Daniel the prophet stand in the holy place, then let them which be in Judæa flee into the mountains;" the abomination of desolation being the Roman army with its eagles — abominable to the Jew, desolating to the land. When the eagles appeared, all might flee for their life; resistance would be vain, obstinacy and bravery utterly unavailing.   The calamity would be so sudden that there would be no time to save any thing.   It would be as when a house is on fire ; people would be glad to escape with their life.[1]   It would be a fearful time of tribulation, unparalleled before or after.[2]   Woe to poor nursing mothers in those horrible days, and to such as were with child!   What barbarities and inhumanities awaited them !   The calamities that were coming would spare nobody, not even Christians. They would find safety only in flight, and they would have cause to be thankful that they escaped at all.   But their flight, though unavoidable, might be more or less grievous according to circumstances ; and they should pray for what might appear small mercies, even for such alleviations as that they might not have to flee to the mountains in winter, when it is cold and comfortless, or on the Sabbath, the day of rest and peace.[3]

After giving this brief but graphic sketch of the awful days approaching, intolerable by mortal men were they not shortened " for the elect's sake," Jesus repeated His warning word against deception, as if in fear that His disciples, distracted by such calamities, might think " surely now is the

[1] Matt. xxiv. 17, 18.
[2] Ver. 21.
[3] Vers. 19, 20.   Keim (*Geschichte*, iii. 199) thinks it improbable that Christ should so speak of the Sabbath, and fancies that the language betrays a Judaist author.   This is very minute and very German criticism.

end." He told them that violence would be followed by apostasy and falsehood, as great a trial in one way as the destruction of Jerusalem in another. False teachers should arise, who would be so plausible as almost to deceive the very elect. The devil would appear as an angel of light ; in the desert as a monk, in the shrine as an object of superstitious worship. But whatever men might pretend, the Christ would not be there ; nor would His appearance take place then, nor at any fixed calculable time, but suddenly, unex- pectedly, like the lightning flash in the heavens. When moral corruption had attained its full development, then would the judgment come.[1]

In the following part of the discourse, the end of the world seems to be brought into immediate proximity to the destruction of the holy city.[2] If a long stretch of ages was to intervene, the perspective of the prophetic picture seems at fault. The far-distant mountains of the eternal world, visible beyond and above the near hills of time in the foreground, want the dim-blue haze, which helps the eye to realize how far off they are. This defect in Matthew's narrative, which we have been taking for our text, is supplied by Luke, who interprets the tribulation ($\theta\lambda\hat{\iota}\psi\iota\varsigma$) so as to include the subsequent long-lasting dispersion of Israel among the nations.[3] The phrase he employs to denote this period is significant, as implying the idea of lengthened duration. It is "the times of the Gentiles" ($\kappa\alpha\iota\rho o\grave{\iota}\ \dot{\epsilon}\theta\nu\hat{\omega}\nu$). The expression means, the time when the Gentiles should have their opportunity of enjoying divine grace, correspond- ing to the time of gracious visitation enjoyed by the Jews referred to by Jesus in His lament over Jerusalem.[4] There is no reason to suppose Luke coined these phrases ; they bear the stamp of genuineness upon them. But if we assume, as we are entitled to do, that not Luke the Pauline universalist, but Jesus Himself, spoke of a time of merciful visitation of the Gentiles, then it follows that in His eschatological discourse He gave clear intimation of a lengthened period during

---

[1] Vers. 23-28.

[2] Matt. xxiv. 29.

[3] Luke xxi. 24.

[4] Luke xix. 44, $\tau\grave{o}\nu\ \kappa\alpha\iota\rho\grave{o}\nu\ \tau\hat{\eta}\varsigma\ \dot{\epsilon}\pi\iota\sigma\kappa o\pi\hat{\eta}\varsigma\ \sigma o\upsilon$. For the use of the verb $\dot{\epsilon}\pi\iota\sigma\kappa\acute{\epsilon}\pi\tau o\mu\alpha\iota$ in the sense of to visit graciously, *vide* Luke i. 78.

which His gospel was to be preached in the world; even as He did on other occasions, as in the parable of the wicked husbandman, in which He declared that the vineyard should be taken from its present occupants, and given to others who would bring forth fruit.[1] For it is incredible that Jesus should speak of a time of the Gentiles analogous to the time of merciful visitation enjoyed by the Jews, and imagine that the time of the Gentiles was to last only some thirty years. The Jewish *kairos* lasted thousands of years: it would be only mocking the poor Gentiles to dignify the period of a single generation with the name of a season of gracious visitation.

The parable of the fig-tree, employed by Jesus to indicate the sure connection between the signs foregoing and the grand event that was to follow, seems at first to exclude the idea of a protracted duration, but on second thoughts we shall find it does not. The point of the parable lies in the comparison of the signs of the times to the first buds of the fig-tree. This comparison implies that the last judgment is not the thing which is at the doors. The last day is the harvest season, but from the first buds of early summer to the harvest there is a long interval. The parable further suggests the right way of understanding the statement: " This generation shall not pass till all these things be fulfilled." Christ did not mean that the generation then living was to witness the end, but that in that generation all the things which form the incipient stage in the development would appear. It was the age of beginnings, of shoots and blossoms, not of fruit and ingathering. In that generation fell the beginnings of Christianity and the new world it was to create, and also the end of the Jewish world, of which the symbol was a fig-tree covered with leaves, but without any blossom or fruit, like that Jesus Himself had cursed, by way of an acted prophecy of Israel's coming doom. The buds of most things in the church's history appeared in that age: of gospel preaching, of antichristian tendencies, of persecutions, heresies, schisms, and apostasies. All these, however, had to grow to their legitimate issues before the end came. How long the development would take, no man could tell,

[1] Matt. xxi. 41.

not even the Son of man.[1] It was a state secret of the Almighty, into which no one should wish to pry.

This statement, that the time of the end is known alone to God, excludes the idea that it can be calculated, or that data are given in Scripture for that purpose. If such data be given, then the secret is virtually disclosed. We therefore regard the calculations of students of prophecy respecting the times and seasons as random guesses unworthy of serious attention. The death-day of the world needs to be hid for the purposes of providence as much as the dying-day of individuals. And we have no doubt that God has kept His secret; though some fancy they can cast the world's horoscope from prophetic numbers, as astrologers were wont to determine the course of individual lives from the positions of the stars.

Though the prophetic discourse of Jesus revealed nothing as to times, it was not therefore valueless. It taught effectively two lessons, — one specially for the benefit of the twelve, and the other for all Christians and all ages. The lesson for the twelve was, that they might dismiss from their minds all fond hopes of a restoration of the kingdom to Israel. Not reconstruction, but dissolution and dispersion, was Israel's melancholy doom.

The general lesson for all in this discourse is: "Watch, for ye know not what hour your Lord doth come." The call to watchfulness is based on our ignorance of the time of the end, and on the fact that, however long delayed the end may be, it will come suddenly at last, as a thief in the night. The importance of watching and waiting, Jesus illustrated by two parables, *the Absent Goodman* and *the Wise and Foolish Virgins.*[2] Both parables depict the diverse conduct of the professed servants of God during the period of delay. The

---

[1] Mark xiii. 32. Colani is of opinion that Jesus made this profession of ignorance in direct reply to the original question of the disciples, When will these things (the destruction of Jerusalem) be? He thinks that the actual facts connected with the eschatological discourse are reducible to these: — The disciples asked, When will the destruction of the temple take place? Jesus replied, I do not know, no one knows, and added some simple counsels concerning watching. All the rest of the discourse is an interpolation, reflecting the apocalyptic creed of the Judaistic Christians. A very summary method of solving a difficult problem. *Vide Jésus Christ et les Croyances messianiques de Son Temps,* 2ième. ed. pp. 203-209.

[2] Matt. xxiv. 45-51, xxv. 1-13.

effect on some, we are taught, is to make them negligent, they being eye-servants and fitful workers, who need over-sight and the stimulus of extraordinary events. Others, again, are steady, equal, habitually faithful, working as well when the master is absent as when they are under his eye. The treatment of both on the master's return corresponds to their respective behavior, — one class being rewarded, the other punished. Such is the substance of the parable of the Absent Goodman. Luke gives an important appendix, which depicts the conduct of persons in authority in the house of the absent Lord.[1] While the common servants are for the most part negligent, the upper servants play the tyrant over their fellows. This is exactly what church dignitaries did in after ages; and the fact that Jesus con-templated such a state of things, requiring from the nature of the case the lapse of centuries to bring it about, is another proof that in this discourse His prophetic eye swept over a vast tract of time. Another remark is suggested by the great reward promised to such as should not abuse their authority: " He will make him ruler over all that he hath." The greatness of the reward indicates an expectation that fidelity will be rare among the stewards of the house. Indeed, the Head of the church seems to have apprehended the prevalence of a negligent spirit among all His servants, high and low; for He speaks of the lord of the household as so gratified with the conduct of the faithful, that he girds himself to serve them while they sit at meat.[2] Has not the apprehension been too well justified by events?

The parable of the Ten Virgins, familiar to all, and full of instruction, teaches us this peculiar lesson, that watching does not imply sleepless anxiety and constant thought con-cerning the future, but quiet, steady attention to present duty. While the bridegroom tarried, all the virgins, wise and foolish alike, slumbered and slept, the wise differing from their sisters in having all things in readiness against a sudden call. This is a sober and reasonable representa-tion of the duty of waiting by one who understands what is possible; for, in a certain sense, sleep of the mind in reference to eternity is as necessary as physical sleep is to

[1] Luke xii. 41–48.   [2] Luke xii. 37.

the body. Constant thought about the great realities of the future would only result in weakness, distraction, and madness, or in disorder, idleness, and restlessness ; as in Thessalonica, where the conduct of many who watched in the wrong sense made it needful that Paul should give them the wholesome counsel to be quiet, and work, and eat bread earned by the labor of their own hands.[1]

The great prophetic discourse worthily ended with a solemn representation of the final judgment of the world, when all mankind shall be assembled to be judged either by the historical gospel preached to them for a witness, or by its great ethical principle, the law of charity written on their hearts ; and when those who have loved Christ and served Him in person, or in His representatives, — the poor, the destitute, the suffering, — shall be welcomed to the realms of the blessed, and those who have acted contrariwise shall be sent away to keep company with the devil and his angels.

---

[1] 2 Thess. iii. 12.

21

THE MASTER SERVING;
or, Another Lesson in Humility

SECTION I —THE WASHING

John 13:1-11

Up to this point the fourth evangelist has said very little indeed of the special relations of Jesus and the twelve. Now, however, he abundantly makes up for any deficiency on this score. The third part of his Gospel, which begins here, is, with the exception of two chapters relating the history of the passion, entirely occupied with the tender, intimate intercourse of the Lord Jesus with " His own," from the evening before His death to the time when He departed out of the world, leaving them behind ! The thirteenth and four following chapters relate scenes and discourses from the last hours spent by the Saviour with His disciples, previous to His betrayal into the hands of His enemies. He has uttered His final word to the outside world, and withdrawn Himself within the bosom of His own family ; and we are privileged here to see Him among His spiritual children, and to hear His farewell words to *them* in view of His decease. It becomes us to enter the supper chamber with deep reverence. " Put off thy shoes from off thy feet, for the place whereon thou standest is holy ground."

The first thing we see, on entering, is Jesus washing His disciples' feet. Marvellous spectacle ! and the evangelist has taken care, in narrating the incident, to enhance its impressiveness by the manner in which he introduces it. He has put the beautiful picture in the best light for being seen to advantage. The preface to the story is indeed a little puzzling to expositors, the sentences being involved, and the sense somewhat obscure. Many thoughts and feelings crowd into the apostle's mind as he proceeds to relate the *memora-bilia* of that eventful night; and, so to speak, they jostle one another in the struggle for utterance. Yet it is not very difficult to disentangle the meaning of these opening sentences. In the first, John adverts to the peculiar tenderness with which Jesus regarded His disciples on the eve of His crucifixion, and in prospect of His departure from the earth to heaven. "Before the feast of the Passover, when Jesus knew that His hour was come that He should depart out of this world" — how at such an hour did He feel towards those who had been His companions throughout the years of His public ministry, and whom He was soon to leave behind Him? "He loved them unto the end." Not selfishly engrossed with His own sorrows, or with the prospect of His subsequent joys, He found room in His heart for His followers still; nay, His love burned out towards them with extraordinary ardor, and His whole care was by precept and example, by words of comfort, warning, and instruction, to prepare them for future duty and trial, as the narrative here commencing would abundantly demonstrate.

The second verse of the preface alludes parenthetically to a fact which served as a foil to the constancy of Jesus: "The devil having already put it into the heart of Judas Iscariot, Simon's son, to betray Him." John would say: "Jesus loved His disciples to the end, though they did not all so love Him. One of them at this very moment entertained the diabolic purpose of betraying his Lord. Yet that Lord loved even him, condescending to wash even his feet; so endeavoring, if possible, to overcome his evil with good."

The aim of the evangelist, in the last sentence of his preface, is to show by contrast what a wondrous condescension it was in the Saviour to wash the feet of any of the disciples. Jesus knowing these things, — these things being true of Him: that "the Father had given all things into His hands" — sovereign power over all flesh; "that He was come from God" — a divine being by nature, and entitled to divine honors; "and that He was about to return to God," to enter on the enjoyment of such honors, — did as is here recorded. He, the August Being who had such intrinsic dignity, such a consciousness, such prospects — even "He riseth from supper and layeth aside His garments, and took a towel and girded Himself. After that He poureth water into a basin, and began to wash the disciples' feet, and to wipe them with the towel wherewith He was girded."

The time when all this took place was, it would seem, about the commencement of the evening meal. The words of the evangelist rendered in the English version " supper being ended," may be translated supper being begun, or better, supper-time having arrived ; [1] and from the sequel of the narrative, it is evident that in this sense they must be understood here. The supper was still going on when Jesus introduced the subject of the traitor, which He did not only after He had washed the feet of His disciples, but after He had resumed His seat at the table, and given an explanation of what He had just done.[2]

That explanation will fall to be more particularly considered afterwards ; but meantime it bears on its face that the occasion of the feet-washing was some misbehavior on the part of the disciples. Jesus had to condescend, we judge, because His disciples would not condescend. This impression is confirmed by a statement in Luke's Gospel, that on the same evening a strife arose among the twelve which of them should be accounted the greatest. Whence that new strife arose we know not, but it is possible that the old quarrel about place was revived by the words uttered by Jesus as they were about to sit down to meat : " With desire I have desired to eat this Passover with you before I suffer. For I say unto you, I will not any more eat thereof until it be fulfilled in the kingdom of God." [3] The allusion to the kingdom was quite sufficient to set their imaginations on fire and re-awaken old dreams about thrones, and from old dreams to old feuds and jealousies the transition was natural and easy ; and so we can conceive how, even before the supper

---

[1] Alford, *in loco*, gives as examples of a similar use of γενομένος, Matt. xxvi. 6 ; John xxi. 4 ; Mark vi. 2. Hofmann (*Schriftbeweis*, iii. 207, 208) renders the phrase as in the Auth. Ver., and reconciles this view with the narrative concerning Judas by assuming that vers. 26, 27 relate a transaction distinct from and subsequent to the supper. The R. V. has " during supper."

[2] John xiii. 21.

[3] Luke xxii. 15, 16. The R. V. reads, " I will not eat it," in place of, " I will not any more eat thereof," omitting οὐκέτι from their text. Westcott and Hort also omit this word ; Tischendorf retains it.

began, the talk of the brethren had waxed noisy and warm. Or the point in dispute may have been in what order they should sit at table, or who should be the servant for the occasion, and wash the feet of the company. Any one of these suppositions might account for the fact recorded by Luke ; for it does not require much to make children quarrel.

The expedient employed by Jesus to divert the minds of His disciples from unedifying themes of conversation, and to exorcise ambitious passions from their breasts, was a most effectual one. The very preliminaries of the feet-washing scene must have gone far to change the current of feeling. How the spectators must have stared and wondered as the Master of the feast rose from His seat, laid aside His upper garment, girt Himself with a towel, and poured out water into a basin, doing all with the utmost self-possession, composure, and deliberation !

With which of the twelve Jesus made a beginning we are not informed ; but we know, as we might have guessed without being told, who was the first to speak his mind about the singular transaction. When Peter's turn came, he had so far recovered from the amazement, under whose influence the first washed may have yielded passively to their Lord's will, as to be capable of reflecting on the indecency of such an inversion of the right relation between master and servants. Therefore, when Jesus came to him, that outspoken disciple asked, in astonishment, " Lord, washest *Thou my* feet ? " His spirit rose in rebellion against the proposal, as one injurious to the dignity of his beloved Lord, and as an outrage upon his own sense of reverence. This impulse of instinctive aversion was by no means discreditable to Peter, and it was evidently not regarded with disapprobation by his Master. The reply of Jesus to his objection is markedly respectful in tone : " What I do," He said, "thou knowest not now, but thou shalt know hereafter," virtually admitting that the proceeding in question needed explanation, and that Peter's opposition was, in the first place, perfectly natural. " I acknowledge," He meant to say, "that my present action is an offence to the feelings of reverence which you rightly cherish towards me. Nevertheless, suffer it. I do this for reasons which you do not comprehend now, but which you shall understand ere long."

Had Peter been satisfied with this apologetic reply, his conduct would have been entirely free from blame. But He was not content, but persisted in opposition after Jesus had distinctly intimated His will, and vehemently and stubbornly exclaimed : " Thou shalt *never* wash my feet ! " The tone here changes utterly. Peter's first word was the expression of sincere reverence ; his second is simply the language of unmitigated irreverence and downright disobedience. He rudely contradicts his Master, and at the same time, we may add, flatly contradicts himself. His whole behavior on this occasion presents an odd mixture of moral opposites : self-abasement and self-will, humility and pride, respect and disrespect for Jesus, to whom he speaks now as one whose shoe-latchet he is not worthy to unloose, and anon as one to whom he might dictate orders. What a strange man ! But, indeed, how strange are we all !

Peter having so changed his tone, Jesus found it needful to alter His tone too, from the apologetic mildness of the first reply to that of magisterial sternness. " If I wash thee not," He said gravely, " thou hast no part with me ; " meaning, " Thou hast taken up a most serious position, Simon Peter, the question at issue being simply, Are you, or are you not, to be admitted into my kingdom — to be a true disciple, and to have a true disciple's reward ? "

On a surface view, it is difficult to see how this could be the state of the question. One is tempted to think that Jesus was indulging in exaggeration, for the purpose of intimidating a refractory disciple into compliance with His will. If we reject this method of interpretation as incompatible with the character of the speaker and the seriousness of the occasion, we are thrown back on the inquiry, What does washing in this statement mean ? Evidently it signifies more than meets the ear, more than the mere literal washing of the feet, and is to be regarded as a symbol of the washing of the soul from sin, or still more comprehensively, and in our opinion more correctly, *as representing all in Christ's teaching and work which would be compromised by the consistent carrying out of the principle on which Peter's opposition to the washing of his feet by Jesus was based.* On either supposition the statement of Jesus was true : in the former case obviously ; in the latter not so obviously, but not less really, as we proceed to show.

Observe, then, what was involved in the attitude assumed by Peter. He virtually took his stand on these two positions : that he would admit of nothing which seemed inconsistent with the personal dignity of his Lord, and that he would adopt as his rule of conduct his own judgment in preference to Christ's will ; the one position being involved in the question, Dost Thou wash my feet ? the other in the resolution, Thou shalt never wash my feet. In other words, the ground taken up by this disciple compromised the whole sum and substance of Christianity, the former principle sweeping away Christ's whole state and experience of *humiliation*, and the latter not less certainly sapping the foundation of Christ's *lordship*.

That this is no exaggeration on our part, a moment's reflection will show. Look first at the objection to the feet washing on the score of reverence. If Jesus might not wash the feet of His disciples because it was beneath His dignity, then with equal reason objection might be taken to any act involving self-humiliation. One who said, Thou shalt not wash my feet, because the doing of it is unworthy of Thee, might as well say, Thou shalt not wash my soul, or do aught towards that end, because it involves humiliating experiences. Why, indeed, make a difficulty about a trifling matter of detail ? Go to the heart of the business at once, and ask, " Shall the Eternal Son of God become flesh, and dwell among us ? shall He who was in the form of God lay aside His robes of state, and gird Himself with the towel of humanity, to perform menial offices for His own creatures ? shall the ever-blessed One become a curse by enduring crucifixion ? shall the Holy One degrade Himself by coming into close companionship with the depraved sons of Adam ? shall the Righteous One pour His life-blood into a basin, that there may be a fountain wherein the unrighteous may be cleansed from their guilt and iniquity ? " In short, incarnation, atonement, and Christ's whole earthly experience of temptation, hardship, indignity, and sorrow, must go if Jesus may not wash a disciple's feet.

Not less clearly is Christ's lordship at an end if a disciple may give Him orders, and say, " Thou shalt never wash my feet." If Peter meant any thing more by these words than a display of temper and caprice, he meant this : that he would not submit to the proposed operation, because his moral feelings and his judgment told him it was wrong. He made his own reason and conscience the supreme rule of conduct. Now, in the first place, by this position the *principle* of obedience was compromised, which requires that the will of the Lord, once known, whether we understand its reason or perceive its goodness or not, shall be supreme. Then there are other things much more important than the washing of the feet, to which objection might be taken on the score of reason or conscience with equal plausibility. For example, Christ tells us that those who would be His disciples, and obtain entrance into His kingdom, must be willing to part with earthly goods, and even with nearest and dearest friends. To many men this seems unreasonable ; and on Peter's prin- ciple they should forthwith say, "I will never do any such thing." Or again, Christ tells us that we must be born again, and that we must eat His flesh and drink His blood. To me these doctrines may seem incomprehensible, and even absurd ; and therefore, on Peter's principle, I may turn my back on the great Teacher, and say, "I will not have this speaker of dark, mystic sayings for my master." Once more, Christ tells us that we must give the kingdom of God the first place in our thoughts, and dismiss from our hearts carking care for to-morrow. To me this may appear in my present mood simply impossible ; and therefore, on Peter's principle, I may set aside this moral requirement as utopian, however beautiful, without even seriously attempting to comply with it.

Now that we know whither Peter's refusal tends, we can see that Jesus spake the simple truth when He said : " If I wash thee not, thou hast no part with me." Look at that refusal as an objection to Christ humbling Himself. If Christ may not humble Himself, then, in the first place, He can have no part with us. The Holy Son of God is forbidden by a regard to His dignity to become in any thing like unto His brethren, or even to acknowledge them as His brethren.

The grand paternal law, by which the Sanctifier is identified with them that are to be sanctified, is disannulled, and all its consequences made void.   A great impassable gulf separates the Divine Being from His creatures.   He may stand on the far-off shore, and wistfully contemplate their forlorn estate ; but He cannot, He dare not — His majesty forbids it — come near them, and reach forth a helping hand.

But if the Son of God may have no part with us, then, in the second place, we can have no part with Him.   We cannot share His fellowship with the Father, if He come not forth to declare Him.   We can receive no acts of brotherly kindness from Him.   He cannot deliver us from the curse of the law, or from the fear of death ; He cannot succor us when we are tempted ; He cannot wash our feet ; nay, what is a far more serious matter, He cannot wash our souls.   If there is to be no fountain opened for sin in the human nature of Emmanuel, sinners must remain impure.   For a God afar off is not able, even if He were willing, to purify the human soul.   A God whose majesty, like an iron fate, kept Him aloof from sinners, could not even effectively forgive them.   Still less could He sanctify them.   Love alone has sanctifying virtue, and what room is there for love in a Being who cannot humble Himself to be a servant ?

Look now at Peter's refusal as resistance to Christ's will.   In this view also it justified the saying, "Thou hast no part with me."   It excluded from salvation ; for if Jesus is not to be Lord, He will not be Saviour.[1]   It excluded from fellow-ship ; for Jesus will have no communion with self-will.   His own attitude towards His Father was, "Not my will, but Thine ;" and He demands this attitude towards Himself in turn from all His disciples.   He will be the Author of eternal salvation, only *to them that obey Him.*   Not that He would have us be always servants, blindly obeying a Lord whose will we do not understand.   His aim is to advance us ultimately to the status of friends,[2] doing His will intelligently and freely — not as complying mechanically with an outward commandment, but as being a law to ourselves.   But we can

---

[1] Peter the *apostle* understood this well.   Four times in his second epistle he conjoins *Lord* and *Saviour* in naming Christ   (i. 11, ii. 20. iii. 2, 18).

[2] John xv. 15.

attain that high position only by beginning with a servant's obedience. We must do, and suffer to be done to us, what we know not now, in order that we may know hereafter the philosophy of our duty to our Lord, and of our Lord's dealings with us. And the perfection of obedience lies in doing that which reverence unenlightened finds peculiarly hard, viz. in letting the Lord change places with us, and if it seem good to Him, humble Himself to be our servant.

It was a serious thing, therefore, to say, "Thou shalt never wash my feet." But Peter was not aware how serious it was. He knew not what he said, or what he did. He had hastily taken up a position whose ground and consequences he had not considered. And his heart was right, though his temper was wrong. Therefore the stern declaration of Jesus at once brought him to reason, or rather to unreason in an opposite direction. The idea of being cut off from his dear Master's sympathy or favor through his waywardness drove him in sheer fright to the opposite extreme of overdone compliance ; and he said in effect, " If my interest in Thee depends on my feet being washed, then, Lord, wash my whole body — hands, head, feet, and all." How characteristic ! how like a child, in whose heart is much foolishness, but also much affection, and who can always be managed by the bands of love ! There is as yet a sad want of balance in this disciple's character : he goes, swinging like a pendulum, from one extreme to another ; and it will take some time ere he settle down into a harmonious equipoise of all parts of his being — intellect, will, heart, and conscience. But the root of the matter is in him : he is sound at the core ; and after the due amount of mistakes, he will become a wise man by and by. He is clean, and needs not more than to have his feet washed. Jesus Himself admits it of him, and of all his brother-disciples — save one, who is unclean all over.

SECTION II — THE EXPLANATION

JOHN xiii. 12-20

Peter's resistance overcome, the washing proceeded without further interruption. When the process had come to an end, Jesus, putting on again His upper garment, resumed His seat, and briefly explained to His disciples the purport of the action. "Know ye," He inquired, "what I have done unto you?" Then, answering His own question, He went on to say: "Ye call me Master and Lord: and ye say well; for so I am. If I, then, your Lord and Master, have washed your feet, ye also ought to wash one another's feet. For I have given you an example, that ye should do as I have done to you."

It was another lesson in humility which Jesus had been giving "His own," — a lesson very similar to the earlier ones recorded in the synoptical Gospels. John's Christ, we see here, teaches the same doctrine as the Christ of the three first evangelists. The twelve, as they are depicted in the fourth Gospel, are just such as we have found them in Matthew, Mark, and Luke — grievously needing to be taught meekness and brotherly kindness; and Jesus teaches them these virtues in much the same way here as elsewhere — by precept and example, by symbolic act, and added word of interpretation. Once He held up a little child, to shame them out of ambitious passions; here He rebukes their pride, by becoming the menial of the household. At another time He hushed their angry strife by adverting to His own self-humiliation, in coming from heaven to be a minister to men's needs in life and in death; here He accomplishes the same end, by expressing the spirit and aim of His whole earthly ministry in a representative, typical act of condescension.

This lesson, like all the rest, Jesus gave with the authority of one who might lay down the law. In the very act of playing the servant's part, He was asserting His sovereignty. He reminds His disciples, when the service is over, of the titles they were wont to give Him, and in a marked, emphatic manner He accepts them as His due. He tells them distinctly that He is indeed their Teacher, whose doctrine it is their business to learn, and their Lord, whose will it is their duty to obey. His humility, therefore, is manifestly not an affectation of ignorance as to who and what He is. He knows full well who He is, whence He has come, whither He is going ; His humility is that of a king, yea, of a Divine Being. The pattern of meekness is at the same time one who prescribes Himself to His followers as a pattern, and demands that they fix their attention on His behavior, and strive to copy it.

In making this demand, Jesus is obviously very thoroughly in earnest. He is not less earnest in requiring the disciples to wash one another's feet, than He was in insisting that He Himself should wash the feet of one and all. As He said to Peter in express words, " If I wash thee not, thou hast no part with me ; " so He says to them all in effect, though not in words, " If ye wash not each other, if ye refuse to serve one another in love, ye have again no part with me." This is a hard saying ; for if it be difficult to believe in the humiliation of Christ, it is still more difficult to humble ourselves. Hence, notwithstanding the frequency and urgency with which the Saviour declares that we must have the spirit manifested in His humiliation *for* us dwelling *in* us, and giving birth in our life to conduct kindred to His own, even sincere disciples are constantly, though it may be half unconsciously, inventing excuses for treating the example of their Lord as utterly inimitable, and therefore in reality no example at all. Even the apparently unanswerable argument employed by Jesus to enforce imitation does not escape secret criticism. " Verily, verily," saith He, "a servant is not greater than his lord, neither he that is sent greater than he that sent him." " It may," say we, " be more incumbent on the servant to humble himself than on the master, but in some respects it is also more difficult. The master can afford to condescend : his action will not be misunderstood, but will be taken for what it is. But the servant cannot afford to be humble : he must assert himself, and assume airs, in order to make himself of any consequence."

The great Master knew too well how slow men would ever be to learn the lesson He had just been teaching His disciples.

Therefore He appended to His explanation of the feet-washing this reflection : " If ye know these things, happy are ye if ye do them," hinting at the rarity and difficulty of such high morality as He had been inculcating, and declaring the blessedness of the few who attained unto it.   And surely the reflection is just ! Is not the morality here enjoined indeed rare ?   Are not the virtues called into play by acts of conde-scension and charity most high and difficult ?   Who dreams of calling them easy ?   How utterly contrary they are to the native tendencies of the human heart ! how alien from the spirit of society ! Is it the way of men to be content with the humblest place, and to seek their felicity in serving others ?   Doth not the spirit that is in us lust unto envy, strive ambitiously for positions of influence, and deem it the greatest happiness to be served, and to be exempt from the drudgery of servile tasks ?   The world itself does not dispute the difficulty of Christ-like virtue ; it rather exaggerates its difficulty, and pronounces it utopian and impracticable — merely a beautiful, unattainable ideal.

And as for the sincere disciple of Jesus, no proof is needed to convince him of the arduousness of the task appointed him by his Lord.   He knows by bitter experience how far con-duct lags behind knowledge, and how hard it is to translate admiration of unearthly goodness into imitation thereof.   His mind is familiarly conversant with the doctrine and life of the Saviour ; he has read and re-read the Gospel story, fondly lingering over its minutest details ; his heart has burned as he followed the footsteps of the Blessed One walking about on this earth, ever intent on doing good : sweeter to his ear than the finest lyric poems are the stories of the woman by the well, the sinner in the house of Simon, and of Zacchæus the publican ; those touching incidents of the little child upheld as a pattern of humility, and of the Master washing quarrelsome disciples' feet, and the exquisite parables of the Lost Sheep, the Prodigal, and the Good Samaritan.   But when he has to close his New Testament, and go away into the rude, ungodly, matter-of-fact world, and *be* there a Christ-like man, and *do* the things which he knows so intimately, and counts himself blessed in knowing, alas, what a descent ! It is like a fall from Eden into a state of mere sin and misery.

And the longer he lives, and the more he gets mixed up with life's relations and engagements, the further he seems to himself to degenerate from the gospel pattern ; till at length he is almost ashamed to think or speak of the beauties of holiness exhibited therein, and is tempted to adopt a lower and more worldly tone, out of a regard to sincerity, and in fear of becoming a mere sentimental hypocrite like Judas, who kissed his Master at the very moment he was betraying Him.

In proportion to the difficulty and the rarity of the virtue prescribed is the felicity of those who are enabled to practise it. Theirs is a threefold blessedness. First, they have the joy connected with the achievement of an arduous task. Easy undertakings bring small pains, but they also bring small pleasures ; rapturous delight is reserved for those who attempt and accomplish that which passes for impossible. And what raptures can be purer, holier, and more intense than those of the man who has at length succeeded in making the mind of the meek and lowly One his own ; who, after long climbing, has reached the alpine summit of self-forgetful, self-humbling love ! Those who practise the things here enjoined further win for themselves the approbation of their Lord. A master is pleased when a pupil understands his lesson, but a lord is pleased only when his servants do his bidding. Christ, being Lord as well as Master, demands that we shall not only *know* but *do*. And in proportion to the preremptoriness of the demand is the satisfaction with which the Lord of Christians regards all earnest efforts to comply with His will and to follow His example. And to all who make such efforts it is a great happiness to be assured of the approval of Him whom they serve. The thought, " I am guided in my present action by the spirit of Jesus, and He approves what I do," sustains the mind in peace, even when one has not the happiness to win the approbation of his fellow-men ; which is not an impertinent remark here, for it will often happen to us to please men least when we are pleasing the Lord *most*. You shall please many men by a prudent selfishness much more readily than by a generous uncalculating devotion to what is *right*. " Men will praise thee when thou doest well to thyself ; " and they will wink at very considerable deviations from the line of pure Christian morality in the prosecution of self-interest, provided you be successful. Even religious people will often vex and grieve you by advices savoring much more of worldly wisdom than of Christian simplicity and godly sincerity. But if Christ approve, we may make shift to do without the sympathy and approbation of men. Their approbation is at most but a comfort ; His is matter of life and death.

The third element in the felicity of the man who is not merely a forgetful hearer, but a doer of the perfect law of Christ, is that he escapes the guilt of unimproved knowledge. It is a religious commonplace that to sin against light is more heinous than to sin in ignorance. " To him that knoweth to do good, and doeth it not, to him it is sin." And, of course, the clearer the light the greater the responsibility. Now, in no department of Christian truth is knowledge clearer than in that which belongs to the department of ethics. There are some doctrines which the church, as a whole, can hardly be said to know, they are so mysterious, or so disputed. But the ethical teaching of Jesus is simple and copious in all its leading features ; it is universally understood, and as universally admired. Protestants and Papists, Trinitarians, Socinians, and Deists, are all at one here. Happy then are they, of all sects and denominations, who do the things which all know and agree in admiring ; for a heavy woe lies on those who do them not. The woe is not indeed expressed, but it is implied in Christ's words. The common Lord of all believers virtually addresses all Christendom here, saying : " Ye behold the sunlight of a perfect example ; ye have been made acquainted with a high and lovely ideal of life, such as pagan moralists never dreamed of. What are ye doing with your light ? Are ye merely looking at it, and writing books about it, and boasting of it, and talking of it, meanwhile allowing men outside the pale of the church to surpass you in humane and philanthropic virtue ? If this is all the use you are making of your knowledge, it will be more tolerable for pagans at the day of judgment than for you."

Having made the reflection we have been considering, Jesus followed it up with a word of apology for the tone of suspicion with which it was uttered, and which was no doubt felt by the disciples. "I speak not," He said, "of you all :

I know whom I have chosen : but that the scripture may be fulfilled, He that eateth bread with me hath lifted up his heel against me." The remark may be thus paraphrased : "In hinting at the possibility of a knowledge of right, unaccompanied by corresponding action, I have not been indulging in gratuitous insinuation. I do not indeed think so badly of you all as to imagine you capable of deliberate and habitual neglect of known duty. But there is one among you who is capable of such conduct. I have chosen you twelve, and I know the character of every one of you ; and, as I said a year ago, after asking a question which hurt your feelings, that one of you had a devil,[1] so now, after making a suspicious reflection, I say there is one among you whose character illustrates negatively its meaning ; one who knows, but will not do ; who puts sentiment in place of action, and admiration in place of imitation ; one who, having eaten bread with me as a familiar friend, will repay me for all my kindness, not by loving obedience, but by lifting up his heel against me." The infirmity of sincere disciples Jesus could patiently bear with : but the Judas-character — in which correct thinking and fine sentiment are combined with falseness of heart and practical laxity, in which to promise is put in place of performance, and to utter the becoming word about a matter is substituted for doing the appropriate deed — such a character His soul utterly abhorred.

Who can doubt that it was not in vain that sincere disciples had been so long in the society of One who was so exacting in His ideal, and that they really did strive in after years to fulfil their Master's will, and serve one another in love ?

---

[1] John vi. 66-70. The words of Jesus on the present occasion become clearer when viewed in the light of the earlier occurrence, comparing the two passages together. We are satisfied that the words, "I speak not of you all," mean, "I do not suspect you all of the sin of knowing and not doing, rather than, "You shall not all partake of the happiness of those who both know and do."

22

IN MEMORIAM;
or, Fourth Lesson on the Doctrine of the Cross

Matt. 26:26-29; Mark 14:22-25; Luke 22:17-20 (1 Cor. 11:23-26)

THE Lord's Supper is a monument sacred to the memory of Jesus Christ. "This do in remembrance of me." In Bethany Jesus had spoken as if He desired that Mary should be kept in remembrance in the preaching of His Gospel; in the supper chamber He expressed His desire to be remembered Himself. He would have Mary's deed of love commemorated by the rehearsal of her story; He would have His own deed of love commemorated by a symbolic action, to be often repeated throughout the ages to the end of the world.

The rite of the Supper, besides commemorating, is likewise of use to *interpret* the Lord's death. It throws important light on the meaning of that solemn event. The institution of this symbolic feast was in fact the most important contribution made by Jesus during His personal ministry to the doctrine of atonement through the sacrifice of Himself. Therefrom more clearly than from any other act or word performed or spoken by Him, the twelve might learn to conceive of their Master's death as possessing a *redemptive* character. Thereby Jesus, as it were, said to His disciples: My approaching passion is not to be regarded as a mere calamity, or dark disaster, falling out contrary to the divine purpose or my expectation; not as a fatal blow inflicted by ungodly men on me and you, and the cause which is dear to us all; not even as an evil which may be overruled for good; but as an event fulfilling, not frustrating, the purpose of my mission, and fruitful of blessing to the world. What men mean for evil, God means for good, to bring to pass to save much people alive. The shedding of my blood, in one aspect the crime of wicked Jews, is in another aspect my own voluntary act. I pour forth my blood for a gracious end, even for the remission of sins. My death will initiate a new dispensation, and seal a new testament; it will fulfil the purpose, and therefore take the place, of the manifold sacrifices of the Mosaic ritual, and in particular of the paschal lamb, which is even now being eaten. I shall be the Paschal Lamb of the Israel of God henceforth; at once protecting them from death, and feeding their souls with my crucified humanity, as the bread of eternal life.

These truths are very familiar to us, however new and strange they may have been to the disciples; and we are more accustomed to explain the Supper by the death, than the death by the Supper. It may be useful, however, here to reverse the process, and, imagining ourselves in the position of the twelve, as witnesses to the institution of a new religious symbol, to endeavor to rediscover therefrom the meaning of the event with which it is associated, and whose significance it is intended to shadow forth. Let us, then, take our stand beside this ancient monument, and try to read the Runic inscription on its weather-worn surface.

I. First, then, we perceive at once that it is to the *death* of Jesus this monument refers. It is not merely erected to His memory in general, but it is erected specially in memory of His decease. All things point forward to what was about to take place on Calvary. The sacramental acts of breaking the bread and pouring out the wine manifestly look that way. The words also spoken by Jesus in instituting the Supper all involve allusions to His death. Both the fact and the manner of His death are hinted at, by the distinction He makes between His body and His blood : " This is my body," " This is my blood." Body and blood are one in life, and become separate things only by death; and not by every kind of death, but by one whose manner involves blood-shedding, as in the case of sacrificial victims. The epithets applied to the body and the blood point at death still more clearly. Jesus speaks of His body as " given " — as if to be slain or " broken " [1] in sacrifice, and of His blood as " shed." Then,

---

[1] 1 Cor. xi. 24.

finally, by describing the blood about to be shed as the blood of a new testament, the Saviour put it beyond all doubt what He was alluding to. Where a testament is, there must also be the death of the testator. And though an ordinary testator may die an ordinary death, the Testator of the *new* testament must die a sacrificial death ; for the epithet *new* implies a reference to the old Jewish covenant, which was ratified by the sacrifice of burnt-offerings and peace-offerings of oxen, whose blood was sprinkled on the altar and on the people, and called by Moses "the blood of the covenant."

2. The mere fact that the Lord's Supper commemorates specially the Lord's *death*, implies that that death must have been an event of a very important character. By instituting a symbolic rite for such a purpose, Jesus, as it were, said to His disciples and to us : " Fix your eyes on Calvary, and watch what happens there. That is the great event in my earthly history. Other men have monuments erected to them because they have lived lives deemed memorable. I wish you to erect a monument to me because I have died : not forgetful of my life indeed, yet specially mindful of my death ; commemorating it for its own sake, not merely for the sake of the life whereof it is the termination. The memory of other men is cherished by the celebration of their birthday anniversaries ; but in my case, better is the day of my death than the day of my birth for the purpose of a commemorative celebration. My birth into this world was marvellous and momentous ; but still more marvellous and momentous is my exit out of it by crucifixion. Of my birth no festive commemoration is needed ; but of my death keep alive the memory by the Holy Supper till I come again. Remembering it well, you remember all my earthly history ; for of all it is the secret, the consummation, and the crown."

But why, in a history throughout so remarkable, should the death be thus singled out for commemoration ? Was it its tragic character that won for it this distinction ? Did the Crucified One mean the Supper which goes by His Name to be a mere dramatic representation of His passion, for the purpose of exciting our feelings, and eliciting a sympathetic tear, by renewing the memory of His dying sorrows ? So

to think of the matter were to degrade our Christian feast to
the level of the pagan festival of Adonis,

> "Whose annual wound in Lebanon allured
> The Syrian damsels to lament his fate
> In amorous ditties all a summer's day."

Or was it the foul wrong and shameful indignity done to the
Son of God by the wicked men who crucified Him that Jesus
wished to have kept in perpetual remembrance? Was the
Holy Supper instituted for the purpose of branding with
eternal infamy a world that knew no better use to make of
the Holy One than to nail Him to a tree, and felt more
kindness even for a robber than for Him? Certainly the
world well deserved to be thus held up to reprobation; but
the Son of man came not to condemn sinners, but to save
them; and it was not in His loving nature to erect an
enduring monument to His own resentment or to the dishonor of His murderers. *The blood of Jesus speaketh better
things than that of Abel.*

Or was it because His death on the cross, in spite of its
indignity and shame, was *glorious*, as a testimony to His
invincible fidelity to the cause of truth and righteousness,
that Jesus instructed His followers to keep it ever in mind,
by the celebration of the new symbolic rite? Is the festival
of the Supper to be regarded as a solemnity of the same
kind as those by which the early church commemorated
the death of the martyrs? Is the *Coenâ Domini* simply the
natalitia of the great Protomartyr? So Socinians would
have us believe. To the question why the Lord wished the
memory of His crucifixion to be specially celebrated in His
church the Racovian Catechism replies: "Because of all
Christ's actions, it (the voluntary enduring of death) was
the greatest and most proper to Him. For although the
resurrection and exaltation of Christ were far greater, these
were acts of God the Father rather than of Christ."[1] In
other words, the death above all things deserves to be
remembered, because it was the most signal and sublime act
of witness-bearing on Christ's part to the truth, the glorious

[1] *De Coenâ Domini*, Quæstio iv.

copestone of a noble life of self-sacrificing devotion to the high and perilous vocation of a prophet.

That Christ's death was all this is of course true, and that it is worthy of remembrance as an act of martyrdom is equally true; but whether Jesus instituted the Holy Supper for the purpose of commemorating His death exclusively, principally, or at all as a martyrdom, is a different question. On this point we must learn the truth from Christ's own lips. Let us return, then, to the history of the institution, to learn His mind about the matter.

3. Happily the Lord Jesus explained with particular clearness in what aspect He wished His death to be the subject of commemorative celebration. In distributing to His disciples the sacramental bread, He said, " This is my body, given, or broken, *for you ;* " [1] thereby intimating that His death was to be commemorated because of a benefit it procured for the communicant. In handing to the disciples the sacramental cup, He said, " Drink ye all of it ; for this is my blood of the new testament, shed (for you [2] and) for many for the remission of sins ; " [3] thereby indicating the nature of the benefit procured by His death, on account of which it was worthy to be remembered.

In this creative word of the new dispensation Jesus represents His death as a sin-offering, atoning for guilt, and purchasing forgiveness of moral debt. His blood was to be shed for the remission of sins. In view of this function the blood is called the blood of the new testament, in apparent allusion to the prophecy of Jeremiah, which contains a promise of a new covenant to be made by God with the house of Israel, — a covenant whose leading blessing should be the forgiveness of iniquity, and called new, because, unlike the old, it would be a covenant of pure grace, of promises unclogged with legal stipulations. [4] By mentioning

---

[1] Luke and Paul.   [2] Luke.

[3] Matthew. On the genuineness of these words, see Neander, *Life of Christ ;* also Keim, *Jesu von Nazara.*

[4] Jer. xxxi. 31–34. Such a covenant is on man's side hardly a covenant at all. See Witsius, *De Œc. Fid.* lib. iii. cap. i. 8–12. The blessings of the new covenant as described by the prophet are these three — (1) The law written on the *heart*, instead of on tables of stone = regeneration — moral renewal ; (2) the knowledge of God simplified, and made accessible to all = abolition of elaborate Levitical ritual ; (3) forgiveness of sins.

His blood and the *new* covenant together, Jesus teaches that, while annulling, He would at the same time fulfil the old, in introducing the new. The new covenant would be ratified by sacrifice, even as was the old one at Sinai, and remission of sin would be granted after blood-shedding. But in bidding His disciples drink the cup, the Lord intimates that after His death there will be no more need of sacrifices. The sin-offering of blood will be converted into a thank-offering of wine, a cup of salvation, to be drunk with grateful, joyful hearts by all who through faith in His sacrifice have received the pardon of their sins. Finally, Jesus intimates that the new covenant concerns the *many*, not the few — not Israel alone, but all nations : it is a gospel which He bequeaths to sinners of mankind.

Well may we drink of this cup with thankfulness and joy ; for the "new covenant" (new, yet far older than the old), of which it is the seal, is in all respects well ordered and sure. Well ordered ; for surely it is altogether a good and God-worthy constitution of things which connects the blessing of pardon with the sacrificial death of Him through whom it comes to us. It is good in the interests of righteousness : for it provides that sin shall not be pardoned till it has been adequately atoned for by the sacrifice of the sinner's Friend ; and it is just and right that without the shedding of the Righteous One's blood there should be no remission for the unrighteous. Then this economy serves well the interest of divine love, as it gives that love a worthy career, and free scope to display its magnanimous nature, in bearing the burden of the sinful and the miserable. And yet once more, the constitution of the new covenant is admirably adapted to the great practical end aimed at by the scheme of redemption, viz. the elevation of a fallen, degraded race out of a state of corruption into a state of holiness. The gospel of forgiveness through Christ's death is the moral power of God to raise such as believe it out of the world's selfishness, and enmities, and baseness, into a celestial life of devotion, self-sacrifice, patience, and humility. If by faith in Christ be understood merely belief in the *opus operatum* of a vicarious death, the power of such a faith to elevate is more than questionable. But when faith is taken in its true scriptural sense, as implying not only belief in a certain transaction, the endurance of death by one for others, but also, and more especially, hearty appreciation of the spirit of the deed and the Doer, then its purifying and ennobling power is beyond all question. "The love of Christ constraineth me;" and "I am crucified with Christ," as the result of such faith.

How poor is the Socinian scheme of salvation in comparison with this of the new covenant! In that scheme pardon has no real dependence on the blood of Jesus: He died as a martyr for righteousness, not as a Redeemer for the unrighteous. We are forgiven on repenting by a simple word of God. Forgiveness cost the Forgiver no trouble or sacrifice; only a word, or stroke of the pen signing a document, "Thus saith the Lord." What a frigid transaction! What cold relations it implies between the Deity and His creatures! How vastly preferable a forgiveness which means a giving for,[1] and costs the Forgiver sorrow, sweat, pain, blood, wounds, death — a forgiveness coming from a God who says in effect: "I will not, to save sinners, repeal the law which connects sin with death as its penalty; but I am willing for that end to become myself the law's victim." Such a forgiveness is at once an act of righteousness and an act of marvellous love; whereas forgiveness without satisfaction, though at first sight it may appear both rational and generous, manifests neither God's righteousness nor His love. A Socinian God, who pardons without atonement, is destitute alike of a passionate abhorrence of sin and of a passionate love to sinners.

Jesus once said, "He loveth much who hath much forgiven him." It is a deep truth, but there is another not less deep to be put alongside of it: we must feel that our forgiveness has cost the Forgiver much in order to love Him much. It is because they feel this that true professors of the catholic faith exhibit that passionate devotion to Christ which forms such a contrast to the cold intellectual homage paid by the Deist to his God. When the catholic Christian thinks of the tears, agonies, bloody sweat, shame, and pain endured by the Redeemer, of His marred vision, broken heart, pierced side, lacerated hands and feet, his bosom burns with devoted love. The story of the passion opens all the fountains of

[1] This idea is well put in Bushnell's *Vicarious Sacrifice*.

feeling; and by no other way than the *via dolorosa* could Jesus have ascended the throne of His people's hearts.

The new covenant inaugurated by Christ's death is sure as well as orderly. It is reliably sealed by the blood of the Testator. For, first, what better guarantee can we have of the good-will of God? "Greater love hath no man than this, that a man lay down his life for his friends." "Hereby perceive we the love of God, because He laid down His life for us." Looking at the matter in the light of justice, again, this covenant is equally sure. God is not unrighteous, to forget His Son's labor of love. As He is true, Christ *shall* see of the travail of His soul. It cannot be otherwise under the moral administration of Jehovah. Can the God of truth break His word? Can the Judge of all the earth permit one, and especially His own Son, to give Himself up, out of purest love, to sorrow, and pain, and shame, for His brethren, without receiving the hire which He desires, and which was promised Him — many souls, many lives, many sinners saved? Think of it: holiness suffering for righteousness' sake, and yet not having the consolation of doing something in the way of destroying unrighteousness, and turning the disobedient to the obedience of the just; love, by the impulse of its nature, and by covenant obligations, laid under a necessity of laboring for the lost, and yet doomed by the untowardness, or apathy, or faithlessness of the Governor of the universe to go unrewarded; — love's labor lost, nobody the better for it, things remaining as before: no sinner pardoned, delivered from the pit and restored to holiness; no chosen people brought out of darkness into marvellous light! Such a state of things cannot be in God's dominions. The government of God is carried on in the interest of Holy Love. It gives love free scope to bear others' burdens: it arranges that if she will do so, she shall feel the full weight of the burden she takes upon her; but it also arranges, by an eternal covenant of truth and equity, that when the burden has been borne, the Burden-bearer shall receive His reward in the form He likes best — in souls washed, pardoned, sanctified, and led to everlasting glory by Himself as His ransomed brethren or children.

The principle of vicarious merit involved in the doctrine

that we are pardoned simply because Christ died for our sins, when looked at with unprejudiced eyes, commends itself to reason as well as to the heart. It means practically a premium held out to foster righteousness and love. This offered premium carried Jesus through His heavy task. It was because, relying on His Father's promise, He saw the certain joy of saving many before Him, that He endured the cross. It is the same principle, in a restricted application of it, which stimulates Christians to fill up that which is behind of the sufferings of their Lord. They know that, if they be faithful, they shall not live unto themselves, but shall benefit Christ's mystic body the church, and also the world at large. If the fact were otherwise, there would be very little either of moral fidelity or of love in the world. If the moral government of the universe made it impossible for one being to benefit another by prayer or loving pains, impossible for ten good men to be a shield to Sodom, for the elect to be a salt to the earth, men would give up trying to do it; generous concern about public wellbeing would cease, and universal selfishness become the order of the day. Or if this state of things should not ensue, we should only have darkness in a worse form: the inscrutable enigma of Righteousness crucified without benefit to any living creature, — a scandal and a reproach to the government and character of God. If, therefore, we are to hold fast our faith in the divine holiness, justice, goodness, and truth, we must believe that the blood of Jesus doth most certainly procure for us the remission of sins; and likewise, that the blood of His saints, though neither available nor necessary to obtain for sinners the blessing of pardon before the divine tribunal — Christ's blood alone being capable of rendering us that service, and having rendered it effectually and once for all — is nevertheless precious in God's sight, and makes the people precious among whom it is shed, and is by God's appointment, in manifold ways, a source of blessing unto a world unworthy to number among its inhabitants men whom it knows not how to use otherwise than as lambs for the slaughter.

4. The sacrament of the Supper exhibits Christ not merely as a Lamb to be slain for a sin-offering, but as a Paschal Lamb to be eaten for spiritual nourishment. "Take, eat,

this is my body." By this injunction Jesus taught the twelve, and through them all Christians, to regard His crucified humanity as the bread of God for the life of their souls. We must eat the flesh and drink the blood of the Son of man spiritually by faith, as we eat the bread and drink the wine literally with the mouth.

In regarding Christ as the Bread of Life, we are not to restrict ourselves to the one benefit mentioned by Him in instituting the feast, the remission of sins, but to have in view all His benefits tending to our spiritual nourishment and growth in grace. Christ is the Bread of Life in all His offices. As a Prophet, He supplies the bread of divine truth to feed our minds; as a Priest, He furnishes the bread of righteousness to satisfy our troubled consciences; as a King, He presents Himself to us as an object of devotion, that shall fill our hearts, and whom we may worship without fear of idolatry.

As often as the Lord's Supper is celebrated we are invited to contemplate Christ as the food of our souls in this comprehensive sense. As often as we eat the bread and drink the cup we declare that Christ has been, and is now, our soul's food in all these ways. And as often as we use this Supper with sincerity we are helped to appropriate Christ as our spiritual food more and more abundantly. Even as a symbol or picture — mysticism and magic apart — the Holy Supper aids our faith. Through the eye it affects the heart, as do poetry and music through the ear. The very mysticism and superstition that have grown around the sacraments in the course of ages are a witness to their powerful influence over the imagination. Men's thoughts and feelings were so deeply stirred they could not believe such power lay in mere symbols; and by a confusion of ideas natural to an excited imagination they imputed to the sign all the virtues of the things signified. By this means faith was transferred from Christ the Redeemer, and the Spirit the Sanctifier, to the rite of baptism and the service of the mass. This result shows the need of knowledge and spiritual discernment to keep the imagination in check, and prevent the eyes of the understanding from being put out by the dazzling glare of fancy. Some, considering how thoroughly the eyes of the understanding have been put out by theories of sacramental grace, have been tempted to deny that sacraments are even *means* of grace, and to think that institutions which have been so fearfully abused ought to be allowed to fall into desuetude.   This is a natural re-action, but it is an extreme opinion.   The sober, true view of the matter is, that sacraments are means of grace, not from any magic virtue in them or in the priest administering them, but as helping faith by sense, and still more by the blessing of Christ and the working of His Spirit, as the reward of an intelligent, sincere, believing use of them.

This, then, is what we have learned from the monumental stone.   The Lord's Supper commemorates the Lord's *death;* points out that death as an event of transcendent importance ; sets it forth, indeed, as the ground of our hope for the pardon of sin ; and finally exhibits Christ the Lord, who died on the Cross, as all to us which our spirits need for health and salvation — our mystic bread and wine.   This rite, instituted by Jesus on the night on which He was betrayed, He meant to be repeated not merely by the apostles, but by His believing people in all ages till He came again.   So we learn from Paul ; so we might have inferred, apart from any express information.   An act so original, so impressive, so pregnant with meaning, so helpful to faith, once performed, was virtually an enactment.   In performing it, Jesus said in effect : " Let this become a great institution, a standing observance in the community to be called by my Name."

The meaning of the ordinance determines the spirit in which it should be observed.   Christians should sit down at the table in a spirit of humility, thankfulness, and brotherly love ; confessing sin, devoutly thanking God for His covenant of grace, and His mercy to them in Christ, loving Him who loved them, and washed them from their sins in His own blood, and who daily feedeth their souls with heavenly food, and giving Him all glory and dominion ; and loving one another — loving all redeemed men and believers in Jesus as brethren, and taking the Supper together as a family meal ; withal praying that an ever-increasing number may experience the saving efficacy of Christ's death.   After this

fashion did the apostles and the apostolic church celebrate
the Supper at Pentecost, after Jesus had ascended to glory.
Continuing daily with one accord in the temple, and breaking bread from house to house, they did eat their meat with
gladness and singleness of heart. Would that we now could
keep the feast as they kept it then ! But how much must be
done ere that be possible ! The moss of Time must be cleared
away from the monumental stone, that its inscription may
become once more distinctly legible ; the accumulated *débris*
of a millennium and a half of theological controversies about
sacraments must be carted out of sight and mind ;[1] the truth
as it is in Jesus must be separated from the alloy of human
error ; the homely rite of the Supper must be divested of the
state robes of elaborate ceremonial by which it has been
all but stifled, and allowed to return to congenial primitive
simplicity. These things, so devoutly to be wished, will
come at last, — if not on earth, in that day when the Lord
Jesus will drink new wine with His people in the kingdom
of His Father.[2]

---

[1] The history of these controversies is very humiliating, and their consequences most
disastrous. Through them the symbol of union has been turned into a chief cause of
division. The church has remembered her Lord, and obeyed His commandment of love,
as members of families sometime remember a deceased parent, casting angry glances at
each other across his grave, and retiring to the house, whose head they have buried, to
squabble about the meaning of his will.

[2] We may here note the *momenta* of the doctrine of the cross as set forth in the four
lessons given by Jesus to His disciples, in order to bring them together in one view.
They are these : —

1. *First Lesson.* — Christ suffered for righteousness' sake : herein an example to all
His followers (Matt. xvi. 24-28, *et parall. vide* p. 183).
2. *Second Lesson.* — Christ suffered for the unrighteous — gave His life a ransom
for the sinful : herein our example so far as He stooped to conquer (Matt. xx.
28, *vide* p. 291).
3. *Third Lesson.* — Christ suffered in the spirit of self-sacrificing love, exemplified
by Mary of Bethany (Matt. xxvi. 6-13, *et parall. vide* p. 301).
4. *Fourth Lesson.* — Christ suffered to inaugurate a new covenant of grace, and
procure for sinners the forgiveness of sin (Matt. xxvi. 26-29, *et parall. vide*
p. 360).

23

JUDAS ISCARIOT

Matt. 26:20-23; Mark 14:17-21; Luke 22:21-23; John 13:21-30

BESIDES the feet-washing and the institution of the Supper, yet another scene occurred on the night preceding the Lord's death, helping to render it forever memorable. On the same night, during the course of the evening meal,[1] Jesus exposed and expelled the false disciple, who had undertaken to deliver his Master into the hands of those who sought His life. Already, while occupied with the washing, He had made premonitory allusions to the fact that there was a traitor among the twelve, hinting that they were not all clean, and insinuating that there was one of them who *knew* and would not *do*. Having finished and explained the service of lowly love, He next proceeded to the unwelcome task of indicating distinctly to which of the disciples He had been alluding. With spirit troubled at thought of the painful duty, and shuddering in presence of such satanic wickedness, He introduced the subject by making the general announcement : "Verily, verily, I say unto you, that one of you shall betray me." Thereafter, in answer to inquiries, He indicated the particular individual, by explaining that the traitor was he to whom He should give a sop or morsel after He had dipped it.[2]

The fact then announced was new to the disciples, but it was not new to their Master. Jesus had known all along that there was a traitor in the camp. He had even hinted as

[1] Whether before or after the institution of the Supper has been much discussed, and is of no theological importance, though it has been thought to be so in connection with the question of strict communion.

[2] On the harmony of this subject, see Ebrard, *Gospel History ;* and also Stier, *Reden Jesu,* who reconciles the Synoptics with John by supposing two announcements of the traitor, with the Lord's Supper intervening, which he brings in between vers. 22 and 23 of John's narrative.

much a full year before. But, excepting on that one occasion, He had not spoken of the matter hitherto, but had patiently borne it as a secret burden on His own heart. Now, how-ever, the secret may be hid no longer. The hour is come when the Son of man must be glorified. Judas, for his part, has made up his mind to be the instrument of betraying his Lord to death ; and such bad work, once resolved on, should by all means be done without delay. Then Jesus wants to be rid of the false disciple's company. He desires to spend the few last hours of His life in tender, confidential fellow-ship with His faithful ones, free from the irritation and distraction caused by the presence of an undeclared yet deadly enemy. Therefore He does not wait till it pleases Judas to depart ; He bids him go, asserting His authority over him even after he has renounced his allegiance and given himself up to the devil's service. Reaching the sop, He says to him in effect : "I know thee, Judas ; thou art the man : thou hast resolved to betray me : away, then, and do it." And then He says expressly : "That thou doest, do quickly." It was an order to go, and go at once.

Judas took the hint. He "went immediately *out*," and so finally quitted the society of which he had been an unworthy member. One wonders how such a man ever got *in*, — how he ever was admitted into such a holy fellowship, — how he came to be chosen one of the twelve. Did Jesus not know the real character of this man when He chose Him ? The words of our Lord, spoken just before, forbid us to think this. "I know," said He, while expounding the feet-washing, "whom I have chosen," meaning, evidently, to claim knowledge of them all, Judas included, at the time He chose them. Did He then choose Judas, knowing what he was, that He might have among the twelve one by whom He might be betrayed, and the Scriptures in that particular be fulfilled ? So He seems to hint in the declaration just alluded to ; for He goes on to say : "But that the scripture may be fulfilled, He that eateth bread with me hath lifted up his heel against me." [1] But it is not credible that Iscariot was chosen merely to be a traitor, as an actor might be chosen by a theatre manager to play the part of Iago. The end pointed at in the scripture

[1] John xiii. 18

quoted might be ultimately served by his being chosen, but that end was not the motive of the choice. We may regard these two points as certain : on the one hand, that Judas did not become a follower of Jesus with treacherous intentions ; and on the other, that Jesus did not elect Judas to be one of the twelve because He foreknew that he would eventually become a traitor.

If the choice of the false disciple was not due either to ignorance or to foreknowledge, how is it to be explained? The only explanation that can be given is, that, apart from secret insight, Judas was to all appearance an eligible man, and could not be passed over on any grounds coming under ordinary observation. His qualities must have been such, that one not possessing the eye of omniscience, looking on him, would have been disposed to say of him what Samuel said of Eliab : "Surely the Lord's anointed is before him." [1] In that case, his election by Jesus is perfectly intelligible. The Head of the church simply did what the church has to do in analogous instances. The church chooses men to fill sacred offices on a conjunct view of ostensible qualifications, such as knowledge, zeal, apparent piety, and correctness of outward conduct. In so doing she sometimes makes unhappy appointments, and confers dignity on persons of the Judas type, who dishonor the positions they fill. The mischief resulting is great ; but Christ has taught us, by His example in choosing Judas, as also by the parable of the tares, that we must submit to the evil, and leave the remedy in higher hands. Out of evil God often brings good, as He did in the case of the traitor.

Supposing Judas to have been chosen to the apostleship on the ground of apparent fitness, what manner of man would that imply? A vulgar, conscious hypocrite, seeking some mean by-end, while professedly aiming at a higher? Not necessarily ; not probably. Rather such an one as Jesus indirectly described Judas to be when He made the reflection : "If ye know these things, happy are ye if ye do them." The false disciple was a sentimental, plausible, self-deceived pietist, who knew and approved the good, though not conscientiously practising it ; one who, in æsthetic feeling, in fancy,

[1] 1 Sam. xvi. 6

and in intellect, had affinities for the noble and the holy, while in will and in conduct he was the slave of base, selfish passions; one who, in the last resource, would always put self uppermost, yet could zealously devote himself to well-doing when personal interests were not compromised — in short, what the Apostle James calls a two-minded man.[1] In thus describing Judas, we draw not the picture of a solitary monster. Men of such a type are by no means so rare as some may imagine. History, sacred and profane, supplies numerous examples of them, playing an important part in human affairs. Balaam, who had the vision of a prophet and the soul of a miser, was such a man. Robespierre, the evil genius of the French Revolution, was another. The man who sent thousands to the guillotine had in his younger days resigned his office as a provincial judge, because it was against his conscience to pronounce sentence of death on a culprit found guilty of a capital offence.[2] A third example, more remarkable than either, may be found in the famous Greek Alcibiades, who, to unbounded ambition, unscrupulous-ness, and licentiousness, united a warm attachment to the greatest and best of the Greeks. The man who in after years betrayed the cause of his native city, and went over to the side of her enemies, was in his youth an enthusiastic admirer and disciple of Socrates. How he felt towards the Athenian sage may be gathered from words put into his mouth by Plato in one of his dialogues — words which invol-untarily suggest a parallel between the speaker and the unworthy follower of a greater than Socrates: "I experience towards this man alone (Socrates) what no one would believe me capable of, a sense of shame. For I am conscious of an inability to contradict him, and decline to do what he bids me; and when I go away I feel myself overcome by the desire of popular esteem. Therefore I flee from him, and avoid him. But when I see him, I am ashamed of my admis-sions, and oftentimes I would be glad if he ceased to exist among the living; and yet I know well, that were that to happen, I should be still more grieved."[3]

---

[1] Jas. i. 8, ἀνὴρ δίψυχος; that is, a man with two minds; not one real, the other feigned, but with two minds both real so far as they go, only the wrong mind strongest, and ultimately prevailing.

[2] Carlyle, *French Revolution*, i. 170, 171.

[3] Plato, Συμπόσιον: Alcibiades *loquitur*.

The character of Judas being such as we have described, the *possibility* at least of his turning a traitor becomes comprehensible.   One who loves himself more than any man, however good, or any cause, however holy, is always capable of bad faith more or less heinous.   He is a traitor at heart from the outset, and all that is wanted is a set of circumstances calculated to bring into play the evil elements of his nature.   The question therefore arises, What were the circumstances which converted Judas from a possible into an actual traitor ?

This is a question very hard indeed to answer.   The crime committed by Iscariot, through which he has earned for himself "a frightful renown," remains, in spite of all the discussion whereof it has been the subject, still mysterious and unaccountable.   Many attempts have been made to assign probable motives for the nefarious deed, some tending to excuse the doer, and others to aggravate his guilt ; all more or less conjectural, and none perfectly satisfactory. As for the Gospel narratives, they do not explain, but merely record, the wickedness of Judas.   The synoptical evangelists do indeed mention that the traitor made a bargain with the priests, and received from them a sum of money for the service rendered ; and John, in his narrative of the anointing at Bethany, takes occasion to state that the faultfinding disciple was a thief, appropriating to his own uses money out of the common purse, of which he had charge.[1]   These facts, of course, show Iscariot to have been a covetous man. None but a man of greedy, covetous spirit could have taken money for such a service.   A vindictive man, whose vanity had been wounded, or who fancied himself in some way wronged, might play the traitor for love of revenge, but he would scorn to be paid for his work.   The petty pilfering from the bag was also a sure sign of a mean, sordid soul. Perhaps the very fact of his being the purse-bearer to the company of Jesus may be regarded as an indication that his heart hankered after greed.   He got the bag to carry, we imagine, because the other disciples were all supremely careless about money matters, while he had decided proclivities towards finance, and showed a desire to have charge of

[1] John xii. 6.

the superfluous funds. All the rest would be only too glad to find a brother willing to take the trouble ; and having imbibed the spirit of their Master's precept, Take no thought for the morrow, they would not think of presenting themselves as rival candidates for the office.

The evangelists do therefore most distinctly represent Judas as a covetous man. But they do not represent his covetousness as the sole, or even as the principal, motive of his crime. That, indeed, it can hardly have been. For, in the first place, would it not have been a better speculation to have continued pursebearer, with facilities for appropriating its contents, than to sell his Master for a paltry sum not exceeding five pounds ?[1] Then what could induce a man whose chief and ruling passion was to amass money to become a disciple of Jesus at all ? Surely following Him who had no place where to lay His head was not a likely way to money-making ! Then, finally, how account for the repentance of the traitor, so great in its vehemence, though most unholy in its nature, on the hypothesis that his sole object was to gain a few pieces of silver ? Avarice may make a man of splendid talents thoroughly mercenary and unscrupulous, as is said to have been the case with the famous Duke of Marlborough ; but it is rarely, indeed, that a man given up to avaricious habits takes seriously to heart the crimes committed under their influence. It is the nature of avarice to destroy conscience, and to make all things, however sacred, venal. Whence, then, that mighty volcanic upheaving in the breast of Judas ? Surely other passions were at work in his soul when he sold his Lord than the cold and hardening love of gain !

Pressed by this difficulty, some have suggested that, in betraying Jesus, Judas was actuated principally by feelings of jealousy or spite, arising out of internal dissensions or imagined injuries. This suggestion is in itself not improbable. Offences might very easily come from various sources. The mere fact that Judas was not a Galilean,[2] but a native of another province, might give rise to misunderstanding. Human sympathies and antipathies depend on very little things. Kinsmanship, a common name, or a common birth-

---

[1] Renan, *Vie de Jésus*, p. 394.   [2] *Vide* cap. iv.

place, have far more power than the grand bonds which connect us with all the race. In religion the same remark holds good. The ties of a common Lord, a common hope, and a common spiritual life, are feeble as compared with those of sect and sectional religious custom and opinion. Then who knows what offences sprang from those disputes among the disciples who should be the greatest in the kingdom? What if the man of Kerioth had been made to feel that, whoever was to be the greatest, he at least had no chance, not being a Galilean? The mean, narrow habits of Judas as treasurer would be a third cause of bad feeling in the apostolic company. Supposing his dishonesty to have escaped observation, his tendency to put the interest of the bag above the objects for which its contents were destined, and so to dole out supplies either for the company or for the poor grudgingly, would be sure to be noticed, and, being noticed, would certainly, in such an outspoken society, not fail to be remarked on.[1]

These reflections show how ill-feeling might have arisen between Judas and his fellow-disciples ; but what we have to account for is the hatred of the false disciple against his Master. Had Jesus, then, done any thing to offend the man by whom He was betrayed? Yes! He had seen through him, and that was offence enough! For, of course, Judas knew that he was seen through. Men cannot live together in close fellowship long without coming to know with what feelings they are regarded by each other. If I distrust a brother, he will find it out, even should I attempt to conceal it. But the guileless and faithful One would make no attempt at concealment. He would not, indeed, offensively obtrude His distrust on the notice of Judas, but neither would He studiously hide it, to make matters go smoothly between them. He who so faithfully corrected the faults of the other disciples would do His duty to this one also, and make him aware that

---

[1] Renan, *Vie de Jésus*, p. 395.

The poor were not forgotten by Jesus and His disciples (John xii. 5, xiii. 29). When supplies overflowed, they were not hoarded for to-morrow, but for the destitute. That they had more than they needed was the result of the love of grateful souls (Luke viii. 1-3), and the bag was kept that nothing might be wasted; for the ethics of Jesus condemn waste as strongly as they discountenance carefulness. " Gather up the fragments," etc.

he regarded his spirit and evil habits with disapprobation, in order to bring him to repentance. And what the effect of such dealing would be it is not difficult to imagine. On a Peter, correction had a most wholesome influence; it brought him at once to a right mind. In the case of a Judas the result would be very different. The mere consciousness that Jesus did not *think* well of him, and still more the shame of an open rebuke, would breed sullen resentment and ever-deepening alienation of heart; till at length love was turned to hatred, and the impenitent disciple began to cherish *vindictive* passions.

The manner in which the betrayal was gone about supports the idea that the agent was actuated by malicious, revengeful feelings. Not content with giving such information as would enable the Jewish authorities to get their Victim into their hands, Judas conducted the band that was sent to apprehend his Master, and even pointed Him out to them by an affectionate salutation. To one in a vengeful mood that kiss might be sweet; but to a man in any other mood, even though he were a traitor, how abhorrent and abominable! The salutation was entirely gratuitous: it was not necessary for the success of the plot; for the military detachment was furnished with torches, and Judas could have indicated Jesus to them while he himself kept in the background. But that way would not satisfy a bosom friend turned to be a mortal enemy.[1]

Along with malice and greed, the instinct of self-preservation may have had a place among the motives of Judas. Perfidy might be recommended by the suggestions of selfish prudence. The traitor was a shrewd man, and believed that a catastrophe was near. He understood better than his single-minded brethren the situation of affairs; for the children of this world are wiser in their generation than the children of light. The other disciples, by their generous enthusiasms and patriotic hopes, were blinded to the signs of the times; but the false disciple, just because he was less noble, was more discerning. Disaster, then, being imminent,

[1] Renan, *Vie de Jésus*, favors the idea that Judas was actuated by spite. He remarks, on the number of denunciators connected with secret societies: " Un léger dépit," he says, " suffisait pour faire d'un sectaire un traître " (p. 395).

what was to be done ?   What but turn king's evidence, and
make terms for himself, so that Christ's loss might be his
gain ?   If this baseness could be perpetrated under pretence
of provocation, why then, so much the better !

These observations help to bring the crime of Judas
Iscariot within the range of human experience, and on this
account it was worth our while to make them ; for it is not
desirable that we should think of the traitor as an absolutely unique character, as the solitary perfect incarnation
of satanic wickedness.[1]   We should rather so think of his
crime as that the effect of contemplating it on our minds
shall be to make us, like the disciples, ask, Is it I ?[2]   "Who
can understand his errors ?   Keep back Thy servant from
presumptuous sins."   There have been many traitors besides
Judas, who, from malice or for gain, have played false to
noble men and noble causes ; some of them perhaps even
worse men than he.   It was his unenviable distinction to
betray the most exalted of all victims ; but many who have
been substantially guilty of his sin have not taken it so
much to heart, but have been able to live happily after their
deed of villany was wrought.

Yet, while it is important for our warning not to conceive
of Judas as an isolated sinner, it is also most desirable that
we should regard his crime as an incomprehensible mystery
of iniquity.   It is in this light that the fourth evangelist
would have us look at it.   He could have told us much about
the mutual relations of Judas and Jesus tending to explain
the deed of the former.   But he has not chosen to do so.
The only explanation he gives of the traitor's crime is, that
Satan had taken possession of him.   This he mentions twice
over in one chapter, as if to express his own horror, and to
awaken similar horror in his readers.[3]   And to deepen the
impression, after relating the exit of Judas, he adds the suggestive reflection that it took place after nightfall :   "He

---

[1] Such is the view of Daub in his *Judas Iscariot, oder Das Böse in Verhältniss
zum Guten*.

[2] The disciples first trembled, each one for himself ; then, after recovering their
composure, began to wonder who it could be ; and finally, Peter made a sign to John,
who was next to Jesus, to inquire.

[3] John xiii. 2, 27.   Satan entered Judas first as the Satan of wicked purpose ; then,
after the sop (Christ's challenge to Judas), as the Satan of action.

then, having received the sop, went immediately out : *and it was night."* Fit time for such an errand !

Judas went out and betrayed his Lord to death, and then he went and took his own life. What a tragic accompaniment to the crucifixion was that suicide ! What an impressive illustration of the evil of a double mind ! To be happy in some fashion, Judas should either have been a better man or a worse. Had he been better, he would have been saved from his crime ; had he been worse, he would have escaped torment before the time. As it was, he was bad enough to do the deed of infamy, and good enough to be unable to bear the burden of its guilt. Woe to such a man ! Better for him, indeed, that he had never been born !

What a melancholy end was that of Judas to an auspicious beginning ! Chosen to be a companion of the Son of man, and an eye and ear witness of His work, once engaged in preaching the gospel and casting out devils ; now possessed of the devil himself, driven on by him to damnable deeds, and finally employed by a righteous Providence to take vengeance on his own crime. In view of this history, how shallow the theory that resolves all moral differences between men into the effect of circumstances ! Who was ever better circumstanced for becoming good than Judas ? Yet the very influences which ought to have fostered goodness served only to provoke into activity latent evil.

What a bitter cross must the constant presence of such a man as Judas have been to the pure, loving heart of Jesus ! Yet how patiently it was borne for years ! Herein He is an example and a comfort to His true followers, and for this end among others had He this cross to bear. The Redeemer of men had a companion who lifted up his heel against Him, that in this as in all other respects He might be like unto, and able to succour, His brethren. Has any faithful servant of Christ to complain that his love has been requited by hatred, his truth with bad faith ; or that he is obliged to treat as a true Christian one whom he more than suspects to be a hypocrite ? It is a hard trial, but let him look unto Jesus and be patient !

24

THE DYING PARENT AND THE LITTLE ONES

SECTION I — WORDS OF COMFORT AND COUNSEL TO THE SORROWING
CHILDREN

John 13:31-35; 14:1-4; 15-21

THE exit of Judas into the darkness of night, on his still
darker errand, was a summons to Jesus to prepare for death.
Yet He was thankful for the departure of the traitor. It
took a burden off His heart, and allowed Him to breathe and
to speak freely; and if it brought Him, in the first place,
near to His last sufferings, it brought Him also near to the
ulterior joy of resurrection and exaltation to glory. Therefore His first utterance, after the departure took place, was

---

[1] Our readers will find at the end of chapter xxvi. of this work an analysis of the
contents of the farewell discourse and intercessory prayer recorded in John xiii 31-38,
xiv.-xvii , which, though placed at the end of our exposition, may perhaps profitably be
consulted here. We have been led to prepare this table partly on account of the length
of the exposition, which is apt to divert attention from the natural divisions of the
subject, and prevent the impression of appropriateness to the situation, which it has been
our aim to produce in connection with this part of John's record, from being as strong as
we should wish. Partly also, however, from observing how much of the criticism on this
farewell discourse, designed to show that it is not an historical record so much as a free
composition, seems to arise out of defective insight into its import. We have had
occasion to notice this even in writers who admit Johannine authorship, and recognize
logia of our Lord as the germs of all John's free expansions ; as, *e.g.* Dr. Sanday in his
thoughtful work on the *Authorship and Historical Character of the Fourth Gospel.*
Admitting the legitimacy of the view taken by this writer of the Johannine discourses in
the abstract, we maintain that he has failed to see *into* the discourses, and very specially
into the farewell discourse, has looked too much at the surface, and so has made criticisms
which he would not have made had he looked more below the surface. It appears to us
intrinsically credible that Jesus spoke words of comfort to His disciples such as are
considered in Section I. of this chapter : words of exhortation, warning, and encouragement respecting their work as *apostles*, such as we find in John xv., xvi. ; and words of
prayer for men on whom so much depended. The children's questions, considered in
Section II. of this chapter, seem to rise naturally out of the previously spoken words of
Jesus, and the answers to them ought to be kept apart from what Jesus meant to say,
irrespective of interruptions.

an outburst of unfeigned gladness. When the false disciple was gone out, and the sound of his retiring footsteps had died away, Jesus said : " *Now* is the Son of man glorified : and God is glorified in Him ; and God shall glorify Him in Himself, yea, He shall straightway glorify Him." [1]

But while, by a faith which substantiated things hoped for, and made evident things not visible, Jesus was able to see in present death coming glory, He remembered that He had around Him disciples to whom, in their weakness, His decease and departure would mean simply bereavement and desolation. Therefore He at once turned His thoughts to them, and proceeded to say to them such things as were suitable to their inward state and their outward situation.

In His last words to His own the Saviour employed two different styles of speech. First, He spoke to them as a dying parent addressing his children ; and then He assumed a loftier tone, and spoke to them as a dying Lord addressing His servants, friends, and representatives. The words of comfort and counsel spoken by Jesus in the former capacity, we find in the passages cited from the thirteenth and fourteenth chapters of John's Gospel ; while the directions of the departing Lord to His future Apostles are recorded in the two chapters which follow. We have to consider in this chapter the dying Parent's last words to His sorrowing children.

These, it will be observed, were not spoken in one continuous address. While the dying Parent spake, the children kept asking Him child's questions. First one, then another, then a third, and then a fourth, asked Him a question, suggested by what He had been saying. To these questions Jesus listened patiently, and returned answer as He could. The answers He gave, and the things He meant to say without reference to possible interrogations, are mixed up together in the narrative. It will be convenient for our purpose to separate these from those, and to consider first, taken together, the words of comfort spoken by Jesus to His disciples, and then their questionings of Him, with the replies which these elicited. This method will make these words stand out in all their exquisite simplicity and appropriateness.

---

[1] John xiii. 31, 32. The words εἰ ὁ Θεὸς ἐδοξάσθη ἐν αὐτῷ are regarded as spurious by Luthardt and other critics.

To show how very simple and suitable they were, we may
here state them in the fewest possible words. They were
these: 1. I am going away; in my absence find comfort in
one another's love (xiii. 31–35). 2. I am going away; but it
is to my Father's house, and in due season I will come back
and take you thither (xiv. 1–49). 3. I am going away; but
even when I am away I will be with you in the person of my
alter ego, the Comforter (xiv. 15–21).

Knowing to whom He speaks, Jesus begins at once with
the nursery dialect. He addresses His disciples not merely
as children, but as "little children;" by the endearing name
expressing His tender affection towards them, and His compassion for their weakness. Then He alludes to His death
in a delicate roundabout way, adapted to childish capacity
and feelings. He tells them He is going a road they cannot
follow, and that they will miss Him as children miss their
father when he goes out and never returns. "Yet a little
while I am with you. Ye shall seek me: and as I said unto
the Jews, Whither I go, ye cannot come; so now I say to
you."

After this brief, simple preface Jesus went on to give His
little ones His *first* dying counsel, viz. that they should *love
one another in His absence.* Surely it was a counsel well
worthy to come first! For what solace can be greater to
orphaned ones than mutual love? Let the world be ever
so dark and cheerless, while brothers in affliction are true
brothers to each other in sympathy and reciprocal helpful-
ness, they have an unfailing well-spring of joy in the desert
of sorrow. If, on the other hand, to all the other ills of life
there be added alienation, distrust, antagonism, the bereaved
are desolate indeed; their night of sorrow hath not even a
solitary star to alleviate its gloom.[1]

Anxious to secure due attention to a precept in itself most
seasonable, and even among the disciples needing enforcement, Jesus conferred on it all the dignity and importance of

[1] Sanday, *Authorship and Historical Character of the Fourth Gospel*, p. 219, says.
"Verses 34, 35 (the *mandatum*) come in curiously as a parenthesis"! This is the first
instance of several in which this author seems to show a want of insight into the structure
of the last discourse in its relation to the solemn circumstances of speaker and hearers.
The *mandatum* surely deserved the first place among the words of consolation to the
bereaved family.

a new commandment, and made the love enjoined therein the distinctive mark of Christian discipleship. " A new commandment," said He, " I give unto you, that ye love one another ; " thus, on that memorable night, adding a third novelty to those already introduced — the new sacrament and the new convenant. The commandment and the covenant were new in the same sense ; not as never having been heard of before, but as now for the first time proclaimed with the due emphasis, and assuming their rightful place of supremacy above the details of Mosaic moral legislation and the shadowy rites of the legal religious economy. *Now* love was to be the outstanding royal law, and free grace was to antiquate Sinaitic ordinances. And why now ? In both cases, because Jesus was about to die. His death would be the seal of the New Testament, and it would exemplify and ratify the new commandment. Hence He goes on to say, after giving forth that new law, " as I have loved you." The past tense is not to be interpreted strictly here : the perfect must be taken as a *future perfect*, so as to include the death which was the crowning act of the Saviour's love. " Love one another," Jesus would say, " as I shall have loved you, and as ye shall know that I have loved you when ye come to need the consolation of so loving each other." So understanding His words, we see clearly why He calls the law of love new. His own love in giving His life for His people was a new thing on earth ; and a love among His followers, one towards another, kindred in spirit and ready to do the same thing if needful, would be equally a novelty at which the world would stare, asking in wonder whence it came, till at length it perceived that the men who so loved had been with Jesus.

The *second* word of comfort spoken by Jesus to the little ones He was about to leave was, in its general aspect, an exhortation to faith : " Let not your heart be troubled ; believe in God, and believe in me ; " in its more special aspect a promise that He would return to take them to be with Him for ever.[1] The exhortation embraces in its scope

---

[1] John xiv. 1. The verb πιστεύετε in either clause may be either imperative or indicative, and four different renderings are possible. The rendering in the Eng. Ver. and that given above come practically to the same thing. Even in the indicative, Ye believe in God, an imperative is implied : Exercise and draw comfort from your faith in God.

the whole interests of the disciples, secular and spiritual, temporal and eternal. Their dying Master recommends them first to exercise faith in God, mainly with reference to temporal anxieties. He says to them, in effect : " I am going to leave you, my children ; but be not afraid. You shall not be in the world as poor orphans, defenceless and unprovided for ; God my Father will take care of you ; trust in Divine Providence, and let peace rule in your hearts." Having thus exhorted them to exercise faith in God the Provider, Jesus next exhorts His little ones to believe in Himself, with special reference to those spiritual and eternal interests for the sake of which they had left all and followed Him. " Believing in God for food and raiment, believe in me too, and be assured that all I said to you about the kingdom and its joys and rewards is true. Soon ye will find it very hard to believe this : it will seem to you as if the promises I made were deceptive, and the kingdom a dream and a hallucination. But do not allow such dark thoughts to take possession of your minds : recollect what you know of me ; and ask yourselves whether it is likely that He whose companions you have been during these years would deceive you with romantic promises that were never to be fulfilled."

The kingdom and its rewards ; these were the things which Jesus had encouraged His followers to expect. Of these, accordingly, He proceeded next to speak, in the style suited to the character he had assumed, — that, viz., of a dying parent addressing his children. " In my Father's house," said He, " are many mansions. I go to prepare a place for you, and I will come again, and receive you unto myself." Such, in its more specific form, was the second word of consolation. What a cheering prospect it held out to the disciples ! In the hour of despondency the little ones would think themselves orphans, without a home either in earth or in heaven. But their Friend assures them that they should not merely have a home, but a splendid one ; not merely a humble shed to shelter them from the storm, but a glorious palace to reside in, in a region where storms were unknown,— a house with a great many rooms in it, supplying abundant accommodation for them all, incomparably more capacious than the temple which had been the earthly dwelling-place of God. His own death, which would appear to them so great a calamity, would simply mean His going before to prepare for them a place in that splendid mansion, and in due season His departure would be followed by a return to take them to be with Himself.[1] What was implied in preparing a place when He should come again, He did not explain. He only added, as if coaxing them to take a cheerful view of the situation, " Whither I go ye know, and the way ye know ; " meaning, Think whither I go, to the Father, and think of my death as merely the way thither : and so let not my absence from the world make you sad, nor my death seem something dreadful.

To the student of New Testament theology, interested in tracing the resemblances and contrasts in different types of doctrine, this second word of consolation spoken by Christ to His disciples has special interest, as containing substantially the idea of a Forerunner, one of the striking thoughts of the Epistle to the Hebrews. The writer of that epistle tells his Hebrew readers that Jesus has gone into heaven not merely as a High Priest, but as a Forerunner,[2] this being one of the

[1] The words of ver. 3 are the Johannine equivalent for the promise of the second coming to set up the kingdom in glory, and to make the disciples partakers in the glory, which forms a conspicuous feature in the synoptical representation of Christ's teaching. They are similar in import to words reported in Luke as spoken by Jesus on the same evening : " Ye are they which have continued with me in my temptations, and I appoint unto you a kingdom, as my Father hath appointed unto me, that ye may eat and drink at my table in my kingdom, and sit on thrones judging the twelve tribes of Israel." Eschatology, and the doctrine of the kingdom generally, retires into the background in John's Gospel. The idea of a divine kingdom is not altogether wanting indeed ; we find it in John iii. 3, xviii. 36, and in the inscription on the cross · " Jesus of Nazareth, the King of the Jews." The Johannine equivalent for the idea of the kingdom is eternal life, an idea found in the synoptical Gospels (Matt. xvi. 25, xix. 17, xix. 29, xxv. 46), but as little prominent there as the idea of the kingdom is in John. The relation between the two ideas is this : the one, the idea of the kingdom, regards man as the member of a society ; the other, the idea of eternal life, regards man as an individual. The former denotes the highest good as the joint possession of all its citizens ; the latter as the separate possession of each individual soul. The retirement of the idea of the kingdom, with all the sensuous coloring with which it is painted in the synoptical narratives, may be accounted for by the late origin of the Fourth Gospel at the close of the first century, when the destruction of Jerusalem, and the spread of the gospel among the heathen, lay behind the aged apostle as historical facts. If it be asked, Could Jesus speak of the same thing on the same occasion so differently as He is represented doing in John xiv. 2, 3, and in Luke xxii. 28 30? we may reply by asking another question, Could Jesus speak to the same hearers on the same occasion so differently as in John xiv. and John xv.? The point of view changing involves a change of style. The house of many mansions and the thrones are both figures or parables, and might both occur in one conversation or discourse.

[2] The point is missed in the A. V. by the use of the article. The R. V. gives it correctly. See its version of Heb. vi. 20.

novelties and glories of the new dispensation ; for no high priest of Israel went into the Most Holy Place as a forerunner, but only as a substitute, going for the people into a place whither they might not follow him. Jesus, on the other hand, goes into the heavenly sanctuary, not only for us, but before us, going into a place whither we may follow Him ; no place being screened off, barred, or locked against us. Similar is the thought which the fourth evangelist puts into the mouth of Jesus here, speaking as the great High Priest of humanity.

These child-like yet profound sayings of the Lord Jesus are not only cheering, but most stimulating to the imagination. The "many mansions" suggest many thoughts. We think with pleasure of the vast numbers which the many-mansioned house is capable of containing. We may too, harmlessly, though perhaps fancifully, with the saints of other ages, think of the lodgings in the Father's house as not only many in number, but also as many in kind, corresponding to the classes or ranks of the residents.[1] But to some the most comfortable thought of all suggested by this pregnant poetic word is the certainty of an eternal life. To men who have doubted concerning the life beyond, the grand desideratum is not detailed information respecting the site, and the size, and the architecture of the celestial city, but to know for certain that there is such a city, that there is an house not made with hands eternal in the heavens. This desideratum is supplied in this word of Christ. For whatever the many mansions may mean besides, they do at the least imply that there is a state of happy existence to be reached by believers, as He in whom they believe reached it, viz. through death. The life everlasting, whatever its conditions, is undoubtedly taught here. And it is taught with authority. Jesus speaks as one who knows, not (like Socrates) as one who merely has an opinion on the subject. At his farewell meeting with his friends before he drank the hemlock cup, the Athenian sage discussed with them the question of the immortality

---

[1] For Cyprian's opinion, see p. 256 of this work. The same idea occurs in Irenæus, *Hæres.* v. 36. No doubt there is a truth in this view. There will be Christians of various ranks in heaven — princes and doorkeepers ; also of various schools, High Church, Broad Church, and Low Church, able at last to believe each other to *be* Christians.

of the soul. On that question he strongly maintained the affirmative ; but still only as one who looked on it as a fair subject for discussion, and knew that there was a good deal to be said on both sides. But Jesus does more than maintain the affirmative on the subject of the life to come. He speaks thereon with oracular confidence, offering to us not the frail raft of a probable opinion, whereon we may perilously sail down the stream of life towards death ; but the strong ship of a divine word, wherein one may sail securely, for which Socrates and his companions sighed.[1] And He so speaks with a full sense of the responsibility He thereby takes upon Himself. " If it were not so," He remarked to His disciples, " I would have told you ;" which is as much as to say, that one should not encourage such expectations as He had led them to entertain unless he were sure of his ground. It was not enough to have an opinion about the world to come : one who took the responsibility of asking men to leave this present world for its sake should be quite certain that it was a reality, and not a dream. What condescension to the weakness of the disciples is shown in this self-justifying reflection of their Lord ! What an aid also it lends to our faith in the reality of future bliss ! For such an one as Jesus Christ would not have spoken in this way unless He had possessed authentic information about the world beyond.

In the *third* word of consolation, the leading thought is the promise of another Comforter, who should take the place of Him who was going away, and make the bereaved feel *as if He were still with them.* In the second word of comfort Jesus had said that He was going to provide a home for the little ones, and that then He would return and take them to it. In this third final word He virtually promises to be present with them by substitute, even when He is absent. " I will pray the Father," He says, "and He shall give you another Comforter, that He may abide with you for ever "[2] (not for a season, as has been the case with me). Then He

---

[1] *Phædo.* cap. xxxv.: " One must do one of two things (in reference to the question of a future state) : either learn how the case stands, or find out ; or if these are impossible, taking the best and least easily refuted of human opinions, and embarking on it as on a raft (σχεδίας), sail perilously through life ; unless one could more securely and less perilously sail upon a stronger vessel or some divine word (λόγου θείου τινος)."

[2] John xiv. 16.

tells them who this wonderful Comforter is : His name is "the *Spirit of Truth.*" [1]   Then, lastly, He gives them to understand that this Spirit of Truth will be a Comforter to them, by restoring, as it were, the consciousness of His own presence, so that the coming of this other Comforter will just be, in a sense, His own spiritual return. " I will not leave you comfortless," He assures them : " I will not leave you *orphans, I* will come to you ; " [2] promising thereby not a different thing, but the same thing which He had promised just before, in different terms.   How the other Comforter would make Himself an *alter ego* of the departed one, He does not here distinctly explain.[3]   At a subsequent stage in His discourse He did inform His disciples how the wonder would be achieved.   The Spirit would make the absent Jesus present to them again, by bringing to their remembrance all His words,[4] by testifying of Him,[5] and by guiding them into an intelligent apprehension of all Christian truth.[6]   All this, though not said here, is sufficiently hinted at by the name given to the new Paraclete.   He is called the Spirit of Truth, not the Holy Spirit, as elsewhere, because He was to comfort by enlightening the minds of the disciples in the knowledge of Christ, so that they should see Him clearly by the spiritual eye, when He was no longer visible to the eye of the body.

This spiritual vision, when it came, was to be the true effectual consolation for the absence of the Jesus whom the eleven had known after the flesh.   It would be as the dawn of day, which banishes the fears and discomforts of the night. While the night lasts, all comforts are but partial alleviations of discomfort.   A father's hand and voice have a reassuring effect on the timid heart of his child, as they walk together by night ; but while the darkness lasts, the little one is liable to be scared by objects dimly seen, and distorted by fear-stricken fancy into fantastic forms.   " In the night-time men (much more children) think every bush a thief ; " and all can sympathize with the sentiment of Rousseau, " It is my nature to be afraid of darkness."   Light is welcome, even

---

[1] Ver. 17.   [2] Ver. 18.

[3] The identity of the doctrine of the Spirit in the farewell discourse with that of Paul may be noted. With Paul also the Spirit is the *alter ego* of Christ. The Lord is the Spirit, he twice declares : 2 Cor. iii. 17, 18 ; *vide* the passage in R. V.

[4] Ver. 26.   [5] John xv. 26.   [6] John xvi. 13, 14.

when it only reveals to us the precise nature and extent of our miseries. If it do not in that case drive sorrow away, it helps at least to make it calm and sober. Such cold comfort, however, was not what Jesus promised His followers. The Spirit of Truth was not to come merely to show them their desolation in all its nakedness, and to reconcile them to it as inevitable, by teaching them to regard their early hopes as romantic dreams, the kingdom of God as a mere ideal, and the death of Jesus as the fate that awaits every earnest attempt to realize that ideal. Miserable comfort this ! to be told that all earnest religion must end in infidelity, and all enthusiasm in despair !

The third word of consolation was introduced by an injunction laid by Jesus on His disciples. "If ye love me," said He to them, "keep my commandments." It is probable that the speaker meant here to set the true way of showing love over against an unprofitable, bootless one, which His hearers were in danger of taking; that, namely, of grieving over His loss. We may paraphrase the words so as to indicate the connection of thought somewhat as follows : " If ye love me, show not your love by idle sorrow, but by keeping my commandments, whereby ye shall render to me a real service. Let the precepts which I have taught you from time to time be your concern, and be not troubled about yourselves. Leave your future in my hands ; I will look after it : for I will pray the Father, and he will send you another Comforter." [1]

But this paraphrase, though true so far as it goes, does not exhaust the meaning of this weighty word. Jesus prefaces the promise of the Comforter by an injunction to keep His commandments, because He wishes His disciples to understand that the fulfilment of the promise and the keeping of the commandments go together. This truth is hinted at by the word "and," which forms the link of connection between precept and promise ; and it is reiterated under various modes of expression in the passage we are now con-

---

[1] The words of Germanicus dying (at Antioch, A.D. 19 : supposed to be poisoned by direction of Tiberius) to his friends occur to the mind here : " Non hoc præcipuum amicorum munus est, prosequi defunctum ignavo quæstu : sed quæ voluerit meminisse, quæ mandaverit exsequi : flebunt Germanicum etiam ignoti : vindicabitis vos, si me potius quam fortunam meam fovebatis." — TACITI *Annal.* ii. 71.

sidering. The necessity of moral fidelity in order to spiritual illumination is plainly taught when the promised Comforter is described as a Spirit "whom the *world* cannot receive, because it seeth Him not, neither knoweth Him."[1] It is still more plainly taught in the last verse of this section : "He that hath my commandments, and keepeth them, he it is that loveth me ; and he that loveth me shall be loved of my Father ; and I will love him, and will manifest myself to him."[2] As in His first great sermon (on the mount) Jesus had said, "Blessed are the pure in heart, for they shall see God ;" so, in His farewell discourse to His own, He says in effect : Be pure in heart, and through the indwelling Spirit of Truth ye shall see me, even when I am become invisible to the world.[3]

Life and light go together : such is the doctrine of the Lord Jesus, as of all Scripture. Keeping in mind this great truth, we comprehend the diverse issues of religious perplexities ; in one resulting in the illuminism of infidelity ; in another, in an enlightened, unwavering faith. The "illumination" which consists in the extinction of the heavenly luminaries of faith and hope is the penalty of not faithfully keeping Christ's commandments ; that which consists in the

[1] John xiv. 17.

[2] John xiv. 21.

[3] John xiv. 19. Sanday (*Fourth Gospel*, p. 230) says the connection in ch. xiv. 12-17, though difficult, is real, but thinks there is hardly a place in this connection for ver. 15 : "If ye love me," etc. He has prevented himself from seeing its relevancy by treating ch. xiv. 12-17 as one continuous train of thought, instead of finding at ver. 15 the beginning of a new independent thought, the second of the three words of consolation. Another of this author's mistaken criticisms on the last discourse may here be adverted to. He complains that the different subjects are not kept apart, but are continually crossing and entangling one another, later subjects being anticipated in the course of the earlier, and the earlier returning in the later. As an illustration of this, he refers to the description of the functions of the Paraclete, which he thinks unnecessarily broken up into five fragments (ch. xiv. 16, 17 ; 25, 26 ; xv. 26 ; xvi. 8-16 ; 23-25). The fact is undoubted ; but instead of making against the historical accuracy of John's record, it rather is in favor of it. If the farewell discourse had been a didactic composition, mainly the product of the writer's mind, the doctrine of the Paraclete probably would have been given in one continuous paragraph. But in a familiar conversation, such as the discourse is given out for, such occasional and fragmentary references to the Comforter are to be expected. The only question that can be properly raised is, Does what is said at each place fit into the connection of thought ? We trust our exposition will satisfy our readers on that point. Certainly, if our view of the discourse, as divided into two parts, in which Jesus addressed the disciples first as children, then as His future representatives, be correct, references to the Comforter were sure to be made in both parts : in the former, to the Comforter as in the place of the absent Head of the family ; in the latter, to the same Comforter as the illuminator and fellow-worker of the apostles.

restoration of spiritual lights after a temporary obscuration by the clouds of doubt is the reward of holding fast moral integrity when faith is eclipsed, and of fearing God while walking in darkness. A man, *e.g.*, who, having believed for a time the divinity of Christ and the life to come, ends by believing that Jesus was only a deluded enthusiast, and that the divine kingdom is but a beautiful dream, will not be found to have made any great effort to realize his own ideal, certainly not to have been guilty of the folly of suffering for it. To many, the creed which resolves all religion into impracticable ideals is very convenient. It saves a world of trouble and pain; it permits them to think fine thoughts, without requiring them to do noble actions, and it substitutes romancing about heroism in the place of being heroes.

Section II — The Children's Questions, and the Adieu

John xiii. 36-38, xiv. 5-7, 8-14, 22-31

The questions put successively by four of the little ones to their dying Parent now invite our attention.

The *first* of these was asked by the disciple who was ever the most forward to speak his mind — Simon Peter. His question had reference to the intimation made by Jesus about His going away. Peter had noted and been alarmed by that intimation. It seemed to hint at danger; it plainly spoke of separation. Tormented with uncertainty, terrified by the vague presentiment of hidden peril, grieved at the thought of being parted from his beloved Master, he could not rest till he had penetrated the mystery; and at the very first pause in the discourse he abruptly inquired, "Lord, whither goest Thou?" thinking, though he did not say, "Where Thou goest, I will go."

It was to this unexpressed thought that Jesus directed His reply. He did not say where He was going; but, leaving that to be inferred from His studied reserve, and from the tone in which He spoke, He simply told Peter: "Whither I go, thou canst not follow me now, but thou shalt follow me afterwards." By this answer He showed He had not forgotten that it was with children He had to deal. He does not look for heroic behavior on the part of Peter and his brother disciples at the approaching crisis. He does indeed expect that they shall play the hero by and by, and follow Him on the martyr's path bearing their cross, in accordance with the law of discipleship proclaimed by Himself in connection with the first announcement of His own death. But meantime He expects them to behave simply as little children, running away in terror when the moment of danger arrives.

While this was the idea Jesus had of Peter, it was not the idea which Peter had of himself. He thought himself no child, but a man every inch. Dimly apprehending what following his Master meant, he deemed himself perfectly competent to the task *now*, and felt almost aggrieved by the poor opinion entertained of his courage. "Why," he therefore asked in a tone of injured virtue, "Lord, why cannot I follow Thee now?" Is it because there is danger, imprisonment, death, in the path? If that be all, it is no good reason, for "I will lay down my life for Thy sake." Ah, that "why," how like a child; that self-confidence, what an infallible mark of spiritual weakness!

If the answer of Jesus to Peter's first question was indirect and evasive, that which He gave to his second was too plain to be mistaken. "Wilt thou," He said, taking up the disciple's words, — "Wilt thou lay down thy life for my sake? Verily, verily, I say unto thee, The cock shall not crow till thou hast denied me thrice." [1] Better for Peter had he been content with the first reply! Yet no: not better, only pleasanter for the moment. It was good for Peter to be thus bluntly told what his Lord thought of him, and to be shown once for all his own picture drawn by an unerring hand. It was just what was needed to lead him to self-knowledge, and to bring on a salutary crisis in his spiritual history. Already more than once he had been faithfully dealt with for faults springing from his characteristic vices of forwardness and self-confidence. But such correction in detail had produced no deep impression, no decisive lasting effect on his mind. He was still ignorant of himself, still as

---

[1] So substantially in the synoptical Gospels (Matt. xxvi. 33-35; Mark xiv. 30; Luke xxii. 34). The harmony of this subject is difficult. Some suppose two allusions to Peter's denial, once in the upper chamber, and a second time on the way to Gethsemane. See Stier for this view.

forward, self-confident, and self-willed as ever, as the declaration he had just made most clearly showed. There was urgent need, therefore, for a lesson that would never be forgotten ; for a word of correction that would print itself indelibly on the erring disciple's memory, and bear fruit throughout his whole after life. And here it is at last, and in good season. The Lord tells His *brave* disciple that he will forthwith play the coward ; He tells His *attached* disciple, to whom separation from his Master seems more dreadful than death, that he will, ere many hours are past, deny all acquaintance or connection with Him whom he so fondly loves. He tells him all this at a time when the prophecy must be followed by its fulfilment almost as fast as a flash of lightning is followed by its peal of thunder. The prediction of Jesus, so minutely circumstantial, and the denial of Peter, so exactly corresponding, both by themselves so remarkable, and coming so close together, will surely help to make each other impressive ; and it will be strange indeed if the two combined do not, by the blessing of God, in answer to the Master's intercessory prayer, make of the fallen disciple quite another man. The result will doubtless prove the truth of another prophetic word reported by Luke as having been spoken by the Lord to His disciple on the same occasion.[1] The chaff will be separated from the wheat in Peter's character ; he will undergo a great change of spirit ; and being converted from self-confidence and self-will to meekness and modesty, he will be fit at length to strengthen others, to be a shepherd to the weak, and, if needful, to bear his cross, and so follow his Master through death to glory.

The *second* question proceeded from Thomas, the melancholy disciple, slow to believe, and prone to take sombre views of things. The mind of this disciple fastened on the statement wherewith Jesus concluded His second word of consolation : "Whither I go, the way ye know." That statement seemed to Thomas not only untrue, but unreasonable. For himself, he was utterly unconscious of possessing the knowledge for which the speaker had given His hearers credit ; and, moreover, he did not see how it was possible for any of them to possess it. For Jesus had never yet dis-

[1] Luke xxii. 31.

tinctly told them whither He was going ; and not knowing
the *terminus ad quem*, how could any one know the road
which led thereto ?　Therefore, in a dry, matter-of-fact,
almost cynical tone, this second interlocutor remarked :
" Lord, we know not whither Thou goest, and how can we
know the way ? " [1]

This utterance was thoroughly characteristic of the man, as
we know him from John's portraiture.[2]　While the practical-
minded Peter asks Jesus where He is going, determined if
possible to follow Him, Thomas does not think it worth his
while to make any such inquiry.　Not that he is unconcerned
about the matter.　He would like well to know whither his
Lord is bound ; and, if it were possible, he would be as ready
as his brother disciple to keep Him company.　Danger would
not deter him.　He had said once before, " Let us go, that
we may die with Him," and he could say the same thing
honestly again; for though he is gloomy, he is not selfish or
cowardly.　But just as on that earlier occasion, when Jesus,
disregarding the warnings of His disciples, resolved to go
from Peræa to Judæa on a visit to the afflicted family of
Bethany, Thomas took the darkest view of the situation, and
looked on death as the certain fate awaiting them all, so now
he resigns himself to a hopeless, desponding mood.　The
thought of the Master's departure makes him so sad that
he has no heart to ask questions concerning the why or
the whitherward.　He resigns himself to ignorance on these
matters as an inevitable doom.　Whither? whither? I know
not ; who can tell?　The future is dark.　The Father's house
you spoke of, where in the universe can it be?　Is there
really such a place at all?

Even the question put by Thomas, " How can we know
the way ? " is not so much a question as an apology for not
asking questions.　It is not a demand for information, but a
gentle complaint against Jesus for expecting His disciples to
be informed.　It is not the expression of a desire for knowledge, but an excuse for ignorance.　The melancholy disciple
is for the present hopeless of knowing either *end* or *way*, and
therefore he is incurious and listless.　Far from seeking
light, he is rather in the humor to exaggerate the darkness.

---

[1] John xiv. 5.　　　　　　　　[2] John xi. 16, xx. 24–29.

As Jonah in his angry mood indulged in querulousness, so Thomas in his sadness delights in gloom. He waits not eagerly for the dawn of day ; he rather takes pleasure in the night, as congenial to his present frame of mind. Good men of melancholic temperament are, at the best, like men walking amid the solemn gloom of a forest. Sadness is the prevailing feeling in their souls, and they are content to have occasional broken glimpses of heaven, like peeps of the sky through the leafy roof of the wood. But Thomas is so heavy-hearted that he hardly cares even for a glimpse of the celestial world ; he looks not up, but walks through the dark forest at a slow pace, with his eyes fixed upon the ground.

The argumentative proclivities [1] of this disciple appear in his words as well as his proneness to despondency. Another man in despairing mood might have said : We know neither end nor way ; we are utterly in the dark both as to whither you are going, and as to the road by which you are to go thither. But Thomas must needs reason ; his mental habit leads him to represent one piece of ignorance as the necessary consequence of another : We know not the *terminus ad quem*, and therefore it is impossible that we can know the way. This man is afflicted with the malady of thought ; he gives reasons for every thing, and he will demand reasons for every thing. Here he demonstrates the impossibility of a certain kind of knowledge ; at another crisis we shall find him insisting on palpable demonstration that his Lord is indeed risen from the dead.

How does Jesus reply to the lugubrious speech of Thomas ? Most compassionately and sympathetically, now as at another time. To the curious question of Peter He returned an evasive answer ; to the sad-hearted Thomas, on the other hand, He vouchsafes information which had not been asked. And the information given is full even to redundancy. The disciple had complained of ignorance concerning the end, and especially concerning the way ; and it would have been a sufficient reply to have said, The Father is the end, and I am the way. But the Master, out of the fulness of His heart, said more than this. With firm, emphatic tones He uttered this oracular response, meant for the ear not o.

---

[1] On the so-called Rationalism of Thomas, see cap. xxviii. sec. 3.

Thomas alone, but of all the world: "I am the way, and the truth, and the life. No man cometh unto the Father but by me."

Comparing this momentous declaration with the preceding word of consolation, we observe a change in the mode of presenting the truth. The Father Himself takes the place of the Father's house with its many mansions, as the end; and Jesus, instead of being the guide who shall one day lead His children to the common home, becomes Himself the *way*. The kind Master alters His language, in gracious accommodation to childish capacities. Of Christians at the best it may be said, in the words of Paul, that now, in this present time-life, they see the heavenly and the eternal as through a glass, in enigmas.[1] But the disciples at this crisis in their history were not able to do even so much. Jesus had held up before their eyes the brightly-polished mirror of a beautiful parable concerning a house of many mansions, and they had seen nothing there; no image, but only an opaque surface. The future remained dark and hidden as before. What, then, was to be done? Just what Jesus did. Persons must be substituted for places. Disciples weak in faith must be addressed in this fashion: Can ye not comprehend whither I am going? Think, then, to *whom* I go. If ye know nothing of the place called heaven, know at least that ye have a Father there. And as for the way to heaven, let that for you mean *me*. Knowing me, ye need no further knowledge; believing in me, ye may look forward to the future, even to death itself, without fear or concern.

On looking more narrowly into the response given by Jesus to Thomas, we find it by no means easy to satisfy ourselves as to how precisely it should be expounded. The very fulness of this saying perplexes us; it is dark with excess of light. Interpreters differ as to how the Way, the Truth, and the Life are to be distinguished, and how they are related to each other. One offers, as a paraphrase of the text: I am the beginning, the middle, and the end of the ladder which leads to heaven; another: I am the example, the teacher, the giver of eternal life; while a third subordinates the two last attributes to the first, and reads: I am

---

[1] ἐν αἰνίγματι, 1 Cor. xiii. 12.

the true way of life.[1]   Each view is true in itself, yet one
hesitates to accept either of them as exhausting the meaning
of the Saviour's words.

Whatever be the preferable method of interpreting these
words of our Lord, two things at least are clear from them.
Jesus sets Himself forth here as all that man needs for
eternal salvation, and as the only Saviour.   He is way, truth,
life, every thing ; and He alone conducts to the Father.   He
says to men in effect : "What is it you want ?   Is it light ?
I am the light of the world, the revealer of the Father : for
this end I came, that I might declare Him.   Or is it reconciliation you want ?   I by that very death which I am about
to endure am the *Reconciler*.   My very end in dying is to
bring you who are for off nigh to God, as to a forgiving,
gracious Father.   Or is it life, spiritual, never-ending life,
you seek ?   Believe in me, and ye shall never die ; or though
ye die, I will raise you again to enter on an inheritance that
is incorruptible, undefiled, and that fadeth not away, eternal
in the heavens.   Let all who seek these things look to *me*.
Look to me for light, not to rabbis or philosophers ; not even
to nature and providence.   These last do indeed reveal God,
but they do so dimly.   The light of creation is but the
starlight of theology, and the light of providence is but its
moonlight, while I am the sunlight.   My Father's Name is
written in hieroglyphics in the works of creation ; in providence and history it is written in plain letters, but so far
apart that it takes much study to put them together, and so
spell out the divine Name : in me the divine Name is written
so that he may read who runs, and the wisdom of God is
become milk for babes.[2]   Look to me also for reconciliation,
not to legal sacrifices.   That way of approaching God is
antiquated now.   I am the new, the living, the eternal way
into the holy of holies, through which all may draw near to
the divine presence with a true heart, in full assurance of
faith.   Look to me, finally, for eternal blessedness.   I am He
who, having died, shall rise again, and live forevermore, and

---

[1] Luther, Grotius, Augustine, quoted in Lange, *Bibelwerk, das Evang. Johan.*
[2] Verbum caro factum est, ut infantiæ nostræ lactesceret sapientia tua, per quam
creasti omnia. — August. *Conf.* vii. 18.   The idea that Christ became man to be the
Revealer of God is made very prominent in the tract of Athanasius, περὶ τῆς 'ενανθρωπή-
σεως τοῦ λόγου.

shall hold in my hands the keys of Hades and of death, and shall open the kingdom of heaven to all believers."

The doctrine that in Christ is the fulness of grace and truth is very comforting to those who know Him; but what of those who know Him not, or who possess only such an implicit, unconscious knowledge as hardly merits the name? Does the statement we have been considering exclude such from the possibility of salvation? It does not. It declares that no man cometh to the Father but by Christ, but it does not say how much knowledge is required for salvation.[1] It is possible that some may be saved by Christ, and for His sake, who know very little about Him indeed. This we may infer from the case of the disciples themselves. What did they know about the way of salvation at this period? Jesus addresses them as persons yet in ignorance concerning Himself, saying: "If ye had known me, ye should have known my Father also." Nevertheless, He has no hesitation in speaking to them as persons who should be with Him in the Father's house. And what shall we say of Job, and the Syro-Phœnician woman, and the Ethiopian eunuch, and Cornelius, and we may add, after Calvin, the Syrian courtier Naaman? We cannot say *more* than the great theologian of Geneva has himself said concerning such cases : "I confess," he writes, "that in a certain respect their faith was implicit, not only as to the person of Christ, but as to His virtue and grace, and the office assigned Him by the Father. Meanwhile it is certain that they were imbued with principles which gave some taste of Christ, however slight."[2] It is doubtful whether even so much can be said of Naaman;

---

[1] The doctrine of the Westminster Confession is ambiguous on this point. Its words are : "Much less can men not professing the Christian religion be saved in any other way whatsoever, be they ever so diligent to frame their lives according to the light of nature, and the law of that religion they do profess." This statement may mean either that the persons in question absolutely cannot be saved, — their non-profession of the Christian religion excluding them from being saved in the true way, and all other ways being unavailable; or that they cannot be saved by any other way : if saved, it must be in spite of other ways, and through the one true way — Christ. The statement in the first chapter, *Of the Holy Scripture*, seems to make the balance incline towards the former view. In that chapter the insufficiency of the light of nature to give that knowledge of God which is necessary for salvation is affirmed, and the affirmation is made the basis of the doctrine of revelation. The strongest statement of all is in the *Larger Catechism*, Q. 60, which seems to affirm positively that none can be saved who have not heard the gospel.

[2] Calv. *Inst.* iii. ii. 32.

though Calvin, without evidence, and merely to meet the exigencies of a theory, argues that it would have been too absurd, when Elisha had spoken to him of little matters, to have been silent on the most important subject. Or if we grant to Naaman the slight taste contended for, must we not grant it also, with Justin Martyr [1] and Zwingli, to Socrates and Plato and others, on the principle that all true knowledge of God, by whomsoever possessed and however obtained, whether it be sunlight, moonlight, or starlight, is virtually Christian; in other words, that Christ, just because He is the only light, is the light of every man who hath any light in him?

This principle, while it has its truth, may very easily be preverted into an argument against a supernatural revelation. Hence in its very first chapter, *Of the Holy Scripture*, the Westminster Confession broadly asserts that the light of nature and the works of creation and providence are not sufficient to give that knowledge of God and of His will which is necessary unto salvation. While strongly maintaining this truth, however, we must beware of being drawn into a tone of disparagement in speaking of what way be learnt of God from those lower sources. While walking in the sunlight, we must not despise the dimmer luminaries of the night, or forget their existence, as in the day-time men forget the moon and the stars. By so doing we should be virtually disparaging the Scriptures themselves. For much that is in the Bible, especially in the Old Testament, is but a record of what inspired men had learned from observation of God's works in creation, and of His ways in providence. All cannot, indeed, see as much there as they saw. On the contrary, a revelation was needed not only to make known truths lying beyond the teachings of natural religion, but even to direct men's dim eyes to truths which, though visible in nature, were in fact for the most part not seen. The Bible, in the

---

[1] Χριστῷ δὲ τῷ καὶ ὑπὸ Σωκράτου ἀπὸ μέρους γνωσθέντι (λόγος γὰρ ἦν, καὶ ἔστιν ὁ ἐν παντὶ ὤν). — *Apol.* ii. 10; so also *Apol.* i. 5. The anticipations of Christian thought in Plato and in Euripides are familiar to scholars. The following opinion on the salvation of the heathen from Richard Baxter deserves notice: — " I am not so much inclined (as he once was) to pass a peremptory sentence of damnation upon all that never heard of Christ, having some more reasons than I knew of before to think that God's dealing with such is much unknown to us." — *Reliquiæ Baxterianæ*, lib. i. part i., comparing his earlier and later religious views.

quaint language of Calvin, is a pair of spectacles, through which our weak eyes see the glory of God in the world.[1] Yet what is seen through the spectacles by weak eyes is in many passages just what might be seen by strong eyes without their aid, — "nothing being placed there which is not visible in the creation." [2]

These observations may help us to cherish hope for those whose opportunities of knowing Him who is "the way, the truth, and the life" are small.   They do not, however, justify those who, having abundant facilities for knowing Christ, are content with the minimum of knowledge.   There is more hope for the heathen than for such men.   To their number no true Christian can belong.   A genuine disciple may know little to begin with : this was the case even with the apostles themselves ; but he will not be satisfied to be in the dark. He will desire to be enlightened in the knowledge of Christ, and will pray, "Lord, show us the Father."

Such was the prayer of Philip, the *third* disciple who took part in the dialogue at the supper-table.   Philip's request, like Thomas's question, was a virtual denial of a statement previously made by Jesus.   "If ye had known me, " Jesus had said to Thomas, "ye should have known my Father also ;" and then He had added, "and from henceforth ye know Him, and have seen Him."   This last statement Philip felt himself unable to homologate.   "Seen the Father! would it were so! nothing would gratify us more : Lord, show us the Father, and it sufficeth us."

In itself, the prayer of this disciple was most devout and praiseworthy.   There can be no loftier aspiration than that which seeks the knowledge of God the Father, no better index of a spiritual mind than to account such knowledge the *summum bonum*, no more hopeful symptom of ultimate arrival at the goal than the candor which honestly confesses present ignorance.   In these respects the sentiments uttered

---

[1] Sicuti senes vel lippi, et quicunque oculis caligant si vel pulcherrimum volumen illis objicias quamvis agnoscant esse aliquid scriptum, vix tamen duas voces contexere poterunt ; specillis autem interpositis adjuti distincte legere incipient : ita Scriptura confusam alioqui Dei notitiam in mentibus nostris colligens, discussa caligine liquido nobis verum Deum ostendit. — *Inst*. i. vi. 1.

[2] Nihil tamen illic (Ps. cxlv., etc.) ponitur quod non liceat in creaturis contemplari. — CALV. *Inst*. i. x. 2.

by Philip were fitted to gratify his Master. In other respects, however, they were not so satisfactory. The ingenuous inquirer had evidently a very crude notion of what seeing the Father amounted to. He fancied it possible, and he appears to have wished, to see the Father as he then saw Jesus — as an outward object of vision to the eye of the body. Then, supposing that to be his wish, how foolish the reflection, "and it sufficeth us"! What good could a mere external vision of the Father do any one? And finally that same reflection painfully showed how little the disciples had gained hitherto from intercourse with Jesus. They had been with Him for years, yet had not found rest and satisfaction in Him, but had still a craving for something beyond Him; while what they craved they had, without knowing it, been getting from Him all along.

Such ignorance and spiritual incapacity so late in the day were very disappointing. And Jesus was disappointed, but, with characteristic patience, not irritated. He took not offence either at Philip's stupidity, or at the contradiction he had given to His own statement (for He would rather be contradicted than have disciples pretend to know when they do not), but endeavored to enlighten the little ones somewhat in the knowledge of the Father. For this end He gave great prominence to the truth that the knowledge of the Father and of Himself, the Son, were one; that He that hath seen the Son hath seen the Father. The better to fix this great principle in the minds of His hearers, He put it in the strongest possible manner, by treating their ignorance of the Father as a virtual ignorance of Himself. "Have I," He asked, "been so long time with you, and yet hast thou not known *me*, Philip?" Then He went on to reason, as if to be ignorant of the Father was to be so far ignorant of Himself as in effect to deny His divinity. "Believest thou not," He again asked, "that I am in the Father, and the Father in me?" and then He followed up the question with a reference to those things which went to prove the asserted identity — His *words* and His *works*.[1] Nor did He stop even here, but proceeded next to speak of still more convincing proofs of His identity with the Father, to be supplied in the marvel-

[1] John xiv. 10, 11.

lous works which should afterwards be done by the apostles themselves in His Name, and through powers granted to them by Himself in answer to their prayers.[1]

The first question put by Jesus to Philip, " Hast thou not known *me* ? " was something more than a logical artifice to make stupid disciples reflect on the contents of the knowledge they already possessed. It hinted at a real fact. The disciples had really not yet *seen* Jesus, for as long as they had been with Him. They knew Him, and they did not know Him : they knew not *that* they knew, nor *what* they knew. They were like children, who can repeat the Catechism without understanding its sense, or who possess a treasure witout being capable of estimating its value. They were like men looking at an object through a telescope without adjusting the focus, or like an ignorant peasant gazing up at the sky on a winter night, and seeing the stars which compose a constellation, such as the Bear or Orion, yet not recognizing the constellation itself. The disciples were familiar with the words, parables, discourses, etc., spoken, and with the miraculous works done, by their Master, but they knew these only as isolated particulars ; the separate rays of light emanating from the fountain of divine wisdom, power, and love in Jesus, had never been gathered into a focus, so as to form a distinct image of Him who came in the flesh to reveal the invisible God. They had seen many a star shine out in the spiritual heavens while in Christ's company ; but the stars had not yet assumed to their eye the aspect of a constellation. They had no clear, full, consistent, spiritual conception of the mind, heart, and character of the man Christ Jesus, in whom dwelt all the fulness of Godhead bodily. Nor would they possess such a conception till the Spirit of Truth, the promised Comforter, came. The very thing He was to do for them was to show them Christ ; not merely to recall to their memories the details of His life, but to show them the one mind and spirit which dwelt amid the details, as the soul dwells in the body, and made them an organic whole, and which once perceived, would of itself recall to recollection all the isolated particulars at present lying latent in their consciousness. When the apostles had

[1] Vers. 12–14.

got that conception, they would know Christ indeed, the same Christ whom they had known before, yet different, a new Christ, because a Christ comprehended, — seen with the eye of the spirit, as the former had been seen with the eye of the flesh. And when they had thus seen Christ, they would feel that they had also seen the Father. The knowledge of Christ would satisfy them, because in Him they should see with unveiled face the glory of the Lord.

The soul-satisfying vision of God being a future good to be attained after the advent of the Comforter, it could not have been the intention of Jesus to assure the disciples that they possessed it already, still less to force it on them by a process of reasoning. When He said, "From henceforth ye know Him (the Father), and have seen Him," He evidently meant : "Ye now know how to see Him, viz. by reflecting on your intercourse with me. And the sole object of the statements made to Philip concerning the close relations between the Father and the speaker evidently was to impress upon the disciples the great truth that the solution of all religious difficulties, the satisfaction of all longings, was to be found in the knowledge of Himself. "Know me," Jesus would say, "trust me, pray to me, and all shall be well with you. Your mind shall be filled with light, your heart shall be at rest ; you shall have every thing you want ; your joy shall be full."

A most important lesson this ; but also one which, like Philip and the other disciples, all are slow to learn. How few, even of those who confess Christ's divinity, do see in Him the true perfect Revealer of God ! To many Jesus is one Being, and God is another and quite a different Being ; though the truth that Jesus is divine is all the while honestly acknowledged. That great truth lies in the mind like an unfructifying seed buried deep in the soil, and we may say of it what has been said of the doctrine of the soul's immortality : "One may believe it for twenty years, and only in the twenty-first, in some great moment, discover with astonishment the rich contents of this belief, the warmth of this naphtha spring."[1] Impressions of God have been received from one quarter, impressions of Christ from another ; and

---

[1] Jean Paul Richter, *Siebenkäs, Erstes Blumenstück.*

the two sets of impressions lie side by side in the mind, incompatible, yet both receiving house-room. Hence, when a Christian begins to carry out consistently the principle that, Jesus being God, to know Jesus is to know God, he is apt to experience a painful conflict between a new and an old class of ideas about the Divine Being. Two Gods — a christianized God, and a sort of pagan divinity — struggle for the place of sovereignty; and when at last the conflict ends in the enthronement in the mind and heart of the God whom Jesus revealed, the day-dawn of a new spiritual life has arrived.

One most prominent idea in the conception of God as revealed by Jesus Christ is that expressed by the name Father. According to the doctrine of our Lord and Saviour, God is not truly known till He is thought of and heartly believed in as a Father; neither can any God who is not regarded as a Father satisfy the human heart. Hence His own mode of speaking concerning God was in entire accordance with this doctrine. He did not speak to men about the Deity, or the Almighty. Those epithets which philosophers are so fond of applying to the Divine Being, the Infinite, the Absolute, etc., never crossed His lips. No words ever uttered by Him could suggest the idea of the gloomy arbitrary tyrant before whom the guilty conscience of superstitious heathenism cowers. He spake evermore, in sermon, parable, model prayer, and private conversation, of a Father. Such expressions as "the Father," "my Father," "your Father," were constantly on His tongue; and all He taught concerning God harmonized perfectly with the feelings these expressions were fitted to call forth.

Yet notwithstanding all His pains, and all the beauty of His utterances concerning the Being whom no man hath seen, Jesus, it is to be feared, has only imperfectly succeeded in establishing the worship of the Father. From ignorance or from preference, men still extensively worship God under other names and categories. Some deem the paternal appellation too homely, and prefer a name expressive of more distant and ceremonious relations. The Deity, or the Almighty, suffices them. Philosophers dislike the appellation Father, because it makes the personality of God too prominent. They prefer to think of the Uncreated as an Infinite, Eternal Abstraction — an object of speculation rather than of faith and love. Legal-minded professors of religion take fright at the word Father. They are not sure that they have a right to use it, and they deem it safer to speak of God in general terms, which take nothing for granted, as the Judge, the Taskmaster, or the Lawgiver. The worldly, the learned, and the religious, from different motives, thus agree in allowing to fall into desuetude the name into which they have been baptized, and only a small minority worship the *Father* in spirit and in truth.

Superficial readers of the gospel may cherish the idea that the name Father, applied to God by Jesus, is simply or mainly a sentimental poetic expression, whose loss were no great matter for regret. There could not be a greater mistake. The name, in Christ's lips, always represents a definite thought, and teaches a great truth. When He uses the term to express the relation of the Invisible One to Himself, He gives us a glimpse into the mystery of the Divine Being, telling us that God is not abstract being, as Platonists and Arians conceived Him ; not the absolute, incapable of relations ; not a passionless being, without affections ; but one who eternally loves, and is loved, in whose infinite nature the family affections find scope for ceaseless play — One in three : Father, Son, and Holy Ghost, three persons in one divine substance. Then again, when He calls God Father, in reference to mankind in general, as He does repeatedly, He proclaims to men sunk in ignorance and sin this blessed truth : " God, my Father, is your Father too ; cherishes a paternal feeling towards you, though ye be so marred in moral vision that He might well not know you, and so degenerate that He might well be ashamed to own you ; and I His Son am come, your elder brother, to bring you back to your Father's house. Ye are not worthy to be called His sons, for ye have ceased to bear His image, and ye have not yielded Him filial obedience and reverence ; nevertheless, He is willing to be a Father unto you, and receive you graciously in His arms. Believe this, and become in heart and conduct sons of God, that ye may enjoy the full, the spiritual and eternal, benefit of God's paternal love." When, finally, He calls God Father, with special reference to His own disciples, He assures them that they are the objects of God's constant, tender, and effective care ; that all His power, wisdom, and love are engaged for their protection, preservation, guidance, and final eternal salvation ; that their Father in heaven will see that they lack no good, and will make all things minister to their interest, and in the end secure to them their inherit- ance in the everlasting kingdom. "Fear not," is His comforting message to His little chosen flock, "it is your Father's good pleasure to give you the kingdom."

We have now to notice the fourth and last of the chil- dren's questions, which was put by Judas, "not Iscariot" (he is otherwise occupied), but the other disciple of that name, also called Lebbæus and Thaddæus.[1]

In His third word of consolation Jesus had spoken of a re-appearance (after His departure) specially and exclusively to "His own." "The world," He had said, "seeth me no more ; but ye see me," that is, shall see after a little while. Now two questions might naturally be asked concerning this exclusive manifestation : How was it possible ? and what was the reason of it ? How could Jesus make Himself visible to His disciples, and yet remain invisible to all others ? and granting the possibility, why not show Himself to the world at large ? It is not easy to decide which of these two difficulties Judas had in his mind, for his question might be interpreted either way. Literally translated, it was to this effect : "Lord, what has happened, that Thou art about to manifest Thyself unto us, and not unto the world ?" The disciple might mean, like Nicodemus, to ask, "How can these things be ?" or he might mean, "We have been hoping for the coming of Thy kingdom in power and glory, visible to the eyes of all men : what has led Thee to change Thy plans ?"

In either case the question of Judas was founded on a misapprehension of the nature of the promised manifestation. He imagined that Jesus was to re-appear corporeally, after His departure to the Father, therefore so as to be visible to the outward eye, and not of this one or that one, but of all, unless He took pains to hide Himself from some while

---

[1] *Vide* chap. iv. of this work.

revealing Himself to others.[1]   Neither Judas nor any of his brethern was capable as yet of conceiving a spiritual manifestation, not to speak of finding therein a full compensation, for the loss of the corporeal presence.   Had they grasped the thought of a spiritual presence, they could have had no difficulty in reconciling visibility to one with invisibility to another; for they would have understood that the vision *could* be enjoyed only by those who possessed the inward sense of sight.

How was a question dictated by incapacity to understand the subject to which it referred to be answered? Just as you would explain the working of the electric telegraph to a child.   If your child asked you, Father, how is it that you can send a message by the telegraph to my uncle or aunt in America, so far, far away? you would not think of attempting to explain to him the mysteries of electricity.   You would take him to a telegraph office, and bid him look at the man actually engaged in sending a message, and tell him, that as the man moved the handle, a needle in America pointed at letters of the alphabet, which, when put together, made up words which said just what you wished to say.

In this way it was that Jesus answered the question of Judas.   He did not attempt to explain the difference between a spiritual and a corporeal manifestation, but simply said in effect: Do you so and so, and what I have promised will come true.   "If a man love me, he will keep my words ; and my Father will love him, and we will come unto him, and make our abode with him."   It is just the former statement repeated, in a slightly altered, more pointed form.   Nothing new is said, because nothing new can be said intelligibly. The old promise is simply so put as to arrest attention on the condition of its fulfilment.   "*If* a man love me, he will keep my words :" attend to that, my children, and the rest will follow.   The divine Trinity — Father, Son, and Spirit — will verily dwell with the faithful disciple, who with trembling solicitude strives to observe my commandments.   As

---

[1] Luthardt (*Das Johan. Evang.* ii. 313) contends that a corporeal manifestation (at the end of the world) is meant, and weakly argues, that if only a spiritual presence were meant, Jesus would have said ἐν αὐτῷ instead of παρ' αὐτῷ in ver. 23.   Παρά suits the parabolic style of speech ; ἐν would be an *interpretation* of the figure.

for those who love me not, and keep not my sayings, and believe not on me, it is simply impossible for them to enjoy such august company. The pure in heart alone shall see God.

Jesus had now spoken all He meant to say to His disciples in the capacity of a dying parent addressing his sorrowing children. It remained now only to wind up the discourse, and bid the little ones adieu.

In drawing to a close, Jesus does not imagine that He has removed all difficulties and dispelled all gloom from the minds of the disciples. On the contrary, He is conscious that all He has said has made but a slight impression. Nevertheless, He will say no more in the way of comfort. There is, in the first place, no time. Judas and his band, the prince of this world, whose servants Judas and all his associates are, may now be expected at any moment, and He must hold Himself in readiness to go and meet the enemy.[1] Then, secondly, to add any thing further would be useless. It is not possible to make things any clearer to the disciples in their present state by any amount of speech. Therefore He does not attempt it, but refers them for all other explanations to the promised Comforter,[2] and proceeds to utter the words of farewell: "Peace I leave with you, my peace I give unto you,"[3] — words touching at all times, unspeakably affecting in the circumstances of the Speaker and hearers. We know not but they did more to comfort the dispirited little ones than all that had been said before. There is a pathos and a music in the very sound of them, apart from their sense, which are wonderfully soothing. We can imagine, indeed, that as they were spoken, the poor disciples were overtaken with a fit of tenderness, and burst into tears. That, however, would do them good. Sorrow is healed by weeping: the sympathy which melts the heart at the same time comforts it.

This touching sympathetic farewell is more than a good wish: it is a promise — a promise made by One who knows that the blessing promised is within reach. It is like the cheering word spoken by David to brothers in affliction:

---

[1] John xiv. 30, 31.   [2] Vers. 25, 26.   [3] Ver. 27.

"Wait on the Lord: be of good courage, and He shall strengthen thine heart: wait, I say, on the Lord." David spoke that word from experience, and even so does Jesus speak here. The peace He offers His disciples is His own peace — "my peace:" not merely peace of His procuring, but peace of His experiencing. He has had peace in the world, in spite of sorrow and temptation, — perfect peace through faith. Therefore He can assure them that such a thing is possible. They, too, can have peace of mind and heart in the midst of untoward tribulation. The world can neither understand nor impart such peace, the only peace it knows any thing about being that connected with prosperity, which trouble can destroy as easily as a breath of wind agitates the calm surface of the sea. But there is a peace which is independent of outward circumstances, whose sovereign virtue and blessed function it is to keep the heart against fear and care. Such peace Jesus had Himself enjoyed; and He gives His disciples to understand that through faith and singleness of mind they may enjoy it also.

The farewell word is not only a promise made by One who knows whereof He speaks, but the promise of One who can bestow the blessing promised. Jesus does not merely say: Be of good cheer; ye may have peace, even as I have had peace, in spite of tribulation. He says moreover, and more particularly, Such peace as I have had I bequeath to you as a dying legacy, I bestow on you as a parting gift. The inheritance of peace is made over to the little ones by a last will and testament, though, being minors, they do not presently enter into actual possession. When they arrive at their majority they shall inherit the promise, and delight themselves in the abundance of peace. The after-experience of the disciples proved that the promise made to them by their Lord had not been false and vain. The apostles, as Jesus foretold, found in the world much tribulation; but in the midst of all they enjoyed perfect peace. Trusting in the Lord, and doing good, they were without fear and without care. In every thing, by prayer and supplication, with thanksgiving, they made their requests known unto God; and the peace of God, which passeth understanding, did verily keep their hearts and minds in Christ Jesus.

Jesus had not yet said His last word to the little ones. Seeing in their faces the signs of grief, in spite of all that He had spoken to comfort them, He abruptly threw out an additional remark, which gave to the whole subject of His departure quite a new turn. He had been telling them, all through His *farewell* address, that though He was going away, He would come again to them, either personally or by deputy, in the body at last, in the Spirit meanwhile. He now told them, that apart from His return, His departure itself should be an occasion of joy rather than of sorrow, because of what it signified for Himself. " Ye have heard how I said unto you, I go away, and come again unto you :" extract comfort from that promise by all means. But "if ye loved me (as ye ought), ye would rejoice because I said, I go unto the Father," [1] forgetting yourselves, and thinking what a happy change it would be for me. Then he added : " For my Father is greater than I." The connection between this clause and the foregoing part of the sentence is somewhat obscure, as is also its theological import. Our idea, however, is, that when Jesus spake these words He was thinking of His death, and meeting an objection thence arising to the idea of rejoicing in His departure. " You are going to the Father," one might have said — " yes ; but by what a way !" Jesus replies : The way is rough, and abhorrent to flesh and blood ; but it is the way my Father has appointed, and that is enough for me ; for my Father is greater than I. So interpreting the words, we only make the speaker hint therein at a thought which we find Him plainly expressing immediately after in His concluding sentence, where He represents His voluntary endurance of death as a manifestation to the world of His love to the Father, and as an act of obedience to His commandment.

And now, finally, by word and act, Jesus strives to impress on the little children the solemn reality of their situation. First, He bids them mark what He has told them of His departure, that when the separation takes place they may not be taken by surprise. " Now I have told you before it come

<hr />

[1] John xiv. 28.

to pass, that when it is come to pass ye might believe."[1] Then He gives them to understand that the parting hour is at hand. Hereafter He will not talk much with them; there will not be opportunity; for the prince of this world cometh. Then He adds words to this effect : " Let him come; I am ready for him. He has indeed nothing in me; no claim upon me ; no power over me ; no fault which he can charge against me. Nevertheless, I yield myself up into his hands, that all men may see that I love the Father, and am loyal to His will: that I am ready to die for truth, for righteous- ness, for the unrighteous."[2] Then, lastly, with firm, resolute voice, He gives the word of command to all to rise up from the couches on which they have been reclining, doubt- less suiting His own action to the word : " Arise, let us go hence."[3]

From the continuation of the discourse, as recorded by John, as well as from the statement made by him at the commencement of the eighteenth chapter of his Gospel (" When Jesus had spoken these words, He went forth," etc.), we infer that the company did not at this point leave the supper-chamber. They merely assumed a new attitude, and exchanged the recumbent for a standing posture, as if in readiness to depart. This movement was, in the circum- stances, thoroughly natural. It fitly expressed the resolute temper of Jesus ; and it corresponded to the altered tone in which He proceeded to address His disciples. The action of rising formed, in fact, the transition from the first part of His discourse to the second. Better than words could have done, it altered the mood of mind, and prepared the disciples for listening to language not soft, tender, and familiar as heretofore, but stern, dignified, impassioned. It struck the keynote, if we may so express it, by which the speaker passed from the lyric to the heroic style. It said, in effect : Let us have done with the nursery dialect, which, continued longer, would but enervate : let me speak to you now for a brief space as men who have got to play an important part in the world. Arise ; shake off languor, and listen, while I utter words fitted to fire you with enthusiasm, to inspire you with courage, and to impress you with a sense of the

---

[1] Ver. 29. [2] John xiv. 30, 31. [3] Ver. 31.

responsibilities and the honors connected with your future position.

So understanding the rising from the table, we shall be prepared to listen along with the disciples, and to enter on the study of the remaining portion of Christ's farewell discourse, without any feeling of abruptness.

25

DYING CHARGE TO THE FUTURE APOSTLES

John 15:1-15

THE subject of discourse in these chapters is the future work of the apostles, — its nature, honors, hardships, and joys. Much that is said therein admits of application to Christians in general, but the reference in the first place is undoubtedly to the eleven then present; and only by keeping this in mind can we get a clear idea of the import of the discourse as a whole.

The first part of this charge to the future apostles has for its object to impress upon them that they have a great work before them.[1] The keynote of the passage may be found in the words: "Ye have not chosen me, but I have chosen you, and ordained you, that ye should go and bring forth fruit, and that your fruit should remain."[2] Jesus would have His chosen ones understand that He expects more of them than that they shall not lose heart when He has left the earth. They must be great actors in the world, and leave their mark permanently on its history: they must, in fact, take His place, and be in His stead, and carry on the work He had begun, in His name and through His aid.

To put their duty clearly before the minds of His disciples, Jesus made large use of a beautiful figure drawn from the vine-tree, which He introduced at the very outset of His discourse. "I am the true vine;" that is the theme, which in the sequel is worked out with considerable minuteness of detail, — figure and interpretation being freely mixed up together in the exposition. The question has often been

---

[1] John xv. 1-17.   [2] Ver. 16.

asked, What led Jesus to adopt this particular emblem as the vehicle of His thoughts? and many conjectural answers have been hazarded.   In absence of information in the narrative, however, we must be content to remain in ignorance on this point, without attempting to supply the missing link in the association of ideas.   This is no great hardship; for, after all, what does it matter how a metaphor is suggested (a thing which even the person employing the metaphor often does not know), provided it be in itself apt to the purpose to which it is applied?   Of the aptness of the metaphor *here* employed there can be no doubt in the mind of any one who attentively considers the felicitous use which the speaker made of it.[1]

Turning our attention, then, to the discourse of Jesus on His own chosen text, we cannot but be struck with the manner in which He hurries on at once to speak of fruit. We should have expected that, in introducing the figure of the vine, He would in the first place state fully in terms of the figure how the case stood.   After hearing the words, "I am the true vine, and my Father is the husbandman," we expect to hear, "and ye, my disciples, are the branches, through which the vine brings forth fruit."   That, however, is not said here; but the speaker passes on at once to tell His hearers how the branches (of which no mention has been made) are dealt with by the divine Husbandman; how the fruitless branches, on the one hand, are lopped off, while the fruitful ones are pruned that they may become still more productive.[2]   This shows what is uppermost in the mind of Jesus.   His heart's desire is that His disciples may be spiritually fruitful.   "Fruit, fruit, my disciples," He exclaims in effect; "ye are useless unless ye bear fruit: my Father desires fruit, even as I do; and His whole dealing with you will be regulated by a purpose to increase your fruitfulness."

While urgent in His demand for fruit, Jesus does not, we

---

[1] Sanday (*Fourth Gospel*, p. 231) speaks of the allegory of the vine as belonging to a different and more didactic period in the life of Christ, and represents it as breaking the thread and having little bearing on the object of the discourse, which is to comfort the disciples in the prospect of their Lord's departure.   That was certainly *one* object, but not the only one.   The allegory is very apt to the other principal object of the discourse, viz. to bring before the hearers their responsibilities as apostles of the Christian faith.

[2] John xv. 2.

observe, in any part of this discourse on the vine, indicate wherein the expected fruit consists. When we consider to whom He is speaking, however, we can have no doubt as to what He principally intends. The fruit He looks for is the spread of the gospel and the ingathering of souls into the kingdom of God by the disciples, in the discharge of their apostolic vocation. Personal holiness is not overlooked; but it is required rather as a means towards fruitfulness than as itself the fruit. It is the purging of the branch which leads to increased fertility.

The next sentence ("Now ye are clean through the word which I have spoken unto you "[1]) it seems best to regard as a parenthesis, in which for a moment the figure of the vine is lost sight of. The mention of branches which, as unproductive, are cut off, recalls to the Lord's thoughts the case of one who had already been cut off, — the false disciple Judas, — and leads Him naturally to assure the eleven that He hopes better things of them. The process of excision had already been applied among them in one instance: therefore they should not be high-minded, but fear. But, on the other hand, as He had said before in connection with the feet-washing, that they were clean, with one exception; so now He would say they were all clean, without exception, through the word which He had spoken to them. As branches they might need pruning, but there would be no occasion for cutting off.

Having strongly declared the indispensableness of fruit-bearing in order to continued connection with the vine, Jesus proceeded next to set forth the conditions of fruitfulness, and (what we should have expected at the very commencement of the discourse) the relation subsisting between Himself and His disciples. "I am the vine," He said (to take the latter first), "ye are the branches."[2] By this statement He explains why He is so urgent that His disciples should be fruitful. The reason is, that they are the media through which He Himself brings forth fruit, serving the same purpose to Him that the branches serve to the vine. His own personal work had been to choose and train them, — to fill them, so to speak, with he sap of divine truth; and their

[1] John xv. 3.   [2] Ver. 5.

work was now to turn that sap into grapes. The Father in heaven, by sending Him into the world, had planted Him in the earth, a new, mystic, spiritual vine; and He had produced them, the eleven, as His branches. Now His personal ministry was at an end; and it remained for the branches to carry on the work to its natural consummation, and to bring forth a crop of fruit, in the shape of a church of saved men believing in His name. If they failed to do this, His labor would be all in vain.

Returning now to the conditions of fruitfulness, we find Jesus expressing them in these terms: "Abide in me, and I in you."[1] These words point to a dependence of the disciples on their Lord under two forms, which by help of the analogy of a tree and its branches it is easy to distinguish. The branch abides in the vine *structurally;* and the vine abides in the branch through its sap, *vitally.* Both of these abidings are necessary to fruit-bearing. Unless the branch be organically connected with the stem, the sap which goes to make fruit cannot pass into it. On the other hand, *although* the branch be organically connected with the stem, yet if the sap of the stem do not ascend into it (a case which is possible and common in the natural world), it must remain as fruitless as if it were broken off and lying on the ground.

All this is clear; but when we ask what do the two abidings signify in reference to the mystic vine, the answer is not quite so easy. The tendency here is to run the two into one, and to make the distinction between them merely nominal. The best way to come at the truth is to adhere as closely as possible to the natural analogy. What, then, would one say most nearly corresponded to the structural abiding of the branch in the tree? We reply, abiding in the doctrine of Christ, in the doctrine He taught; and acknowledging Him as the source whence it had been learned. In other words, "Abide in me" means, Hold and profess the truth I have spoken to you, and give yourselves out merely as my witnesses. The other abiding, on the other hand, signifies the indwelling of the Spirit of Jesus in the hearts of those who believe. Jesus gives His disciples to understand that, while abiding in His doctrine, they must also have His Spirit

[1] John xv. 4.

abiding in them ; that they must not only hold fast the truth, but be filled with the Spirit of truth.

As thus distinguished, the two abidings are not only different in conception, but separable in fact. On the one hand, there may be Christian orthodoxy in the letter where there is little or no spiritual life ; and there may, on the other hand, be a certain species of spiritual vitality, a great moral, and in some respects most Christian-like earnestness, accompanied with serious departure from the faith. The one may be likened unto a dead branch on a living tree, bleached, bark-less, moss-grown, and even in summer leafless, stretching out like a withered arm from the trunk into which it is inserted, and with which it still maintains an organic structural connection. The other is a branch cut off by pride or self-will from the tree, full of the tree's sap, and clothed with verdure at the moment of excision, and foolishly imagining, because it does not wither at once, that it can live and grow and blossom independently of the tree altogether. Have such things never been since Christianity began ? Alas, would it were so ! In the grand primeval forest of the Church too many dead orthodoxies have ever been visible ; and as for branches setting up for the themselves, their name is legion.

The two abidings, which we have seen to be not only separable, but often separated, cannot be separated without fatal effects. The result ever is in the end to illustrate the truth of Christ's words, "Without, or severed from, me ye can do nothing." [1] Dead orthodoxy is notoriously impotent. Feeble, timid, torpid, averse to any thing arduous, heroic, stirring in thought or conduct at best, it becomes at last insincere and demoralizing : salt without savor, fit only to be thrown out ; worthless vine-wood, good for nothing except for fuel, and not worth much even for that purpose. Heresies, not abiding in the doctrine of Christ, are equally helpless. At first, indeed, they possess a spurious ephemeral vitality, and make a little noise in the world ; but by and by their leaf begins to wither, and they bring forth no abiding fruit.

The conception of a dead branch, applied to individuals as distinct from churches or the religious world viewed collectively, is not without difficulty. A dead branch on a tree was

[1] John xv. 5.

not always dead : it was produced by the vital force of the tree, and had some of the tree's life in it.   Does the analogy between natural and spiritual branches hold at this point? Not in any sense, as we believe, that would compromise the doctrine of perseverance in grace, nowhere taught more clearly than in the words of our Lord.   At the same time, it cannot be denied that there is such a thing as abortive religious experience.   There are blossoms on the tree of life which are blasted by spring frosts, green fruits which fall off ere they ripen, branches which become sickly and die. Jonathan Edwards, a high Calvinist, but also a candid, shrewd observer of facts, remarks : "I cannot say that the greater part of supposed converts give reason by their conversation to suppose that they are true converts.   The proportion may perhaps be more truly represented by the proportion of the blossoms on a tree which abide and come to mature fruit, to the whole number of blossoms in spring." [1] The permanency of many spiritual blossoms is here denied, but the very denial implies an admission that they were blossoms.

That some branches should become unfruitful, and even die, while others flourish and bring forth fruit, is a great mystery, whose explanation lies deeper than theologians of the Arminian school are willing to admit.   Yet, while this is true, the responsibility of man for his own spiritual character cannot be too earnestly insisted on.   Though the Father, as the husbandman, wields the pruning-knife, the process of purging cannot be carried on without our consent and co-operation.   For that process means practically the removal of moral hinderances to life and growth, — the cares of life, the insidious influence of wealth, the lusts of the flesh, and the passions of the soul, — evils which cannot be overcome unless our will and all our moral powers be brought to bear against them.   Hence Jesus lays it upon His disciples as a *duty* to abide in Him, and have Him abiding in them, and resolves the whole matter at last, in plain terms, into keeping His commandments.[2]   If they diligently and

---

[1] See memoir by Sereno E. Dwight, prefixed to English edition of the Works of Edwards, in two volumes : vol. i. p. clxxii.

[2] John xv. 10.

faithfully do their part, the divine Husbandman, He assures them, will not fail to give them liberally all things needful for the most abundant fruitfulness.   " Ye shall ask what ye will, and it shall be done unto you." [1]

The doom of branches coming short in either of the two possible ways, is very plainly declared by Jesus.   The doom of the branch which, while in Him structurally, beareth not fruit, either because it is absolutely dead and dry, or because it is afflicted with a vice which makes it barren, is to be taken away — judicially severed from the tree.[2]   The doom of the branch which *will* not abide in the vine, is not to be cut off, — for that it does itself, — but to be thrown out of the vineyard, there to lie till it be withered, and at length, at a convenient season, to be gathered, along with all its self-willed, erratic brethren, into a heap, and burned in a bonfire like the dry rubbish of a garden.[3]

In the latter portion of the discourse on the vine,[4] Jesus expresses His high expectations with respect to the fruitfulness of the apostolic branches, and suggests a variety of considerations which, acting on the minds of the disciples as motives, might lead to the fulfilment of His hopes.   As to the former, He gave the disciples to understand that He expected of them not only fruit, but much fruit,[5] and fruit not only abundant in quantity, but good in quality;[6] fruit that should remain, grapes whose juice should be worthy of preservation as wine in bottles; a church that should endure till the world's end.

These two requirements, taken together, amount to a very high demand.   It is very hard indeed to produce fruit at once *abundant* and *enduring*.   The two requirements to a certain extent limit each other.   Aiming at high quality leads to undue thinning of the clusters, while aiming at quantity may easily lead to deterioration in the quality of the whole. The thing to be studied is to secure as large an amount of fruit as is consistent with permanence; and, on the other hand, to cultivate excellence as far as is consistent with obtaining a fair crop which will repay labor and expense. This is, so to speak, the ideal theory of vine culture; but in

---

[1] Ver. 7.   [3] Ver. 6.   [5] Ver. 8.
[2] John xv. 2.   [4] Vers. 8-17.   [6] Ver. 16.

practice we must be content with something short of the
perfect realization of our theory.   We cannot, for example,
rigorously insist that all the fruit shall be such as can endure.
Many fruits of Christian labor are only transient means
towards other fruits of a permanent nature ; and if we satisfy
the law of Christ so far as to produce much fruit, *some* of
which shall remain, we do well.   The permanent portion
of a man's work must always be small in proportion to the
whole.   At highest, it can only bear such a proportion to
the whole as the grape-juice bears to the grapes out of which
it is pressed.   A small cask of wine represents a much larger
bulk of grapes ; and in like manner the perennial result of a
Christian life is very inconsiderable in volume compared with
the mass of thoughts, words, and deeds of which that life was
made up.   One little book, for instance, may preserve to all
generations the soul and essence of the thoughts of a most
gifted mind, and of the graces of a noble heart.   Witness
that wondrous book the *Pilgrim's Progress*, which contains
more wine in it than may be found in the ponderous folios of
some wordy authors, whose works are but huge wine-casks
with very little wine in them, and sometimes hardly even the
scent of it.

To satisfy these two requirements, two virtues are above
all needful, viz. diligence and patience, — the one to insure
quantity, the other to insure superior quality.   One must
know both how to labor and how to wait ; never idle, yet
never hurrying.   Diligence alone will not suffice.   Bustling
activity does a great many things badly, but nothing well.
On the other hand, patience unaccompanied by diligence
degenerates into indolence, which brings forth no fruit at
all, either good or bad.   The two virtues must go together ;
and when they do, they never fail to produce, in greater or
less abundance, fruit that remaineth in a holy exemplary life
whose memory is cherished for generations, in an apostolic
church, in books or in philanthropic institutions, in the
character of descendants, scholars, or hearers.

When the two requirements are taken as applying to all
believers in Christ, the term "much" must be understood
relatively.   It is not required of all indiscriminately to
produce an absolutely large quantity of fruit, but only of

those who, like the apostles, have been chosen and endowed to occupy distinguished positions. Of him to whom little is given shall little be required. For men of few talents it is better not to attempt much, but rather to endeavor to do well the little for which they have capacity. Aspiration is good in the abstract ; but to aspire to exceed the appointed dimensions of our career, is to supply a new illustration of the old fable of the frog and the ox. The man who would be and do more than he is fit for, is worse than useless. He brings forth, not the sweet, wholesome fruits of the Spirit, but the inflated fruits of vanity, which, like the apples of Sodom, are fair and delicious to the eye and soft to the touch, but are yet full of wind, and, being pressed, explode like a puff-ball.[1]

The demand for much fruit, while very exacting as towards the apostles, to whom it in the first place refers, has a gracious aspect towards the world. The fruit which Jesus expected from His chosen ones was the conversion of men to the faith of the gospel — the ingathering of souls into the kingdom of God. A demand for much fruit in this sense is an expression of good-will to mankind, a revelation of the Saviour's loving compassion for a world lying in sin, and error, and darkness. In making this demand, Jesus says in effect to His apostles : Go into the world, bent on evangelizing all the nations ; be fruitful and multiply, and replenish the earth, and subdue it. Ye cannot bring too many to the obedience of faith ; the greater the number of those who believe on me through your word, the better I shall be pleased. We have here, in short, but an echo of the impassioned utterances of that earlier occasion, when Jesus welcomed death as the condition of abundant fruitfulness, and the cross as a power by whose irresistible attraction He should draw all unto Him.[2]

From the high requirements of the Lord, we pass on to the arguments with which He sought to impress on the disciples the duty of bringing forth much and abiding fruit. Of these there are no less than six, grouped in pairs. The first pair we find indicated in the words : " Herein is my Father glorified, that ye bear much fruit, and that ye may be

---

[1] Robinson, *Biblical Researches*, i. 523.   [2] John xii. 24, 33.

my disciples."[1] In other words, Jesus would have His chosen ones remember that the credit, both of the divine Husbandman, and of Himself, the vine, largely depended on their behavior. The world would judge by results. If they, the apostles, abounded in fruitfulness, it would be remarked that God had not sent Christ into the world in vain ; and their success would be ascribed to Him whose disciples they had been. If they failed, men would say : God planted a vine which has not thriven ; and the vine produced branches which have borne no fruit ; or in plain terms, Christ chose agents who have done nothing.

The force of these arguments for fruitfulness is more obvious in the case of these apostles, the founders of the Church, than in reference to the present condition of the Church, when the honor of Christ and of God the Father seems to depend in a very small measure on the conduct of individuals. The whole stress then lay on eleven men. Now it is distributed over millions. Nevertheless, there is great need, even yet, for spiritually fruitful life in the Church, to uphold the honor of Christ's name ; for there is a tendency at the present time to look on Christianity as used up. The old vine stock is considered by many to be effete, and past fruit-bearing ; and a new plant of renown is called for. This idea can be exploded effectually only in one way, viz. by the rising up of a generation of Christians whose life shall demonstrate that the "true vine" is not one of the things that wax old and vanish away, but possesses eternal vitality, sufficient not only to produce new branches and new clusters, but to shake itself clear of dead branches, and of all the moss by which it may have become overgrown in the course of ages.

A second pair of motives to fruitfulness we find hinted at in the words : " These things have I spoken unto you, that my joy might remain in you, and that your joy might be fulfilled."[2] Jesus means to say, that the continuance of His joy in the disciples, and the completion of their own joy as believers in Him, depended on their being fruitful. The

---

[1] John xv. 8. *Vide* various reading, γένησθε instead of γενήσεσθε. The sense is the same ultimately, whichever reading we prefer.

[2] John xv. 11.

emphasis in the first clause lies on the word "remain." Jesus has joy in His disciples even now, though spiritually crude, even as the gardener hath joy in the clusters of grapes when they are green, sour, and uneatable. But He rejoices in them at present, not for what they are, but because of the promise that is in them of ripe fruit. If that promise were not fulfilled, He should feel as the gardener feels when the blossom is nipped by frost, or the green fruit destroyed by mildew ; or as a parent feels when a son belies in his man-hood the bright promise of his youth. He can bear delay, but He cannot bear failure. He can wait patiently till the process of growth has passed through all its stages, and can put up with all the unsatisfactory qualities of immaturity, for the sake of what they shall ripen into. But if they never ripen, — if the children never become men, if the pupils never become teachers, — then He will exclaim, in bitter disappointment : " Woe is me ! my soul desired ripe fruit ; and is this what I find after waiting so long ? "

In the second clause the stress lies on the word "fulfilled." It is not said or insinuated that a Christian can have no joy till his character be matured and his work accomplished. The language of Jesus is quite compatible with the assertion that even at the very commencement of the spiritual life there may be a great, even passionate, outburst of joy. But, on the other hand, that language plainly implies that the joy of the immature disciple is necessarily precarious, and that the joy which is stable and full comes only with spiritual maturity. This is a great practical truth, which it concerns all disciples to bear in mind. Joy in the highest sense is one of the *ripe* fruits of the Holy Spirit, the reward of persever-ance and fidelity. Rejoicing at the outset is good, so far as it goes ; but all depends on the sequel. If we stop short and grow not, woe to us ; for failure in all things, and specially in religion, is misery. If we be comparatively unfruitful, we may not be absolutely unhappy, but we can never know the fulness of joy ; for it is only to the faithful servant that the words are spoken : " Enter thou into the joy of thy Lord." The perfect measure of bliss is for the soldier who hath won the victory, for the reaper celebrating harvest-home, for the athlete who hath gained the prize of strength, skill, and swiftness.

The two last considerations by which Jesus sought to impress on His disciples the duty of being fruitful, were — the honorable nature of their apostolic calling, and the debt of gratitude they owed to Him who had called them, and who was now about to die for them. The dignity of the apostleship, in contrast to the menial position of the disciple, He described in these terms : " Henceforth I call you not servants ; for the servant knoweth not what his lord doeth : but I have called you friends ; for all things that I have heard of my Father I have made known unto you." [1] In other words, the disciples had been apprentices, the apostles would be partners : the disciples had been as government clerks ; the apostles would be confidential ministers of the king : the disciples had been pupils in the school of Jesus ; the apostles would be the treasurers of Christian truth, the reporters and expositors of their Master's doctrine, the sole reliable sources of information concerning the letter and spirit of His teaching. What office could possibly be more important than theirs ? and how needful that they should realize their responsibilities in connection with it !

While endeavoring to walk worthy of so high a vocation, it would become the apostles also to bear in mind their obligations to Him who had called them to the apostolic office. The due consideration of these would be an additional stimulus to diligence and fidelity. Hence Jesus is careful to impress on His disciples that they owe all they are and will be to Him. " Ye did not choose me, but I chose you," [2] He tells them. He wishes them to understand that they had conferred no benefit on Him by becoming His disciples : the benefit was all on their side. He had raised them from obscurity to be the lights of the world, to be the present companions and future friends and representatives of the Christ. Having done so much for them, He was entitled to ask that they would earnestly endeavor to realize the end for which He had chosen them, and to fulfil the ministry to which they were ordained.

One thing more is noteworthy in this discourse on the true vine, — the reiteration of the commandment to love one another. At the commencement of the farewell address,

[1] John xv. 15.   [2] Ver. 16.

Jesus enjoined on the disciples brotherly love as a source of consolation under bereavement; here He re-enjoins it once and again as a condition of fruitfulness.[1] Though He does not say it in so many words, He evidently means the disciples to understand that abiding in each other by love is just as necessary to their success as their common abiding in Him by faith. Division, party strife, jealousy, will be simply fatal to their influence, and to the cause they represent. They must be such fast friends that they will even be willing to die for each other. Had Christians always remembered the commandment of love, on which Christ so earnestly insisted, what a different history the Church would have had! how much more fruitful she would have been in all the great results for which she was instituted!

SECTION II — APOSTOLIC TRIBULATIONS AND ENCOURAGEMENTS

JOHN xv. 18–27, xvi. 1–15

From apostolic duties Jesus passed on to speak of apostolic tribulations. The transition was natural; for all great actors in God's cause, whose fruit remains, are sure to be more or less men of sorrow. To be hated and evil entreated is one of the penalties of moral greatness and spiritual power; or, to put it differently, one of the privileges Christ confers on His "friends."

Hatred is very hard to bear, and the desire to escape it is one main cause of unfaithfulness and unfruitfulness. Good men shape their conduct so as to keep out of trouble, and through excess of cowardly prudence degenerate into spiritual nonentities. It was of the first importance that the apostles of the Christian faith should not become impotent through this cause. For this reason Jesus introduces the subject of tribulation here. He would fortify His disciples for the endurance of sufferings by speaking of them beforehand. "These things," saith He, in the course of His address on the unpleasant theme, as if apologizing for its introduction, " have I spoken unto you that ye should not be scandalized,"[2] that is, be taken by surprise when the time of trouble came.

---

[1] Vers. 12, 17.   [2] John xvi. 1; see also ver. 4.

To nerve the young soldiers of the cross, the Captain of salvation has recourse to various expedients, among which the first is to tell them, without disguise, what they have to expect, that familiarity with the dark prospect may make it less terrible. Of the world's hatred Jesus speaks as an absolutely certain matter, not even deeming it necessary to assert its certainty, but assuming that as a thing of course: "If the world hate you"[1] — as of course it will. Farther on He describes, without euphemism or circumlocution, the kind of treatment they shall receive at the world's hands: "They shall put you out of the synagogues; yea, but the time cometh, that whosoever killeth you will think that he offereth service unto God."[2] Harsh, appalling words; but since such things were to be, it was well to know the worst.

Jesus further tells His disciples that whatever they may have to suffer, they can be no worse off than He has been before them. "If the world hate you, ye know that it has hated me before you." Poor comfort, one is disposed to say; yet it is not so poor when you consider the relative position of the parties. He who has already been hated is the Lord; they who are to be hated are but the servants. Of this Jesus reminds His disciples, repeating and recalling to their remembrance a word He had already spoken the same evening.[3] The consideration ought at least to repress murmuring; and, duly laid to heart, it might even become a source of heroic inspiration. The servant should be ashamed to complain of a lot from which his Master is not, and does not wish to be, exempted; he should be proud to be a companion in tribulations with One who is so much his superior, and regard his experience of the cross not as a fate, but as a privilege.

A third expedient employed by Jesus to reconcile the apostles to the world's hatred, is to represent it as a necessary accompaniment of their *election*.[4] This thought, well weighed, has great force. Love ordinarily rests on a community of interest. Men love those who hold the same opinions, occupy

---

[1] John xv. 18.

[2] John xvi. 2; so in R. V. The idea is that the murderers will imagine they are offering an acceptable religious service or sacrifice unto God.

[3] John xv. 20; comp. xiii. 16, also xii. 26.

[4] John xv. 19.

the same position, follow the same fashions, pursue the same ends with themselves; and they regard all who differ from them in these respects with indifference, dislike, or positive animosity, according to the degree in which they are made sensible of the contrast. Hence arises a dilemma for the chosen ones. Either they must forfeit the honor, privileges, and hope of their election, and descend into the dark world which is without God and without hope; or they must be content, while retaining their position as called out of darkness, to accept the drawbacks which adhere to it, and to be hated by those who love the darkness rather than the light, because their life is evil. What true child of light will hesitate in his choice?

To show the disciples that they have no alternative but to submit patiently to their appointed lot as the chosen ones, Jesus enters yet more deeply into the philosophy of the world's hatred. He explains that what in the first place will be hatred to them, will mean in the second place hatred to Himself; and in the last place, and radically, ignorance of and hostility to God His Father.[1] In setting forth this truth, He takes occasion to make some severe reflections on the unbelieving world of Judæa, in which He had Himself labored. He puts the worst construction on its unbelief; declares it to be utterly without excuse; accuses those who have been guilty of it, of hating Him without a cause, that is, of hating one whose whole character and conduct, words and works, should have won their faith and love; and in their hatred of Him He sees revealed a hatred of that very God for whose glory they professed to be so zealous.[2]

How painful is the view here given of the world's enmity to truth and its witnesses! One would like to see, in the bitterness with which the messengers of truth have been received (not excepting the case of Jesus), the result of a pardonable misunderstanding. And without doubt this is the origin of not a few religious animosities. There have been many sins committed against the Son of man, and those like-minded, which were only in a very mitigated degree sins against the Holy Ghost. Were it otherwise, alas for us all! For who has not persecuted the Son of man or His interest,

---

[1] John xv. 21.   [2] Vers. 22–25.

cherishing ill-feeling and uttering bitter words against His members, if not against Him personally, under the influence of prejudice ; yea, it may be, going the length of inflicting material injury on the apostles of unfamiliar, unwelcome truths, in obedience to the blind impulses of panic fear or selfish passion ?

If there be few who have not in one way or another persecuted, there are perhaps also few of the persecuted who have not taken too sombre views of the guilt of their persecutors. Men who suffer for their convictions are greatly tempted to regard their opponents as in equal measure the opponents of God. The wrongs they endure provoke them to think and speak of the wrong-doers as the very children of the devil. Then it gives importance to one's cause, and dignity to one's sufferings, to conceive of the former as God's, and of the latter as endured for God's sake. Finally, broadly to state the question at stake as one between God's friends and God's foes, satisfies both the intellect and the conscience, — the former demanding a *status quæstionis* which is simple and easily understood ; the latter, one which puts you obviously in the right, and your adversaries obviously in the wrong.

All this shows that much candor, humility, and patience of spirit, is needed before one can safely say, "He that hateth me hateth God." Nevertheless, it remains true that a man's real attitude towards God is revealed by the way in which he treats God's present work and His living servants. On this principle Jesus judged His enemies, though He cherished no resentment, and was ever ready to make due allowance for ignorance. In spite of His charity, He believed and said that the hostility He had encountered sprang from an evil will, and a wicked, godless heart. He had in view mainly the leaders of the opposition who organized the mob of the ignorant and the prejudiced into a hostile army. These men He unhesitatingly denounced as haters of God, truth, and righteousness ; and He pointed to their treatment of Himself as the conclusive evidence of the fact. His appearance and ministry among them had stripped off the mask, and shown them in their real character as hypocrites, pretending to sanctity, but inwardly full of baseness and impiety, who hated genuine goodness, and could not rest till they had got it flung out of the world and nailed to a cross. With the history and the sayings of Christ before our eyes, we must beware lest we carry apologies for unbelief too far.

Jesus having spoken, as in a brief digression, of His bitter experience in the past, very naturally goes on next to express the hope which He cherishes of a brighter future. Hitherto He has been despised and rejected of men, but He believes it will not always be so. The world, Jewish and Gentile, will ere long begin to change its mind, and the Crucified One will become an object of faith and reverence. This hope He builds on a strong and sure foundation, even the combined testimony of the Spirit of truth and of His own apostles. "But," saith He, His face brightening as He speaks, "when the Comforter (of whom He had spoken to His little ones, and to whom He now alludes as His own Comforter not less than theirs) is come, whom I will send unto you from the Father, even the Spirit which proceedeth from the Father, He shall testify of me." [1] What results the Spirit would bring about by His testimony He does not here state. To that point He speaks shortly after, on discovering that His hearers have not apprehended His meaning, or at least have failed to find in His words any comfort for themselves. Meantime He hastens to intimate that the disciples as well as the Spirit of truth will have a share in the honorable work of redeeming from disgrace their Master's name and character. They also should bear witness, as they were well qualified to do, having been with Him from the beginning of His ministry,[2] and knowing fully His doctrine and manner of life.

In this future witness-bearing of the Spirit and of the apostles, Jesus sought comfort to His own heart under the depressing weight of a gloomy retrospect, and the immediate prospect of crucifixion. But not the less did He mean the disciples also to seek from the same quarter strength to encounter their tribulations. In truth, no considerations could tend more effectually to reconcile generous minds to a

---

[1] John xv. 26.
[2] Ver. 27. Hofmann takes μαρτυρεῖτε in ver. 27 as an imperative: And do ye also bear witness of me: tell the world what I am. — *Schriftbeweis*, 2te Hälfte, 2te Abtheilung, p. 19.

hard lot, than those implied in what Jesus had just said, viz. that the apostles would suffer in a cause favored by Heaven, and tending to the honor of Him whom they loved more than life. Who would not choose to be on the side for which the Divine Spirit fights, even at the risk of receiving wounds? Who would not be happy to be reproached and evil-entreated for a name which is worthy to be above every name, especially if assured that the sufferings endured contributed directly to the exaltation of that blessed name to its rightful place of sovereignty? It was just such considerations which more than any thing else supported the apostles under their great and manifold trials. They learned to say: "For Christ's sake we are killed all the day long; we are accounted as sheep for the slaughter. But what does it matter? The Church is spreading; believers are multiplying on every side, springing up an hundred-fold from the seed of the martyrs' blood; the name of our Lord is being magnified. We will gladly suffer, therefore, bearing witness to the truth."

Having premised these observations concerning the aids to endurance, Jesus proceeded at length to state distinctly, in words already quoted, what the apostles would have to endure.[1] On these words we make only one additional remark, viz., that the disciples would learn from them not only the nature of their future tribulations, but the quarter whence they were to come. The world, against whose hatred their Master forewarns them in this part of His discourse, is not the irreligious, sceptical, easy-going, gross-living world of paganism. It is the world of antichristian Judaism; of synagogue-frequenting men, accustomed to distinguish themselves from "the world" as the people of God, very zealous after a fashion for God's glory, fanatically in earnest in their religious opinions and practices, utterly intolerant of dissent, relentlessly excommunicating all who deviated from established belief by a hair's-breadth, and deeming their death no murder, but a religious service, an acceptable sacrifice to the Almighty. To this Jewish world is assigned the honor of representing the entire *kosmos* of men alienated from God and truth; and if hatred to the good be the central characteristic of worldliness, the honor was well

[1] John xvi. 2.

earned, for it was among the Jews that the power of hating attained its maximum degree of intensity. No man could hate like a religious Jew of the apostolic age : he was renowned for his diabolic capacity of hating. Even a Roman historian, Tacitus, commemorates the "hostile odium" of the Jewish race against all mankind ; and the experience of the Christian apostles fully justified the prominence given to the Jew by Jesus in discoursing on the world's hatred. It was to the unbelieving Jews they mainly owed their knowledge of what the world's hatred meant. The pagan world despised them rather than hated them. The Greek laughed, and the Roman passed by in contemptuous indifference, or at most opposed temperately, as one who would rather not. But the persevering, implacable, malignant hostility of the Jewish religionist ! — it was bloodthirsty, it was pitiless, it was worthy of Satan himself. Truly might Jesus say to the Jews, with reference thereto, " Ye are of your father the devil, and the lusts of your father ye will do."

What a strange fruit was this wicked spirit of hatred to grow upon the goodly vine which God had planted in the holy land ! Chosen to be the vehicle of blessing to the world, Israel ends by becoming the enemy of the world, "contrary to all men," so as to provoke even the humane to regard and treat her as a nuisance, whose destruction from the face of the earth would be a common cause of congratulation. Behold the result of election abused ! Peculiar favors minister to pride, instead of stirring up the favored ones to devote themselves to their high vocation as the benefactors of mankind ; and a divine commonwealth is turned into a synagogue of Satan, and God's most deadly foes are those of His own house. Alas ! the same phenomenon has re-appeared in the Christian Church. The world that is most opposed to Christ, Antichrist itself, is to be found not in heathendom, but in Christendom ; not among the irreligious and the sceptical, but among those who account themselves the peculiar people of God.

The announcement made by Jesus concerning their future tribulations, produced, as was to be expected, a great sensation among the disciples. The dark prospect revealed by the momentary lifting of the veil utterly appalled them. Consternation appeared in their faces, and sorrow filled their hearts. To be forsaken by their Master was bad enough, but to be left to such a fate was still worse, they thought. Jesus noticed the impression He had produced, and did what He could to remove it, and help the poor disciples to recover their composure.

First, He makes a sort of apology for speaking of such painful matters, to this effect: " I would gladly have been silent concerning your coming troubles, and I have been silent as long as possible; but I could not think of leaving you without letting you know what was before you, which accordingly I have done now, as the hour of my departure is at hand." [1]   The kind feeling which dictated the statement thus paraphrased is manifest; but the statement itself appears inconsistent with the records of the other Gospels, from which we learn that the hardships connected with discipleship in general, and with the apostleship in particular, were a frequent subject of remark in the intercourse of Jesus with the twelve.   The difficulty has been variously dealt with by commentators.   Some admit the contradiction, and assume that such earlier discourses concerning persecutions as are found — *e.g.* in the tenth chapter of Matthew — are introduced by the evangelist out of their chronological order. Others insist on the difference between the earlier utterances and the present in respect to *plainness:* representing the former as vague and general, like the early illusions made by Jesus to His own death; the latter as particular, definite, and unmistakeable, like the announcements which Jesus made respecting His passion towards the end of His ministry.   A third class of expositors make the novelty of this discourse on the world's hatred lie in the explanation given therein of its cause and origin; [2] while a fourth class insist that the grand distinction between this discourse and all that went before is to be found in the fact that it is a farewell discourse, and therefore one which, owing to the situation, made quite a novel impression. [3]

Where so much difference of opinion prevails, it would be unbecoming to dogmatize.   Our own opinion, however, is, that the peculiarity of the present utterance concerning

[1] John xvi. 4.   [2] Stier.   [3] Luthardt.

apostolic tribulations lies in the manner or style, rather than in the matter. On former occasions, especially on the occasion of the trial mission of the twelve, Jesus had said much the same things: He had spoken of scourging in synagogues at least, if not of excommunication from them, and had alluded to death by violence as at least a possible fate for the apostles of the kingdom. But He had said all things in a different way. There He *preached* concerning persecution; here He makes an awfully real *announcement*. There is all the difference between that discourse and the present communication that there would be between a sermon on the text, "It is appointed unto men once to die," and a special intimation to an individual, "This year thou shalt die." The sermon may say far more about death than the intimation, but in how different a manner, and with what a different effect!

The next expedient for curing grief to which Jesus has recourse is friendly remonstrance. He gently taunts the disciples for their silence, which He regards as a token of hopeless, despairing sorrow. "But now I go my way to Him that sent me; and none of you asketh me, Whither goest Thou? But because I have said these things unto you, sorrow hath filled your heart." [1] "Why," He means to say, "are you so utterly cast down? have you no questions to ask me about my departure? You were full of questions at the first. You were curious to know whither I was going. I would be thankful to have that question asked over again, or indeed to have any question put to me, whether wise or foolish. The most childish interrogations would be better than the gloom of speechless despair."

As the question, "Whither goest Thou?" had been sufficiently answered already, it might have been superfluous to ask it again. There were, however, other questions, neither superfluous nor impertinent, which the disciples might have taken occasion to ask from the communication just made to them concerning their future lot, and which they probably would have asked had they not been so depressed in spirit. "If," they might have said, "it is to fare so ill with us after

[1] John xvi. 5, 6. Olshausen joins the first part of ver. 5 to the preceding, and supposes a pause after the words were uttered.

you go, why do not you stay? While you have been with us you have sheltered us from the world's hatred, and you tell us that when you, our leader and head, are gone, that hatred will be directed against us, your followers. If so, how can we possibly regard your departure as any thing but a calamity?"

These unspoken questions Jesus proceeds in the next place to answer. He boldly asserts that whatever they may think, it is for their good that He should go away.[1] The assertion, true in other respects also, is made with special reference to the work of the apostleship. In the early part of His farewell address, Jesus had explained to His disciples how His departure would affect them as *private persons* or individual believers. He had assured them that when "the Comforter" came, He would make them feel as if their departed Master were returned to them again; yea, as if He were more really present to them than ever He had been. Here His object is to show the bearing of His departure on their work as *apostles*, and to make them understand that His going away would be good for them as public functionaries.

The proof of this assertion follows;[2] its substance is to this effect: "When I leave you and go to my father,[3] two *desiderata* of essential importance for the success of your work as apostles will be supplied. Then you will have *receptive hearers*, and you yourselves will be *competent to preach*. Neither of these *desiderata* exists for the present. The world has rejected me and my words; and you, though sincere, are very ignorant, and understand not what I have taught you. After my ascension, there will be a great alteration in both respects: the world will be more ready to hear the truth, and you will be able to declare it intelligently. The change cannot come till then; for it will be brought about by the work of the Comforter, the Spirit of truth, and He cannot come till I go."

In the section of His discourse of which we have given the general meaning, Jesus sketches in rapid outline, first the Spirit's converting work in the world,[4] and then His enlight-

---

[1] John xvi. 7.
[2] John xvi. 7-15.
[3] ἀπέλθω, πορευθῶ.
[4] John xvi. 8-11.

ening work in the minds of the apostles.[1] The former He describes in these terms: "When He is come, He will convince (produce serious thought and conviction in) the world about sin, righteousness, and judgment." Then He explains in what special aspects the Spirit will bring these great moral realities before men's minds; and here He but expounds what He has already said concerning the Spirit's testimony in His own behalf.[2] He tells His disciples that the Comforter, witnessing for Himself in the hearts and consciences of men, will convince them of sin specially as unbelievers in Him; of righteousness in connection with His departure to the Father; and of judgment (to come), because the prince of this world is judged already (that is, shall have been, when the Comforter commences His work).

The second and third explanatory remarks are enigmatical, and instead of throwing light on the subject in hand, seem rather to involve it in darkness. They have given rise to so much dispute and diversity of opinion, that to expatiate on them were vain, and to dogmatize presumption. One great point of dispute has been: What righteousness does Jesus allude to, — His own, or that of sinners? Does He mean to say that the Spirit will convince the world, after He has left the earth, that He was a righteous man? or does He mean that the Spirit will teach men to see in the Crucified One the Lord their righteousness? Our own opinion is, that He means neither, and both. Righteousness is to be taken in its undefined generality: and the idea is, that the Spirit will make use of the exaltation of Christ to make men think earnestly on *the whole subject of righteousness;* to show them the utterly rotten character of their own righteousness, whose crowning feat was to crucify Jesus; to bring home to their hearts the solemn truth that the Crucified One was the Just One; and ultimately to put them on a track for finding in Jesus their true righteousness, by raising in their minds the question, Why then did the Just One suffer?

The meaning of the third explanatory remark we take to be to this effect: "When I am crucified, the god of this world shall have been judged. Both this world and its god, indeed, but the latter only finely and irreversibly, — the world, though

---

[1] John xvi. 12-15.   [2] John xv. 26.

presently following Satan, being convertible. When I am ascended, the Spirit will use the then past judgment of Satan to convince men of a judgment to come ; teaching them to see therein a prophecy of a final separation between me and all who obstinately persist in unbelief, and so, by the terrors of perdition, bringing them to repentance and faith."

What Jesus says of the enlightening work of the Spirit on the minds of the disciples, amounts to this : He will fit you to be intelligent and trustworthy witnesses to me, and to be guides of the Church in doctrine and practice. For these high purposes two things would be necessary : that they should understand Christian truth, and that they should possess the gift of prophecy, so as to be able to fortell in its general outlines the future, for the warning and encouragement of believers. Both these advantages Jesus promises them as fruits of the Spirit's enlightening influence. He assures them that, when the Comforter is come, He will guide them unto all the truth He had himself taught them, recalling things forgotten, explaining things not understood, developing germs into a system of doctrine which was entirely above their present power of comprehension.[1] He further informs them that this same Spirit will show them things to come, — such as the rise of heresies and apostasies, the coming of Antichrist, the conflict between light and darkness, and their final issue, as described in the Book of Revelation.

Such were the changes to be brought about in the world and in the disciples by the advent of the Comforter. Great beneficent changes truly ; but *why cannot they take place before Jesus leaves the world?* The answer to this question is hinted at by Jesus, when He says of the Spirit : " He shall not speak of Himself,"[2] and " He shall receive of mine, and shall show it unto you."[3] The personal ministry of Jesus behoved to come to an end before the ministry of the Spirit began, because the latter is merely an application of the former. The Spirit does not speak as from Himself : He simply takes of the things relating to Christ, and shows them to men, — to unbelievers, for their conviction and conversion ; to believers, for their enlightenment and sanctifica-

---

[1] John xvi. 12.   [2] Ver. 13.   [3] Ver. 14.

tion. But till Jesus had died, risen, ascended, the essentials about Him would remain incomplete; the materials for a gospel would not be ready to hand. There could be neither apostolic preaching, nor the demonstration of the Spirit with power accompanying it. It must be possible for the apostles and the Spirit to bear witness of One who, though perfectly holy, had been crucified, to show the world the heinousness of its sin. They must have it in their power to declare that God hath made that same Jesus whom they have crucified both Lord and Christ, exalted to heavenly glory, before their hearers can be pricked in the heart, and made to exclaim in terror, "Men and brethren, what shall we do?" Only after Jesus had ascended to glory, and become invisible to mortal eyes,[1] could men be made to understand that He was not only personally a righteous man, but the Lord their righteousness. Then the question would force itself upon their minds: What could be the meaning of the Lord of glory becoming man, and dying on the cross? and by the teaching of the Spirit they would learn to reply, not as in the days of their ignorance, "He suffers for His own offences," but, "Surely He hath borne our griefs and carried our sorrows; He was wounded for our transgressions."

Finally, not till the apostles were in a position to say that their Lord was gone to heaven, could they bring to bear with full effect on the impenitent the doctrine of a judgment. Then they could say, Christ is seated on the heavenly throne a Prince and a Saviour to all who believe, but also a Judge to those who continue in rebellion and unbelief. "Kiss the Son, lest He be angry, and ye perish from the way, when His wrath is kindled but a little. Blessed are all they that put their trust in Him."

All this the disciples for the present did not understand. Of the Spirit's work on the conscience of the world and in their own minds, and of the relation in which the third person of the Trinity[2] stood to the second, they had simply no conception. Hence Jesus does not enlarge on these topics,

---

[1] Ver. 10: "And ye see me no more," = I am no longer seen on earth; suggesting the idea that earth was Christ's place of sojourn, heaven His home, therefore inferentially asserting His divinity.

[2] The personality of the Holy Ghost is assumed throughout this discourse. See ver. 13, ἐκεῖνος.

but restricts Himself to what is barely necessary to indicate the truth. But the time came when the disciples did get to understand these matters, and then they fully appreciated the eulogium of their Lord on the dispensation of the Comforter. Then they acknowledged that the assertion was indeed true that it was expedient for them that He should go away, and smiled when they remembered that they had once thought otherwise ; yea, they perceived that the word "expedient," far from being too strong, was rather a weak expression, chosen in gracious accommodation to their feeble spiritual capacity, instead of the stronger one "indispensable." Then they felt, as we imagine good men feel about death when they have got to heaven. On this side the grave

> "Timorous mortals start and shrink
> To cross the narrow sea ;
> And linger, shivering, on the brink,
> And fear to launch away."

But to those on the other side how insignificant a matter must death seem, and how strange must it appear to their purged vision, that it should ever have been needful to prove to them that it was better to depart to heaven than to remain in a world of sin and sorrow !

SECTION III —THE LITTLE WHILE, AND THE END OF THE DISCOURSE

JOHN xvi. 16-33

The eulogium on the dispensation of the Comforter winds up with a paradox. Jesus has been telling His disciples that His departure will be beneficial for them in various respects, but particularly in this, that they shall attain thereafter to a clear, full comprehension of Christian truth. In effect, what He has said is : It is good for you that I go, for not till I become invisible physically, shall I be visible to you spiritually : I must be withdrawn from the eye of your flesh, before I can be seen by the eye of your mind. Hence He fitly ends His discourse on the Comforter by repeating a riddle, which He had propounded in a less pointed form in His first farewell address : "A little while, and ye no longer see me : and again a little while, and ye shall see me ; because I go to the Father."

This riddle, like all riddles, is very simple when we have the key to it. As in that other paradoxical saying of Jesus, concerning losing and saving life,[1] the principal word, "see," is used in two senses,[2] — first in a physical, and then, in the second clause, in a spiritual sense. Hence the possibility of one event, the departure of Christ to the Father, becoming a cause at once of not seeing and of seeing. When Jesus ascended to heaven, the disciples saw Him no more as they saw Him then in the supper-chamber. But immediately thereafter they began to see Him in another way. The idea of His life did sweetly creep into the eye and prospect of their soul. And the sight was satisfying: it justified the glowing language in which their Master had spoken of it before He left them. Though they saw Him no more in the flesh, yet, believing in Him, to quote the words of the Apostle Peter, they rejoiced with joy unspeakable and full of glory.

For the present, however, the disciples have no conception of the vision and the joy which await them. Their Lord's words have no meaning for them ; they are a riddle indeed, yea, a contradiction. Standing around the inspired speaker, they whisper remarks to each other concerning the strange enigmatical words He has just uttered about a little while, and about seeing and not seeing, and about going to the Father. The riddle has evidently served one purpose at least : it has roused the disciples out of the stupor of grief, and awakened for a little their curiosity. That, however, is the amount of the service it has rendered : it has created surprise, but it has conveyed no sense ; the hearers are constrained to confess, "We cannot tell what He saith."[3] Yet we observe, they ask no questions of Jesus. They would like to do so at this point, but they do not feel able to take the liberty ; restrained, we imagine, by respect for the lofty sustained tone in which their Master has been addressing them in the second part of His farewell discourse. Jesus, however, reads a question in their countenances, and kindly favors them with a word of explanation.[4]

That word does not, strictly speaking, explain the riddle.

---

[1] Matt. xvi. 25.
[2] There are two words in the Greek — θεωρεῖτε, ὄψεσθε.
[3] John xvi. 18.
[4] Vers. 19-21.

Jesus does not tell His disciples what the little while means, nor does He distinguish the two kinds of seeing : He leaves the enigma to be solved, as it only can be, by experience. All He attempts is to make it conceivable how the same event which in immediate prospect causes sorrow, may, after its occurrence, be a cause of joy.   For this purpose He compares the crisis through which the disciples are about to pass, not, as we have already done, to the solemn event by which a Christian makes his exit out of this world into a better, but to the event with which human life begins.[1]

The comparison is apt to the purpose for which it is introduced ; but we cannot with certainty, not to say propriety, pursue it into detail.   Interpreters who aspire to understand all mysteries and all knowledge, have raised many questions thereanent, such as : Who is represented by the mother in the parable — Christ, or the disciples ?   When does the sorrow begin, and when and in what does it end ?   The answers given to these questions are very various.   According to one, Jesus Himself is the new man, and the sorrow He alludes to is His own death, viewed as the redemption of sinful humanity.   Another will have it that Jesus represents His own disciples as with child of a spiritual Christ, who will be born when the Comforter comes.   Most make the time of sorrow begin with Christ's passion, but there is much difference of opinion as to when it ends.   One makes the joy date from the resurrection, which, after a little while of painful separation, restored Jesus to His sorrowing disciples ; another extends the " little while " to Pentecost, when the Church was born into the world a new man in Christ ; a third makes the little while a long while indeed, by making the words " I will see you again " refer to Christ's second coming, and to the blessed era when the new heavens and the new earth, wherein dwelleth righteousness, for which the whole creation groans, shall at length come into being.[2]

We do not think it necessary to pronounce on these disputed points.   As little do we think it necessary to give the analogy a doctrinal turn, and find in it a reference to

[1] Vers. 20-22.
[2] See, for the various opinions on these points, Stier, Luthardt, Lange, Olshausen, Alford, etc.

regeneration. What Jesus has in view throughout this part of His discourse is not the new birth, either of the disciples or of the Church, but the spiritual illumination of the apostles; their transition from the chrysalis into the winged state, from an ignorant implicit faith to a faith developed and intelligent; their initiation into the highest grade of the Christian mysteries, when they should see clearly things presently unintelligible, and be *Epopts* in the kingdom of heaven.[1] For them, as for Christians generally (for there is a sense in which the experience of the apostles repeats itself in the spiritual history of many believers), this crisis is not less important than the initial one by which men pass from death into life. It is a great thing to be regenerated, but it is a not less great thing to be illuminated. It is a great, ever-memorable time that, when Christ first enters the heart, an object of faith and love; but it is an equally important crisis when Christ, after having departed perhaps for a season, leaving the mind clouded with doubt and the heart oppressed with sorrow, returns never to depart, driving away wintry frosts and darkness, and bringing light, gladness, summer warmth, and spiritual fruitfulness to the soul. Verily one might be content that Christ, as he first knew Him, should depart, for the sake of having his sorrow after a little while turned into such joy!

Having shown, by a familiar and pathetic analogy, the possibility of present sorrow being transmuted into great joy, Jesus proceeds next to describe, by a few rapid strokes, the characteristics of the state at which the apostles will ere long arrive.[2] First among these He mentions an *enlarged comprehension of truth;* for it is to this He refers when He says, "In that day ye shall ask me nothing." He means that they will then ask Him no questions such as they had been asking all along, and especially that night, — child's questions, asked with a child's curiosity, and also with a child's incapacity to understand the answers. The questioning spirit of childhood would be replaced by the understanding

---

[1] One who had been introduced into the highest (third) grade of the Eleusinian mysteries was called ἐπόπτης. See Plato, *Convivium* (Socrates reporting discourse of Diotime on Ἑρως).

[2] John xvi. 23, 24.

spirit of manhood. The truths of the kingdom would no
longer, as heretofore, be inscrutable mysteries to them : they
should have an unction from the Holy One, and should know
all things.

Some think this too much to be said of any Christian, not
even excepting the apostles themselves, while in the earthly
state, and therefore argue that the day alluded to here is that
of Christ's second coming, or of His happy reunion with His
own in the kingdom of His Father.[1]   And without doubt, it
is true that in that final day only shall Christians know as
they are known, and have absolutely no need to ask any
questions.   Then,

> " 'Midst power that knows no limit,
>   And wisdom free from bound,
> The beatific vision
>   Shall glad the saints around,"

as it can never gladden them here below.   Still, the statement
before us has a relative truth in reference to this present
life.   While, in comparison with the perfect state, the clear-
est vision of any Christian is but a seeing in a glass darkly,
the degree of illumination attained by the apostles might be
described, without exaggeration, in contrast to their ignorance as disciples, as that of men who needed not any longer to
ask questions.   In promising His disciples that they would
ere long attain this high degree, Jesus was but saying in
effect, that as apostles they would be teachers, not scholars, —
doctors of divinity, with titles conferred by Heaven itself,
— capable of answering questions of young disciples, similar
to those which they once asked themselves.

The second feature of the apostolic illumination mentioned
by Jesus is *unlimited influence with God through prayer.*   Of
this He speaks with much emphasis : "Verily, verily, I say
unto you, Whatsoever ye shall ask the Father in my name,
He will give it you."[2]   That is to say, the apostles were to

[1] So Luthardt, ii. 348, who holds that the first clause of ver. 23 refers to the final condition of the Church, and the second to its imperfect state, on the ground that the two
cannot be contemporaneous. He says where there is praying there is asking, and *vice
versâ.* Yet it is also true that the less a man needs to ask questions, that is, the more
enlightened he is, the more he will *pray.*

[2] John xvi. 23. The verb translated *ask* in this clause is not the same as that rendered by the same English word in the first. In the first clause it is ἐρωτήσατε; in the
second, αἰτήσητε.

have at command the whole power of God : the power of
miracles, to heal diseases ; of prophecy, to foretell things to
come bearing on the Church's interest, and which it was
desirable that believers should know ; of providence, to make
all events subservient to their well-being, and that of the
cause in which they labored. The promise in its substance,
though not in its miraculous accidents, is made to all who
aspire to Christian manhood, and is fulfilled to all who reach it.

In the next sentence, Jesus, if we mistake not, particular-
izes a third feature in the state of spiritual maturity to which
He would have His disciples aspire. It is a *heart enlarged*
to desire, ask, and expect great things for themselves, the
Church, and the world. "Hitherto," He says to them, "have
ye asked nothing in my name." There was a reason for this,
distinct from the spiritual state of the twelve. The time
had not yet come for asking any thing in Christ's name :
they could not fitly or naturally make "Christ's sake" their
plea till Christ's work was completed, and He was glorified.
But Jesus meant more than this by His remark. He meant
to say, what was in fact most true, that hitherto His disciples had asked little in any name. Their desires had been
petty, their ideas of what to ask obscure and crude ; any
wishes of large dimensions they had cherished had been of
a worldly character, and therefore such as God could not
grant. They had been like children, to whom a penny
appears greater than a thousand pounds does to a wealthy
man. But Jesus hints, though He does not plainly say, that
it will be otherwise with the apostles after the advent of the
Comforter. Then they will be poor boys grown to rich mer-
chants, whose ideas of enjoyment have enlarged with their
outward fortunes. Then they will be able to pray such
prayers as that of Paul in his Roman prison in behalf of the
Ephesian Church, and of the Church in all ages ; able to
pray the Lord's prayer, and especially to say, "Thy kingdom
come," with a comprehensiveness of meaning, a fervency of
desire, and an assurance of faith, whereof at present they
have simply no conception. Hitherto they have been but as
children, asking of their father trifles, toys, pence : then they
shall make large demands on the riches of God's grace, for
themselves, the Church, and the world.

Along with this enlargement, Jesus promises, will come fulness of joy. What is asked, the Father will grant; and the answer to prayer will fill the cup of joy to the brim. Hope may be deferred for a season, but in the end will come the unspeakable joy of hope fulfilled. "Ask, and ye shall receive, that your joy may be full." So it turned out in the experience of the apostles. They had fulness of joy in the Holy Ghost, in His work in their own hearts and in the world. The law ought to hold good still. But why, then, is the cause of Christianity not progressing, but rather, one might almost say, retrograding? We must answer this question by asking others : How many have large hearts cherishing comprehensive desires? How many with their whole soul desire for themselves above all things sanctification and illumination? How many earnestly, passionately desire the conversion of the heathen, the unity and peace and purity of the Church, the prevalence of righteousness in society at large? We are straitened in our own hearts, not in God.

The farewell discourse is now at an end. Jesus has said to His disciples what time permits, and what they are able to hear. He does not imagine that He has conveyed much instruction to their minds, or that He has done much for them in the way of consolation. He has a very humble idea of the character and practical effect of the address He has just delivered. Casting a glance backwards at the whole, while perhaps specially alluding to what had been said just before, He remarks : "These things have I spoken unto you in proverbs." A few parables or figurative sayings about the house of many mansions, and about the Divine Trinity coming to make their abode with the faithful, and about the vine and its branches, and about maternal sorrows and joys : such, in the speaker's view, is the sum of His discourse.

Conscious of the inevitable deficiency not only of the present discourse, but of His whole past teaching, Jesus takes occasion for the third time to repeat the promise of future spiritual illumination, this time speaking of Himself as the illuminator, and representing the doctrine of the Father as the great subject of illumination. "The time cometh when *I* shall no more speak unto you in proverbs, but *I* shall show you plainly of the Father." The time referred to is still the era dating from the ascension. Shortly thereafter the disciples would begin to experience the fulfilment of Philip's prayer, to understand what their Lord meant by His going to the Father, and to realize its blessed consequences for themselves. Then would their exalted Lord, through the Spirit of truth, speak to them plainly of these and all other matters ; plainly in comparison with His present mystic, hidden style of speech, if not so plainly as to falsify the statements in other places of Scripture concerning the partiality and dimness of all spiritual knowledge in this earthly state of being.

Of the good time coming Jesus has yet another thing to say ; not a new thing, but an old thing said in a new, wondrously kind, and pathetic way. It has reference to the hearing of prayer, and is to this effect: "In the day of your enlightenment you will, as I have already hinted, pray not less than heretofore, but far more, and you will use my name as your plea to be heard. Let me once more assure you that you *shall* be heard. In support of this assurance, I might remind you that I will be in heaven with the Father, ever ready to speak a word in your behalf, saying, ' Father, hear them for my sake, whose name they plead in their petitions.' But I do not insist on this, not only because I believe you do not need to be assured of my continued interest in your welfare, but more especially because my intercession will not be necessary. My Father will not need to be entreated to hear *you*, the men who have been with me in all my temptations,[1] who have loved me with leal-hearted affection, who have believed in me as the Christ, the Son of the living God, while the world at large has regarded me as an impostor and a blasphemer. For these services to His Son my Father loves you, is grateful to you — in a sense accounts Himself your debtor."[2] What heart, what humanity, what poetry is in all this ! — poetry, and also truth ; truth unspeakably comforting not only to the eleven faithful companions of Jesus, but to all sincere believers in Him.

Having alluded to the faith of His disciples, — so merito-

---

[1] Luke xxii. 28. *Vide* p. 18, note.   [2] John xvi. 26, 27.

rious, because so rare, — Jesus takes occasion, in closing His discourse, and at the close of His life, solemnly to declare its truth. " I came forth from the Father, and am come into the world : again I leave the world, and go to the Father." [1] The first part only of this statement the disciples believed ; the second they did not yet understand : but Jesus puts both together, as the two halves of one whole truth, either of which necessarily implies the other. The declaration is a most momentous one : it sums up the history of Christ ; it is the substance of the Christian faith ; it asserts doctrines utterly incompatible with a merely human view of Christ's person, and makes His divinity the fundamental article of the creed.

These last words of Jesus burst on the disciples like a star suddenly shining out from the clouds in a dark night. At length one luminous utterance had pierced through the haze of their Master's mysterious discourse, and they fancied that now at last they understood its import. Jesus had just told them that He came forth from the Father into the world. That, at least, they understood ; it was because they believed it that they had become disciples. Delighted to have heard something to which they could give a hearty response, they make the most of it, and inform their Master that the intelligible, plain speaking on His part, and the intelligent apprehending on theirs which He had projected into the future, were already in existence. " Lo," said they, with emphasis on the temporal particle, " *now* Thou speakest plainly, and speakest no proverb. *Now* are we sure that Thou knowest all things, and needest not that any man should ask Thee : in this we believe that Thou camest forth from God."

Alas, how impossible it is for children to speak otherwise than as children ! The disciples, in the very act of professing their knowledge, betray their utter ignorance. The statement begining with the second " now " indicates an almost ludicrous misapprehension of what Jesus had said about their asking Him no questions in the day of their enlightenment. He meant they would not then need to ask questions as learners : they took Him to mean that He Himself had no need to be asked questions as to who He

[1] Ver. 28.

was and whence He came, His claim to a heavenly descent being already admitted, at least by them. And as to the inference drawn from that statement, "By this we believe," we can make nothing of it. After many attempts to understand the logic of the disciples, we must confess ourselves utterly baffled. The only way by which we can put a tolerable sense on the words, is to regard the phrase translated by "this" as an adverb of time, and to read "at this present moment:" Meanwhile, whatever additional light may be in store for us in the future, we even now believe that Thou camest forth from God. This translation, however, is not favored, or even suggested, by any of the critics.[1]

That the disciples did honestly believe what they professed to believe, was true. Jesus had just before admitted as much. But they did not understand what was involved in their belief. They did not comprehend that the coming of Jesus from the Father implied a going thither again. They had not comprehended that at the beginning of the discourse ; they did not comprehend it when the discourse was finished ; they would not comprehend it till their Lord had taken His departure, and the Spirit had come who should make all things plain. In consequence of this ignorance, their faith would not carry them through the evil hour that was now very near. The death of their Master, the first step in the process of His departure, would take them by surprise, and make them flee panic-stricken like sheep attacked by wolves. So Jesus plainly told them. "Do ye now believe?" He said ; "behold, the hour cometh, yea, is now come, that ye shall be scattered, every man to his own, and shall leave me alone."[2]

Stern fact sternly announced ; but however stern, Jesus is not afraid to look it in the face. His heart is in perfect peace, for He has two great consolations. He has a good conscience: He can say, "I have overcome the world."

[1] Winer, *Neutest. Grammatik,* states that he knows no clear example of the use of ἐν τούτῳ = by this, or because of. Of its use = intereâ he gives several examples from classic authors, pp. 361-2 (Moulton's translation, p. 484).

[2] The commentators tell us that ἄρτι πιστεύετε is not a question. If not, why is there no adversative particle in next clause (ἔρχεται δὲ)? The clause is undoubtedly interrogative in effect. Christ calls in question not the reality, indeed, but the sufficiency, of the faith of His disciples.

He has held fast His moral integrity against incessant temptation. The prince of this world has found none of his spirit in Him, and for that very reason is going to crucify Him. But by that proceeding Satan will not nullify, but rather seal, His victory. Outward defeat by worldly power will be but the index and measure of His spiritual conquest. The world itself knows well that putting Him to death is but the second best way of overcoming Him. His enemies would have been much better pleased if they had succeeded in intimidating or bribing Him into compromise. The ungodly powers of the world always prefer corruption to persecution as a means of getting rid of truth and righteousness ; only after failing in attempts to debauch conscience, and make men venal, do they have recourse to violence.

Christ's other source of consolation in prospect of death is the approval of His Father : " I am not alone, because the Father is with me." The Father has been with Him all along. On three critical occasions — at the baptism, on the hill of transfiguration, in the temple a few days ago — the Father had encouraged Him with an approving voice. He feels that the Father is with Him still. He expects that He will be with Him when He is deserted by His chosen ones, and all through the awful crisis at hand, even in that darkest, bitterest moment, when the loss of His Father's sensible presence will extort from Him the cry : " My God, my God, why hast Thou forsaken me ? " He expects that His Father will be with Him then, not to save Him from the *sense* of desertion (He would not wish to be saved from that, for He would know by experience that sorest of all sorrows, that in this, as in all other respects, He might be like His brethren, and be able to succor them when they are tempted to despair), but to sustain Him under the sore affliction, and enable Him with filial faith to cry "*My* God " even when complaining of being forsaken.

Free from all anxiety for Himself, Jesus bids His disciples also be of good cheer ; and for the same reason why He Himself is without fear, viz., because He has overcome the world. He will have them understand that His victory is theirs too. "Be of good cheer : I have overcome the world, therefore so have ye in effect ; " — such is His meaning.

Men of Socinianizing tendencies would interpret the words differently. They would read : I have overcome the world, therefore so may ye. Follow my example, and manfully fight the battle of righteousness in spite of tribulations.[1] The meaning is good enough, so far as it goes. It does nerve one for the battle of life to know that the Lord of glory has been through it before him. It is an inspiring thought that He has even been a combatant at all ; for who would not follow when the divine Captain of salvation leads through suffering to glory ? Then, when we think that this august combatant has been completely victorious in the fight, His example becomes still more cheering. His victory shows that the god of this world is not omnipotent ; that it is always in the power of any one to overcome him simply by being willing to bear the cross. Looking at Jesus enduring the contradiction of sinners even unto death, and despising the shame of crucifixion, His followers get more heart to fight the good fight of faith.

But while this is true, it is the smallest part of the truth. The grand fact is that Christ's victory is the victory of His followers, and insures that they too shall conquer. Jesus fought His battle not as a private person, but as a public character, as a representative man. And all are welcome to claim the benefits of His victory, — the pardon of sin, power to resist the evil one, admission into the everlasting kingdom. Because Christ hath overcome, we may say to all, Be of good cheer. The victory of the Son of God in human nature is an available source of consolation for all who partake of that nature. It is the privilege of every man (as well as the duty) to acknowledge Christ as his representative in this great battle. "The Head of every man is Christ." All who sincerely recognize the relationship will get the benefit of it. Claim kindred with the High Priest, and you shall receive from Him mercy and grace to help in your hour of need. Lay it to heart that men are not isolated units, every one fighting his own battle without help or encouragement. We are members one of another, and above all, we have in Christ an elder brother. We have at least a human

---

[1] On the Socinian theory of Atonement, *vide The Humiliation of Christ* (sixth series of *Cunningham Lectures*), Lect. VII. p. 296, 2d ed.

relationship to Him, if not a regenerate one. Let us therefore look up to Him as our Head in all things : as our King, and lay down the weapons of our rebellion ; as our Priest, and receive from Him the pardon of our sins ; as our Lord, to be ruled by His will, defended by His might, and guided by His grace. If we do this, the accuser of the brethren will have no chance of prevailing against us. The words of St. John in the Apocalypse will be fulfilled in our history : "They overcame him by the blood of the Lamb, and by the word of their testimony ; and they loved not their lives unto the death."

26

THE INTERCESSORY PRAYER

John 17

THE prayer uttered by Jesus at the close of His farewell address to His disciples, of unparalleled sublimity, whether we regard its contents or the circumstances amid which it was offered up, it was for years our fixed purpose to pass over in solemn, reverent silence, without note or comment. We reluctantly depart from our intention now, constrained by the considerations that the prayer was not offered up mentally by Jesus, but in the hearing and for the instruction of the eleven men present ; that it has been recorded by one of them for the benefit of the Church in all ages ; and that what it hath pleased God to preserve for our use we must endeavor to understand, and may attempt to interpret.

The prayer falls naturally into three divisions, in the first of which Jesus prays for Himself, in the second for His disciples, and in the third for the Church which was to be brought into existence by their preaching.

The prayer of Jesus for Himself (vers. 1–5) contains just one petition, with two reasons annexed. The petition is, "Father, the hour is come, glorify Thy Son ;" in which the manner of address, simple, familiar, confidential, is note-worthy. "Father!"—such is the first word of the prayer, six times repeated in its course, with or without epithet attached, and the name which Jesus gives to Him to whom His prayer is addressed. He speaks to God as if He were already in heaven, as indeed He expressly says He is a little farther on : "Now I am no more in the world."

The significant phrase, "the hour is come," is it not less worthy of notice. How much it expresses !—filial obedience, filial intimacy, filial hope and joy. The hour ! It is the

hour for which He has patiently waited, which He has looked
forward to with eager expectation, yet has never sought to
hurry on ; the hour appointed by His Father, about which
Father and Son have always had an understanding, and of
which none but they have had any knowledge. That hour
is come, and its arrival is intimated as a plea in support of
the petition : " Thou knowest, Father, how patiently I have
waited for what I now ask, not wearying in well-doing, nor
shrinking from the hardships of my earthly lot. Now that
my work is finished, grant me the desire of my heart, and
glorify me."

"Glorify me," that is, "take me to be with Thyself."
The prayer of Jesus is that His Father would be pleased
now to translate Him from this world of sin and sorrow into
the state of glory He left behind when He became man.
Thus He explains His own meaning when He repeats His
request in a more expanded form, as given in the fifth verse :
"And now, O Father, glorify Thou me with Thine own self,
with the glory I had with Thee before the world was," *i.e.*
with the glory He enjoyed in the bosom of the Father before
His incarnation as God's eternal Son.

It is observable that in this prayer for Himself Jesus makes
no allusion to His approaching sufferings. Very shortly
after, in Gethsemane, He prayed : "O my Father, if it be
possible, let this cup pass from me !" But here is no mention of the cup of sorrow, but only of the crown of glory. For
the present heaven is in full view, and its anticipated glories
make Him oblivious of every thing else. Not till He is gone
out into the night do the sulphurous clouds begin to gather
which overshadow the sky and shut out the celestial world
from sight. Yet the coming passion, though not mentioned,
is virtually included in the prayer. Jesus knows that He
must pass through suffering to glory, and that He must
behave Himself worthily under the last trial, in order to
reach the desired goal. Therefore the uttered prayer includes
this unuttered one : "Carry me well through the approaching
struggle ; let me pass through the dark valley to the realms
of light without flinching or fear." [1]

[1] Reuss (*Theologie Chrétienne*, ii. 455) maintains that the Gospel of John knows
nothing of a state of humiliation, and in proof alludes to the fact that in this Gospel

The first reason annexed to the prayer is, "That Thy Son also may glorify Thee." Jesus seeks His own glorification merely as a means to a higher end, the glorification of God the Father. And in so connecting the two glorifyings as means and end, He but repeats to the Father what He had said to His disciples in His farewell address. He had told them that it was good for them that He should go, as not till His departure would any deep impression be made on the world's conscience with respect to Himself and His doctrine. He now tells His Father in effect: "It is good for Thy glory that I leave the earth and go to heaven; for henceforth I can promote Thy glory in the world better there than by a prolonged sojourn here." To enforce the reason, Jesus next declares that what He desires is to glorify the Father in His office as the Saviour of sinners: "As Thou hast given Him power over all flesh, that He should give eternal life to as many as Thou hast given Him." [1] Interpreted in the light of this sentence, the prayer means: "Thou sentest me into the world to save sinners, and hitherto I have been constantly occupied in seeking the lost, and communicating eternal life to such as would receive it. But the time has come when this work can be best carried on by me lifted up. Therefore exalt me to Thy throne, that from thence, as a Prince and a Saviour, I may dispense the blessings of salvation."

It is important to notice how Jesus defines His commis-

Christ's death is represented as a glorification. On this view *vide The Humiliation of Christ*, p. 34, 2d ed. On the theological import of ver. 5, *vide* the same work, p. 359.

[1] John xvii. 2. The R. V. has "Thou gavest." The revisers have carried out their views of the rendering of the aorist too rigidly in this chapter. There can be little doubt that some of the aorists are in effect perfects. We may here quote the following sentences from Buttmann's *Grammar of the New Testament Greek:* "That the aorist may stand for the perfect, has been denied by many grammarians in reference to ordinary Greek usage, and by Winer in reference to the New Testament also, yet with too little qualification. As in so many other instances, the question depends simply upon our connecting the correct idea with the grammatical terminology; that is to say, inasmuch as the relation of time expressed by the perfect is compounded, as it were, of that of the aorist and that of the present, in cases where the aorist is used in the sense of the perfect, we must take this view of the matter, — that the aorist was not intended to express both relations of the perfect at once, but that the writer for the moment withdraws from the present and places himself in the past, consequently in the position of a narrator. This position is uniformly the most natural for the act of composition, and from it there results of itself, if not a positive aversion to the perfect, yet a greater preference for the aorist. The continuance of the action, therefore, and its effect down to the present time, resides, not indeed in the tense, but in the connection; and the necessary insertion of this relation is left in every case to the hearer." — Pp. 197-8, American Edition.

sion as the Saviour.   He represents it at once as concerning
all flesh, and as specially concerning a select class, thus
ascribing to His work a general and a particular reference,
in accordance with the teaching of the whole New Testament, which sets forth Christ at one time as the Saviour of
all men, at another as the Saviour of His people, of the elect,
of His sheep, of those who believe.   This style of speaking
concerning the redeeming work of our Saviour it is our duty
and our privilege to imitate, avoiding extremes, both that of
denying or ignoring the universal aspects of Christ's mission,
and that of maintaining that He is in the same sense the
Saviour of all, or that He will and must eventually save all.
Both extremes are excluded by the carefully selected words
of Jesus in His intercessory prayer.   On the one hand, He
speaks of all flesh as belonging to His jurisdiction as the
Saviour of humanity at large as the mass into which the
leaven is to be deposited, with a view to leavening the whole
lump.   On the other hand, there is an obvious restriction on
the universality of the first clause in the terms of the second.
The advocates of universal restoration have no support for
their tenet here.   They may indeed ask : If Jesus has power
over all flesh, is it credible that He will not use it to the
uttermost ?   In reply, we shall not seek to evade the question, by resolving the power claimed into a mere mediatorial
sovereignty over the whole solely for the sake of a part,
because we know that the elect part is chosen not *merely* for
its own sake, but also for the sake of the whole, to be the
salt of the earth, the light of the world, and the leaven to
leaven the corrupt mass.[1]   We simply observe that the power
of the Saviour is not compulsory.   Men are not saved by
force as machines, but by love and grace as free beings ; and
there are many whom brooding love would gather under its
wings who prefer remaining outside to their own destruction.
     The essence of eternal life is defined in the next sentence
of the prayer, and represented as consisting in the knowledge of the only true God, and of Jesus Christ His messenger, knowledge been taken comprehensively as including
faith, love, and worship, and the emphasis lying on the *objects*

---

[1] On this see Martensen, *Die Christliche Dogmatik*, § 215 (translated in Foreign
Theological Library).

of such knowledge. The Christian religion is here described in opposition to paganism on the one hand, with its many gods, and to Judaism on the other, which, believing in the one true God, rejected the claims of Jesus to be the Christ. It is further so described as to exclude by anticipation Arian and Socinian views of the person of Christ. The names of God and of Jesus are put on a level as objects of religious regard, whereby an importance is assigned to the latter incompatible with the dogma that Jesus is a mere man. For eternal life cannot depend on knowing any man, however wise and good : the utmost that can be said of the benefit derivable from such knowledge is that it is helpful towards knowing God better, which can be affirmed not only of Jesus, but of Moses, Paul, John, and all the apostles.

It may seem strange that, in addressing His Father, Jesus should deem it needful to explain wherein eternal life consists ; and some, to get rid of the difficulty, have supposed that the sentence is an explanatory reflection interwoven into the prayer by the evangelist. Yet the words were perfectly appropriate in the mouth of Jesus Himself. The first clause is a confession by the man Jesus of His own faith in God His Father as the supreme object of knowledge ; and the whole sentence is really an argument in support of the prayer, Glorify Thy Son. The force of the declaration lies in what it implies respecting the existing ignorance of men concerning the Father and His Son. It is as if Jesus said : Father, Thou knowest that eternal life consists in knowing Thee and me. Look around, then, and see how few possess such knowledge. The heathen world knoweth Thee not — it worships idols : the Jewish world is equally ignorant of Thee in spirit and in truth ; for, while boasting of knowing Thee, it rejects me. The whole world is overspread with a dark veil of ignorance and superstition. Take me out of it, therefore, not because I am weary of its sin and darkness, but that I may become to it a sun. Hitherto my efforts to illuminate the darkness have met with small success. Grant me a position from which I can send forth light over all the earth.

But why does the Saviour here alone, in the whole Gospel history, call Himself *Jesus Christ ?* Some see in this compound name, common in the apostolic age, another proof that this verse is an interpolation. Again, however, without reason, for the style in which Jesus designates Himself exactly suits the object He has in view. He is pleading with the Father to take Him to glory, that He may the more effectually propagate the true religion. What more appropriate in this connection than to speak of Himself objectively under the name by which He should be known among the professors of the true religion?

The second reason pleaded by Jesus in support of His prayer, is that His appointed service has been faithfully accomplished, and now claims its guerdon: "I have glorified Thee on the earth: I have finished the work which Thou gavest me to do. Now, therefore, glorify Thou me." [1] The great Servant of God speaks here not only with reference to the past, but by anticipation with reference to His passion already endured in purpose; so that the "I have finished" of the prayer is equivalent in meaning to the "It is finished" spoken from the cross. And what He says concerning Himself is true; the declaration, though one which no other human being could make without abatement, is on His part no exaggerated, boastful piece of self-laudation, but the sober, humble utterance of a conscience void of offence towards God and towards men. Nor can we say that the statement, though true, was ultroneous and uncalled for. It was necessary that Jesus should be able to make that declaration; and though the fact declared was well known to God, it was desirable to proclaim in the hearing of the eleven, and unto the whole Church through their record, the grounds on which His claim to be rewarded with glory rested, for the strengthening of faith. For as our faith and hope towards God are based on the fact that Jesus Christ was able to make the declaration in question, so they are confirmed by the actual making of it, His protestation that He has kept His covenant of work being to us, as it were, a seal of the covenant of grace, serving the same end as the sacrament of the Supper.

Having offered this brief petition for Himself, Jesus proceeded to pray for His disciples at much greater length, all that follows having reference to them mainly, and from the

[1] John xvii. 4

sixth to the twentieth verse referring to them exclusively. The transition is made by a special declaration, applying the general one of the preceding sentence to that part of Christ's personal work which consisted in the training of these men: "I have manifested Thy name unto the men whom Thou gavest me out of the world."[1] After this introductory statement follows a short description of the persons about to be prayed for. Jesus gives His disciples a good character. First, scrupulously careful not to exaggerate the importance of the service He has rendered in training them for the apostolate, He acknowledges that they were good when He got them: "Thine they were, and Thou gavest them me:" they were pious, devout men, God-taught, God-drawn, God-given. Then He testifies that since they had been with Him they had sustained the character they had when they joined His company: "They have kept Thy word." And finally, He bears witness that the men whom His Father had given Him had been true believers in Himself, and had received all His words as the very truth of God, and Himself as one sent forth into the world by God.[2] Here, surely, is a generous eulogy on disciples, who, while sincere and devoted to their Master, were, as we know, exceedingly faulty in conduct, and slow to learn.

Having thus generously praised His humble companions, Jesus intimates His intention to pray for them: "I pray for them." But the prayer comes not just yet; for some prefatory words must be premised, to give the prayer more emphasis when it does come. First, the persons prayed for are singled out as for the moment the sole objects of a concentrated solicitude. "I pray for them: I pray not for the world."[3] The design of Jesus in making this statement is not, of course, to intimate the absolute exclusion of the world from His sympathies. Not exclusion, but *concentration in order to eventual inclusion*, is His purpose here. He would have His Father fix His special regards on this small band of men, with whom the fortunes of Christianity are bound up. He prays for them as a mother dying might pray exclusively for her children, — not that she is indifferent to the interest of all beyond, but that her family, in her solemn situa-

---

[1] Ver. 6.   [2] Vers. 7, 8, cf. Luke xxii. 28, 29.   [3] Ver. 9.

tion, is for her the natural legitimate object of an absorbing, all-engrossing solicitude. He prays for them as the precious fruit of His life-labor, the hope of the future, the founders of the Church, the Noah's ark of the Christian faith, the missionaries of the truth to the whole world ; for them *alone*, *but* for the world's sake, — it being the best thing He can do for the world meantime to commend them to the Father's care.

What Jesus means to ask for the men thus singled out, we can now guess for ourselves. It is that His Father would keep them, now that He is about to leave them. But before the request come two reasons why it should be granted. The first is expressed in these terms : " They are Thine : and all mine are Thine, and Thine are mine ; and I am glorified in them ;" [1] — and means in effect this : " It is Thy business, Thy interest, to keep these men. They are Thine ; Thou gavest them me : keep Thine own. Although since they became my disciples they have been mine, that makes no difference : they are still Thine ; for between me and Thee is no distinction of *meum* and *tuum*. Then I am glorified in them : my cause, my name, my doctrine, are to be henceforth identified with them ; and if they miscarry, my interest will be shipwrecked. Therefore, as Thou valuest the honor of Thy Son, keep these men." The other reason why the request about to be proffered should be granted is : " And now I am no more in the world." [2] The Master, about to depart from the earth, commends to His Father's care those whom He is leaving behind without a head.

And now at length comes the prayer for the eleven, ushered in with due solemnity by a new emphatic address to the Hearer of prayer : " Holy Father, keep in Thine own name those whom Thou hast given me, that they may be one, as we are." [3] The epithet " holy " suits the purport of the prayer, which is that the disciples may be kept pure in faith and practice, separate from all existing error and sin, that they may be eventually a salt to the corrupt world in which their Lord is about to leave them. The prayer itself embraces two particulars. The first is that the disciples may be kept *in* the name of the Father, which Jesus has manifested to

[1] Ver. 10.   [2] Ver. 11.   [3] Ver. 11.

them ; that is, that they may continue to believe what He had taught them of God, and so become His instruments for diffusing the knowledge of the true God and the true religion throughout the earth. The second is, that they may be one, that is, that they may be kept in love to each other, as well as in the faith of the divine name ; separate from the world, but not divided among themselves.[1] These two things, truth and love, Jesus asks for His own, as of vital moment : truth as the badge of distinction between His Church and the world ; love as the bond which unites believers of the truth into a holy brotherhood of witness-bearers to the truth. These two things the Church should ever keep in view as of co-ordinate importance : not sacrificing love to truth, dividing those who should be one by insisting on too minute and detailed a testimony ; nor sacrificing truth to love, making the Church a very broad, comprehensive society, but a society without a vocation or *raison d'être*, having no truth to guard and teach, or testimony to bear.

Having commended His disciples to His Father's care, Jesus next gives an account of His own stewardship as their Master, and protests that He has faithfully kept them in divine truth.[2] He claims to have done His duty by them all, not even excepting Judas, in whose case He admits failure, but at the same time clears Himself of blame. The reference to the false disciple shows how conscientious He is in rendering His account. He feels, as it were, put on His defence with reference to the apostate ; and supposing Himself to be asked the question, What have you to say about this man ? He replies in effect : " I admit I have not been able to keep him from falling, but I have done all I could. The son of perdition is not lost through my fault." [3] We know how well entitled Jesus was to make this protestation.

In the next part of the prayer [4] Jesus defines the sense in which He asks that His disciples may be kept, and in doing this virtually offers new reasons why the petition should be heard. He commends them to His Father's care as the depositaries of truth, worth keeping on that account, and needing to be kept, because of the world's dislike of the truth.[5] And He explains that by keeping He means not

[1] Ver. 11.   [2] Ver. 12.   [3] Ver. 12.   [4] Vers. 14-20.   [5] Ver. 14.

translation out of the world, but preservation in the world from its moral evil, their presence there as a salt being necessary, and their purity not less needful, that the salt might not be without savor and virtue. This explanation He meant not for the ear of His Father alone, but also for the ears of His disciples. He wished them to understand that two things were equally to be shunned, — conformity to the world, and weariness of the world. They must abide in the truth, and they must abide in the world for the truth's sake ; mindful, for their consolation, that when they felt the world's hatred most, they were doing most good, and that the weight of their cross was the measure of their influence.

The keeping asked by Jesus for His own is but the continuance and perfecting of an existing moral condition. He needs not to ask His Father now for the first time to separate His disciples in spirit and character from the world. That they are already ; that they were when first they joined His society ; that they have continued to be. This, in justice to them, their Master is careful to state twice over in this portion of His prayer. "They," He testifies, "are not of the world, even as I am not of the world,"[1] putting them on a level with Himself with characteristic magnanimity, and not without truth ; for the persons thus described, though in many respects defective, were very unworldly, caring nothing for the world's trinity, — riches, honors, and pleasures, — but only for the words of eternal life.

Yet, notwithstanding their sincerity, the eleven still needed not only keeping, but *perfecting ;* and therefore their Master went on to pray for their sanctification in the truth, having in view not only their perseverance, growth, and maturity in grace as private Christians, but more especially their spiritual equipment for the office of the apostleship. Hence He goes on in the next breath to make mention of their apostolic vocation, showing that that is principally in His eye : "As Thou hast sent me into the world, even so have I also sent them into the world."[2] That they may be fitted for their mission is His intense desire. Hence He proceeds to speak of His own sanctification as a means towards their apostolic sanctification as the end, as if His own ministry were merely

---

[1] John xvii. 14, 16.　　　　[2] Ver. 18.

subordinate to theirs. For their sakes I sanctify myself, that they also might be sanctified through the truth." [1] Remarkable words, whose meaning is obscure, and has been much debated, but in which we may at least with confidence discover a singular display of condescension and love. Jesus speaks here like a parent who lives for the sake of His children, having a regard to their moral training in all His personal habits, denying Himself pleasures for their benefit, and making it His chief end and care to form their characters, perfect their education, and fit them for the duties of the position which they are destined to fill.

The remainder of the prayer (with exception of the two closing sentences) [2] respects the Church at large, — those who should believe in Christ through the word of the apostles, heard from their lips, or reported in their writings. What Jesus desires for the body of believers is partly left to be inferred; for when He says, "I pray not for these *alone*," He intimates that He desires for the parties next to be prayed for the same things He has already asked for his disciples: preservation in the truth, and from the evil in the world, and sanctification by the truth. The one blessing He expressly asks for the Church is "unity." His heart's desire for believers in Him is "that they all may be one." His ideal of the Church's unity is very high, its divine exemplar being the unity subsisting between the persons in the Godhead, and specially between the Father and the Son, and its ground the same divine unity: "one *as* we are one, and *in* us who are one," bound together as closely and harmoniously by the common name into which they are baptized, and by which they are called. [3]

This unity, desirable for its own sake, Jesus specially desiderates, because of the moral power which it will confer on the Church as an institute for propagating the Christian faith: "That the world may believe that Thou hast sent me." [4] Now this end is one which cannot be promoted unless the unity of believers be in some way made manifest. A unity which is not apparent can have no effect on the world, but must needs be as a candle under a bushel, which gives no light, nay, ceases to be a light, and goes out. There

[1] Ver. 19.   [2] Vers. 20-24.   [3] Ver. 21.   [4] Vers. 21, 23.

can be no doubt, therefore, that our Lord had a visible unity in view ; and the only question is how that is to be reached. The first and most obvious way is by union in one church organization, with appointed means for representing the whole body, and expressing its united mind ; such, *e.g.*, as the œcumenical councils of the early centuries. This, the most complete manifestation of unity, was exhibited in the primitive Church.

In our day incorporating union on a great scale [1] is not possible, and other methods of expressing the feeling of catholicity must be resorted to. One method that might be tried is that of confederation, whereby independent church organizations might be united after the fashion of the United States of America, or of the Greek republics, which found a centre of unity in the legislative and judicial assembly called the Amphictyonic Council. But whatever may be thought of that, one thing is certain, that the unity of believers in Christ must be made more manifest as an undeniable fact somehow, if the Church is to realize her vocation as a holy nation called out of darkness to show forth the virtues of Him whose name she bears, and win for Him the world's homage and faith. It is true, indeed, that the unity of the Church does find expression in its creed ; by which we mean not the sectional creed of this or that denomination, but the creed within the creeds, expressive of the *catholic* orthodoxy of Christendom, and embracing the fundamentals, and only the fundamentals, of the Christian faith. There is a Church within all the churches to which this creed is the thing of value, all else being, in the esteem of its members, but the husk containing the precious kernel. But the existence of that Church is a fact known by faith, not by sight : its influence is little felt by the world ; and however thankful we may be for the presence in the midst of ecclesiastical organizations of this holy commonwealth, we cannot accept it as the realization of the ideal which the Saviour had in His mind when He uttered the words, " That they all may be one."

[1] This remark is meant to apply to the whole visible Church, divided not only by diversity of opinion on doctrines of cardinal importance, but by incompatible forms of church government. Local and partial incorporating unions of bodies really allied in doctrine and government, are not only practicable, but obligatory.

In the next two sentences [1] Jesus fondly lingers over this prayer, repeating, expanding, enforcing the petition in language too deep for our fathoming line, but which plainly conveys the truth that without unity the Church can neither glorify Christ, commend Christianity as divine, nor have the glory of Christ abiding on herself. And this is a truth which, on reflection, approves itself to reason. Wrangling is not a divine thing, and it needs no divine influence to bring it about. Anybody can quarrel; and the world, knowing that, has little respect for a quarrelling Church. But the world opens its eyes in wonder at a community in which peace and concord prevail, saying, Here is something out of the common course, — selfishness and self-will rooted out of human nature: nothing but a divine influence could thus subdue the centrifugal forces which tend to separate men from each other.

The endearing name Father, with which the next sentence begins, marks the commencement of a new final paragraph in the prayer of the great High Priest.[2] Jesus at this point casts a glance forward to the end of things, and prays for the final consummation of God's purpose with regard to the Church: that the Church militant may become the Church triumphant; that the body of saints, imperfectly sanctified on earth, may become perfectly sanctified and glorified in heaven, with Himself where He will be, beholding His glory, and changed into the same image by the Spirit of God.

Then comes the conclusion, in which Jesus returns from the distant future to the present, and gathers in His thoughts from the Church at large to the company assembled in the supper-chamber, Himself and His disciples.[3] These two closing sentences serve the same use in Christ's prayer that the phrase "for Christ's sake" serves in ours. They contain two pleas, — the service of the parties prayed for, and the righteousness of the Being prayed to, — the last coming first, embodied in the title, "O righteous Father." The services, merits, and claims of Jesus and His disciples are specifically mentioned as matters to which the righteous Father will doubtless attach the due weight. The world's ignorance of God is alluded to, to enhance the value of the acknowledg-

[1] John xvii. 22, 23.   [2] Ver. 24.   [3] Vers. 25, 26.

ment which He has received from His Son and His Son's
companions. That ignorance explains why Jesus deems it
necessary to say, "I have known Thee." Even *His* knowledge was not a thing of course in such a world. It was an
effort for the man Jesus to retain God in His knowledge,
quite as much as to keep Himself unspotted from the world's
corruptions. It was as hard for Him to know and confess
God as Father in a world that in a thousand ways practically denied that Fatherhood, as to live a life of love amid
manifold temptations to self-seeking. In truth, the two
problems were one. To be light in the midst of darkness,
love in the midst of selfishness, holiness in the midst of
depravity, are in effect the same thing.

While pleading His own merit, Jesus forgets not the claims
of His disciples. Of them He says in effect : They have
known Thee at second-hand through me, as I have known
Thee at first-hand by direct intuition.[1] Not content with
this statement, He expatiates on the importance of these
men as objects of divine care, representing that they are
worth keeping, as already possessing the knowledge of God's
name, and destined ere long to know it yet more perfectly, so
that they shall be able to make it known as an object of
homage to others, and God shall be able to love them even
as He loved His own Son, when He was in the world faithfully serving His heavenly Father. "And I have declared
unto them Thy name, and will declare it ; that the love
wherewith Thou hast loved me may be in them, and I in
them."[2] Wonderful words to be uttered concerning mere
earthen vessels !

<hr>

[1] John xvii. 25.   [2] Ver. 26.

APPENDIX TO CHAPTERS 24–26

We append here an analysis of the farewell discourse and accompanying prayer.

PART I — John xiii. 31–xiv. 31

> Div. I — Words of comfort to disciples as *children*, ten (or at most thirteen) sentences in all : —
>> 1. *First* word, xiii. 34, 35: Love one another in my absence.
>> 2. *Second* word, xiv. 1–4: Have faith in God and in me.   I will be looking after your interest while absent, and will come for you.
>> 3. *Third* word, xiv. 15–18: Even while away I will be with you *per* the Holy Spirit (19–21, enlargement).
>
> Div. II — Children's questions with the answers : —
>> 1. Peter's question, xiii. 36–38 : Whither goest Thou ?
>> 2. Thomas's question, xiv. 5–7 : How can we know the way ?
>> 3. Philip's request, xiv. 8–14 : Show us the Father.
>> 4. Judas's question, xiv. 22–24 : How canst Thou appear to us and not to the world ?

PART II — John xv., xvi. : Dying charge to the future *apostles* (style changed).

> 1. Allegory of the Vine, xv. 1–16 : The apostles Christ's means of working in the world.   They work through His life dwelling in them.
> 2. Apostolic tribulations and encouragements, xv. 18–27, xvi. 1–15 : The world will hate, but the Spirit will convince the world, and enlighten them.
> 3. The little while, and end of discourse, xvi. 16–33 : Paradox of seeing and not seeing = physical absence, but spiritual presence.   Adieu.

PART III — John xvii. : Intercessory prayer.

> 1. Prays for Himself, vers. 1 ·5.
> 2. Prays for disciples, vers. 6–19.
> 3. Prays for Church, vers. 20–23.
> 4. Conclusion of prayer, vers. 24–26.

27

THE SHEEP SCATTERED

Section I — "All the Disciples forsook Him, and fled."

Matt. 26:36-41; 55, 56, 69-75; John 18:15-18

From the supper-chamber, in which we have lingered so long, we pass into the outside world, to witness the behavior of the eleven in the great final crisis. The passages cited describe the part they played in the solemn scenes connected with their Master's end. That part was a sadly unheroic one. Faith, love, principle, all gave way before the instincts of fear, shame, and self-preservation. The best of the disciples — the three who, as most reliable, were selected by Jesus to keep Him company in the garden of Gethsemane — utterly failed to render the service expected of them. While their Lord was passing through His agony, they fell asleep, as they had done before on the Mount of Transfiguration. Even the picked men thus proved themselves to be raw recruits, unable to shake off drowsiness while they did duty as sentinels. "What! could ye not watch with me one hour?" Then, when the enemy appeared, both these three and the other eight ran away panic-stricken. "All the disciples forsook Him, and fled." And finally, that one of their number who thought himself bolder than his brethren, not only forsook, but denied his beloved Master, declaring with an oath, "I know not the man."

The conduct of the disciples at this crisis in their history, so weak and so unmanly, naturally gives rise to two questions: How should they have acted? and why did they act as they did — what were the causes of their failure?

Now, to take up the former of these questions first, when we try to form to ourselves a distinct idea of the course of action demanded by fidelity, it is not at once quite apparent wherein the disciples, Peter of course excepted, were at fault. What could they do when their Lord was apprehended, but run away? Offer resistance? Jesus had positively forbidden that just immediately before. On the appearance of the band of armed men, "when they which were about Him saw what would follow, they said unto Him, Lord, shall we smite with the sword?"[1] Without waiting for a reply, one of them smote the servant of the high priest, and cut off his right ear. The fighting disciple, John informs us, was Simon Peter. He had brought a sword with him, one of two in the posssession of the company, from the supper-chamber to Gethsemane, thinking it might be needed, and fully minded to use it if there was occasion; and, coward as he proved himself afterwards among the serving-men and maids, he was no such arrant coward in the garden. He used his weapon boldly if not skilfully, and did some execution, though happily not of a deadly character. Thereupon Jesus interposed to prevent further bloodshed, uttering words variously reported, but in all the different versions clearly inculcating a policy of non-resistance. "Put up again thy sword into his place," He said to Peter, adding as His reason, "for all they that take the sword shall perish with the sword;" which was as much as to say, "In this kind of warfare we must necessarily have the worst of it." Then He went on to hint at higher reasons for non-resistance than mere considerations of prudence or expediency. "Thinkest thou," He asked the warlike disciple, "that I cannot now pray to my Father, and He shall presently give me more than twelve legions of angels? But how then shall the Scriptures be fulfilled, that thus it must be?"[2] He could meet human force by superior, divine, celestial force if He chose, but He did not choose; for to overpower His enemies would be to defeat His own purpose in coming to the world, which was to conquer, not by physical force, but by truth and love and godlike patience; by drinking the cup which His Father had put into His hands, bitter though it was to flesh and blood.[3]

Quite in harmony with these utterances in Gethsemane are the statements made by Jesus on the same subject ere

[1] Luke xxii. 49.   [2] Matt. xxvi. 52–54.   [3] John xviii. 11.

He left the supper-room, as recorded by Luke.[1]   In the letter, indeed, these statements seem to point at a policy the very opposite of non-resistance.   Jesus seems to say that the great business and duty of the hour, for all who are on His side, is to furnish themselves with swords : so urgent is the need, that he who wants a weapon must sell his garment to buy one.   But the very emphasis with which He speaks shows that His words are not to be taken in the literal prosaic sense.   It is very easy to see what He means.   His object is by graphic language to convey to His disciples an idea of the gravity of the situation.   " Now," He would say, " now is the day, yea, the hour of battle : if my kingdom be one of this world, as ye have imagined, now is the time for fighting, not for dreaming ; now matters have come to extremities, and ye have need of all your resources : equip yourselves with shoes and purse and knapsack, and above all, with swords and warlike courage."

The disciples did not understand their Lord's meaning. They put a stupid, prosaic interpretation upon this part, as upon so many other parts, of His farewell discourse.   So, with ridiculous seriousness, they said : " Lord, behold, here are two swords."   The foolish remark provoked a reply which should surely have opened their eyes, and kept Peter from carrying the matter so far as to take one of the swords with him.   " It is enough," said Jesus, probably with a melancholy smile on His face, as He thought of the stupid simplicity of those dear childish and childlike men : " It is enough."   Two swords : well, they are enough only for one who does not mean to fight at all.   What were two swords for twelve men, and against a hundred weapons of offence ?   The very idea of fighting in the circumstances was preposterous : it had only to be broadly stated to appear an absurdity.

The disciples, then, were not called on to fight for their Master, that He might not be delivered to the Jews.   What else, then, should they have done ?   Was it their duty to suffer with Him, and, carrying out the professions of Peter, to go with Him to prison and to death ?   This was not required of them either.   When Jesus surrendered Himself into the hands of His captors, He proffered the request that, while

[1] Luke xxii. 35–38.

taking Him into custody, they should let His followers go their way.[1] This He did not merely out of compassion for them, but as the Captain of salvation making the best terms for Himself and for the interests of His kingdom ; for it was not less necessary to these that the disciples should live than that He Himself should die. He gave Himself up to death, that there might be a gospel to preach ; He desired the safety of His disciples, that there might be men to preach it. Manifestly, therefore, it was not the duty of the disciples to expose themselves to danger : their duty lay rather, one would say, in the direction of taking care of their life for future usefulness.

Where, then, if not in failing to fight for or suffer with their Lord, did the fault of the eleven lie ? It lay in their lack of faith. " Believe in God, and believe in me," Jesus had said to them at the commencement of His farewell address, and at the critical hour they did neither. They did not believe that all would yet end well both with them and their Master, and especially that God would provide for *their* safety without any sacrifice of principle, or even of dignity, on their part. They put confidence only in the swiftness of their feet. Had they possessed faith in God and in Jesus, they would have witnessed their Lord's apprehension without dismay, assured both of His return and of their own safety ; and, as feeling might incline, would either have followed the officers of justice to see what happened, or, averse to exciting and painful scenes, would have retired quietly to their dwellings until the tragedy was finished. But wanting faith, they neither calmly followed nor calmly retired ; but faithlessly and ignominiously forsook their Lord, and *fled*. The sin lay not so much in the outward act, but in the inward state of mind of which it was the index. They fled in unbelief and despair, as men whose hope was blasted, from a man whose cause was lost, and whom God had abandoned to His enemies.

Having ascertained wherein the disciples were at fault, we have now to inquire into the causes of their misconduct ; and here, at the outset, we recall to mind that Jesus anticipated the breakdown of His followers. He did not count

---

[1] John xviii. 8.

on their fidelity, but expected desertion as a matter of course. When Peter offered to follow Him wheresoever He might go, He told him that ere cock-crowing next morning he would deny Him thrice. At the close of the farewell address He told all the disciples that they would leave Him alone. On the way to the Mount of Olives He repeated the statement in these terms: "All ye shall be offended because of me this night; for it is written, I will smite the Shepherd, and the sheep of the flock shall be scattered abroad."[1]   And on all these occasions the tone in which He spoke was rather prophetic than reproachful.   He expected His disciples to be panic-stricken, just as one should expect sheep to flee on the appearance of a wolf, or women to faint in presence of a scene of carnage.   From this leniency we should infer that, in the view of Jesus, the sin of the disciples was one of infirmity; and that this was the view which He took thereof, we *know* from the words He addressed to the three drowsy brethren in Gethsemane.   "Watch and pray," He said to them, "that ye enter not into temptation: the spirit indeed is willing, but the flesh is weak."[2]   The kind judgment thus expressed, though pronounced with special reference to the shortcoming of Peter, James, and John in the garden, manifestly applies to the whole conduct of all the disciples (not even excepting Peter's denial) throughout the terrible crisis.   Jesus regarded the eleven as men whose attachment to Himself was above suspicion, but who were liable to fall, through the weakness of their flesh, on being exposed to sudden temptation.

But what are we to understand by the weakness of the flesh?   Mere instinctive love of life, dread of danger, fear of man?   No; for these instincts continued with the apostles through life, without leading, except in one instance, to a repetition of their present misconduct.   Not only the flesh of the disciples, but even the willing spirit, was weak. Their spiritual character at this season was deficient in certain elements which give steadiness to the good impulses of the heart, and mastery over the infirmities of sentient nature. The missing elements of strength were: *forethought, clear perceptions of truth, self-knowledge, and the discipline of experience.*

[1] Matt. xxvi. 31.   [2] Ver. 41.

For want of forethought it came to pass that the apprehension of their Lord took the eleven by surprise. This may seem hardly credible, after the frequent intimations Christ had given them of His approaching death ; after the institution of the Supper, the farewell address, the reference to the traitor, the prophetic announcement concerning their own frailty, and the discourse about the sword, which was like a trumpet-peal calling to battle. Yet there can be no doubt that such was the fact. The eleven went out to Gethsemane without any definite idea of what was coming. These raw recruits actually did not know that they were on the march to the battle-field. The sleep of the three disciples in the garden is sufficient proof of this. Had the three sentinels been thoroughly impressed with the belief that the enemy was at hand, weary and sad though they were, they would not have fallen asleep. Fear would have kept them awake. "Know this, that if the goodman of the house had known in what watch the thief would come, he would have watched, and would not have suffered his house to be broken up."

The breakdown of the disciples at the final crisis was due in part also to the want of clear perceptions of truth. They did not understand the doctrine concerning Christ. They believed their Master to be the Christ, the Son of the living God ; but their faith was twined around a false theory of Messiah's mission and career. In that theory the cross had no place. So long as the cross was only spoken about, their theory remained firmly rooted in their minds, and the words of their Master were speedily forgotten. But when the cross at length actually came, when the things which Jesus had foretold began to be fulfilled, then their theory went down like a tree suddenly smitten by a whirlwind, carrying the woodbine plant of their faith along with it. From the moment that Jesus was apprehended, all that remained of faith in their minds was simply a regret that they had been mistaken : "We trusted that it had been He who should have redeemed Israel." How could any one act heroically in such circumstances ?

A third radical defect in the character of the disciples was self-ignorance. One who knows his weakness may become strong even at the weak point ; but he who knows not his

weak points cannot be strong at any point.   Now the followers of Jesus did not know their weakness.   They credited
themselves with an amount of fidelity and valor which existed
only in their imagination, all adopting as their own the sentiment of Peter: "Though I should die with Thee, yet will I
not deny Thee." [1]   Alas! they did not know how much fear
of man was in them, how much abject cowardice in presence
of danger.   Of course, when danger actually appeared, the
usual consequence of self-conscious valor followed.   All these
stout-hearted disciples forsook their Master, and fled.

The last, and not the least, cause of weakness in the disciples was their inexperience of such scenes as they were
now to pass through.   Experience of war is one great cause
of the coolness and courage of veteran soldiers in the midst
of danger.   Practical acquaintance with the perils of military
life makes them callous and fearless.   But Christ's disciples
were not yet veterans.   They were now but entering into
their first engagement.   Hitherto they had experienced only
such trials as befall even the rawest recruits.   They had been
called on to leave home, friends, fishing-boats, and their
earthly all, to follow Jesus.   But these initial hardships do
not make a soldier; no, nor even the discipline of the drill-
sergeant, nor the donning of a uniform.   For behold the
green soft youth with his bright uniform brought face to face
with the stern reality of battle.   His knees smite each other,
his heart sickens, perchance he faints outright, and is carried
to the rear, unable to take any part in the fight.   Poor lad,
pity him, do not scorn him; he may turn out a brave soldier
yet.   Even Frederick the Great ran away from his first
battle.   The bravest of soldiers probably do not feel very
heroic the first time they are under fire.

These observations help us to understand how it came to
pass that the little flock was scattered when Jesus their shepherd was smitten.   The explanation amounts in substance to
a proof that the disciples were sheep, not yet fit to be shepherds of men.   That being so, we do not wonder at the
leniency of Jesus, to which reference has already been made.
No one expects sheep to do any thing else than flee when
the wolf cometh.   Only in shepherds is craven fear severely

---

[1] Matt. xxvi. 35.

reprehensible. Bearing this in mind, we shall more readily forgive Peter for denying his Lord in an unguarded moment, than for his cowardice at Antioch some years after, when he gave the cold shoulder to his Gentile brethren, through fear of the Jewish sectaries from Jerusalem. Peter was a shepherd then, and it was his duty to lead the sheep, or even to carry them against their inclination into the wide green pastures of Christian liberty, instead of tamely following those who, by their scrupulosity, showed themselves to be but lambs in Christ's flock. His actual behavior was very culpable and very mischievous. For though in reality not leading, but led, he, as an apostle, enjoyed the reputation and influence of a chief shepherd, and therefore had no option but either to lead or to mislead; and he did mislead, to such an extent that even Barnabas was carried away by his dissimulation. It is a serious thing for the Church when those who are shepherds in office and influence are sheep in opinion and heart; leaders in name, led in fact.

Section II — Sifted as Wheat

Luke xxii. 31, 32

This fragment of the conversation at the supper-table is important, as showing us the view taken by Jesus of the crisis through which His disciples were about to pass. In form an address to Peter, it is really a word in season to all, and concerning all. This is evident from the use of the plural pronoun in addressing the disciple directly spoken to. "Satan," says Jesus, "hath desired to have (not thee, but) you:" thee, Simon, and also all thy brethren along with thee. The same thing appears from the injunction laid on Peter to turn his fall to account for the benefit of his *brethren*. The brethren, of course, are not the other disciples then present alone, but all who should believe as well. The apostles, however, are not to be excluded from the brotherhood who were to be benefited by Peter's experience; on the contrary, they are probably the parties principally and in the first place intended.

Looking, then, at this utterance as expressive of the judgment of Jesus on the character of the ensuing crisis in the history of the future apostles, we find in it three noticeable particulars.

1. First, Jesus regards the crisis as a *sifting*-time for the disciples. Satan, the accuser of the brethren, sceptical of their fidelity and integrity, as of Job's and of all good men's, was to sift them as wheat, hopeful that they would turn out mere chaff, and become apostates like Judas, or at least that they would make a miserable and scandalous breakdown. In this respect this final crisis was like the one at Capernaum a year before. That also was a sifting-time for Christ's discipleship. Chaff and wheat were then, too, separated, the chaff proving to be out of all proportion to the wheat, for " *many* went back, and walked no more with Him."

But alongside of this general resemblance between the two crises, — the minor and the major we may call them, — an important difference is to be observed. In the minor crisis, the chosen few were the pure wheat, the fickle multitude being the chaff ; in the major, they are both wheat and chaff in one, and the sifting is not between man and man, but between the good and the bad, the precious and the vile, in the same man. The hearts of the eleven faithful ones are to be searched, and all their latent weakness discovered : the old man is to be divided asunder from the new ; the vain, self-confident, self-willed, impetuous Simon son of Jonas, from the devoted, chivalrous, heroic, rock-like Peter.

This distinction between the two crises implies that the later was of a more searching character than the earlier ; and that it was so indeed, is obvious on a moment's reflection. Consider only how different the situation of the disciples in the two cases ! In the minor crisis, the multitude go, but Jesus remains ; in the major, Jesus Himself is taken from them, and they are left as sheep without a shepherd. A mighty difference truly, sufficiently explaining the difference in the conduct of the same men on the two occasions. It was no doubt very disappointing and disheartening to see the mass of people who had lately followed their Master with enthusiasm, dispersing like an idle mob after seeing a show. But while the Master remained, they would not break their hearts about the defection of spurious disciples. They loved Jesus for His own sake, not for His popularity or for any other by-end. He was their teacher, and could give them the bread of eternal truth, which, and not the bread that perisheth, was what they were in quest of: He was their Head, their Father, their Elder Brother, their spiritual Husband, and they would cling to Him through all fortunes, with filial, brotherly, wifely fidelity, He being more to them than the whole world outside. If their prospects looked dark even with Him, where could they go to be any better? They had no choice but to remain where they were.

Remain accordingly they did, faithfully, manfully; kept steadfast by sincerity, a clear perception of the alternatives, and ardent love to their Lord. But now, alas! when it is not the multitude, but Jesus Himself, that leaves them, — not forsaking them, indeed, but torn from them by the strong hand of worldly power, — what are they to do? Now they may well ask Peter's question, "To whom shall we go?" despairing of an answer. He whose presence was their solace at a trying, discouraging season, who at the worst, even when His doctrine was mysterious and His conduct incomprehensible, was more to them than all else in the world at its best; even He is reft from their side, and now they are utterly forlorn, without a master, a champion, a guide, a friend, a father. Worse still, in losing Him they lose not merely their best friend, but their faith. They could believe Jesus to be the Christ, although the multitude apostatized; for they could regard such apostasy as the effect of ignorance, shallowness, insincerity. But how can they believe in the Messiahship of one who is led away to prison in place of a throne; and instead of being crowned a king, is on His way to be executed as a felon? Bereft of Jesus in this fashion, they are bereft of their Christ as well. The unbelieving world asks them, "Where is thy God?" and they can make no reply.

"Christ and we against the world;" "Christ in the world's power, and we left alone:" such, in brief, was the difference between the two sifting seasons. The results of the sifting process were correspondingly diverse. In the one case, it separated between the sincere and the insincere; in the other, it discovered weakness even in the sincere. The men who on the earlier occasion stood resolutely to their colors, on the later fled panic-stricken, consulting for their safety without dignity, and, in one case at least, with shameful disregard of truth. Behold how weak even good men are without faith! With faith, however crude or ill-informed, you may overcome the whole world; without the faith that places God consciously at your side, you have no chance. Satan will get possession of you and sift you, and cause you to equivocate with Abraham, feign madness with David, dissemble and swear falsely or profanely with Peter. No one can tell how far you may fall if you lose faith in God. The just live justly, nobly, only by their faith.

2. Jesus regards the crisis through which His disciples are to pass as one which, though perilous, shall not prove deadly to their faith. His hope is that though they fall, they shall not fall away; though the sun of faith be eclipsed, it shall not be extinguished. He has this hope even in regard to Peter, having taken care to avert so disastrous a catastrophe. "I have prayed for thee, that thy faith fail not." And the result was as He anticipated. The disciples showed themselves weak in the final crisis, but not wicked. Satan tripped them up, but he did not enter into and possess them. In this respect they differed *toto cælo* from Judas, who not only lost his faith, but cast away his love, and, abandoning his Lord, went over to the enemy, and became a tool for the accomplishment of their wicked designs. The eleven, at their worst, continued faithful to their Master in heart. They neither committed, nor were capable of committing, acts of perfidy, but even in fleeing identified themselves with the losing side.

But Peter, what of him? was not he an exception to this statement? Well, he certainly did more than fail in faith; and we have no wish to extenuate the gravity of his offence, but would rather see in it a solemn illustration of the close proximity into which the best men may be brought with the worst. At the same time, it is only just to remark that there is a wide difference between denying Christ among the servants of the high priest, and betraying Him into the hands of the high priest himself for a sum of money. The latter act is the crime of a traitor knave; the former might be committed by one who would be true to his master on all occasions in which his interests seemed seriously involved. In denying Jesus, Peter thought that he was saving himself by dissimulation, without doing any material injury to his Lord. His act resembled that of Abraham when he circulated the lying story about his wife being his sister, to protect himself from the violence of licentious strangers. That was certainly a very mean, selfish act, most unworthy of the father of the faithful. Peter's act was not less mean and selfish, but also not more. Both were acts of weakness rather than of wickedness, for which few, even among good men, can afford to throw stones at the patriarch and the disciple. Even those who play the hero on great occasions will at other times act very unworthily. Many men conceal and belie their convictions at the dinner-table, who would boldly proclaim their sentiments from the pulpit or the platform. Standing in the place where Christ's servants are expected to speak the truth, they draw their swords bravely in defence of their Lord; but, mixing in society on equal terms, they too often say in effect, "I know not the man." Peter's offence, therefore, if grave, is certainly not uncommon. It is committed virtually, if not formally, by multitudes who are utterly incapable of public deliberate treason against truth and God. The erring disciple was much more singular in his repentance than in his sin. Of all who in mere acts of weakness virtually deny Christ, how few, like him, go out and weep bitterly!

That Peter did not fall as Judas fell, utterly and irrevocably, was due in part to a radical difference between the two men. Peter was at heart a child of God; Judas, in the core of his being, had been all along a child of Satan. Therefore we may say that Peter could not have sinned as Judas sinned, nor could Judas have repented as Peter repented. Yet, while we say this, we must not forget that Peter was kept from falling away by *special* grace granted to him in answer to his Master's prayers. The precise terms in which Jesus prayed for Peter we do not know; for the prayer in behalf of the one disciple has not, like that for the whole eleven, been recorded. But the drift of these special intercessions is plain, from the account given of them by Jesus to Peter. The Master had prayed that His disciple's faith might not fail. He had not prayed that he might be exempt from Satan's sifting process, or even kept from falling; for He knew that a fall was necessary, to show the self-confident disciple his own weakness. He had prayed that Peter's fall might not be ruinous; that his grievous sin might be followed by godly sorrow, not by hardening of heart, or, as in the case of the traitor, by the sorrow of the world, which worketh death: the remorse of a guilty conscience, which, like the furies, drives the sinner headlong to damnation. And in Peter's repentance, immediately after his denials, we see the fulfilment of his Master's prayer, special grace being given to melt his heart, and overwhelm him with generous grief, and cause him to weep out his soul in tears. Not by his piety or goodness of heart was the salutary result produced, but by God's Spirit and God's providence conspiring to that end. But for the cock-crowing, and the warning words it recalled to mind, and the glance of Jesus' eye, and the tender mercy of the Father in heaven, who can tell what sullen devilish humors might have taken possession of the guilty disciple's heart! Remember how long even the godly David gave place to the devil, and harbored in his bosom the demons of pride, falsehood, and impenitence, after his grievous fall; and see how far it was from being a matter of course that Peter, immediately after denying Christ, should come under the blessed influence of a broken and contrite spirit, or even that the spiritual crisis through which he passed had a happy issue at all. By grace he was saved, as are we all.

3. Jesus regards the crisis about to be gone through by His disciples as one which shall not only end happily, but result in spiritual benefit to themselves, and qualify them for being helpful to others. This appears from the injunction He lays on Peter: "When thou art converted, strengthen thy brethren." Jesus expects the frail disciple to become strong in grace, and so able and willing to help the weak. He cherishes this expectation with respect to all, but specially in regard to Peter, assuming that the weakest might and ought eventually to become the strongest; the last first, the greatest sinner the greatest saint; the most foolish the wisest, most benignant, and sympathetic of men.

How encouraging this genial, kindly view of moral shortcoming to such as have erred! The Saviour says to them in effect, There is no cause for despair : sin cannot only be for-given, but it can even be turned to good account both for yourselves and for others. Falls, rightly improved, may become stepping-stones to Christian virtue, and a training for the office of a comforter and guide. How healing such a view to the troubled conscience! Men who have erred, and who take a serious thought of their sin, are apt to con-sume their hearts and waste their time in bitter reflections on their past misconduct. Christ gives them more profitable work to do. "When thou art converted," He says to them, "strengthen thy brethren :" cease from idle regrets over the irrevocable past, and devote thyself heart and soul to labors of love ; and let it help thee to forgive thyself, that from thy very faults and follies thou mayest learn the meekness, patience, compassion, and wisdom necessary for carrying on such labors with success.

But while very encouraging to those who have sinned, Christ's words to Simon contain no encouragement *to* sin. It is a favorite doctrine with some, — that we may do evil that good may come ; that we must be prodigals in order to be good Christians ; that a *mud bath* must precede the wash-ing of regeneration and the baptism of the soul in the Redeemer's blood. This is a false, pernicious doctrine, of which the Holy One could not be the patron. Do evil that good may come, say you? And what if the good come not? It does not come, as we have seen, as a matter of course ; nor is it the likelier to come that you make the hope of its coming the pretext for sinning. If the good ever come, it will come through the strait gate of repentance. You can become wise, gracious, meek, sympathetic, a burden-bearer to the weak, only by going out first and weeping bitterly. But what chance is there of such a penitential melting of heart appearing in one who adopts and acts on the principle that a curriculum of sin is necessary to the attainment of insight, self-knowledge, compassion, and all the humane virtues? The probable issue of such a training is a hardened heart, a seared conscience, a perverted moral judg-ment, the extirpation of all earnest convictions respecting the difference between right and wrong ; the opinion that

evil leads to good insensibly transforming itself into the idea
that evil is good, and fitting its advocate for committing sin
without shame or compunction.

> " And dare we to this fancy give,
>   That had the wild-oat not been sown,
>   The soil, left barren, scarce had grown
> The grain by which a man may live ?
>
> Oh, if we held the doctrine sound,
>   For life outliving heats of youth ;
>   Yet who would preach it as a truth
> To those that eddy round and round ?
>
> Hold thou the good : define it well :
>   For fear divine Philosophy
>   Should push beyond her mark, and be
> Procuress to the lords of hell." [1]

In Peter's case good did come out of evil.   The sifting
time formed a turning-point in his spiritual history : the sifting process had for its result a second conversion more
thorough than the first, — a turning from sin, not merely in
general, but in detail ; from besetting sins, in better informed
if not more fervent repentance, and with a purpose of new
obedience less self-reliant, but just on that account more
reliable.   A child hitherto, — a child of God, indeed, yet
only a child, — Peter became a man strong in grace, and fit
to bear the burden of the weak.   Yet it is worthy of notice,
as showing how little sympathy the Author of our faith had
with the doctrine that evil may be done for the sake of good,
that Jesus, while aware how Peter's fall would end, did not
on that account regard it as desirable.   He said not, " *I* have
desired to sift thee," but assigns the task of sifting the disciple to the evil spirit who in the beginning tempted our
first parent to sin by the specious argument, " Ye shall be
as gods, knowing good and evil," reserving to Himself the
part of an intercessor, who prays that the evil permitted
may be overruled for good.   " Satan hath desired to have
you :" " I have prayed for thee."   What words could more
strongly convey the idea of guilt and peril than these, which
intimate that Simon is about to do a deed which is an object

---

[1] Tennyson, *In Memoriam*, liii.

of desire to the evil one, and which makes it necessary that he should be specially prayed for by the Saviour of souls? Men must go elsewhere in quest of support for apologetic or pantheistic views of sin.

But it may be thought that the reference to Satan tends in another way to weaken moral earnestness, by encouraging men to throw the blame of their falls on *him*. Theoretically plausible, this objection is practically contrary to fact; for the patrons of lax notions of sin are also the unbelievers in the personality of the devil. "The further the age has removed from the idea of a devil, the laxer it has become in the imputation and punishment of sin. The older time, which did not deny the temptations and assaults of the devil, was yet so little inclined on that account to excuse men, that it regarded the neglect of resistance against the evil spirit, or the yielding to him, as the extreme degree of guilt, and exercised against it a judicial severity from which we shrink with horror. The opposite extreme to this strictness is the laxity of recent criminal jurisprudence, in which judges and physicians are too much inclined to excuse the guilty from physical or psychical grounds, while the moral judgment of public opinion is slack and indulgent. It is undeniable that to every sin not only a bad will, but also the spell of some temptation, contributes; and when temptation is not ascribed to the devil, the sinner does not on that account impute blame to his bad will, but to temptations springing from some other quarter, which he does not derive from sin, but from *nature*, although nature tempts only when under the influence of sin. The world and the flesh are indeed powers of temptation, not through their natural substance, but through the influence of the bad with which they are infected. But when, as at present, the seduction to evil is referred to sensuality, temperament, physical lusts and passions, circumstances, or fixed ideas, monomanias, etc., guilt is taken off the sinner's shoulders, and laid upon something ethically indifferent or simply natural." [1]

The view presented by Jesus of His disciple's fall cannot therefore be charged with weakening the sense of responsibility; on the contrary, it is a view tending at once to inspire

---

[1] Sartorius, *Die Lehre von der heiligen Liebe*, pp. 79, 80.

hatred of sin and hope for the sinner. It exhibits sin about to be committed as an object of fear and abhorrence; and, already committed, as not only forgivable, being repented of, but as capable of being made serviceable to spiritual progress. It says to us, on the one hand, Trifle not with temptation, for Satan is near, seeking thy soul's ruin, — "fear, and sin not;" and, on the other hand, "If any man sin, we have an Advocate with the Father, Jesus Christ the righteous," — despair not: forsake thy sins, and thou shalt find mercy.

SECTION III — PETER AND JOHN

JOHN xviii. 15-18, xix. 25-27

Though all the disciples, without exception, forsook Jesus at the moment of His apprehension, two of them soon recovered their courage sufficiently to return from flight, and follow after their Master as He was being led away to judgment. One of these was Simon Peter, ever original both in good and in evil, who, we are told, followed Jesus "afar off unto the high priest's palace, to see the end." [1] The other, according to the general, and we think correct, opinion of interpreters, was John. He is indeed not named, but merely described as another, or rather the other, disciple; but as John himself is our informant, the fact is almost certain evidence that he is the person alluded to. "The other disciple," who "was known unto the high priest, and went in with Jesus into the palace of the high priest," [2] is the well-known unnamed one who so often meets us in the fourth Gospel. Had the man whose conduct was so outstanding been any other than the evangelist, he would certainly not have remained nameless in a narrative so minutely exact, that even the name of the servant whose ear Peter cut off is not deemed too insignificant to be recorded. [3]

These two disciples, though very different in character, seem to have had a friendship for each other. On various occasions besides the present we find their names associated in a manner suggestive of a special attachment. At the supper-table, when the announcement concerning the traitor

[1] Matt. xxvi. 58.   [2] John xviii. 15.   [3] John xviii. 10.

had been made, Peter gave the disciple whom Jesus loved a sign that he should ask who it should be of whom He spake. Three times in the interval between the resurrection and the ascension the two brethren were linked together as companions. They ran together to the sepulchre on the resurrection morning. They talked together confidentially concerning the stranger who appeared at early dawn on the shores of the Sea of Galilee, when they were out on their last fishing expedition, the disciple whom Jesus loved, on recognizing the Risen One, saying unto Peter, "It is the Lord." They walked together shortly after on the shore, following Jesus, — Peter by commandment, John by the voluntary impulse of his own loving heart. An intimacy cemented by such sacred associations was likely to be permanent, and we find the two disciples still companions after they had entered on the duties of the apostleship. They went up together into the temple at the hour of prayer; and, having got into trouble through the healing of the lame man at the temple gate, they appeared together before the ecclesiastical tribunal, to be tried by the very same men, Annas and Caiaphas, who had sat in judgment upon their Lord, companions now at the bar, as they had been before in the palace, of the high priest.

Such a friendship between the two disciples as these facts point to, is by no means surprising. As belonging to the inner circle of three whom Jesus honored with His confidence on special occasions, they had opportunities for becoming intimate, and were placed in circumstances tending to unite them in the closest bonds of spiritual brotherhood. And, notwithstanding their characteristic differences, they were fitted to be special friends. They were both men of marked originality and force of character, and they would find in each other more sources of interest than in the more commonplace members of the apostolic band. Their very peculiarities, too, far from keeping them apart, would rather draw them together. They were so constituted that each would find in the other the complement of himself. Peter was masculine, John was feminine, in temperament; Peter was the man of action, John the man of thought and feeling; Peter's part was to be a leader and a champion, John's was to cling, and trust, and be loved ; Peter was the hero, and John the admirer of heroism.

In their respective behavior at this crisis, the two friends were at once like and unlike each other. They were like in this, that they both manifested a generous solicitude about the fate of their Master. While the rest retired altogether from the scene, they followed to see the end. The common action proceeded in both probably from the same motives. What these motives were we are not told, but it is not difficult to guess. A certain influence may be assigned, in the first place, to natural activity of spirit. It was not in the nature either of Peter or of John to be listless and passive while such grave events were going on. They could not sit at home doing nothing while their Lord was being tried, sentenced, and treated as a malefactor. If they cannot prevent, they will at least witness, His last sufferings. The same irrepressible energy of mind which, three days after, made these two disciples run to see the empty grave, now impels them to turn their steps towards the judgment-hall to witness the transactions there.

Besides activity of mind, we perceive in the conduct of the two disciples a certain spirit of daring at work. We learn from the Acts of the Apostles, that when Peter and John appeared before the council in Jerusalem, the rulers were struck with their boldness. Their boldness then was only what was to be expected from men who had behaved as they did at this crisis. By that time, it is true, they had, in common with all their brethren, experienced a great spiritual change ; but yet we cannot fail to recognize the identity of the characters. The apostles had but grown to such spiritual manhood as they gave promise of in the days of their discipleship. For it was a brave thing in them to follow, even at a distance, the band which had taken Jesus a prisoner. The rudiments at least of the martyr character were in men who could do that. Mere cowards would not have acted so. They would have eagerly availed themselves of the virtual sanction given by Jesus to flight, comforting their hearts with the thought that, in consulting for their safety, they were but doing the duty enjoined on them.

But the conduct of the two brethren sprang, we believe,

mainly from their ardent love to Jesus. When the first paroxysm of fear was past, solicitude for personal safety gave place to generous concern about the fate of one whom they really loved more than life. The love of Christ constrained them to think not of themselves, but of Him whose hour of sorrow was come. First they slacken their pace, then they halt, then they look round ; and as they see the armed band nearing the city, they are cut to the heart, and they say within themselves, " We cannot leave our dear Master in His time of peril ; we must see the issue of this painful business." And so with anguished spirit they set out towards Jerusalem, Peter first, and John after him.

The two brethren, companions thus far, diverged widely on arriving at the scene of trial and suffering. John clung to his beloved Lord to the last. He was present, it would appear, at the various examinations to which Jesus was subjected, and heard with his own ears the judicial process of which he has given so interesting an account in his Gospel. When the iniquitous sentence was executed, he was a spectator. He took his stand by the foot of the cross, where he could see all, and not only be seen, but even be spoken to, by his dying Master. There he saw, among other things, the strange phenomenon of blood and water flowing from the spear-wound in the Saviour's side, which he so carefully records in his narrative. There he heard Christ's dying words, and among them those addressed to Mary of Nazareth and himself : to her, " Woman, behold thy son ; " to him, " Behold thy mother."

John was thus persistently faithful throughout. And Peter, what of him ? Alas ! what need to tell the familiar story of his deplorable weakness in the hall or inner court of the high priest's palace ? how, having obtained an entrance through the street door by the intercession of his brother disciple, he first denied to the portress his connection with Jesus ; then repeated his denial to other parties, with the addition of a solemn oath ; then, irritated by the repetition of the charge, and perhaps by the consciousness of guilt, a third time declared, not with a solemn oath, but with the degrading accompaniment of profane swearing, " I know not the man ; " then, finally, hearing the cock crow, and catching

Jesus' eye, and remembering the words, "Before the cock crow thou shalt deny me thrice," went out to the street and wept bitterly!

What became of Peter after this melancholy exhibition we are not informed. In all probability he retired to his lodging, humbled, dispirited, crushed, there to remain overwhelmed with grief and shame, till he was roused from stupor by the stirring tidings of the resurrection morn.

This difference in conduct between the two disciples corresponded to a difference in their characters. Each acted according to his nature. It is true, indeed, that the circumstances were not the same for both parties, being favorable for one, unfavorable for the other. John had the advantage of a friend at court, being somehow known to the high priest. This circumstance gained him admission into the chamber of judgment, and gave him security against all personal risk. Peter, on the other hand, not only had no friends at court, but might not unnaturally fear the presence there of personal foes. He had made himself obnoxious by his rash act in the garden, and might be apprehensive of getting into trouble in consequence. That such fears would not have been altogether groundless, we learn from the fact stated by John, that one of the persons who charged Peter with being a disciple of Jesus was a kinsman of the man whose ear Peter had cut off, and that he brought his charge against the disciple in this form: "Did I not see thee in the garden with Him?" It is therefore every way likely that the consciousness of having committed an offence which might be resented, made Peter anxious to escape identification as one of Christ's disciples. His unseasonable courage in the garden helped to make him a coward in the palace-yard.

Making all due allowance for the effect of circumstances, however, we think that the difference in the behavior of the two disciples was mainly due to a difference in the men themselves. Though he had been guilty of no imprudence in the garden, Peter, we fear, would have denied Jesus in the hall; and, on the other hand, supposing John had been placed in Peter's position, we do not believe that he would have committed Peter's sin. Peter's disposition laid him open to temptation, while John's, on the other hand, was a protection against temptation. Peter was frank and familiar, John was dignified and reserved ; Peter's tendency was to be on hail-fellow-well-met terms with everybody, John could keep his own place and make other people keep theirs. It is easy to see what an important effect this distinction would have on the conduct of parties placed in Peter's position. Suppose John in Peter's place, and let us see how he might have acted. Certain persons about the court, possessing neither authority nor influence, interrogate him about his connection with Jesus. He is neither afraid nor ashamed to acknowledge his Lord, but nevertheless he turns away and gives the interrogators no answer. They have no right to question him. The spirit which prompts their questions is one with which he has no sympathy, and he feels that it will serve no good purpose to confess his discipleship to such people. Therefore, like his Master when confronted with the false witnesses, he holds his peace, and withdraws from company with which he has nothing in common, and for which he has no respect.

To protect himself from inconvenient interrogation by such dignified reserve, is beyond Peter's capacity. He cannot keep people who are not fit company for him at their distance; he is too frank, too familiar, too sensitive to public opinion, without respect to its quality. If a servant-maid ask him a question about his relation to the Prisoner at the bar, he cannot brush past her as if he heard her not. He must give her an answer ; and as he feels instinctively that the animus of the question is against his Master, his answer must needs be a lie. Then, unwarned by this encounter of the danger arising from too close contact with the hangers-on about the palace, the foolish disciple must involve himself more inextricably into the net, by mingling jauntily with the servants and officers gathered around the fire which has been kindled on the pavement of the open court. Of course he has no chance of escape here ; he is like a poor fly caught in a spider's web. If these men, with the insolent tone of court menials, charge him with being a follower of the man whom their masters have now got into their power, he can do nothing else than blunder out a mean, base denial. Poor Peter is manifestly not equal to the situation. It would have been wiser in him to have staid at home, restraining his curiosity to see the end. But he, like most men, was to learn wisdom only by bitter experience.

The contrast we have drawn between the characters of the two disciples suggests the thought, What a different thing growth in grace may be for different Christians! Neither John nor Peter was mature as yet, but immaturity showed itself in them in opposite ways. Peter's weakness lay in the direction of indiscriminate cordiality. His tendency was to be friends with everybody. John, on the other hand, was in no danger of being on familiar terms with all and sundry. It was rather *too easy* for him to make a difference between friends and foes. He could take a side, and keep it; he could even hate with fanatical intensity, as well as love with beautiful womanly devotion. Witness his proposal to call down fire from heaven to consume the Samaritan villages! That was a proposal which Peter could not have made; it was not in his nature to be so truculent against any human being. So far, his good nature was a thing to be commended, if in other respects it laid him open to temptation. The faults of the two brethren being so opposite, growth in grace would naturally assume two opposite forms in their respective experiences. In Peter it would take the form of concentration; in John, of expansion. Peter would become less charitable; John would become more charitable. Peter would advance from indiscriminate goodwill to a moral decidedness which should distinguish between friends and foes, the Church and the world; John's progress, on the other hand, would consist in ceasing to be a bigot, and in becoming imbued with the genial, humane, sympathetic spirit of his Lord. Peter, in his mature state, would care much less for the opinions and feelings of men than he did at the present time; John, again, would care much more.

We add a word on the question, Was it right or was it wrong in these two disciples to follow their Lord to the place of judgment? In our view it was neither right nor wrong in itself. It was right for one who was able to do it without spiritual harm; wrong for one who had reason to believe that, by doing it, he was exposing himself to harm. The latter was Peter's case, as the former seems to have been

John's. Peter had been plainly warned of his weakness; and, had he laid the warning to heart, he would have avoided the scene of temptation. By disregarding the warning, he wilfully rushed into the tempter's arms, and of course he caught a fall. His fall reads a lesson to all who, without seeking counsel of God or disregarding counsel given, enter on undertakings beyond their strength.

28

THE SHEPHERD RESTORED

SECTION I — TOO GOOD NEWS TO BE TRUE

Matt. 28:17; Mark 16:11-15; Luke 24:11, 13-22, 36-42;
John 20:20, 24-29

THE black day of the crucifixion is past; the succeeding
day, the Jewish Sabbath, when the Weary One slept in His
rock-hewn tomb, is also past; the first day of a new week
and of a new era has dawned, and the Lord is risen from the
dead. The Shepherd has returned to gather His scattered
sheep. Surely a happy day for hapless disciples! What
rapturous joy must have thrilled their hearts at the thought
of a reunion with their beloved Lord! with what ardent hope
must they have looked forward to that resurrection morn!

So one might think; but the real state of the case was not
so. Such ardent expectations had no place in the minds of
the disciples. The actual state of their minds at the resurrection of Christ rather resembled that of the Jewish exiles
in Babylon, when they heard that they were to be restored
to their native land. The first effect of the good news was
that they were as men that dreamed. The news seemed too
good to be true. The captives who had sat by the rivers of
Babylon, and wept when they remembered Zion, had ceased
to hope for a return to their own country, and indeed to be
capable of hoping for any thing. "Grief was calm and hope
was dead" within them. Then, when the exiles had recovered from the stupor of surprise, the next effect of the
good tidings was a fit of over-joy. They burst into hysteric
laughter and irrepressible song.[1]

---

[1] Ps. cxxxvii. The experience of the exiles and of the apostles recalls the lines of
the Greek poet Euripides —

> " πολλαὶ μορφαὶ τῶν δαιμονίων
> πολλὰ δ' ἀελπτως κραινουσι θεοί
> καὶ τὰ δοκηθεντ' οὐκ ἐτελέσθη
> τῶν δ' ἀδοκήτων πόρον εὗρε θεός,"

Very similar was the experience of the disciples in connection with the rising of Jesus from the dead. Their grief was not indeed calm, but their hope was dead. The resurrection of their Master was utterly unexpected by them, and they received the tidings with surprise and incredulity. This appears from the statements of all the four evangelists. Matthew states that on the occasion of Christ's meeting with His followers in Galilee after He was risen, some doubted, while others worshipped.[1] Mark relates that when the disciples heard from Mary Magdalene that Jesus was alive, and had been seen of her, "they believed not;"[2] and that when the two disciples who journeyed toward Emmaus told their brethren of their meeting with Jesus on the way, "neither believed they them."[3] He further relates how, on a subsequent occasion, when Jesus Himself met with the whole eleven at once, He "upbraided them with their unbelief and hardness of heart, because they believed not them which had seen Him after He was risen."[4]

In full accordance with these statements of the two first evangelists are those of Luke, whose representation of the mental attitude of the disciples towards the resurrection of Jesus is very graphic and animated. According to him, the reports of the women seemed to them "as idle tales, and they believed them not."[5] The two brethren vaguely alluded to by Mark as walking into the country when Jesus appeared to them, are represented by Luke as sad in countenance, though aware of the rumors concerning the resurrection; yea, as so depressed in spirits, that they did not recognize Jesus when He joined their company and entered into conversation with them.[6] The resurrection was not a fact for them : all they knew was that their Master was dead, and that they had vainly trusted that it had been He who should have redeemed Israel. The same evangelist also informs us that on the first occasion when Jesus presented Himself in the midst of His disciples, they did recognize the resemblance of the apparition to their deceased Lord, but thought it was only His ghost, and accordingly were terrified and affrighted ; insomuch that, in order to charm away their fear, Jesus

---

[1] Matt. xxviii. 17.   [3] Mark xvi. 13.   [5] Luke xxiv. 11.
[2] Mark xvi. 11.   [4] Mark xvi. 14.   [6] Luke xxiv. 16.

showed them His hands and feet, and besought them to handle His body, and so satisfy themselves that He was no ghost, but a substantial human being, with flesh and bones like another man.[1]

Instead of general statements, John gives an example of the incredulity of the disciples concerning the resurrection, as exhibited in its extreme form by Thomas. This disciple he represents as so incredulous, that he refused to believe until he should have put his finger into the prints of the nails, and thrust his hand into the wound made by the spear in the Saviour's side. That the other disciples shared the incredulity of Thomas, though in a less degree, is implied in the statement made by John in a previous part of his narrative, that when Jesus met His disciples on the evening of the day on which He rose, "He showed unto them His hands and His side."[2]

The women who had believed in Christ had no more expectation of His resurrection than the eleven. They set forth towards the sepulchre on the morning of the first day of the week, with the intention of embalming the dead body of Him whom they loved. They sought the living among the dead. When the Magdalene, who was at the tomb before the rest, found the grave empty, her idea was that some one had carried away the dead body of her Lord.[3]

When the incredulity of the disciples did at length give place to faith, they passed, like the Hebrew exiles, from extreme depression to extravagant joy. When the doubt of Thomas was removed, he exclaimed in rapture, "My Lord and my God!"[4] Luke relates that when they recognized their risen Lord, the disciples "believed not for joy,"[5] as if toying with doubt as a stimulus to joy. The two disciples with whom Jesus conversed on the way to Emmaus, said to each other when He left them, "Did not our heart burn within us while He talked with us by the way, and while He opened to us the Scriptures?"[6]

In yet another most important respect did the eleven resemble the ancient Hebrew exiles at the time of their recall. While their faith and hope were palsied during the interval

[1] Luke xxiv. 36, 37.   [3] John xx. 2.   [5] Luke xxiv. 41.
[2] John xx. 20.   [4] John xx. 28.   [6] Luke xxiv. 32.

between the death and the resurrection of Jesus, their love remained in unabated vitality. The expatriated Jew did not forget Jerusalem in the land of strangers. Absence only made his heart grow fonder. As he sat by the rivers of Babylon, listless, motionless, in abstracted dreamy mood, gazing with glassy eyes on the sluggish waters, the big round tears stole quietly down his cheeks, because he had been thinking of Zion. The exile of poetic soul did not forget what was due to Jerusalem's honor. He was incapable of singing the Lord's songs in the hearing of a heathen audience, who cared nothing for their meaning, but only for the style of execution. He disdained to prostitute his talents for the entertainment of the voluptuous oppressors of Israel, even though thereby he might procure his restoration to the beloved country of his birth, as the Athenian captives in Sicily are said to have done by reciting the strains of their favorite poet Euripides in the hearing of their Sicilian masters.[1]

The disciples were not less true to the memory of their Lord. They were like a " widow indeed," who remains faithful to her deceased husband, and dotes on his virtues, though his reputation be at zero in the general esteem of the world. Call Him a deceiver who might, they could not believe that Jesus had been a deceiver. Mistaken He as well as they might have been, but an impostor — *never!* Therefore, though He is dead and their hope gone, they still act as men who cherish the fondest attachment to their Master whom they have lost. They keep together like a bereaved family, with blinds down, so to speak, shutting and barring their doors for fear of the Jews, identifying themselves with the Crucified, and as His friends dreading the ill-will of the unbelieving world. Admirable example to all Christians how to behave themselves in a day of trouble, rebuke, and blasphemy, when the cause of Christ seems lost, and the powers of darkness for the moment have all things their own way. Though faith be eclipsed and hope extinguished, let the heart ever be loyal to its true Lord !

The state of mind in which the disciples were at the resurrection of Jesus Christ from the dead, is of great moment in

---

[1] The story is told by Plutarch in his Παράλληλα (*Nikias*), and quoted and commented on by Gillies, *History of Greece*, cap. xx.

an apologetic point of view.   Their despair after their Lord's crucifixion gives great weight to the testimony borne by them to the *fact* of His resurrection.   Men in such a mood were not likely to believe in the latter event except because it could not reasonably be disbelieved.   They would not be lightly satisfied of its truth, as men are apt to be in the case of events both desired and expected: they would sceptically exact superabundant evidence, as men do in the case of events desirable but not expected.   They would be slow to believe on the testimony of others, and might even hesitate to believe their own eyes.   They would not be able, as M. Renan supposes, to get up a belief in the resurrection of Jesus, from the simple fact that His grave was found empty on the third day after His death, by the women who went to embalm His body.   That circumstance, on being reported, might make a Peter and a John run to the sepulchre to see how matters stood; but, after they had found the report of the women confirmed, it would still remain a question how the fact was to be explained; and Mary Magdalene's theory, that some one had carried off the corpse, would not appear at all improbable.

These inferences of ours, from what we know concerning the mental condition of the disciples, are fully borne out by the Gospel accounts of the reception they gave to the risen Jesus at His first appearances to them.   One and all of them regarded these appearances sceptically, and took pains to satisfy themselves, or made it necessary that Jesus should take pains to satisfy them, that the visible object was no ghostly apparition, but a living man, and that man none other than He who had died on the cross.   The disciples doubted now the substantiality, now the identity, of the person who appeared to them.   They were therefore not content with seeing Jesus, but at His own request handled Him. One of their number not only handled the body to ascertain that it possessed the incompressibility of matter, but insisted on examining with sceptical curiosity those parts which had been injured by the nails and the spear.   All perceived the resemblance between the object in view and Jesus, but they could not be persuaded of the identity, so utterly unprepared were they for seeing the Dead One alive again; and their theory at first was just that of Strauss, that what they saw was a ghost or spectre. And the very fact that they enter-tained that theory makes it impossible for us to entertain it. We cannot, in the face of that fact, accept the Straussian dogma, that "the faith in Jesus as the Messiah, which by His violent death had received an apparently fatal shock, was subjectively restored by the instrumentality of the mind, the power of imagination and nervous excitement." The power of imagination and nervous excitement we know can do much. It has often happened to men in an abnormal, excited state to see projected into outward space the crea-tions of a heated brain. But persons in a crazy state like that — subject to hallucination — are not usually cool and rational enough to *doubt* the reality of what they see ; nor is it necessary in their case to take pains to overcome such doubts. What they need rather, is to be made aware that what they think they see is *not* a reality : the very reverse of what Christ had to do for the disciples, and *did*, by solemn assertion that He was no spirit, by inviting them to handle Him, and so satisfy themselves of His material substanti-ality, and by partaking of food in their presence.

When we keep steadily before our eyes the mental condi-tion of the eleven at the time of Christ's resurrection, we see the transparent falsehood and absurdity of the *theft* theory invented by the Jewish priests. The disciples, according to this theory, came by night, while the guards were asleep, and stole the dead body of Jesus, that they might be able to circulate the belief that He was risen again. Matthew tells that even before the resurrection the murderers of our Lord were afraid this might be done ; and then, to prevent any fraud of this kind, they applied to Pilate to have a guard put upon the grave, who accordingly contemptuously granted them permission to take what steps they pleased to prevent all resurrectionary proceedings on the part either of the dead or of the living, scornfully replying, " Ye have a watch : go your way, make it as sure as ye can." This accordingly they did, sealing the stone and setting a watch. Alas ! their precautions prevented neither the resurrection nor belief in it, but only supplied an illustration of the folly of those who attempt to manage providence, and to control the course of the world's history. They gave themselves much to do, and it all came to nothing. Not that we are disposed to deny the astuteness of these ecclesiastical politicians. Their scheme for preventing the resurrection was very prudent, and their mode of explaining it away afterhand very plausible. The story they invented was really a very respectable fabrication, and was certain to satisfy all who wanted a decent theory to justify a foregone conclusion, as in fact it seems to have done; for, according to Matthew, it was commonly reported in after years.[1] It was not improbable that soldiers should fall asleep by night on the watch, especially when guarding a dead body, which was not likely to give them any trouble; and in the eyes of the unbelieving world, the followers of the Nazarene were capable of using any means for promoting their ends.

But granting all this, and even granting that the Sanhedrists had been right in their opinion of the character of the disciples, their théft theory is ridiculous. The disciples, even if capable of such a theft, so far as scruples of conscience were concerned, were not in a state of mind to think of it, or to attempt it. They had not spirit left for such a daring action. Sorrow lay like a weight of lead on their hearts, and made them almost as inanimate as the corpse they are supposed to have stolen. Then the motive for the theft is one which could not have influenced them then. Steal the body to propagate a belief in the resurrection! What interest had they in propagating a belief which they did not entertain themselves? "As yet they knew not the Scriptures, that He must rise again from the dead;"[2] nor did they remember aught that their Master had said on this subject before His decease. To some this latter statement has appeared hard to believe; and to get over the difficulty, it has been suggested that the predictions of our Lord respecting His resurrection may not have been so definite as they appear in the Gospels, but may have assumed this definite form after the event, when their meaning was clearly understood.[3] We see no occasion for such a supposition. There can be no doubt that Jesus spoke plainly enough about His death at least; and yet His death, when it happened, took the disciples as

---

[1] Matt. xxviii. 15.   [2] John xx. 9.   [3] See Neander, *Life of Jesus.*

much by surprise as did the resurrection.[1] One explanation
suffices in both cases. The disciples were not clever, quick-
witted, sentimental men such as Renan makes them. They
were stupid, slow-minded persons; very honest, but very un-
apt to take in new ideas. They were like horses with blind-
ers on, and could see only in one direction, — that, namely,
of their prejudices. It required the surgery of events to
insert a new truth into their minds. Nothing would change
the current of their thoughts but a damwork of undeniable
fact. They could be convinced that Christ must die only by
His dying, that He would rise only by His rising, that His
kingdom was not to be of this world, only by the outpouring
of the Spirit at Pentecost and the vocation of the Gentiles.
Let us be thankful for the honest stupidity of these men.
It gives great value to their testimony. We know that
nothing but facts could make such men believe that which
nowadays they get credit for inventing.

The apologetic use which we have made of the doubts of
the disciples concerning the resurrection of Christ is not
only legitimate, but manifestly that which was intended by
their being recorded. The evangelists have carefully chroni-
cled these doubts that we might have no doubt. These
things were written that we might believe that Jesus really
did rise from the dead; for the apostles attached supreme
importance to that fact, which they had doubted in the days
of their disciplehood. It was the foundation of their doctrinal edifice, an essential part of their gospel. The Apostle
Paul correctly summed up the gospel preached by the men
who had been with Jesus, as well as by himself, in these
three items: "that Christ died for our sins according to the
Scriptures; and that He was buried; and that He rose again
the third day, according to the Scriptures." All the eleven
thoroughly agreed with Paul's sentiment, that if Christ were

---

[1] Colani (*Jésus Christ et les Croyances messianiques de son Temps*, 2ième ed.
p. 164) endeavors to weaken the force of this argument by the remark that the death of
Jesus, being an unwelcome event, was a thing the disciples did not wish to remember or
believe in, as involving the ruin of their Messianic hopes: whereas, the resurrection
being a joyful event, would most gladly have been believed in had it really been prean-
nounced. The author forgets that the resurrection implied death as its antecedent, and
that if believed in, it would have made death appear in an altogether different light,
and that if it failed to do that, it would beforehand share the same fate as the death, that,
viz., of being disregarded; and afterhand would seem "too good news to be true."

not risen, their preaching was vain, and the faith of Christians was also vain. There was no gospel at all, unless He who died for men's sins rose again for their justification. With this conviction in their minds, they constantly bore witness to the resurrection of Jesus wherever they went. So important a part of their work did this witness-bearing seem to them, that when Peter proposed the election of one to fill the place of Judas he singled it out as the characteristic function of the apostolic office. "Of these men," he said, "which have companied with us all the time that the Lord Jesus went in and out among us, . . . must one become a witness with us of His resurrection."

With this supreme value attached to the fact of Christ's rising again in apostolic preaching, it is our duty most heartily to sympathize. Modern unbelievers, like some in the Corinthian church, would persuade us that it does not matter whether Jesus rose or not, all that is valuable in Christianity being quite independent of mere historical truth. With these practically agree many believers addicted to an airy spiritualism, who treat mere supernatural facts with contemptuous neglect, deeming the high doctrines of the faith as alone worthy of their regard. To persons of this temper such studies as those which have occupied us in this chapter seem a mere waste of time ; and if they spoke as they feel, they would say, "Let these trifles alone, and give us the pure and simple gospel." Intelligent, sober, and earnest Christians differ *toto cælo* from both these classes of people. In their view Christianity is in the first place a religion of supernatural facts. These facts occupy the principal place in their creed. They know that if these facts are honestly believed, all the great doctrines of the faith must sooner or later be accepted; and, on the other hand, they clearly understand that a religion which despises, not to say disbelieves, these facts, is but a cloudland which must soon be dissipated, or a house built on sand which the storm will sweep away. Therefore, while acknowledging the importance of all revealed truth, they lay very special stress on revealed facts. Believing with the heart the precious truth that Christ died for our sins, they are careful with the apostles to include in their gospel these items of fact, that He was buried, and that He rose again the third day.[1]

SECTION II — THE EYES OF THE DISCIPLES OPENED

MARK xvi. 14; LUKE xxiv. 25–32, 44–46; JOHN xx. 20–23

Jesus showed Himself alive after His passion to His disciples in a body, for the first time, on the evening of His resurrection day. It was the fourth time He had made Himself visible since He rose from the dead. He had appeared in the morning first of all to Mary of Magdala. She had earned the honor thus conferred on her by her pre-eminent devotion. Of kindred spirit with Mary of Bethany, she had been foremost among the women who came to Joseph's tomb to embalm the dead body of the Saviour. Finding the grave empty, she wept bitter tears, because they had taken away her Lord, and she knew not where they had laid Him. Those tears, sure sign of deep true love, had not been unobserved of the Risen One. The sorrows of this faithful soul touched His tender heart, and brought Him to her side to comfort her. Turning round in distress from the sepulchre, she saw Him standing by, but knew Him not. "Jesus saith to her, Woman, why weepest thou? whom seekest thou? She, supposing Him to be the gardener, replies, Sir, if thou hast borne Him hence, tell me where thou hast laid Him,

---

[1] Baur, denying, or tacitly ignoring the *fact* of the resurrection, admits that the *belief* in it by the apostles was the necessary presupposition of the whole historical development of Christianity. How that belief arose in their minds he does not attempt to explain, but rather declares to be inexplicable by psychological analysis (*vide Kirchengeschichte der Drei Ersten Jahrhunderte*, 3te Ausg., p. 40). Keim's view is peculiar. Holding with Baur and Strauss the impossibility of a resurrection in the ordinary sense, he yet differs from Strauss in regarding the appearances of Jesus after His death as something more than hallucinations, as objective occurrences, "telegraphic" communications from the spirit-world to let the dispirited disciples know that all was well (*Jesu von Nazara*, Band iii. p 605). This hypothesis, which seems to have been suggested by the phenomena of modern spiritualism, adds a fourth to the list of the naturalistic attempts to dispose of the great cardinal fact considered in this chapter. For the reader's benefit we may here give the list: —

    1. Jesus never was dead: resurrection was merely reanimation after a swoon.

    2. The dead body was stolen, and the lie circulated that Jesus had risen.

    3. The disciples honestly believed that Jesus was risen, but their belief was a pure hallucination bred by a heated brain.

    4. Jesus after death made spiritualistic communications to His disciples, which naturally led to the belief that He was risen.

and I will take Him away. Jesus saith unto her, Mary."[1]
Startled with the familiar voice, she looks more attentively,
and forthwith returns the benignant salutation with an expressive word of recognition, "Rabboni." Thus "to holy
tears, in lonely hours, Christ risen appears."

The second appearance was vouchsafed to Peter. Concerning this private meeting between Jesus and His erring
disciple we have no details : it is simply mentioned by Paul
in his Epistle to the Corinthians, and by Luke in his
Gospel; but we can have no doubt at all as to its object.
The Risen Master remembered Peter's sin; He knew how
troubled he was in mind on account of it ; He desired without delay to let him know he was forgiven ; and out of delicate consideration for the offender's feelings He contrived
to meet him for the first time after his fall, *alone.*

In the course of the day Jesus appeared, for the third
time, to the two brethren who journeyed to Emmaus. Luke
has given greater prominence to this third appearance than
to any other in his narrative, probably because it was one of
the most interesting of the anecdotes concerning the resurrection which he found in the collections out of which he
compiled his Gospel. And, in truth, any thing more interesting than this beautiful story cannot well be imagined.
How vividly is the whole situation of the disciples brought
before us by the picture of the two friends walking along
the way, and talking together of the things which had happened, the sufferings of Jesus three days ago, and the
rumors just come to their ears concerning His resurrection ;
and as they talked, vibrating between despair and hope, now
brooding disconsolately on the crucifixion of Him whom till
then they had regarded as the Redeemer of Israel, anon
wondering if it were possible that He could have risen
again ! Then how unspeakably pathetic the behavior of
Jesus throughout this scene ! By an artifice of love He
assumes the *incognito,* and, joining the company of the two
sorrowful men, asks them in a careless way what is the subject about which they are talking so sadly and seriously ;
and on receiving for reply a question expressive of surprise
that even a stranger in Jerusalem should not know the

[1] John xx. 15, 16.

things which have come to pass, again asks dryly and indif-
ferently, "What things?" Having thereby drawn out of
them their story, He proceeds in turn to show them that an
intelligent reader of the Old Testament ought not to be surprised at such things happening to one whom they believed
to be Christ, taking occasion to expound unto them "in
all the Scriptures the things concerning Himself," without
saying that it is of Himself He speaks. On the arrival of
the travellers at the village whither the two brethren were
bound, the unknown One assumes the air of a man who is
going farther on, as it would not become a stranger to
thrust himself into company uninvited ; but receiving a pressing invitation, He accepts it, and at last the two brethren
discover to their joy whom they have been entertaining
unawares.

This appearing of Jesus to the two brethren by the way
was a sort of prelude to that which He made on the evening
of the same day in Jerusalem to the eleven, or rather the
ten. As soon as they had discovered whom they had had
for a guest, Cleopas and his companion set out from Emmaus
to the Holy City, eager to tell the friends there the stirring
news. And, behold, while they are in the very act of telling
what things were done in the way, and how Jesus became
known to them in the breaking of bread, Jesus Himself
appeared in the midst of them, uttering the kindly salutation, "Peace be unto you!" He is come to do for the future
apostles what He has already done for the two friends : to
show Himself alive to them after His passion, and to open
their understandings that they might understand the Scriptures, and see that, according to what had been written
before of the Christ, it behooved Him to suffer, and to rise
from the dead the third day.

While the general design of the two appearances is the
same, we observe a difference in the order of procedure followed by Jesus. In the one case He opened the eyes of the
understanding first, and the eyes of the body second ; in
the other, He reversed this order. In His colloquy with the
two brethren He first showed them that the crucifixion and
the rumored resurrection were in perfect accordance with
Old Testament Scriptures, and then at the close made

Himself visible to their bodily eyes as Jesus risen. In other words, He first taught them the true scriptural theory of Messiah's earthly experience, and then He satisfied them as to the *matter of fact.* In the meeting at night with the ten, on the other hand, he disposed of the matter of fact first, and then took up the theory afterwards. He convinced His disciples, by showing them His hands and His feet, and by eating food, that He really was risen ; and then He proceeded to show that the fact was only what they ought to have expected as the fulfilment of Old Testament prophecy.

In thus varying the order of revelation, Jesus was but adapting His procedure to the different circumstances of the persons with whom He had to deal. The two friends who journeyed to Emmaus did not notice any resemblance between the stranger who joined their company and their beloved Lord, of whom they had been thinking and speaking. "Their eyes were holden, that they should not know Him." [1] The main cause of this, we believe, was sheer heaviness of heart. Sorrow made them unobserving. They were so engrossed with their own sad thoughts that they had no eyes for outward things. They did not take the trouble to look who it was that had come up with them ; it would have made no difference though the stranger had been their own father. It is obvious how men in such a mood must be dealt with. They can get outward vision only by getting the inward eye first opened. The diseased mind must be healed, that they may be able to look at what is before them, and see it as it is. On this principle Jesus proceeded with the two brethren. He accommodated Himself to their humor, and led them on from despair to hope, and then the outward senses recovered their perceptive power, and told who the stranger was. "You have heard," He said in effect, "a rumor that He who was crucified three days ago is risen. You regarded this rumor as an incredible story. But why should you ? You believe Jesus to be the Christ. If He was the Christ, His rising again was to be expected as much as the passion, for both alike are foretold in the Scriptures which ye believe to be the Word of God." These thoughts having taken hold of their minds, the hearts of the two

[1] Luke xxiv. 16.

brethren begin to burn with the kindling power of a new truth; the day-dawn of hope breaks on their spirit; they waken up as from an oppressive dream; they look outward, and, lo, the man who has been discoursing to them is Jesus Himself!

With the ten the case was different. When Jesus appeared in the midst of them, they were struck at once with the resemblance to their deceased Master. They had been listening to the story of Cleopas and his companion, and were in a more observing mood. But they could not believe that what they saw really was Jesus. They were terrified and affrighted, and supposed that they had seen a spirit — the ghost or spectre of the Crucified. The first thing to be done in this case, therefore, manifestly was to allay the fear awakened, and to convince the terrified disciples that the being who had suddenly appeared was no ghost, but a man: the very man He seemed to be, even Jesus Himself. Not till that has been done can any discourse be profitably held concerning the teaching of the Old Testament on the subject of Messiah's earthly history. To that task accordingly Jesus forthwith addressed Himself, and only when it was successfully accomplished did He proceed to expound the true Messianic theory.

Something analogous to the difference we have pointed out in the experience of the two and the ten disciples in connection with belief in the resurrection may be found in the ways by which different Christians now are brought to faith. The evidences of Christianity are commonly divided into two great categories — the external and the internal; the one drawn from outward historical facts, the other from the adaptation of the gospel to man's nature and needs. Both sorts of evidence are necessary to a perfect faith, just as both sorts of vision, the outward and the inward, were necessary to make the disciples thorough believers in the fact of the resurrection. But some begin with the one, some with the other. Some are convinced first that the gospel story is true, and then perhaps long after waken up to a sense of the importance and preciousness of the things which it relates. Others, again, are like Cleopas and his companion; so engrossed with their own thoughts as to be incapable of appreciating or seeing facts, requiring first to have the eyes of their understanding enlightened to see the beauty and the worthiness of the truth as it is in Jesus.   They may at one time have had a kind of traditional faith in the facts as sufficiently well attested.   But they have lost that faith, it may be not without regret.   They are sceptics, and yet they are sad because they are so, and feel that it was better with them when, like others, they believed.   Yet, though they attempt it, they cannot restore their faith by a study of mere external evidences.   They read books dealing in such evidences, but they are not much impressed by them.   Their eyes are holden, and they know not Christ coming to them in that outward way.   But He reveals Himself to them in another manner.   By hidden discourse with their spirits He conveys into their minds a powerful sense of the moral grandeur of the Christian faith, making them feel that, true or not, it is at least *worthy to be true.*   Then their hearts begin to burn: they hope that what is so beautiful may turn out to be objectively true; the question of the external evidences assumes a new interest to their minds; they inquire, they read, they look; and, lo, they see Jesus revived, a true historical person for them: risen out of the grave of doubt to live for evermore the sun of their souls, more precious for the temporary loss; coming

> "Apparelled in more precious habit,
> More moving, delicate, and full of life,
> Into the eye and prospect of their soul,"

than ever He did before they doubted.

From these remarks on the order of the two revelations made by Jesus to His disciples, — of Himself to the eye of their body, and of the scriptural doctrine of the Messiah to the eye of their mind, — we pass to consider the question, What did the latter revelation amount to?   What was the precise effect of those expositions of Scripture with which the risen Christ favored His hearers?   Did the disciples derive therefrom such an amount of light as to supersede the necessity of any further illumination?   Had Jesus Himself done the work of the Spirit of Truth, whose advent He had promised before He suffered, and led them into all truth? Certainly not. The opening of the understanding which took place at this time did not by any means amount to a full spiritual enlightenment in Christian doctrine. The disciples did not yet comprehend the moral grounds of Christ's sufferings and resurrection. Why He underwent these experiences they knew not; the words "ought" and "behooved" meant for them as yet nothing more than that, according to Old Testament prophecies rightly understood, the things which had happened might and should have been anticipated. They were in the same state of mind as that in which we can conceive the Jewish Christians to whom the Epistle to the Hebrews was addressed to have been after perusing the contents of that profound writing. These Christians were ill grounded in gospel truth: they saw not the glory of the gospel dispensation, nor its harmony with that which went before, and under which they had been themselves educated. In particular, the divine dignity of the Author of the Christian faith seemed to them incompatible with His earthly humiliation. Accordingly, the writer of the epistle set himself to prove that the divinity, the temporary humiliation, and the subsequent glorification of the Christ were all taught in the Old Testament Scriptures, quoting these liberally for that purpose in the early chapters of his epistle. He did, in fact, by his written expositions for his readers, what Jesus did by His oral expositions for His hearers. And what shall we say was the immediate effect of the writer's argument on the minds of those who attentively perused it? This, we imagine, that the crude believer on laying down the book would be constrained to admit: "Well, he is right: these things are all written in the Scriptures of the Messiah; and therefore no one of them, not even the humiliation and suffering at which I stumble, can be a reason for rejecting Jesus as the Christ." A very important result, yet a very elementary one. From the bare concession that the real life of Jesus corresponded to the ideal life of the Messiah as portrayed in the Old Testament, to the admiring, enthusiastic, and thoroughly intelligent appreciation of gospel truth exhibited by the writer himself in every page of his epistle, what a vast distance!

Not less was the distance between the state of mind of the

disciples after Jesus had expounded to them the things in the law, and the prophets, and the psalms concerning Himself, and the state of enlightenment to which they attained as apostles after the advent of the Comforter. Now they knew the alphabet merely of the doctrine of Christ; then they had arrived at perfection, and were thoroughly initiated into the mystery of the gospel. Now a single ray of light was let into their dark minds; then the daylight of truth poured its full flood into their souls. Or we may express the difference in terms suggested by the narrative given by John of the events connected with this first appearance of the risen Jesus to His disciples. John relates, that, at a certain stage in the proceedings, Jesus breathed on the disciples, and said unto them, "Receive ye the Holy Ghost." We are not to understand that they then and there received the Spirit in the promised fulness. The breath was rather but a sign and earnest of what was to come. It was but an emblematic renewal of the promise, and a first instalment of its fulfilment. It was but the little cloud like a man's hand that portended a plenteous rain, or the first gentle puff of wind which precedes the mighty gale. Now they have the little breath of the Spirit's influence, but not till Pentecost shall they feel the rushing wind. So great is the difference between now and then: between the spiritual enlightenment of the disciples on the first Christian Sabbath evening, and that of the apostles in after days.

It was but the day of small things with these disciples yet. The small things, however, were not to be despised; nor were they. What value the *ten* set on the light they had received we are not indeed told, but we may safely assume that their feelings were much of kin to those of the two brethren who journeyed towards Emmaus. Conversing together on the discourse of Jesus after His departure, they said one unto another, "Did not our heart burn within us while He talked with us by the way, and while He opened to us the Scriptures?" The light they had got might be small, but it was *new* light, and it had all the heart-kindling. thought-stirring power of new truth. That conversation on the road formed a crisis in their spiritual history. It was the dawn of the gospel day; it was the little spark which kindles a great fire; it deposited in their minds a thought which was to form the germ or centre of a new system of belief; it took away the veil which had been upon their faces in the reading of the Old Testament, and was thus the first step in a process which was to issue in their beholding with open face, as in a glass, the glory of the Lord, and in their being changed into the same image, from glory to glory, by the Lord the Spirit. Happy the man who has got even so far as these two disciples at this time!

Some disconsolate soul may say, Would that happiness were mine! For the comfort of such a forlorn brother, let us note the circumstances in which this new light arose for the disciples. Their hearts were set a-burning when they had become very dry and withered: hopeless, sick, and life-weary, through sorrow and disappointment. It is always so: the fuel must be dry that the spark may take hold. It was when the people of Israel complained, "Our bones are dried and our hope is lost, we are cut off for our parts," that the word went forth: "Behold, O my people, I will open your graves, and cause you to come up out of your graves, and bring you into the land of Israel." So with these disciples of Jesus. It was when every particle of the sap of hope had been bleached out of them, and their faith had been reduced to this, "We trusted that it had been He which should have redeemed Israel," that their hearts were set burning by the kindling power of a new truth. So it has been in many an instance since then. The fire of hope has been kindled in the heart, never to be extinguished, just at the moment when men were settling down into despair; faith has been revived when a man seemed to himself to be an infidel; the light of truth has arisen to minds which had ceased to look for the dawn; the comfort of salvation has returned to souls which had begun to think that God's mercy was clean gone for ever. "When the Son of man cometh shall He find faith on the earth?"

There is nothing strange in this. The truth is, the heart needs to be dried by trial before it can be made to burn. Till sorrow comes, human hearts do not catch the divine fire; there is too much of this world's life-sap in them. That was what made the disciples so slow of heart to believe all that the prophets had spoken.   Their worldly ambition prevented them from learning the spirituality of Christ's kingdom, and pride made them blind to the glory of the cross.   Hence Jesus justly upbraided them for their unbelief and their mind-less stupidity.   Had their hearts been pure, they might have known beforehand what was to happen.   As it was, they comprehended nothing till their Lord's death had blighted their hope and blasted their ambition, and bitter sorrow had prepared them for receiving spiritual instruction.

SECTION III — THE DOUBT OF THOMAS

JOHN xx. 24-29

"Thomas, one of the twelve, called Didymus, was not with them when Jesus came" on that first Christian Sabbath evening, and showed Himself to His disciples.   One hopes he had a good reason for his absence ; but it is at least possi-ble that he had not.   In his melancholy humor he may simply have been indulging himself in the luxury of solitary sadness, just as some whose Christ is dead do now spend their Sab-baths at home or in rural solitudes, shunning the offensive cheerfulness or the drowsy dulness of social worship.   Be that as it may, in any case he missed a good sermon ; the only one, so far as we know, in the whole course of our Lord's ministry, in which He addressed Himself formally to the task of expounding the Messianic doctrine of the Old Testament. Had he but known that such a discourse was to be delivered that night !   But one never knows when the good things will come, and the only way to make sure of getting them is to be always at our post.

The same melancholy humor which probably caused Thomas to be an absentee on the occasion of Christ's first meeting with His disciples after He rose from the dead, made him also sceptical above all the rest concerning the tidings of the resurrection.   When the other disciples told him on his return that they had just seen the Lord, he replied with vehemence : "Except I shall see in His hands the print of the nails, and put my fingers into the print of the nails, and put my hand into His side, I will not believe."[1]

[1] Ver. 25.

He was not to be satisfied with the testimony of his brethren : he must have palpable evidence for himself. Not that
he doubted their veracity ; but he could not get rid of the
suspicion that what they said they had seen was but a mere
ghostly appearance by which their eyes had been deceived.

The scepticism of Thomas was, we think, mainly a matter
of temperament, and had little in common with the doubt of
men of rationalistic proclivities, who are inveterately incredulous respecting the supernatural, and stumble at every thing
savoring of the miraculous. It has been customary to call
Thomas the Rationalist among the twelve, and it has even
been supposed that he had belonged to the sect of the Sadducees before he joined the society of Jesus. On mature
consideration, we are constrained to say that we see very
little foundation for such a view of this disciple's character,
while we certainly do not grudge modern doubters any comfort they may derive from it. We are quite well aware that
among the sincere, and even the spiritually-minded, there
are men whose minds are so constituted that they find it
very difficult to believe in the supernatural and the miraculous : so difficult, that it is a question whether, if they had
been in Thomas's place, the freest handling and the minutest
inspection of the wounds in the risen Saviour's body would
have availed to draw forth from them an expression of *unhesitating* faith in the reality of His resurrection. Nor do
we see any reason *à priori* for asserting that no disciple of
Jesus *could* have been a person of such a cast of mind. All
we say is, there is no evidence that Thomas, as a matter of
fact, was a man of this stamp. Nowhere in the Gospel history do we discover any unreadiness on his part to believe
in the supernatural or the miraculous *as such*. We do not
find, *e.g.* that he was sceptical about the raising of Lazarus :
we are only told that, when Jesus proposed to visit the
afflicted family in Bethany, he regarded the journey as
fraught with danger to his beloved Master and to them all,
and said, " Let us also go, that we may die with Him."
Then, as now, he showed Himself not so much the Rationalist as the man of gloomy temperament, prone to look upon
the dark side of things, living in the pensive moonlight
rather than in the cheerful sunlight. His doubt did not

spring out of his system of thought, but out of the state of his feelings.

Another thing we must say here concerning the doubt of this disciple.   It did not proceed from *unwillingness* to believe.   It was the doubt of a sad man, whose sadness was due to this, that the event whereof he doubted was one of which he would most gladly be assured.   Nothing could give Thomas greater delight than to be certified that his Master was indeed risen.   This is evident from the joy he manifested when he was at length satisfied.   " My Lord and my God ! " that is not the exclamation of one who is forced reluctantly to admit a fact he would rather deny.   It is common for men who never had any doubts themselves to trace all doubt to bad motives, and denounce it indiscriminately as a crime. Now, unquestionably, too many doubt from bad motives, because they do not wish and cannot afford to believe. Many deny the resurrection of the dead, because it would be to them a resurrection to shame and everlasting contempt. But this is by no means true of all.   Some doubt who desire to believe ; nay, their doubt is due to their excessive anxiety to believe.   They are so eager to know the very truth, and feel so keenly the immense importance of the interests at stake, that they cannot take things for granted, and for a time their hand so trembles that they cannot seize firm hold of the great objects of faith — a living God ; an incarnate, crucified, risen Saviour ; a glorious eternal future.   Theirs is the doubt peculiar to earnest, thoughtful, pure-hearted men, wide as the poles asunder from the doubt of the frivolous, the worldly, the vicious : a holy, noble doubt, not a base and unholy ; if not to be praised as positively meritorious, still less to be harshly condemned and excluded from the pale of Christian sympathy — a doubt which at worst is but an infirmity, and which ever ends in strong, unwavering faith.

That Jesus regarding the doubt of the heavy-hearted disciple as of this sort, we infer from His way of dealing with it. Thomas having been absent on the occasion of His first appearing to the disciples, the risen Lord makes a second appearance for the absent one's special benefit, and offers him the proof desiderated.   The introductory salutation

being over, He turns Himself at once to the doubter, and
addresses him in terms fitted to remind him of his own statement to his brethren, saying : " Reach hither thy finger, and
behold my hands ; and reach hither thy hand, and thrust it
into my side : and be not faithless, but believing." There
may be somewhat of reproach here, but there is far more of
most considerate sympathy. Jesus speaks as to a sincere
disciple, whose faith is weak, not as to one who hath an evil
heart of unbelief. When demands for evidence were made
by men who merely wanted an excuse for unbelief, He met
them in a very different manner. " A wicked and adulterous
generation," He was wont to say in such a case, "seeketh
after a sign, and there shall no sign be given unto it but the
sign of the Prophet Jonas."

Having ascertained the character of Thomas's doubt, let
us now look at his faith.

The melancholy disciple's doubts were soon removed.
But how ? Did Thomas avail himself of the offered facilities
for ascertaining the reality of his Lord's resurrection ? Did
he actually put his fingers and hand into the nail and spear
wounds ? Opinions differ on this point, but we think the
probability is on the side of those who maintain the negative.
Several things incline us to this view. First, the narrative
seems to leave no room for the process of investigation.
Thomas answers the proposal of Jesus by what appears to be
an immediate profession of faith. Then the form in which
that profession is made is not such as we should expect the
result of a deliberate inquiry to assume. " My Lord and my
God ! " is the warm, passionate language of a man who has
undergone some sudden change of feeling, rather than of one
who has just concluded a scientific experiment. Further, we
observe there is no allusion to such a process in the remark
made by Jesus concerning the faith of Thomas. The disciple is represented as believing because he has seen the
wounds shown, not because he has handled them. Finally,
the idea of the process proposed being actually gone through
is inconsistent with the character of the man to whom the
proposal was made. Thomas was not one of your calm, cold-
blooded men, who conduct inquiries into truth with the
passionless inpartiality of a judge, and who would have

examined the wounds in the risen Saviour's body with all
the coolness with which anatomists dissect dead carcasses.
He was a man of passionate, poetic temperament, vehement
alike in his belief and in his unbelief, and moved to faith or
doubt by the feelings of his heart rather than by the reasonings of his intellect.

The truth, we imagine, about Thomas was something like
this. When, eight days before, he made that threat to his
brother disciples, he did not deliberately mean all he said.
It was the whimsical utterance of a melancholy man, who
was in the humor to be as disconsolate and miserable as
possible. "Jesus risen! the thing is impossible, and there's
an end of it. I won't believe except I do so and so. I don't
know if I shall believe when all's done." But eight days
have gone by, and, lo, there is Jesus in the midst of them,
visible to the disciple who was absent on the former occasion
as well as to the rest. Will Thomas still insist on applying
his rigorous test? No, no! His doubts vanish at the very
sight of Jesus, like morning mists at sunrise. Even *before*
the Risen One has laid bare His wounds, and uttered those
half-reproachful, yet kind, sympathetic words, which evince
intimate knowledge of all that has been passing through His
doubting disciple's mind, Thomas is virtually a believer; and
after he has seen the ugly wounds and heard the generous
words, he is ashamed of his rash, reckless speech to his
brethren, and, overcome with joy and with tears, exclaims,
"My Lord and my God!"

It was a noble confession of faith, — the most advanced,
in fact, ever made by any of the twelve during the time they
were with Jesus. The last is first; the greatest doubter
attains to the fullest and firmest belief. So has it often
happened in the history of the Church. Baxter records it
as his experience, that nothing is so firmly believed as that
which hath once been doubted. Many Thomases have said,
or could say, the same thing of themselves. The doubters
have eventually become the soundest and even the warmest
believers. Doubt in itself is a cold thing, and, as in the case
of Thomas, it often utters harsh and heartless sayings. Nor
need this surprise us; for when the mind is in doubt the
soul is in darkness, and during the chilly night the heart

becomes frozen. But when the daylight of faith comes, the frost melts, and hearts which once seemed hard and stony show themselves capable of generous enthusiasm and ardent devotion.

Socinians, whose system is utterly overthrown by Thomas's confession naturally interpreted, tell us that the words " My Lord and my God " do not refer to Jesus at all, but to the Deity in heaven. They are merely an expression of astonishment on the part of the disciple, on finding that what he had doubted was really come to pass. He lifts up his eyes and his hands to heaven, as it were, and exclaims, My Lord and my God ! it is a fact : The crucified Jesus is restored to life again. This interpretation is utterly desperate. It disregards the statement of the text, that Thomas, in uttering these words, was answering and speaking to Jesus, and it makes a man bursting with emotion speak frigidly ; for while the one expression " My God " might have been an appropriate utterance of astonishment, the two phrases, " My Lord and my God," are for that purpose weak and unnatural.

We have here, therefore, no mere expression of surprise, but a profession of faith most appropriate to the man and the circumstances ; as pregnant with meaning as it is pithy and forcible. Thomas declares at once his acceptance of a miraculous fact, and his belief in a momentous doctrine. In the first part of his address to Jesus he recognizes that He who was dead is alive : My Lord, my beloved Master ! it is even He, — the very same person with whom we enjoyed such blessed fellowship before He was crucified. In the second part of his address he acknowledges Christ's divinity, if not for the first time, at least with an intelligence and an emphasis altogether new. From the fact he rises to the doctrine : My Lord risen, yea, and therefore my God ; for He is divine over whom death hath no power. And the doctrine in turn helps to give to the fact of the resurrection additional certainty ; for if Christ be God, death *could* have no power over Him, and His resurrection was a matter of course. Thomas having reached the sublime affirmation, " My God," has made the transition from the low platform of faith on which he stood when he demanded sensible evidence, to the higher, on which it is felt that such evidence is superfluous.

We have now to notice, in the last place, the remark made by the Lord concerning the faith just professed by His disciple. "Jesus saith unto him, Thomas, because thou hast seen me, thou hast believed : blessed are they that have not seen, and yet have believed."

This reflection on the blessedness of those who believe without seeing, though expressed in the past tense, really concerned the future. The case supposed by Jesus was to be the case of all believers after the apostolic age. Since then no one has seen, and no one can believe because he has seen, as the apostles saw. They saw, that we might be able to do without seeing, believing on their testimony.

But what does Jesus mean by pronouncing a beatitude on those who see not, yet believe?

He does not mean to commend those who believe without any inquiry. It is one thing to believe without seeing, another thing to believe without consideration. To believe without seeing is to be capable of being satisfied with something less than absolute demonstration, or to have such an inward illumination as renders us to a certain extent independent of external evidence. Such a faculty of faith is most needful ; for if faith were possible only to those who see, belief in Christianity could not extend beyond the apostolic age. But to believe without consideration is a different matter altogether. It is simply not to care whether the thing believed be true or false. There is no merit in doing that. Such faith has its origin in what is base in men, — in their ignorance, sloth, and spiritual indifference ; and it can bring no blessing to its possessors. Be the truths credited ever so high, holy, blessed, what good can a faith do which receives them as matters of course without inquiry, or without even so much as knowing what the truths believed mean ?

The Lord Jesus, then, does not here bestow a benediction on credulity.

As little does He mean to say that all the felicity falls to the lot of those who have never, like Thomas, doubted. The fact is not so. Those who believe with facility do certainly enjoy a blessedness all their own. They escape the torment of uncertainty, and the current of their spiritual life flows on very smoothly. But the men who have doubted, and now at length believe, have also their peculiar joys, with which no stranger can intermeddle. Theirs is the joy experienced when that which was dead is alive again, and that which was lost is found. Theirs is the rapture of Thomas when he exclaimed, with reference to a Saviour thought to be gone for ever, "My Lord and my God." Theirs is the bliss of the man who, having dived into a deep sea, brings up a pearl of very great price. Theirs is the comfort of having their very bygone doubts made available for the furtherance of their faith, every doubt becoming a stone in the hidden foundation on which the superstructure of their creed is built, the perturbations of faith being converted into confirmations, just as the perturbations in the planetary motions, at first supposed to throw doubt on Newton's theory of gravitation, were converted by more searching inquiry into the strongest proof of its truth.

What, then, does the Lord Jesus mean by these words? Simply this : He would have those who must believe without seeing, understand that they have no cause to envy those who had an opportunity of seeing, and who believed only after they saw. We who live so far from the events, are very apt to imagine that we are placed at a great disadvantage as compared with the disciples of Jesus. So in some respects we are, and especially in this, that faith is more difficult for us than for them. But then we must not forget that, in proportion as faith is difficult, it is meritorious, and precious to the heart. It is a higher attainment to be able to believe without seeing, than to believe because we have seen ; and if it cost an effort, the trial of faith but enhances its value. We must remember, further, that we never reach the full blessedness of faith till what we believe shines in the light of its own self-evidence. Think you the disciples were happy men because they had seen their risen Lord and believed? They were far happier when they had attained to such clear insight into the whole mystery of redemption, that proof of this or that particular fact or doctrine was felt to be quite unnecessary.

To that felicity Jesus wished His doubting disciple to aspire ; and by contrasting his case with that of those who believe without seeing, He gives us to know that it is

attainable for us also.   We, too, may attain the blessedness
of a faith raised above all doubt by its own clear insight into
divine truth.   If we are faithful, we may rise to this from
very humble things.   We may begin, in our weakness, with
being Thomases, clinging eagerly to every spar of external
evidence to save ourselves from drowning, and end· with a
faith amounting almost to sight, rejoicing in Jesus as our
Lord and God, with a joy unspeakable and full of glory.

29

THE UNDER-SHEPHERDS ADMONISHED

John 21:15-17

"I go a-fishing," said Simon to his companions, some time after they and he had returned from Jerusalem to the neighborhood of the Galilean lake. "We also go with thee," replied Thomas and Nathanael, and James and John, and two others unnamed, making with Peter seven, probably all of the eleven who were fishermen by trade. One and all went on that fishing expedition *con amore*. It was an expedition, we presume, in the first place, in quest of food, but it was something more. It was a return to dear old ways, amid familiar scenes, which called up pleasing reminiscences of bygone times. It was a recreation and a solace, most welcome and most needful to men who had passed through very painful and exciting experiences ; a holiday for men fatigued by sorrow, and surprise, and watching. Every student with overtasked brain, every artisan with overstrained sinews, can conceive the *abandon* with which those seven disciples threw themselves into their boats, and sailed out into the depths of the Sea of Tiberias to ply their old craft.

Out on the waters that night, what were these men's thoughts? From the significant allusion made by Jesus to Peter's youth in the colloquy of next morning, we infer they were something like the following : — "After all, were it not better to be simple fishermen than to be apostles of the Christian religion? What have we got by following Jesus? Certainly not what we expected. And have we any reason to expect better things in the future? Our Master has told us that our future lot will be very much like His own, — a life of sorrow, ending probably in martyrdom. But here, in our native province of Galilee, pursuing our old calling, we might think, believe, act as we pleased, shielded by obscurity from all danger. Then how delightfully free and independent this rustic life by the shores of the lake! In former days, ere we left our nets and followed Jesus, we girded ourselves with our fishermen's coats, and walked whither we would. When we shall have become apostles, all that will be at an end. We shall be burdened with a heavy load of responsibility ; obliged continually to think of others, and not to please ourselves ; liable to have our personal liberty taken away, yea, even our very life."

In putting such words into the mouths of the disciples, we do not violate probability ; for such feelings as the words express are both natural and common in view of grave responsibilities and perils about to be incurred. Perhaps no one ever put his hand to the plough of an arduous enterprise, without indulging for at least a brief space in such a looking back. It is an infirmity which easily besets human nature.

Yet, natural as it comes to men to look back, it is not wise. Regretful thoughts of the past are for the most part delusive ; they were so, certainly, in the case of the disciples. If the simple life they left behind them was so very happy, why did they leave it ? Why so prompt to forsake their nets and their boats, and to follow after Jesus? Ah! fishing in the blue waters of the Sea of Galilee did not satisfy the whole man. Life is more than meat, and the kingdom of God is man's chief end. Besides, the fisherman's life has its drawbacks, and is by no means so romantic as it seems at the distance of years. You may sometimes go out with your nets, and toil all night, and catch nothing.

This was what actually happened on the present occasion. "That night they caught nothing." [1] The circumstance probably helped to break the spell of romance, and to waken the seven disciples out of a fond dream. Be that as it may, there was One who knew all their thoughts, and who would see to it that they did not indulge long in the luxury of reactionary feeling. "When the morning was now come, Jesus stood on the shore." [2] He is come to show Himself for the third time [3]

---

[1] John xxi. 3.   [2] John xxi. 4.   [3] The *sixth* appearance since He was risen.

to His disciples, — not, as before, to convince them that He is risen, but to induce them to dedicate their whole minds and hearts to their future vocation as fishers of men, and as under-shepherds of the flock, preparatory to His own departure from the world. His whole conduct on this occasion is directed to that object. First, He gives them directions for catching a great haul of fish, to remind them of their former call to be His apostles, and to be an encouraging sign or symbol of their success in their apostolic work. Then He invites them to dine on fish which He had procured,[1] roasted on a fire of His own kindling on the shore, to cure them of earthly care, and to assure them that if they seek to serve the kingdom with undivided heart, all their wants will be attended to. Finally, when the morning meal is over, He enters into conversation, in the hearing of all, with the disciple who had been the leader in the night adventure on the lake, and addresses him in a style fitted to call forth all his latent enthusiasm, and intended to have a similar effect on the minds of all present.

On the surface, the words spoken by Jesus to Peter seem to concern that disciple alone ; and the object aimed at appears to be to restore him to a position as an apostle, which he might not unnaturally think he had forfeited by his conduct in the high priest's palace. This, accordingly, is the view commonly taken of this impressive scene on the shore of the lake. And whether we agree with that view or not, we must admit that, for some reason or other, the Lord Jesus wished to recall to Peter's remembrance his recent shortcomings. Traces of allusion to past incidents in the disciple's history during the late crisis are unmistakable. Even the time selected for the conversation is significant. It was when they had dined that Jesus asked Peter if he loved Him ; it was after they had supped Jesus gave His disciples His new commandment of love, and that Peter made his vehement protestation of devotion to his Master's cause and person. The name by which the risen Lord addressed His disciple — not Peter, but Simon son of Jonas — was fitted to remind him of his weakness, and of that other occasion on

---

[1] When the disciples landed, they saw the fire and fish *already* laid on it, and bread set near by.

which, calling him by the same name, Jesus warned him that Satan was about to sift him as wheat. The thrice-repeated question, "Lovest thou me?" could not fail painfully to remind Peter of his threefold denial, and so to renew his grief. The form in which the question was first put — "Lovest thou me more than these?" — contains a manifest allusion to Peter's declaration, "Though all shall be offended 'because of Thee, yet will I never be offended." The injunction, "Feed my sheep," points back to the prophetic announcement made by Jesus on the way to the Mount of Olives, "All ye shall be offended because of me this night; for it is written, I will smite the Shepherd, and the sheep of the flock shall be scattered abroad," and means, Suffer not the sheep to be scattered, as ye were for a season scattered yourselves. The injunction, "Feed my *lambs*," associated with the first question, "Lovest thou me more than these?" makes us think of the charge, "When thou art converted, strengthen thy brethren;" the idea suggested in both cases being the same, viz. that the man who has fallen most deeply, and learned most thoroughly his own weakness, is, or ought to be, best qualified for strengthening the weak, — for feeding the lambs.

Notwithstanding all these allusions to Peter's fall, we are unable to acquiesce in the view that the scene here recorded signified the formal restoration of the erring disciple to his position as an apostle. We do not deny that, after what had taken place, that disciple needed restoration for his own comfort and peace of mind. But our difficulty is this: Had he not been restored already? What was the meaning of that private meeting between him and Jesus, and what its necessary result? Who can doubt that after that meeting the disciple's mind was at ease, and that thereafter he was at peace, both with himself and with his Master? Or if evidence is wanted of the fact, look at Peter's behavior on recognizing Jesus from the boat, as He stood on the shore in the gray morning, casting himself as he was into the sea, in his haste to get near his beloved Lord. Was that the behavior of a man afflicted with a guilty conscience? But it may be replied, There was still need for a formal public restoration, the scandal caused by Peter's sin being public.

This we doubt; but even granting it, what then? Why did the restoration not take place sooner, at the first or second meeting in Jerusalem? Then, does the scene by the shores of the lake really look like a formal transaction? Can we regard that casual, easy, familiar meeting and colloquy after breakfast with two-thirds of the disciples as an ecclesiastical diet, for the solemn purpose of restoring a fallen brother to church fellowship and standing? The idea is too frigid and pedantic to be seriously entertained. Then one more objection to this theory remains to be stated, viz. that it fails to give unity to the various parts of the scene. It may explain the questioning to which Jesus subjected Peter, but it does not explain the prophetic reference to his future history with which He followed it up. Between "I allow you, notwithstanding past misdemeanors, to be an apostle," and "I forewarn you that in that capacity you shall not have the freedom of action in which you rejoiced in former days," there is no connection traceable. Peter's fall did not suggest such a turn of thought; for it sprang not from the love of freedom, but from the fear of man.

Not the restoration of Peter to a forfeited position, but his recall to a more solemn sense of his high vocation, do we find in this scene. Not "I allow you," but "I urge you," seems to us to be the burthen of Christ's words to this disciple, and through him to all his brethren. By all considerations He would move them to address themselves heart and soul to their apostolic work, and let boats and nets and every thing else alone for ever. "By the memory of thine own weakness," He would say to Simon for that end; "by my forgiving love, and thy gratitude for it; by the need of brother disciples, which thine own past frailty may teach thee to understand and compassionate; by the ardent attachment which I know you cherish towards myself: by these and all kindred considerations, I charge thee, on the eve of my departure, be a hero, play the man, be strong for others, not for thyself, 'feed the flock of God, taking the oversight thereof, not by constraint, but willingly.' Shrink not from responsibility, covet not ease, bend thy neck to the yoke, and let love make it light. Sweet is liberty to thy human heart; but patient, burden-bearing love, though less pleasant, is far more noble."

Such being the message which Jesus meant for all present, Peter was most appropriately selected as the medium for conveying it. He was an excellent text on which to preach a sermon on self-consecration. His character and conduct supplied all the poetry, and argument, and illustration necessary to give pathos and point to the theme. How dear to his impetuous, passionate spirit, unrestrained freedom! And what heart is not touched by the thought of such a man schooling his high, mettlesome soul into patience and submission? The young, frolicsome, bounding fisherman, girding on his coat, and going hither and thither at his own sweet will; the aged saintly apostle, meek as a lamb, stretching forth his arms to be bound for the martyr's doom: what a moving contrast! Had that passionate man, in some senses the strongest character among the twelve, been in other senses the weakest, then who could better illustrate men's need of shepherding? Had he learnt his own weakness, and through his knowledge thereof grown stronger? Then how better state the general duty of the strong to help the weak, than by assigning to this particular disciple the special duty of taking care of the weakest? To say to Peter, "Feed my lambs," was to say to all the apostles, "Feed my sheep."

In requiring Peter to show his love by performing the part of shepherd to the little flock of believers, Jesus adapted His demand to the spiritual capacity of the disciple. Love to the Saviour does not necessarily take the form of feeding the sheep; in immature and inexperienced disciples, it rather takes the form of being sheep. It is only after the weak have become strong, and established in grace, that they ought to become shepherds, charging themselves with the care of others. In laying on Peter and his brethren pastoral duties, therefore, Jesus virtually announces that they have now passed, or are about to pass, out of the category of the weak into the category of the strong. "Hitherto," He virtually says to them, "ye have been as sheep, needing to be guided, watched over, and defended by the wisdom and courage of another. Now, however, the time is arrived when ye must become shepherds, able and willing to do for the weak what I have done for you. Hitherto ye have left me to care for you; henceforth you must accustom yourselves to be looked to as guardians, even as I have been by you. Hitherto ye have been as children under me, your parent; henceforth ye must yourselves be parents, taking charge of the children. Hitherto ye have been as raw recruits, liable to panic, and fleeing from danger; henceforth ye must be captains superior to fear, and by your calm determination inspire the soldiers of the cross with heroic daring." In short, Jesus here in effect announces to Peter and to the rest that they are now to make the transition from boyhood to manhood, from pupilage to self-government, from a position of dependence and exemption from care to one of influence, authority, and responsibility, as leaders and commanders in the Christian community, doing the work for which they have been so long under training. Such a transition and transformation did accordingly take place shortly after in the history of the disciples. They assumed the position of Christ's deputies or substitutes after His ascension, Peter being the leading or representative man, though not the Pope, in the infant Church; and their character was altered to fit them for their high functions. The timid disciples became bold apostles. Peter, who weakly denied the Lord in the judgment-hall, heroically confessed Him before the Sanhedrim. The ignorant and stupid disciples, who had been continually misunderstanding their Master's words, became filled with the spirit of wisdom and understanding, so that men listened to their words as they had been wont to listen to the words of Jesus Himself.

We have said that love to Christ does not impose on all His disciples the duty of a shepherd; showing itself rather in by far the larger number in simply hearing the shepherd's voice and following him, and generally in a willingness to be guided by those who are wiser than themselves. We must add, that all who are animated by the spirit of love to the Redeemer, will be either shepherds or sheep, actively useful in caring for the souls of others, or thankfully using the provision made for the care of their own souls. Too many, however, come under neither designation. Some are sheep indeed, but sheep going astray; others are neither sheep nor shepherds, being self-reliant, yet indisposed to be helpful;

too self-willed to be led, yet disinclined to make their strength and experience available for their brethren, utilizing all their talents for the exclusive service of their own private interests. Such men are to be found in Church and State, sedulously holding back from office and responsibility, and severely criticising those who have come under the yoke; animadverting on their timidity and bondage, as unbroken colts, if they could speak, might animadvert on the tameness of horses in harness, the bits and bridles that form a part of church harness, in the shape of formulas and confessions, coming in for a double share of censure.[1]

Now, it is all very well to be wild colts, rejoicing in unrestrained liberty, for a season in youth; but it will not do to be spurning the yoke all one's lifetime. " Ye, then, that are strong ought to bear the infirmities of the weak, and not to please yourselves." It is no doubt most agreeable to be free from care, and to walk about unfettered in opinion and action, and, shaking off those who would hang on our skirts, to live the life of gods, careless of mankind. But it is not the chief end of any man, least of all of a wise and strong man, to be free from care or trouble. He who has a Christian heart must feel that he is strong and wise for the sake of others who want strength and wisdom; and he will undertake the shepherd's office, though shrinking with fear and trembling from its responsibilities, and though conscious also that in so doing he is consenting to have his liberty and independence greatly circumscribed. The yoke of love which binds us to our fellows is sometimes not easy, and the burden of caring for them not light; but, on the whole, it is better and nobler to be a drudge and a slave at the bidding of love, than to be a free man through the emancipating power of selfishness. Better Peter a prisoner and martyr for the gospel, than Simon inculcating on his Lord the selfish policy, "Save Thyself," or lying in luxurious ease on the hill of Transfiguration, exclaiming, "Lord, it is good to be here." Better Peter bound

---

[1] It is a fair question whether our venerable Confession is not too minute and stringent, a sort of double bridle, even for ministers; and whether subscription should be required at all for lay elders, who do not teach, want the professional knowledge necessary to intelligent subscription to all details, and are as amenable to discipline for belief as for *conduct* without subscription. No man signs an obligation to keep the ten commandments in order to be subject to discipline for immorality.

by others, and led whither he would not, as a good shepherd to be sacrificed for the sheep, than Simon girding on his own garment, and walking along with the careless jaunty air of a modern *pococurantist*. A life on the ocean wave, a life in the woods, a life in the mountains or in the clouds, may be fine to dream and sing of; but the only life out of which genuine heroism and poetry comes, is that which is spent on this solid prosaic earth in the lowly work of doing good.

Note now, finally, the evidence supplied in Peter's answers to his Lord's questions, that he is indeed fitted for the responsible work to which he is summoned. It is not merely that he can appeal to Jesus Himself, as one who knows all things, and say, " Thou knowest that I love Thee;" for, as we have already hinted, every sincere disciple can do that. Two specific signs of spiritual maturity are discernible here, not to be found in those who are weak in grace, not previously found in Peter himself. There is, first, marked modesty, — very noticeable in so forward a man. Peter does not now make any comparisons between himself and his brethren as he had done previously. In spite of appearances, he still protests that he does love Jesus; but he takes care not to say, " I love Thee more than those." He not only does not say this, but he manifestly does not think it: the bragging spirit has left him; he is a humble, subdued, wise man, spiritually equipped for the pastorate, just because he has ceased to think himself supremely competent for it.

The second mark of maturity discernible in Peter's replies is godly sorrow for past shortcoming: " Peter was grieved because He (Jesus) said unto him the third time, Lovest thou me?" He was grieved because by the threefold interrogation he was reminded that the threefold denial of which he had been guilty afforded ground for calling his love in question. Observe particularly the feeling produced by this delicate reference to his former sins. It was *grief*, not irritation, anger, or shame. There is no pride, passion, vanity in this man's soul, but only holy, meek contrition; no sudden coloring is observable in his countenance, but only the gracious softened expression of a penitent, chastised spirit. The man who can so take allusions to his sins is not only fit to tend the sheep, but even to nurse the lambs. He will restore those who have fallen in a spirit of meekness. He will be tender towards offenders, not with the spurious charity which cannot afford to condemn sin strongly, but with the genuine charity of one who has himself received mercy for sins sincerely repented of. By his benignant sympathy sinners will be converted unto God in unfeigned sorrow for their offences, and in humble hope of pardon; and by his watchful care many sheep will be kept from ever straying from the fold.

SECTION II — PASTOR PASTORUM

JOHN xxi. 19-22

To be a dutiful under-shepherd is, in another view, to be a faithful sheep, following the Chief Shepherd whithersoever He goes. Pastors are not lords over God's heritage, but mere servants of Christ, the great Head of the Church, bound to regard His will as their law, and His life as their model. In the scene by the lake Jesus took pains to make His disciples understand this. He did not allow them to suppose that, in committing to their pastoral charge His flock, He was abdicating His position as Shepherd and Bishop of souls. Having said to Peter, "Feed my lambs," "Feed my sheep," He said to him, as His final word, "Follow me."

It is implied in the narrative, that while Jesus said this, He arose and walked away from the spot where the disciples had just taken their morning meal. Whither He went we are not told, but it may have been towards that "mountain in Galilee," the preappointed rendezvous where the risen Saviour met "above five hundred brethren at once." The sheep have doubtless been wending thither to meet their divine Shepherd, as in a secluded upland fold; and it is more than possible that the object of the journey in which Peter is invited to join his Master, is to introduce him to the flock which had just been committed to his care.

Be this as it may, Peter obeyed the summons, and rose at once to follow Jesus. His first impression probably was that he was to be the solitary attendant of his Lord, and a natural wish to ascertain the state of the case led him to look behind to see what his companions were doing. On turning round, he observed the disciple whom Jesus loved, and whom he too loved, following close in his footsteps ; and the question forthwith rose to his lips, " Lord, and what of this man ? " The question was elliptical, but it meant : John is coming after us ; Is the same lot in store for him that you have prophesied for me ? Shall he too be bound and led whither he would not ; or shall he, as the disciple most dearly beloved, be exempted from the hardships I am fated to endure ?

That another and a happier fortune was reserved for John seemed, we believe, probable to Peter. He could not but recall to mind that memorable scene in which John's mother made her ambitious request for her two sons ; and in spite of what Jesus had said to them about tasting of His cup, and being baptized with His baptism, he, Peter, might well imagine that John's desire would be fulfilled, and that he would live to see the kingdom come, and to share its glories ; especially as one and all of the disciples, down to the very last day of their Lord's sojourn on earth, still expected the kingdom to be restored to Israel very soon. If such was Peter's thought, it is not surprising that he should ask, if not with envy, at least with a sadder sense of his own loss, " Lord, what of this man ? " Adversity is hard to bear at best, but hardest of all when personal ill-fortune stands in glaring contrast with the prosperity of a brother who started on his career at the same time, and with no better prospects than the man whom he has far outstripped in the race.

To such considerations, however, Jesus paid little respect in His reply to Peter's question. " If I will," He said, " that he tarry till I come, what is that to thee ? Follow thou me." " How stern and unfeeling ! " one is tempted to exclaim. Might not Jesus at least have reminded Simon, for his comfort, of the words He once uttered to James and John : " Ye shall drink of my cup " ? Would it not have helped Peter more cheerfully to follow his Master in the arduous path of the cross, to have told him that, in whatever manner John might die, he too would have to suffer for the gospel ; that his life, whether long or short, would be full of tribulation ; that participation in the glory of the king-

dom did not depend on longevity; that, in fact, the first to
die would be the first to enter into glory? But no, it might
not be. To administer such comfort would have been to
indulge the disciple's weakness. One who has to play a
soldier's part must be trained with military rigor. Effemi-
nacy, sighing after happiness, brooding over the felicity we
have missed, are out of place in an apostle's character; and
Jesus, to whom such dispositions are most abhorrent, will
take good care not to give them any countenance. He will
have all His followers, and specially the heads of His people,
to be heroes, — "Ironsides," prompt to do bidding, fearless
of danger, patient of fatigue, without a trace of selfish soft-
ness. He will give no quarter even to natural weaknesses,
disregards present pain, cares not how we smart under
rebuke, provided only He gain His end, — the production of
character temptation-proof.

Having this end in view, Jesus took no trouble to correct
Peter's misapprehensions about his brother disciple. Misapprehensions, we say, for such they indeed were. John
did not tarry till the Lord came in the sense in which Peter
understood the words. He lived, indeed, till the close of
the first Christian century, therefore long after the Lord's
coming to execute judgment on Jerusalem. But except for
the longevity he enjoyed, the last of the apostles was in no
respect to be envied. The Church was militant all his days:
he took part in many of its battles, and received therein
many scars. Companion with Peter in the Church's first
conflict with the world, he was a prisoner in Patmos for the
word of God, and for the testimony of Jesus Christ, after
Peter had fallen asleep. One might perhaps say that, owing
to temperament, the life of John was less stirring than that
of his brother apostle. He was a man of less impetuosity,
though not of less intensity; and there was, perhaps, not
so much in his character provocative of the world's opposition. Both by his virtues and by his infirmities Peter was
predestined to be the *champion* of the faith, the Luther of
the apostolic age, giving and receiving the hardest blows,
and bearing the brunt of the battle. John, on the other
hand, was the Melanchthon among the apostles, without,
however, Melanchthon's tendency to yield; and as such,

enjoyed probably a quieter, and, on the whole, more peaceful life. But this difference between the two men was, after all, quite subordinate ; and, all things considered, we may say that John drank not less deeply of Christ's cup than did Peter. There was nothing glorious or enviable in his lot on earth, except the vision in Patmos of the glory yet to be revealed.

Yet while all this was clear to His prescient eye, Jesus did not condescend to give any explanations concerning the appointed lot of the beloved disciple, but allowed Peter to think what he pleased about the future of his friend. "If I will," He said, "that he tarry till I come, what is that to thee?" not meaning to give any information, as contemporary believers imagined, but rather refusing to give any in the bluntest and most peremptory manner. "Suppose" — such is the import of the words — "Suppose it were my pleasure that John should remain on the earth till I return to it, what is that to thee? Suppose I were to grant him to sit on my right hand in my Messianic kingdom, what, I ask again, is that to thee? Suppose John were not to taste of death, but, surviving till my second advent, were, like another Elijah, to be wafted directly into heaven, or to be endowed in his body with the power of an endless life, still what is that to thee? FOLLOW THOU ME."

The emphatic repetition of this injunction is very significant. It shows, for one thing, that when Jesus said to Peter, "Feed my sheep," He had no intention of making him a pastor of pastors, a shepherd or bishop over his fellow-disciples. In Roman Catholic theology the lambs are the lay members of the church, and the sheep are the under-shepherds — the whole body of the clergy, the Pope excepted. How strange, if this be true, that Peter should be checked for looking after one of the flock, and asking so simple a question as that, "Lord, and what shall this man do?" Jesus replies to him as if he were a busybody, meddling with matters with which he had no concern. And, indeed, busy-bodyism was one of Peter's faults. He was fond of looking after and managing other people ; he tried once and again to manage the Lord Himself. Curiously enough, it is from this apostle that the Church gets the needful warning against the too common vice just named. "Let none of you," he writes in his first epistle, "suffer as a murderer, or as a thief, or as an evil-doer, or *as a busybody in other men's matters;*" literally, as a bishop intruding into another's diocese.[1] Evidently the frequent rebukes administered to Peter by his Master had made a lasting impression on him.

Heavy as was the load of responsibility laid upon this disciple at this time, it did not amount to any thing so formidable as that involved in being a visible Christ, so to speak, to the whole Church. Neither Peter nor any other man is able to bear that burden, and happily no one is required to do so. The responsibility of even the highest in the Church is restricted within comparatively narrow limits. The main business, even of the chief under-shepherds, is not to make others follow Christ, but to follow Him themselves. It is well that our Lord made this plain by the words addressed to the representative man among the apostles; for Christians of active, energetic, and earnest natures are very apt to have very exaggerated ideas of their responsibilities, and to take on themselves the care of the whole world, and impose on themselves the duty of remedying every evil that is done under the sun. They would be defenders-general of the faith wherever assailed, redressers-general of all wrongs, curates-general of all souls. There is something noble as well as quixotic in this temper; and it were not the best sign of a man's moral earnestness if he had not at some time of his life known somewhat of this fussy, over-zealous spirit. Still it should be understood that the Head of the Church imposes on no man such unlimited responsibility, and that, when self-imposed, it does not conduce to a man's real usefulness. No one man can do all other men's work, and no one man is responsible for all other men's errors and failures; and each man contributes most effectually and surely to the good of the whole by conducting his own life on godly principles. The world is full of evils — scepticism, superstition, ignorance, immorality, on every side — a sight saddening in the extreme. What, then, am I to do?" This one thing above all: Follow thou Christ. Be thou a believer, let who will be infidels. Let thy religion be reasonable, let who will

---

[1] 1 Pet. iv. 15: ἀλλοτριοεπίσκοπος is the Greek word.

pin their faith to a fallible human authority, and place their religion in fantastic ritualisms and gross idolatries. Be thou holy, an example of sobriety, justice, and godliness, though all the world should become a sweltering chaos of impurity, fraud, and impiety. Say with Joshua of old, "If it seem good unto you to serve the Lord, choose you this day whom ye will serve; but as for me and my house, *we* will serve the Lord."

The repeated injunction, "Follow thou me," whilst restricting individual responsibility, prescribes undivided attention to personal duty. Christ demands of His disciples that they follow Him with integrity of heart, without distraction, without murmuring, envy, or calculations of consequences. Peter was, it is to be feared, not yet up to the mark in this respect. There was yet lingering in his heart a vulgar hankering after *happiness* as the chief end of man. Exemption from the cross still appeared to him supremely desirable, and he probably fancied that special favor on Christ's part towards a particular disciple would show itself in granting such exemption. He did not yet understand that Christ oftenest shows special favor to His followers by making them in a remarkable degree partakers of His bitter cup and His bloody baptism. The grand enthusiasm of Paul, which made him desire to know Jesus in the fellowship of His sufferings, had not yet taken possession of Simon's breast. When an arduous and perilous piece of service was to be done, those who were selected to be the forlorn hope seemed to him objects of pity rather than of envy. Far from volunteering for such a service, he would rather congratulate himself on having escaped it; and the highest conceivable virtue, in case one were so unlucky as not to escape, would, in his opinion, be submission to the inevitable.

Peter was deficient also as yet in the military virtue of unquestioning obedience to orders, which is the secret of an army's strength. A general says to one, Go, and he goeth; to another, Come, and he cometh: he appoints to one *corps* its station here, and to another its station there; and no one ventures to ask why, or to make envious comparisons. There is an absolute surrender of the individual will to the will of the commander; and so far as thoughts of preference are concerned, each man is a machine, having a will, a head, a hand, a heart, only for the effective performance of his own appointed task. Peter had not yet attained to this pitch of self-abnegation. He could not do simply what he was bidden, but must needs look round to see what another was doing. Nor let us think this a small offence in him. It was a breach of discipline which could not be overlooked by the Commander of the faithful. Implicit obedience is as necessary in the Church as it is in the army. The old soldier Loyola understood this, and hence he introduced a system of military discipline into the constitution of the so-called " Society of Jesus." And the history of that society shows the wisdom of the founder ; for whatever we may think of the quality of the work done, we cannot deny the energy of the Jesuitic fraternity, or the devotion of its members. Such devotion as the Jesuit renders to the will of his spiritual superior Christ demands of all His people ; and to none except Himself can it be rendered without impiety. He would have every believer give himself up to His will in cheerful, exact, habitual obedience, deeming all His orders wise, all His arrangements good, acknowledging His right to dispose of us as He pleases, content to serve Him in a little place or in a large one, by doing or by suffering, for a long period or a short, in life or by death, if only He be glorified.

This is our duty, and it is also our blessedness. So minded, we shall be delivered from all care of consequences, from ambitious views of our responsibilities, from imaginary grievances, from envy, fretfulness, and the restlessness of self-will. We shall no longer be distracted or tormented with incessant looking round to see what is become of this or that fellow-disciple, but be able to go on with our own work in composure and peace. We shall not trouble ourselves either about our own future or about that of any other person, but shall healthily and happily live in the present. We shall get rid for ever of fear, and care, and scheming, and disappointment, and chagrin, and, like larks at heaven's gate, sing : —

> " Father, I know that all my life
>   Is portioned out by Thee,
> And the changes that will surely come
>   I do not fear to see ;
> But I ask Thee for a present mind,
>   Intent on serving Thee.

> I would not have the restless will
>   That hurries to and fro,
> Seeking for some great thing to do,
>   Or secret thing to know ;
> I would be treated as a child,
>   And guided where I go."

Thus, brother, "go thou thy way till the end be ;" and "thou shalt rest, and stand in thy lot at the end of the days."

30

POWER FROM ON HIGH

Matt. 28:18-20; Mark 16:15; Luke 24:47-53; Acts 1:1-8

FROM Galilee the disciples, of their own accord or by direction, found their way back to Jerusalem, where their risen Lord showed Himself to them once more, and for the last time, to give them their final instructions, and to bid them farewell.

Of this last meeting no distinct notice is taken in the Gospels. Each of the synoptical evangelists, however, has preserved some of the last words spoken by Jesus to His disciples ere He ascended to heaven. Among these we reckon the closing verses of Matthew's Gospel, where we read : "All authority hath been given unto me in heaven and in earth. Go ye therefore, and make disciples of all nations, baptizing them into the name of the Father, and of the Son, and of the Holy Ghost ; teaching them to observe all things whatsoever I have commanded you : and, lo, I am with you alway, even unto the end of the world." [1] Of this last word Mark gives, in the close of his Gospel, an abbreviated version, in these terms : "Go ye into all the world, and preach the gospel to the whole creation." [2] In Luke's narrative the words spoken by Jesus on the occasion of His final appearance to the eleven are so interwoven with those which He spoke to them on the evening of His resurrection day, that, but for the supplementary and more circumstantial account given by the same author in the Book of the Acts, we should never have thought of making a distinction, far

---

[1] Matt. xxviii. 18–20.
[2] Mark xvi. 15. So in R. V. the rendering in A. V. " to every creature " answers to πάσῃ κτίσει, without the article. We do not here enter into the question of the authenticity of Mark xvi. 9-20.

less have known where to place the boundary line. On comparing the two accounts, however, we can see that words spoken at two different times are construed together into one continuous discourse ; and we have no great difficulty in determining what belongs to the first appearance and what to the last. According to the Book of Acts, Jesus, in His last conversation with His disciples, spoke to them of their apostolic duties as witnesses unto Himself and preachers of His gospel ; of the promise of the Spirit, whose descent was to fit them for their work ; and of what they should do till the promise should be fulfilled. Now these are just the topics adverted to in the verses cited from the last chapter of Luke's Gospel. There is first the apostolic commission to preach repentance and remission of sins in the name of Jesus among all nations, beginning at Jerusalem ; and a virtual injunction laid on the disciples to be faithful witnesses to all things they had seen and heard in their Lord's company, and especially to His resurrection from the dead. Then there is the renewal of this promise, here called the " promise of my Father." Then, finally, there is the direction to wait for the promised blessing in the holy city : " But tarry ye at Jerusalem until ye be clothed with power from on high."

All these sayings bear internal evidence of being last words, from their fitness to the situation. It was natural and needful that Jesus should thus speak to His chosen agents at the hour of His final departure, giving them instructions for their guidance in their future apostolic labors, and in the short interval that was to elapse before those labors began. Even the business-like brevity and matter-of-fact tone of these last words betray the occasion on which they were uttered. On first thoughts, we should perhaps have expected a more pathetic style of address in connection with a farewell meeting ; but, on reflection, we perceive that every thing savoring of sentimentality would have been beneath the dignity of the situation. In the farewell address before the passion, pathos was in place ; but in the farewell words before the ascension, it would have been misplaced. In the former case, Jesus was a parent speaking His last words of counsel and comfort to His sorrowing children; in the latter, He was "as a man taking a far journey, who left his house, and gave authority to his servants, and to every man his work, and commanded the porter to watch;"[1] and His manner of speech was adapted to the character He sustained.

And yet the tone adopted by Jesus in His last interview with the eleven was not purely magisterial. The Friend was not altogether lost in the Master. He had kind words as well as commands for His servants. What could be kinder and more encouraging than that word: "And, lo, I am with you alway, even unto the end of the world"? And is there not an accent of friendship in that utterance, in which Jesus, now about to ascend to glory, seems by anticipation to resume the robe of divine majesty, which He laid aside when He became man: "All power is given unto me in heaven and in earth"? Why does He say that now? Not for the purpose of self-exaltation; not to put a distance between Himself and His quondam companions, and, as it were, degrade them from the position of friends to that of mere servants. No; but to cheer them on their way through the world as the messengers of the kingdom; to make them feel that the task assigned them was not, as it might well seem, an impossible one. "I have all power," saith He in effect, "in heaven, and jurisdiction over all the earth: go ye therefore[2] into all the world, making disciples of all the nations, nothing doubting that all spiritual influences and all providential agencies will be made subservient to the great errand on which I send you."

Jesus had kind actions as well as kind words for His friends at parting. There was indeed no farewell kiss, or shaking of hands, or other symbolic act in use among men who bid each other adieu; but the manner of the ascension was most gracious and benignant towards those whom the ascending One left behind. Jesus moved upwards as if lifted from the earth by some celestial attraction, with His face looking downwards upon His beloved companions, and with His hand stretched out in an attitude of benediction. Hence the eleven grieved not for their Lord's disappearance.

---

[1] Mark xiii. 34.

[2] Οὖν is a disputed reading, but the idea it expresses is implied in the connection.

They marvelled indeed, and gazed eagerly and wonderingly towards the skies, as if trying to penetrate the cloud which received their Master's person ; but the parting left no sadness behind. They bowed their heads in worship towards the ascended Christ, and returned to Jerusalem with great joy, as if they had *gained*, not *lost* a friend, and as if the ascension were not a *sunset*, but a *sunrise* — as indeed it was, not for them alone, but for the whole world.

Of that miraculous event, by which our High Priest passed within the veil into the celestial sanctuary, we may not speak. Like the transfiguration, it is a topic on which we know not what to say ; an event not to be explained, but to be devoutly and joyfully believed, in company with the kindred truth declared by the two men in white apparel to the disciples, who said : " Ye men of Galilee, why stand ye gazing into heaven ? This same Jesus, which was taken up from you into heaven, shall so come in like manner as ye have seen Him go into heaven." [1] Wherefore we pass from the ascension to make some observations on the great commission given by the Lord to His apostles for the last time, just before He was taken up into glory.

That commission was worthy of Him from whom it emanated, whether we regard Him as Son of God or as Son of man. " Go ye into all the world, and preach the gospel to the whole creation." Surely this is the language of a Divine Being. What mere man ever entertained a plan of beneficence embracing the whole human race within its scope ? and who but one possessing all power in heaven and on earth could dare to hope for success in so gigantic an undertaking ? Then how full of grace and love the matter of the commission ! The errand on which Jesus sends His apostles is to preach repentance and remission of sins in His name, and to make a peaceful conquest of the world to God by the word of reconciliation through His death. Such philanthropy approves itself to be at once divine and most intensely human. And mark, as specially characteristic of the gracious One, the direction, " beginning at Jerusalem." The words indicate a plan of operations adapted at once to the circumstances of the world, and to the capacities and

---

[1] Acts i. 11.

idiosyncrasies of the agents ; but they do more.   They open
a window into the heart of Jesus, and show Him to be the
same who prayed on the cross : " Father, forgive them ; for
they know not what they do."   Why begin at Jerusalem ?
Because " Jerusalem sinners " most need to repent and to be
forgiven ; and because Jesus would show forth in them at
the outset the full extent of His long-suffering, for a pattern
to them who should afterwards believe, in Samaria, Antioch,
and the uttermost parts of the earth.

It was in every way a commission worthy of Jesus, as the
Son of God and Saviour of sinners, to give.   But what a
commission for poor Galilean fishermen to *receive!* what
a burden of responsibility to lay upon the shoulders of any
poor mortal !   Who is sufficient for these things ?   Jesus
knew the insufficiency of His instruments.   Therefore,
having invested them with official authority, He proceeded
to speak of an investment with another kind of power, without which the official must needs be utterly ineffectual.
" And, behold," He said, " I send the promise of my Father
upon you ; but tarry ye at Jerusalem till ye be clothed with
power from on high."

" Power from on high : " the expression has a mystical
sound, and its sense seems difficult to define ; yet the general
meaning is surely plain enough.   The thing signified is not
altogether or chiefly a power to work miracles, but just what
Jesus had spoken of at such length in His farewell address
before His death.   " Power from on high " means : All that
the apostles were to gain from the mission of the Comforter
— enlightenment of mind, enlargement of heart, sanctification of their faculties, and transformation of their characters,
so as to make them whetted swords and polished shafts for
subduing the world unto the truth ; these, or the effect of
these combined, constituted the power for which Jesus
directed the eleven to wait.   The power, therefore, was a
spiritual power, not a *magical;* an inspiration, not a possession ; a power which was not to act as a blind fanatical
force, but to manifest itself as a spirit of love and of a
sound mind.   After the power descended, the apostles were
to be not less rational, but more ; not mad, but sober-
minded ; not excited rhapsodists, but calm, clear, dignified

expositors of divine truth, such as they appear in Luke's history of their ministry. In a word, they were to be less like their past selves and more like their Master : no longer ignorant, childish, weak, carnal, but initiated into the mysteries of the kingdom, and habitually under the guidance of the Spirit of grace and holiness.

Such being the power promised, it was evidently indispensable to success. Vain were official titles — apostles, evangelists, pastors, teachers, rulers ; vain clerical robes, without this garment of divine power to clothe the souls of the eleven. Vain then, and equally vain now. The world is to be evangelized, not by men invested with ecclesiastical dignities and with parti-colored garments, but by men who have experienced the baptism of the Holy Ghost, and who are visibly endued with the divine power of wisdom, and love, and zeal.

As the promised power was indispensable, so it was in its nature a thing simply to be waited for. The disciples were directed to tarry till it came. They were neither to attempt to do without it, nor were they to try to *get it up*. And they were wise enough to follow their instructions. They fully understood that the power was needful, and that it could not be got up, but must come down. All are not equally wise. Many virtually assume that the power Christ spake of can be dispensed with, and that in fact it is not a reality, but a chimera. Others, more devout, believe in the power, but not in man's impotence to invest himself with it. They try to get the power up by working themselves and others into a frenzy of excitement. Failure sooner or later convinces both parties of their mistake, showing the one that to produce spiritual results something more than eloquence, intellect, money, and organization àre required ; and showing the other that true spiritual power cannot be produced, like electric sparks, by the friction of excitement, but must come sovereignly and graciously down from on high.

31

WAITING

Acts 1:12-14[1]

AFTER that the Lord was parted from them, and carried up into heaven, the eleven returned to Jerusalem, and did as they had been commanded. They assembled together in an upper room in the city, and, in company with the believing women, and Mary the mother of Jesus, and His kinsmen and other brethren, amounting in all to one hundred and twenty, waited for Power and for Light as men who wait for the dawn; or as men who have come to see a panorama wait for the lifting of the curtain that hides from view scenes which their eyes have not seen, nor their ears heard of, nor hath it entered into their hearts to conceive. These verses from the first chapter of the " Acts " show us the disciples and the rest in the act of so waiting.

How solemn is the situation of these men at this crisis in their history! They are about to undergo a spiritual transformation; to pass, so to speak, from the chrysalis to the winged state. They are on the eve of the great illumination promised by Jesus before His death. The Spirit of Truth is about to come and lead them into all Christian truth. The day-star is about to arise in their hearts, after the dreary, pitchy night of mental perplexity and despairing sorrow through which they have recently passed. They are about to be endowed with power of utterance and of character proportional to their enlarged comprehension of the words and work of Christ, so that men hearing them shall be

---

[1] The portions of the evangelic history and of the Acts of the Apostles referred to in this chapter contain much debatable matter. But as it would be quite unsuitable to the character of this work to enter into disputed questions at length, we give our own construction of events without reference to the sceptical views of many modern critics.

amazed, and say one to another : " Behold, are not all these which speak Galileans ? And now hear we every man in our own tongue wherein we were born the wonderful works of God." [1] With a dim presentiment of what is coming, with hearts which throb and swell under the excitement of expectation, and heaving with wondering thoughts of the great things about to be revealed, they sit there in that upper room for ten long days, and wait for the promise of the Father. Verily it is an impressive, a sublime scene.

But how do they wait ? Do they sit still and silent, Quaker fashion, all that time expecting the descent of the Power ? No ; the meeting in the upper room was not a Quaker meeting. They prayed, they even transacted business ; for in those days Peter stood up and proposed the election of a new apostle in the room of Judas, gone to his own place. Nor was their meeting a dull one, as those may imagine who have never passed through any great spiritual crisis, and to whom waiting on God is a synonym for listless indolence. The hundred and twenty believers did not, we may be sure, suffer from *ennui*. Prayers and supplications alone filled up many blessed hours. For to men in the situation of the disciples prayer is not the dull "devotional" form with which we in these degenerate days are too familiar. It is rather a wrestling with God, during which hours passed unobserved, and the day breaks before one is aware. "These all continued with one accord in prayer and supplication." They prayed without fainting, without wearying, with one heart and mind.

Besides praying, the waiting disciples doubtless spent part of their time in reading the Scriptures. This is not stated; but it may be assumed as a matter of course, and it may also be inferred from the manner in which Peter handled Old Testament texts in his address to the people on the day of Pentecost. That pentecostal sermon bears marks of previous preparation. It was in one sense an extempore effusion, under the inspiration of the Holy Ghost, but in another it was the fruit of careful study. Peter and his brethren had, without doubt, reperused all those passages which Jesus had expounded on the evening of the day on which He rose from

[1] Acts ii. 7-11.

the dead, and among them that psalm of David, whose words the apostle quoted in his first gospel sermon, in support of the doctrine of Christ's resurrection. We may find evidence of the minute, careful attention bestowed on that and other Messianic portions of Scripture in the exactness with which the quotation is given. The four verses of the psalm stand word for word in Peter's discourse as they do in the original text — a fact all the more remarkable that New Testament speakers and writers do not, as a rule, slavishly adhere to the *ipsissima verba* in their Old Testament citations, but quote texts somewhat freely.

The spiritual exercises of those ten days would be further diversified by religious conversation. The reading of Scripture would naturally give rise to comments and queries. The brethren who had been privileged to hear Jesus expound the things which were written in the law, and in the prophets, and in the psalms concerning Himself, on the night of His resurrection-day, would not fail to give their fellow-believers the benefit of instructions through which their own understandings had been opened. Peter, who was so prompt to propose the election of a new witness to the resurrection of Jesus, would be not less prompt to tell the company in the upper room what the risen Jesus had said about these Old Testament texts. He would freely speak to *them* of the meaning Jesus taught him to find in the sixteenth Psalm, just as he took the liberty of doing afterwards in addressing the multitude in the streets of Jerusalem. When that psalm had been read, he would say : " Men and brethren, thus and thus did the Lord Jesus interpret these words ;" just as, when the 109th Psalm had been read, he stood up and said : " Men and brethren, this scripture must needs have been fulfilled, which the Holy Ghost by the mouth of David spake before concerning Judas : for it is written, Let his habitation be desolate, and let no man dwell therein ; and his bishopric let another take. Wherefore" — let us choose another to fill his place.

Thus did the brethren occupy themselves during these ten days. They prayed, they read the Scriptures, they conferred together on what they read and on what they expected to see. So they continued waiting with one accord in one

place till the day of Pentecost was fully come, when suddenly there came a sound from heaven as of a rushing
mighty wind, filling all the house where they were sitting;
and there appeared unto them cloven tongues like as of fire,
and they were all filled with the Holy Ghost, and began to
speak with other tongues, as the Spirit gave them utterance.
Then the promise was fulfilled, the Power had come down
from on high, in a manner illustrating the words of the
prophet : " Since the beginning of the world men have not
heard, nor perceived by the ear, neither hath the eye seen,
O God, beside Thee, what he hath prepared for him that
waiteth for him."

The events of Pentecost were the answer to the prayers
offered up during those ten days, which we may call the
incubation period of the Christian Church.   And that the
lesson of encouragement to be learned from this fact may
not be lost, it may be well to remember that the prayers of
those assembled in the upper room were not essentially different from the prayers of saints at any other period in the
Church's history.   They had reference to much the same
objects.   The eleven and the others prayed for the promised
Power, for additional light on the meaning of Scripture, for
the coming of the divine kingdom on earth.   And while they
prayed for these things, we believe, with peculiar fervor,
they did not pray for them with extraordinary intelligence.
Of them, perhaps more emphatically than of most, it might
be said that they knew not what to pray for as they ought.
They had very indistinct ideas, we believe, of the "power,"
of its nature, and of the effects it was to produce.   That
they had crude, and even erroneous ideas of the "kingdom,"
we know; for it is recorded that on the very day of His
ascension they asked Jesus the question, "Dost Thou at this
time restore the kingdom to Israel?" [1]   In this brief question three gross misconceptions are contained.   It is assumed that Christ was to reign personally on the earth, a
great king, like David.   The disciples had no idea whatever
of an ascension into heaven.   Then the kingdom they expect
is merely a national Jewish one.   "Dost Thou," they ask,
"restore the kingdom *to Israel?*"   Finally, the kingdom

[1] Acts i. 6.

looked for by them is political, not spiritual : it is not a new creation, but a kingdom of earth *restored* from a present prostrate condition to former power and splendor.

The notions of the eleven concerning the kingdom continued to be much the same to the day of Pentecost as they had been on the day of the ascension. It is true that Jesus had, in His reply to their question, made a statement which, if rightly understood, was fitted to correct their misconceptions. Formally a declinature to give information on the subject about which the disciples were curious, that reply afforded a sufficiently clear and full explanation of the real state of the case. When He spoke of the power which *they* should receive, Jesus not obscurely hinted that the work of inaugurating the kingdom was to be done by the apostles as His commissioners, not by Himself in person. And the same thing is implied in the words, " Ye shall be witnesses unto me," for witnesses would be needed only for one who was himself unseen. By connecting the "power " with the descent of the Holy Ghost, Jesus in effect corrected the third mistake of the eleven concerning the kingdom — the notion, viz., that it was to be of a political nature. Power arising out of a baptism of the Spirit is moral, not political, in its character ; and a kingdom founded through such power is not a kingdom of this world, but one whose subjects and citizens consist of men believing the truth : " of the truth," as Jesus Himself put it in speaking of His kingdom before Pilate. And, in the last place, the words, " Witnesses unto me, both in Jerusalem, and in all Judæa, and in Samaria, and unto the uttermost parts of the earth," were certainly fitted to banish from the minds of the eleven the dream of a merely national Jewish kingdom. If it was but the kingdom of Israel that was to be restored, to what purpose bear witness to Jesus to the world's end ? Such witness-bearing speaks to a kingdom of a universal nature, embracing people of every tongue and kindred under heaven.

From the reply of their Lord the disciples might thus have gathered the true idea of the kingdom, as one founded on faith in Christ ; presided over by a king, no longer present bodily, but omnipresent spiritually ; not limited to one country, but embracing all who were of the truth in all parts of the world. This great idea, however, they did not take out of the words on which we have been commenting. They were to learn the nature of the kingdom, not from the teaching of Jesus, but from the events of providence. The panorama of the kingdom of God was to be hid from their eyes till the curtain was lifted in three distinct historical movements — the *ascension*, the *descent of the Spirit* at Pentecost on the multitude who had come to keep the feast, and the *conversion of Samaritans and the Gentiles*.[1] The first of these movements had already taken place when the disciples assembled themselves together in the upper room to wait for the promise of the Father. Jesus had ascended, so that they now knew that the seat of empire, the capital of the kingdom, was to be in heaven, not in Jerusalem. This was a valuable piece of knowledge, but it was not all that was needed. Only a small part of the panorama was yet visible to the spectators, and they were still in the dark as to the nature and extent of the coming kingdom. They expected to see a panorama of a new Palestine, not of a new heaven and a new earth wherein should dwell righteousness ; and they doubtless continued to cherish this expectation till the curtain was uplifted, and facts showed what they had unwittingly been praying for, when they at length learned that the Hearer of prayer not only does for His people what they ask, but far above what they even think.

This waiting scene, looked at in relation to the subsequent events recorded in the Acts of the Apostles, not to say the whole history of the Church, suggests another observation. We may learn therefrom what significance may lie in things apparently very insignificant. We had occasion to make this remark in connection with the first meeting of Jesus with five of those who afterwards became members of the chosen band of twelve, and we think it seasonable to repeat it here now. To the contemporary Jewish world that meeting in the upper room, if they knew of its existence, would appear a very contemptible matter, yet it was the only thing of perennial interest in Judæa at the time. The hope of

---

[1] Compare remarks on p. 495 on the slow-mindedness of the disciples, preventing them from understanding the words of Christ till these were interpreted and illuminated by events.

Israel, yea, of the world, lay in that small congregation. For small as it was, God was with those who formed it. Infidels who believe not in supernatural influence smile at such words; but even they must acknowledge that some source of power was centred in that little community, for they multiplied with a rapidity surpassing that of the Israelites in Egypt. Those who reject divine influence impose on themselves the burden of a very laborious explanation of the fact. For those who believe in that influence it is enough to say the little flock grew great, not by might, nor by power of this world, but by God's Spirit. It was their Father's good pleasure to give them the kingdom.

And now, in taking leave of those men with whom we have so long held goodly fellowship, it may be well here to indicate in a sentence, by way of *résumé*, the sum of the teaching they had received from their Master. By such a summary, indeed, it is impossible to convey an adequate idea of the training for their future career which they had enjoyed, seeing that by far the most important part of that training consisted in the simple fact of being for years *with such an one as Jesus.* Yet it may be well to let our readers see at a glance that, unsystematic and occasional as was the instruction communicated by Jesus to His disciples, therein differing utterly from the teaching given in theological schools, yet in the course of the time during which He and they were together lessons of priceless worth were given by the Divine Master to His pupils on not a few subjects of cardinal importance. To enumerate the topics, as far as possible in the order in which they have been considered in this work, Jesus gave His disciples lessons on the nature of the divine kingdom;[1] on prayer;[2] on religious liberty, or the nature of true holiness;[3] on His own Person and claims;[4] on the doctrine of the cross and the import of His death;[5] on humility and kindred virtues, or on the right Christian temper required of disciples both in their private life and in their ecclesiastical life;[6] on the doctrine of self-sacrifice;[7] on the leaven of

---

[1] Chaps. v., viii.   [2] Chap. vi.   [3] Chap. vii.
[4] Chap. xi.   [5] Chaps. xii., xvii., xviii., xxii., and also ix.
[6] Chaps. xiv., xv., xvii., xxi., xxix.   [7] Chap. xvi.

Pharisaism and Sadduceeism, and the woes it was to bring on the Jewish nation;[1] on the mission of the Comforter, to convince the world and to enlighten themselves.[2] The teaching conveyed, assuming that we have even an approximately correct account of it in the Gospels, was fitted to make the disciples what they were required to be as the apostles of a spiritual and universal religion: enlightened in mind, endowed with a charity wide enough to embrace all mankind, having their conscience tremulously sensitive to all claims of duty, yet delivered from all superstitious scruples, emancipated from the fetters of custom, tradition, and the commandments of men, and possessing tempers purged from pride, self-will, impatience, angry passions, vindictiveness, and implacability. That they were slow to learn, and even when their Master left them were far from perfect, we have frankly admitted; still they were men of such excellent moral stuff, that it might be confidently anticipated that having been so long with Jesus they would prove themselves exceptionally good and noble men when they came before the world as leaders in a great movement, called to act on their own responsibility. Not, certainly, as we believe, without the aid of the promised power from on high, not without the enlightening, sanctifying influence of the Paraclete; yet even those who have no faith in supernatural influence must admit on purely psychological grounds, that men who had received such an exceptional training were likely to acquit themselves wisely, bravely, heroically as public characters. According to the actual narrative in the Acts of the Apostles, they did so acquit themselves. According to a well-known school of critics, they acquitted themselves very poorly indeed — in a manner utterly unworthy of their great Master. Which view is the more credible, that of the evangelist Luke, or that of Dr. Baur?

---

[1] Chaps. vii., x., xx.   [2] Chaps. xxix., xxv.

INDEX

AKIBA, Rabbi, story of, 82.

Alcibiades, character of, by Plato, 371.

Alford, on harmony of first and second evangelists in reference to instructions connected with Galilean mission, 112; on reading in John vi 69, 148; on Matt. xviii. 11, 206; on reading in Mark x. 24, 254; date of anointing, 298; on meaning of γενομένου in John xiii. 2. 343.

Amphictyonic Council (modern Utopian), 238; a method of exhibiting unity of the Catholic Church, 460.

Andrew, first meeting with Jesus, 1; call to apostolate, 11; applied to by Greek strangers, 319; inquires concerning the end of the world, 332.

Anointing in Bethany, 297; emblem of Christ's love, 299-307.

Antony, St., story of his conversion, 257.

Apologies, Christ's, for loving sinners, 26; three distinguished, 26; contain germ of universalism, 28.

Apostles (see The Twelve), all the apostles good witnesses, 39; pillar apostles, 39; apostolic estimate of the parables, 46; salting of, 201; instructed with regard to church discipline, 207; salting process at length effectual, 222; parable of extra service spoken to, 260; position of, in Christian church, 265; in heaven, 267; Christ's dying charge to, 410; compared to branches of a vine, 410; apostolic tribulations, 423; apostolic illumination, 437; Epopts in divine kingdom, 439; their commission, 535; power from on high, what, 536.

Aristotle, quoted, 25, 305.

Arnold, Matthew, on "moral therapeutics," 50

Athanasius, Life of Antony by, quoted, 257; design of incarnation, 395.

Augustine, on Jewish mode of keeping the Sabbath, 90; on sense of eating Christ's flesh, 142; on way, truth, and life, 395; on incarnation, 396.

BALAAM, example of a two-minded man, 371.

Barnabas. See Paul.

Baur, on the mission of the seventy, 32, 104; Matthew's Gospel the oldest and most historical, 166; opinion regarding Book of Revelation, 242; doubts authenticity of Matt. xx. 28, 293; importance of the belief in the resurrection of Jesus, 497; psychologically inexplicable, 497; opinion of the apostles contrasted with Luke's, 545.

Baxter, Richard, on fixed forms of prayer, 58; opinion of Sir Matthew Hale, 232; salvability of heathen, 397; on uses of doubt, 510.

Bethsaida Julias, distinct from native town of Peter and Andrew, 121; scene of miracle of feeding, 121.

Bethsaida, native town of Peter and Andrew, 12.

Bingham, Origines Ecclesiasticæ referred to in connection with celebration of the first day of week, "the Lord's day," as a day of rest and worship, 97; on ancient church discipline, 214.

Buddhism, a universal religion, 28; its doctrine of Nirvana, 268.

Bunyan, John, an effective "apostle," 38; his concern in gaol for wife and child, 270; worth of his Pilgrim's Progress, 418.

Buttmann, on the use of the aorist, 451.

Bushnell, forgiving a giving for, 362.

Buxtorf, on Jewish fasts, 72; on rabbinical observance of ceremonial washings, 82; their notions, of Sabbath-breaking, 90; Sabbath-day journey, 92.

CÆSAREA PHILIPPI, the scene of Peter's confession, 163; the situation described, 163.

Calvin, difference between eating and believing, 143; on knowledge of Christ as necessary to salvation, 397; Bible a pair of spectacles, 398.

Capernaum, centre of Christ's operations and His home, 12; Matthew, a tax-gatherer in, 20; sermon in synagogue of, 135; Christ's residence there known to the fourth evangelist, 136.

Carlyle, on Robespierre, 371.

Church, first mentioned at Cæsarea Philippi,

TABLE OF PASSAGES FROM THE GOSPELS